D1526064

Beliefs and the Dead
in Reformation England

Beliefs and the Dead in Reformation England

PETER MARSHALL

OXFORD
UNIVERSITY PRESS

OXFORD
UNIVERSITY PRESS

Great Clarendon Street, Oxford OX2 6DP

Oxford University Press is a department of the University of Oxford.
It furthers the University's objective of excellence in research, scholarship,
and education by publishing worldwide in

Oxford New York

Auckland Bangkok Buenos Aires Cape Town Chennai
Dar es Salaam Delhi Hong Kong Istanbul Karachi Kolkata
Kuala Lumpur Madrid Melbourne Mexico City Mumbai Nairobi
São Paulo Shanghai Taipei Tokyo Toronto

Oxford is a registered trade mark of Oxford University Press
in the UK and in certain other countries

Published in the United States
by Oxford University Press Inc., New York

© Peter Marshall 2002

The moral rights of the author have been asserted
Database right Oxford University Press (maker)

First published 2002
First published in paperback 2004

British Library Cataloguing in Publication Data
Data available

Library of Congress Cataloging in Publication Data
Data available
ISBN 0-19-820773-5
ISBN 0-19-927372-3 (Pbk.)

1 3 5 7 9 10 8 6 4 2

Printed in Great Britain
on acid-free paper by
Biddles Ltd,
King's Lynn, Norfolk

in memory of
MICHAEL KRÖHL

Acknowledgements

THIS BOOK DESERVES its own table of benefactors. Some of these are institutional: the University of Warwick granted me two periods of sabbatical leave to work on this project, the British Academy/Humanities Research Board helped with research and travel expenses, and the Arts and Humanities Research Board funded an additional period of study leave. But mostly my debts are personal ones, and not all of them can be recorded here. Particular thanks are due to those friends who shouldered the burden of reading the manuscript. Will Coster, Bruce Gordon, Sasha Handley, Trevor Johnson, Beat Kümin, and Alec Ryrie provided incisive commentary on particular chapters; Susan Brigden and Bernard Capp heroically read the text in full. My book has benefited greatly from the wide knowledge and wise criticism of all these scholars, though they bear no responsibility for the errors and infelicities that remain.

Experiencing the generosity of fellow historians has been one of the principal consolations of working on this project. Ian Archer, Margaret Aston, Richard Cust, and Roberta Gilchrist were all kind enough to send me copies of important work in advance of its publication. Many useful pointers and references, either solicited or gratuitously offered, were supplied by Virginia Bainbridge, Clive Burgess, Eric Carlson, Patrick Collinson, Peter Davidson, Eamon Duffy, Tom Freeman, Steve Gunn, Steve Hindle, Norman Jones, Judith Maltby, Diarmaid MacCulloch, Chris Marsh, Anthony Milton, John Newton, Michael Questier, Mike Riordan, Ethan Shagan, Tony Shaw, Andrew Spicer, Brett Usher, Alexandra Walsham, Heather Wardle, Robyn White, and Bill Wizeman SJ: I thank them all. I would also like to thank several of the other scholars concerned with cultural aspects of death in early modern England (a larger group than I anticipated at the outset!) for encouragement and shared insights: Jonathan Finch, Jacob Helt, David Hickman, Ralph Houlbrooke, Peter Sherlock, Sir Keith Thomas. Ruth Parr at OUP has been an extremely sympathetic and enthusiastic editor, and Richard Parker at Warwick University Library an invaluable source of logistical support.

In the midst of reflection on death and loss, my daughters Isabel, Maria, and Catherine have supplied a continual reminder of the joy and potential of young life. They have helped me to finish this book, even when they did not seem to be doing so. Throughout the period of writing, their mother, Ali Marshall, has supported and encouraged me in ways too numerous to describe, and impossible to repay. The dedication recalls a debt of friendship from another time.

P.M.

Leamington
Advent 2001

Contents

Abbreviations

ACC	Alcuin Club Collections
BI	Borthwick Institute, York
BL	British Library
Cressy, *Birth, Marriage, and Death*	D. Cressy, *Birth, Marriage, and Death: Ritual, Religion, and the Life-Cycle in Tudor and Stuart England* (Oxford, 1997)
CS	Camden Society
CSPD	*Calendar of State Papers Domestic*
Duffy, *Altars*	E. Duffy, *The Stripping of the Altars: Traditional Religion in England 1400–1580* (New Haven and London, 1992)
EEA	W. P. M. Kennedy (ed.), *Elizabethan Episcopal Administration*, 3 vols., ACC (1924)
EETS	Early English Text Society
EHR	*English Historical Review*
ES	extra series
Foxe	J. Foxe, *Acts and Monuments*, ed. S. R. Cattley and G. Townsend, 8 vols. (1837–41)
HJ	*Historical Journal*
Houlbrooke, *Death*	R. Houlbrooke, *Death, Religion, and the Family in England, 1480–1750* (Oxford, 1998)
HRO	Hampshire Record Office
JEH	*Journal of Ecclesiastical History*
Kreider, *Chantries*	A. Kreider, *English Chantries: The Road to Dissolution* (Cambridge, Mass., 1979)
LP	J. S. Brewer *et al.* (eds.), *Letters and Papers, Foreign and Domestic, of the Reign of Henry VIII*, 21 vols. (1862–1932)
NS	new series
OED	*Oxford English Dictionary*
Place of the Dead	B. Gordon and P. Marshall (eds.), *The Place of the Dead: Death and Remembrance in Late Medieval and Early Modern Europe* (Cambridge, 2000)
PP	*Past and Present*
PRO	Public Record Office
PS	Parker Society
SCH	Studies in Church History

SCJ	*Sixteenth Century Journal*
SS	Surtees Society
TRHS	*Transactions of the Royal Historical Society*
TRP	P. L. Hughes and J. F. Larkin (eds.), *Tudor Royal Proclamations*, 3 vols. (New Haven and London, 1964–9)
VAI	W. H. Frere and W. P. M. Kennedy (eds.), *Visitation Articles and Injunctions of the Period of the Reformation*, 3 vols., ACC (1910)
VAIESC	K. Fincham (ed.), *Visitation Articles and Injunctions of the Early Stuart Church*, Church of England Record Society, 1/5 (1994–8)
YAJ	*Yorkshire Archaeological Journal*
YASRS	Yorkshire Archaeological Society Record Series

In quotations from primary sources, the original spelling has been retained, though the letters u and v have been made to conform to modern usage, and the archaic letter 'thorn' has been transcribed as 'th'. Punctuation and capitalization have been modernized, except where sense or emphasis seemed to require non-intervention. Abbreviations and contractions have been silently expanded. Dates are in Old Style, but the year has been taken to begin on 1 January. Unless otherwise noted, place of publication is London in all citations from published sources.

Introduction

WHY STUDY THE dead? It is a question which all historians might be
asked, or ask themselves, but one of particular relevance to the author, and
potential reader, of this book. For my subject is the cultural importance of
the dead in English society, and the ways in which beliefs about the dead
reflected and shaped patterns of reform in England (with occasional glances
at Wales) over the century and a half from around 1480 to around 1630. The
aim is twofold: to attempt the first comprehensive survey of an important
aspect of the English Reformation, and to use the findings in order to deepen
our understanding of the nature and experience of religious change over the
course of the long period during which England moved from being a cohe-
sively Catholic nation to become an emphatically Protestant one.

A generation ago, the social history of death was an undiscovered country
to historians of early modern England. But following directions suggested by
the pioneering work of French scholars such as Philippe Ariès, Pierre
Chaunu, and Michel Vovelle, considerable progress has been made in map-
ping its landmarks and contours.[1] Recent work by Clare Gittings, Nigel
Llewellyn, David Cressy, Jennifer Woodward, and (particularly) Ralph
Houlbrooke has dramatically improved our understanding of the mortuary
culture of sixteenth- and seventeenth-century England, and 'death in the
Middle Ages' has become a thriving cottage industry in its own right.[2] I am
greatly indebted to this scholarship, but have aimed here to do something
rather different; the focus is not 'death', but 'the dead', a subject whose
scope is more specific, yet potentially expansive. For the dead in this period,
as in other cultures and times, constituted not merely an ever-growing army
of corpses, but an elaborate cultural construction and a complex social

---

[1] P. Ariès, L'Homme devant la mort (Paris, 1977), tr. H. Weaver as The Hour of Our Death
(1981); P. Chaunu, La Mort a Paris: XVIe, XVIIe et XVIIIe siècles (Paris, 1978); M. Vovelle, La
Mort et l'Occident de 1300 à nos jours (Paris, 1983).

[2] C. Gittings, Death, Burial and the Individual in Early Modern England (1984); N. Llewel-
lyn, The Art of Death: Visual Culture in English Death Ritual c. 1500–c.1800 (1991); Cressy,
Birth, Marriage, and Death; J. Woodward, The Theatre of Death: The Ritual Management of
Royal Funerals in Renaissance England (Woodbridge, 1997); Houlbrooke, Death; id. (ed.),
Death, Ritual, and Bereavement (1989); P. Jupp and C. Gittings (eds.), Death in England: An
Illustrated History (Manchester, 1999). See also a forthcoming study of burial practices in
London and Paris by Vanessa Harding. On the medieval period: H. Braet and W. Verbecke
(eds.), Death in the Middle Ages (Louvain, 1983); S. Bassett (ed.), Death in Towns: Urban
Responses to the Dying and the Dead, 400–1600 (Leicester, 1992); P. Binski, Medieval Death:
Ritual and Representation (1996); C. Daniell, Death and Burial in Medieval England (1997); D.
Hadley, Death in Medieval England (Stroud, 2001). A great deal of important work has also
appeared in article form, some in the recently founded interdisciplinary journal, Mortality.

presence. Writing about modern 'thanatology' (the scientific study of death), the early medieval scholar Patrick Geary complains that 'the vast literature on death and dying ignores the dead to focus exclusively on the dying and then on the survivors'.[3] The charge is slightly less true of historical scholarship, but attitudes towards the dead, especially the longer-term dead, are seldom the primary concern of historical thanatologists. Particular aspects (bereavement, funeral ritual, burial patterns, the iconography of tombs) have received attention in recent years, but the theme has never been approached in an overarching or integrated way.

The primacy of 'beliefs' in my title calls for some explanation. Orthodox Marxist historiography has traditionally regarded religious belief as an 'epiphenomenon', a barely disguised correlate of economic structures and power relationships. Even among social historians who take religion seriously, there is often a greater concern with the 'functions' of belief than with its inner logic, and its contemporary meanings and contradictions. Such approaches sometimes take their bearings from the work of social anthropologists, a point of considerable interest here, since many of the latter have for decades been investigating 'relationships' between the living and the dead, in a variety of traditional and developing societies across the world.[4] In a classic study of Amazonian peoples in the immediate pre-war period, the French anthropologist Claude Lévi-Strauss concluded that 'the image a society evolves of the relationship between the living and the dead is, in the final analysis, an attempt, on the level of religious thought, to conceal, embellish or justify the actual relationships which prevail among the living'.[5] Yet it would seem reasonable to expect that such dependences require to be demonstrated on a case-by-case basis, rather than granted a priori status as universal ethnographic law. It would certainly be crass to pretend that, historically, religion has not often been made to serve the interests of the rich and powerful, or to justify the revolutionary aspirations of the economically dispossessed, but I have not begun this study with the conviction that beliefs about the dead demand to be explained and codified in terms of direct correspondence to either fixed or shifting patterns of social structure. Readers will look in vain for much social anthropology in the footnotes to

---

[3] P. Geary, *Living with the Dead in the Middle Ages* (Ithaca and London, 1994), 1.

[4] Among the most interesting works here are R. Hertz, *Death and the Right Hand*, tr. R. and C. Needham (New York, 1960); J. Goody, *Death, Property, and the Ancestors: A Study of the Mortuary Customs of the Lodagaa of West Africa* (Palo Alto, 1962); M. Bloch, *Placing the Dead: Tombs, Ancestral Villages and Kinship Organization in Madagascar* (1971); L. Danforth, *The Death Rituals of Rural Greece* (Princeton, 1982); H. G. Nutini, *Todos Santos in Rural Tlaxcala: A Syncretic, Expressive, and Symbolic Analysis of the Cult of the Dead* (Princeton, 1988). C. Lévi-Strauss, *Tristes tropiques*, tr. J. and D. Weightman (Harmondsworth, 1973), ch. 23, 'The Living and the Dead'.

[5] Lévi-Strauss, *Tristes tropiques*, 320. For some incisive comments on this work, see C. Geertz, 'The Cerebral Savage: On the Work of Claude Lévi-Strauss', in his *The Interpretation of Cultures* (New York, 1973).

this book. Cross-cultural comparisons can illuminate, but they can also predetermine conclusions and encourage circularity in argument.

I start rather with an almost instinctive orientation: that the beliefs of the people of the past are strange and interesting, and that since they were (or appear to have been) very important to those who held them, they are *ipso facto* of importance to historians as well. I would further contend that it is possible, albeit very imperfectly, to reconstruct their beliefs and place them in a meaningful historical context. Despite the strictures of post-modernists, I hold unrepentantly to the view that 'texts' had 'authors', and refer in significant ways to a social reality outside of themselves. It is important here to note that the object of investigation is 'beliefs' not 'belief'. The latter implies the reconstruction of a uniform 'world-view', yet cross-currents, contradictions, complexities, and conflicts are all important components of the narrative that follows. Despite a determination to take belief seriously, this is not a work of historical theology, valuable though such approaches often are. A central aim of the study is to investigate how religious and cultural ideas about the dead interacted with political processes and ecclesiastical politics, with representations and reaffirmations of the social order, with notions of 'community' and 'identity'. The emphasis on interaction allows, however, for the possibility that beliefs could enjoy a degree of real cultural autonomy, and exercise a genuine causal power.

It would, of course, be naïve, if not disingenuous, to pretend to an ultra-objective honest brokerage, merely enabling the people of the past to have their say, and on their own terms. Historians select, they periodize, they follow some lines of enquiry and abandon others. John McManners has wryly observed that 'the historian ... when he writes about death always turns out to be writing about something else'.[6] This book has been conceived primarily as a contribution to the social history of early modern English religion, and more particularly as a means of bringing a new perspective to bear on assessments of the English Reformation as an agent of social and cultural transformation. Put simply, the theme might be defined as the role of the Reformation in shaping attitudes towards the dead, and the role that attitudes towards the dead played in determining the shape and outcomes of the Reformation. I hope to demonstrate not only that the dead can be regarded as a significant 'marker' of religious and cultural change, but that a persistent concern with their status did a great deal to fashion the distinctive appearance of the English Reformation as a whole, and to create its peculiarities and contradictory impulses. In the process attention is paid to a number of important historiographical questions which are currently engaging Reformation scholars: questions of the popular appeal, functions, and dysfunctions of pre-Reformation Catholicism; of the motivation and

[6] J. McManners, 'Death and the French Historians', in J. Whaley (ed.), *Mirrors of Mortality: Studies in the Social History of Death* (1981), 130.

importance of early reformers and their influence on the formulation of official policy; of the conceptual utility and integrity of the notion of a 'long Reformation'; of the emotional temperature of the growing fissures within English Protestantism in the early seventeenth century.[7]

Somewhere near the heart of this story is the process we can call (inverting the title of a seminal study by the medievalist Jacques Le Goff) 'the death of purgatory'.[8] On the face of things, this has a good claim to be considered the most radical and complete of all the disjunctures brought about by Reformation in the sixteenth century. The doctrine of purgatory, the 'middle place' where souls were purged of their sins, supplied the official rationale for remembering the dead, and actively praying for them. The effect of its repudiation, it has recently been suggested, was 'to sever the relationship between the dead and the living'.[9] If this was so, it was a social and cultural upheaval of profound moment: another historian writes that the abolition of purgatory and consequent loss of prayers for the dead 'constituted one of the great unchartable revolutions of English history'.[10] I make the attempt to chart it, or some aspects of it, in this book, and to compare the results to the larger-scale maps on which recent scholarship has plotted the progress of the English Reformation.

Over a period which corresponds roughly to the coming of age of the social history of death, readings of the social history of the English Reformation have also been transformed. A narrative which emphasized the relative speed and popularity of religious change in the sixteenth century has been progressively replaced since the 1970s by a 'revisionist' account which has highlighted the destructive impact of change on a vibrant religious culture, and produced evidence of widespread resistance giving way to slow and sullen acceptance.[11] More recently, a movement towards 'post-revisionism' in English Reformation studies has insisted on extending the chronology of 'Reformation' into the seventeenth century in order to understand the gradual yet thorough accommodation of the people to modes of reformed religion, as well as to discern patterns of deep underlying continu-

---

[7] The relevant works of recent scholarship will be cited in the notes as occasion demands. As extreme shorthand here, these four topic areas speak to issues and problems raised, respectively, by Duffy, *Altars*; C. Haigh, *English Reformations: Religion, Politics, and Society under the Tudors* (Oxford, 1993); N. Tyacke (ed.), *England's Long Reformation 1500–1800* (1998); A. Milton, *Catholic and Reformed: The Roman and Protestant Churches in English Protestant Thought, 1600–1640* (Cambridge, 1995).

[8] J. Le Goff, *La Naissance du purgatoire* (Paris, 1981), tr. A. Goldhammer as *The Birth of Purgatory* (Aldershot, 1984).

[9] Cressy, *Birth, Marriage, and Death*, 396.

[10] R. Houlbrooke, 'Death, Church and Family in England between the Late Fifteenth and the Early Eighteenth Centuries', in id. (ed.), *Death, Ritual, and Bereavement*, 36. Houlbrooke's own work has contributed greatly to the charting process.

[11] A. G. Dickens, *The English Reformation*, 2nd edn. (1989) may stand as representative of the first school; J. J. Scarisbrick, *The Reformation and the English People* (Oxford, 1984), Duffy, *Altars*, and Haigh, *English Reformations*, of the second.

ity between the religious cultures of 'Catholic' and 'Protestant' England.[12] I began this research without feeling a prior allegiance to any of these positions (which are in any case loose and convenient labels rather than fixed historiographical 'parties'[13]) and concluded it without discovering the need to declare one. By attempting to track changes across a period approximating to the lives of five generations of Tudor and Stuart people, I hope in some measure to close the gap between revisionist approaches, which tend to focus on the years before 1580, and 'post-revisionist' ones, nearly always commencing post-1560. By taking with equal seriousness the beliefs of advocates of religious change and of its opponents, as well as the beliefs of those stranded in the middle, I hope to give everyone their due, and to avoid suspicions of partisanship or special pleading.

The structure adopted in this book is in broad terms a chronological one, as seems appropriate for a study attempting to map a process of religious and cultural change over time. But an unswervingly linear approach would not allow particular themes to be elucidated with the care which they deserve. The opening chapter explores the range of attitudes towards the dead to be discerned in pre-Reformation religious culture, drawing on evidence from the later fifteenth and early sixteenth centuries. Chapters 2–4 exhibit a stronger narrative thrust, tracing the development of an attempted 'reformation of the dead' through the reigns of Henry VIII, Edward, Mary, Elizabeth, James I, and into the reign of Charles I, though in each case the tracking camera following the progress of official reform initiatives is intercut with close-focus study of the ideas of intellectuals, and the responses of the people. Chapter 5 is concerned with (predominantly) Protestant perceptions of the afterlife in Elizabethan and early Stuart England, and Chapter 6 with the cultural meanings of the appearance of ghosts over the same period. The final chapter revisits, a century on, several of the themes and issues of the first one, evaluating the ways of remembering and forgetting the dead which seem characteristic of Protestant (or 'post-Reformation') England. Three broad themes resurface throughout the book: memory, commemoration, and the afterlife. Shifts in the social and personal imperative to remember the dead, and in the language of memory, are related to rituals and structures of commemoration; while conditioning, and at times constraining, both were beliefs about the most unfathomable of all human questions: the nature of life after death.

---

[12] Among the best and most suggestive of post-revisionist works are D. Cressy, *Bonfires and Bells: National Memory and the Protestant Calendar in Elizabethan and Stuart England* (1989); T. Watt, *Cheap Print and Popular Piety 1560–1640* (Cambridge, 1991); C. Marsh, *Popular Religion in Sixteenth-Century England* (Basingstoke, 1998); A. Walsham, *Providence in Early Modern England* (Oxford, 1999).

[13] Useful surveys of the recent historiography are provided by P. Collinson, 'The English Reformation, 1954–1995', in M. Bentley (ed.), *Companion to Historiography* (1997); P. Marshall, 'Introduction', in id. (ed.), *The Impact of the English Reformation 1500–1640* (1997).

I

The Presence of the Dead:
Memory and Obligation Before
the Reformation

THE DEAD OCCUPY a space, or series of spaces, close to the heart of late medieval English religious culture. Their fate in the afterlife was the hub around which the theology of the Church revolved, and evolved. Their demands for memory and intercession shaped the liturgy, moulded the fabric and furnishing of churches, provided employment for an army of massing-priests, and, so reformers would claim, made the Church a great deal of money. Their physical remains resided in and around places of worship, with varying degrees of emblematic display. The dead were silent, and not silent. Their demands were articulated by the living, both the soon to be dead and the longer-term survivors. Collectively, these representations comprise a discourse that is extraordinarily revealing about the concerns and aspirations of a world far removed from our own. In this opening chapter I hope to explore some of the lineaments of that world, and also to make some preliminary suggestions as to why its beliefs and institutions were open to particular forms of disparagement and assault.

Medievalists sometimes complain that historians of the Reformation tend to look at fifteenth- and early sixteenth-century religion through the lens of later religious change, a view that distorts rather than focuses understanding.[1] As if to give the lie to that assessment, the most persuasive recent work on the mortuary culture of late medieval England by a historian of the Tudor Reformations has not sought to find there any seeds of discontent with the old religious world.[2] But to enquire about the social etymology of tumultuous change is not necessarily to applaud or endorse the process. The Refor-

[1] For example, C. Burgess, '"A Fond Thing Vainly Invented": An Essay on Purgatory and Pious Motive in Later Medieval England', in S. J. Wright (ed.), Parish, Church and People (1988), 69; N. Tanner, 'The Reformation and Regionalism: Further Reflections on the Church in Late Medieval Norwich', in J. A. F. Thomson (ed.), Towns and Townspeople in the Fifteenth Century (Gloucester, 1988), 129; C. Carpenter, 'The Religion of the Gentry of Fifteenth-Century England', in D. Williams (ed.), England in the Fifteenth Century (Woodbridge, 1987), 72.
[2] Duffy, Altars, chs. 9–10.

mation was not 'about' one single issue or set of issues, whether theological, social, or political. But, as I hope to substantiate in the chapters which follow, across all three organizing categories a concern with the placing of the dead looms very large. Furthermore, it is the contention here that the ways in which late medieval Catholicism articulated its relationship with the dead may serve as a kind of synecdoche for that religious system as a whole; one that helps us to understand both its remarkable vitality and tenacity, and also its sometimes perplexing brittleness facing the chill winds of religious reform.

LANDS OF THE DEAD

The prominence of the dead in late medieval Latin Christianity was a result of the conjunction of two compelling ideas. The first was the gradual evolution of the belief that the majority of the faithful dead did not proceed immediately to the Beatific Vision of God in heaven, but underwent a painful purgation of the debt due for their sins in the intermediary state (and place) of purgatory. The second was the conviction, predicated upon the theory that all faithful Christians in this world and the next were incorporated in a single 'communion of saints', that the living had the ability (and the duty) to ease the dead's sufferings. As a result, there is a good case for claiming both that (in A. N. Galpern's words) late medieval Catholicism was in large measure 'a cult of the living in the service of the dead', and that (in Eamon Duffy's) '*the* defining doctrine of late medieval Catholicism was purgatory'.[3] It is with the conceptual landscape of purgatory and its significance as the primary habitation of the dead that the first part of this chapter will be concerned.

The doctrine of purgatory 'had been creeping up on Western Christendom since the early Middle Ages'.[4] Whether the idea of purgatory as a distinct 'place' only became firmly established in the later twelfth century, as claimed in an influential book by Jacques Le Goff, or whether the development happened earlier, is not really to the purpose here.[5] By the later fifteenth century, the idea of purgatory as one of a series of linked territories comprising a 'geography' of the other world was firmly established both in ecclesiastical teaching and, so far as we can tell, in the religious imagination of the people. This was a development of considerable importance. It

---

[3] A. N. Galpern, 'The Legacy of Late Medieval Religion in Sixteenth-Century Champagne', in C. Trinkaus and H. O. Oberman (eds.), *The Pursuit of Holiness in Late Medieval and Renaissance Religion* (Leiden, 1974), 149: Duffy, *Altars*, 8.

[4] J. Bossy, *Christianity in the West 1400–1700* (Oxford, 1985), 30.

[5] J. Le Goff, *The Birth of Purgatory*, tr. A. Goldhammer (Aldershot, 1984), whose chronology is questioned by R. W. Southern, 'Between Heaven and Hell', *Times Literary Supplement* (18 June 1982), and B. P. McGuire, 'Purgatory, the Communion of Saints, and Medieval Change', *Viator*, 20 (1989).

was precisely because 'the dead became objectified as beings existing in an identifiable place' that their problems impinged so directly upon the living.[6]

And yet both the exterior boundaries and interior topography of this 'place' of purgatory remained remarkably hazy. The Councils of Lyons (1274) and Florence (1439) had formally defined the theological rationale of purgatory (the painful purgation of satisfaction due for sins), and described some means of relieving its pains (offering of the mass, prayer, alms, and other works of piety), but they offered no more circumstantial detail.[7] Not even this minimal official sanction was provided for the Church's teaching on other territorial subdivisions of the next life: the *limbus infantium* which received the souls of children dying before baptism, and the *limbus patrum* for the souls of prophets and patriarchs who died before the Incarnation, and which Christ was widely held to have visited after the crucifixion in the so-called 'harrowing of hell'. The devotional imagination thrived on this paucity of doctrinal definition. The extensive vision literature of the early and high Middle Ages anticipated theological certitude with vivid first-hand accounts of the contours of the afterlife and lurid descriptions of its punishments.[8] A number of such well-established works were put into print in England at the end of the fifteenth century: *The Vision of the Monk of Evesham*; *The Pilgrimage of the Soul*; *The Gast of Guy*. Compilations of otherworldly visions were also to be found in the famous collection of saints' lives known as *The Golden Legend* (printed by Caxton in 1483) and in *The Floure of the Commaundements of God* (1510).[9] As old as Christianity itself, the motif of the otherworldly journey was not moribund in the later fifteenth century. In 1465 Edmund Leversedge of Frome, Somerset, visited, and returned from, the next life during a plague fever. The experience was repeated by a Cheshire draper, John Newton, in 1492.[10]

[6] J. R. Banker, *Death in the Community: Memorialization and Confraternities in an Italian Commune in the Late Middle Ages* (Athens, Ga. and London, 1988), 2.

[7] The Florentine decree virtually reproduced verbatim that of 1274: see G. Marc'hadour, 'Introduction', in Thomas More, *The Supplication of Souls*, ed. F. Manley *et al* (New Haven and London, 1990), pp. xcii–iii.

[8] On medieval vision literature, see T. Wright, *St Patrick's Purgatory: An Essay on the Legends of Purgatory, Hell, and Paradise, Current During the Middle Ages* (1844); H. R. Patch, *The Other World According to Descriptions in Medieval Literature* (New York, 1970); J. Le Goff, 'The Learned and Popular Dimensions of Journeys in the Otherworld in the Middle Ages', in S. Kaplan (ed.), *Understanding Popular Culture: Europe from the Middle Ages to the Nineteenth Century* (Berlin, 1984); A. Gurevich, *Medieval Popular Culture: Problems of Belief and Perception*, tr. J. Bak and P. Hollingsworth (Cambridge, 1988), ch. 4; A. Morgan, *Dante and the Medieval Other World* (Cambridge, 1986); R. Easting, '"Send Thine Heart into Purgatory": Visionaries of the Other World', in H. Cooper and S. Mapstone (eds.), *The Long Fifteenth Century: Essays for Douglas Gray* (Oxford, 1997).

[9] For the publishing history, see R. White, 'Early Print and Purgatory: The Shaping of an Henrician Ideology', Australian National University Ph.D. thesis (1994), ch. 2.

[10] A. D. Brown, *Popular Piety in Late Medieval England: The Diocese of Salisbury 1250–1550* (Oxford, 1995), 1; P. Morgan, 'Of Worms and War: 1380–1558', in P. C. Jupp and C. Gittings (eds.), *Death in England* (Manchester, 1999), 131.

The status of this material as either 'fiction' or objective 'truth' confounds the categories familiar to modern (i.e. pre-post-modern) minds. Aaron Gurevich has argued that the *Divine Comedy* of Dante (not printed in England in this period) was virtually unique in recognizing its own status as a distinctly allegorized version of religious truth, though the fifteenth-century English translator of William de Deguilleville's *Pilgrimage of the Soul* had conceded that the work was in places 'over fantastyk, noughte grounded, nor foundable in holy scripture, ne in doctoures wordes'.[11] Such an overt sense of sceptical distance was highly uncharacteristic of the genre as a whole, though it is suggestive that manuscript versions of visions were often included with romances.[12] Accounts of the afterlife in vision literature (as well as in the *ars moriendi* tracts, sermons, and more sober theological treatises which drew upon it) were certainly 'revelations', lightning-flash glimpses into a normally hidden other-reality. But at the same time, in itemizing gruesome torments, they were designed to deter people from sin, and to comprise didactic treatises on its nature and taxonomy. The result was a positively baroque exuberance in representation, and a gloriously untidy popular theology.

The conciliar decrees had said nothing about actual locations, but there was no shortage of authorities willing to 'map' the afterlife and establish a schema for the geographic relations of the constituent parts. In the poetic imagination of Deguilleville or Dante, purgatory was a mountainous region on the borders of heaven, but more commonly it was assigned a subterranean location in the vicinity of hell.[13] Aquinas surmised that 'the place of purgatory is situated below and in proximity to hell, so that it is the same fire which torments the damned in hell and cleanses the just in purgatory'.[14] *The Ordynare of Crysten Men* (1502), stated that purgatory was 'one part of hell'.[15] Thomas More, reflecting on the credal formula that Christ 'descended into hell', maintained that *limbus patrum* and purgatory are 'two placys amonge other taken and comprehended under the name of hell ... habytacyons of sowlys byneth or under us in the low placys under the ground'.[16] Still more categorical was a *Lytel Boke, that speketh of Purgatorye*, appearing on the very eve of Henry VIII's break with Rome. This laid down that hell, *limbus infantium*, purgatory, and *limbus patrum* were situated under the earth, stacked one on top of the other in that ascending

[11] Gurevich, *Medieval Popular Culture*, 144; G. Edwards, 'The Idea of Post Mortem Purgation in the Western Church to the End of the Middle Ages', University of Exeter Ph.D. thesis (1983), 228.

[12] A point noted by G. Keiser, 'The Progress of Purgatory: Visions of the Afterlife in Later Middle English Literature', *Analecta Cartusiana*, 117 (1987), 90–1.

[13] Le Goff, *Birth of Purgatory*, 205–8, 252, 310–15.

[14] Aquinas, *Summa Theologica*, cited in M. Joseph, 'Discerning the Ghost in Hamlet', *Publications of the Modern Language Association of America*, 76 (1961), 497.

[15] *The Ordynare of Crysten Men* (1502), ll2ʳ.

[16] More, *Supplication*, 186.

order.[17] Yet the location of purgatory was a highly contingent issue, one that was at times, literally, up in the air. *The Golden Legend*, source-book for countless homilists, summarized the issues thus:

be it said that the souls are purged in some place located near hell and called purgatory. This is the opinion held by most learned men, although others think the place is in the air and in the torrid zone. However, by divine dispensation different places are sometimes appointed for different souls, and this for a number of reasons—either because their punishment is lighter or their liberation faster, or for our instruction, or because their sin was committed in this particular place, or on account of the prayer of some saint.[18]

The existence of an aerial purgatory, though condemned as a 'fantastical fiction' by Bonaventure, was promoted by the *Gast of Guy*, and the notion that there were actually two purgatories, one under the earth and the other at an earthly location appropriate to the punishment of the individual, was a popular one.[19] There was also a long-standing association of places in this world with entrances to the netherworld. Volcanoes, particularly Mount Etna in Sicily, seemed obvious candidates for this role, though closer to home there was St Patrick's Purgatory at Lough Derg in Ireland, a cave in which penitents were granted visions of the next life.[20] The theme of localized purgatories on this earth was closely linked with the appearance of the dead to the living, a theme to which we will return shortly.

Varying assessments of the location of purgatory were matched by differing views on what awaited souls there. Fire was by far the most commonly imagined instrument of punishment and purgation, but the vision literature typically provided a wider range of horrors, both environmental (frozen lakes, icy storms), and more directly corporeal (serpents, skewers, hooks), with disembodied souls often tormented in ways appropriate to sins committed in life.[21] Whether the pains of purgatory were ministered by angels or demons was a disputed point. Some of the visionaries fell in with the view of Aquinas, and of early Tudor England's foremost theologian John Fisher, that purgatory was in the keeping of the angels, though others, perhaps finding this too counter-intuitive, insisted that fiends were the agents of God's justice there. The latter view was shared by Thomas More and the *Lytel Boke*. *The Golden Legend* similarly taught that 'purgation and punishment are the work of wicked angels, not of good ones', though good angels

---

[17] *Here begynneth a Lytel Boke that speketh of Purgatorye* (?1531), sig. A2ᵛ. This was taken from the fourteenth-century didactic poem 'The Pricke of Conscience'.

[18] J. de Voragine, *The Golden Legend*, tr. W. Ryan, 2 vols. (Princeton, 1993), ii. 282.

[19] Edwards, 'The Idea of Post-Mortem Purgation', 228; *Lytel Boke*, A3ᵛ. For the suggestion that Catholic cosmographies of the afterlife may have become more systematic in the later sixteenth century as a consequence of Protestant challenges, see C. Eire, 'The Good Side of Hell: Infernal Meditations in Early Modern Spain', *Historical Reflections / Réflexions Historiques*, 26 (2000), 288–9.

[20] Le Goff, *Birth of Purgatory*, 193–205.

[21] White, 'Early Print and Purgatory', 27–44; Duffy, *Altars*, 338–9.

would frequently visit purgatory to comfort souls and exhort them to suffer patiently.[22] A disputed question of arguably greater theological weight was that of whether the souls in purgatory were aware of their status as saved souls. Aquinas's view that they were was upheld on the eve of the Reformation by Thomas More. But the fourteenth-century visionary saint Bridget of Sweden had thought otherwise, and the popular Brigittine devotional writer Richard Whitford conceded that in some cases, for special punishment, God 'doth hyde, and kepe that knowledge from them'.[23] *The Ordynare of Crysten Men* and *The Golden Legend* taught that it was a great consolation for the souls in purgatory that 'they await with certainty the glory to come', but the *Lytel Boke* suggested pains so intense that 'they take no kepe, that god wyll them save'.[24] There was lack of unanimity too as to whether souls in purgatory might effectually pray for the living. More urged his readers to remember those who 'there pray for us as we praye here for theym'. But in this he contradicted John Fisher's dictum that 'no creature beynge in purgatorye may have the in remembraunce as he sholde'. Souls would reciprocate the prayers offered on their behalf only when they entered the kingdom of heaven.[25] A poem in the commonplace book of the London merchant Richard Hill urged prayers and masses for kinsfolk in purgatory with the thought 'in hevyn they shall do for thee the same', and a number of inscriptions on early sixteenth-century tombs proclaimed 'For Jhus love pray for me, I may not pray nowe pray ye'.[26] Given the lack of unanimity about where purgatory was, and what precisely souls experienced there, it is perhaps less surprising than it might seem that the doctrine made little direct mark on the visual culture of later medieval England. Scenes of purgatory were occasionally included in devotional books and manuscripts, but only rarely in the public space of churches, where the dominant visual image was of the 'doom', the Last Judgement at the end of time when purgatory would be no more.[27] In this context, the art historian Paul Binski has helpfully pointed to the difficulties

---

[22] Duffy, *Altars*, 344–5; J. Fisher, *The English Works*, ed. J. Mayor, EETS ES 27 (1876), 9; *A Critical Edition of Two Fruytfull Sermons of Saint John Fisher*, ed. M. D. Sullivan (Ann Arbor, 1974), 30; *Lytel Boke*, B4ʳ; *Golden Legend*, ii. 282.

[23] Duffy, *Altars*, 346.

[24] *Ordynare of Crysten Men*, ll2ᵛ; *Golden Legend*, ii. 282; *Lytel Boke*, A4ʳ, B3ᵛ.

[25] T. More, *The Debellation of Salem and Bizance*, ed. J. Guy et al. (New Haven and London, 1987), 231; Fisher, *English Works*, 16; *Two Fruytfull Sermons*, 29. Fisher's position had been that of Jean Gerson: cf. G. Marc'hadour, 'Introduction', in More, *Supplication*, p. xcvii. See also *Ordynare of Crysten Men*, ll2ᵛ.

[26] R. Dyboski (ed.), *Songs, Carols, and Other Miscellaneous Poems, from ... Richard Hill's Commonplace Book*, EETS 101 (1908), 71; C. Litzenberger, *The English Reformation and the Laity: Gloucestershire, 1540–1580* (Cambridge, 1997), 24; T. F. Ravenshaw, *Antiente Epitaphs* (1878), 22.

[27] M. Driver, 'Pictures in Print: Late Fifteenth- and Early Sixteenth-Century English Religious Books for Lay Readers', in M. Sargent (ed.), *De Cella in Seculum: Religious and Secular Life and Devotion in Late Medieval England* (Woodbridge, 1989), 238–9; BL Add. MS 37049, 24ᵛ, 27ᵛ–28ʳ. An exception to prove the rule about churches is the early thirteenth-century wall-painting of a 'purgatorial ladder' in the church of Chaldon, Surrey, reproduced as the cover illustration to M. Aston, *Faith and Fire: Popular and Unpopular Religion, 1350–1600* (1993).

of portraying purgatory within a representational system that was most comfortable with absolute binary oppositions.[28] Yet the failure of the Church to establish a fixed and universally accepted set of iconographic conventions for the representation of purgatory must surely also have been a reason for the doctrine's dissemination in primarily aural and textual contexts.

To say that late medieval mystics, homilists, and scholars 'disagreed' about purgatory would be to overstate the case. The basic rationale of post-mortem purgation was well understood, and certain structuring motifs were widely propagated. Yet while purgatory may well have been the 'defining doctrine' of pre-Reformation Catholicism, it was also arguably of all major doctrines the least clearly and authoritatively defined. The world of the dead seems to have been at once vivid and vague, a nexus of objectified theological and cultural values, visionary speculation, and calculating didacticism. The mix was in many ways a highly creative one, and the possibilities for widely variant representations of purgatory did not self-evidently undermine its credibility in the eyes of contemporaries. Even the Lollards, those self-appointed guardians of the godly conscience of later medieval England, do not seem to have singled out the doctrine for much criticism.[29]

Yet at the same time, the multiplication of minor discrepancies, the sketchiness of theological parameters, and the absence of authoritative texts and approved images presaged a fundamental pregnability. Later reformers would seize on all these issues to argue that purgatory and the limbos were imaginary places, fantasies and frauds. But both they and the defenders of tradition had to deal with the fact that there was a further source of testimony to the shape of the next life. For the dead sometimes returned to the living and told of their experiences there.

ENCOUNTERS WITH THE DEAD

The realms of the living and of the dead in the late medieval imagination were not merely contiguous, but coinciding. In spite of occasional disap-

---

[28] P. Binski, *Medieval Death: Ritual and Representation* (1996), 70, 188–99. The scarcity of visual representations is also noted by T. Matsuda, *Death and Purgatory in Middle English Didactic Poetry* (Cambridge, 1997), 94. Examples of visual representations of purgatory are given in S. Greenblatt, *Hamlet in Purgatory* (Princeton, 2001), 52–61, though mainly from non-English sources, and Greenblatt accepts (p. 61) that 'it was in narrative even more than in pictures that the purgatorial poem was created and maintained'.

[29] Anne Hudson notes that purgatory does not appear to have concerned Wyclif or his early followers, though it had begun to feature in trials by the 1460s: *The Premature Reformation: Wycliffite Texts and Lollard History* (Oxford, 1988), 193–4, 309–11. Nonetheless, only one of the heretics caught up in Archbishop Warham's sweep in Kent in 1511 seems to have attacked the doctrine: N. Tanner (ed.), *Kent Heresy Proceedings 1511–12*, Kent Records, 26 (1996), 46. This lack of concern on the part of Lollards (or their persecutors) seems to have been matched in other parts: Kreider, *Chantries*, 94–6. As late as 1528, the Essex Lollard John Tyball held that 'the sowles of synners and yvell doers go to purgatory', though he had believed for a while that there was no such place: J. Strype *Ecclesiastical Memorials*, 3 vols. (1721), i (2), 36.

proval from ecclesiastical authorities, churchyards were sites for the conviv-
ial secular activities of the living as well as resting-places of the dead.[30] The
visible and invisible worlds touched at points which were variously temporal, physical, and cognitive. Historians attuned to the language of social
anthropology will wish here to speak of 'liminality'. Thomas More's Uto-
pians believed that the dead walked invisibly among them, witnessing their
words and actions, and in this they may not have differed so greatly from the
mentality of European peoples.[31]

Points of contact between the living and the dead were at least in part
defined by difficulties of separating the categories in the first place. Medieval
representational systems may have been based on 'a binary rhetorical order
of absolute distinctions',[32] but cultural constructions of life and death fit
somewhat uneasily into the model. Members of religious orders were,
conventionally, and in theory more than practice, 'dead to the world', but
lepers underwent a ritual of separation from society taking the form of a
mock burial service, and those who had received the sacrament of anointing
for the sick ('extreme unction') occupied a similarly transitional position
between the living and the dead. Against popular instincts, ecclesiastical
authority was obliged to maintain that the sacrament could be administered
more than once, and that those who recovered were not barred permanently
from the consumption of meat or bound to a life of chastity.[33] Even outside
these special cases, the boundaries of life and death can appear to us blurred,
not least because contemporaries possessed no infallible test for diagnosing
when death had actually occurred. From the deathbed through to the interment in consecrated ground, dying evinced more of the character of an
extended ritual performance rather than of a single transformative 'event'.
Students of medieval funeral ritual have usually interpreted it as a transitional process, serving gradually to relocate the departed in the society of the
dead, and concluding with a commensal funeral feast that re-established
the solidarity of the living.[34] But even when the body had been placed in the

---

[30] D. Dymond, 'God's Disputed Acre', *JEH* 50 (1999), 464–97. For Continental parallels, see
P. Ariès, *The Hour of Our Death*, tr. H. Weaver (1981), 62–71; J. Delumeau, *Sin and Fear: The
Emergence of a Western Guilt Culture*, tr. E. Nicholson (New York, 1990), 38–9; R.
Muchembled, *Popular Culture and Elite Culture in France 1400–1750*, tr. L. Cochrane
(Baton Rouge and London, 1985), 64.

[31] T. More, *Utopia*, ed. E. Surtz and J. H. Hexter (New Haven and London, 1965), 225.

[32] Binski, *Medieval Death*, 194.

[33] R. Finucane, 'Sacred Corpse, Profane Carrion: Social Ideals and Death Rituals in the Later
Middle Ages', in J. Whaley (ed.), *Mirrors of Mortality: Studies in the Social History of Death*
(1981), 42–55; R. Gilchrist, 'Christian Bodies and Souls: The Archaeology of Life and Death in
Later Medieval Hospitals', in S. Bassett (ed.), *Death in Towns: Urban Responses to the Dying
and the Dead, 100–1600* (1992), 115; Duffy, *Altars*, 313.

[34] M. Aston, 'Death', in R. Horrox (ed.), *Fifteenth-Century Attitudes: Perceptions of Society
in Late Medieval England* (1994), 220–2; R. Dinn, 'Death and Rebirth in Late Medieval Bury St
Edmunds', in Bassett (ed.), *Death in Towns*, 151–69; Binski, *Medieval Death*, 29–30; V. Bain-
bridge, 'The Medieval Way of Death: Commemoration and the Afterlife in Pre-Reformation
Cambridgeshire', SCH Subsidia, 10 (1994), 200–1. These works all owe a debt to A. Van
Gennep, *The Rites of Passage*, tr. M. Vizedum and G. Caffee (1960), 146–65.

earth, a final categorical disconnection might not be achieved. Orthodox piety stressed the natural reluctance of the soul to be severed from the body, but popular belief may have entertained the more naturalistic conception that the souls of the dead lingered for a time in the vicinity of their graves, a 'liminal' period during which their spirits were most likely to appear to the living.[35] The permeability of the barrier between life and death was further underscored by the perception that, even before the Last Judgement, death was not a final sentence with no possibility of reprieve. Among the miracles of Christ, the raising of Lazarus seems to have exercised a particular fascination for late medieval English people.[36] The ability to raise the dead, moreover, was not unique to Christ's earthly ministry, but had been franchised to certain powerful intercessors. The miracle collection compiled to support the canonization of Henry VI contained numerous examples of drowned children and careless workmen restored to life through the mediation of the royal saint-in-waiting.[37] In the early sixteenth century, Richard Whitford averred that alongside Lazarus 'many have ben reysed by myracle'. More remarkably, he went on to add 'I knewe, and spake with one suche my selfe'.[38]

The most culturally conspicuous moment of 'slippage' between the parallel worlds of living and dead was calendrically defined. The twin feasts of All Saints and All Souls at the beginning of November constituted a temporal window through which the souls of the dead might pass back to their earthly habitations. Whether or not the feast had direct pre-Christian antecedents, the association of death and approaching winter invested it with a particularly intense sensibility.[39] In some places bonfires were lit, and special foods, 'soul cakes' were distributed for the benefit of the dead.[40] But the most prominent seasonal custom, and the one that has left most mark on the records, was the ringing of church bells, usually on the eve of All Souls, but sometimes on the feast itself. The foremost historian of the practice, Ronald Hutton, is able to count twenty-nine parishes whose accounts made

---

[35] C. Gittings, *Death, Burial and the Individual in Early Modern England* (1984), 162–3; R. Finucane, *Appearances of the Dead: A Cultural History of Ghosts* (1982), 65–6; C. Daniell, *Death and Burial in Medieval England* (1997), 61. Robert Fossier makes the more sweeping and questionable assertion that country-dwellers believed that 'until the sound of the Last Trumpet they wandered without repose, asexual and joyless, where they had lived, round the church where they had been baptised': *Peasant Life in the Medieval West*, tr. J. Vale (Oxford, 1988), 27.

[36] Daniell, *Death and Burial*, 10–11, 82; Wright, *Patrick's Purgatory*, 167; Duffy, *Altars*, 81–2, 340–1, pl. 127–8; G. England and A. W. Pollard (eds.), *The Towneley Plays*, EETS 71 (1897), 387–93.

[37] R. Finucane, *Miracles and Pilgrims: Popular Beliefs in Medieval England* (1977), 73–4, 195.

[38] R. Whitford, *A Dayly Exercyse and Experyence of Dethe* (1537), A7ᵛ–8ʳ.

[39] For suggestions that All Souls customs were indebted to a prehistoric belief in the potency of supernatural forces at the turning of pastoral seasons, see R. Hutton, *The Stations of the Sun: A History of the Ritual Year in Britain* (Oxford, 1996), 366; E. Muir, *Ritual in Early Modern Europe* (Cambridge, 1997), 71–2.

[40] See below, 137–8.

payments for ringing in the fifteenth and early sixteenth centuries.[41] Where
the accounts are silent, arrangements for paying the ringers may have been
less formalized. At Holy Trinity, Coventry, for example, it was the deacon's
task to go 'on All halowe day, at evyn, a mong the pepyll, in the northesyde
of the churche, and gedyr money off them, for the ryngars that ryng for all
crystyn souls'.[42] The reference to ringing 'for all crystyn souls' raises the
question of whether the practice was primarily intercessory or apotropaic.
Hutton is in no doubt that the point of the ringing was 'to comfort those
departed souls which were enduring the torments of purgatory', but Natalie
Davis has seen its function as 'to keep the dead at bay'.[43] Nowhere in
ecclesiastical sources does it seem to say that bells were an effectual instrument of intercession for the dead, though it is revealing that *The Golden
Legend* praises their efficacy as 'Christ's trumpets' for frightening off
demons.[44] Later reformers, however, were convinced that bell-ringing was
one of many foolish popish remedies 'to ease the pain of the dead'.[45] The
impulse to assist the dead is not incompatible with a desire to propitiate
them and guard against their precipitate return. Cultural historians have
identified a range of strategies that late medieval and early modern communities might adopt to protect themselves against revenants, of which the
profane rites (staked body, burial at crossroads) that accompanied the
interment of suicides are the best attested for England.[46]

Despite precautionary measures, the dead sometimes did return, their
presence a distinctly problematic feature on the conceptual map of late
medieval religion. It was orthodox teaching that the dead could not appear
to the living of their own volition, but only under the special providence of
God. Yet, as Thomas More put it, 'no cuntrey ys there in crystendome in
whych he shall not here credably reported of such apparycyons dyvers tymys
there sene and apperyng'.[47] The sources for late medieval ghostly apparitions include didactic visions, exempla from collections of sermons, and
occasionally more circumstantial accounts in chronicles or other sources,

[41] R. Hutton, *The Rise and Fall of Merry England: The Ritual Year 1400–1700* (Oxford, 1994), 305 n.
[42] C. Phythian-Adams, *Desolation of a City: Coventry and the Urban Crisis of the Late Middle Ages* (Cambridge, 1979), 94.
[43] Hutton, *Rise and Fall of Merry England*, 45; N. Z. Davis, 'Ghosts, Kin, and Progeny: Some Features of Family Life in Early Modern France', *Daedalus*, 106 (1977), 93.
[44] *Golden Legend*, i. 287.
[45] J. Hooper, *Early Writings*, ed. S. Carr (PS, 1843), 571, and see below, 128–32, 161.
[46] M. MacDonald and T. Murphy, *Sleepless Souls: Suicide in Early Modern England* (Oxford, 1990), 44–9; Davis, 'Ghosts, Kin, and Progeny', 94; N. Caciola, 'Wraiths, Revenants and Ritual in Medieval Culture', *PP* 152 (1996); 29; E. Musgrave, 'Memento Mori: The Function and Meaning of Breton Ossuaries 1450–1750', in P. Jupp and G. Howarth (eds.), *The Changing Face of Death* (Basingstoke, 1997), 68; R. Scribner, 'The Impact of the Reforma-tion on Daily Life', in *Mensch und Objekt im Mittelalter und in der frühen Neuzeit* (Vienna, 1990), 336–40. For a broader comparative perspective, see P. Barber, *Vampires, Burial, and Death: Folklore and Reality* (New Haven and London, 1988).
[47] More, *Supplication*, 196.

including a vivid compilation of local hauntings by a monk of Byland, North
Yorkshire, from the early fifteenth century.[48] On the basis of these it is
possible to construct a typology of apparitions of the dead (excluding visions
of saints, which present a rather different set of issues). A few souls returned
(temporarily) from hell to exemplify the consequences of sin, but the typical
medieval ghost was a soul from purgatory, often known to the percipient,
and making quite specific requests for assistance from the living.[49] The
ghosts who populated the pages of collections such as *The Golden Legend*
or Mirk's *Festial* were somewhat stereotypical figures whose exploits and
utterances conformed to orthodox templates about the importance of confession, the sanctity of vows, the value of intercessory prayer.[50] Yet attempts
to draw a clear line between the didactic apparitions of preachers' exempla,
and 'real' ghosts are likely to prove as problematic as attempts to disentangle
pristine categories of 'elite' and 'popular' culture. Ecclesiastical exempla
were usually at the end of a chain of transmission that began with an
experienced supernatural event, and in turn they shaped the ways in which
subsequent phenomena would be interpreted and reported. We should pay
attention here to Jean-Claude Schmitt's insight that it is wrong to think of an
immutable 'belief in ghosts' in traditional societies, which the documents
merely record or reflect. Recorded accounts of apparitions were themselves a
constitutive 'part of the process of believing'.[51] Nonetheless, a neatly functionalist model in which ghosts merely objectify Church teaching about the
afterlife, well-ordered social relations, and the taxonomy of sin does not do
justice to the complexity of the theme. Nancy Caciola's important work on
the laity and the 'dangerous dead' in later medieval Europe introduces us to
revenants who were distinctly theologically incorrect—reanimated corpses,
and bodies of the living possessed by wandering spirits of the dead.[52] Most
of the Byland Abbey ghosts were not well-behaved supplicants from purgatory, but grotesque spectres who wrestled with the living, and required
conjuring with invocations and holy water.[53] There are also cases where
recorded apparitions defy any convenient rationalization, and where, to

[48] The standard work on late medieval ghosts is now J.-C. Schmitt, *Ghosts in the Middle
Ages: The Living and the Dead in Medieval Society*, tr. T. Fagan (Chicago and London, 1998).
For the Yorkshire cases, see M. R. James, 'Twelve Medieval Ghost Stories', *EHR* 37 (1922),
translation in J. Shinners (ed.), *Medieval Popular Religion 1000–1500* (Peterborough, Ontario,
1997), 229–37.
[49] It has been estimated that 75% of the ghosts in vision literature were souls from purgatory:
G. Walters, 'Visitacyons, Prevytes, and Deceytys: The Vision in Late Medieval English Popular
Piety', University of Cambridge Ph.D. thesis (1992), 93. Though note the view of one fifteenth-
century writer that 'comonly swyche sprytis arn fendys': P. Barnum (ed.), *Dives and Pauper*,
EETS 275 (1976), 171.
[50] *Golden Legend*, ii. 280–90; T. Erbe (ed.), *Mirk's Festial*, EETS ES 96 (1905), 269–71.
[51] Schmitt, *Ghosts in the Middle Ages*, 221.
[52] Caciola, 'Wraiths, Revenants and Ritual'; 'Spirits Seeking Bodies: Death, Possession and
Communal Memory in the Middle Ages', in *Place of the Dead*.
[53] James, 'Twelve Medieval Ghost Stories', 413–22.

quote Ronald Finucane, 'supernatural beings assume bizarre forms and take to frightening people for no apparent reason'.[54]

Yet the recurrent themes of ghost tales are disjuncture, imbalance, malfunction. Ghosts seem often to have been those who had made a bad end, dying unshriven, or in a violent, sudden manner before the end of their natural span.[55] Or they were those for whom rites of burial or intercession had been inadequately or negligently performed. Almost always, they were the recently dead, fresh in the memory and (sometimes guilty) consciences of those who had known them and their affairs.[56] Encounters with an identifiable dead person were most commonly directed towards 'laying' the ghost, and fixing it irrevocably within its proper spiritual location. If there is any consistent narrative running through the apparition stories of the late Middle Ages, it is not one about maintaining contact between the living and the dead, but about ensuring the finality of their separation. The appearance of a ghost, numinous, portentous, terrifying, was a sign that something, somewhere had gone wrong.

Direct encounters with the dead were only ever the experience of a small minority. We will never know how many late medieval English people thought they had seen a ghost, or knew someone who had. But all our sources stress that apparitions were exceptional not normative occurrences. Thomas More tempered his reflections on the appearance of ghosts throughout the Christian world with a recognition of God's goodness in providing 'that such apparycyons, revelacyons, and myracles, shold not be to copyouse and commune', thereby diluting the merits of simple faith.[57] Yet ghosts are more than a trivial epiphenomenon of pre-Reformation culture. We should take note here of Peter Brown's comment on late antiquity: 'the supernatural becomes the depository of the objectified values of the group'.[58] Late medieval people did not see ghosts because of a conscious desire to maintain personalized contact with dead friends, in the manner of nineteenth-century spiritualists. Rather, ghosts bring sharply into focus a paradox that did much to frame the association between 'society' and 'the dead'—the obligations due to the departed and to their memory, on the one hand, and the desire to forget them, to dissolve their hold on the living, on the other. By their irregular and unpredictable intrusions into the mainstream of contemporary

[54] Finucane, *Appearances of the Dead*, 79–80.

[55] The type is exemplified by the fifteenth-century gentleman Richard Baynard of Messing, Essex, who while out hunting suddenly 'felle downe and dyed with owte howsill and shrifte [communion and confession] and a non after he walkyd and yit doth and hath don moche harme': C. Carpenter (ed.), *The Armburgh Papers: The Brokholes Inheritance in Warwickshire, Hertfordshire and Essex c.1417–c.1453* (Woodbridge, 1998), 62.

[56] Caciola, 'Wraiths, Revenants and Ritual', 27–9; 'Spirits Seeking Bodies', 66–7, 75–9; R. Scribner, 'Elements of Popular Belief', in T. Brady, H. Oberman, and J. Tracey (eds.), *Handbook of European History 1400–1600*, 2 vols. (Leiden, 1994–5), i. 237; Schmitt, *Ghosts in the Middle Ages*, 172.

[57] More, *Supplication*, 197.

[58] Peter Brown, *Society and the Holy in Late Antiquity* (Berkeley, 1982), 318.

religious culture, ghosts provide us with a point of entry into the broader
theme of how the requirement to remember the dead was negotiated in pre-
Reformation communities.

IDIOMS OF MEMORY

In wishing to be remembered after their deaths, the people of late medieval
England did not have in mind some fond, passive recollection, shared among
a restricted circle of family and friends. To 'remember' the dead meant
primarily to include them in one's prayers, and memory in this context
was not an involuntary reflex, or a mental straining after an enacted past.
Rather, it involved a prescribed and understood set of rules and practices for
'calling to mind' in a more formal sense, for refiguring the social presence of
the dead, a virtual re-membering. This had developed over the course of the
Middle Ages in the theory of *memoria*, the naming of the dead in a liturgical
context by the communities charged with praying for them.[59] A leading
scholar of the theme writes that '*memoria* not only commemorated the
departed but made them present through the manipulation of words (especially names) and objects'.[60] Yet this was neither a straightforwardly finite
nor a predictably cyclical process. In the cultural environment of pre-
Reformation England, memory was most often a layered fabric whose
warp and weft involved the living and the dead in a complex pattern of
exchanges and transactions.

Memorialization began with the funeral.[61] Funerals, medieval or otherwise, have generally interested historians because of their obvious typo-
logical significance as 'rites of passage', and because of their equally
evident utility for articulating to us patterns of social and hierarchical
relations. But contemporaries most probably saw them in other terms:
handled correctly, funerals unleashed the 'first massive updraught of prayers
of intercession'.[62] Late medieval funerals were drawn-out affairs, which
began on the eve of the burial with the vespers of the office of the dead
(*placebo*), followed the next day by matins of the dead (*dirige*), and a
requiem mass. The services were intersected by processions with the corpse:
beween *placebo* and *dirige* from the home of the deceased to the church, and

---

[59] On *memoria*, see P. Geary, *Living with the Dead in the Middle Ages* (Ithaca and London,
1994),87–91; id., *Phantoms of Remembrance: Memory and Oblivion at the End of the First
Millennium* (Princeton, 1994), 15–19, 54, 131; D. L. d'Avray, *Death and the Prince: Memorial
Preaching before 1350* (Oxford, 1994), 60, 69–70; O. G. Oexle, 'Die Gegenwart der Toten', in
H. Braet and W. Verbecke (eds.), *Death in the Middle Ages* (Louvain, 1983); K. Schmid and J.
Wollasch (eds.), *Memoria. Der geschichtliche Zeugniswert des liturgischen Gedenkens im
Mittelalter* (Munich, 1984).
[60] Geary, *Phantoms of Remembrance*, 18.
[61] Though this is not an absolute rule. Some tombs were constructed in the lifetime of the
testator, and occasionally chantries were up and running before the death of the founder.
[62] Morgan, 'Of Worms and War', 134.

after mass from the church to the grave.[63] The obsequies were often repeated a month later, at a so-called 'month's mind', and some testators sought to link the two commemorations by arranging for bells to be rung for them every day in the month after their demise.[64] Arrangements for funerals often seem driven by a desire to maximize attendance. In many parishes impending funerals were announced by a bell-man, who would walk the streets with a handbell, identifying the deceased and calling on people to pray for his or her soul.[65] Two categories of strangers seem to have been particularly welcome: priests, and the poor. It was common for small sums to be left to every priest prepared to come to the burial and month's mind and say a mass, and even more so for doles to the poor to be explicitly earmarked for distribution on these occasions.[66] Such posthumous largesse had a quasi-contractual character so well understood that it sometimes did not need to be explicitly articulated. In an archetypal 'gift exchange', recipients would pray for the benefactor, and the prayers of the poor, like those of priests and religious, were believed to be particularly pleasing to the ears of the Lord.[67]

The intitial impetus supplied by a collective local response to the rites of burial was subsequently maintained by the 'professionals' of the chantry system, priests appointed to keep up a daily stream of masses for specified dead individuals. Ideally, a chantry represented a self-perpetuating engine of prayer, fuelled by landed endowment lavish enough to support an unceasing succession of 'soul priests'. However, from the end of the fourteenth century onwards, royal mortmain legislation made it increasingly difficult and expensive to alienate lands permanently into the hands of the Church.[68] There were ways to get round this: some late fifteenth-century Bristol testators employed the legal expedient of the enfeoffment to 'use', and some founders,

[63] Useful summaries in Dinn, 'Death and Rebirth', 153–5; Gittings, *Death, Burial and the Individual*, 31–2.

[64] C. Burgess, '"By Quick and By Dead": Wills and Pious Provision in Late Medieval Bristol', *EHR* 102 (1987), 841; H. Thurston, *The Memory of Our Dead* (1915), 237. See also C. Richmond, 'The Sulyard Papers: The Rewards of a Small Family Archive', in D. Williams (ed.), *England in the Fifteenth Century* (Woodbridge, 1987), 217.

[65] C. Burgess, 'A Service for the Dead: The Form and Function of the Anniversary in Late Medieval Bristol', *Transactions of the Bristol and Gloucestershire Archaeological Society*, 105 (1987), 189; Dinn, 'Death and Rebirth', 154; Duffy, *Altars*, 359; P. Heath, 'Urban Piety in the Later Middle Ages: The Evidence of Hull Wills', in R. B. Dobson (ed.), *The Church, Politics and Patronage in the Fifteenth Century* (Gloucester, 1984), 217; D. Crouch, 'Death in Medieval Scarborough', *YAJ* 72 (2000), 68.

[66] P. Marshall, *The Catholic Priesthood and the English Reformation* (Oxford, 1994), 54; R. B. Dinn, 'Popular Religion in Late Medieval Bury St Edmunds', University of Manchester Ph.D. thesis (1990), 662; Gittings, *Death, Burial, and the Individual*, 37–8; P. H. Cullum and P. J. Goldberg, 'Charitable Provision in Late Medieval York: "To the Praise of God and the Use of the Poor"', *Northern History*, 29 (1993), 24–39.

[67] On the social functions of gift and counter-gift, see M. Mauss, *The Gift: Forms and Functions of Exchange in Archaic Societies*, tr. I. Cunnison (1966); Geary, *Living with the Dead*, 77–92; N. Z. Davis, *The Gift in Sixteenth-Century France* (Oxford, 2000).

[68] S. Raban, *Mortmain Legislation and the English Church 1297–1500* (Cambridge, 1982).

particularly in the north, seem simply to have ignored the restrictions. In Lancashire and Yorkshire (where chantry priests fulfilled important pastoral roles in spread-out moorland parishes), chantry foundation was at its height around 1500; elsewhere it seems to have peaked a century earlier.[69] Attempts to deploy these statistics, and calculations of the volume of intercession in wills more generally, in a positivistic manner to illuminate supposed regional patterns in the intensity of 'belief' in purgatory on the eve of the Reformation, are largely unconvincing.[70] Across all parts of England the testamentary evidence for the early sixteenth century suggests that securing intercessory prayer was a priority for the great majority of those facing death. Where a perpetual chantry was not an option, testators established temporary ones, requiring that a priest should 'sing' for them for a specified period, most commonly a year, but often longer. Alternatively (or additionally) they might call for a specific number of masses, usually the series of thirty known as a trental.[71] These bequests are suggestive of a particular concern with the fate of the soul in the short term, but they do not necessarily reflect a conviction that this provision would be sufficient to ease their soul through purgatory, and many of the soon to be dead planned complementary strategies.

One of the most common of these was the institution of an 'obit'.[72] These annual celebrations, also called anniversaries and 'years-minds', involved an exact re-creation of the funeral rites on the anniversary of the death, with the bell-man going forth once more, candles, mass and *dirige*, doles to the poor,

---

[69] C. Burgess, 'Strategies for Eternity: Perpetual Chantry Foundation in Late Medieval Bristol', in C. Harper-Bill (ed.), *Religious Belief and Ecclesiastical Careers in Late Medieval England* (Woodbridge, 1991), 14; D. MacCulloch, 'England', in A. Pettegree (ed.), *The Early Reformation in Europe* (Cambridge, 1992), 178; Kreider, *Chantries*, 71–92.

[70] This is attempted by R. Whiting, 'Local Responses to the Henrician Reformation', in D. MacCulloch (ed.), *The Reign of Henry VIII: Politics, Policy and Piety* (Basingstoke, 1995), 214, and, more surprisingly, by an early incarnation of the arch-revisionist Christopher Haigh: *Reformation and Resistance in Tudor Lancashire* (Cambridge, 1975), 74–5, where it is suggested that in the early sixteenth century southern England was already 'disillusioned with traditional Catholicism', and diverting resources from intercession to other uses. Local studies do suggest variations, while pointing to an impressive overall level of investment nationally through the first three decades of the sixteenth century. Yet discrepancies in methodology, and in the size and social composition of historians' samples, do much to make regional comparisons rather meaningless. Cf. N. Tanner, *The Church in Late Medieval Norwich 1370–1532* (Toronto, 1984), 101; J. Helt, 'Purgatory, Policy, and Piety in Sixteenth-Century Essex', Vanderbilt University Ph.D. thesis (1996), 26; S. Brigden, *London and the Reformation* (Oxford, 1989), 34; L. Attreed, 'Preparation for Death in Sixteenth-Century Northern England', *SCJ* 13 (1982), 46; R. Whiting, *The Blind Devotion of the People* (Cambridge, 1989), 20; J. J. Scarisbrick, *The Reformation and the English People* (Oxford, 1984), 5–6; Marshall, *Catholic Priesthood*, 51. One should take note here also of Clive Burgess's convincing demonstration that wills significantly underestimate the overall volume of intercession: '"For the Increase of Divine Service": Chantries in the Parish in Late Medieval Bristol', *JEH* 36 (1985), 52; 'Late Medieval Wills and Pious Convention: Testamentary Evidence Reconsidered', in M. A. Hicks (ed.), *Profit, Piety and the Professions* (Gloucester, 1990), 14–33; '"By Quick and By Dead"', 856.

[71] Marshall, *Catholic Priesthood*, 50–4.

[72] The essential guide here is Burgess, 'A Service for the Dead'.

even the presence of a hearse in the parish church. Administered both by parishes and guilds, obits were much cheaper to endow than chantries, typically costing 5s., as opposed to £5 per annum, and were usually intended to last longer. In rural Suffolk, 39 per cent of obits were to continue 'as long as the world stondyth', as were 64 per cent of those founded in fifteenth-century Bristol.[73] The performative and mimetic character of the obit was intended to jog memories, and to draw as many as possible into the collective business of intercessory prayer; they were (in Burgess's phrase) 'obtrusive' celebrations. In towns particularly, obits regularly punctuated the quotidian business of the living, taking place at least once a fortnight in early sixteenth-century Bristol.

The vivid, representational character of obits in bringing the needs of the dead to the attention of the living was shared by tombs and monuments, albeit in a more static manner. Just as obits combined what we might term primary and secondary effects—a mass for the deceased, and inducement to others to pray—the placing and marking of graves involved a series of overlapping calculations. According to the *Festial*, the rationale of burial in consecrated ground was that 'alle schuldon have parte of the suffrages of the masse and of holy chyrch', and patterns of church burial in the late Middle Ages clearly suggest the hope for distinct spiritual benefits from being buried close to the relics, image, or altar of a particular saint, or to the high altar of the church.[74] One Buckinghamshire testator in 1521 seems to be setting up a direct line to heaven in requesting burial 'within the chuncell of Hartwell bifore the myddys of the high awter so that the prist may stande apon my feete in the sacryng of the masse' (i.e. the elevation of the host).[75] But a more conspicuous role of pre-Reformation funeral monuments, made explicit in their iconography and inscriptions, was to serve as foci of intercessory prayer. The fates of the body and of the soul were not divorced; they would be reunited at the Last Day, and in the interim it was hoped that the presence of the body, and its physical memorial, under the eyes of the living would serve to channel remembrance for the soul. The great majority of chantries were established in the parish where the founder was buried, and in addition to saying masses chantry priests were often required to visit the tomb, recite the *De profundis*, and sprinkle it with holy water.[76] Some testators

[73] Dinn, 'Popular Religion in Late Medieval Bury St Edmunds', 564; Burgess, 'A Service for the Dead', 194.

[74] *Mirk's Festial*, 296. Aston, 'Death', 216; Daniell, *Death and Burial in Medieval England*, 97–115; R. Dinn, '"Monuments Answerable to Mens Worth": Burial Patterns, Social Status and Gender in Late Medieval Bury St Edmunds', *JEH* 46 (1995), 237–55.

[75] E. M. Elvey (ed.), *The Courts of the Archdeaconry of Buckingham 1483–1523*, Buckinghamshire Record Society, 19 (1975), 344.

[76] PRO, SP 1/123, 202ᵛ (*LP* xii (2), 436); R. B. Dobson, 'The Foundation of Perpetual Chantries by the Citizens of York', SCH 4 (1967), 35; Heath, 'Urban Piety in the Later Middle Ages', 220; Brigden, *London and the Reformation*, 35; A. Hussey (ed.), *Kent Obit and Lamp Rents*, Kent Records, 14 (1936), 27; F. Skillington, 'Enclosed in Clay: A Study in Leicester Wills', *Leicestershire Archaeological and Historical Society Transactions*, 42 (1966–7), 39.

clearly gave thought to how to draw attention to their monument. Making his will in 1487, the London goldsmith Edmund Shaa directed that whenever common assemblies of the mayor, aldermen, and commons were held in the church of St Thomas of Acres, the door of his chapel was to be opened, 'to the intent that his fellowship might among their devout meditations remember the poor soul of his body there lying interred'.[77] The growing popularity in early sixteenth-century London of tomb-chests doubling as Easter sepulchres (where crucifix and sacrament were symbolically interred between Good Friday and Easter Sunday) similarly suggests an impulse to link the individual's memorial with the corporate worship of the community.[78]

Tombs and monuments were multi-media productions, combining text, representational realism, and iconographic symbolism. Most included some depiction of the deceased person, either in the three dimensions of effigial sculpture, or the two of the engraved brass plate: 'it was the human form which prompted commemoration and jogged the memory'.[79] Though there was no iconographic tradition of depicting the deceased in purgatory, tombs sometimes focused on the fate of the post-mortem body. Brasses depicting the bodies of the deceased in their shroud became common in the last quarter of the fifteenth century, and a significant minority of both brasses and sculpted tombs represented the corpse in a state of advancing physical decay, skeletal and worm-eaten.[80] Though art historians have puzzled over the precise range of meanings of these 'cadaver tombs', a primary purpose was surely the employment of 'shock tactics' to arouse the pity of spectators, and move them to prayer. Some monuments combined such representation with the motto 'suche as we are, such schall ye be / And suche as we were, suche be ye', a classic memento mori, which asserted the common destiny and identity of living and dead.[81]

Indirect methods of eliciting prayer were usually accompanied by overt requests, a development accelerated in the fifteenth century by the growing affordability of monumental brasses allowing for the incorporation of more

[77] K. L. Wood-Legh, *Perpetual Chantries in Britain* (Cambridge, 1965), 305 n.

[78] B. Cherry, 'An Early Sixteenth-Century London Tomb Design', *Architectural History*, 27 (1984), 89–90.

[79] J. Middleton-Stewart, 'Personal Commemoration in Late Medieval Suffolk: The Deanery of Dunwich 1370–1547', University of East Anglia Ph.D. thesis (1995), 282.

[80] M. Norris, *Monumental Brasses: The Memorials*, 2 vols. (1977), i. 206–8; P. King, 'The English Cadaver Tomb in the Late Fifteenth Century: Some Indications of a Lancastrian Connection', in J. Taylor (ed.), *Dies Illa: Death in the Middle Ages* (Liverpool, 1984); id., 'The Cadaver Tomb in England: Novel Manifestations of an Old Idea', *Church Monuments*, 5 (1990), 26–36; K. Cohen, *Metamorphosis of a Death Symbol: The Transi Tomb in the Late Middle Ages and the Renaissance* (Berkeley, Calif., 1973); Binski, *Medieval Death*, 139–52.

[81] Norris, *Monumental Brasses: The Memorials*, i. 175. The phrase originated with the medieval legend of 'The Three Living and the Three Dead', which told of a party of three carefree young nobles confronted in a cemetery by three decaying corpses: see Daniell, *Death and Burial in Medieval England*, 69; Binski, *Medieval Death*, 134–8; Caciola, 'Wraiths, Revenants and Ritual', 24–6.

textual material into the overall design. As Richard Rex has pointed out, the dominance of English over Latin as the predominant language of inscriptions predates the Reformation and seems designed to maximize their ability to garner prayers.[82] Pre-Reformation epitaphs usually began with the phrase 'orate pro anima...' or 'pray for the soul of...' (in Norfolk, in the first decade of the sixteenth century, 86 per cent did so), or concluded poignantly 'cuius anima propitietur deus...', 'on whose soul God have pardon...'.[83] Though occasionally florid and discursive, pre-Reformation epitaphs were usually brief and to the point. They include the name and rank of the deceased and usually the date of their death—in order to encourage prayer on the anniversary. A study of requests for brass memorials in Norfolk wills has demonstrated that testators usually wanted their monuments in place within one year, to increase the impact of an anniversary celebration.[84] Inscriptions were not all sparsely functional. They could provide scope for individual pious and devotional expression, and also for the celebration of worldly 'fame'. A memorial board in St Mary Redcliffe, Bristol, commemorating the merchant William Canynges (d. 1474) itemized in great detail his earthly accomplishments, including the tonnage of his ten ships, and concluded that 'no age nor time can wear out well-woon fame'.[85] Eulogistic descriptions of worldly achievement were appearing on a growing minority of tombs by the early sixteenth century, but can hardly be regarded as a harbinger of theological change.[86] In many cases, the recording of good deeds was designed to underline particular worthiness for prayer, as with the inscription for Thomas Gray and his wife Benet (1520) in the parish church of Cople, Bedfordshire:

> Yit, we trust to be had in memory,
> As longe as the paryshe of Coople shall last
> For our benefitis don to it largely,
> As witnesse xx^{ti} pownd with other giftis many,
> Wherfor all cristen men that goo by this way
> Pray for the soulis of Benet and Thomas Gray.[87]

The idiom of memory was thus generically an importunate one, serving to assert the (competing?) claims of individuals among the virtuous dead. In

[82] Houlbrooke, *Death*, 345; R. Rex, 'Monumental Brasses and the Reformation', *Transactions of the Monumental Brass Society*, 15 (1990), 386.

[83] J. Finch, *Church Monuments in Norfolk before 1830: An Archaeology of Commemoration* (Oxford, 2000), 71–2; Rex, 'Monumental Brasses'; S. Brigden, 'Religion and Social Obligation in Early Sixteenth-Century London', *PP* 103 (1984), 68.

[84] J. R. Greenwood, 'Wills and Brasses: Some Conclusions from a Norfolk Study', in J. Bertram (ed.), *Monumental Brasses as Art and History* (Stroud, 1996), 92–4.

[85] I. M. Roper, *The Monumental Effigies of Gloucestershire and Bristol* (Gloucester, 1931), 122–5.

[86] A point made by Duffy, *Altars*, 333.

[87] G. Isherwood, *Monumental Brasses in the Bedfordshire Churches* (1906), 21–2. See also F. A. Greenhill, *Incised Effigial Slabs: A Study of Engraved Stone Memorials in Latin Christendom c.1100 to c.1700*, 2 vols. (1976), i. 319, 324.

addition to tombs and brasses, the fabric and furnishings of the parish church itself comprised a field of memory, on which parishioners could inscribe a post-mortem presence through the pious donation of objects personalized with names and coats of arms. Where, as was often the case, the gifts involved were requisite to the liturgy—missals, vestments, chalices—individuals hoped to achieve a perpetual linkage of their own names with the corporate worship of the community.[88] In the words of Colin Richmond, 'to walk into a parish church around 1500 was to enter (as it were) an ante-chamber of purgatory. Almost everything was labelled with the names of local souls who required assistance; almost everything in use was an *aide-mémoire*'.[89] The interior fittings of the church might well conform to this typology. The rood screen, 'the most important single focus of imagery in the people's part of the church', frequently declared the identity of the donor, as did stained-glass windows.[90]

Gifts to the parish church often generated an additional textual record, in the claims of the donor to be included on the parochial bede-roll, an instrument of commemoration which perhaps more than any other exemplifies the logic of *memoria*. Bede-rolls were lists of benefactors with details of the bequests they had left, and were maintained by virtually all parishes and by many guilds. They were usually recited at least once a year in full, and in a shortened form during the priest's bidding prayers at the weekly Sunday mass. Payments to the curate for their annual recitation (clearly a laborious task) pepper the accounts of a number of pre-Refomation parishes.[91] Bede-rolls served a dual function, providing benefactors with an opportunity to become the focus of intercessory prayer, and parishes with a means for

---

[88] On this theme, see Burgess, 'The Benefactions of Mortality', 72–3; id., '"Longing to be Prayed For": Death and Commemoration in an English Parish in the Later Middle Ages', in *Place of the Dead*, 64; Middleton-Stewart, 'Personal Commemoration in Late Medieval Suffolk', 181; Duffy, *Altars*, 330, who notes that inscribed liturgical books, vessels, and vestments, intended in the first instance for use in temporary chantries, usually subsequently passed into parochial use.

[89] C. Richmond, 'Religion', in Horrox (ed.), *Fifteenth-Century Attitudes*, 186.

[90] E. Duffy, 'The Parish, Piety, and Patronage in Late Medieval East Anglia: The Evidence of Rood Screens', in K. French, G. Gibbs, and B. Kümin (eds.), *The Parish in English Life 1400–1600* (Manchester, 1997), 136; C. R. Councer (ed.), *Lost Glass from Kent Churches*, Kent Records, 22 (1980).

[91] H. Littlehales (ed.), *The Medieval Records of a London City Church (St Mary at Hill)*, EETS 128 (1905), 21, 149, 184, 213, 229, 263, 309, 339, 342, 349, 381; A. Hanham (ed.), *Churchwardens' Accounts of Ashburton 1479–1580*, Devon and Cornwall Record Society, NS 18 (1970), 2, 8, 38, 44, 95; E. Hobhouse (ed.), *Churchwardens' Accounts of Croscombe, Pilton, Yatton, Tintinhull, Morebath, and St Michael's, Bath, 1349–1560*, Somerset Record Society, 4 (1890), 192, 229; Cox, *Churchwardens' Accounts*, 62; Whiting, *Blind Devotion of the People*, 19–20. For examples of parochial bede-rolls, see J. Williams, 'The Black Book of Swaffham', *Norfolk Archaeology*, 33 (1965), 243–53; Hobhouse (ed.), *Churchwardens' Accounts*, 210–19; C. Burgess (ed.), *The Pre-Reformation Records of All Saints', Bristol: Part 1*, Bristol Record Society, 46 (1995), 4–30. Further discussion in F. Gasquet, *Parish Life in Medieval England* (1906), 222–5; Duffy, *Altars*, 334–7; Burgess '"Longing to be Prayed For"'.

advertising the benefits of generosity to the church. For both purposes, naming was essential. In the little Devon parish of Morebath, a bede-roll was begun in 1520 so that the parishioners might see 'how this churche was prevaylyd by the dethe of all those persons that here after ys expressyd by name'.[92] The more elaborate benefaction list of the Bristol parish of All Saints included a lengthy prefatory section showing why it was important that the good deeds of benefactors 'be rehearsed and shown yearly unto you by name ... that they shall not be forgotten but be had in remembrance and be prayed for of all this parish that be now and all of them that be to come, and also for an example to all you that be now living'.[93]

Any attempt to bring about a pure distillation of motives here seems likely to be frustrated. Did the dying (a category which includes any who reflected on their own mortality) choose particular strategies of remembrance out of purely utilitarian calculations about what would maximize benefit for their soul, or were their choices shaded either by a vainglorious desire to leave their mark, or by an altruistic impulse to assist the living? Revisionist scholarship on these themes has tended to stress the seamless dovetailing of self-interest and altrusim, and the reciprocal character of a flow of spiritual and material benefits between living and dead members of the community.[94] Yet an alternative historiographical tradition maintains that it was individuals' fear of punishment in the next life which was the essential motor of the whole intercessory industry. The official abrogation of purgatory in the mid-sixteenth century, suggests Alan Kreider, must have 'brought joyful release from an acutely existential dread'.[95]

That the representation of purgatory in contemporary religious culture constituted a fearsome prospect can hardly be denied. It was a homilists' cliché that the pains of purgatory were worse than any earthly pain that could be imagined or experienced (even by the martyrs of the Church); that they were equal to the pains of hell.[96] Yet such accounts must be read contextually. Preachers certainly sought to instil fear, but not a fear without remedy. Fear of God's punishment was intended to be a dynamic process

[92] Hobhouse (ed.), *Churchwardens' Accounts*, 210.

[93] Burgess (ed.), *Pre-Reformation Records of All Saints'*, 4.

[94] Burgess, '"A Fond Thing Vainly Invented"', 56–84; Duffy, *Altars*, 364; B. Kümin, *The Shaping of a Community: The Rise and Reformation of the English Parish c.1400–1560* (Aldershot, 1996), 109, 223–4; J. A. Goodall, *God's House at Ewelme: Life, Devotion and Architecture in a Fifteenth-Century Almshouse* (Aldershot, 2001), 205.

[95] Wood-Legh, *Perpetual Chantries*, 313; Kreider, *Chantries*, 41, 93. See also A. G. Dickens, *The English Reformation*, 2nd edn. (1989), 29–30, and the recent survey by Christopher Marsh, *Popular Religion in Sixteenth-Century England* (Basingstoke, 1998), 66, which maintains that the fear of purgatory 'has been unhelpfully dismissed in recent analyses'.

[96] *Ordynare of Crysten Men*, Il2ʳ; *Lytel Boke, that Speketh of Purgatorye*, A1ᵛ, A4ʳ–B4ʳ; *Golden Legend*, i. 179, ii. 282; *A Devout Treatyse called the Tree and xii Frutes of the Holy Goost*, ed. J. Vaissier (Groningen, 1960), 27; More, *Supplication*, 225–6; Fisher, *English Works*, 10, 54–5; *Two Fruytfull Sermons*, 24–6, 34–5.

leading to contrition and amendment.[97] A wide range of sources stressed that good works performed in this life were highly efficacious for reducing time in purgatory. John Fisher, for example, evoked the 'grevouse paynes of purgatory' explicitly in order to 'quycken and styre theym so to lyve here, that after our departure hence we be not arested by the waye'.[98] The conclusion of Carlos Eire, in a recent study of the mortuary culture of sixteenth-century Spain, seems apposite here: 'belief in purgatory lessened anxiety over death by means of a paradox and by setting in motion a dialectic between terror and confidence'.[99] Preaching on the pains of purgatory was not usually *ad hominem*. The case of Thomas Kyrkeby, parish priest of Halsall in Lancashire, who told his parishioners from the pulpit in 1531 that the souls of their fathers and mothers were 'brennyng in the payne of purgatorie or hell', was clearly exceptional, albeit many were reported to have taken his words for true and been much distressed by them.[100]

The extent to which people may have 'felt' fear in the contemplation of purgatory is epistemologically and methodologically difficult to establish. The *Lytel Boke, that Speketh of Purgatorye* rhetorically justified its concern with post-mortem punishment by noting that 'fewe it drede'.[101] Wills, of course, provide the most obvious point of entry here, and it is not hard to multiply examples of testators wanting large numbers of masses (usually a thousand) to be said in the period shortly after death, and demanding that such intercessions begin 'as soon after my departyng as may be done', 'immediately as by man erthly it may be perceyved that my soule shuld be from my body separate'.[102] Recent studies, however, have usually concluded that these types of bequests were not normative.[103] While some testators evidently hoped to take the citadel of heaven by sudden storm, rather more

[97] For contemporary typologies of fear, see my 'Fear, Purgatory and Polemic in Reformation England', in W. G. Naphy and P. Roberts (eds.), *Fear in Early Modern Society* (Manchester, 1997), 150–66. Note here also the perceptive comment of Matsuda, *Death and Purgatory*, 236–7, that the doctrine 'provided an ideological context within which what had been biblical or patristic aphorisms of a general nature could function as specific pieces of pragmatic wisdom for an individual making preparations for death'.

[98] Fisher, *Two Fruytfull Sermons*, 3. See also *The Interpretacyon and Sygnyfycacyon of the Masse* (1532), K1[r]; More, *Supplication*, 219; *Lytel Boke*, A2[r], B2[v]; E. Arber (ed.), *The Revelation to the Monk of Evesham* (1901), 39. The *Ordynare of Crysten Men*, ll2[r], taught that one tear of penitence shed in this life was of more effect that ten years in the pains of purgatory.

[99] C. Eire, *From Madrid to Purgatory: The Art and Craft of Dying in Sixteenth-Century Spain* (Cambridge, 1995), 520. For a parallel argument, see L. J. Taylor, 'God of Judgement, God of Love: Catholic Preaching in France, 1460–1560', *Historical Reflections / Réflexions Historiques*, 26 (2000), 247–68.

[100] H. Fishwick (ed.), *Pleadings and Depositions in the Duchy Court of Lancaster*, Lancashire and Cheshire Record Society, 32 (1896), 199.

[101] *Lytel Boke*, A1[r].

[102] For example, J. Weaver and A. Beardwood (eds.), *Some Oxfordshire Wills Proved in the Prerogative Court of Canterbury, 1393–1510*, Oxfordshire Record Society (1958), 96; J. Raine (ed.), *Testamenta Eboracensia*, V, SS 79 (1884), 33; F. W. Weaver (ed.), *Somerset Medieval Wills 1501–30*, Somerset Record Society, 19 (1903), 72.

[103] Tanner, *The Church in Late Medieval Norwich*, 102–3; Heath, 'Urban Piety in the Later Middle Ages', 227; Duffy, *Altars*, 346–7; Marshall, *Catholic Priesthood*, 54.

envisaged a drawn-out siege, opting for a combination of the short-, medium-, and long-term devices that have been elaborated above. It seems unlikely that the people of early Tudor England were walking around in a state of 'acute existential dread', but the evidence does suggest that (among the will-making classes, at least), the Church's teaching on purgatory and the need for intercession had been widely internalized. The fact that such a broad range of strategies was employed indicates how closely the commemoration of the dead was bound up with wider patterns of social and religious organization. But the sheer variety of idioms of memory suggests, if not a lack of clarity, at least an extreme broad-mindedness about how intercession for the dead was actually believed to work. It is worth reflecting on this a little further, not least because it was a theme which was to be central to the reformers' attempt to undermine the entire system.

In the view of hostile observers, in the sixteenth century and since, medieval Catholic teaching on the attainment of salvation has appeared highly mechanistic, to represent, in the memorable phrase of J. T. Rosenthal, 'the purchase of paradise'.[104] But in fact a closer look reveals a system which was anything but straightforwardly and predictably 'mechanistic' in its operation. Preaching at the month's mind of Lady Margaret Beaufort in 1509, John Fisher adduced a host of reasons for the 'evydent lyklyhode and coniecture' that her soul was already in heaven: 'Yf the herty prayer of many persons, yf her owne contynuall prayer in her lyf tyme, yf the sacraments of the chirche orderly taken, yf indulgences and pardons graunted by divers popes, yf true repentaunce and teeres, yf fayth and devocyon in Criste Ihesu, yf charyte to her neyghbours, yf pyte upon the poore, yf forgyveness of iniuries, or yf good workes'—if all of these were 'avaylable' [i.e. efficacious], then her attainment of paradise was 'almoost certayne'.[105] This was, in a sense, a report on the successful management of a portfolio of different types of intercessory options. Fisher had no direct interest in advancing the claims of one of them over the others, but many devotional writers, like rival financial advisers, offered guidance on how to maximize the return on spiritual, and indeed monetary, investment.

According to *The Golden Legend*, there were three reasons why suffrages offered for the souls in purgatory actually helped them: their merits, having deserved such suffrages in life; their need, being unable to help themselves; and their unity with the living: 'the dead are one body with the Church militant, and the goods of the latter must be common to all'.[106] On the eve of the Reformation it was usually taught that three things were most beneficial to the dead—prayers, alms-giving, and masses—a schema variously attributed to St Augustine or St Gregory, and endorsed in the Council

---

[104] J. T. Rosenthal, *The Purchase of Paradise: Gift Giving and the Aristocracy 1307–1485* (1972).
[105] Fisher, *English Works*, 309.
[106] *Golden Legend*, ii. 289.

of Florence's decree of 1439. Often, fasting was added to the list.[107] Of these there was a broad consensus that the mass was most efficacious. John Lydgate's poem *The Vertue of the Masse*, printed twice in the early sixteenth century, suggested that 'a masse is egall to crystes passion / To help soules out of purgatory'.[108] This was in a sense sound theology, rather than gross hyperbole, given the orthodox teaching that the sacrifice of the mass was substantially identical to that of Calvary, the application in space and time of the merits of Christ's redemptive passion. Yet if a single mass was of such efficacy, why was it necessary to multiply them, and to direct their efficacy to certain individuals? The issue had been squarely faced, if not entirely clearly resolved, by Archbishop Pecham's constitutions of 1281, which taught that though the sacrifice of Christ is of infinite virtue 'nevertheless in the sacrament or sacrifice it does not operate in the fullness of its immensity; otherwise there would never be need to say more than one mass for a deceased person. For in these mysteries He is operative by a certain distribution of his fullness which He himself fixed to them'.[109] The mass in other words, operated as a quantifiable unit of merit, whose effectuality could be diluted or intensified. Once this principle had been established, questions of how to maximize its efficacy were bound to be considered. All masses were equal, but some were more equal than others.

Though it was the universal teaching of orthodox theologians that the mass worked *ex opere operato* not *ex opere operantibus* (that is, by virtue of the work itself not the moral condition of the priest celebrating it), the distinction was clouded by the claims some devotional writers made for new priests' first masses, when they were 'wont to prepare themself more devoutly'.[110] That many laypeople may not have understood or completely accepted the *operato/operantibus* distinction is suggested by the frequency with which testators imposed moral qualifications on the priests to celebrate for them—'an honest priest', one 'of good name and fame'.[111]

Other laypeople evinced an interest in particular votive masses: masses of the Trinity, of the name of Jesus, of the Five Wounds, or the seven so-called 'golden masses', which could produce souls 'flyeng out of purgatorye as

[107] *Mirk's Festial*, 269, 296; *Lytel Boke*, D1ᵛ; *Golden Legend*, ii. 284; S. Powell and A. Fletcher, '"In Die Sepulture seu Trigintale": The Late Medieval Funeral and Memorial Sermon', *Leeds Studies in English*, 12 (1981), 197; Marc'hadour, 'Introduction', in More, *Supplication*, p. xciii.

[108] H. Huth and W. Hazlitt (eds.), *Fugitive Tracts* (1875), no. 3. See also *The Interpretacyon and Sygnyfycacyon of the Masse*, E2ʳ, E4ᵛ.

[109] Cited in Wood-Legh, *Perpetual Chantries*, 307–8.

[110] *The Interpretacyon and Sygnyfycacyon of the Masse*, B4ʳ, which went on to claim that God reserved certain souls to be released from purgatory on these occasions, perhaps as many as there were folk hearing the mass.

[111] In the first three decades of the sixteenth century, almost half the testators requesting masses specified either an individual or a particular type of priest to celebrate: Marshall, *Catholic Priesthood*, 50–9.

thycke as sparkes of fyre'.[112] Of these the most popular appears to have been the Trental of St Gregory. The associated legend maintained that after her (unshriven) death, Gregory's mother had appeared to him and begged for the special series of thirty masses; requests for the trental can be found in wills from all parts of England in the early sixteenth century.[113] Duffy attributes its appeal to the fact that it defined a recognizable genre, 'the revelation of the secrets of the other world by a suffering spirit . . . who reveals a specially privileged form of devotion'. In this it resembled the revelation to St Bridget of the potency of the prayers known as the 'Fifteen Oes'; the efficacy of the penitential psalms advocated in the *Gast of Guy*, and the elaborate series of 300 masses interspersed with recitations of the psalm *Miserere mei deus* and the hymn *Veni creator spiritus* in the 'Revelacyone schewed to ane holy woman'.[114] Some of these privileged sequences can seem obscure at this remove, such as 'the same masses that Pope Innocent did syng for his mother wich be xiii masses', requested by a Cheshire testator in 1526.[115] Another de luxe model was 'masses of scala coeli', which drew their special potency from an indulgence attached to a church outside Rome, where St Bernard had enjoyed a vision of souls ascending a ladder to heaven. By around 1470, an English guidebook to Rome was reporting that if a mass was said for a soul in the chapel it would 'at once be free from the pains of purgatory'. In 1476 the indulgence was transferred to a royal chapel within the palace of Westminster, a grant renewed by Henry VII in 1500, and in around 1516 the indulgence was acquired by the wealthy guild of St Mary at Boston, Lincolnshire.[116]

There was a distinct, if patchy, interest in all these forms of 'quick-fix' intercession. Trentals, for example, particularly the St Gregory Trental, seem to have been very popular in Bury St Edmunds, reasonably so in Hull and Colchester, and less so in Norwich and Scarborough.[117] In all places, the majority of testators seemed content to ask for 'regular' requiem masses. Yet the inflated claims made for privileged devotions were attracting hostile attention long before the Reformation. At the end of the fourteenth century

---

[112] *Interpretacyon and Sygnyfycacyon of the Masse*, C1ᵛ.

[113] For example, Weaver (ed.), *Somerset Medieval Wills 1501–30*, 72, 223; C. W. Foster (ed.), *Lincoln Wills 1505–1530*, Lincoln Record Society, 10 (1918), 141, 207; A. Cirket (ed.), *English Wills, 1498–1526*, Befordshire Historical Record Society, 37 (1956), 47; J. Raine (ed.), *The Injunctions and Other Ecclesiastical Proceedings of Richard Barnes, Bishop of Durham*, SS 22 (1850), p. v; G. M. Benton (ed.), *Essex Wills at Canterbury*, Transactions of the Essex Archaeological Society, 21 (1937), 261.

[114] Duffy, *Altars*, 370–3, 218, 249–56; C. Horstman (ed.), *Yorkshire Writers*, 2 vols. (1895), i. 384–91.

[115] G. Piccope (ed.), *Lancashire and Cheshire Wills and Inventories from the Ecclesiastical Court, Chester*, Chetham Society, 33 (1857), 11.

[116] N. Morgan, 'The Scala Coeli Indulgence and the Royal Chapels', in B. Thompson (ed.), *The Reign of Henry VII* (Stamford, 1995), 87–91; Duffy, *Altars*, 375–6.

[117] Dinn, 'Death and Rebirth in Late Medieval Bury St Edmunds', 164; Heath, 'Urban Piety in the Later Middle Ages', 219; Marshall, *Catholic Priesthood*, 54; Tanner, *The Church in Late Medieval Norwich*, 102–3; Crouch, 'Death in Medieval Scarborough', 70.

Wyclif had attacked prelates who 'maken the peple to bileve or triste that if a prest seye a masse at scala celi for a soule it schal onoon ben out of purgatorie'.[118] The St Gregory Trental was attacked by the fifteenth-century moralistic treatise *Dives and Pauper* (printed in the early 1530s), which insisted that it was wrong for priests to abandon masses of the day to say special masses or trentals, and particularly castigated the advocates of the Gregorian Trental for deceiving souls and bringing about 'moche simony and moche hypocrisie, and moche foly'.[119] Such condemnations are a back-handed compliment to the devotion's fashionable appeal. But the consumer-ist interest in the various offers of super-potent intercession inevitably raised something of a question mark over the credibility of the system as a whole. If the St Gregory Trental and other votive masses really fulfilled the claims that were made for them, then what was point in persisting with ordinary masses for the dead?[120] This was a question some contemporaries considered even more pertinent with regard to the theory and practice of indulgences.

Indulgences were certificates issued by the Church declaring that part or all of the penances incurred by a sinner had been remitted. They did not forgive sins per se (this was achieved by sacramental confession), but the penalties or punishment due for sins which would otherwise have to be paid in this world, or in purgatory.[121] To date, there has been no comprehensive study of indulgences in the religious culture of late medieval England, and this is not the place to attempt it. Recent work has made clear, however, that Christopher Haigh's contention that 'indulgences did not play a big part in English religion' requires considerable qualification.[122] It is noteworthy that the earliest datable piece of printing undertaken in England was Sixtus IV's bull of 1476, which for the first time explicitly extended the benefits of indulgences to the souls in purgatory.[123] Almost fifty indulgences are known to have been printed in England in the 1520s alone, and many more must not have survived.[124] Masses of Scala Coeli or the Name of

---

[118] Morgan, 'The Scala Coeli Indulgence', 85.

[119] *Dives and Pauper* (1534), 266ᵛ–68ʳ.

[120] The recipient of the early fifteenth-century 'revelacyone schewed to ane holy woman' asked the ghost appearing to her 'what prophete it was for a saule to say mo messis of the trynyte and of oure lady and of saynt Petir, thane it was of requiem[?]' She received a demonstration, but no convincing explanation: Horstman (ed.), *Yorkshire Writers*, i. 385.

[121] A useful summary of the role of indulgences within the Church's penitential system is supplied by E. Cameron, *The European Reformation* (Oxford, 1991), 79–83.

[122] C. Haigh, *English Reformations: Religion, Politics, and Society under the Tudors* (Oxford, 1993), 70. Cf. Morgan, 'The Scala Coeli Indulgence'; R. N. Swanson, *Church and Society in Late Medieval England* (Oxford, 1989), 293–4; id. (ed.), *Catholic England* (Manchester, 1993), 201–10; N. Orme, 'Indulgences in the Diocese of Exeter 1100–1536', *Reports and Transactions of the Devonshire Association*, 120 (1988), 15–32; Duffy, *Altars*, 288–92. See also K. W. Cameron, *The Pardoner and his Pardons: Indulgences Circulating in England on the Eve of the Reformation* (Hartford, Conn., 1965); C. Holdworth, 'On Some Pardons or Indulgences Preserved in Yorkshire, 1412–1527', *YAJ* 16 (1902), 369–423.

[123] Marc'hadour, 'Introduction', in More, *Supplication*, p. lxx.

[124] White, 'Early Print and Purgatory', 90.

Jesus had indulgences attached to them, as did certain places of burial, most notably the 'pardon churchyard' of St Paul's Cathedral in London.[125] In the Norfolk parish of Swaffham, a list of papal indulgences granted for various acts of piety was bound together with the fifteenth-century bede-roll.[126] The most striking evidence for their ubiquity has been uncovered as historians have begun to explore the print culture of late fifteenth- and early sixteenth-century England. In the prayer books for use of the laity known as primers or books of hours, offers of pardon abounded, often associated with the saying of specified prayers in front of a devotional picture of the instruments of Christ's passion, the 'Image of Pity'.[127] There was a distinctly unregulated, 'free-market' feel about this. The amounts of indulgence specified were frequently implausibly large, 26,000 years or more, and were offered for each successive repetition of the prayers. Such promises clearly enjoyed no episcopal or papal sanction, but there was little attempt to crack down, and the availability of often apocryphal indulgences was commonly displayed on colophons and title pages as an inducement to purchase. As Eamon Duffy has pointed out, some indulgence rubrics mangled the already somewhat arcane theology of penal remission, offering different tariffs for mortal and venial sins, and promising to commute the pains of hell into those of purgatory, and those of purgatory into the joys of heaven.[128]

The impression of a genuine popular enthusiasm for collecting indulgences is confirmed by the phenomenon of so-called 'pardon brasses', whereby the subjects of memorials attempted to induce more bystanders to pray for their soul. Some of these were clearly as spurious as the Image of Pity indulgences. The 1506 brass to Roger and Elizabeth Legh in the Savage Chapel in Macclesfield offered, in return for five pater nosters, five aves, and a creed, 26,000 years and twenty-six days of remission in purgatory. Others provided considerably more modest incentives, but with stronger guarantees of authenticity. The brass of John Marsham (1525) in St John Maddermarket, Norwich concluded 'Ye shall not lose your charitable devotion; xii cardinals have granted you xii days of pardon', and another Norwich citizen, Robert Gardener, made a bequest in 1508 for an indulgence to be purchased from Rome granting 300 days of pardon to every well-disposed person who prayed at his grave for his and his two wives' souls.[129]

Even before Luther took his celebrated stand on the issue, there were figures in the Church who were concerned and perplexed by indulgences.

---

[125] On indulgenced masses, see R. W. Pfaff, *New Liturgical Feasts in Later Medieval England* (Oxford, 1970), 62–6; on the pardon churchyard, see below, 107.

[126] Williams, 'The Black Book of Swaffham', 253.

[127] Swanson, *Church and Society*, 293–4; Duffy, *Altars*, 288–9.

[128] Duffy, *Altars*, 290–1.

[129] M. Norris, *Monumental Brasses: The Craft* (1978), 62; Tanner, *The Church in Late Medieval Norwich*, 102. See also Norris, *Monumental Brasses*, i. 175; Orme, 'Indulgences in the Diocese of Exeter', 26; Greenhill, *Incised Effigial Slabs*, i. 319.

Although the 'years' and 'days' specified by pardons expressed an equivalence to periods of earthly penance, there was an understandably widespread perception that what was on offer was a reduction of that length of time in purgatory. Erasmus condemned as self-delusionists those who 'measure the length of their time in purgatory as if by water-clock, counting centuries, years, months, days and hours as though there were a mathematical table to calculate them accurately', though he prudently restricted his critique to 'imaginary pardons'.[130] Yet the legitimate acquisition of large numbers of years of remission, and especially plenary indulgences (which granted a complete remission of penalties for sin), might seem to make the laborious business of endowing prayers, obits, and masses (even special votive masses) distinctly otiose. In the main, however, people do not appear to have believed that it did. For all their prominence in later Protestant polemic, indulgences appear to have played a rather subsidiary role in the overall drama of good works performed for the dead, and popular attitudes towards them remain hard to fathom. There may even have been something of a 'flag-day' attitude to the issue of some indulgences, in which small sums were gladly given in the service of good causes, such as the upkeep of churches.[131] As fast as some authorities (including, of course, the papacy itself) sought to promote indulgences, others played them down, advising that it was foolhardy to rely on them exclusively. In official theology at least, indulgences were far from being 'magically' efficacious. They depended on proper confession and contrition, and one could never be sure that some moral fault on the part either of the purchaser or the beneficiary might not have impeded their validity, making them as worthless as the paper on which they had been printed.[132]

Whether or not it was a source of persistent anxiety, the successful negotiation of their fate in the afterlife was clearly a matter of paramount concern to the people of late medieval England—how could it not have been? The key to success (after a virtuous life in this world) was a facility for mastering the social, cultural, and theological grammar of remembrance. The language of post-mortem commemoration was rich and complex, its

[130] Erasmus, *Praise of Folly*, ed. A. Levi, tr. B. Radice (Harmondsworth, 1971), 126–7. There were side-swipes at indulgences in the *Colloquies* also, the folly of pinning one's hopes of salvation 'on a piece of parchment instead of on a moral life': *The Colloquies of Erasmus*, tr. C. R. Thompson (Chicago, 1965), 7, 627.

[131] This is suggested by Orme, 'Indulgences in the Diocese of Exeter', 16. See also Swanson, *Church and Society*, 227–8; B. Nilson and R. H. Frost, 'The Archiepiscopal Indulgences for the City of York 1450–1500', in D. M. Smith (ed.), *The Church in Medieval York* (York, 1999), 113–22.

[132] W. Bonde, *Pylgrimage of Perfection*, cited in White, 'Early Print and Purgatory', 84; T. More, *The Confutation of Tyndale's Answer*, ed. L. A. Schuster et al. (New Haven, 1973), 289–90; *Lytel Boke*, E1ʳ⁻ᵛ, E2ᵛ. The same point was made by St Catherine of Genoa, *Treatise on Purgatory*, tr. C. Balfour and H. Irvine, new edn. (1976), 31. The rubrics themselves usually confined themselves to specifying that the requisite prayers were to be said 'devoutly': see e.g. Duffy, *Altars*, pl. 85; Cameron, *Pardoner and his Pardons*, 56.

idioms cut across each other, and at times appeared contradictory. Its valid-ating principle was an internal logic of agreed social and ritual convention. As with the doctrine of purgatory itself, its inconsistencies were a direct function of its popular appeal and its 'consumer-led' character. Under the harsh mortality regime of pre-industrial England, the demands of the dead for memory were potentially insatiable. In practice they had to be managed, prioritized, and limited. The following section explores how this was achieved, and in the process it will attempt to add light and shade to the familiar insight that, before the onset of the Reformation, the living and the dead comprised a single 'community'.

THE LIMITS OF REMEMBRANCE

As an imagined social presence, the dead of late medieval England mirrored the living in some fairly evident ways. Most obviously, though preachers and painters might present death as the great social leveller, dragging the great and the little along together in the 'Dance of Death', the ability to perpetuate one's memory bore a direct relationship to worldly wealth and status. The explicit commodification of endowed masses as the most potent instrument of intercession made the point, as did the expense of permanent memorials. Drawing up a contract with the Lincoln marbler John Hippis in 1515 for a tomb in Wollaton church for himself and his wife, the Nottinghamshire gentleman Sir John Willoughby laid due emphasis on the 'scucuions of ther armys' that were to emblazon the monument, and was insistent that the construction be 'of the same stone that my lorde Phitzhugh is of'. At around the same time, the wealthy Suffolk widow Dame Anne Sulyard prescribed for herself a tomb 'made to the degre that god hathe of his grete grace called me to'.[133] The placing as well as the magnificence of tombs spoke to the living of social power. By the early sixteenth century most London parishes were levying fees for church burial, and some had estab-lished scales of charges to reflect the desirability of specific locations.[134] In some more stable communities, burial in the church, particularly the chancel, might be the prerogative of local gentry: in parishes with resident gentry, the wills of other parishioners were much less likely to request intramural burial.[135] We should not offer too restrictive an account

---

[133] J. Hodson (ed.), 'An Agreement for the Construction of a Tomb in Wollaton Church, 1515', *Thoroton Society RS*, 21 (1962), 1–2; Richmond, 'The Sulyard Papers', 221.

[134] V. Harding, 'Burial Choice and Burial Location in Later Medieval London', in Bassett (ed.), *Death in Towns*, 129–31.

[135] Middleton-Stewart, 'Personal Commemoration in Late Medieval Suffolk', 84–5. For an impressive demonstration of the links between monuments and the articulation of status in a particular local setting, see N. Saul, *Death, Art, and Memory in Medieval England: The Cobham Family and their Monuments, 1300–1500* (Oxford, 2000), though Saul warns (p. 243) against an overemphasis on the secular aspects of commemoration.

here. Though marbled figure sculpture was undoubtedly the preserve of
gentry and higher ecclesiastics, funerary monuments per se had a broader
social base. By the last decades of the fifteenth century, London and provincial workshops were turning out small (typically two-foot) brass memorials
at a fraction of what they had cost at the beginning of the century, to the
despair of some modern art historians, who remark on their 'quantity,
monotony, and carelessness of execution'.[136] Recent research has made it
clear also that an absolute distinction between individuated, marked graves
within the church, and anonymous burial in the collective space of the
churchyard where 'individual burial-places were not marked or remembered',[137] is an over-simplification. Examples can be multiplied from late
medieval wills of gravestones, and even brasses, sited in churchyards, though
it is likely that many extramural markers were impermanent wooden
crosses.[138] The purpose-built chantry chapel was a realistic aspiration only
for a tiny social elite, but there was, as we have seen, a range of cheaper
commemorative options—registration on a bede-roll, or membership of one
or more of the many guilds and fraternities which littered the religious
landscape of late medieval England. A primary *raison d'être* of the latter
was to provide masses for defunct brethren, and they have been characterized as 'communal chantries'.[139] It was, quite literally, never too late to
join—many guilds accepting the registration of new members already dead,
sometimes at a reduced rate.[140] Nonetheless, the language of memory was
firmly punctuated by the marks of hierarchy and degree, late fifteenth-
century testators in Hull requesting the ringing of the great bell 'as is
accustomed for the souls of notable men of the town'.[141] Similarly, the
practice of instituting funeral and memorial sermons was largely restricted
to a social elite, Thomas More satirizing those who arranged for 'some
doctour to make a sermon at our masse in our monthys mynde, and there

[136] S. Badham, 'London Standardisation and Provincial Idiosyncrasy: The Organisation and
Working Practices of Brass-Engraving Workshops in Pre-Reformation England', *Church Monuments*, 5 (1990), 3–25 (quote at p. 7); M. Norris, 'Later Medieval Monumental Brasses: An
Urban Funerary Industry and its Representation of Death', in Bassett (ed.), *Death in Towns*,
184–209.

[137] Bossy, *Christianity in the West*, 31.

[138] Dinn, '"Monuments Answerable to Mens Worth"', 244–5; Harding, 'Burial Choice and
Burial Location', 129; Middleton-Stuart, 'Personal Commemoration in Late Medieval Suffolk',
285; Norris, *Monumental Brasses: The Craft*, 66; Greenwood, 'Wills and Brasses', 85–91.

[139] C. Barron, 'The Parish Fraternities of Medieval London', in C. Barron and C. Harper-Bill
(eds.), *The Church in Pre-Reformation Society* (Woodbridge, 1985), 23. See also Scarisbrick,
The Reformation and the English People, 19–39; Bainbridge, 'The Medieval Way of Death',
191–6; R. Whiting, '"For the Health of my Soul": Prayers for the Dead in the Tudor South-
West', in P. Marshall (ed.), *The Impact of the English Reformation 1500–1640* (1997), 123–4.
Dinn, 'Death and Rebirth in Late Medieval Bury St Edmunds', 163, suggests that, since guild
masses for dead members tended to be annual rather than daily, 'communal obits' is a more apt
description than 'communal chantries'.

[140] Brigden, 'Religion and Social Obligation', 98–101; Scarisbrick, *Reformation and the
English People*, 25.

[141] Heath, 'Urban Piety in the Later Middle Ages', 217.

to preche to our prayse'.[142] Despite the contemporary truism that the rich needed intercession more than the poor, it is possible to detect signs of unease with the brute realities of the economy of salvation. An impoverished London priest dying in 1519 left a small legacy to a fellow 'to pray for my soule, desiring hyme to take itt in worth for my substance is no bettyr', and begged his executor to 'ordeyne for my soule a lowe *dirige* and a masse of requiem becawse I have but smalle goodes'.[143]

On the basis of the many thousands of extant wills, a strong case can certainly be made for the socially flexible and versatile characteristics of late medieval commemoration. But will-makers constituted a minority of the population as a whole. The majority were remembered at their funeral, albeit with very little of the pomp that graced the exequies of the wealthy, but thereafter they had little or no opportunity to leave a record of their existence. In a culture which laid such emphasis on *memoria*, we might well think that, in Margaret Aston's words, 'the countless corporation of the dead seemed disadvantaged by their very anonymity'.[144]

Contemporaries were aware of this disparity, and concerned by it. Late medieval culture possessed a twofold conceptualization of the dead. Ghosts might be identifiable individuals with specific social attributes, or they might be (literally) faceless representatives of a broad collectivity. In a local context, the latter were often remembered at an annual parochial obit, or general mind, and by an 'alms light' or 'All Souls Light' burning during services before the rood.[145] The most imposing collective representation of the dead, however, was on the feast of All Souls itself, when, as we have seen, local communities rang the church bells in honour of all the faithful departed. The more formal procedure comprised a requiem for the parish dead, a procession round the churchyard, and the blessing of the graves. As John Bossy has pointed out, the impulse behind the solemnity was a growing concern in pious circles about the post-mortem fate of those lacking

---

[142] More, *Supplication*, 220. Like other commemorative instruments, funeral sermons undoubtedly made a statement about the status of the founder, but the main impulse behind them seems to have been an intercessory one, testators specifying that the preacher was to urge auditors to pray for their souls: S. Wabuda, 'The Provision of Preaching during the Early English Reformation: With Special Reference to Itineration, c.1530 to 1547', University of Cambridge Ph.D. thesis (1992), 191–3. The first printed English example was Fisher's 1509 sermon for Henry VII, but, as David d'Avray notes, 'its content does not include very much about his qualities and personality, and could without too many difficulties be turned into a miniature treatise on the difficulty of dying': 'The Comparative Study of Memorial Preaching', *TRHS* 5th ser., 40 (1990), 28. See also Powell and Fletcher, '"In Die Sepulture seu Trigintale"'; Marshall, *Catholic Priesthood*, 95; Heath, 'Urban Piety in the Later Middle Ages', 226 (noting the complete absence of bequests for sermons in a sample of 355 Hull wills).

[143] I. Darlington (ed.), *London Consistory Court Wills, 1492–1547*, London Record Society, 3 (1967), 52.

[144] Aston, 'Death', 228.

[145] Burgess '"Longing to be Prayed For"', 64; Hobhouse (ed.), *Churchwardens' Accounts*, 1; E. Duffy, *The Voices of Morebath: Reformation and Rebellion in an English Village* (New Haven and London, 2001), 25.

sufficient 'friends' to pray for them.[146] The Sarum missal provided texts for votive masses 'for those at rest in a cemetery', and devotional works supplied the texts of prayers to be said in or when passing a churchyard for 'all christen souls'. In exchange for these prayers, some primers promised as many years' pardon as there were corpses buried there. *The Golden Legend* reported that when a man who had always recited *De profundis* for the dead was pursued by enemies through a churchyard, 'the buried, each one armed with the tool proper to his craft, quickly rose and defended the fleeing man with might and main'.[147] A desire that the benefits of intercessory prayer be widely shared was reflected in the order of bidding the bedes, recited weekly in parish churches. This laid down a hierarchy of souls, beginning with the clergy and defunct royalty, and proceeding through benefactors of the church, fathers, mothers, godparents, siblings, friends, and 'souls that we be bound to pray for', before concluding with a plea for 'al the soules that be in the paines of purgatory, there abydynge the mercy of almyghty god. And in especyal, for them that have moost nede, and leest help'.[148]

Gauging the level and enthusiasm of response to such exhortations is difficult. It has been suggested that the founders of chantries sought prayer not only for their own souls and those of their kin, but 'invariably specified that their Masses were to be for the profit of all the faithful departed'.[149] Yet this is too lavish a claim. In the mortmain licences for chantries of fifteenth-century nobles analysed by J. T. Rosenthal, the emphasis is firmly on the immediate rather than extended family, and only 3 per cent make reference to all Christian souls.[150] Considerably more frequent were prayers for ancestors, the neglect of whose souls might imply a carelessness about ancestral title to lands.[151] The concern with lineage was less marked at lower social levels, but here too testators most usually associated themselves with networks of kinship rather than the more theological category of souls 'abydynge the mercy of almyghty god'. In a study of late medieval Bury St Edmunds and its rural hinterland, Robert Dinn found that only about 10 per cent of wills included all Christian souls in their bequests for prayers and masses.[152] Of all groups one might expect the London parish

---

[146] Bossy, *Christianity in the West*, 32.

[147] *Golden Legend*, ii. 285.

[148] J. Strype, *Ecclesiastical Memorials* (1721), i (2), 98–100.

[149] Burgess, '"A Fond Thing Vainly Invented"', 67. See also Aston, 'Death', 216; Duffy, *Altars*, 352.

[150] Rosenthal, *The Purchase of Paradise*, 11–30.

[151] Carpenter, 'Religion of the Gentry', 69.

[152] Dinn, 'Popular Religion in Late Medieval Bury St Edmunds', 714–15, 732. The figure seems to have been rather higher among testators in early sixteenth-century York, seven of twenty-nine testators requesting prayers or obits: C. C. Webb, '"Toward the Salary and Fyndyng of Jhesu Masse": The Obit of Robert Dale, Shipman and Citizen of York, in 1503', in Smith (ed.), *Church in Medieval York*, 130. Cf. also H. R. Mosse, *The Monumental Effigies of Sussex*, 2nd edn. (Hove, 1933): of twenty-four inscriptions on tombs from 1476 to 1535 requesting prayers or asking for pardon, only three extend this to all Christian souls.

clergy to be most divorced from the claims of immediate family and most receptive to teachings about the solidarity of all souls. In the 1510s, 11 per cent of London curates requesting prayers or masses associated their own intercession with prayer for the soul of their parents (twice as many laypeople in Bury did so), and around a third identified themselves with all Christian souls. But even here the impulse was clearly not ubiquitous.[153]

The perception that in later medieval Europe the dead consituted an 'age group' in society to set alongside youth, the married, and the elderly is an extremely appealing one.[154] But as an age group the dead seem to belong as much within the structures of the ongoing family as to an aggregate demographic category.[155] Devotional writers employed the most affective language to depict the hapless 'prisoners' in purgatory as fathers, mothers, wives, and husbands, looking to their living kinsfolk to take pity on them and alleviate their sufferings.[156] For the poorest, however, family survival strategies were most likely of necessity focused on this world rather than the next. If the social limits of remembrance were fixed variably, according to social status, and between a duty to all the faithful departed and a priority to the particularity of kin, we need also to consider how they were positioned in time, somewhere between the transience of bereavement and the eternal perspectives of Christian eschatology.

Chantries or obits guaranteeing intercession 'as long as the world standeth' required a level of investment beyond what most testators could afford. Just as endowed masses usually had a circumscribed duration, so did other more 'communal' methods of securing remembrance. The ordinances of the guild of St Mary, Lichfield, laid down that the names of brothers and sisters, along with benefits they had given, be recorded in a book at the time of their death 'so that ther may be a perpetuall memory of ther departing'.[157] But, with a heavy throughput of members, the enactment of such 'perpetual memory' may have been rather contingent. Philip Morgan

[153] Darlington (ed.), *London Consistory Court Wills*. For a Kentish priest who in 1521 wished his obit to be held not on his anniversary, but on the feast of All Souls, see Hussey (ed.), *Kent Obit and Lamp Rents*, 28.

[154] The concept has been popularized by Natalie Davis, who attributes it to André Varagnac: N. Z. Davis, 'Some Tasks and Themes in the Study of Popular Religion', in Trinkaus and Oberman (eds.), *The Pursuit of Holiness*, 327–8; 'Ghosts, Kin, and Progeny', 92. See also Bossy, *Christianity in the West*, 30; Muchembled, *Popular and Elite Culture*, 55; R. Dinn, 'Death and Rebirth in Late Medieval Bury St Edmunds', 161; Geary, *Living with the Dead*, 36; Caciola, 'Wraiths, Revenants and Ritual', 7.

[155] Further confirming this impression is that most testators expressing a preference about whom they wished to be buried near designated a spouse, parent, or child: Dinn, '"Monuments Answerable to Mens Worth"', 253–5; Daniell, *Death and Burial in Medieval England*, 101–2; Harding, 'Burial Choice and Burial Location', 127. Freedom of choice in the matter of burial, notes Bossy, sustained a 'sense of family property in the dead': *Christianity in the West*, 33.

[156] More, *Supplication*, 223–8; Fisher, *Two Fruytfull Sermons*, 21, 26; *Ordynarye of Crysten Men*, ll3ʳ.

[157] F. J. Furnivall (ed.), *The Gild of St Mary, Lichfield*, EETS ES 114 (1920), 5.

has written that 'guild members seem to have retained their individuality at the moment of joining, during their membership and perhaps for a time after their death, but weight of numbers drove further commemoration into a subsumed collective identity in which prayers were directed on behalf of all dead members'.[158] Parish bede-rolls, which Eamon Duffy has described as 'a social map of the community, often stretching over centuries, and promising a continuing place in the consciousness of the parish' did not necessarily guarantee permanent memorialization.[159] The public recitation of a bene-factor's name seems in some places to have been explicitly commodified. Testators in fifteenth-century Bury paid for 'sangredes' to have their name 'sung-read' by the parish priest weekly from the pulpit, but usually only for the period of a year.[160] A London priest in 1516 left 4d. a year for three years 'to those who use bede rolls and will pray for my soul with others named in their bede rolls on Sundays'.[161] Other testators in Suffolk, Hull, and London paid for inclusion on the weekly bede-roll for periods of seven, eight, sixty, or eighty years.[162]

Parishioners were not always able so precisely to prescribe the period during which they would remain in the consciousness of the community. Time and chance might erase the identity of long-dead benefactors. In the late 1540s chantry commissioners in Kent found numerous instances of lamps and obits where the endowment had been given 'many yeres past, by whome it is unknown'.[163] Testators who provided for grave markers and monuments in the church or churchyard must have hoped that these would indefinitely perpetuate their social presence and activate bursts of charitable prayer. But this was not always to be. At Dorchester in Oxfordshire, the Henrician antiquary John Leland recorded the tomb of a knight 'whos name is there oute of remembrance'.[164] As we shall see, funeral monuments were to suffer considerably at the hands of iconoclasts in the course of the sixteenth century. Yet, in the absence of any ideological impulse, medieval communities could prove quite pragmatic and utilitarian in their approach to the monuments of past generations. Fourteenth-century rebuilding work at Helpston, Northamptonshire, and at Bakewell, Derbyshire involved the

[158] Morgan, 'Of Worms and War', 132–3.

[159] Duffy, *Altars*, 335.

[160] Dinn, 'Death and Rebirth in Late Medieval Bury St Edmunds', 164.

[161] Darlington (ed.), *London Consistory Court Wills*, 19.

[162] Middleton-Stewart, 'Personal Commemoration in Late Medieval Suffolk', 101; Little-hales (ed.), *The Medieval Records of a London City Church*, 80, 149; Heath, 'Urban Piety in the Later Middle Ages', 226; Brigden, *London and the Reformation*, 35.

[163] Hussey (ed.), *Kent Obit and Lamp Rents*, 22, 16, 34–5, 38, 42, 44–6, 51, 55, 59–60, 66, 69–74, 76–8, 80, 85–6, 89, 91, 93, 98, 103, 105, 107, 115–16, 122. Burgess's analysis of the various redactions of the benefaction list of All Saints', Bristol shows that the memory of even generous benefactors might 'fade', the record of their generosity becoming terser in successive versions of the bede-roll: *Pre-Reformation Records of All Saints'*, pp. xxiii–xxv.

[164] *The Itinerary of John Leland*, ed. L. Toulmin Smith, 5 vols. (1964), i. 117. Throughout the record of his journeys, Leland notes the presence of 'fair tombs' in churches, whose subject he could not identify.

use as masonry of large numbers of gravestones and inscribed slabs.[165] Slabs were recycled as window lintels at Bradbourne in Derbyshire, and at Wath-upon-Dearne and Baslow in Yorkshire; in the latter place five were also employed in the construction of a fifteenth-century clerestory.[166] Between 1457 and 1533, churchwardens' accounts of the London parishes of St Michael Cornhill, St Mary at Hill, St Andrew Hubbard, St Stephen Coleman, All Hallows Staining, St Lawrence Pountney, and St Mary Magdalen Milk Street show periodic sales of old gravestones.[167] The practice was not unique to London (where pressure on churchyard space was greatest), though it may have been harder to justify elsewhere: in the mid-fifteenth century the sub-sacrist of Bury St Edmunds Abbey was reprimanded by the abbot for 'removing stones with which the tombs of the dead in the abbey's cemeteries are covered...a bad and pernicious example for all faithful Christians who wish, for the remedy of their souls, to place such stones over the tombs of their predecessors, kinsmen and benefactors.'[168] It was not only monuments exterior to churches which were liable to summary eviction, according to the anti-mendicant satire *Pierce the Ploughmans Crede*, which accused friars of encouraging the building of tombs, 'to chargen her chirche-flore, and chaungen it ofte'.[169] But where the tombs of the dead shared space with the worshipping community of the living, venality was not necessarily the motive for seeking to renegotiate the terms of coexistence. In 1511 the churchwardens of Minster-in-Sheppey, Kent, made a presentation to the episcopal visitors:

That where, of long tyme agoo, in the said chapelle, a knight and his wif buried, and theire pictures upon theym very sore worne and brokene, that they may take awey the pictures [i.e. effigies], and lay in the place a playne stone, with an epitaphy who is there buried, that the people may make setts and pewys, where they may more quietly serve God, and that it may less cowmber the rowme.[170]

Rather different, however, was the practice of appropriating monuments, particularly brasses, and reinscribing them on the reverse to commemorate a newly dead person. A memorial of *c.*1480 at St Giles Lincoln, for example, has been shown to be an appropriation of a thirteenth-century effigial slab.[171] This represents at least a decent interval, but a brass commemorating Elizabeth Echyngham (d. 1452) and Agnes Oxenbride (d. 1480) in the

---

[165] F. Burgess, *English Churchyard Memorials* (1963), 29; Greenhill, *Incised Effigial Slabs*, i. 59–60.

[166] D. Hadley, *Death in Medieval England: An Archaeology* (Stroud, 2001), 148.

[167] Harding, 'Burial Choice and Burial Location', 129, 135 n.; Littlehales (ed.), *The Medieval Records of a London City Church*, 78, 222; C. Burgess (ed.), *The Church Records of St Andrew Hubbard Eastcheap c.1450–c.1570*, London Record Society, 34 (1999), 49.

[168] Dinn, '"Monuments Answerable to Mens Worth"', 246.

[169] W. Skeat (ed.), *Pierce the Ploughmans Crede*, EETS 30 (1867), 19.

[170] K. Wood-Legh (ed.), *Kentish Visitations of Archbishop William Warham and his Deputies, 1511–1512*, Kent Records (1984), 256.

[171] Greenhill, *Incised Effigial Slabs*, i. 64–5.

parish church of Etchingham in Sussex has on the reverse an inscription to a
London mercer, Thomas Austin, who had died only around half a century
earlier, in 1405.[172] Thomas Broke's brass (1493) at Baring in Essex reused a
1442 memorial to a London vintner.[173] Even before the onset of doctrinal
change, a number of sixteenth-century persons reused brasses dating from
no earlier than the mid-to late-fifteenth century.[174] These 'palimpsests' do
not seem in the main to have been 'waste' (engravers' reuse of discarded
workshop 'seconds'), but must have become available through rebuilding
work, or perhaps even theft. Their existence serves to remind us that late
medieval people did not necessarily regard the monuments of the dead with
superstitious awe, that in a very real sense the dead might be in competition
with each other for the attention of the living, and that it was the longer-term
dead who were most likely to lose out.

The yielding of place to the more recent dead could be a physical as well as
a mnemonic displacement. In urban areas particularly, the capacity of graveyards was finite, and the bones of the older dead were periodically harvested
to make way for the new. Repositories for these bones – charnel houses – are
known to have existed, either as free-standing chapels or as vaults under the
church, at Bury St Edmunds, Cambridge, Coventry, Norwich, and Worcester.[175] In addition, at least seven late medieval London parishes used them,
probably on an ad hoc rather than systematic basis, though occasional
payments for removal of large amounts of earth and rubbish from cemeteries
must have involved the disturbance of considerable numbers of skeletons.[176]
It is tempting to co-opt charnel houses into an anthropological reading of
liminal stages in the death process, the final extinction of vestigial 'life force'
as the 'wet' enfleshed cadaver transmutes into 'dry' bones.[177] Later medieval
England might seem superficially to equate to a number of societies – such as
that of twentieth-century rural Greece or the Merina people of Madagascar –
where after the decay of the flesh the dead are exhumed and placed in a
permanent new location.[178] But the employment of charnel houses seems
neither systematic nor ritualized enough to justify invoking the concept of
'secondary burial' identified by the anthropologist Robert Hertz.[179] None-

[172] Mosse, *The Monumental Effigies of Sussex*, 80–1.
[173] R. H. D'Elboux (ed.), *The Monumental Brasses of Essex*, 2 vols. (Ashford, 1948–51), i.
26.
[174] Norris, *Monumental Brasses: The Memorials*, i. 275–6. See also J. Page-Phillips, *Palimpsests: The Backs of Monumental Brasses*, 2 vols. (1980), i. 17.
[175] Aston, 'Death', 204–6; J. Cox, *Churchwardens' Accounts* (1913), 169; *Itinerary of John
Leland*, ii. 107; Houlbrooke, *Death*, 332–3.
[176] Harding, 'Burial Choice and Burial Location', 128. There was no English equivalent to
the regular transfer of remains from churches to charnels practised in sixteenth-century Brit-
tany: Musgrave, 'Memento Mori: The Function and Meaning of Breton Ossuaries', 66–7.
[177] On these categories, see Caciola, 'Wraiths, Revenants and Ritual', 33.
[178] L. Danforth, *The Death Rituals of Rural Greece* (Princeton, 1982), 37; M. Bloch, *Placing
the Dead: Tombs, Ancestral Villages and Kinship Organization in Madagascar* (1971), 145–70.
[179] R. Hertz, 'Contribution to the Study of Collective Representations of Death', in *Death
and the Right Hand*, tr. R. and C. Needham (New York, 1960).

theless, where it took place the process was not a casual or irreverent one: the bones on display in charnel chapels served as memento mori, and as focuses of prayer. At the final resurrection they would be knit together and re-encased with the flesh they had shed in the ground. Yet, in the meantime, the inhabitants of charnels had been thoroughly collectivized and anonymized, no longer threatening the living or making insistent demands on their recollection.[180] The medieval dead, remarks Jean-Claude Schmitt, are subject to 'a triple progressive disappearance: of their physical remains in the grave, of their soul beyond purgatory, and of their memory in the minds of the living'.[181]

We seem here to have something like a natural process, the memory of the dead a biodegradable product of culture, as the claims of one dead generation gradually give way to those of the next. And yet in pre-Reformation England the expectations of the dead (as anticipated by their still-living selves) conformed unwillingly to a paradigm of gradual social erasure and assimilation into a vast collectivity of souls. As we have seen, the lifeblood of the memorializing impulse was a process of naming and renaming, the preservation of an individuated social persona (albeit that it was something only the wealthy had a realistic hope of sustaining). This was a consequence not only of *amour propre*, but also of the eschatological teachings of the Church, as they were received in lay circles. The nature of 'time' in purgatory was an ontologically and theologically complex question, but there is no doubting that late medieval Christians were taught to expect that the experience of the next life was to be a temporal, diachronic one, measurable in that highly potent quantity, 'thousands' of years. They also understood that the sources of relief available to them from this world partook of an essentially quantifiable and attritional character. In these circumstances the aspiration for a 'perpetual memory' made sense. The logic of purgatory wove assertions of perpetual remembrance across the fabric of 'natural' processes of forgetting. The concluding section of this chapter will examine this dialectic as a point of tension in late medieval communities, as the claims of remembering and forgetting competed both culturally and (crucially) for material resources.

THE WEIGHT OF THE DEAD

The dead in Thomas More's *Supplication of Souls* complain that even before the advent of heresy 'we have bene wyth many folke mych forgoten of

---

[180] We should note here Susan Karant-Nunn's suggestion that German charnels usually housed only the skulls and femurs of the dead; these were the 'dangerous' parts corpses required to move around, and charnels thus served an apotropaic function: *The Reformation of Ritual: An Interpretation of Early Modern Germany* (1997), 177. This, however, runs counter to the usual perception of cultural historians that it is the recent dead who pose a threat as potential revenants: see Barber, *Vampires, Burial, and Death*, 196–7.

[181] Schmitt, *Ghosts in the Middle Ages*, 200.

neglygence'. It was a case of 'that olde sayd saw, owte of syght owte of mynde', and it was the sport of the 'evyll aungellys' who presided in purgatory to show to their charges widows 'sone waxen wanton, and forgetyng us theyre old husbands' and children piping and dancing who 'no more thynke on theyre fathers soulys then on theyre olde shone [shoes]'. The only exception to this sorry familial neglect was that a wife sometimes 'in chydynge with her secunde husbande to spyghte hym wyth all' would exclaim 'god have mercy...on my fyrst husbandes sowle', a very characteristic Morean touch.[182] A polemical work of the opening stages of the Reformation, More's *Supplication* is sometimes regarded as an unreliable guide to late medieval teaching on purgatory.[183] But in this respect it was recycling a well-worn theme. The *Arte or Crafte to Deye Well* (1505) imagined souls in purgatory remonstrating against those on whom they had bestowed benefices and who ceased to remember them, those who inherited their goods and showed no compassion in return, executors who were negligent in fulfilling testaments, and clerical intercessors who were insufficiently devout in their prayers.[184] When we die, thought Richard Whitford, 'than comunely feyned frendes done sone forget'.[185] In the fifteenth century, the untrustworthiness of executors had become practically proverbial: 'Have in mynd, in mynd, in mynd, secuters be ofte onekynd'.[186] In the early sixteenth century, a version of this couplet was recorded in the commonplace book of Richard Hill, and was even included on monumental inscriptions: there are examples at St Edmund Lombard Street, London; Hampden-in-Arden, Warwickshire; and Kelshall in Hertfordshire.[187] Variants on the theme include a 1526 inscription from St Leonard, Foster Lane: 'When the bels be merily roong / And the masse devoutly sung, And the meat merily eaten, / Then shall Robert Traps his wives / And children be forgotten'.[188] One of the most widely recycled ghost stories in popular sermon collections was of the negligent executor carried off to hell.[189]

[182] More, *Supplication*, 111, 218–19, 222. The stereotype of the negligent widow appears in an incident involving the fifteenth-century mystic Margery Kempe. She was able to discern that a certain man's soul would be thirty years less in purgatory if his widow were to spend £3 on masses and alms for the poor, but the widow 'toke lytyl hede at hir wordys and let it passyn forth': *The Book of Margery Kempe*, ed. S. B. Meech, EETS 212 (1940), 46.
[183] Burgess, '"A Fond Thing Vainly Invented"', 58–9; White, 'Early Print and Purgatory', 105–10, both of whom protest too much on this theme.
[184] *The Arte or Crafte to Deye Well* (1505), cited in White, 'Print and Purgatory', 37.
[185] Whitford, *Dayly Exercyse and Experyence of Dethe*, E5ᵛ.
[186] R. L. Greene (ed.), *The Early English Carols* (Oxford, 1977), 226; *The Towneley Plays*, 392.
[187] Dyboski (ed.), *Songs, Carols, and Other Miscellaneous Poems*, 138; Ravenshaw, *Antiente Epitaphs*, 15; E. W. Badger, *The Monumental Brasses of Warwickshire* (Birmingham, 1895), 24; Norris, *Monumental Brasses: The Craft*, 64.
[188] J. Stow, *A Survey of London*, ed. C. L. Kingsford, 2 vols. (Oxford, 1908), i. 306–7
[189] *Mirk's Festial*, 270; *Golden Legend*, ii. 290; Walters, 'Visitacyons, Prevytes, and Deceytys', 98.

There was a distinct element of cliché to all this. Monuments bemoaning the negligence of executors would not have been erected at all had the phenomenon been quite so universal. Visitation evidence suggests that though parishes very regularly complained that executors were withholding legacies to the Church, relatively few of these were explicitly for obit provision.[190] Preachers had a vested interest in stressing that the dead would be soon forgotten in order to exhort people to prepare for death, and to emphasize that meritorious works in this life were the most reliable means of profiting a man's soul.[191] Yet the perception that the dead were alarmingly dependent on the good offices of the living seems to have been real enough. A Kentish priest dying in 1526 insisted that there should be an annual presentation to the visiting archdeacon 'that my obit is kept, performed, and observed'.[192] Wills quite often charged executors to fulfil their promises as they would have to answer 'at the dredfull daie of dome', and, more practically, testators commonly made the establishment of masses or obits a condition of inheritance for their heirs. On occasion formal indentures were drawn up between parents and children binding the latter to provide intercession for the former.[193]

People were sometimes wise not to rely completely on filial devotion, for that might turn out to be distinctly wanting, as illustrated by fifteenth-century England's most famous gentry family. In the 1440s and 1450s, John Paston I failed in his duty to establish chantries for his father William Paston in Norwich Cathedral and for his patron, Sir John Fastolf, at Caister.[194] In his turn, John Paston I was poorly served by his son, Sir John Paston II. Five years after his father's death in 1466 no start had been made on his tomb at Bromholm, which his widow reported to be 'a sheme and a thing that is much spoken of in this contry'. John Paston himself acknowledged in 1476 'the ill speech which is in the country now of new that the tomb is not made', but only finally made arrangements to begin construction two years later.[195] The Pastons provide the best-known cases of negligence

---

[190] Brown, *Popular Piety in Late Medieval England*, 100. Wood-Legh (ed.), *Kentish Visitations*, supplies only four cases of executors witholding obit money: see pp. 170, 202, 253, 254. It was clearly a source of considerable scandal at Kennington (p. 205) that John May 'hathe brokene an obite that hathe bene used long seasone'.

[191] These points were made forcefully by John Fisher in a sermon of around 1520: *Two Fruytfull Sermons*, 39–42. He returned to the theme in a 'spiritual consolation' written in the Tower: Fisher, *English Works*, 362–3. See also the treatise on death compiled some years later by the conservative priest Robert Parkyn: A. G. Dickens (ed.), *Tudor Treatises*, YASRS, 125 (1959), 65.

[192] Hussey (ed.), *Kent Obit and Lamp Rents*, 16.

[193] Duffy, *Altars*, 350–1; Dinn, 'Popular Religion in Late Medieval Bury St Edmunds', 707–8; Burgess, '"By Quick and By Dead"', 853–4; 'A Service for the Dead', 199–202; 'Late Medieval Wills and Pious Convention', 22–3; David Lamburn, *The Laity and the Church: Religious Developments in Beverley in the First Half of the Sixteenth Century*, University of York, Borthwick Paper No. 97 (2000), 7.

[194] Morgan, 'Of Worms and War', 138.

[195] Aston, 'Death', 213–15.

by gentry heirs, but they are not unique ones: the magnificent tomb begun in his lifetime by Sir Ralph Shelton (d. 1498) at Shelton, Norfolk, appears to have been left unfinished by his son Sir John Shelton, despite precise instructions for the completion of the work in Sir Ralph's will.[196]

If, within the confines of two adjoining generations, the demands of the dead could be found unacceptably burdensome, the sense of obligation might become increasingly attenuated over the longer term. It is clear that a considerable number of the 'perpetual' chantries of the late Middle Ages turned out to be anything but. The reason for their disappearance was usually the decline in the value of the lands comprising the original endowment, and chantries were amalgamated, or confiscated by descendants of the original founders. Fewer than half the institutions for which mortmain licences had been acquired were still functioning in the 1540s; predictably, those furthest from their date of foundation were most likely to have fallen by the wayside. Few chantries set up before the 1360s made it intact into the mid-sixteenth century, though more recent ones might be vulnerable too. In Bury St Edmunds, for example, those of John Edward (1441) and Adam Newhouse (1496) had decayed by the 1540s.[197] Obits might appear to be less vulnerable to these processes than chantries, as the cost to parishes of maintaining the anniversaries of benefactors was often considerably less than the annual income from the endowment. In towns in particular (where burgage tenure allowed greater flexibility in the devising of property by will), parish finances at the close of the fifteenth century were increasingly reliant on income 'from the dead'.[198] In so far as failure by the churchwardens to fulfil the wishes of benefactors might result in loss of the property to other beneficiaries, there was an incentive scrupulously to maintain them. But this cut both ways; the incentive was there only so long as the dead were able 'to pay their way'.[199] In 1472 the city councillors of Salisbury declared that if any tenement tied to an obit they were bound to perform was vacant or dilapidated in a particular year, then the obit was not to be celebrated. At Reading, and at Wimborne Minster, individual obits were amalgamated into

---

[196] J. Finch, 'Fragments of Ambition: the Monuments of the Shelton Family at Shelton, Norfolk', in C. Rawcliffe, R. Virgoe, and R. Wilson (eds.), *Counties and Communities: Essays on East Anglian History Presented to Hassell Smith* (Norwich, 1996), 92–3. See also M. Hicks, 'Chantries, Obits and Almshouses: The Hungerford Foundations 1325–1478', in Barron and Harper-Bill (eds.), *The Church in Pre-Reformation Society*, for a very marked neglect of the chantries of their predecessors on the part of the fifteenth-century Hungerford family.

[197] Kreider, *Chantries*, 76, 87–9, supplies the most comprehensive information on attrition rates. See also Dobson, 'Foundation of Perpetual Chantries'; Burgess, 'Strategies for Eternity', 29; Dinn, 'Popular Religion in Late Medieval Bury St Edmunds', 698.

[198] Kümin, *Shaping of a Community*, 109–20; C. Burgess and B. Kümin, 'Penitential Bequests and Parish Regimes in Late Medieval England', *JEH* 44 (1993), 611–30; C. Burgess, 'Shaping the Parish: St Mary at Hill, London, in the Fifteenth Century', in J. Blair and B. Golding (eds.), *The Cloister and the World: Essays in Medieval History in Honour of Barbara Harvey* (Oxford, 1996), 251–2; R. Tittler, *The Reformation and the Towns in England: Politics and Political Culture, c.1540–1640* (Oxford, 1998), 37–8.

[199] The formulation is Andrew Brown's: *Popular Piety in Late Medieval England*, 242.

a single annual service for the dead, a collectivizing impulse that would undoubtedly have dismayed the founders.[200] Even conscientious churchwardens could not always keep up the full panoply of what testators intended. In the early 1450s Thomas and Joan Halleway endowed a perpetual chantry and anniversary in All Saints church, Bristol. The latter was to be attended every year by twenty priests and all four orders of friars, with 50s. being distributed to the poor. Nonetheless, rising costs ensured that over the next half-century the stipulated number of priests was never reached, the friars were irregular attenders, and little more than 7s. or 8s. was available for the poor.[201]

The sufficiency of endowments aside, pressures of time, administration, and convenience might encourage a rationalization and curtailment of the wishes of the dead. In 1489 the vicar and churchwardens of St Nicolas's, Bristol, ruled that the church bells would not be rung for anyone during the month after their burial, whether they were parishioners or not.[202] In 1480 the Salisbury authorities decided to amalgamate obits in their charge, thereafter celebrating only three annually for the souls of civic benefactors, though maintaining the same overall level of expenditure.[203] In late fifteenth-century London, members of the Goldsmiths Company were obliged to attend twenty-five obits, a level of commitment which by 1497 they considered to be 'to the great unease and trouble of the wardens and of all the livery'. The number of commemorations was cut to fourteen, bringing together 'dry' and 'wet' obits (i.e. those at which drink was provided).[204] The solution here suggests a problem with attendances. This was explicitly acknowledged by the Drapers' Company in 1519, allowing that only half the fellowship need attend any particular obit. But the expectations on the London craft guilds remained heavy. In the latter part of Henry VIII's reign, the Grocers attended twelve obits per annum, the Merchant Taylors, twenty-seven. In London as a whole over 360 obits were still being performed.[205] Conceivably, this level of familiarity may have bred a degree, if not of contempt, then of formalism and occasional cynicism. The parishioners of St Mary's Dover complained to the visitors in 1511 that they lacked masses on Wednesdays and Fridays 'if there be any mind within the town where our curate may get a groat'.[206]

To ask whether the obligation to remember the dead constituted a considerable burden on the living is to invite the response that it unquestionably did. Whether in a personal capacity, as sons, daughters, and legatees, or ex

---

[200] Ibid. 166, 96.
[201] Burgess, 'A Service for the Dead', 185.
[202] Burgess, 'The Benefactions of Mortality', 75.
[203] Brown, *Popular Piety in Late Medieval England*, 168.
[204] C. Platt, *King Death: The Black Death and its Aftermath in Late-Medieval England* (1996), 106.
[205] Brigden, *London and the Reformation*, 388–9.
[206] Marshall, *Catholic Priesthood*, 180.

officio, as churchwardens, guild officers, or aldermen, huge numbers of late medieval people inherited obligations towards past generations which were contractually binding as well as customary and affective. In towns in particular, as Charles Phythian-Adams remarks in a related context, there was a heavy economic price involved in 'ceremonialising the traditional social structure'.[207] Whether these obligations were generally *experienced* as onerous, oppressive, or unbearable is a rather different question.[208] It would be crass to suggest that early sixteenth-century society was in some way groaning under the weight of its dead, whether psychologically or economically. But the heavy-handed grasp of memory was acceptable only so long as there was a fairly universal adherence to the belief system which provided its rationale, and under which the living could expect in their turn to need and get the same treatment.

The disintegration, resilience, and mutability of that belief system is the core subject of the rest of this book. I remain firmly unconvinced that it was 'waning' or in obvious crisis in the early years of the sixteenth century, but at the same time I would want to claim that how late medieval Catholicism imagined and constructed the 'presence of the dead' exemplifies in certain unmistakable ways its vulnerability to sustained political and intellectual assault. Like the wider religious culture it inhabited, and very substantially shaped, the commemoration of the dead before the Reformation was at the same time eminently functional, and riven by paradoxes. Even by the generous standards of late medieval religious thought, the world of purgatory and intercession was both elastic and capacious, combining a slender core of doctrinal definition and authoritative text with a lavish layering of the prescriptive and the speculative. Within its orbit, spiritual, social, economic, and political interests were endlessly intertwined. As a cultural and social presence, the dead hovered in the spaces separating a succession of shifting polarities: allegory and realism; remembering and forgetting; particularity and collectivity; self-interest and altruism; fear and hope; the spiritual and the material. These were the themes that would play and replay, as the symbolic landscapes of the dead became some of the principal battlegrounds of the early Reformation.

---

[207] Phythian-Adams, *Desolation of a City*, 287, where it is suggested that the abrogation of Corpus Christi pageants and other ceremonies must have been regarded with relief.

[208] There are suggestive comments here in R. N. Swanson, *Religion and Devotion in Europe, c.1215–c.1515* (Cambridge, 1995), 233–4; Burgess, ' "By Quick and By Dead" ', 857; Brown, *Popular Piety in late Medieval England*, 241–2. See also the remark of Natalie Davis, 'Ghosts, Kin, and Progeny', 103, that 'the cyclical exchange with souls in purgatory was somewhat in tension with the arrow of family history'.

2

Debates Over the Dead:
Purgatory and Polemic in
Henrician England

THE status of the dead was among the most divisive issues of the early
Reformation; it was also arguably the theological terrain over which in
the reign of Henry VIII official reform travelled furthest and fastest. The
focus of this chapter is on the early evangelical critique of purgatory
and customary intercessory practice, and on identifying its points of coinci-
dence and convergence with the emergent reform agenda sanctioned by the
Henrician state. Controversies over the doctrine of purgatory can seem a
rather peripheral aspect of contemporary religious thought, a side-issue in
the Reformation's great debates about free will, grace, justification, and
sacraments.[1] Yet they demand a closer reading than is sometimes accorded
them, being tied up inextricably with the most fundamental questions of
soteriology and authority, while at the same time touching issues of great
pastoral sensitivity. To debate the existence and rationale of purgatory was
to raise questions about the nature of the Church, the extent of papal
prerogative and scriptural imperative, the human response to God's offer
of redemption, and the priorities of popular religion. Beliefs and practices
pertaining to the dead represented a thread visibly protruding from the
theological and devotional apparel of traditional religion. It did not take
long for both defenders and assailants of the old order to understand that if
this thread were pulled upon vigorously enough, the entire fabric might start
to unravel.

OPENING SALVOS: FISH, FRITH, AND MORE

A conventional starting date for the Protestant Reformation is appropriate
to our purposes here. Martin Luther's Ninety-Five Theses of 1517

---

[1] There is, for example, no index entry for purgatory in Alistair McGrath's otherwise
excellent *Reformation Thought: An Introduction* (Oxford, 1988), and only two in Bernard
Reardon's *Religious Thought in the Reformation*, 2nd edn. (1995).

disavowed neither the existence of purgatory nor the legitimacy of praying for the dead, but in denying the efficacy of papal indulgences to remit canonical penalties they served to open up all these issues for public debate. Luther held that indulgences were an obstacle to true repentance, and thus immensely spiritually harmful. The dead were free of the jurisdiction of canon law, and (a point clarified in his subsequent explications of the theses) their experience in purgatory was one of purification, rather than the performance of satisfactory penance. The polemical impact of the Ninety-Five Theses was heightened by Luther's inclusion of what he termed 'shrewd questionings of the laity': if the pope has the power to empty purgatory, why does he not out of charity do so? If indulgences are of such efficacy, why should requiems and anniversary masses continue to be said?[2]

At the Leipzig disputation of 1519 Luther still protested a belief in purgatory, but he denied that there was any scriptural sanction for the doctrine, and by 1522 he was denouncing masses for the dead and agnostic about their whereabouts. Other early reformers, notably Zwingli and Karlstadt, had already completely rejected the idea, and in 1530 Luther finally caught up with the publication of his *Widerruf vom Fegefeuer* (Repeal of Purgatory).[3] In the meantime, both purgatory and papal indulgences had been defended in the writings of Luther's leading English opponents, in Henry VIII's *Assertio Septem Sacramentorum*, John Fisher's *Assertionis Lutheranae Confutatio*, and Thomas More's *Responsio ad Lutherum*.[4] In October 1528, *The Obedience of a Christian Man* by Luther's disciple William Tyndale included the first systematic attacks on purgatory and intercessory practices in an English book.[5] Yet it was not Tyndale who ignited the first major literary controversy on these issues within England.

While Luther was still feeling his way towards a complete rejection of purgatory, a short work appeared in England which, page for page, proved as influential as any other text of the early English Reformation. *A Supplicacyon for the Beggers* by the exiled common lawyer Simon Fish was printed in Antwerp in late 1528 or early 1529, and in February copies were scattered in the street in Westminster. Modern commentators have not been inclined to take the *Supplicacyon* seriously as a work of religious polemic, seeing it as an anti-clerical philippic largely innocent of theological sophistication or

---

[2] The most accessible version of the theses is in E. G. Rupp and B. Drewery (eds.), *Martin Luther* (1970), 19–25.

[3] A. F. Mayne, 'Disputes about Purgatory in the Early Sixteenth Century', University of London M.Phil. thesis (1975), 10–13; C. M. Koslofsky, *The Reformation of the Dead: Death and Ritual in Early Modern Germany, 1450–1700* (Basingstoke, 2000), 19–39.

[4] Henry VIII, *Miscellaneous Writings*, ed. F. Macnamara (1924), 44; J. Fisher, *Assertionis Lutheranae Confutatio* (1523), article 37; T. More, *Responsio ad Lutherum*, ed. J. M. Headley (New Haven and London, 1969), 257–9, 327–9.

[5] W. Tyndale, *Doctrinal Treatises and Introductions to Different Portions of the Holy Scriptures*, ed. H. Walter (PS, 1848), 148, 158, 235–8, 243–9, 268–72, 302–3, 318–21.

intent.[6] Yet this may be to underestimate both the radicalism of the tract and the intense contemporary interest it aroused. For Fish's central contention was an explosive one: that excessive clerical wealth and power was inextricably bound up with intercession for the dead. Fish drew attention to the 'multitude of money', the 'yerely exaccions' which went into the hands of pardoners and priests for dirges and masses. There were, he insidiously observed, 'many men of great litterature and iudgement' prepared to risk their lives for the opinion 'that there is no purgatory, but that it is a thing invented by the covitousnesse of the spiritualtie'. These unnamed authorities further observed that there was no mention of purgatory in the Bible, and that the doctrine, and specifically the pardons issued by the pope, was the reason the wealth of the whole kingdom was slipping so rapidly into the hands of the clergy.[7] While Fish's pamphlet devoted only a couple of pages to the direct disparagement of purgatory, it managed unerringly to highlight the characteristics which made the doctrine most vulnerable, and which would be rehearsed repeatedly in subsequent attacks: its lack of scriptural foundation, and its potential for association with clerical abuses, and with the authority of the pope.

Whether or not John Foxe was right in claiming that Anne Boleyn placed a copy of the tract in the hands of the king, Fish's work made an immediate splash.[8] The *Supplicacyon* was condemned at an assembly at Westminster presided over by Archbishop Warham and Bishop Tunstal on 24 May 1530, and the prohibition was repeated in a royal proclamation of the following month.[9] Fish's pithy pamphlet also earned the distinction of a disproportionately long refutation by England's leading Catholic polemicist, Thomas More, which appeared from the press in September 1529 – a *Supplication of Souls* in which the tormented souls in purgatory put their case against the arguments of Fish's 'Beggers'.[10] More well understood the significance of Fish's insinuations. If there were no purgatory, the entire fabric of intercession was unnecessary, and the result would be a sundering of the Christian community, which for More comprised both the living and the dead. His

---

[6] See, for example, A. Fox, *Thomas More: History and Providence* (Oxford, 1982), 167; J. A. Guy, *The Public Career of Sir Thomas More* (New Haven and London, 1980), 109; R. Marius, *Thomas More* (1984), 353–4; W. A. Clebsch, *England's Earliest Protestants 1520–1535* (New Haven and London, 1964), 244; D. Daniell, *William Tyndale: A Biography* (New Haven and London, 1994), 219.

[7] S. Fish, *A Supplicacyon for the Beggers*, in T. More, *The Supplication of Souls*, ed. F. Manley *et al.* (New Haven and London, 1990), 413, 419–20

[8] Foxe, iv. 657. Anne's biographer is disinclined to accept the story: E. Ives, *Anne Boleyn* (Oxford, 1986), 163 n.

[9] D. Wilkins, *Concilia Magna Britanniae et Hiberniae*, 4 vols. (1737), iii. 733, 736, 740; *TRP*, i. 194.

[10] The supposition of Alistair Fox, *Thomas More*, 180, that More delayed his reply hoping that the commotion caused by the tract would die a natural death is less plausible than the suggestion by the modern editor of the *Supplication of Souls* that More was tied up until midsummer finishing his *Dialogue Concerning Heresies*: More, *Supplication*, p. lxv.

treatise is pervaded by a vivid sense of the nearness of souls in purgatory to the living, opening with an appeal 'to all good Crysten people' from 'your late aquayntaunce, kindred, spouses, companions, play felowes, and frendes', and closing with a petition to remember 'familier frendship', and 'how nature and crystendom byndeth you to remember us'. Fish's unnamed 'wyse men', whom More identifies as 'Luther and Tyndall and [Fish] him self' are faithless people, 'fallen from all crysten charyte' and 'from all humanitie and felyng of eny good affeccyon naturall'. Because of their fanatical hatred of priesthood they 'wolde make you beleve that there were no purgatory, and wold rather wysh by theyr wyllys that theyr owne fathers shuld lye here in fyre tyll the day of doome, then eny man shulde geve a preste one peny to pray for them'.[11]

More's book was followed from the presses within a few months by a second, very different, treatise: *A New Boke of Purgatory whiche is a Dyaloge & Dysputacyon betwene one Comyngo an Almayne a Christen man & one Gyngemyn a Turke*. This curious text, the work of More's brother-in-law the printer John Rastell, employed the very Morean touch of an infidel defending Catholic orthodoxy against a heterodox German. This approach constrained Rastell to combat 'a new opinyon spronge amonge the people, that there is no purgatory' with 'naturall reason and good philosophye', eschewing scriptural or patristic citation. After applying the method to the existence of God, and the immortality of the soul, Rastell argued that God's justice demands the existence of purgatory, likening him to a prince who will neither condemn every offender to death nor completely free him from punishment. Rastell's methodology took him some way from traditional devotional concerns. On the question of the location of purgatory, he remarked 'me thynketh it is a great folyshnes to demaunde that questyon'. Similarly, men would never be able to know in this life what kind of pains were suffered there 'nor how, nor in what maner that soule is able to suffer that payne'. Much was made of the pragmatic argument that purgatory was necessary to discourage vice and instil 'the drede of god'.[12] Rastell wrote with considerable flair and ingenuity, but the enduring impression from his work is of how hollow the doctrine of purgatory looked, severed from the traditional pieties and social customs that sustained it. As a work of theology, it was to be significantly outclassed by a response from an opponent almost thirty years younger, John Frith's *Disputation of Purgatory* (1531).

Frith was a junior canon of Wolsey's Cardinal College, and friend of Tyndale's, who had fled to Antwerp in 1528. Friends in England sent him More's *Supplication* and Rastell's *New Boke*, and having checked what Fisher had to say on purgatory in the *Assertionis Lutheranae Confutatio*,

[11] More, *Supplication*, 111, 228, 177, 206.
[12] J. Rastell, *A New Boke of Purgatory* (1530), F1^v–2^v, G3^{r-v}, H3^v–4^r.

he resolved on a triple-decked confutation: a philosophical treatment against Rastell, and a debate over the scriptural sources with More, and over the patristic authorities with Fisher. His aim was to prove 'that this their painful purgatory was but a vain imagination, and that it hath of long time but deceived the people, and milked them from their money'.[13] Returning to England in 1532, Frith was arrested and placed in the Tower where, before he was burned for his sacramentarian views in July 1533, he composed *Another Book Against Rastell* in response to a rejoinder of Rastell's which has not survived. More, too, seems to have contemplated a refutation of Frith.[14]

Frith's opponents mocked him as 'yong father Fryth'; an 'arrogant fole nothyng doutynge the iudgement of the hole worlde' who 'toke upon hym to teache the hole chyrche of chryste revokynge us from our errour (as he calleth yt) of purgatorye, wherin we have this XV hundred yeres contynued'.[15] But his *Disputation of Purgatory* was a formative text for the first generation of English evangelicals. In the spate of heresy trials that marked Thomas More's last months as chancellor in 1531–2, Frith's *Disputation* cropped up repeatedly as a book in the possession of the defendants. When, in the early 1540s, William Tolwyn was charged with possession of 'a boke of frythes', John Bale assumed that the *Disputation* was meant. Many years later, the Elizabethan archdeacon of Nottingham John Louthe recalled the impact the book had had on him as a schoolboy in the early 1530s: he had been lent it to read for two days, 'but I begged it and craved it for twenty-three days'.[16] Frith's second book against Rastell was supposed to have converted his opponent, making him an advocate of radical reform in the last few years of his life.[17]

A work often found alongside Frith's *Disputation* in the possession of suspected heretics was the testament of William Tracy, a Gloucestershire gentleman who died in October 1530 and achieved posthumous fame by virtue of having his exhumed corpse burnt (illegally) for heresy by the chancellor of Worcester diocese. By 1531 copies of Tracy's will were circulating in manuscript in London, and in 1535 it was printed in Antwerp with commentaries by Frith and William Tyndale.[18] The document began with

[13] Clebsch, *England's Earliest Protestants*, 78–94; J. Frith, *A Disputation of Purgatory*, in *The Work of John Frith*, ed. N. T. Wright (Oxford, 1978), 87–8, 90.

[14] D. Birch, *Early Reformation English Polemics* (Salzburg, 1983), 84.

[15] T. More, *The Confutation of Tyndale's Answer*, ed. L. A. Schuster *et al.* (New Haven, 1973), 969; G. Gardiner, *A Letter of a Yonge Gentylman ... Wherin Men May Se the Demeanour & Heresy of John Fryth* (1534), A3ʳ⁻ᵛ.

[16] C. Haigh, *English Reformations: Religion, Politics, and Society under the Tudors* (Oxford, 1993), 66–7; Foxe, v. 38; J. Bale, *Yet a Course at the Romysh Foxe* (Zurich [i.e. Antwerp], 1544), 46ᵛ–47ᵛ; J. G. Nichols (ed.), *Narratives of the Days of the Reformation*, CS 77 (1859), 5. 'Frythe his book', perhaps the *Disputation*, was among the works cast on a bonfire at Louth in 1536 at the outbreak of the Lincolnshire Rebellion: LP xi. 828.

[17] Frith, *Disputation*, 211. See the introduction by A. J. Geritz to his edition of *The Pastyme of People and a New Boke of Purgatory* (New York, 1985).

[18] J. Craig and C. Litzenberger, 'Wills as Religious Propaganda: The Testament of William Tracy', *JEH* 44 (1993), 424–5.

the assertion that there was no mediator between God and man but Jesus Christ, and in consequence 'will I bestow no part of my goods for that intent, that any man should say or do to help my soul'. As to the disposal of his body, Tracy left it entirely to the discretion of his executors, citing a passage from Augustine's *De cura agenda pro mortuis* to the effect that funeral ceremonies were rather the solace of those still living than of any help to the dead.[19]

As these works circulated in evangelical networks, the denial of purgatory became an increasingly public matter. In 1531 Edward Crome, Hugh Latimer, and Nicholas Shaxton, three preachers who were to have distinguished careers as evangelical activists, were all in trouble for casting doubt on the existence of purgatory.[20] Having abjured in March 1532, Latimer proceeded again to undermine traditional pieties in a series of Lenten sermons given in Bristol early the following year, asserting that 'the souls that be in purgatory ... have no need of our prayers'. Local conservatives furiously denounced Latimer's views, in one of the first 'pulpit wars' of the English Reformation. In an indication of how the political atmosphere was changing, the resultant commission of inquiry appointed by Thomas Cromwell vindicated Latimer, and his chief opponent, William Hubbardine, was sent to the Tower.[21] These exchanges were perhaps responsible for an unusually doctrinaire tone in the bequests of some Bristol testators, requesting masses and *dirige* 'as a true cristen man ought to have'.[22]

By the time Henry VIII was formalizing his rupture with the papacy in 1533–4, the status of purgatory and post-mortem intercession had emerged as a major fault-line in an increasingly contentious religious landscape. Big guns on both sides of the debate had laid down their barrage: Fisher, More, Rastell, Hubbardine, and others in the cause of tradition; Fish, Tyndale, Frith, and Latimer, in the service of new-found conviction. Purgatory, a devotional and customary belief, was becoming a controversial opinion. This in itself was highly significant. The anonymous author (probably George Joye) of the 1533 *Souper of the Lorde* bullishly asserted that had not More, Fisher, and Rastell stirred the matter in print, 'purgatory paradventure had served them yet another yere, nether had it so sone have ben quenched'.[23]

---

[19] W. Tyndale, *An Answer to Sir Thomas More's Dialogue*, ed. H. Walter (PS, 1850), 272. The passage from Augustine was later to be a particular favourite of Protestant commentators. See below, 150, 268.

[20] Kreider, *Chantries*, 100–1; H. Latimer, *Sermons and Remains*, ed. G. E. Corrie (PS, 1845), 218.

[21] Kreider, *Chantries*, 102–3; M. C. Skeeters, *Community and Clergy: Bristol and the Reformation c.1530–c.1570* (Oxford, 1993), 38–45.

[22] T. P. Wadley (ed.), *Notes or Abstracts of...the Great Orphan Book and Book of Wills* (Bristol, 1886), 180, 184.

[23] George Joye(?), *The Souper of the Lorde*, in T. More, *The Answer to a Poisoned Book*, ed. S. M. Foley and C. H. Miller (New Haven and London, 1985), 336.

But why were evangelicals so confident that they had quenched it? At this point it is appropriate to trace in more detail the recurrent themes that had emerged in polemic against purgatory and intercession for the dead by the mid-1530s, to examine why evangelicals found these beliefs theologically so offensive, and to consider why they became a defining issue for the first generation of English reformers. We can then begin to investigate the ways in which their ideas came to intersect with the development of official policy from the mid-1530s onwards, and the consequences for the emergent shape of the English Reformation.

THE DECONSTRUCTION OF A DOCTRINE

First and foremost, reformers rejected purgatory because they could not find it in the Bible. There was, Simon Fish opined, 'not one word spoken of hit in al holy scripture'.[24] The point was elaborated in Frith's *Disputation*: if such a thing had been ordained by God 'then I am sure that Christ and all his Apostles would not have forgotten to have remembered us of it'.[25] In the early evangelical satire *The Burial of the Mass*, Thomas More is mocked for his device of bringing forth souls from purgatory to attack Fish: 'It was the suerest waye by seynt Ihone / For had they to playne scripture gone / I wousse they hadde be taken tardye.'[26]

Of course, defenders of purgatory denied that the doctrine was unscriptural. In his *Assertionis Lutheranae Confutatio*, John Fisher remarked that, Scripture being a kind of treasure-chest of necessary truths, 'nobody can doubt that the truth of purgatory is contained in it'.[27] Thomas More dedicated a considerable part of his *Supplication of Souls* to the scriptural proofs for purgatory, explicating ten different passages, and concluding with the claim 'by playn scripture [to] have provyd you purgatory'.[28] In a Bristol sermon of 1536–7, the preacher Roger Edgeworth described it as 'very easy...to declare and prove Purgatory by scriptures with the expositions of autenticall doctours'.[29] Naturally, traditionalists recognized that the *word* 'purgatory' was not to be found in Scripture, but then, as Johan Eck had pointed out in his controversy with Luther, neither was the word 'Trinity'.[30]

Yet Catholic controversialists were understandably reluctant to fight this battle entirely on the chosen ground of their opponents. It was characteristic

[24] Fish, *Supplicacyon*, 419.
[25] Frith, *Disputation*, 104.
[26] J. Barlow, *The Burial of the Mass*, in E. Arber (ed.), *English Reprints* (1871), 144.
[27] R. Rex, *The Theology of John Fisher* (Cambridge, 1991), 98.
[28] More, *Supplication*, pp. lxxiv–lxxxvii, 195.
[29] R. Edgeworth, *Sermons very Fruitfull, Godly and Learned*, ed. J. Wilson (Cambridge, 1993), 128.
[30] Mayne, 'Disputes about Purgatory', 18.

of heretics, thought More, to 'make lyttel force of reason and ever aske for scripture'. Even if there were no proof-texts for the doctrine it was necessary to believe it 'syth the catholyque churche of cryste hath allway so fermely byleved yt for a playne trowthe'.[31] For their part, evangelical writers were entirely dismissive of the suggestion that purgatory should be believed on the Church's authority alone, or because it was an 'unwritten verity' of the faith.[32] Moreover, claims to have proven the doctrine from the Bible seemed to them to epitomize all that was wrong with scholastic methods of exegesis, which 'corrupteth the scripture, and fashioneth it after his own imagination'.[33] The most unambiguous scriptural endorsement of prayer for the dead, in the second book of Maccabees, was dismissed on the grounds that this was an uncanonical text.[34] In these debates, the status of the name 'purgatory' itself was not a side issue, and, as we shall see, it was to assume considerable significance in the development of official policy from the late 1530s. In an extremely grudging abjuration made in 1531, Edward Crome admitted there was a place where souls were punished, but he stressed that he could not find the word purgatory in Scripture, adding disingenuously 'my thynk theye hurte purgatorye sore, whych goo abowte to bryng in scriptures to prove purgatorye withall: whych doo make rather agaynst purgatorye then with ytt'.[35]

The absence of scriptural sanction came up repeatedly in heresy trials. In 1531 James Bainham said that if the idea of purgatory had been put to St Paul, 'he thought St Paul would have condemned it for a heresy'. When John Lambert appeared before Archbishop Warham the following year, he denied that purgatory could be proved by Scripture 'unless it be by one place of the same, which, well examined I trow, shall make but little against me'.[36] This perception that Maccabees was the exception proving the rule was echoed at the 1533–4 trial of Thomas Hoth, precentor of the Augustinian New Priory in Hastings, who admitted saying 'that the most I have red in scripture of purgatory is in *Libro machabeorum* xii capt'.[37] In April 1540 Humfrey Grynshill, a weaver from Stonehouse in Gloucestershire,

was redyng the byble in englyshe in Cryste Church in Gloucester. . . and immediately aftre he had redde . . . he dyd affirme and saye . . . hit can not be proved nether founde

---

[31] More, *Supplication*, 176, 195. See also id., *Confutation*, 374, 1033–4; *A Dialogue of Comfort*, ed. L. Martz and F. Manley (New Haven, 1976), 38; Rex, *Theology of Fisher*, 99.

[32] P. Marshall, 'The Debate over "Unwritten Verities" in Early Reformation England', in B. Gordon (ed.), *Protestant Identity and History in Sixteenth-Century Europe*, vol. i: *The Medieval Inheritance* (Aldershot, 1996), 60–77.

[33] Tyndale, *Doctrinal Treatises*, 158.

[34] Frith, *Disputation*, 156–62; D. B. Knox, *The Doctrine of Faith in the Reign of Henry VIII* (1961), 218.

[35] J. Strype, *Ecclesiastical Memorials*, 3 vols. (1721), iii (2), 20–1.

[36] Foxe, iv. 699, v. 195.

[37] C. E. Welch, 'Three Sussex Heresy Trials', *Sussex Archaeological Collections*, 95 (1957), 60–1.

in any part of the hole scriptur, that there is any moo places wherin christen soules departed may be, but only hell and heven, and therfore he sayde that he wolde have no prayers sayde for his sowle when so ever he shall dye.[38]

In making the Bible available in English in 1538, the government had given a green light to DIY hermeneutics of this sort.

If there was no purgatory in Scripture, reformers had their own explanations of how it had become so central a feature of the Church's teaching. Foremost among these was the theme that had dominated Fish's *Supplication*: the doctrine of purgatory and the entire associated paraphernalia of intercession had been invented to serve the financial interests of the clergy. The theme was much to the fore in Tyndale's *Obedience of a Christen Man*. Trentals, bede-rolls, *diriges*, month's minds and year's minds were all means for priests to fleece the laity. Purporting to eat the people's sin, the clergy 'thereof wax fat', and took away, not sin, but God's Word, and also 'house and land, rent and fee, tower and town, goods and cattle, and the very meat out of men's mouths... When other weep for their friends, they sing merrily; when other lose their friends, they get friends.' Purgatory, Tyndale concluded, only serves 'to purge thy purse, and to poll thee'.[39] John Bale similarly suggested that priests, canons, and monks 'do but fyll their bely / With my swett and labour for ther popych purgatory'.[40] In an ironic gloss on the traditional commonplace that the fire of purgatory was hotter than any earthly fire, Frith conceded that it must be so, for 'it hath alone melted more gold and silver, for our spiritualty's profit, out of poor men's purses, than all the goldsmiths' fires within England'.[41] Similar claims were advanced by Hugh Latimer, whose provocative convocation sermon of 1536 reprised the connection Simon Fish had made between clerical exactions and the derogation of royal fiscal rights. Purgatory was 'a pleasant fiction, and from the beginning so profitable to the feigners of it, that almost, I dare boldly say, there hath been no emperor that hath gotten more taxes and tallages of them that were alive, then these... got by dead men's tributes and gifts'.[42] Such allegations were highly partisan propaganda. Simon Fish's precise figures on the huge sums garnered by the friars are entirely bogus, and Thomas More was surely right in pointing out that occupation of a chantry was hardly the route to untold clerical wealth.[43] But charges of financially motivated wrongdoing have a perennial tendency to find their mark. Moreover, the allegation was reducible to a single alliterative

---

[38] C. Litzenberger, *The English Reformation and the Laity: Gloucestershire, 1540–1580* (Cambridge, 1997), 40.

[39] Tyndale, *Doctrinal Treatises*, 148, 237–8, 249, 302–3, 318.

[40] J. Bale, *Complete Plays*, ed. P. Happé, 2 vols. (Cambridge, 1985–6), i. 40, 70.

[41] Frith, *Disputation*, 183.

[42] Latimer, *Sermons*, 50.

[43] Fish, *Supplicacyon*, 413; T. More, *The Apology*, ed. J. B. Trapp (New Haven, 1979), 73.

expression, one of the great catchphrases of the early Reformation: 'purga-tory pick-purse'.[44]

Purgatory and post-mortem intercession were thus frequently epitomized in terms of the cupidity and corruption of the clergy, but a related aspect was a stress on their disastrous social effects—again a theme Simon Fish had anticipated in juxtaposing the king's 'poore beedmen' with the 'counterfeit holy and ydell beggers' of the clergy.[45] Tyndale castigated 'the prayers of them that devour widows' houses, and eat the poor out of house and harbour', and the theme was to be a prominent one in early Protestant polemic, paralleling the long-standing Lollard complaint that offering to images robbed the true images of Christ, the poor.[46] In making these points, reformers self-consciously spoke the language of 'charity', the idiom within which the rationale of intercession was conventionally cast. Under investi-gation in 1533, and picking his words with care, Latimer argued that 'the souls in purgatory be so charitable, and of charity so loth to have God dishonoured that they would have nothing withdrawn from the poor here in this world, to be bestowed upon them'.[47] Latimer, now a bishop, returned to the theme in his convocation sermon of 1536, the year in which another evangelical prelate, William Barlow, delivered a sermon in pastiche of trad-itional purgatory preaching, urging his listeners to devote themselves 'to relyve the miserable creatures in the purgatory of thys lyfe, moste wofully paynede with uglie sores and horrible diseases'.[48] A few years later, Henry Brinkelow complained that Londoners were still 'providinge for the deade uncommaunded, and leave providinge for the poore lyvinge which the Scripture most ernestly teacheth'.[49] Traditionalists like More protested that the souls in purgatory and the poor in this life were not in fact in competition for resources, that alms given to the former for the sake of the latter benefited both parties,[50] but evangelical polemic resolutely ignored the argument that purgatory might be a spur to charitable giving.

In any case, the evangelical critique of the social injustice of purgatory was not limited to the circumstances of the poor, and sought to appeal to the self-

---

[44] *OED* attributes the origin of the phrase to Latimer, though in fact it seems to have been coined by Tyndale in 1528: *Doctrinal Treatises*, 342. See also ibid. 424; H. Latimer, *Sermons*, ed. G. E. Corrie (PS, 1844), 49; Bale, *Complete Plays*, i. 71; PRO, SP 6/11, 59ʳ; Kreider, *Chantries*, 100; N. Wyse, *A Consolacyon for Chrysten People to Repayre Agayn the Lordes Temple* (1538), G5ᵛ; *LP* xviii (2), 546 (p. 316); J. Bradford, *Letters, Treatises, Remains*, ed. A. Townsend (PS, 1853), 292; H. Bullinger, *The Decades: The Fourth Decade*, ed. T. Harding (PS, 1851), 395; M. Coverdale, *Remains*, ed. G. Pearson (PS, 1846), 270; Strype, *Ecclesiastical Memorials*, iii (2), 50.

[45] Fish, *Supplicacyon*, 412.

[46] Tyndale, *Doctrinal Treatises*, 122; M. Aston, *England's Iconoclasts* (Oxford, 1988), 124–32.

[47] Latimer, *Remains*, 238.

[48] Latimer, *Sermons*, 36–7; PRO, SP 1/101, 184ʳ (*LP* x. 225).

[49] Henry Brinkelow, *Complaynt of Roderyck Mors and The Lamentacyon of a Christen Agaynst the Cyte of London*, ed. J. M. Cowper, EETS ES 22 (1874), 81.

[50] More, *Supplication*, 119.

interest as well as to the altruism of the groups it was attempting to persuade. In fastening on the connection between purgatory and inheritance, a number of reformers sought to play on long-standing anxieties about the social burden of intercession. In the anonymous *Dyalogue betwene a Gentillman and a Husbandman* (1530), the Gentleman speaks of his 'auncesteres of worthy progeny', who had kept their estates honourably and aided the poor, until persuaded by the clergy that there was a purgatory. Thereafter they made over to the Church the lands 'which shuld pertayne unto us of duete'. The Gentleman denies that these were freely given: 'they ware certeynely therto constreyned / By their couetous disceite and falshod' and by threatening of punishment. 'They have oure auncesters lyvelood and rentes'—a slogan designed to strike a chord, and shiver a spine.[51] William Tyndale played the same tune. The clergy promised benefactors perpetual prayers 'lest the lands should ever return home again unto the right heirs'. 'Their own heirs do men disinherit, to endote them'.[52] If this were not scandalous enough, Tyndale reminded his readers of what they must already have known, that the provisions of founders were not in the long term secure, that the sacrifice expected of heirs might in the end count for nothing. In *The Practice of Prelates*, monks and friars secure papal dispensations to alter ordinances of old founders, 'and because, as they thought, they had prayed and distributed for their souls enough to bring him out of purgatory, they thrust them out of their bead-rolls'. The religious promised a daily mass for 40s. a year, 'of which foundations when they have gotten twenty, they will yet, with an union purchased of the pope, make but one chauntry'. If the orders were actually to honour the undertakings they had given to founders, 'five hundred monks were not enough in many cloisters'.[53] The logic here was unmistakable—a call to disendowment and the reclamation of benefactions obtained by a fraudulent Church.

Evangelical activists of the 1520s and 1530s clearly felt that purgatory was vulnerable on social and economic grounds, but this was ultimately a secondary line of attack. The polemical critique of purgatory and intercession was first and foremost a theological one, predicated upon their fundamental incompatibility with the idea of justification by faith alone. In addition to repeatedly pointing to the lack of scriptural evidence, evangelical polemic excelled at exposing the internal inconsistencies of teaching on purgatory, as well as its baleful effects on the spiritual lives of believers. Polemicists repeatedly seized, for example, upon the dread and fearfulness inhering in the Catholic teaching.[54] Only a desperate fear of fiery punish-

---

[51] Arber (ed.), *English Reprints*, 133–6.

[52] Tyndale, *Doctrinal Treatises*, 244, 249.

[53] W. Tyndale, *Expositions and Notes...together with The Practice of Prelates*, ed. H. Walter (PS, 1849), 287.

[54] The following paragraphs draw on my 'Fear, Purgatory and Polemic in Reformation England', in W. G. Naphy and P. Roberts (eds.), *Fear in Early Modern Society* (Manchester, 1997), 150–66.

ment in store could make sense of the level of investment in clerical services, and it followed that the clergy must be assiduous in promoting this fear. Dying men robbed their heirs of their inheritance, thought Tyndale, because the clergy 'fear them with purgatory', a theme endlessly rehearsed in *The Burial of the Mass*.[55] One adjective more than any other was paired with purgatory, serving at once to explain and to expel the fearfulness with which the concept was held to be indelibly imbued—'feigned'. Frith's *Disputation* observed that the papists had contrived to 'feign a purgatory'.[56] Tyndale excelled in references to 'that terrible and fearful purgatory they have feigned to purge thy purse withal', a purgatory 'as hot as their bellies can feign it', a 'feigned purgatory, where we must suffer seven years for every sin'.[57] Latimer noted that purgatory was infinitely profitable 'to the feigners of it'.[58] In acknowledging the literary conceit of More's *Supplication of Souls*, George Joye portrayed him as 'the proctour of purgatory, fayning to have come fro[m] thence'.[59] In a culture habituated to a heightened polarity of truth and falsehood, the 'feigning' of purgatory was intended to carry profoundly uncomfortable resonances. By revealing that the terrors of purgatory were no more than the hook for an elaborate confidence trick, evangelical writers sought not so much to persuade as to jolt, almost to embarrass their readers into abandoning their belief: 'their painful purgatory was but a vain imagination . . . a vain and childish fear which our forefathers had'.[60] Tyndale stressed that the only foundation for fear of purgatory was the 'poetry' of the bishop of Rome, and concluded severely that 'fools be out of their wits to believe it'.[61]

In responding to this onslaught, traditionalist writers did not attempt to deny that contemplating purgatory ought to strike fear in the believer: this was essential to restrain the people from sin. This argument was a central theme of Rastell's *New Boke of Purgatorye*, which argued that loss of purgatory would 'put away the drede of god from the most parte of the people in the worlde, and gyve them boldness to do and commytte offences and synnes', and it recurred throughout the polemical writings of Thomas More.[62] More's *Confutation of Tyndale's Answer* contained a merciless

[55] Tyndale, *Doctrinal Treatises*, 244; Barlow, *The Burial of the Mass*, 133 ff.
[56] Frith, *Disputation*, 141.
[57] Tyndale, *Doctrinal Treatises*, 302; *Expositions and Notes*, 162, 287.
[58] Latimer, *Sermons*, 50.
[59] G. Joye, *The Subversion of Moris False Foundacion* (Emden, 1534), 36ᵛ.
[60] Frith, *Disputation*, 90, 207.
[61] Tyndale, *Expositions and Notes*, 159, 287. Cf. here Stephen Greenblatt's suggestion that to Protestant critics purgatory was quintessentially 'a poet's fable': *Hamlet in Purgatory* (Princeton, 2001), ch. 1.
[62] Rastell, *New Boke*, H3ᵛ-4ʳ; More, *Supplication of Souls*, 175, 199–200; *A Dialogue Concerning Heresies*, ed. T. M. Lawler *et al.* (New Haven, 1981), 377; *Confutation*, 90, 289–90, 967–8; *The Answer to a Poisoned Book*, 187–8. It had been a cardinal principle of Utopian religion that subjects could not be trusted to obey the king if they had 'nothing to fear but laws and no hope beyond the body': *Utopia*, ed. E. Surtz and J. H. Hexter (New Haven, 1965), 223.

caricature of what would inevitably follow from the teaching of justification by faith:

neyther purgatory nede to be fered when we go hens, nor penauns nede to be done whyle we be here, but synne and be sory and syt and make mery, and then synne agayne and then repent a lytell and ronne to the ale & wasshe away the synne, thynke ones on goddys promyse and then do what we lyste.[63]

After More's death, the argument that denial of purgatory 'bringes a man to carnall libertye' recurred in the preaching of Roger Edgeworth, and could even evoke an echo in those much less committed to upholding traditional orthodoxy: the humanist and Henrician loyalist Thomas Starkey judged it to be folly to deny purgatory its place as 'a holesome tradition to the conseruation of the christian lyfe'. In a letter to Henry VIII in 1536 Starkey warned about the unsettling effects of radical preaching: 'with the despysing of purgatory, they began little to regard hell'.[64]

Given the centrality of such arguments to Catholic defences of purgatory, it is unsurprising that Protestant polemicists went to considerable lengths to deny that belief in purgatory was an effective deterrent against sin. Frith and Tyndale both argued that if the unmistakable monitions of the Old and New Testaments did not induce men to reform themselves, fear of purgatory would hardly do so.[65] Indeed, the specious assurance of ultimate salvation that purgatory conveyed, combined with the myriad possibilities for ameliorating its pains, undermined any restraining effect it could possibly have. Frith envisaged the young saying to themselves, 'I will take my pleasure while I may, and if I may have but one hour's respite to cry God mercy, I care not, for then shall I go but to purgatory'. Meanwhile the older generation clung avariciously to their goods, confident that they too could cry 'God mercy', and that their executors 'shall redeem me thence well enough'. In a sweeping inversion of the argument of Rastell and More, Frith concluded that 'to believe purgatory is rather an occasion of reckless boldness than of the fear of God'.[66] Such arguments seem hardly consistent with the line advanced by these same writers that the effect of purgatory was to terrorize the laity into giving to the clergy. But this perhaps takes us to the crux of the polemical campaign against intercession for the dead. The absurdity of a purgatory which could not exist, and which no one need fear, was best exposed by accentuating the dialectical confusion of fearfulness and easiness which underlay the whole intercessory system. As Tyndale put it, 'what great fear can there be of that terrible fire, which thou mayest quench almost for three half-pence? ... Show the pope a little money, and God is so merciful that there is no purgatory.'[67]

[63] More, *Confutation*, 90–1.
[64] T. Starkey, *Life and Letters*, ed. S. J. Herrtage, EETS 57 (1878), p. liii.
[65] Tyndale, *Answer to More*, 28; Frith, *Disputation*, 122.
[66] Frith, *Disputation*, 132.
[67] Tyndale, *Answer to More*, 28, 143.

The precise logistics of purgation and intercession for the souls in purgatory excited a good deal of evangelical derision. The tradition that each
mortal sin incurred a seven-year tariff, for example, invited charges of
sophistry and 'subtelty',[68] and the belief that the dead fared better in the
next life if they had been buried in a friar's cowl came in for particular
mockery.[69] Referring to the devotional topos that every mass delivered a
soul from purgatory, William Tyndale remarked that even if it took ten
masses to accomplish the feat 'yet were the parish priests and curates of
every parish sufficient to scour purgatory: all the other costly workmen
might be well spared'.[70] A more humble heretic, William Wingrave of the
diocese of Lincoln, arrived at a similar balance sheet: 'If there were any
purgatory and every mass that is said should deliver a soul out of purgatory,
there should be never a soul there, for there be more masses said in a day
than there be bodies buried in a month'.[71]

In this ruthlessly 'rationalist' appraisal of the mechanisms of post-mortem
intercession, evangelical polemicists were helped by the fact that the Church
appeared to be operating two ostensibly incompatible methods. On the one
hand were prayers, alms-givings, and masses, suffrages which, with the
exception of a few special trentals, were understood to work in an essentially
attritional way. On the other were pardons, up to and including papally
sanctioned plenary indulgences, which at a stroke wiped out huge swaths
of 'time' in purgatory.[72] Was it not strange, observed Tyndale, that God
might ordain a soul to lie a thousand years in 'a purgatory as hot as hell',
when 'to purge withal, the pope, for the value of a groat, shall command him
thence full purged in the twinkling of an eye'.[73] In his commentary on Tracy's
will, Frith pointed to the paradox of making elaborate preparations to
alleviate 'the grievous pains of purgatory' when they might 'be quenched
both with less cost and labour' if 'the Pope's pardon is ready at hand'.[74] Hugh

---

[68] PRO, SP 6/11, 59^{r-v}; Latimer, *Remains*, 339; Tyndale, *Doctrinal Treatises*, 271; *Expositions and Notes*, 159; *Answer to More*, 47.

[69] Tyndale, *Doctrinal Treatises*, 48, 122; *Expositions and Notes*, 92; Frith, *Disputation*, 118; Foxe, iv. 651, v. 196; *LP* xii (1), 508, 1147; Latimer, *Sermons*, 50, 51; *Remains*, 239, 332; J. Bale, *Select Works*, ed. H. Christmas (PS, 1849), 329; Wyse, *A Consolacyon for Chrysten People*, H8^v; T. Becon, *Early Works*, ed. J. Ayre (PS, 1843), 315. It is hard to say how common the practice actually was; it doesn't appear much if at all in wills, but isolated examples are noted by G. Williams, *Wales and the Reformation* (Cardiff, 1997), 50; C. Daniell, *Death and Burial in Medieval England 1066–1550* (1997), 156. Interestingly, the 1547 homily 'Of Good Woorkes' suggested that the superstition of being buried in a friar's coat 'hath been lytle used in this realme', though was rife abroad: R. B. Bond (ed.), *Certain Sermons or Homilies (1547)* (Toronto, 1987), 110. The claims made by religious orders for special privileges for those dying wearing their cowls are discussed in R. Copsey, 'Simon Stock and the Scapular Vision', *JEH* 50 (1999), 652–83.

[70] Tyndale, *Doctrinal Treatises*, 303.

[71] Foxe, iv. 584.

[72] See above, 27–32.

[73] Tyndale, *Answer to More*, 141.

[74] Frith, *Disputation*, 250.

Latimer similarly suggested that the pains of purgatory were not greatly to be cared for 'if the bishop's two fingers can shake away a good part... or the pope's pardon, or scala coeli of a groat, can dispatch for altogether', and sarcastically added: 'I will never found abbey, college, nor chantry for that purpose'.[75] How close a correspondence there was between such observations and the spirit in which early Tudor English people set about the business of arranging intercession for the soul is not really the issue here. One evangelical monk claimed in 1535 that 'y have knowyn sum fawle almost yn desparacon be overmyche truste yn perdons', yet Tyndale himself suggested that the clergy did not really trust them, preferring to load their bedemen and chaplains with so many masses and dirges 'that I have known of some of them that have bid the devil take their founder's souls, for very impatiency and weariness of so painful labour'.[76] In fact, evangelical writers did not need to make a consistent case that, objectively considered, the system of intercession was too burdensome or too easy. Rather, they wanted to imply that it was uncertain and contradictory, menacing yet somehow comical, and hopelessly compromised by the base motives of those who administered it.

One question in particular seemed to evangelicals to exemplify the self-subverting nature of the Church's claims about purgatory, Luther's 'shrewd question' about why the pope did not exercise his power to release all the souls thence. Simon Fish reported that 'many men of greate litterature and iudgement' thought the pope 'a cruell tyraunt without all charite' if he had the means to empty purgatory but refused to do so, and John Frith rapidly placed himself in this camp.[77] In a letter of late 1531 Latimer confessed how

I have thought in times past, that the pope could have spoiled purgatory at his pleasure with a word of his mouth: now learning might persuade me otherwise; or else I would marvel why he should suffer so much money to be bestowed that way, which so needful is to be bestowed otherwise, and to deprive us of so many patrons in heaven, as he might deliver out of purgatory.[78]

In 1532 a canon of Exeter, Peter Carslegh, preached that if the pope would not deliver souls charitably from purgatory without money, it was a pity he was not in purgatory himself.[79] Such arguments were effective because they

[75] Latimer, *Remains*, 239, 362.

[76] PRO, SP 1/195, 118ʳ (*LP* ix. 135); Tyndale, *Doctrinal Treatises*, 331.

[77] Fish, *Supplicacyon*, 419; Frith, *Disputation*, 93. The claim that the pope was 'a tresourer most banisschid out of charite' had been made in the Lollard *Twelve Conclusions* posted on the doors of Westminster Hall in 1395: A. Hudson, *The Premature Reformation: Wycliffite Texts and Lollard History* (Oxford, 1988), 300.

[78] Latimer, *Remains*, 332. Foxe, v. 524, later reported how William Button, a soldier in the garrison of Calais (that hotbed of heresy) had delighted in winding up priests and pardoners by demanding why the pope 'doth not... of charity deliver all the souls thereout?' See also Bradford, *Letters, Treatises, Remains*, 292.

[79] N. Orme, 'Indulgences in the Diocese of Exeter 1100–1536', *Reports and Transactions of the Devonshire Association*, 120 (1988), 25. Carslegh seems not to have been an evangelical, though he was employing a distinctively evangelical motif.

turned on its head one of the most powerful supports of intercessory prayer, its status as a deed of charity. Addressing this question in his *Supplication of Souls*, More argued that if the pope were thought cruel on these grounds, 'thys unreasonable rason layeth cruelte to the blame of god, which may undoutedly delyver all sowlys thens and yet he leveth them there'.[80] Yet this may have been to beg the question of the existence of purgatory in precisely the way his opponents wanted.

The ambiguities, doubts, and inconsistencies that evangelicals associated with the traditional teaching on purgatory were, they felt, fairly easily resolved, not merely by recognizing that purgatory did not exist, but by accepting that God's chosen way of reconciling himself with fallen man was quite incompatible with any notion of purgation in the next life. To believe purgatory was to create a perverse image of a vengeful and arbitrary God. No father, thought Tyndale, would punish his son to purge him if he had already forsaken sin and submitted himself to his father's doctrine.[81] An evangelical scriptural commentary of the 1530s suggested that purgatory made God seem like a king pardoning a man for theft, and afterwards hanging him, saying 'Syr I forgave you your thefte but nott your hangynge wch is due unto your thefte'.[82] The *Burial of the Mass* charged that 'of Christ oure mercifull saveoure / They make a iudge full of terroure'.[83] A recurrent theme of Frith's *Disputation* was the incompatibility of purgatory with the mercy of God, 'for the nature of mercy is to forgive, but purgatory will have all paid and satisfied'.[84] The only satisfaction that God required had been made once for all in the sacrifice of the Cross. If there was satisfaction for sins in purgatory, Frith remarked, 'verily then is Christ dead in vain'.[85] By extension, the suffrages conventionally offered for the relief of souls in purgatory were a derogation of Christ's passion. To demand perpetual prayers, claimed John Bale, was 'to thinke Christes deth to be unsufficient'.[86] One of Bale's heroines, the Henrician martyr Anne Askew, told her interrogators that 'it was great idolatry to believe more in [masses for the departed] than in the death that Christ died for us'.[87] Pressed on the existence of purgatory, an earlier Henrician victim, James Bainham, responded obliquely, but clearly enough: 'If we walk in light, even as he is in light, we have society together with him, and the blood of Jesus Christ his Son hath cleansed us from all sin...If we confess our sins, he is faithful

---

[80] More, *Supplication*, 198.
[81] Tyndale, *Answer to More*, 143.
[82] PRO, SP 6/11, 59[r–v].
[83] Barlow, *Burial of the Mass*, 73.
[84] Frith, *Disputation*, 138–9.
[85] Ibid. 142. Brinkelow held that intercession for the dead 'cast Christes meretes asyde': *Lamentacyon of a Christen*, 86.
[86] Bale, *Complete Plays*, i. 41–2.
[87] Bale, *Select Works*, 152.

and just, and will forgive us our sins, and will purge us from all our iniquities.'[88]

Evangelical writers sometimes spoke of a 'true purgatory', by which they meant the cross of Christ and his precious blood.[89] For those who had come to believe in an imputed righteousness arising solely from Christ's vicarious work of satisfaction, the suffrages offered by the living for the welfare of the dead were pointless and futile. If Christians did not recognize God's prom-ises they would perish, admonished Tyndale, even if they had 'a thousand holy candles...a hundred ton of holy water, a ship-full of pardons, a cloth-sack full of friars' coats, and all the ceremonies in the world'.[90] Henry Brinkelow warned the citizens of London that their prayers could help the dead 'no more then a mans brethe blowynge in the sayle, can cause a greate shippe for to sayle', and that their ceremonies 'avayleth the deade no more then the pissinge of a wrenne helpeth to cause the see to flowe at an extreme ebbe'.[91] Equally graphic bestial imagery was employed by a Here-fordshire man, John Cooke, arguing about the value of obits with his neighbours in the house of Richard Tokyr in April 1540. 'Wat avaylyth your babblyng and your syngyng... By Godys blode, no more worth that Tokyrs wyffes cowe to lowe or ellys that my bitch showld take Richard Tokyrs sowe by the yere'.[92] Thomas Fougeler of Rye announced 'that he had rather have a doge to syng for hym then a prest'.[93]

The lineaments of the theological assault on purgatory, as it had de-veloped up to the mid-1530s, have been examined at some length because it is important to understand how central a deep hostility to the doctrine was to the evangelical mentality. Purgatory was not merely an excrescent super-stition (though it had bred its share of those), but a linchpin of the whole anti-Christian system. Belief in purgatory, or in any notion of post-mortem purgation, seemed to epitomize the merit-theology espoused by a corrupt Church, and it was incompatible with the central theological insight of the Reformation: justification by faith alone. It exalted the principle of extra-scriptural traditions against the purity of God's Word; it underscored the power of a sacramental priesthood pronouncing absolution from sin (but not the penalties due for sin) in confession; and by providing a rationale for

[88] Foxe, iv. 697. Bainham was here engaged in the common ploy of quoting bare Scripture to interrogators, a direct recital of 1 John 1: 7, 9.

[89] Frith, *Disputation*, 90–1; Tyndale, *Answer to More*, 214; Foxe, v. 11; S. B. House, 'Literature, Drama and Politics', in D. MacCulloch (ed.), *The Reign of Henry VIII: Politics, Policy and Piety* (Basingstoke, 1995), 188. See also C. R. Trueman, *Luther's Legacy: Salvation and English Reformers 1525–1556* (Oxford, 1994), 131, 142. Calvin's ultimate objection to purgatory was that 'it makes void the cross of Christ...the blood of Christ is the only satisfac-tion, expiation, and cleansing for the sins of believers': *Institutes of the Christian Religion*, tr. H. Beveridge, 2 vols. in 1 (Grand Rapids, Mich. 1989), ii. 576.

[90] Tyndale, *Doctrinal Treatises*, 48.

[91] Brinkelow, *Lamentacyon of a Christen*, 81, 88.

[92] PRO, E 36/120, 71ʳ (*LP* xv. 587).

[93] PRO, SP 1/113, 92ʳ (*LP* xi. 1424).

celebrations of the eucharist as a propitiatory application of the merits of Christ's passion, it was a central prop of that great 'idol', the mass. At the same time, however, the perceived vulnerability of the doctrine on scriptural, historical, and psychological, as well as social and economic grounds made it the ideal stalking-horse for a broader programme of reform.[94] Demolish purgatory, and the rest—good works, auricular confession, the sacrificial doctrine of the mass—would surely follow in time. This presents us with a paradox and a conundrum. Henry VIII never abandoned his faith in the mass, and he explicitly set his face, and committed his Church, against justification by faith. Yet, as will be shown, his ecclesiastical policy after 1534 was profoundly influenced by the views surveyed above, and in this area his Church made significant departures from traditional orthodoxy. The vulnerability of purgatory was a Trojan horse of the English Reformation.[95]

PURGATORY, PAPACY, AND PARDONS

Between the break with Rome in 1533–4, and 1536, when the Ten Articles provided the first doctrinal formulation for the Henrician Church, traditional views on purgatory and the value of prayer for the dead came under increasingly fierce attack, and did so with a considerable degree of official encouragement. An entirely new set of parameters within which these questions could be judged was provided by the 'order taken for preaching and bidding of the beads' issued by Archbishop Cranmer in June 1534. This prescribed prayers for the whole Catholic Church 'as well quick as dead', and laid down that the bidding of beads should finish in time-honoured fashion with prayers 'for the souls of all them that be dead, and specially of such as it shall please the preacher to name'. But 'to keep unity and quietness in this realm' it was also ordained that preachers should not openly contend with one another, and 'that no preachers for a year shall preach neither with nor against purgatory, honouring of saints, that priests may have wives, that faith only justifieth, to go on pilgrimages, to forge miracles', all matters that 'have caused dissension amongst the subjects of this realm'.[96] The implications of this eirenic-sounding proposal are worth

[94] Note here the evangelical William Marshall's translation of Erasmus's *A Playne and Godly Exposition or Declaration of the Comune Crede* (1533), O4ᵛ–5ʳ, which remarked that 'it was lawfull also more than C.C.C. yeres after the incarnation of Christ / to doute whyther there were any clensynge fyre, or fyre of purgatory which certayn men dyd iudge to be charite'.

[95] Did Henry himself understand this? According to an account which John Foxe claimed to have received from one of Henry's footmen, Edmund Moddis, the king asked to have Fish's *Supplicacyon* read to him, and then put the pamphlet in his desk, with the gnomic comment that 'If a man should pull down an old stone wall, and begin at the lower part, the upper part thereof might chance to fall upon his head': Foxe, iv. 658.

[96] T. Cranmer, *Miscellaneous Writings*, ed. J. E. Cox (PS, 1846), 460–1.

reflecting upon. At a stroke, the existence of purgatory, a given of late medieval religion, had been relegated to the status of a contentious opinion. In retrospect, this looks remarkably like the 'preaching mandates' which presaged the implementation of full-scale reformation in a number of German towns.[97]

The preaching order expired in the summer of 1535, but contemporaries remained unsure of their freedom to uphold traditional doctrine. The conservative archbishop of York, Edward Lee, took no chances, and continued to inhibit both radicals and traditionalists from preaching about purgatory.[98] The experience of Lee's episcopal colleague, John Stokesley of London, suggested he was right to be cautious. In the spring and early summer of 1535, Stokesley prohibited Latimer and John Hilsey from preaching at Paul's Cross, fearing, with good reason, that they would preach against intercession for the dead. At the end of the year, Cromwell struck back, taking responsibility for licensing preachers at Paul's Cross away from Stokesley and giving it to Hilsey, now bishop of Rochester. Early the next year both Latimer and Cranmer inveighed against purgatory from this most famous of English pulpits.[99] Meanwhile, traditionalists who preached in favour of purgatory and intercession were reported to the authorities, and in March 1536 a monk of Syon who interrupted an anti-purgatory sermon in the presence of the king was threatened with execution.[100]

The pole around which much of the agitation against purgatory revolved was the king's new vice-gerent in spirituals, Thomas Cromwell. In August 1534 Cromwell was sent a set of reform proposals, including the proposition that 'that the prayers of men that be here living can in no wise be profitable for the souls of them that be dead'. The leading author was John Rastell, now thoroughly disabused of his former opinions. Other radicals, such as Clement Armstrong and Thomas Swinnerton, sent the minister manuscript treatises which denounced purgatory.[101] Towards the end of 1534, a member of Cromwell's office drew up a memorandum of abuses he hoped parliament would proscribe, which included the following propositions:

[97] E. Cameron, *The European Reformation* (Oxford, 1991), 235–7.

[98] Kreider, *Chantries*, 108.

[99] S. Wabuda, 'The Provision of Preaching during the Early English Reformation: With Special Reference to Itineration, *c.*1530 to 1547', University of Cambridge Ph.D. thesis (1992), 115–16; Kreider, *Chantries*, 108–13; S. Brigden, *London and the Reformation* (Oxford, 1989), 258–9.

[100] PRO, SP 6/2, 88ʳ; Kreider, *Chantries*, 109, 113.

[101] Kreider, *Chantries*, 116–17. Swinnerton was licensed as a preacher by Cranmer in June 1535, in which capacity he seems to have preached 'ayenste prayer to be said for sowllys departed and ayenste purgatory': D. MacCulloch, *Thomas Cranmer: A Life* (New Haven, 1996), 139 n.; PRO, SP 1/113, 92ʳ (*LP* xi. 1424). Other protégés of the archbishop, including Thomas Garrett and Thomas Lawney, were preaching against purgatory in 1535–6, the latter complaining 'that people have a communicacion and beleve that sowllys have dyvers paynes in purgatory as of fire and other': ibid.

that it cannot be proved by Scripture that the Busshopis of Rome may deliver soulis out of purgatorie: ne that ther is any purgatory. That if there be a purgatorye, that there is neyther payne of fire ne heat, nor sight of devillys. That it is a more necessarye and more cheritable prayor to pray for theym that be a live than for theym that be dead. That god only forgivethe synne.[102]

This was an effective thumbnail summary of the main lines of evangelical criticism. In 1535 a monk of Winchcombe, John Horwood alias Placet, was writing to Cromwell requesting sponsorship for his scheme to counter the 'drye dremes, fansis and fables' to be found in 'syche bokys as trete off purgatory'. He was clearly given encouragement, for some time later he wrote again, noting 'I have dyligencely remembryde every thynge that ye spake to me, the kynges grace lying at Waltam', and he reported that he had sought out many 'wolde bokys and ragyde pawmphylions' containing old doctors' opinions of purgatory, 'pro et contra'.[103] A more influential client of Cromwell's, William Marshall, published the first English version of the primer 'cum gratia et privilegio regali' in 1534, omitting the *dirige* which had always been a central feature of these texts, and including no other prayers for the dead. The *dirige* was restored in a second edition of 1535, but hardly with ringing endorsement, denouncing as superstition the fact 'that we have rung and sung, mumbled, murmured and piteously puled forth a certain sort of psalms ... for the souls of our christian brethren and sistern that be departed out of this world'.[104] The same year saw the appearance of Marshall's translation of Marsiglio of Padua's *Defensor Pacis*, its marginal notes making clear the translator's scepticism: 'This geare must be iudged by higher judges, whether there be a purgatory after this lyfe or no'; 'Yf the preeste do his dutie as he is bounde, who goeth to purgatorie? and then wherfore shuld we beleve that there is one'; 'We be not agreed as yet of any purgatorye after this lyfe'.[105] At the start of 1536 the question seemed genuinely to be up in the air. According to Chapuys, when parliament met for its last session on 4 February the government had supplied members with books against both the adoration of saints and purgatory.[106]

The extent to which the Henrician regime tolerated, even encouraged, quite radical attacks on the traditional theology of intercession and the afterlife is remarkable. The presence of leading evangelicals in positions of authority of course supplies part of the explanation, but the reformers among the crew in the ship of state did not get their way on all issues, and could not steer in a direction in which the captain fundamentally did not wish to go. The question of Henry VIII's own attitudes towards the commemoration of the dead is an intriguing one, and will be considered

[102] BL, Cotton Cleo E vi. 330ᵛ (*LP* vii. 1383).
[103] PRO, SP 1/95, 118ʳ; 98, 131ʳ (*LP* ix. 135, 723).
[104] Duffy, *Altars*, 382.
[105] Marsiglio, *The Defence of Peace*, tr. William Marshall (1535), 62ᵛ, 65ʳ.
[106] Kreider, *Chantries*, 117.

in more detail below. But for the moment it can be noted that, in those critical years when the English Church was disengaging itself from Rome, attacks upon traditional modes of intercession dovetailed with the needs of the royal supremacy. As Alan Kreider was undoubtedly correct to observe, 'the whole issue of purgatory was inextricably intertwined with the papacy'.[107]

Evangelical writers lost few opportunities to point out the connections between purgatory and the usurped authority of the papacy. 'The pope, with all his pardons, is grounded on purgatory', observed Tyndale, while Frith's translation of Luther's *The Revelation of Antichrist* included the memorable image of the pope as 'the Kinge of them that are dead and raigneth in purgatorye'.[108] In Bale's play *King Johan*, purgatory is called 'the Popes kychyne'. King John's nemesis, Stephen Langton, metonymically termed 'Sedicyon' in the play, comes armed with a papal bull, promising the clergy 'absolucyon / A pena et culpa, with a thowsand dayes of pardon.'[109] An officially sanctioned tract of 1534, the *Litel Treatise ageynste the mutterynge of some papistes in corners*, made reference to the huge sums popes had polled out of England for dispensations, citations, and pardons, a clear echo of the rhetoric of Fish's *Supplicacyon*.[110]

It was not just radical evangelicals who harped on the connection. In *An Exhortation to the People, Instructynge them to Unitie and Obedience* (1536), Thomas Starkey supplied an account of the growth of papal authority which identified the time when 'purgatorie after a newe facion was invented' as a pivotal moment: 'therby chiefelye beganne his reygne, thenne came in pardones and reservation to his owne see, than crope in the difinition of thynges by his hye authoritie, than entred excommunication and intedytes upon all princis and christen nations'. Starkey was no evangelical. Indeed, he specifically rebuked those who 'repute folyshe simplicite . . . purgatory and praying for them which be deed'. Although popes had misused purgatory to their own glory 'yet the thynge in it selfe was of no pope inventyd', being rather a venerable patristic tradition with at least some claim to scriptural support. But repeated reference to the abuse of pardons and to the pope's 'pluckyng soules out of purgatory' was hardly calculated to bolster confidence in the traditional teaching. Starkey also threw in what was rapidly becoming an established *obiter dictum* in reformist vocabulary: if the pope has power to deliver souls out of torment, yet demurs from doing

---

[107] Ibid. 104.

[108] Tyndale, *Doctrinal Treatises*, 303; More, *Supplication*, p. lxxii.

[109] Bale, *Complete Plays*, i. 82, 61. Papal claims to offer pardon 'a poena et culpa' were regarded as particularly offensive: Tyndale, *Doctrinal Treatises*, 268, 27; R. Barnes, *A Supplicacion unto the Most Gracyous Prince H. the VIII* (1531), 30ᵛ. Attacks on pardons granted by the pope feature prominently in the attacks on purgatory being made in 1529–31 subsequently recorded by Foxe, v. 28, 33, 39.

[110] N. Pocock (ed.), *Records of the Reformation: The Divorce 1527–1533*, 2 vols. (1870), ii. 549.

so, then 'he is pleyn more then a tiranne'.[111] The issue was summarized more
bluntly in a 1536 draft treatise against the power of Rome, apparently
drawn up by Thomas Wriothesley: 'thoppinion that there is a purgatory
meynteyneth a favour to Rome for that oppinion hath been maynteyned by
the power of Rome'.[112]

The essential link between the theology of purgatory and the political
authority of the pope was of course the latter's claim to administer a
'treasury of merit' which allowed him to issue indulgences remitting penalties due in purgatory. In his *Assertio Septem Sacramentorum* of 1521, Henry
VIII argued that 'if, as Luther says, indulgences have no efficacy at all but are
mere impostures, then it is necessary that we consider as impostors not only
the present pontiff, Leo X... but also all the Roman pontiffs through so
many ages past'.[113] These words must have seemed ironically prophetic to
the Henry of 1534. The Dispensations Act of that year forbade the seeking
of indulgences from Rome, and while it did not annul papal indulgences
acquired before March 1534, it did not empower the king or the archbishop
of Canterbury to issue them in future. Moreover, it reserved to the king
the right to reform all manner of indulgences obtained at the see of Rome,
and 'the abuses of such indulgences'.[114] The issue was revisited in a proclamation of January 1536, which complained of the activity of pardoners
still peddling 'divers indulgences and pardons corruptly and deceitfully
obtained of the Bishop of Rome'. Henceforth no such pardons were to be
published. The measure was presented in crime and disorder terms: pardoners were said to be typically 'confederate with the great errant thieves of this
realm', leading them to the houses of the rich to commit robbery. The alleged
misdeeds of licensed indulgence-sellers or pardoners were a familiar theme,
almost a late medieval cliché, given definitive literary expression by Chaucer
in *The Canterbury Tales*.[115] But in 1536 a theological rationale was also
provided for curtailing their activities. The effect of indulgences was to
encourage subjects 'to commit sin and to withdraw their faith, hope, and
devotion from God', a sentiment that would have been applauded by Tyndale or Frith.[116] Papal pardons were also condemned in the Ten Articles later
that year. Indulgences as such were not formally prohibited, and as late as
December 1536 Bishop Veysey of Exeter offered forty days of pardon to

[111] T. Starkey, *An Exhortation to the People, Instructynge them to Unitie and Obedience*
(1536), 63ʳ, 24ᵛ, 76ʳ–77ʳ, 66ᵛ, 64ʳ.
[112] PRO, SP 1/105, 60ʳ (*LP* xi. 86 (2)).
[113] Cited in More, *Responsio*, 327–9.
[114] H. Gee and W. J. Hardy (eds.), *Documents Illustrative of English Church History* (1896),
229–30.
[115] *The Riverside Chaucer*, ed. L. D. Benson, (3rd edn. (Oxford, 1988), 34–5, 194–6.
Unauthorized pardoners were placed in the pillory in London in 1494 and 1497, and their
activities were attacked by the Vagrancy Act of 1531: K. W. Cameron, *The Pardoner and his
Pardons: Indulgences Circulating in England on the Eve of the Reformation* (Hartford, Conn.,
1965), 7; *The Statutes of the Realm*, 11 vols. (1830–52), 330 (2 Hen. VIII c. 12).
[116] *TRP* i. 235–7.

contributors towards the upkeep of a bridge in his diocese.[117] Effectively, however, the trade in indulgences was closed down in that year.[118] An evangelical sermon preached in Oxford in 1537 rejoiced that the devil 'can no more make men to putt trust and confydence in pardons', and mocked the past achievements of that great saint, Money, that 'coulde do with a becke all his pleasure as well in hevyn as in erth and for neade brynge a sowle owt of the popis purgatorye'.[119] But an evangelical tract of the same year complaining of things begun by the power of Rome and 'yet used among the people', noted 'that pardons are still granted from Rome for the souls of deceased persons'.[120]

There seemed to be compelling political reasons in the mid-1530s for cracking down on the people's appetite for indulgences. In 1535 the apostate friar Robert Ward was writing to Cromwell about the cycle depicting the life of St Thomas Becket in the windows of the church of St Thomas of Acres. This included such inappropriate scenes as the king kneeling naked at St Thomas's shrine. Ward had seen this style in other places too, 'and have heard pardoners set forth, in the dedication of the pardon of St Thomas, divers points whereof he was slain in that he did resist the King'.[121] Ward's view that indulgences represented an open invitation to treason was not entirely without force. In Lent 1536, at the Crutched Friars in London, the priest George Rowland was urging his penitents in confession to recognize the pope as head of the universal Church of Christ, and to believe that his pardons were as effectual as ever they were, adjoining to this the conventional, though now contested, wisdom that 'they that make not satysfacyon in this world for ther synnes must be punyshed in purgatory'.[122] In June of that year, the vicar of Loose in Kent was reported by some of his parishioners for promising indulgences to those who came to the first evensong of Corpus Christi, indulgences he ascribed to '"the Holy Bishop Urban" (naming him at first Pope)'.[123] Similar promises were made in an intemperate sermon by one Mr Lovell at Sturminster Newton in Dorset that same Corpus Christi.

---

[117] Orme, 'Indulgences in the Diocese of Exeter 1100–1536', 26.

[118] Paul Ayris has drawn attention to an apparent revival of the practice in the summer of 1543, when an exhortation (possibly the work of Cranmer) was ordered to be read out in churches promising (rather indeterminate) spiritual rewards to those who contributed towards Ferdinand's campaign to halt the Turks in eastern Europe. But this document stressed that it was not an indulgence in the traditional sense, noting that 'ye were wonte to be abused with vayne tales, and for counterfaite pardons departyd with yor moneye'. It insisted that it provided nothing 'to the preiudyce or derogation of the effecte of Chrystys passion, whiche ys the very purgation and redemption of all synne'. P. Ayris, 'Preaching the Last Crusade: Thomas Cranmer and the "Devotion" Money of 1543', *JEH* 49 (1998), 683–701.

[119] PRO, SP 1/120, 251ᵛ (*LP* xii (1), 1325).

[120] *LP* xii (1), 791.

[121] PRO, SP 1/92, 128–9 (*LP* viii. 626). The windows were taken down on Cromwell's orders in 1538: C. Wriothesley, *A Chronicle of England*, ed. W. D. Hamilton, 2 vols., CS NS 11, 20 (1875–7), i. 87.

[122] PRO, SP 1/102, 73ʳ–74ʳ (*LP* x. 346).

[123] *LP* x. 1125.

He urged the people to keep holidays, to offer candles, and to beware of the New Testament in English, and concluded with the highly implausible claim that forty days of pardon had been granted by the archbishop of Canterbury, and the bishops of Salisbury and Exeter, to all who heard his sermon. Afterwards, he was heard to remark, vis-à-vis the diplomatic situation in Europe, that since the pope supported the French king in his quarrel with the emperor, there would be a blessing on all who took the French side, 'and that if our King and the Emperor after their departing went not to Hell, the devil is not in Hell'.[124] A few months later, participants in the greatest single challenge to Henry's rule, the Pilgrimage of Grace, believed that they were eligible for the 'crusade indulgence', which remitted all sin.[125]

This was heady stuff, but links between conservative disaffection from the royal supremacy and support for traditional ideas about the dead had been apparent from the beginning of Henry's break with Rome. This was certainly the case with perhaps the most dangerous of Henry's early opponents, the visionary 'Nun of Kent', Elizabeth Barton, who prophesied Henry's death if he persisted with his plan to divorce Queen Catherine. Nicholas Heath's December 1533 sermon denouncing Barton and her supporters made much of a book of the Nun's revelations compiled by her spiritual advisor, the Benedictine Edward Bocking. It singled out for condemnation supposed insights into the condition of departed souls. Barton was said to have discerned that Wolsey had died fifteen years before God would have him, and that sentence on him was deferred until this time was up. She had been thanked by a soul who, were it not for her prayers, 'had been utterly damned and gone to the pit of hell'. Mary Magdalene herself had acknowledged to her that her petitions had saved one 'which was sometimes my servant' from everlasting damnation. Heath also drew attention to a sentence in the book 'concerning the soul of a certain dead man': 'he was delivered from that place ... where he was punished—a place of no salvation—unto purgatory, a place of salvation'.[126] It is significant that the campaign to discredit Barton felt the need to disparage revelations of this sort: since her first emergence into public prominence in 1525–6, a prominent part of the Nun's 'charism' had been her ability to discern the state of departed souls, and report their place and condition to the living.[127]

---

[124] Ibid. 1140.

[125] E. H. Shagan, 'Popular Politics and the English Reformation, *c.*1525–1553', Princeton University Ph.D. thesis (2000), 170.

[126] L. E. Whatmore (ed.), 'The Sermon against the Holy Maid of Kent and her Adherents', *EHR* 59 (1943), 468–70.

[127] A. Neame, *The Holy Maid of Kent: The Life of Elizabeth Barton, 1506–1534* (1971), 36–7, 147–8; Cranmer, *Miscellaneous Writings*, 272–3. The reception of special foreknowledge of people in the afterlife seems to be characteristic of a number of female visionaries in late medieval Europe and underlines a very distinctive and powerful mediatory role. Others include the fifteenth-century English mystic Margery Kempe and the fourteenth-century Bavarian nun Margaretha von Ebner, as well as St Catherine of Siena and St Bridget of Sweden: *The Book of Margery Kempe*, ed. S. B. Meech, EETS 212 (1940), 46, 53; U. Rublack, 'Female Spirituality

Barton's was not the only case where visions relating the condition of the dead acquired a distinctly political tinge. In June 1534 the Carthusian John Darley confessed to having received a vision of a deceased brother, Fr. Raby. As the old Carthusian lay dying, Darley had said to him 'good ffather Raby, yff the dede may come to the qwyke, I besuch yow to com to me', and so it had transpired. In the evening of the feast of St John the Baptist (24 June) Raby appeared to Darley in his cell and urged him to follow the example of 'our ffather' (the recently executed Prior Houghton), whom Raby announced to be a 'marter in hevyn next unto angelles'. During a second visitation, Raby confirmed that Bishop Fisher was in the same case. Darley, who understood how the percipient of a ghostly vision was supposed to behave, asked his former confrere, 'ffather, shall I pray ffor yow?' As a saint in heaven, Raby had no need of prayers, but he advised that 'prayer both for yow and other doith good'.[128] In March the following year, the Suffolk rector Robert Creukehorne was hauled in front of Archbishop Cranmer and Bishops Shaxton and Latimer to give an account of a vision of the Trinity and the Blessed Virgin, during which the latter had urged him 'to preche abrode that she wold be honorid at Eppiswhiche and at Willisdon as she hath bee in old tymes'. In the course of the interrogation, Creukehorne offered to prove purgatory from a certain place in the psalter, a provocative challenge to the three evangelical bishops. The weight of their combined learning was too much for Creukehorne to overcome, for he could not find the passage in question, protesting rather lamely that 'my lord of London saide that it made well for it'.[129]

Connections between opposition to the government's religious policies and traditionalist attitudes towards purgatory and the dead manifested themselves in more prosaic ways as well, for example in the reports of priests who from the pulpit failed to denounce the pope or declare the royal supremacy, but continued to pray for the souls in purgatory.[130] In other cases, the link between papalism and the defence of purgatory was more overt. In October 1537 a layman in Norwich greeted the dissolution of a local abbey with the defiant words, 'Rome shall uppe ageyne, and purgatorie is found'.[131]

---

and the Infant Jesus in Late Medieval Dominican Convents', in B. Scribner and T. Johnson (eds.), *Popular Religion in Germany and Central Europe, 1400–1800* (Basingstoke, 1996), 30–1; D. Watt, 'The Prophet at Home: Elizabeth Barton and the Influence of Bridget of Sweden and Catherine of Siena', in R. Voaden (ed.), *Prophets Abroad: The Reception of Continental Holy Women in Late-Medieval England* (Cambridge, 1996), 173.

[128] T. Wright (ed.), *Three Chapters of Letters relating to the Suppression of Monasteries*, CS 26 (1843), 34–5.

[129] Ibid. 36–7. Stokesley's advocacy of purgatory is well documented. In 1540 Bishop Richard Sampson of Chichester reported how the bishop of London had been 'very earnest with me for old usages', in particular 'praying for souls, and that by prayers they were delivered from pains'. Strype, *Ecclesiastical Memorials*, i (2), 257.

[130] *LP* viii. 480, xiii (1), 603, 981.

[131] *LP* xii (2), 864. As I shall show, this was a rather optimistic reading of the theology of the 1537 Bishops' Book.

Another layman, Richard James of Harwich, was in April 1539 reported to
have said that 'he trusted there should be a pope where there should be no
king', a prospect he linked with a robust (if confused) affirmation of traditional belief about the dead: 'the soul that was departed should go to St
James, or he went to purgatory and mett with the body at the churchgate'.[132]
Some of the most uncompromising attitudes were to be found in that most
religiously polarized of all King Henry's possessions, the garrison town of
Calais. In 1537 a priest there, William Mynstreley, was executed after
preaching that priests ought to have no temporal prince in authority over
them, a teaching he combined with defences of purgatory. In January 1538
the chaplain to the High Marshal in Calais was reported to have shown to the
soldiers there a book to prove purgatory, and that it was right to pray for the
pope.[133]

    Purgatory also played a role in one of the most bizarre cases of clerical
dissidence in Henrician England, that of the Franciscan Observant John
Forest, who in May 1538 achieved the unique distinction of being burned
as a heretic for upholding the authority of the pope. One of the articles
alleged against Forest was that he had taught that 'a priest maie turne and
change the paines of hell of a sinner, trulie penitent, contrite of his sinns, by
certaine pennance enjoyned him in the paines of purgatorie'.[134] This was a
version of familiar orthodox teaching. The *Exoneratorium Curatorum*, a
popular clerical handbook of the 1520s, explained that by virtue of the
sacrament of penance pains of hell which sinners deserved were changed
to 'temporall payne of this worlde or of purgatory'.[135] But in the circumstances of 1538 it seemed a dangerously reactionary teaching. Forest's claim
directly echoed one of the 'revelations' of Elizabeth Barton. Moreover, the
regime had just put down a focus for 'superstitious' pilgrimage in North
Wales, the great wooden statue of Dderfel Gadarn. According to the com-
missary-general of the diocese of St Asaph, the Welsh believed that if anyone
made an offering to the image 'he hathe power to fetch hym or them that so
offers out of hell when they be dampned'.[136] Appropriately, the friar and the
'abused image' were burned together. The catalyst for Forest's arrest was his
pro-papal utterances during confession, and the case conjoins a number of
themes that were alarming the government in the late 1530s: popular
'superstition', the papalism of conservative clergy, the potential of confession as a medium for spreading their treason, and the exaggerated claims for
theological powers they exercised therein. Drawing all of these threads

---

[132] *LP* xiv (1), 863.

[133] Kreider, *Chantries*, 142; *LP* xiii (1), 108.

[134] Wriothesley, *Chronicle*, i. 79. I discuss the case in greater detail in 'Papist as Heretic: The
Burning of John Forest, 1538', *HJ* 41 (1998), 351–74.

[135] Cited in R. White, 'Early Print and Purgatory: The Shaping of an Henrician Ideology',
Australian National University Ph.D. thesis (1994), 84. See also More, *Confutation*, 289.

[136] Wright, *Three Chapters of Letters*, 190–1.

together was the question of purgatory, and traditional suffrages for the dead.

In July 1536, with the promulgation of the Ten Articles, Henry VIII's Church provided the first clear statement of what the people were now to believe. The tenth article was headed 'Of Purgatory'. Its wording is suggestive in a number of ways, and is worth reproducing in its entirety:

Forasmuch as due order of charity requireth, and the Book of Maccabees, and divers ancient doctors plainly shewen, that it is a very good and charitable deed to pray for souls departed, and forasmuch also as such usage hath continued in the church so many years, even from the beginning, we will that all bishops and preachers shall instruct and teach our people committed by us unto their spiritual charge, that no man ought to be grieved with the very due order of charity, a Christian man to pray for souls departed, and to commit them in our prayers to God's mercy, and also to cause others to pray for them in masses and exequies, and to give alms to others to pray for them, whereby they may be relieved, and holpen, of some part of their pain: but forasmuch as the place where they be, the name thereof, and kind of pains there, also be to us uncertain by scripture; therefore this with all other things we remit to God Almighty, unto whose mercy it is meet and convenient for us to commend them, trusting that God accepteth our prayers for them, referring the rest wholly to God, to whom is known their estate and condition; wherefore it is much necessary that such abuses be put clearly away, which under the name of purgatory hath been advanced, as to make men believe that through the bishop of Rome's pardon souls might clearly be delivered out of purgatory, and all the pains of it, or that masses said at scala coeli, or otherwise, in any place, or before any image, might likewise deliver them from all their pain, and send them straight to heaven; and other like abuses.[137]

Did this represent a victory or a defeat for evangelicals seeking to undermine purgatory? Historians' views on this have been divided.[138] Contemporaries too had differing assessments of the article's significance. The emperor's proctor at Rome, Pedro Ortiz, wrote in June 1536 that 'purgatory is preached again', while Reginald Pole conceded that the Ten Articles dealt with purgatory 'much after the old manner'.[139] But there is an alternative reading in the 'insider's view' provided by Bishop William Barlow of St Davids in a sermon later that year. Exasperated by 'slanderous rumures ...that the olde popisshe purgatorie is founde agayne', Barlow supplied

---

[137] C. Lloyd (ed.), *Formularies of Faith* (Oxford, 1825), 16–17.

[138] White, 'Early Print and Purgatory', 128, and J. Helt, 'Purgatory, Policy, and Piety in Sixteenth-Century Essex', Vanderbilt University Ph.D. thesis (1996), 61, 97, 101, regard the tenth article as fundamentally conservative. Contrast Kreider, *Chantries*, 122–4; Duffy, *Altars*, 393; MacCulloch, *Cranmer*, 162.

[139] *LP* x. 1043, xi. 376.

his auditors with a first-hand account of the bishops' deliberations over the tenth article. Having surveyed the scriptural passages traditionally held to support purgatory, they found that they served nothing to that purpose and that only the second book of Maccabees ('moste suspectyd to be of leste auctorite') gave any sanction to prayers, suffrages, and sacrifices for the dead. The patristic testimony too was found to be contradictory and inconclusive. Nonetheless, because prayer for the dead had been taught by diverse fathers as a 'custome of longe continuaunce', the bishops agreed it was 'mete and expedient' for it to continue, but 'withoute determinacion of eny specialle place or expressyd assertion of any name eyther to be callyd sinus abrahe [Abraham's Bosom] or other wise, referringe hyt to god'. Nothing was further from their minds than to revive a 'popisshe purgatory'.[140] A similar gloss was provided by another insider, Archbishop Cranmer, in a stinging letter to the Kentish conservative Sir Thomas Cheyney, furious that after the issuing of the 1537 Bishops' Book (which repeated the tenth article verbatim) Cheyney's servants had been reporting 'that all things are restored by this new book to their old use, both of ceremonies, pilgrimages, purgatory, and such other'. Cranmer warned that 'if men will indifferently read these late declarations, they shall well perceive that purgatory, pilgrimages...and such other, be not restored to their late accustomed abuses; but shall evidently perceive that the word of God hath gotten the upper hand of them all'.[141]

A closer consideration of the phraseology of the article suggests that Cranmer had a point. Though it commended prayer for the dead as a charitable deed, the article was notable in insisting that Scripture had nothing certain to teach about the place or condition of departed souls. The book of Maccabees was cited, alongside 'divers ancient doctors', but nothing certain was said about its canonical status. In an echo of the recent proclamation about indulgences, the belief that papal pardons might deliver souls out of purgatory was explicitly condemned. So was the placing of any trust in 'masses of scala coeli'. We may be looking here at the fingerprints of purgatory's most vocal critic among the bench of bishops, Hugh Latimer.[142] In 1533 Latimer had mocked the ability of 'the pope's pardon, or scala coeli of a groat' to dispense with the pains of purgatory, and addressing convoca-

---

[140] PRO, SP 1/101, 184^r–185^r (*LP* x. 225, which attributes the sermon to Bishop Rawlins, who died in February 1536; his successor Barlow is clearly the author).

[141] Cranmer, *Miscellaneous Writings*, 351. Cranmer threatened to proceed against Cheyney's servants 'as against heretics' if they continued to 'maintain either pilgrimage, purgatory, images, or saints...as they have been heretofore by many both taught and used'. It may also have been in the immediate aftermath of the Ten Articles that Robert Wymond of Rye rejoiced that 'there ys no purgatorye for purgatorye ys pissed owte': PRO, SP 1/113, 90^r (*LP* xi. 1424).

[142] A point made by Duffy, *Altars*, 393. It is worth noting that the draft brought to convocation in June was sharpened up in these areas. The place and pains being 'uncertayne' received the added qualification 'by scripture', and a reference to prayers 'wherby they may be deliveryd and holpen of theyre paynes' was changed to 'relieved and holpen', probably to tighten the association of 'delivery' with bogus papal pardons: PRO, SP 6/1, 4^v–5^r.

tion in 1536 he condemned 'scalary loosings' and metonymically termed the pope himself 'that scalary'.[143]

It is significant that in the article these are described as abuses 'advanced under the name of purgatory'. In retrospect, the article's agnosticism about the name purgatory ('uncertain by scripture') seems its most significant feature. As we have seen, evangelicals made much of the fact that 'purgatory' was not to be found in Scripture, and contemporaries showed themselves well aware that a third place by any other name might not burn as bright. In his address to convocation, Latimer noted that some that love 'this monster, purgatory...earnestly endeavour them to restore him his old name. They would not set an hair by the name, but for the thing. They be not so ignorant, (no, they be crafty), but that they know if the name come again, the thing will come after'.[144] The perception was shared by the editor who in or shortly after 1537 added a prologue to Frith's *Another Book Against Rastell*, berating some persons 'which triumphed of late, and with much joy and clapping of hands sent tidings into all parts, that purgatory was found again; because they read in a book named the Institution of a Christian man, this word purgatory'.[145] That rescinding the name purgatory might be the first step towards undermining the structures of intercession themselves was recognized by the author of a manuscript treatise of 1536, even though he doubted the utility of the strategy. For as long as preachers were permitted to pray for dead souls, 'the oppinion that there is a purgatory wyll not be put away, and that conveniaunce to turn the name of purgatory in to the name of a third place helpeth lytle'.[146]

Of course, the Ten Articles did not deliver all that the evangelicals wanted, on purgatory or on any other key theological issue, but it is hard to resist the conclusion that they represented a decisive turning away from the priorities and ethos of traditional religion. The placing of the article is itself significant. The preface to the Articles introduced a crucial distinction between those 'commanded expressly by God, and necessary to our salvation', and those which were merely 'prudently instituted and used in the churches of our realm'. The article on purgatory was tacked on to the end of the latter group.[147]

The ethos of the article shines through another text of 1536, Starkey's *Exhortation to Unitie*. Starkey portrayed purgatory as essentially a piece of

---

[143] Latimer, *Remains*, 239; *Sermons*, 51. On backgound to scala coeli masses, see above, 29–30. For other hostile Henrician references, see F. J. Furnivall (ed.), *Ballads from Manuscripts*, Ballad Society (1868–72), 171, 261; Becon, *Early Works*, 191; L. Ridley, *A Commentary in Englyshe upon Sayncte Paules Epystle to the Ephesyans* (1540), B2^v; BL, Harleidn 425, 7^r; J. Bale, *A Mysterye of Inyquyte* (Geneva [i.e. Antwerp], 1545), 17^r. M. Bowker, *The Henrician Reformation: The Diocese of Lincoln under John Longland 1521–1547* (Cambridge, 1981), 166.

[144] Latimer, *Sermons*, 51.

[145] Frith, *Disputation*, 207.

[146] PRO, SP 1/105, 60^r (*LP* xi. 86 (2)).

[147] See Marshall, 'Unwritten Verities', 68.

adiaphora, neither proved nor disproved by Scripture, belief in which was
not necessary to salvation. It did not follow that prayer for the dead was
wrong; on the contrary it was 'a convenient thynge, and to charitie conform-
able, that every man shulde desyre after death good to his frende'. Indeed,
the very uncertainty of what awaited the dead reinforced a natural desire to
pray for them. For Starkey, whether such prayer was effectual was hardly the
issue; in performing it we 'can not doo but wel, in as moch as we declare
therby to god the charitie of our hartes'. Even if it profited the dead not at all,
God would delight in it 'and taketh to his honour our aboundante devotyon
and fervent charytie'.[148] This approach, humanist in several senses of the
term, had its own (rather touching) rationale, but it moves us a world away
from the vivid representations and ideas of spiritual efficacy that had
hitherto characterized discussions of intercession for the dead.

In terms of purgatory and intercession for the dead, the Ten Articles were
not a high water mark of evangelical advance, but rather a pointer to the
channels through which government policy would henceforth ineluctably
flow. Towards the end of 1536 Latimer thought it was worthwhile, and safe,
to send a memorandum to the king arguing the non-existence of purgatory;
he was rebuffed, for the moment.[149] That year Henry ordered houses of
friars to celebrate masses for the soul of his illegitimate son, the duke of
Richmond, and in 1537 he had 1,200 masses said for Jane Seymour, and
went on to re-found an abbey at Bisham to pray for her soul.[150] Yet
purgatory was denounced in the marginalia of the 'Matthew Bible' published under royal licence in 1537.[151] The Bishops' Book of that year
recycled the tenth article of 1536 without amendment, but the provisional
status of that text was soon to become apparent. As Alan Kreider has shown,
at the end of 1537 Henry systematically examined and rewrote the article on
purgatory from the Bishops' Book, at the same time soliciting advice on the
topic from Cranmer and a range of other theologians. The king's final
manuscript departed significantly from the original text. The heading 'Of
Purgatory' became of 'the souls of them which be departed from this life'.
The scriptural critique of purgatory and intercession became yet more
searching, it being noted that nowhere do the Scriptures speak of a place
where souls are continually cleansed, their condition being the secret knowledge of God and 'not necessary for us to know'. The silence of Scripture was
proof that it could not be necessary for salvation. The status of the book of
Maccabees was overtly downgraded, the purgation of the dead being 'un-

---

[148] Starkey, *Exhortation*, 79ᵛ–78ʳ (*sic*).

[149] BL, Cotton MS Cleo. E. v., 140ʳ–142ʳ; Latimer, *Remains*, 245–9.

[150] J. Martin, 'Leadership and Priorities in Reading during the Reformation', in P. Collinson
and J. Craig (eds.), *The Reformation in English Towns* (Basingstoke, 1998), 115; G. Constant,
The Reformation in England: I. The English Schism, tr. R. E. Scantlebury (New York, 1934),
407; MacCulloch, *Cranmer*, 207 n.

[151] N. Tyacke, 'Introduction', in id. (ed.), *England's Long Reformation 1500–1800* (1998),
87–8.

discussed and undetermined in the canon of the bible'. 'Abuses' were further castigated, and there was an emphasis on repentance in this life, with the suggestion that people were deceived who trusted in the good works of others after their death. On the other hand, the king concurred with the Bishops' Book in encouraging prayer for the dead on the basis of patristic testimony and ancient usage. He argued further (in a distinct echo of Starkey's arguments) that survivors' love towards the departed 'maketh us to wish well unto them to pray to God for them', and that our very uncertainty about their state underlined the status of prayer for them as a charitable deed.[152] What Kreider has called 'the King's book of 1538' is a remarkable document. It reveals quite how much of the evangelical critique of purgatory Henry had imbibed and made his own.

In the light of this, it is perhaps less surprising that the Act of Six Articles of 1539, generally regarded as the epitome of orthodox reaction in Henry's reign, made little attempt to reverse the inroads into traditionalist models of intercession. While the fifth of the Six Articles insisted that 'it is meet and necessary that private masses be continued' as agreeable to God's law and a source of 'goodly consolations and benefits' to Christian people, there was no direct mention of what had always been the primary purpose of most private masses, propitiatory sacrifice for the souls of the dead.[153] The point was grasped by that most inveterate of campaigners against prayer for the dead, Edward Crome, who in 1540 was charged with having impugned the Six Articles (a capital offence) by denying the efficacy of masses for the departed. Crome was able to argue, however, that there were other advantages in private masses: commemoration of the passion, and prayer for the living.[154] One of the conservative prebends on the look-out at this time for heresy in Kent placed in his list the contention 'that private masses are not available for souls departed'.[155]

In his introduction to the King's Book of 1543, Henry noted that 'the heads and senses of our people have been embusied, and in these days travailed with the understanding of free will, justification, good works, and praying for the souls departed'.[156] This was hardly less than a statement of fact, and the new formulary aimed to provide definitive statements on all these contentious issues. As far as the first three were concerned, the King's Book largely lived up to the deeply conservative reputation it has enjoyed, then and subsequently. But in its consideration of prayer for the dead, it moved decisively still further away from past certainties. The attack on abuses was extended: in addition to the bishop of Rome's pardons and

---

[152] Kreider, *Chantries*, 132–7.
[153] Gee and Hardy (eds.), *Documents*, 306.
[154] S. Wabuda, 'Equivocation and Recantation During the English Reformation: The "Subtle Shadows" of Dr Edward Crome', *JEH* 44 (1993), 233.
[155] *LP* xviii (2), 546, p. 331.
[156] Lloyd, *Formularies*, 217.

masses of scala coeli, the idea that 'a prescribed number of prayers' would help a petition sooner was 'utterly to be abolished and extinguished'—a condemnation of trentals. Other than in connection with such abuses, the word purgatory had now disappeared. The article was headed 'Of prayer for souls departed', and, in the light of the behaviour of 'supporters and maintainers of the papacy of Rome', it was commanded that people 'abstain from the name of purgatory, and no more dispute or reason thereof'. The uncertainty surrounding the condition of the dead was re-emphasized, though all reference to their undergoing pain was now excised. Most significantly, however, the King's Book laid down that no one could know 'how much, and in what space of time, or to what person particularly the said masses, exequies, and suffrages do profit and avail', and that therefore anyone establishing any such intercessions 'should yet (though their intent be more for one than for another) cause them also to be done for the universal congregation of Christian people, quick and dead'. God alone 'knoweth the measures and times of his own judgement and mercies'. This suggestion that it was somehow improper to ordain masses for the souls of specified individuals (which Henry's own will was egregiously to ignore) was entirely at odds with the rationale which had underlain the whole medieval intercessory system. Prayers for souls departed were still declared to be good deeds which 'declare us to be charitable folk', yet they could now be justified only on the highly generic grounds that the dead remained 'members of the same mystical body of Christ whereunto we pertain'.[157]

There is little doubt that the progressive distancing from the language and mentality of traditional practice in the official formularies set significant constraints on the activity of conservative preachers and writers. In the aftermath of the Ten Articles, the Bristol preacher Roger Edgeworth sought to make the case that that the repudiation of purgatory was an invitation to 'carnall libertye', and he mocked Latimer's concession that if there were any purgatory at all, it were 'a place of ease, quietnesse, and rest'. Yet Edgeworth was obliged to be circumspect, disowning any intention to 'contende about this vocable Purgatory'. Indeed, Edgeworth averred that 'I wold not care thoughe I never called it Purgatorye, but let A. be his name'. Despite the display of insouciance, this sounds remarkably like making a virtue out of necessity.[158] The absence of purgatory by name is also notable in a 1538 sermon before the king by another conservative, John Longland, though it touched upon prayer for the dead and made specific reference to limbo.[159] When the printer Robert Wyer produced an edition of the popular medieval didactic poem *The Pricke of Conscience* in c.1542, he scrupulously excised

---

[157] Ibid. 375–7.
[158] Edgeworth, *Sermons*, 128–9.
[159] Cited in P. O'Grady, *Henry VIII and the Conforming Catholics* (Collegeville, Minn., 1990), 89. Neither is purgatory mentioned in Richard Whitford's *A Dayly Exercyse and Experyence of Dethe* (1537), though the work commends intercessionary prayer.

all uses of the word purgatory and references to undergoing purgation there, replacing them with references to mercy, and doing penance in preparation for heaven.[160] Richard Smyth, one of the most unashamedly traditional of Henrician Catholic writers, devoted a chapter of his 1546 *Defence of the Sacrifice of the Masse* to arguing that 'the masse is profitable to the deade', but he desisted from mentioning purgatory by name. Though he declared an intention to 'set forthe a hoole booke of that matter, against Frithes book compiled of the same', it may be significant that this never appeared in Henry's reign.[161] References to purgatory are also notably absent from the writings of Stephen Gardiner, though in May 1540 Robert Barnes claimed to have clashed with the bishop over the issue.[162] It is revealing also that, though the recantations secured from the evangelicals Edward Crome and Nicholas Shaxton in 1546 included the assertion that the mass was 'a meane to obteyne grace and mercye boothe for quyck and deadde', this was qualified by the recognition that 'yt liethe not in the power of man to lymyte howe mych or in what measure the same doothe avayle'—a formula scrupulously in line with the theology of the King's Book.[163]

Conservatives who stepped beyond the bounds of what the formularies prescribed were liable to be leapt upon by hostile critics. Smyth had learned this in 1537 when, preaching in Evesham parish church, his addition of the phrase 'which is purgatory' to the bidding prayer for souls 'abiding the mercy of god' led to an attempt to arrest him by the sheriff of Worcestershire. In May 1538 a monk preaching in Oxford insisted that 'there was a purgatory as holy fathers hath declared it', thereby offending the mayor and other citizens, who reported him to Cromwell and committed him to the custody of his abbot.[164] In 1540 a Yorkshire butcher, James Hardcastell, was telling his neighbours in Barwick-in-Elmet that 'it was agenst the Kinge's articles to have *dirige* said for a dede body'.[165] During the period of guerrilla warfare between radicals and conservatives in Kent in the early 1540s which historians have termed 'the Prebendaries Plot', the accusation was made against the traditionalist William Gardiner that 'he plainly affirmed the state and condition of the souls departed'—presumably an offence against the studied agnosticism of the formularies. A more explicit charge was made against the executors of a petty canon of Canterbury who had bequeathed 20d. to every vicar of Christ Church to say Our Lady's psalter for his soul,

---

[160] J. F. Preston, 'The Pricke of Conscience (Parts I–III) and its First Appearance in Print', *The Library*, 6th ser., 7/4 (1985), 301–14.

[161] R. Smyth, *A Defence of the Sacrifice of the Masse* (1546), 126ᵛ, 127ʳ.

[162] H. Robinson (ed.), *Original Letters relative to the English Reformation*, 2 vols. (PS, 1846–7), ii. 616. The remarkable absence of purgatory from Henrician traditionalist polemics is noted by Diarmaid MacCulloch in a review of E. A. Macek's book on the latter theme: *JEH* 49 (1998), 361.

[163] Foxe, v, app. nos. xvi, xvii.

[164] Kreider, *Chantries*, 141–2.

[165] A. G. Dickens, *Lollards and Protestants in the Diocese of York* (Oxford, 1959), 45.

'which is thought to be against the King's book last set forth in the article of prayer for the souls departed'.[166] By this reading, the implication of the royal statement that it was impossible to say how suffrages benefited an individual soul, and that they should therefore be made for 'the universal congregation of Christian people', was that all bequests in wills for intercession for the testator were ipso facto illegal. A similar logic may have fuelled the complaint against another Kentish conservative for preaching that venial sins would be punished in the next life 'except they were relieved by masses and diriges after their death'.[167]

Wills did in fact continue to specify masses and prayers for the souls of named beneficiaries, though in the last decade of Henry's reign markedly fewer were doing so than had earlier been the case. Patterns vary across the country, but as a rule of thumb it can be suggested that requests for chantries, obits, and endowed masses were running at roughly half the rate in the 1540s that they had in the 1520s.[168] Bequests to guilds and fraternities, 'corporate chantries', suggest the same pattern of decline.[169] The process is paralleled by the physical evidence of funerary monuments. Epitaphs entreating the onlooker to 'pray for the soul of . . .' are markedly less dominant in the 1540s, and the less imperative formula 'on whose soul God have mercy' seems more in evidence.[170] The extent to which this constitutes unambiguous evidence for a widespread loss of 'belief' in purgatory is debatable.[171] Most historians now accept that throughout the reign of Henry VIII those with genuine evangelical convictions remained a minority. As Eamon Duffy has demonstrated, testators drawing up their will (a public legal document) could be highly sensitive to the requirements of the law and the likely direction of government policy. The impulse is at times made explicit in testaments like that of the Northumbrian John Hynes, who in 1545 requested that his funeral arrangements be made 'accordynge to the kynges Maiesties actes statutes and Iniunctions'.[172] Silences and omissions in wills most likely reflect a climate of uncertainty about official intentions

---

[166] *LP* xviii (2), 546, pp. 293, 304.

[167] Ibid., p. 304.

[168] L. Attreed, 'Preparation for Death in Sixteenth-Century Northern England', *SCJ* 13 (1982), 45–6; Helt, 'Purgatory, Policy, and Piety', 131–2; P. Marshall, *The Catholic Priesthood and the English Reformation* (Oxford, 1994), 51; R. Whiting, '"For the Health of my Soul": Prayers for the Dead in the Tudor South-West', in P. Marshall (ed.), *The Impact of the English Reformation 1500–1640* (1997), 126; Brigden, *London and the Reformation*, 386.

[169] Ibid. 389; Bowker, *Henrician Reformation*, 177; Whiting, '"For the Health of my Soul"', 126.

[170] For examples of late Henrician epitaphs employing only the latter formula, see G. Isherwood, *Monumental Brasses in the Bedfordshire Churches* (1906), 32; T. F. Ravenshaw, *Antiente Epitaphs* (1878), 24; H. R. Mosse, *The Monumental Effigies of Sussex*, 2nd edn (Hove, 1933), 26; J. W. Clay (ed.), *Yorkshire Church Notes 1619–1631*, YASRS, 34 (1904), 48.

[171] As suggested by Dickens, *Lollards and Protestants*, 238, and R. Whiting, *Local Responses to the English Reformation* (Basingstoke, 1998), 72–4. Scepticism is expressed by Brigden, *London and the Reformation*, 386 and Duffy, *Altars*, 513.

[172] Duffy, *Altars*, 510–16.

rather than a radical reorientation of popular mentalities. But this in itself is highly significant. However positivist or deconstructionist one's reading of the statistics generated by serial will-analysis, it is probably a mistake to think in terms of a free standing popular 'belief' independent of the means of its expression or the social and cultural structures and practices that endowed it with meaning. Revisionist historians are undoubtedly right to insist that popular instincts were characteristically neither ahead of nor in sympathy with the reformist direction of government policy. But over the longer term they could hardly remain unscathed by it. If by 1540 the confidence of English people in the traditional structures of intercession for the dead had begun to be shaken, it was with good reason. For by then the regime had gone beyond issuing quasi-reformist formularies to provide an unmistakable signal that the survival of those structures had become a matter of contingency and expediency; it had closed the religious houses.

THE DISSOLUTION AND THE DEAD

Medieval monasteries were 'purgatorial institutions', established to offer masses and prayers for the souls of their founders and benefactors in perpetuity.[173] Yet over the two centuries preceding the break with Rome their importance in the overall provision of post-mortem intercession had become more peripheral. Though the friars and their trentals remained popular, most chantries were established in parish churches, and the task of (usually fixed-term) mass-saying was overwhelmingly undertaken by the secular clergy. By the 1530s, the founders of monasteries had often been dead for centuries, and their families were sometimes extinct. For these reasons, it has been suggested that doubts about the very purpose of monasticism 'could be entertained without challenging belief in purgatory itself'.[174]

Yet so complete a dissociation may well be false to contemporary perceptions. The closeness of the link between the institution of monasticism and the false doctrine of purgatory was regularly identified by Henrician evangelicals. Purgatory, remarked Frith, was 'the foundation of all religions and cloisters'.[175] Francis Bigod's attack on monastic impropriation of benefices imagined the monks defending the practice thus: 'we pray for the souls of them that have improperated [*sic*] such benefyces unto us, and synge masse and diryge for them'.[176] In Bale's *King Johan*, the poisoner of the king is encouraged with the thought that he shall have five monks singing for his

---

[173] R. W. Hoyle, 'The Origins of the Dissolution of the Monasteries', *HJ* 38 (1995), 276.
[174] Ibid. 277.
[175] Frith, *Disputation*, 183.
[176] A. G. Dickens (ed.), *Tudor Treatises*, YASRS, 125 (1959), 50. Impropriation was the practice whereby religious houses assumed responsibility for a parish, collecting the tithes and appointing a vicar.

soul.[177] Friars, wrote Jerome Barlow, were the 'fe fermers of purgatory'.[178] Yet evangelicals might also point out how carelessly the monks performed their obligations in these respects. Fish's *Supplicacyon* reminded the king that his predecessors had given lands to monasteries for daily masses 'wherof they sey never one. If the Abbot of Westminster shulde sing every day as many masses for his founders as he is bounde to do by his foundacion, .M. monkes were to fewe.'[179]

The large-scale closure of monasteries beginning in 1536 was from the outset identified by contemporaries as having vital consequences for the status of purgatory and intercession. The habit of inferring doctrinal statements from royal policy was not a new one. Fish had argued in 1529 that if there were a purgatory 'your people will thinke that your statute of mortmayne was never made with no good conscience' since it had removed the right to buy souls out of purgatory by giving to the spiritualty as freely as in the past.[180] In 1536, in the wake of the act dissolving the smaller monasteries, Hugh Latimer tried the same argument on the king. His paper presenting scriptural and other arguments against the doctrine culminated in a famous syllogism: 'the fowndyng of monastarys arguyd purgatory to be, so the puttyng of them down arguyth it not to be, what uncharitabulnesse of cruellnes semyth it to be, to distrawe monasteryes yf purgatory be'. Henry read the paper with care, annotating it with his own comments, and taking clear pleasure in demolishing Latimer's scriptural and patristic arguments as irrelevant or misdirected, but this final highly sensitive thrust was not so easily brushed aside. To Latimer's contention that 'it semyth nott convenyentt the acte of parliament to preach one thing, and the pulpit another clean contrary', Henry could manage no better than a petulant 'why then do you?'.[181]

Latimer was not alone in arguing that the logical outcome of the dissolution was a complete renunciation of purgatory and intercessory prayer. An anonymous evangelical tract of the late 1530s argued that, as long as praying for the dead was suffered, the people would think there was a purgatory. By closing religious houses without a decisive rejection of postmortem intercession, the king was running a grave political risk, causing 'many to thinke that it is pitie that houses of Relligion sholde be decayed, whose prayers as they thinke proffited muche to sowles departed. And that herafter shall cause the kinges dede in suppressing of houses of religion to be thought uncharitable, and that may be herafter right dangerouse aswell to the kinges supremacye as to his succession.'[182] In a sermon preached in Bristol between July 1536 and early 1537, Roger Edgeworth warned that heretics were 'reasoning agaynst purgatory because they would by that

---

[177] Bale, *Complete Plays*, i. 82.   [178] Barlow, *Burial of the Mass*, 72, 85–6.
[179] Fish, *Supplicacyon*, 422.   [180] Ibid. 420.
[181] BL, Cotton MS Cleo. E. v., 140ʳ–142ʳ; Latimer, *Remains*, 245–9.
[182] PRO, SP 6/3, 79ʳ (*LP* xiv (1), 376).

destroye prayers for the dead, and so consequently put downe abbeys and chauntries which were founded for such praiers'.[183] In 1539 the vicar of Malmesbury was reported to have said that 'yff the kynges grase dyd thynke that massys and dyryggys dyd good to the soles departyd he wolde nott subprese so many howsys or monasterys as he have done, and take there levyng from them. Butt rather to have geve theme more.'[184] A similar inference was drawn by Edward Crome in his advent sermons of 1540: if the mass were profitable to the dead 'then the king's grace hath done evil to put down the abbeys as he hath done'. He was made to recant, but repeated the assertion in a Passion Sunday sermon in 1546.[185]

Opponents of the dissolution also recognized its doctrinal implications. In February 1536 Ambassador Chapuys reported that the king's object was to persuade the people that there was no purgatory 'in order afterwards to seize all the ecclesiastical endowments', a policy 'most strange to the people, and still more to the lords whose predecessors have left foundations for the memory of posterity'. By April Chapuys recognized that the king did not intend to deny that prayers assist the dead, 'yet he will not forbear to throw down the monasteries, and impiously usurp the foundations for the redemption of the dead'.[186] Rather pathetically, the last abbess of Godstow sought to save her house from closure in 1538 by assuring Cromwell that 'there is neither pope, purgatory, images nor pilgrimage, nor praying to dead saints used amongst us'.[187] There is no doubt that the authors of the dissolution policy were aware of the perceived link with purgatory and intercession, though there is no direct evidence for the assertion that the intention to seize monastic assets was a primary motivation for the increasing radicalization of the king's attitude towards purgatory.[188] A draft set of injunctions to be imposed on the religious houses by the royal visitors in 1535 stated they were required to pray for the founder's soul, but this was struck out by Cromwell, and not included in the final version.[189] The apparent misfit between the Crown's words and actions, which Latimer had brought to the king's attention, was reinforced in a letter from another advisor, Thomas Starkey, though to rather different ends. Starkey admitted that the suppression of abbeys had caused 'no smal controversye' among the people, 'specyally seyng that by the consent of al your lernyd clergy hyt ys agreed that

---

[183] Edgeworth, *Sermons*, 16.

[184] PRO, SP 1/156, 60ʳ (*LP* xiv (2), 804).

[185] Wabuda, 'Equivocation and Recantation', 233–4; Robinson (ed.), *Original Letters*, i. 212. Some conservatives attempted to catch a different straw in the wind of official policy—the fact that in 1539 Henry had caused solemnities to be celebrated for the soul of the Empress Isabella: PRO, SP 1/156, 60ʳ (*LP* xiv (2), 804); E 36/120, 71ʳ (*LP* xv. 587).

[186] *LP* x. 282, 752.

[187] L. B. Smith, *Tudor Prelates and Politics* (Princeton, 1953), 168.

[188] A suggestion made by Kreider, *Chantries*, 127, 137. Unlike sexual misdemeanour and the promotion of false relics, intercessory functions did not feature prominently in the government's propaganda against monasticism.

[189] *LP* viii. 76.

such a place ther ys wherein soulys departyd remaynyng may be relevyd by
the prayer and almys dede of ther posteryte'. It followed that there would be
those who would judge the Suppression Act 'bothe to be agayne the order of
charyte and iniuryous to them wych be dede bycause the foundarys therof
and the soulys departyd seme therby to be defraudyd of the benefyte of
prayer and almys dede'. But, Starkey argued, it was a fundamental principle
that no private will might be repugnant to the 'publyke wele', and given the
current deplorable state of religious houses, founders' consent to the alter-
ation of their wills might be presupposed. Moreover, though prayer for the
dead was charitable and pleasing to God, 'yet to converte over much
possessyon to that end and purpos, and to appoynt over many personys to
such offyce and exercyse, can not be wythout grete detryment and hurt to the
chrystian commynwele'. It would in any case do no harm to the dead to turn
their endowments to benefit the living, since the latter would then be bound
to pray for their benefactors, and, if they failed to, the fault would be theirs
not the dead's. There was an obligation to have the departed 'in charytabul
memory', but this pertained to men of all degrees, 'not only of them wych
lyve in monasterys'.[190] One wonders whether this rather pusillanimous
justification for expropriation appealed to Henry more than the robust
response he received from the earl of Arran in 1543 to his advice to seize
the Scottish monasteries: 'he thought that all houses of religion were first
founded to pray for souls in purgatory, and if there was no purgatory (as was
his opinion) these foundations were vain and should be converted to better
use'.[191]

The overall effect of the disappearance of the religious houses on the
status of intercessory prayer is difficult to assess in either quantitative or
qualitative terms. There was certainly, as Robert Aske observed plaintively
in the aftermath of the Pilgrimage of Grace, a 'greate nombre of messes
unsaid'.[192] In addition to the masses of the monks themselves, monasteries
had supported large numbers of secular chantry priests both within and
without their own churches. The Court of Augmentations very often failed
to support these obligations, even though, at the conversion of monastic
cathedrals into secular foundations in 1540, the obits of founders and
benefactors were ordered to be observed.[193] The dissolution of the monas-

[190] Starkey, *Life and Letters*, pp. liv–lvi.
[191] *LP* xviii (1), 391.
[192] A. Fletcher and D. MacCulloch, *Tudor Rebellions*, 4th edn. (1997), 138.
[193] Kreider, *Chantries*, 128; S. E. Lehmberg, *The Reformation of Cathedrals: Cathedrals in English Society, 1485–1603* (Princeton, 1988), 93. Some chantries clearly were transferred to new settings at the dissolution. Three chantries in the Augustinian Priory at Northleach, Gloucestershire, went to the parish church, and the Dacre chantry at Lanercost Priory, Cumberland, to Carlisle Cathedral: *The Itinerary of John Leland*, ed. L. Toulmin Smith, 5 vols. (1964), i. 126; H. Summerson, 'Intersections of Patronage: Rulers and Subjects at Lanercost Priory and Church', paper at conference on 'The Archaeology of Reformation', British Museum, 17 Feb. 2001.

teries did not lead directly to the ending of most intercessory masses, but it undoubtedly raised an alarming (or encouraging) question mark about the future of those that remained.

Yet in terms of that 'charytabul memory' which Starkey extolled in 1536, the dissolution had a significance beyond the silencing of monastic prayers. Religious houses, like parish churches, were physical sites of memory, replete with the burial places, stone monuments, and brasses of both clergy and laity. Though the majority of late medieval testators sought burial in parish church or churchyard, and though the percentage wishing to be interred in religious houses may have been falling in the early sixteenth century, monastic burial continued to be a viable option up to the eve of the dissolution itself, particularly in houses of friars.[194] For considerable numbers of nobles and gentlemen in 1536, monasteries and friaries housed the tombs of ancestors, those tangible indices of lineage, and the social and political capital it conveyed. In the run-up to the dissolution some families made their anxieties plain. In April 1536 Sir Simon Harcourt of Stanton Harcourt, Oxfordshire, wrote to Cromwell about the Augustinian house of Roughton, Staffordshire, asking that it be allowed to continue, and if not, that he be permitted to purchase it. His declared motive was that it was a house 'the whiche my power auncestors dyd buyld . . . for this intent ther to be prayed for perpetually. And so many of them be ther tumulate and buried.'[195] Similarly, Lord La Warre wrote to Cromwell in March requesting a reprieve for Boxgrove Priory in Sussex, a house of which he was founder, where 'lyethe many of my aunsystorys and also my wyffys mother'. The priory church doubled as a place of parish worship, and La Warre had made 'a power chapell' there to be buried in himself.[196] Did the government give much thought to these issues in the evolution of the dissolution process? An intriguing presence among the collection of papers which may once have formed part of Cromwell's archive is a blank folio headed 'Places of sepulture of princes'.[197] Yet in the event the king appeared remarkably relaxed about the implications for his own ancestors and kin. In March 1536 the

---

[194] V. Harding, 'Burial Choice and Burial Location in Later Medieval London', in S. Bassett (ed.), *Death in Towns* (1992), 122–4; J. Middleton-Stewart, 'Personal Commemoration in Late Medieval Suffolk: The Deanery of Dunwich 1370–1547', University of East Anglia Ph.D. thesis (1995), 87–8; N. Tanner, *The Church in Late Medieval Norwich 1370–1532* (Toronto, 1984), 108, 189; A. D. Brown, *Popular Piety in Late Medieval England: The Diocese of Salisbury 1250–1550* (Oxford, 1995), 44, 35. A manuscript catalogue of burials in the London Greyfriars runs to thirty-two pages: J. G. Nichols (ed.), *Chronicle of the Grey Friars of London*, CS (1852), p. xxxi.

[195] PRO, SP 1/103, 72ʳ (*LP* x. 613).

[196] Wright, *Three Chapters of Letters*, 119. La Warre was successful in being allowed to buy the church and acquire a lease of the priory, but after suspected involvement in the Exeter conspiracy had to give this up to the king: H. Miller, *Henry VIII and the English Nobility* (Oxford, 1986), 227–9.

[197] PRO, SP 6/1, 146ʳ. For the suggestion that the papers in SP 6 were once Cromwell's, see Rex, *Theology of John Fisher*, 150 and n.

abbot of Faversham sought to save his house by stressing that it was the foundation of 'one of the kynges most noble progenytours [Stephen] whose very bodye, togither with the bodyes of his deere and welbeloved quene and also the prynce his sonne there lyeth buryed in honourable sepulture'. He added that all these royal personages were there had 'in perpetuall memory with contynuall suffrages'. But none of this weighed with Cromwell, or presumably Henry, as the house went down with the others: Stephen's tomb was completely destroyed, as was that of Henry I at Reading.[198] An appeal from the duke of Norfolk to keep open the Cluniac priory of Thetford on the grounds that there 'doth lye buryed the bodie of the late Duke of Richmond, the king's naturall sonn', might have been expected to exercise a greater emotional pull, but the plea fell on deaf ears.[199] Equally remarkably, the fine alabaster tomb of Henry's sister Mary, in the abbey of Bury St Edmunds was destroyed in 1540.[200] In at least one instance the fate of tombs suggests not indifference, but the deliberate settling of overdue scores. At the dissolution of Canterbury Priory in 1540, Cranmer authorized the putting down of the chantry foundations of bishops Thomas Arundel and John Buckingham and the destruction of their monuments. Both had been notable persecutors of Lollardy.[201]

The dissolution involved the dispersal of dead as well as living inmates from the religious houses, and just as some families took in their relatives among the latter, a few made efforts to rehouse the former as well. Having failed to preserve Thetford as the site of a family mausoleum, the duke of Norfolk eventually arranged the removal of the bones of his father (and of Henry's bastard son) to Framlingham parish church.[202] Lord Lisle's agent arranged in January 1538 for the removal of the first Lady Lisle from Titchfield Abbey to the parish church there, and the earl of Rutland transferred ancestral tombs to Bottesford church, Leicestershire, following the suppressions of Croxton Abbey and Belvoir Priory.[203] In 1537 Lord Stone rescued the tombs of his ancestors from Stone Priory, though with remarkable lack of foresight installing them in the Augustinian house

[198] BL, Cotton MS Cleo. E. iv, 34 (*LP* x. 484); Daniell, *Death and Burial in Medieval England*, 201.

[199] L. Stone and H. Colvin, 'The Howard Tombs at Framlingham, Suffolk', *The Archaeological Journal*, 122 (1965), 160.

[200] P. Sherlock, 'Funeral Monuments: Piety, Honour and Memory in Early Modern England', University of Oxford D.Phil. thesis (2000), 27. Mary's remains were removed to a nearby parish church, but on the initiative of local inhabitants, not the Crown.

[201] MacCulloch, *Cranmer*, 266. John Stow's copy of part of the manuscripts of John Leland notes that the tomb of the fourteenth-century bishop John Dalderby in Lincoln Cathedral was removed 'nomine superstitionis', though it is not clear when this took place: *Itinerary of John Leland*, v. 122.

[202] Stone and Colvin, 'Howard Tombs at Framlingam', 162; R. Marks, 'The Howard Tombs at Thetford and Framlingham: New Discoveries', *The Archaeological Journal*, 141 (1984), 252–68.

[203] *The Lisle Letters*, ed. M. St Clare Byrne, 6 vols. (Chicago, 1981), v. 10, 20; N. Llewellyn, *Funeral Monuments in Post-Reformation England* (Cambridge, 2000), 304.

in Stafford, and the tombs were lost when that house was dissolved the following year.[204] At the London Blackfriars, the corpse of Gerard Danet was dug up and relocated to the parish church of Tiltey in Essex, and there is archaeological evidence suggesting the careful removal of burials from Guildford Friary.[205] On his travels in the early 1540s, the antiquary John Leland noted several other places where swift action had been taken to relocate burials and burial markers. In the West Riding of Yorkshire, an effigy of Margaret Cobham, countess of Westmorland, had been translated from the White Friars, Doncaster, to St George's church, and at Tickhill a number of bodies of the Fitzwilliams had similarly been taken from the friary to the parish church (these included those of the father and grandfather of the current Lord Privy Seal, Sir William Fitzwilliam). At Boston in Lincolnshire, a member of the Huntingfield family in the suppressed Dominican priory 'was a late taken up hole', and, at Godstow nunnery, the tomb of 'Fair Rosamund', mistress of Henry II, was similarly 'taken up a late'.[206] Later accounts add a few more cases. Sir Thomas Shirley's early seventeenth-century family history recounts how 'all the places of sepulchre, for this religious and devoute stocke of Shirley' were 'profained by the lamentable demolition of all the religious houses in England', and how Sir Thomas's ancestor, Francis Shirley, purchased the priory church of Bredon from Henry VIII 'for a buryall place for himselfe and all his successours for ever'.[207] The motive for such translations was not always a dynastic one. The eighteenth-century antiquarian Thomas Hearne, in an account of Abingdon, Berkshire, detailed the charitable endowments of an early fifteenth-century civic benefactor, Geofrey Barbour, who 'was first of all buried in the Abbey Church; but upon the dissolution he was translated from thence in the most solemn manner to St Helen's Church'.[208] At the end of the sixteenth century it was also reported that the first Lord Paget had rescued an Anglo-Saxon monument from the abbey of Burton-on-Trent.[209] The total number of such 'rescue missions' is now difficult to establish with any certainty, though in Charles I's reign the antiquary John Weever praised 'the memory of such, who upon the dissolution, and finall destruction of our religious structures, caused so many funerall monuments, with the bodies therein included, to bee removed into other neighbouring churches'.[210]

[204] P. Morgan, 'Of Worms and War: 1380–1558', in P. C. Jupp and C. Gittings (eds.), *Death in England* (Manchester, 1999), 142.
[205] R. Gilchrist, '"Dust to Dust": Revealing the Reformation Dead', in D. Gaimster and R. Gilchrist (eds.), *The Archaeology of the Reformation* (forthcoming).
[206] *Itinerary of John Leland*, i. 35, 36, iv. 114, i. 328.
[207] BL, MS Harleian 4928, 99^{r–v}.
[208] *Itinerary of John Leland*, v. (app.) 114.
[209] T. Hearne (ed.), *A Collection of Curious Discourses written by Eminent Antiquaries upon several Heads*, 2 vols. (1775), i. 247–8.
[210] J. Weever, *Ancient Funerall Monuments* (1631), 25.

The most portable of funerary monuments were brasses, and a handful were retrieved and placed in parish churches. A 1479 brass to Judge Billyng from Biddlesden Abbey was rehoused at Wappenham; the brass of Prior Langley in the parish church of Horsham St Faith must have been brought from the priory there; a similarly local move seems to have taken place at Little Walsingham. The brass of Walter Curson, placed in the house of Augustine friars in Oxford as recently as 1533 found its way safely to Waterperry; the 1435 brass of Thomas Widvile Esq. was recovered from the monastery of St James, Northampton, and taken to Bromham where, with the addition of a new inscription, it was appropriated for use by a descendant.[211] Such selective resettlements seem, however, to have been exceptions to the rule. The flip-side of brasses' portability was their resale value, and along with other moveable assets, such as bells, they were alienated by the Court of Augmentations. In many places they may have been melted down with bells in on-site furnaces. At Merevale in Warwickshire, six gravestones with brasses were sold for 5s.; at Dieulacres the roof and the church paving with gravestones fetched £13. 6s. 8d.[212] Even when a conventual church was given over to parish use, its monuments were sometimes put up for sale – as at Owston and Kirby Bellars, Leicestershire.[213] Of the large number of mid-Tudor palimpsest brasses some can definitely be identified as originating from dissolved monasteries, and many more must have done so. The leading authority on sixteenth-century brasses, Malcolm Norris, has suggested that the market was flooded as a result of the dissolution and that an overall majority of brasses engraved in 1545–75 may in fact be palimpsests.[214] However many brasses were salvaged and reused, many others were destroyed, and in neither case does the process suggest much concern about the memory of the original donor.

The full extent of the destruction of funeral monuments as a direct consequence of the dissolution is difficult to estimate, but it is likely to have been massive, and to have taken little account of the social eminence of the commemorated. The late sixteenth-century antiquary John Stow listed 127 eminent persons (mainly from the late fifteenth and early sixteenth centuries) buried in the London Greyfriars' church. At the dissolution, nine alabaster tombs and 'seven-score grave stones of Marble' were sold by Alderman

[211] M. Norris, *Monumental Brasses: The Memorials*, 2 vols. (1977), i. 259.

[212] J. Page-Phillips, 'Palimpsests—Re-used Brasses', in J. Bertram (ed.), *Monumental Brasses as Art and History* (Stroud, 1996), 139–40; Norris, *Monumental Brasses: The Memorials*, i. 259.

[213] F. A. Greenhill, *Incised Effigial Slabs: A Study of Engraved Stone Memorials in Latin Christendom c.1100 to c.1700*, 2 vols. (1976), i. 61.

[214] Norris, *Monumental Brasses: The Memorials*, i. 270; J. Page-Phillips, *Palimpsests: The Backs of Monumental Brasses*, 2 vols. (1980), i. 17–18. Although less common than with brasses, there is some evidence for the appropriation and reuse of stone effigies from religious houses: P. Lindley, 'Innovations, Tradition and Disruption in Tomb-Sculpture', in D. Gaimster and P. Stamper (eds.), *The Age of Transition: The Archaeology of English Culture 1400–1600* (Oxford, 1997), 83.

Martin Bowes for £50.[215] For the Cistercian monastery of New Abbey or St Mary Graces, Stow preserved a note of burials from a heraldic visitation of 1533. This listed seventeen tombs of the nobility and gentry, including daughters of Edward duke of Buckingham, Humphrey duke of Buckingham, and the earl of Oxford. The site was acquired by Sir Arthur Darcy in 1542, who pulled down the monastery and replaced it with a storehouse. Stow also recorded that after the house of Austin friars was acquired by Lord Treasurer Sir William Paulet, his son, the marquis of Winchester, 'sold the Monuments of noble men there buried in great number...and in place thereof made fayre stabling for horses'.[216] Funeral monuments in religious houses were not always put up for sale, but sometimes lay undisturbed among the ruins: when the site of Bardney Abbey in Lincolnshire was excavated in 1909–14 much of the floor of the church was found to comprise forty-seven incised slabs.[217]

During interrogations on charges of treason in November 1538, Margaret, countess of Salisbury, was charged that 'she liked not the plucking do[wn] of the abbayes and howeses of religion'. She admitted that she was sorry to see the fall of houses 'where her auncesters lay'. Another 'traitor', Robert Aske, had hated to see 'tombs of honourable and noble men pulled down and sold'.[218] Yet, all things considered, there appears to have been an extraordinary complacency on the part of landed elites regarding the loss of intercessions for ancestors and the destruction of ancestral tombs which took place in 1536–40; the issue is surely one of the deafening silences surrounding the dissolution of the monasteries. The reasons for this are not immediately obvious, though the complicity of elites in the process of expropriation itself must have played a part. It may also have been the case, as has recently been argued by Benjamin Thompson, that the late Middle Ages witnessed a weakening of ties between monasteries and their 'founders', that is, the patron regarded as the living heir of the original benefactor. The identity of founders was scrupulously recorded in the visitation of 1535; many were now neither local nor lineal descendants of the first founder: in Norfolk not a single monastery was still in the hands of the family that had founded it. Founders thus might have little direct interest in the maintenance of prayers for a long-dead original donor.[219] The dissolution of the monasteries was an event of more than economic and social, or even religio-political significance. It represented an

---

[215] J. Stow, *A Survey of London*, ed. C. L. Kingsford, 2 vols. (Oxford, 1908), i. 318–22. His list was by no means complete; cf. the Greyfrairs burial register in BL, Cotton MS Vitellius F. xii. 'Divers tombs in the choir' were among the spoil handed over to the commissioners at the suppression of the Franciscan house at Dorchester in September 1538: *LP* xiii (2), 474.

[216] Stow, *Survey*, i. 125, 176–7, ii. 289.

[217] Greenhill, *Incised Effigial Slabs*, i. 61.

[218] PRO, SP 1/138, 200ʳ (*LP* xiii (2), 818); *LP* xii (1), p. 405.

[219] B. Thompson, 'Monasteries and their Patrons at Foundation and Dissolution', *TRHS* 6th ser., 4 (1994), 103–23.

extraordinary repudiation of the hold of the past, and of past dead generations, on the present and the living. It was a signal of what else it might be
possible to achieve.

Henry's reign was to see no other reform measure as traumatic as the
dissolution of the monasteries. In December 1545, however, an act was
passed, authorizing the king to dissolve any chantries or colleges named in
a commission for that purpose. The Chantries Act of 1545 did not lead
directly to a general dissolution, and was probably not intended to do so.
The preamble to the act justified the measure not on theological grounds, but
on those of financial necessity (Henry's military adventures in France, and
particularly the cost of fortifying Boulogne, were by 1545 putting immense
financial strain on the government). It is probably correct to say that the
basic rationale of the act was 'secular and pragmatic'.[220] An explicit intention was to forestall private dissolutions, which had understandably accelerated in the light of the uncertainty created by monastic suppression; the act
ordered the confiscation of all chantry endowments which had been taken
into private hands between February 1536 and December 1545.[221] Over the
course of 1546, the act was used to dissolve three hospitals, two free chapels,
eight chantries, and (an epilogue to the dissolution of the monasteries) seven
collegiate churches.[222] Nonetheless, the Chantries Act of 1545 was an
important straw in the wind. After the King's Book had impugned the
value of masses for the souls of specified individuals, the vulnerability of
the chantries was glaringly apparent. It is revealing too that the act was
partially justified on the grounds that incumbents of chantries were lax in
carrying out the wishes of their founders, a claim that had been a theme of
evangelical propaganda against intercession from Simon Fish onwards. In
the aftermath of the Chantries Act, evangelicals were ready to draw the same
conclusions they had done in 1536. Preaching at St Mary Aldermary on
Passion Sunday 1546, Edward Crome argued that parliament had done well
to bestow colleges, and chantries on the king, as private masses did nothing
to relieve souls in purgatory.[223]

A final attempt to reform commemoration of the dead in Henry's reign
was made in January 1546. Cranmer drafted a letter for the king to sign
ordering, *inter alia*, that the 'vigil, watching, and ringing of bells all the night
along' on the night of All Hallows Day be abolished as a superstitious
enormity. In a first draft of the letter, Cranmer had allowed for the retention
of one peal before *dirige*, to notify the congregation 'to pray for all Christian
souls departed', but perhaps sensing how far the king was now persuadable

[220] Kreider, *Chantries*, 176; Haigh, *English Reformations*, 163.
[221] For details on such 'anticipatory dissolutions', see Kreider, *Chantries*, 154–64, 211–13.
The main beneficiary had in fact been the Crown itself, which in 1540–5 initiated the dissolution
of around sixty intercessionary institutions.
[222] Kreider, *Chantries*, 183.
[223] Wabuda, 'Equivocation and Recantation', 234.

on this issue, he struck the concession out.[224] Hostility to the ceremonies of All Souls had long been on the evangelical agenda. The 1536 manuscript treatise drafted by Wriothesley had advocated that 'the ceremony of al soules daye be also prohibited. For as long as that ceremonial service contynueth the oppinion of purgatory ne a favour to Rome by whois article yt was first brought upp wyll not owt of the hartes of many of the clergy'.[225] Prohibition of the All Souls ringing with its suggestions of disorder and 'superstition' was precisely the sort of measure Henry might readily countenance, but the scheme seems to have been scotched by a warning from Gardiner, then in Brussels negotiating for an alliance with Charles V, that the emperor would be offended by further reforming moves at this time.[226]

Though detailed prescriptions for post-mortem intercession had begun to disappear from a number of wills in the mid-1540s, Henry VIII's was not one of them. At the end of 1546 the king directed that 1,000 marks be given in alms to the poor, with instruction to pray for his soul; four solemn obits were to be maintained at St George's Chapel Windsor, where also 'an altar shall be furnished for the saying of daily masses while the world shall endure'.[227] This last-minute reversion to type seems epigrammatic of the contradictions, reversals, and confusions which marked Henry's Reformation as a whole.[228] Had the king recovered a wavering belief in the utility of 'attritional' intercessory masses, or were the claims of status-display and ancestral and dynastic convention more decisive? Requiem masses were celebrated for Henry throughout the land in February 1547, but this chapter has questioned the view that, papal headship aside, traditional religion was little disturbed in his reign, or that the Reformation had been 'reversed' in the 1540s.[229] On the contrary, an essentially evangelical critique of post-

---

[224] Cranmer, *Remains*, 414–15; MacCulloch, *Cranmer*, 351–2. This was despite the fact that the value of bells in causing Christians to 'be moved with charity to pray for them so departed' had been explicitly endorsed only a couple of years earlier by the bishops charged with explicating ceremonies: C. S. Cobb (ed.), *The Rationale of Ceremonial 1540–1543*, ACC 18 (1910), 30.

[225] PRO, SP 1/105, 60ᵛ–61ʳ (*LP* xi. 86 (2)). The reflection may have been sharpened by a report reaching Cromwell from Lincolnshire in November 1535, that 'in these very holidays on which the dead are celebrated', a priest had preached in the parish church of Grantham in favour of purgatory and masses for the dead 'and was received with great applause'. The preacher had brought out tried-and-tested arguments, such as 'that any earthly fire as compared with the fire of purgatory was as the picture of a man to a real man': *LP* ix. 740.

[226] Foxe, v. 562.

[227] White, 'Early Print and Purgatory', 201; *LP* xxi (2), 634.

[228] D. MacCulloch, 'Henry VIII and the Reform of the Church', in id. (ed.), *Reign of Henry VIII*, 159–80. See also id., *Tudor Church Militant: Edward VI and the Protestant Reformation* (1999), 58, on the 'radical incoherence' of Henry VIII's theology 'stranded between his loss of purgatory and his rejection of justification by faith'. For a contrasting view, see G. W. Bernard, 'The Making of Religious Policy, 1533–1546: Henry VIII and the Search for the Middle Way', *HJ* 41 (1998).

[229] For a survey of the historiographical tradition of 'Catholicism without the pope', see my 'Is the Pope a Catholic? Henry VIII and the Semantics of Schism', in M. Senna and E. Shagan (eds.), *Catholics and the Protestant Nation* (Manchester, forthcoming). Cf. Haigh, *English Reformations*, ch. 9, 'Reformation Reversed, 1538–1547'.

mortem commemoration continued to be influential in shaping public policy.[230] Though prayer for the dead was still laudable, many of its accustomed forms had become associated with 'superstition' and political disloyalty. The doctrine of purgatory itself, 'cornerstone in the great edifice of Catholic religion', had been shown to be vulnerable on theological, economic, and political grounds.[231] The institutional dissolutions, realized and projected, had demonstrated that the wishes of the dead and the reverence due to their memory were distinctly negotiable entities. By the end of 1546, a hole had been cut clear through the web of customary connections regulating the relations of the living and the dead. In the following years, reformers would rush to exploit the opening, and to reconfigure the threads.

[230] The pattern is paralleled in Henrician policy towards images: Aston, *England's Iconoclasts*, 220–46.
[231] An expression of Clebsch's: *England's Earliest Protestants*, 128. It is revealing that in 1545 John Bale could accuse an opponent of planning 'to sett up purgatorye ageyne, reparinge the broken chest of the churches olde suffrages': *Mysterye of Inyquyte*, 17ʳ.

3

'Rage Against the Dead': Reform, Counter-reform, and the Death of Purgatory

IN 1631 the antiquary John Weever looked back with horror at events in the reign of Edward VI. 'Under a godly pretence of reforming Religion', royal commissioners tore down and defaced tombs and funeral monuments. They were motivated partly by an animus against all religious imagery, but more particularly by a hostility to prayer for the dead. Inscriptions and epitaphs were pulled from sepulchres 'especially if they began with an orate pro anima, or concluded with cuius animae propitietur Deus'. This constituted, thought Weever, nothing less than a 'barbarous rage against the dead'.[1] The language was emotive, but Weever was undoubtedly correct to perceive that after the death of Henry VIII the theological temperature rose sharply, and that a thoroughgoing attempt was made to transform popular views of the requirements of the dead and the appropriate means of commemorating them. Under Mary, the theological bearings were reversed, and the doctrine of purgatory and the practices of intercessory prayer were officially restored. But the reconstitution of a single 'community' embracing the living and the dead had become highly problematic. As the society of the living splintered over religious allegiance, it was increasingly believed that not all of the departed were deserving of respectful memory. To its critics, some of the actions of the Marian regime would seem equally to embody a shameful 'rage against the dead'. The mid-Tudor period did not unambiguously resolve theological questions relating to the condition of the dead in the next life, nor did it definitively settle the liturgical, social, and cultural rules for ordering their commemoration in this world. But in these years the presence of the dead in English society was decisively reshaped into the form that succeeding generations were to inherit. For some, the memory of what had been achieved in the middle decade of the sixteenth century would reverberate as a call to unfinished business; others would shudder at the recollection of how much had been done.

[1] J. Weever, *Ancient Funerall Monuments* (1631), 50–1.

PROHIBITIONS AND DISSOLUTIONS

Four months after the death of Henry VIII his great rival, Francis I of France, followed him to the grave, and the government in England ordered the full traditional ceremonies to be said for him in St Pauls. On the following day, 'the sayd obbyt [was] kepte in every paryche churche in London with the belles ryngyng'.[2] In 1539 the exequies ordered for the Empress Isabella had been interpreted by conservatives as a signal that 'dyryges and massys dyd goode on to the soles departyd', but in the summer of 1547 this later diplomatic nicety turned out not to be a reliable pointer to official thinking.[3] At the end of July, two documents were published which made clear the authorities' attitude towards purgatory and intercessory prayer, and which between them contained a manifesto for action: the new Book of Homilies, and the Royal Visitation Injunctions. Cranmer's 'Homily of Good Works' supplied the first clear and formal repudiation of purgatory in an official statement of the English Church. A list of 'papisticall supersticions and abuses' included purgatory and satisfactory masses, as well as fraternities and pardons and other abused things pretending 'to atteyn to the eternall lyfe, or remission of sinne'.[4] The injunctions which royal commissioners took with them at the end of August did not actually ban prayer for the dead or outlaw requiem masses, but they sought to circumscribe traditional intercessory practice in every way short of this. Pardons and trentals were condemned as 'blind devotions', and giving to the poor was urged in their place. Moreover, the money of guilds and fraternities, along with 'money given or bequeathed to the finding of torches, lights, tapers and lamps', was all to be transferred to the parish poor chest, a preliminary step towards the full dissolution of these institutions and endowments which was to follow a few months later. In the West Country, and most probably in other parts as well, the commissioners went beyond the letter of the injunctions by forbidding ringing for the dead on All Saints' night, thus implementing the proposal which Henry VIII had cautiously vetoed eighteen months earlier.[5]

At the end of 1547 the government moved decisively to dig up the foundations of post-mortem intercession, introducing a bill into parliament which dissolved all chantries, hospitals, and fraternities, and ordered the seizure of all lands, revenues, and rents devoted 'to the finding or mainten-

---

[2] J. G. Nichols (ed.), *Chronicle of the Grey Friars of London*, CS (1852), 54. In the parish of St Andrew Holborn it was recorded that 'the French King's dirge was solemnly kept in the church this year, and cost 3s 4d': T. Bentley, 'Some Monuments of Antiquities worthy memory, collected and gathered out of sundry old Accounts', in E. Griffith, *Cases of Supposed Exemption from Poor-rates, claimed on grounds of extraparochiality, with a preliminary sketch of the ancient history of the parish of St Andrew, Holborn* (1831), p. xvi.

[3] PRO, SP 1/156, 60ᵣ (*LP* xiv (2), 804).

[4] R. B. Bond (ed.), *Certain Sermons or Homilies (1547)* (Toronto, 1987), 112.

[5] *VAI* ii. 127–8; R. Hutton, *The Rise and Fall of Merry England: The Ritual Year 1400–1700* (Oxford, 1994), 79.

ance of any anniversary or obit, or other like thing ... or of any light or lamp in any church or chapel'. The scope of the measure, comprehending all intercessory provisions, however modest, differentiated it from Henry's Chantries Act of 1545, as did the overtly theological rationale. The pre-amble ascribed a great part of the superstition and error in Christian religion to men's ignorance of 'their very true and perfect salvation through the death of Jesus Christ'. At the root of this was the

> devising and phantasing vain opinions of purgatory and masses satisfactory, to be done for them which be departed, the which doctrine and vain opinion by nothing more is maintained and upholden, than by the abuse of trentals, chantries, and other provisions made for the continuance of the said blindness and ignorance.[6]

The process by which the chantries were dissolved has been the subject of detailed study, and does not require recapitulation here.[7] Commissioners were dispatched to oversee the confiscation of the endowments of around 4,000 chantries, colleges, and hospitals, and a probably much larger number of obits and parochial guilds.[8] A few exceptions were made. Oxford, Cam-bridge, Eton, and Winchester were allowed to keep their endowments, the monies spent on obsequies to be converted to other uses. An initial intention to dissolve craft guilds as well as the solely religious ones was abandoned in the face of opposition in the commons, and only the wealth devoted to 'superstitious' purposes was seized.[9] To observe that the motivation behind the Chantries Act was essentially 'secular' is not particularly helpful.[10] The precise timing of the measure, as well as the failure to deliver on promises about the conversion of revenues to education and poor relief, probably was conditioned by the financial requirements of Protector Somerset's war with Scotland. But the abolition of chantries represented the inescapable logic of theological imperatives which had been gathering momentum for a gener-ation. It was unthinkable that the chantries could have survived under an evangelical regime such as that gathered around the young King Edward. Responses to the dissolution will be considered in more detail below, but from the perspective of its sponsors the act represented a moment of cathar-tic triumph, the cutting out from the body Christian of a bloated parasite, which had drained the material substance of believers, and endangered the souls it hypocritically professed to assist.

Along with the chantries, several related forms of intercession were put down in the heady months of 1548. Parochial bede-rolls were suppressed,

---

[6] H. Gee and W. Hardy (eds.), *Documents Illustrative of English Church History* (1896), 328–57.

[7] Kreider, *Chantries*, ch. 8; P. Cunich, 'The Dissolution of the Chantries', in P. Collinson and J. Craig (eds.), *The Reformation in English Towns* (Basingstoke, 1998).

[8] C. Haigh, *English Reformations: Religion, Politics, and Society under the Tudors* (Oxford, 1993), 171; A. G. Dickens, *The English Reformation*, 2nd edn. (1989), 231.

[9] Kreider, *Chantries*, 191–2, 197–9.

[10] As, for example, by Haigh, *English Reformations*, 171.

and efforts were made to expunge any residual hold that indulgences might have. A letter from Somerset and the Council in May 1548 instructed preachers to teach the people 'to flee all old, erroneous superstitions, as the confidence in pardons, pilgrimages, beads'. In the early part of the reign, visitation injunctions enquired whether pardon rubrics had been thoroughly expunged from service books.[11] In the aftermath of the Chantries Act, there was a concerted effort on the part of the bishops to ensure that intercessory masses could not continue in any guise or form. Cranmer's visitation articles for Canterbury in 1548 ordered that curates were not to undertake trentals or other satisfactory masses 'to say or sing for the quick or the dead'.[12] In the summer of that year, seven priests from along the Devon–Cornwall border were indicted in King's Bench for assembling to celebrate 'papisticas missas satisfactorias pro defunctis'.[13] Yet for as long as the mass remained the official form of worship of the Church, it was difficult for the Edwardian authorities to convey a clear message denying any efficacy to post-mortem prayer. In what was supposed to be a sermon of recantation, preached at court on St Peter's Day 1548, Stephen Gardiner attempted to vindicate prayer for the dead and the intercessory role of the mass, without mentioning purgatory, or condemning the dissolution of the chantries. The mass, Gardiner asserted, was a sacrifice, serving *inter alia* for 'commending unto God the souls of such as be dead in Christ'. It was not, however, another redemption, or a means of satisfaction for sins, and if it had been so abused in the chantries then 'I that allow Mass so well, and I, that allow praying for the dead, as indeed the dead are of Christian charity to be prayed for, yet can agree with the realm in the matter of putting down chantries'.[14] This was, in effect, a riposte to the Latimer–Crome argument that the dissolutions represented a clear repudiation of intercessory prayer.

Gardiner was roundly answered the following year, when the Latin mass was abolished and replaced by a communion service in English.[15] But even this was not seen as having solved the problem at a stroke. In a draft set of articles drawn up soon after the Prayer Book came into use, purgatory headed the list of twenty or so abuses which no man was to maintain, and it was reiterated that none should 'buy or sell the Holy Communion as in trentals and such other'. A similar concern with 'trentals of communions' was manifested by Ridley's articles for London in 1550, and Bulkeley's for the very different diocese of Bangor in 1551.[16] Undoubtedly, however, the bishop most alarmed by the potential of even reformed eucharistic rites for

[11] E. Cardwell, *Documentary Annals of the Reformed Church of England*, 2 vols. (Oxford, 1844), i. 65; *VAI* ii. 112, 181.
[12] *VAI* ii. 182.
[13] A. Greenwood, 'A Study of the Rebel Petitions of 1549', University of Manchester Ph.D. thesis (1990), 90.
[14] J. A. Muller, *Stephen Gardiner and the Tudor Reaction* (1926), 178–9.
[15] See below, 109–12.
[16] *VAI* ii. 193–4, 238, 244, 265.

serving syncretist purposes was John Hooper. In his 1551 injunctions and articles for the paired dioceses of Gloucester and Worcester, Hooper anticipated the phraseology of the Forty-Two Articles of 1553 (which he had seen in a draft form late in 1549), attacking 'the doctrine of the schoolmen of purgatory, pardons, prayers for them that are departed out of this world'. A cluster of interrogatories centred around whether clergy 'used the communion as they used trentals of masses'. When communion was celebrated at burials did only small numbers received the sacrament? Was anyone hired to receive communion for another? Was more than one communion celebrated at a burial, or did it invove more than one minister? He also wished to know if any minister was seeking to persuade the people that 'the Psalms appointed for burial in the King's Majesty's Book for thanksgiving unto God for the deliverance of the dead out of this miserable world, be appointed or placed instead of the dirge', and whether any month's minds or anniversaries were kept after the corpse had been buried. Hooper's concerns went beyond the misuse of the Prayer Book, and extended to a minute regulation of funeral ritual and mortuary culture. He proscribed 'knells or forthfares', allowing the ringing of church bells only while the sick person was dying, to solicit the prayers of neighbours, and after his death only short ringing of a single bell to announce the event. He was concerned that curates might permit crosses of wax or wood to be placed on corpses, or pardons or relics to be buried with them. He also insisted that there be no observance of the abrogated feast of All Souls, and that there be no ringing of bells on that day or the night before 'as it was used after the popish and superstitious order'.[17] To Hooper's mind, the degree of prescription was proportionate to the extent of the disease. In a funeral sermon preached the previous year, he had put forward a despairing view of 'the common sort of such as beareth the name of Christianity'. These were the people who 'imagine their friends' souls to be broiled and roasted in the fire of purgatory', and who instinctively turned to 'medicines appointed by man, as mass, *dirige*, peregrinations, pardons, other men's merits, when ye be gone; trentals, anniversaries, invocation and prayers of and to saints departed'.[18] Hooper's were the attitudes of cultural revolution, which brooked no compromise or entanglement with a discredited past. Even the self-consciously godly could be castigated for their negligence in this regard. In 1551 Bishop Robert Ferrar of St Davids, a friend of Hooper who was to be a martyr for the Protestant cause under Mary, found himself accused by a number of the leading clergy in his cathedral chapter of maintaining superstition in the church of Carmarthen. Among the charges was that the bishop 'seeing corpses there within the

[17] Ibid. 269, 277, 287, 296, 301–2, 304. The feast of All Souls had disappeared from the Calendar published with the Prayer Book in 1549: J. Ketley (ed.), *The Two Liturgies... in the Reign of King Edward VI* (PS, 1844), 28. In 1551 Martin Bucer was also complaining about the ringing of bells on 'superstitious festivals', principally All Souls: E. C. Whitaker (ed.), *Martin Bucer and the Book of Common Prayer*, ACC 55 (1974), 138.

[18] J. Hooper, *Early Writings*, ed. S. Carr (PS, 1843), 561, 564.

church with a great number of lights upon them, never spake against any of them'. For his part, Ferrar insisted that when he saw the lights, he rebuked the priests involved 'as cormorants and ravens, flying about the dead carcass for lucre's sake'.[19]

The exchanges at Carmarthen suggest that the condemnation and eradication of 'superstitions' relating to the dead were regarded as vital to the articulation of a distinctly Protestant polity in the reign of Edward VI. Yet how central an issue purgatory remained for Edwardian Protestants might be considered a moot point. With the dissolutions of 1547–8 it is tempting to think of a chapter finally closing, the Chantries Act delivering, as Diarmaid MacCulloch has put it, 'the *coup de grâce* to the moribund purgatory industry'.[20] Yet there are few indications that mid-Tudor reformers felt in any way complacent about what they had achieved. Edwardian England witnessed the publication of only one substantial work against the doctrine of post-mortem purgation, a *Liber de Purgatorio* by the Hamburg Lutheran reformer Johannes Aepinus (or Hoeck), printed at London in 1549, and dedicated to Edward VI. But diatribes against purgatory and intercessory prayer are to be found in many mid-Tudor Protestant works. Purgatory was, according to a verse narrative composed early in the reign by the gentleman pensioner William Palmer, the 'doctryne of the dyvell...whiche ys to be detestyde of all other'.[21] In 1551 the reformers were delighted to advertise that the conservative theologian John Redman had on his deathbed accepted that 'purgatory as the scole men taught it and used it was ungodly, and that there was no soch kynd of purgatory as they phantasyed'.[22] The recurrent interest of Protestant writers reminds us the issue was not a self-contained one, but rather intimately interwoven with the Reformation's central issues of doctrine and authority. In the Forty-Two Articles issued by the Edwardian Church in 1553, the condemnation of purgatory was inserted between articles on authority in the Church and on the sacraments. The phraseology

[19] Foxe, vii. 3, 6, 13. The factionalism among the Protestant clergy of the diocese may have been more a matter of personality and patronage, rather than of doctrine: G. Williams, *Wales and the Reformation* (Cardiff, 1997), 167–8, 172–3.

[20] D. MacCulloch, *Tudor Church Militant: Edward VI and the Protestant Reformation* (1999), 81.

[21] Trinity College Cambridge, MS R.3.33, 74ʳ–76ʳ. See also T. Cranmer, *An Answer to a Crafty and Sophistical Cavillation devised by Stephen Gardiner*, in *Writings and Disputations*, ed. J. E. Cox (PS, 1844), 349–54; id., *Miscellaneous Writings and Letters*, ed. J. E. Cox (PS, 1846), 63–4; H. Latimer, *Sermons and Remains*, ed. G. E. Corrie (PS, 1845), 56–8; J. Bale, *The Vocacyon of Johan Bale*, ed. P Happé and J. N. King (Binghamton, NY, 1990), 51, 60; J. Hooper, *Later Writings*, ed. C. Nevinson (PS, 1852), 31–2; N. Pocock (ed.), *Troubles Connected with the Prayer Book of 1549*, CS (1884), 173–4; J. Olde, *A Confession of the Most Auncient and True Christen Catholike Olde Belefe* (Emden, 1556), D3ʳ; J. Bradford, *Writings*, ed. A. Townsend, 2 vols. (PS, 1848–9), i. 49, 71, ii. 269–71, 279–80. Attacks on purgatory also comprised much of the matter of the first printed Protestant funeral sermons: Hooper, *Early Writings*, 561–72; Robert King, *A Funerall Sermon that was prepared to have bine preached...for a certein honourable lady then almoste deade, but afterward recovered* (1552), E1ᵛ–2ʳ, E7ᵛ–F3ᵛ.

[22] *A Reporte of Maister Doctor Redmans Answeres* (1551), A3ᵛ.

of the article represented a crisp précis of the main themes of evangelical polemic which had been developed from the 1520s onwards. 'The doctrine of school authors concerning purgatory' was said to be 'a fond thing, vainly feigned, and grounded upon no warrant of scripture'.[23] Repeatedly, Protestant writers returned to the point that Cranmer made to the western rebels in 1549: it was a gross injury to Christ 'to affirm that all have not full and perfect purgation by his blood, that die in his faith'.[24] The recurrent emphasis on trentals and communions for the dead in Edwardian visitation articles suggests how closely the issue remained tied to the crux questions of contemporary theological debate: the nature of the eucharist, and whether it could be thought of as a sacrifice. More than anything else, masses for the dead exposed the perverse eucharistic theology of the papists. They were, wrote John Bale, 'a blasphemous profanation of the Lord's holy supper'.[25] Other themes rehearsed in the preceding decades recurred in the Edwardian polemic against purgatory, such as its social injustice. Visitation articles emphasized giving to the poor as the obvious alternative to endowing intercessory prayer, while the Chantries Act spoke (optimistically) of 'better provision for the poor and needy' as a result of the dissolution.[26] Touring the Midlands with the royal enclosure commission in the summer of 1548, Somerset's ally John Hales spoke to local people of the 'insatiable desire' of some uncharitable rich men, and averred that masses and prayers for the dead would not save them from damnation.[27]

Alongside the earnestness, the solemn Catholic exequies for the dead continued to supply an apparently irresistible target for ridicule, humour, and burlesque. Purgatory was 'a fond thing'. Luke Shepherd's *The Upcheringe of the Mass* included a mock *dirige* and *placebo*, mercilessly lampooning the Latin rite: 'Requiem eternam / Lest penam sempiternam / For vitam supernam / And umbram infernam / For vernam lucernam . . .'.[28] In response to the western rebels, Philip Nichols joked that if God had a third place to purge souls before they entered heaven, it was only fair that the devil should have a fourth place to make sure that the damned were 'clene scoured' of any drop of goddness before they descended to hell. 'These are but dreams, good people.'[29] Anyone who believed the mass was a propitiatory sacrifice, scoffed John Bradford, must think 'that the priest is God's fellow, for he may apply it to whom he will. Therefore honour Sir John, and make much of

---

[23] Ketley (ed.), *Two Liturgies*, 532.

[24] Cranmer, *Miscellaneous Writings*, 181.

[25] J. Bale, *Select Works*, ed. H. Christmas (PS, 1849), 152–3.

[26] *VAI* ii. 112, 127, 182, 188; Gee and Hardy, *Documents*, 329.

[27] N. Tyacke, 'Introduction', in id. (ed.), *England's Long Reformation 1500–1800* (1998), 18.

[28] J. N. King, *English Reformation Literature: The Tudor Origins of the Protestant Tradition* (Princeton, 1982), 265–7. See also S. Brigden, *London and the Reformation* (Oxford, 1989), 436–7.

[29] Pocock (ed.), *Troubles Connected with the Prayer Book*, 174.

Sir Thomas.'[30] In a systematic dissection of 'the popish mass', Thomas Becon sneered at the thoughts passing through the minds of priests at the memento for the souls of the dead:

ye pray for Philip and Cheny, more than a good meany, for the souls of your great grand Sir and of your old Beddlam Hurre, for the souls of father Princhard and of mother Puddingwright, for the souls of good-man Rinsepitcher and good-wife Pint-pot, for the souls of Sir John Huslegoose and Sir Simon Sweetlips, and for the souls of all your benefactors, founders, patrons, friends and well-willers, which have given you either dirige-groats, confessional-pence, trentals, year-services, dinner or supper.[31]

Yet, in spite of its intentions, Becon's burlesque reminds us that the Edwardian assault on purgatory brought about not merely an abstract theological transposition, but a disaffirmation of the claims on the memory of the community by known individuals, neighbours and kin, parents and grandparents. This was carried through with a scrupulous disregard for persons. The chantry chaplains of aristocratic families were silenced, just as the obit lamps of the more humble dead were extinguished, and the bede-roll registrations of modest parish benefactors rendered redundant. The confiscations of church plate, vestments, and altar cloths instigated by Northumberland at the end of the reign, and the pre-emptive sales which so many parishes had been making from 1547 onwards to avoid them, involved the dispersal and destruction of commemorative objects inscribed with the names and coats of arms of local donors.[32] How people experienced and reacted to these developments is a question of considerable moment. Is there any evidence that English communities, weighed down by the burden of the dead, saw the Edwardian dissolutions as liberating, or did they regard them as acts of desecration, to be resisted, and, when opportunity allowed, reversed?

RECEPTION, REACTIONS, AND RESPONSE

The outright proscription of purgatory, and of the whole gamut of traditional means of assisting the repose of the souls of the dead, must rank as one of the most audacious attempts at the restructuring of beliefs and values ever attempted in England, a kind of collective cultural de-programming. Yet any clear sense of how people reacted or felt about it is frustratingly elusive

---

[30] Bradford, *Writings*, ii. 290.

[31] T. Becon, *Prayers and Other Pieces*, ed. J Ayre (PS, 1844), 276. Duffy, *Altars*, 495, cites this passage as a parody of the bede-roll—this is perhaps being evoked, though the context is clearly the liturgical one of the memento in the canon of the mass.

[32] E. Duffy, *The Voices of Morebath: Reformation and Rebellion in an English Village* (New Haven and London, 2001), 125. For the extent of parochial sales, see Haigh, *English Reformations*, 182–3.

and intangible. In 1548 chantries and related institutions seem to have gone down not with a bang but a whimper, and a number of historians have commented on the remarkable absence of significant overt opposition, given the magnitude of the cultural and religious revolution that the process represented.[33] There seems something almost epigrammatic about this silence, as if here we held the key to understanding how a palpably unlooked-for Reformation was successfully imposed and ultimately embraced. One approach is to suppose that the actions of the Edwardian government merely lopped the head from an already withering plant. Here, for once, 'traditional' and 'revisionist' assessments concur, A. G. Dickens observing that 'in so far as people ceased to believe in the doctrine of intercessory masses for souls in purgatory, chantries lost their main reason for existence', and Christopher Haigh maintaining that the 1547 act 'killed off institutions and devotions which were already waning'.[34] As we have seen, the testamentary evidence from the last years of Henry VIII's reign goes some way towards supporting this view, and (unsurprisingly) in Edward's reign the percentage of testators requesting masses effectively collapsed: in one nationwide testamentary sample, 97 per cent of Edwardian wills make no such bequest.[35] Of course, from 1548 such investments were effectively illegal, and the large clerical labour force existing to service them had been laid off. We should not read wild fluctuations in the graph of testamentary provision as a surging vote of confidence in government policy, but they do suggest a willingness to acquiesce. Acquiescence was not the invariable response of conservative English people to the dismantling of traditional religion: in 1536–7 tens of thousands rose in the north in defence of monasteries and saints' days, and in the summer of 1549 the abolition of the Latin mass provoked a serious rebellion in the south-west of England, and substantial disorder elsewhere. But in 1548 the dissolution of the chantries triggered no comparable armed protest.

Yet in exploring the interface between compliance and resistance, large-scale popular rebellion can be a somewhat crude instrument of orientation. Neither the Pilgrimage of Grace nor the 1549 'Prayer Book Rising' were monocausal or unproblematically 'religious' movements, and the quiesence of some parts of the country at these times can be attributed to political and structural factors as much as to supposed variations in the temperature of popular religious sentiment.[36] Nor is it in fact the case that no instances of

---

[33] Dickens, English Reformation, 235; C. J. Kitching, 'The Chantries of the East Riding of Yorkshire at the Dissolution in 1548', YAJ 44 (1972), 183; Cunich, 'Dissolution of the Chantries', 161.

[34] Dickens, English Reformation, 235; Haigh, English Reformations, 172.

[35] See above, 80–1; P. Marshall, The Catholic Priesthood and the English Reformation (Oxford, 1994), 51.

[36] M. Bush, The Pilgrimage of Grace (Manchester, 1996); R. Hoyle, The Pilgrimage of Grace and the Politics of the 1530s (Oxford, 2001); J. Youings, 'The South-Western Rebellion of 1549', Southern History, 1 (1979). See also the forthcoming doctoral work of Amanda Jones of the University of Warwick on the rebellions of 1549 outside East Anglia and the south-west.

resistance can be directly associated with the campaign against intercession. At Poole, Dorset, on All Saints, 1547, the new Protestant minister Thomas Hancock ordered the curate to ignore a request from three powerful local Catholics to 'say *dirige* for all solls', and swore that he himself would never say *dirige* 'nott whyle they leved'. In response 'did they all as hytt wer with on mowth call me knav'.[37] Three hundred miles away, in the vicinity of Scarborough on the Yorkshire coast the suppression of chantries led directly to the so-called 'Seamer Rising' of July–August 1549, which involved the participation of at least 3,000, and the murder of one of the Yorkshire chantry commissioners.[38] The Seamer rebels hoped to link up with the rising in the south-west, and it is clear that here too the government's dismantling of the structures of intercessory prayer was part of the background to armed revolt. The murder at Helston in 1548 of the archdeacon of Cornwall, William Body, a riotous prelude to the later disturbances, was in part provoked by his overbearing participation in the chantry commission for the county.[39] The assembled rebels the following summer did not call for the re-establishment of the chantry system as such, but they demanded a partial restoration of monasticism endowed with returned chantry lands. They also asserted that 'we wyll have everye preacher in his sermon, and every pryest at hys masse, praye specially by name for the soules in purgatory, as oure forefathers dyd'.[40] The emphasis on prayer for souls 'by name', in sermons and at mass, is fairly clearly a reference, not to chantries, but to the parochial bede-rolls which had been terminated throughout the south-west in the course of 1548. At Stratton in Cornwall, annual bede-roll registrations had numbered a mere handful through the 1530s and 1540s, but in 1547 a total of thirty-one names were added, parishioners rushing to lay claim to post-mortem memory for themselves and others to pre-empt a feared closing of the books.[41]

Local resistance to the ending of intercessions was not necessarily defiant, overt, or easily detectable. Concealment from the commissioners of chantry lands was a widespread phenomenon.[42] In many cases the motive was to preserve communal endowments to local uses, rather than necessarily to maintain the flow of intercessory prayer, but in a few instances the latter impulse is discernible. At Arnold in Nottinghamshire, Liskeard in Cornwall, and Gainsborough in Lincolnshire, concealed lands which had supported

[37] J. G. Nichols (ed.), *Narratives of the Days of the Reformation*, CS 77 (1859), 78.

[38] A. G. Dickens, 'Some Popular Reactions to the Edwardian Reformation in Yorkshire', in id., *Reformation Studies* (1982), 21–39. The role of chantry chapels in providing basic pastoral care in this region was undoubtedly a major factor in the rising.

[39] A. L. Rowse, *Tudor Cornwall* (1941), 253–8.

[40] A. Fletcher and D. MacCulloch, *Tudor Rebellions*, 4th edn. (1997), 140.

[41] Greenwood, 'Rebel Petitions', 90–1.

[42] C. Burgess and B. Kümin, 'Penitential Bequests and Parish Regimes in Late Medieval England', *JEH* 44 (1993), 629–30; C. J. Kitching, 'The Quest for Concealed Lands in the Reign of Elizabeth I', *TRHS* 24 (1974); E. H. Shagan, 'Popular Politics and the English Reformation, c.1525–1553', Princeton University Ph.D. thesis (2000), 466–8.

obit lamps were restored to that purpose after the accession of Mary, and in Lancaster the priest of an almshouse chantry was able to carry on saying mass till his discovery in 1560.[43] It has also sometimes been suggested that the very testamentary evidence which seems to show such ready compliance may in fact encode a covert subversion of the wishes of the reformers. As the percentage of wills requesting masses fell, that leaving bequests for alms-deeds rose: in the 1540s 42 per cent of Essex testators did so; in 1547–8 this rose to 63 per cent. In Gloucestershire 8 per cent of non-elite testators made gifts to the poor in the 1540s, and 25 per cent in Edward's reign; in London the figures were 12 per cent and 32 per cent.[44] As Eamon Duffy has observed, 'of all the medieval activities held to assist the soul after death, the relief of the poor was the only one permitted and indeed actively encouraged by the Protestant authorities after 1547'.[45] Testators sometimes explicitly laid down that legacies were to go to the poor if masses, prayers, or obits would not stand with the law. Others felt it necessary to insist that this was not their motivation, the Londoner John Maior leaving 20s. to the poor in 1551, 'not to thintente to pray for me but to be thankefull unto God and to pray for the kynge'.[46]

The evidence here is ambiguous to say the least. The suggestion that Edwardian shifts in testamentary provision signal a sudden and widespread repudiation of the deeply rooted notion that good works in this life served to benefit the soul in the next is unconvincing. But equally so is the implication that 'belief' in purgatory was of sufficient resilience and plasticity simply to adapt itself unscathed to new forms of expression. Chantries, obits, bede-rolls, ringing at All Souls—these had given shape to and sustained traditional ideas about the needs and location of the dead, and their abrogation could not but lead to the attenuation of those ideas in their accustomed social context. At the same time, the dissolution and dismantling of traditional structures of intercession was not simply a process imposed on communities from outside, but one in which many were implicated and which created both willing and unwitting collaborators. From the late 1530s onwards, when the dissolution of the monasteries announced the vulnerability of endowed religious institutions to official expropriation, there had been an increasing number of private anticipatory dissolutions of chantries and obits to forestall government action. As the dissolution itself got under way in 1548, some patrons made efforts to resume the lands of their or their ancestors' foundations, and within a short time many of the elites, both

[43] Shagan, 'Popular Politics', 469; Haigh, *English Reformations*, 172.
[44] J. Helt, 'Purgatory, Policy, and Piety in Sixteenth-Century Essex', Vanderbilt University Ph.D. thesis (1996), 190–1; C. Litzenberger, *The English Reformation and the Laity: Gloucestershire, 1540–1580* (Cambridge, 1997), 185; S. Brigden, 'Religion and Social Obligation in Early Sixteenth-Century London', *PP* 103 (1984), 104–5.
[45] Duffy, *Altars*, 505.
[46] Ibid.; Brigden, 'Religion and Social Obligation', 106.

urban and gentry, were purchasing chantry lands.[47] Furthermore, as Ethan
Shagan has recently demonstrated, the dissolution was accompanied by a
fair amount of simple embezzlement, a form of 'resistance' that was hardly
ideologically motivated.[48] All of these actions represented an implicit bol-
stering of the evangelical case against devoting energy and resources to
interceding for the dead, even if their authors were consciously out of
sympathy with it.

The question of the extent to which local patterns of behaviour were
responsive to government policy, both in the sense of following a lead, and
in that of attempting to pre-empt or forestall events, is equally applicable to
the fate of sepulchral monuments of the dead. As we have seen, the monastic
dissolutions of 1536–40 frequently involved the displacement or destruction
of tombs and brasses; the Edwardian Reformation brought this process into
the heart of parish communities. Such memorials had never been entirely
sacrosanct, but the scale of destruction in 1547–53 was entirely unprecedented. In many London parishes an exfoliant hammering and levering sim-
ultaneously removed layers of brass from the church floor, and layers of dead
faces and names from the inherited memory of the parishioners. At St
Andrew Holborn in 1547, churchwarden Oliver Tatam 'took up as much
old copper off the tombs and grave stones in the church as came to one
hundred weight, for which he took 36s'; the following year a further 18s. 6d.
worth was ripped up.[49] The parish of St Faith's sold 'seven score poundes of
olde and broken lattyn' for 46s. in 1552; St Mary Aldermary sold 'plattes
that ware over gravys stonys' to a pewterer for £3. 13s. 54d., as well as
'sundry gravestones sold to four men for 22s'. At All Hallows London Wall
'metell which was upon the grave stones and other monments' went for 3d.
per lb; St Alphage, London Wall sold 202 lb, and a significant quantity was
also sold by St Dunstan in the west. According to the Elizabethan chronicler
John Stow, there was such pulling down of brass monuments at All Hallows,
Stone Church, that 'the church wardens were forced to make a large account, 12. shillings that yeare for Broomes, besides the carriage away of
stone, and brasse of their owne charge'.[50]

London's proximity to the nerve-centres of the Edwardian Reformation,
and the fact that its local elites were typically merchants, rather than landed

[47] Kreider, *Chantries*, ch. 6; Dickens, 'Reactions to the Edwardian Reformation', 25; id., 'A
Municipal Dissolution of Chantries at York, 1536', in *Reformation Studies*, 47–56; Shagan,
'Popular Politics', 450–1.

[48] Shagan, 'Popular Politics', 470–2.

[49] Bentley, 'Some Monuments of Antiquities', pp. xv–xvi.

[50] J. Page-Phillips, *Palimpsests: The Backs of Monumental Brasses*, 2 vols. (1980), i. 18; M.
Norris, *Monumental Brasses: The Memorials*, 2 vols. (1977), i. 259; J. Stow, *A Survey of
London*, ed. C. L. Kingsford, 2 vols. (Oxford, 1908), i. 204. The '74 lb of latten' sold for 3¼d.
per pound at St Andrew Hubbard in 1550–2 seems likely also to have been funeral brasses: C.
Burgess (ed.), *The Church Records of St Andrew Hubbard Eastcheap c.1450–c.1570*, London
Record Society, 34 (1999), 68.

gentry with a vested interest in preserving ancestral tombs, must have made its monuments particularly vulnerable. But the stripping of the burial-markers of the dead from churches, and their sale for re-engraving, or for melting down for other uses, was not confined to the capital. The church-wardens of Ludlow sold 45 lb of 'old brasse' for 15s. in 1551; the accounts of St Thomas the Martyr, Salisbury, list receipts of 36s. in 1547–8 for 'brase which was upon graves and tombes'; those of Thame, Oxfordshire, record the sale of 80 lb of brass in 1550. Yet this was small beer compared to the 3 hundredweight 'in Brasses' sold at Long Melford, Suffolk, in 1548, or the 9 hundredweight at St Martin's Leicester in 1547. St John's Winchester got £2. 3s. 0d. for brasses in 1549–50. Brasses were the most versatile (and remov-able) form of funerary monument, but they were not the only type torn out of the churches in these years. The accounts of Crondall in Hampshire have four separate entries for 'stones sold owte of the churche' in Edward's reign, and those of Ludlow record the sale of 'stones out of the churchyard' in 1551.[51] A host of questions attach themselves to such laconic entries. Were churchwardens disposing of brasses and stones on their own initiative or under direct external pressure? Were monuments of the dead jettisoned selectively (and, if so, by what criteria) or wholesale? To what extent, if any, was the process ideologically motivated? In some cases it seems likely that the intention was to make the most of communal resources before the govern-ment could get its hands on them. At Great Yarmouth, for example, the assembly ordered the town bailiffs to send brasses from St Nicholas church to be cast into weights and measures for the use of the town.[52] The inventories which parishes were required to compile in 1552 as a means of halting further alienation of valuables often record the disposal of brasses over the previous four years, though at Baldock in Hertfordshire there were still 'ii plates of brasse in the store howse'.[53] Yet the wardens of St Martin's Leicester recorded that their disposal of brasses had been undertaken 'by the commaundement of Mr Mayor and his brethren, accordyng to the Kings Injuncyons'.[54]

The direct responsibility of royal commissioners for damage to funeral monuments was emphasized by later commentators. John Weever, with whose strictures this chapter opened, wrote that 'marbles which covered the dead were digged up...tombes hackt and hewne apeeces; images or representations of the defunct, broken, erazed, cut, or dismembered'. Epitaphs were prised off 'for greediness of the brasse, or for that they were thought to be antichristian'. Carcases were cast out of graves 'for gaine

[51] T. Wright (ed.), *Churchwardens' Accounts of the Town of Ludlow*, CS 102 (1869), 48–9; H. W. Macklin, *The Brasses of England*, 3rd edn. (1913), 306; Norris, *Monumental Brasses: The Memorials*, i. 259; Duffy, *Altars*, 495; J. F. Williams (ed.), *The Early Churchwardens' Accounts of Hampshire* (Winchester, 1913), 116–17.

[52] Page-Phillips, *Palimpsests*, i. 18.

[53] Ibid.; A. Palmer, *Tudor Churchwardens' Accounts*, Hertfordshire Record Publications, 1 (1985), 70.

[54] Norris, *Monumental Brasses: The Memorials*, i. 259.

of their stone or lead coffins'.[55] A generation earlier, the Elizabethan Yorkshire rector Michael Sherbrook similarly charged the commissioners with naked self-interest, and 'seeing all things were put to the spoil'. Other persons, 'of the like consciences and condicions to the commissioners', 'plucked up the brass of tombs and gravestones in the church'.[56] There was in fact in the 1547 injunctions no direct sanction for removing or defacing funeral monuments, but the commissioners were charged with overseeing the destruction of shrines, pictures, paintings, 'and all other monuments of feigned miracles, pilgrimages, idolatry and superstition: so that there remain no memory of the same'.[57] Under a broad interpretation of this rubric, monuments with images of the Trinty or of the Virgin, and with inscriptions requesting prayer for the soul in purgatory, were distinctly vulnerable.[58] As far as funerary monuments were concerned, the Edwardian regime seemed consistently to speak with two voices.[59] An act of parliament of 1550, providing for the defacing and destruction of graven, carved, or painted church images, contained an important exemption:

this act or anything therein contained shall not extend to any image or picture set or graven upon any tomb in any church, chapel, or churchyard only for a monument of any king, prince, nobleman, or other dead person, which hath not been commonly reputed and taken for a saint; but ... such pictures and images may stand and continue.[60]

Yet within a year of the act's passing Bishop Hooper was ordering the removal from churches and chapels of 'all places, tabernacles, tombs, sepulchres, tables, footstools, rood-lofts, and other monuments ... where such superstition, idols, images, or other provocation of idolatry have been used'.[61] Meanwhile, the Crown had been showing scant regard for its own admonitions. Just as the royal seizure of the monasteries had involved the physical destruction of memorials, so did the dissolution of chantries and collegiate churches. At Wells Cathedral, the fifteenth-century chantry chapel of Bishop Stillington was demolished in 1552, and two brass images of

---

[55] Weever, Ancient Funerall Monuments, 50–1.

[56] A. G. Dickens (ed.), Tudor Treatises, YASRS, 125 (1959), 139. The Marian preacher Roger Edgeworth had seen the process in similar terms, condemning as contemporary grave-robbers those 'that steale plates of brasse with epitaphies from mens graves or tombes': Sermons very Fruitfull, Godly and Learned, ed. J. Wilson (Cambridge, 1993), 346.

[57] VAI ii. 126.

[58] On the great popularity of devotional panels with images of the Trinity or saints on fifteenth-century brasses, see Norris, Monumental Brasses: The Memorials, i. 202–5. R. Rex, 'Monumental Brasses and the Reformation', Transactions of the Monumental Brass Society, 15 (1990), 378, speculates that 'obit brasses' which recorded details of an obit foundation would have been regarded as part of the endowment and thus seized by chantry commissioners.

[59] For the suggestion that the sending of mixed messages was a conscious reforming strategy of the Edwardian authorities, see MacCulloch, Tudor Church Militant, 61–2.

[60] J. R. Tanner (ed.), Tudor Constitutional Documents, 2nd edn. (Cambridge, 1948), 115.

[61] VAI ii. 284–5.

bishops in the choir were sold for £3. 12s. 1d.[62] One authority asserts that most English cathedrals lost their brasses in Edward's reign.[63] At St Paul's in 1552 the Council managed to restrain Bishop Ridley from pulling down the tomb of John of Gaunt.[64] But elsewhere the Crown's carelessness with regard to the monuments of royal progenitors which had been manifest in the late 1530s was repeated after 1547. The dissolution of the collegiate churches at Fotheringhay and Leicester led in a thoroughly evenhanded way to the destruction of the late medieval tombs of the dukes of York at the former, and of the earls and dukes of Lancaster at the latter.[65]

Without doubt, however, the single largest disturbance of the remains and monuments of the dead took place in London in April 1549: the destruction by order of Protector Somerset of the Pardon Churchyard of St Paul's Cathedral. A generation after the event, it was described in detail by John Stow. The Pardon Churchyard was a great cloister on the north side of the cathedral, in the midst of which stood 'a fair chapel', and around whose walls was painted a dance of death, modelled on that of St Innocents cloister in Paris, with verses by the poet John Lydgate. According to Stow, the funeral monuments in this cloister 'in number and curious workmanship, passed all other that were in that church'. But on 10 April 1549 chapel, cloister, and monuments were pulled down, along with a large charnel house on the north side of the churchyard, leaving nothing but 'the bare plot of ground'. The bones from the charnel were conveyed to Finsbury Field, and there unceremoniously 'laid on a morish ground in short space after raised, by soylage of the citie upon them, to beare three milles'. Stow claimed to have it on good authority (that of the printer Reyner Wolfe, who had paid for the carriage) that the bones amounted to more than a thousand cart-loads. Warehouses and sheds for stationers, Stow wistfully noted, now stood in place of the tombs.[66]

With this massive act of desecration and countless others on a smaller scale, the reformers were signalling a decisive rescheduling of the debts claimed from the living by the dead. The doctrinal rejection of purgatory and intercessory prayer translated in cultural terms into a conscious abroga-tion of the hold of the past, a heedlessness of the wishes of dead ances-tors, and a prioritization of resources towards meeting the needs of this world rather than the next—whether the charitable ends of education and poor relief, or the political and military requirements of Somerset's

[62] S. E. Lehmberg, *The Reformation of Cathedrals: Cathedrals in English Society, 1485–1603* (Princeton, 1988), 112; Norris, *Monumental Brasses: The Memorials*, i. 259.

[63] J. Bertram, 'Introduction', in id. (ed.), *Monumental Brasses as Art and History* (Stroud, 1996), 22.

[64] M. Aston, *England's Iconoclasts* (Oxford, 1988), 270.

[65] H. Colvin, *Architecture and the Afterlife* (New Haven and London, 1991), 174–5, 255.

[66] Stowe, *Survey*, i. 327–30. The Greyfriars chronicler more conservatively estimated 'iiij. or v. C. lode of bones carred in to the feldes and burryd there': J. G. Nichols (ed.), *Chronicle of the Grey Friars of London*, CS (1852), 57.

and Northumberland's foreign policy.[67] There is little evidence that the shift was actively sought or welcomed outside evangelical circles. But since the force of what Robert Tittler has called 'the purgatorial imperative'[68] was so dependent on inherited social convention, institutional structures, and the customary allocation of communal resources, there were few effective strategies for resisting the process, and many were caught up in its logic. The Edwardian campaign against purgatory represents a moment of rupture, perhaps the most abrupt and traumatic of all the cultural apertures opened up in sixteenth-century England.[69] Yet what was intended and achieved between 1547 and 1553 was not merely abandonment, cancellation, obliteration. Reformers did not mean to abolish the memory of the dead but to reform it; their interest in the departed had a scope wider than the defacement of monuments and proscription of traditional intercessions. The Edwardian Church began the process of attempting to construct structures and rituals of remembrance that reflected its axioms of *sola fides* and *sola scriptura*, and did not impinge in any way upon the utter inexorability of God's intentions for the dead. It was to prove a complex and contentious task.

IN PLACE OF PURGATORY

In 1550 royal injunctions were issued remodelling the arrangements for the commemoration of benefactors at St George's Chapel, Windsor. In place of the traditional obsequies, the dean and canons were henceforth to assemble four times a year for a reading of Ecclesiasticus 44 ('Let us now praise famous men'), as well as a sermon commending the benefits of their founder and of Henry VIII, and exhorting the company to use their gifts to the glory of God 'and to the godly intent of the founder and benefactors'. After the sermon, the *Te Deum* was to be sung in English, and the service was to conclude with a prayer glorifying God in his departed servants and asking 'that both they and we may everlastingly reign with Thee in glory'.[70] The ordinances exemplify both the confidence of a new Protestant language of remembrance, and its potential ambiguities. Did the last phrase constitute a prayer for the dead? How might the dead be spoken about in a devotional or liturgical context without intimating that the living continued to assume some responsibility for their fate in the afterlife?

---

[67] See here the suggestive comments of MacCulloch, *Tudor Church Militant*, 134.

[68] R. Tittler, *The Reformation and the Towns in England: Politics and Political Culture, c.1540–1640* (Oxford, 1998), 24.

[69] W. K. Jordan, *Edward VI: The Threshold of Power* (1970), 181; P. Collinson, 'England', in B. Scribner, R. Porter, and M. Teich (eds.), *The Reformation in National Context* (Cambridge, 1994), 88.

[70] *VAI* ii. 220–1.

With respect to commemoration of the dead, the Edwardian Church's first liturgical innovation was a new 'Form of Bidding the Common Prayer', appended to the injunctions of 1547. This was traditional in its form, if not its content. After prayers for the royal family, and leaders of church and state, the people were instructed 'ye shall pray for all them that be departed out of this world in the faith of Christ, that they with us, and we with them at the day of judgement, may rest both body and soul, with Abraham, Isaac, and Jacob in the Kingdom of Heaven'.[71] The formula consciously avoided any suggestion that the present condition of the departed might be ameliorated by prayer; its focus was distinctly prospective ('at the day of judgement'), and its imagery was irreproachably biblical. But nonetheless it clearly offered sanction for a continuing concern on the part of the living for the happiness and ultimate salvation of the dead. This attitude survived into a more momentous liturgical innovation of the English Reformation, Cranmer's Prayer Book of 1549. The 1549 Prayer Book addressed the commemoration of the dead in two contexts, in the texts for the celebration of communion, and in the order of service for the burial itself. Preceding the consecration in the communion service was a prayer 'for the whole state of Christ's church', in which the congregation was invited to

commend unto thy mercy (O Lord) all other thy servants, which are departed hence from us, with the sign of faith, and now do rest in the sleep of peace: Grant unto them, we beseech thee, thy mercy, and everlasting peace, and that, at the day of the general resurrection, we and all they which be of the mystical body of thy Son, may altogether be set on his right hand.

Variations on this formula, a petition that the departed might rise together with the now living on the Last Day, recurred in the burial service:

Grant, we beseech thee, that at the day of judgement his soul and all the souls of thy elect, departed out of this life, may with us, and we with them, fully receive thy promises, and be made perfit altogether... Grant unto this thy servant, that the sins which he committed in this world be not imputed unto him... make him to rise also with the just and righteous, and receive this body again to glory.

As the body was interred, the minister was to cast earth upon the coffin, saying 'I commend thy soul to God the Father Almighty, and thy body to the ground, earth to earth, ashes to ashes, dust to dust, in sure and certain hope of resurrection to eternal life'.[72] Eamon Duffy has remarked that 'the dead could still be spoken to directly, even in 1549, because in some sense they still belonged within the human community'.[73] Yet perhaps the most significant feature of the burial rites of 1549, and their clearest point of connection to previous practice, was their explicit provision for 'the Celebration of the Holy Communion when there is a Burial of the Dead'.[74]

---

[71] Ibid. 130.   [72] Ketley, *Two Liturgies*, 87–8, 145–7.
[73] Duffy, *Altars*, 475.   [74] Ketley, *Two Liturgies*, 147–8.

From the very moment of its appearance, there were those who felt that
the new liturgy was fundamentally compromised by the survival of these
trace elements of intercessory prayer. Reporting on the contents of the
forthcoming Prayer Book to the ministers at Strassburg in April 1549, the
German reformers Martin Bucer and Paul Fagius noted that some concessions had been made to antiquity and 'the infirmity of the present age'. These
included the use of vestments and candles, and 'also in regard to the commemoration of the dead'. But, they had been told, there was no superstition
in these things, and 'they are only to be retained for a time'.[75] Bucer shortly
had the opportunity to recommend the retraction of these concessions. In the
critique of the Prayer Book which he had produced by early 1551 at the
invitation of Bishop Goodrich, Bucer condemned the commendation of
the departed to God in the eucharistic service. Though he admitted that
'this custom of praying for the faithful departed is a very ancient one' with
considerable patristic support, there was no word of it in the Bible. Moreover, any hint of effectual prayer for the departed threatened to reignite the
embers of purgatory in the minds of the pople: 'when prayer is offered for
the dead that the Lord will grant them his mercy and everlasting peace, the
common man supposes that this implies that the departed still feel the want
of that peace . . . and that the primary purpose of our prayers is to gain these
things for them'. His readers scarcely needed reminding of the 'great torrent
of worse than heathen superstition' this false belief had generated in the past.
Bucer was more tolerant of the form of prayer prescribed in the burial
service, which seemed to him to be made 'for the living only'.[76] Other
foreign friends of the English Church added their voice. In a letter to
Somerset of October 1549, John Calvin drew particular attention to the
presence of the prayer for the departed in the Lord's Supper. He was aware
that 'the intention of this was not to sanction a popish purgatory', and also
that 'the ancient custom may be alleged of commemorating the departed,
with a view to unite together all the members of the body'. But against this
he insisted that the Supper of Jesus Christ was an act so sacred 'that it ought
not to be defiled by any human inventions', but stick closely to the Word of
God: 'such a commemoration as implies commendation, is not suitable to
the form of true and proper prayer'.[77]

The leaders of Edward's Church did not need outside experts to tell them
these things. The 1549 liturgy was regarded as a provisional measure of
reform, and the prevalence of concern about the misuse of funeral eucharists
in episcopal injunctions of 1549–51 strongly suggests that this concession

---

[75] H. Robinson (ed.), Original Letters relative to the English Reformation, 2 vols. (PS,
1846–7), ii. 535.

[76] Whitaker (ed.), Martin Bucer and the Book of Common Prayer, 50–2, 126.

[77] G. C. Gorham (ed.), Gleanings of a Few Scattered Ears, during the Period of the Reformation in England (1857), 66–7, redated by M. Bush, The Government Policy of Protector
Somerset (1975), 110 n. 71.

only ever had a limited shelf-life. The potential for some testators blithely to regard the new liturgy as if it were the old is suggested by the will of Bridget, Lady Marney, of September 1549. This made provision for an elaborate sung mass in the traditional manner, attended by large numbers of priests and choristers, but using 'such service as is set out and appointed by the King's Book [i.e. the new Prayer Book] to be used at burials'.[78]

In the revised Edwardian Prayer Book of 1552, there was no provision for a funeral celebration of the eucharist, and the language of the prayers in the burial service was considerably amended. The corpse was now spoken of by the minister in the third rather than second person: 'Forasmuch as it hath pleased almighty God of his great mercy to take unto himself the soul of our dear brother here departed: we therefore commit his body to the ground'. Whereas the bidding prayer of 1547, and the burial service of 1549 had prayed that at the Second Coming *they with us, and we with them* would rise together in glory, this order of priority was now reversed: God was petitioned 'shortly to accomplish the number of thine elect, and to haste thy kingdom, that *we with this* our brother, and all other departed in the true faith of thy holy name, may have our perfect consummation and bliss, both in body and soul'. This was a subtle shift of register, but one that was designed to minimize any suspicion that the Church was engaged in plea-bargaining with God with respect to the soul of the departed.[79]

The message was made more clearly in the changes to the communion service. The prayer for 'the whole state of Christ's Church' now carried the important qualifier 'militant here in earth', and the commendation of the departed was now entirely omitted. The fact that Stephen Gardiner had argued that the prayer for the whole estate of Christ's Church was one of several passages in the first Prayer Book explicitly upholding Catholic doctrine may have been a factor in its demise.[80] To a more humble religious conservative, the Yorkshire curate Robert Parkyn, the 1552 service represented a clear moment of rupture. There were now 'no diriges or other devoutt prayers to be songe or saide for suche as was departtide this transitorie worlde, for thai nedyde none (saide the boyke). Why? By cawsse ther sowlles was immediattlye in blisse and joy after the departtynge from the bodies, and therfor thay nedyde no prayer.'[81]

More modern assessments of the 1552 burial liturgy have tended to be equally unenthusiastic. Writing in the early part of the twentieth century, the Anglo-Catholic R. J. E. Boggis argued (somewhat optimistically) that in 1549 'the ancient and catholic custom of praying for the departed was fully recognised and encouraged'. But he found no such constancy in the

---

[78] D. MacCulloch, *Thomas Cranmer: A Life* (New Haven, 1996), 462.

[79] Ketley, *Two Liturgies*, 318–20 (my italics).

[80] Ibid. 270; Muller, *Gardiner*, 215–16.

[81] A. G. Dickens (ed.), 'Robert Parkyn's Narrative of the Reformation', in *Reformation Studies*, 305.

1552 Prayer Book, a circumstance he ascribed to the (by implication malign) 'influence of foreign Protestantism'.[82] More recently, Eamon Duffy has interpreted the ethos of 1552 as representing a final break with the outlook which saw the living and the dead as part of a single Christian community: 'in the world of the 1552 book the dead were no longer with us. They could neither be spoken to nor even spoken about, in any way that affected their well-being.' The fact that the minister no longer addressed the corpse was emblematic; the dead person was considered 'as one no longer here, but precisely as departed: the boundaries of human community have been re-drawn'.[83] Diarmaid MacCulloch too has seen in the reformed liturgy a desire 'to destroy the sense of continuing communion between living and dead which had been such a striking feature of late medieval religion'. The 1552 rite with its long Scripture readings was designed primarily to edify the living rather than maintain a relationship with the dead.[84]

It is hard to dissent from these assessments, but even this most austere of Protestant liturgies retained a prospective rather than merely commemorative interest in the fate of the body and the soul. The dead continued to be interred 'in sure and certayne hope of resurreccion to eternal lyfe', and in the prayer for God 'shortly to accomplyssh the noumbre of thyne elect' a slender thread of petition for the faithful departed remained. It is a noteworthy fact that prayer for the dead as such has not been condemned by any official formulary of the Church of England. Article 23 ('Of Purgatory') of the Forty-Two Articles drawn up in 1553 roundly declared that 'The Doctrine of School authors concerning purgatory, pardons, worshipping and adoration as well of images as of relics, and also invocation of Saints, is a fond thing, vainly feigned, and grounded upon no warrant of scripture, but rather repugnant to the word of God.'[85] But a draft set of articles approved by the six royal preachers Harley, Bill, Horne, Grindal, Perne, and Knox in October 1552 included an additional article 'de precatione pro defunctis', which was removed by Cranmer in the course of his final revisions.[86] It is possible to make too much of this, and Cranmer's intention was clearly not to sanction or encourage prayer for the deceased. Nonetheless, it must have been in his mind that the 1549 Prayer Book had included explicit commendations of the departed to the mercy of God, and that the recent Act of Uniformity had declared the superseded liturgy to be 'agreeable to the word of God'.[87]

Some leading Edwardian Protestants do not seem to have wished to close the door completely on the possibility of praying for the dead. In the course

[82] R. J. E. Boggis, *Praying for the Dead: An Historical Review of the Practice* (1913), 176–8.
[83] Duffy, *Altars*, 475.
[84] MacCulloch, *Cranmer*, 509.
[85] Ketley, *Two Liturgies*, 532.
[86] E. C. Messenger, *The Reformation, the Mass and the Priesthood*, 2 vols. (1936–7), i. 534, 553–5.
[87] Gee and Hardy, *Documents*, 369.

of a disputation on the issue held at Oxford in 1549, the dean of Christ Church, Richard Cox, argued against Richard Smyth that there was no necessity to believe purgatory simply because the apostles had taught prayer for the dead, thereby implying that the two were in principle separable.[88] Even that veteran campaigner against purgatory and popish intercession Hugh Latimer did not feel that it was wrong to invoke God's blessing upon the dead. In a sermon before the king in April 1549, Latimer urged his auditors 'to remember the souls departed, with lauds and praise to almighty God'; in November the following year at Stamford he commended to the congregation 'the souls departed this life in the faith of Christ, that ye remember to give laud, praise, and thanks to Almighty God for his great goodness and mercy shewed unto them in that great need and conflict against the devil and sin'.[89]

Yet other mid-Tudor Protestants subscribed more apprehensively to the logic of the slippery slope. Thomas Sampson, in a letter addressed in Mary's reign to the 'true professors' in his former parish of All Hallows, Bread Street, denounced all prayer for the dead as vain, a kind of 'curious charity' that had 'no ground in the scripture'. Purgatory, *dirige*, pardons and trentals had all been built 'on this unhappy ground'.[90] A more detailed consideration of the issue was the Marian martyr John Bradford's *An Exhortacion to the Carienge of Chrystes Crosse*, smuggled out of England and published on the Continent in 1555.[91] Bradford opened the treatise by declaring that Christians in England were being persecuted for four points of religion: 'namely, of the sacrament of Christ's body and blood, and for the sacrifice of Christ, for praying for the dead, and praying to the dead, that is, to saints'. The duties of the living towards the dead had been set out by Abraham, Isaac, Jacob, Moses, the prophets, Christ, and the apostles: 'we bury the dead in a convenient place, and mourn in measure'. It was right to give thanks to God for the departed, and to pray that we might depart in the same faith and rise with them at the resurrection. The dead were 'members of the same body mystical of Christ that we be of', yet were to be distinguished from 'militant members' as being at rest and having no need of our help. Charity was better directed towards 'brethren that be alive'. Bradford admitted the truth of the papists' claim that the Fathers 'were accustomed to make memorials for the dead...as we do in our communion. But, to gather that therefore they prayed for them, it no more followeth, than to say that our English Service doth allow it, where it doth not.' There is memorial for the dead, Bradford insisted, in giving thanks to God for them, as well as in praying for them, and it followed that 'to pray for the dead, is a general word, including in it giving

---

[88] J. Strype, *Ecclesiastical Memorials* (1721), ii (1), 208–9. Cox went on to argue that the apostolic injunction was in any case not now binding on Christians.

[89] Latimer, *Sermons*, 217, 284.

[90] Strype, *Ecclesiastical Memorials*, iii (2), 49–50.

[91] Bradford, *Writings*, ii. 269 ff.

of thanks'. Thus when Augustine, Chrysostom, and others seemed to allow praying for the dead, they had no thought of delivering them from purgatory, or bettering their estate. Rather they meant to declare the Church's love to the dead, and pray for the 'more speedy coming of Christ'. Having trumped one of the papists' aces, he proceeded to attempt to do likewise with another: 'they say "charity requireth it"'. Here Bradford rehashed the polemical topos that a truly charitable pope would empty purgatory at a stroke. Moreover, purgatory was a doctrine that led charity to grow cold in this world, encouraging a man 'to live in little love, in wrath even to our death's day' in the expectation that 'when he is gone, he shall find ease and release'.[92]

Bradford's arguments represent a considered summary of orthodox Protestant views on prayer for the dead, yet there is a defensive tone to some of his attacks. The demonstrable practices of the early Church required some swift-footed exegesis, and there was a somewhat tremulous insistence that the phraseologies of the Edwardian liturgy were models of rectitude, not hostages to fortune. Moreover, reading against the grain of Bradford's text gives a sense of the deep-rootedness of the instinct that to pray for the dead was a quintessentially charitable act. This was graphically illustrated in Cambridge in 1557, at the burning of the Protestant minister John Hullier. In a curious inversion of the usual roles, Hullier's sympathizers in the crowd continued to pray for him after he was dead, while enraged papists cried 'he was not to be prayed for; and being but a damned man, it could profit him nothing'.[93]

PURGATORY RESTORED?

The premature death of Edward VI in July 1553 meant a change of regime, a new theology, and another set of royal exequies. Edward's funeral was celebrated on 8 August, Mary desiring a liturgical commemoration according to the ancient rites, but her confidant the imperial ambassador advising against, lest it provoke unrest in the capital. In the event, the burial service was performed for Edward in English in Westminster Abbey, most probably by Cranmer, while the queen attended a solemn requiem in the Tower, celebrated by Gardiner, who 'did all things as in times past'.[94] The bifurcated ritual was an indication of how emblematic the commemoration of the dead had become for the emergent confessional identities of mid-Tudor England. One Suffolk priest, on hearing that 'our good king is buried

[92] Ibid. 269, 279–80, 292–3. For discussion of how later Protestants interpreted the practice of the early Church, see below, 141–8.
[93] Foxe, viii. 380.
[94] Muller, *Gardiner*, 223–4; J. Loach, *Edward VI* (New Haven and London, 1999), 167–9. Cranmer's early biographer reported that it 'was falslye bruted abrode that he offered hymselfe to synge the mase and requiem at the kynges burynge': Nichols (ed.), *Reformation Narratives*, 227.

with a mass by the bishop of Winchester', thought it 'great idolatry and blasphemy', and the bishop a traitor.[95] Though spared the full requiem mass in August, Londoners were soon hearing messages that had not been publicly articulated for over a decade. In October 1553 Dr Hugh Weston preached at Paul's Cross, beginning his sermon by urging his auditors: 'You shall pray for all them that be departed, that be neither in heaven, nor hell, but in a place not yet sufficiently purged to come to heaven, that they may be relieved by your devout prayers.' A fortnight later Leonard Pollard preached at St Michael's, Cambridge, 'and in his sermon approved purgatory'.[96] In visitation articles of 1554, the restored bishop of London, Edmund Bonner, instructed curates to urge testators 'to have due respect to their soul's health', and his new order of bidding the beads prescribed prayers for 'the Catholic Church of Christ, dispersed throughout the whole world, and for the three estates of the same, that is for the spirituality, the temporality, and the souls departed this world in the faith of Christ, abiding the mercy of God, in the pains of purgatory'.[97] Among the articles to which Cambridge scholars were expected to subscribe by the vice-chancellor, Stephen Gardiner, was 'credimus post hanc vitam esse purgatorium, in quo animae defunctorum purgantur'.[98]

As doctrinal verities, purgatory and prayer for the dead were undoubtedly restored after the accession of Mary. But a number of scholars have doubted whether they did or could assume anything like the importance in religious culture that they had enjoyed before 1529, or even whether the reinstatement of these practices was any kind of priority for the Marian authorities.[99] Some contemporaries, too, saw lukewarmness and parsimony where once there had been unquestioning devotion. In the early 1560s the Catholic exile William Allen held that devotion in praying for the dead was 'of late yeres, even before this pitifull overthrowe of vertue [i.e. the accession of Elizabeth], by our negligens and lack of devotion muche decayde'. It comprised 'for the most parte, but twellve-monthes myndes, or monthes for the most: and that commonly but for the first yere of theyre rest: and then afterwarde ether cleane forgotten, or openly not often remembred'.[100]

---

[95] Foxe, viii. 535.
[96] Ibid. vi. 541–2
[97] VAI ii. 336, 370.
[98] Cardwell, *Documentary Annals*, i. 197. ('We believe there to be a purgatory after this life, in which the souls of the dead are purged'.)
[99] Hutton, *Merry England*, 102; D. Loades, 'The Spirituality of the Restored Catholic Church (1553–1558) in the Context of the Counter Reformation', in T. M. McCoog (ed.), *The Reckoned Expense: Edmund Campion and the Early English Jesuits* (Woodbridge, 1996), 16; Duffy, *Altars*, 494–5; P. Morgan, 'Of Worms and War: 1380–1558', in P. C. Jupp and C. Gittings (eds.), *Death in England* (Manchester, 1999), 142; R. White, 'Early Print and Purgatory: The Shaping of an Henrician Ideology', Australian National University Ph.D. thesis (1994), 217.
[100] W. Allen, *A Defense and Declaration of the Catholike Churches Doctrine touching Purgatory* (Antwerp, 1565), 169ᵛ.

There is evidence which seems to bear out Allen's pessimistic assessment. A mere handful of perpetual chantries were founded under Mary, by such prominent figures as Viscount Montague, Sir John Gage, and More's son-in-law William Roper.[101] Like the monastic estates, chantry lands remained in the hands of their lay purchasers, and very few fraternities were founded or refounded in the course of the reign; in London only one of the dozens of pre-Reformation guilds was restored.[102] Surveys of the testamentary evidence suggest that demand for traditional forms of intercession did not return even to the reduced level of the 1540s. In the south-west, 18 per cent of Marian wills requested masses and prayers; in the northern counties, around 15 per cent did so, and in Gloucestershire, only 4 per cent.[103] Plausible explanations for this are not hard to adduce. Two decades of exposure to evangelical strategies of persuasion had undoubtedly worked an effect. There were many (though we cannot say how many) in Marian England who did not believe that prayers and masses would benefit their souls after death. But pragmatism rather than conviction may have been decisive in determining some patterns of testamentary provision. Recent experience had demonstrated how vulnerable the institutional arrangements for upholding intercessory prayer were to the attentions of a permanently impecunious Tudor state, and it was widely understood that the heir presumptive, the Princess Elizabeth, was not an orthodox Catholic. We are provided with a window on a usually hidden calculation of risk and benefit through bequests such as that of Alan Wood, a Kentish yeoman. Wood established a yearly obit in his parish church of Snodland, but instructed that 'if the same obite by order of law be abrogated hereafter, then the money among the poor of Snodland for ever'.[104] The foundation of obits and temporary chantries in Mary's reign must be considered a conscious statement of religious commitment, rather than a customary cultural reflex. Before the 1530s, patterns of commemorating the dead displayed an almost organic dependence on long-standing social convention and locally embedded structures. But in the late 1540s fraternities had been dissolved, bede-roll registrations had been suspended, the army of jobbing mass-priests had been dispersed. The bequest of the

[101] A. Bartholomew, 'Lay Piety in the Reign of Mary Tudor', University of Manchester MA thesis (1979), 110–11; D. Loades, The Reign of Mary Tudor, 2nd edn. (1991), 298–9.

[102] J. J. Scarisbrick, The Reformation and the English People (Oxford, 1984), 37–8; R. Whiting, Local Responses to the English Reformation (Basingstoke, 1998), 50; Brigden, London and the Reformation, 582.

[103] R. Whiting, '"For the Health of my Soul": Prayers for the Dead in the Tudor South-West', in P. Marshall (ed.), The Impact of the English Reformation 1500–1640 (1997), 134; L. C. Attreed, 'Preparation for Death in Sixteenth Century Northern England', SCJ 13 (1982), 46; C. Litzenberger, 'Local Responses to Changes in Religious Policy Based on Evidence from Gloucestershire Wills (1540–1580)', Continuity and Change, 8 (1993), 434. These figures would not, of course, include all who expected to benefit from a requiem mass celebrated at their funeral.

[104] Bartholomew, 'Lay Piety', 111. For other examples of conditional bequests, see Duffy, Altars, 553–4; N. Jones, 'Negotiating the Reformation', in E. Carlson (ed.), Religion and the English People 1500–1640 (Kirksville, Mo., 1998), 273.

Sussex schoolmaster Gabriel Fowlle is a revealing one. He wanted ten priests to sing masses for him, 'if they can be got'.[105] Eamon Duffy has commented upon 'the loss of this vital dimension of continuity', and sees in it the main reason for 'the surprising failure of the Marian laity in many regions to re-establish the cult of the dead on anything like its former footing'.[106]

Nonetheless, it is possible to exaggerate the extent to which the plant had been pulled up by the roots, and to underestimate its potential for new shoots. Though overall testamentary provision for intercession in Mary's reign never returned to pre-Reformation levels, it showed a discernible rise after the initial uncertainty in the parishes attendant upon a contested succession and the immediate memory of waves of predatory commissioners. In Essex, for example, 17 per cent of testators left money for masses in 1554, while 39 per cent did so in 1558. There was a similar pattern in East Sussex, bequests for masses and obits rising nearly fourfold between 1554 and 1558.[107] The middle year of the reign, 1555, seems to mark a turning-point, a time by which the queen had seen off an armed rebellion led by Thomas Wyatt, solemnized her marriage to Philip of Spain, and begun a full-scale purge of heretics. In November 1555 Robert Parkyn and his colleague William Watson, curate of Melton-on-the-Hill, felt confident enough to revive the practice of saying trentals, and the diarist Henry Machyn records that trentals and half-trentals were being sung in a number of London parishes from the end of that year.[108] Cautiously, and patchily, obit-celebration began to resume its accustomed urban habitats. In Salisbury in 1555 the mayor and burgesses restored the traditional three *dirige* for the city's benefactors, and in 1556 the tailors' guild decided once again to 'cause a solemne *dirige* to be kept at St Thomas's church accordyng to the olde custom and the Sunday shalbe kepte the obit masse'.[109] In Doncaster, 1556 was also the year in which the town elites began once more to request *dirige* and mass of requiem at their burials, and to establish obits.[110] Traditional intercessory practices which did not require endowment seem to have been re-established more quickly and easily. Ronald Hutton has found that payments for the ringing of bells on the eve of All Souls are to be found in twenty sets of Marian churchwardens' accounts from all parts of England, urban

[105] G. Mayhew, 'The Progress of the Reformation in East Sussex 1530–1559: The Evidence from Wills', *Southern History*, 5 (1983), 54.

[106] Duffy, *Altars*, 495.

[107] Helt, 'Purgatory, Policy, and Piety', 234; Mayhew, 'Progress of the Reformation in East Sussex', 52–3.

[108] Dickens, *English Reformation*, 30; H. Machyn, *The Diary of Henry Machyn*, ed. J. G. Nichols, CS 42 (1847), 98, 161.

[109] A. D. Brown, *Popular Piety in Late Medieval England: The Diocese of Salisbury 1250–1550* (Oxford, 1995), 238. In London, however, the Grocers' Company cautiously declined an offer of property to maintain an obit in 1556: J. P. Ward, 'Religious Diversity and Guild Unity in Early Modern London', in Carlson (ed.), *Religion and the English People*, 84.

[110] C. Cross, 'Religion in Doncaster from the Reformation to the Civil War', in Collinson and Craig (eds.), *Reformation in English Towns*, 54–5.

and rural—as large a percentage of the surviving total as before the Reformation.[111] Despite the iconoclasm of the previous decade, requests for passers-by to pray for the soul are to be found on a widely dispersed cross-section of later Marian tombs and brasses.[112]

How assiduously did the authorities seek to promote the return of these attitudes and values among the laity? An examination of the religious literature of the mid-1550s dismisses any idea that the opinion-formers of the Marian Church had essentially lost interest in purgatory and intercessory prayer, or had relegated it to the status of a back-burner issue.[113] The necessity of praying for the dead was emphasized in a wide range of Marian devotional and instructional works, including the various editions of the primer, and the catechetical work for children set forth by Bonner, *An Honest Godlye Instruction*.[114] In 1558 Thomas Paynell translated *Certain Godly and Devout Prayers made in Latin by the Reverend Father in God Cuthbert Tuncstall*. This collection included 'a prayer unto god for the dede which have no man that praieth for them', beseeching God to have mercy on all 'which have no intercessors that remembre them ... [or] thrugh the negligence of those whiche are alyve, or the slydynge course of tyme are cleane forgotten of theyr frendes, and posteritie'. Such a prayer was thoroughly traditional, but undoubtedly carried an added poignancy after the dissolutions of Edward's reign and its abrogation of the commemoration of All Souls.[115] Earlier works with a focus on purgatory, such More's *Supplication of Souls* and Fisher's sermons on the seven penitential psalms, were reprinted in the reign, and the issue was discussed in books by Thomas Paynell, John Angel, Roger Edgeworth, William Peryn, Thomas Watson, and Richard Smyth.[116] Smyth's *Bouclier of the Catholike Fayth* devoted a

---

[111] Hutton, *Merry England*, 97. The pre-Reformation practice of a nightly ringing of bells between the death of substantial parishioners and their month's mind had been re-established in the Devon parish of Morebath by the end of Mary's reign: E. Duffy, 'Morebath 1520–1570: A Rural Parish in the Reformation', in J. Devlin and R. Fanning (eds.), *Religion and Rebellion* (Dublin, 1997), 35.

[112] R. H. D'Elboux (ed.), *The Monumental Brasses of Essex*, 2 vols. (Ashford, 1948–51), ii. 56; N. Llewellyn, 'Claims to Status through Visual Codes: Heraldry on Post-Reformation Funeral Monuments', in A. Anglo (ed.), *Chivalry in the Renaissance* (Woodbridge, 1990), 156; D. MacCulloch (ed.), *The Chorography of Suffolk*, Suffolk Records Society, xix (1976), 298; H. R. Mosse, *The Monumental Effigies of Sussex*, 2nd edn. (Hove, 1933), 184, 190; J. Finch, *Church Monuments in Norfolk before 1830: An Archaeology of Commemoration* (Oxford, 2000), 77–8; P. Sherlock, 'Funeral Monuments: Piety, Honour and Memory in Early Modern England', University of Oxford D.Phil. thesis (2000), 36.

[113] As suggested, for example, by White, 'Early Print and Purgatory', 217.

[114] *The Primer in English for Children, after the use of Sarum* (1556), B1ʳ–2ʳ; Duffy, *Altars*, 539; *An Honest Godlye Instruction* (1556), B1ʳ, 2ᵛ, 3ʳ–4ᵛ.

[115] C. Sturge, *Cuthbert Tunstall* (1938), 386–7.

[116] T. More, *Workes* (1557); J. Fisher, *Treatyse concernynge the Fruytfull Sayings of Davyd* (1555); T. Paynell, *Certain Sermons of Sainte Augustines* (1557), L6ʳ–K7ʳ; J. Angel, *The Agrement of the Holye Fathers* (1555), M1ᵛ–5ᵛ; Edgeworth, *Sermons*, 126–30; W. Peryn, *Spiritual Exercyses and Goostly Meditacions* (1557), D1ᵛ, P4ʳ, R7ᵛ, T8ʳ, U1ʳ; T. Watson, *Holsome and Catholyke Doctryne* (1558), 57ᵛ–58ʳ; R. Smyth, *A Bouclier of the Catholike Fayth* (1554), 22ʳ–40ʳ.

chapter to rebutting the view of the Edwardian articles that the doctrine of purgatory was 'the teaching of the schole men and vayne'. He also took the opportunity to settle some personal scores, breaking off from a discussion of patristic testimony to observe 'howe ygnorant were then Doctour Richarde Cox & Christopher Nevensen when they did geve out an Inyunction in their visitacion at Oxford, that no candels, torches, or other lyghtes shuld be usyd at any burialles, seynge S. Athenasius exhorteth men to use them at the tombes & graves of the dead'.[117]

Yet though purgatory and prayer for the dead were by no means neglected in Marian writings, some of the treatment of these issues bore the imprint of recent controversies. As we have seen, the word 'purgatory' had become something of a taboo for conservatives in the 1540s, a self-denying ordinance which had persisted into Edward's reign. In 1549 Cranmer had mocked the western rebels on this score: 'Purgatory was wont to be called a fire as hot as hell, but not so long during. But now the defenders of purgatory within this realm be ashamed so to say: nevertheless they say it is a third place; but where or what it is, they confess themselves they cannot tell.'[118] In 1552 when two traditionalist canons of Worcester, Henry Joliffe and Robert Johnson, vigorously debated matters of doctrine with their bishop, John Hooper, prayer for the dead was firmly on the agenda. But Joliffe and Johnson displayed the characteristic chariness of late Henrician conservatives: 'the name purgatory is none of our business'.[119] Remarkably, such circumspection persisted after 1553. While some Marian writers, such as Peryn or Smyth, were happy to use the traditional appellation for the place of purgation, others displayed a noticeable fastidiousness. The word 'purgatory' did not appear once in the seminal text of Marian religious instruction, Bonner's *Profitable and Necessarye Doctryne*, nor in the complementary set of *Homilies*. In another key work, Thomas Watson's *Holsome and Catholyke Doctryne*, the term is similarly absent, reference being made to the dead 'being for a tyme deteyned in the temporall afflictions and purgacions'. Tunstall's prayer for the forgotten dead petitioned for their deliverance 'from the tormente of paynes'.[120] Duffy's suggestion that leaders of the Marian Church who had been prominent 'Henricians' remained marked by the experience seems apposite here, as does William Wizeman's insight that Marian treatments of purgatory look towards the more measured, even minimalist treatment characteristic of the catechisms and commentaries of the early Continental Counter-Reformation.[121] It is noteworthy that the lavish indulgence rubrics familiar in the early sixteenth century were absent

---

[117] *A Bouclier*, 22[r], 40[r].
[118] Cranmer, *Miscellaneous Writings*, 181.
[119] MacCulloch, *Tudor Church Militant*, 118.
[120] White, 'Early Print and Purgatory', 221; Watson, *Holsome and Catholyke Doctryne*, 57[v]–58[r]; Sturge, *Cuthbert Tunstall*, 387.
[121] Duffy, *Altars*, 533–4. See Wizeman's forthcoming Oxford doctoral thesis.

from the primers produced in Mary's reign.[122] Purgatory was doctrinally significant: in the treatments by Bonner and Watson it was incorporated into sections on the sacrifice of the mass, in marked contrast to the Henrician formularies where it was tacked on to the end of the Articles as an adiaphoristic afterthought.[123] But there is not much evidence of an appetite to revive the dense and vividly material descriptions of the 'third place' that had pertained at the start of Henry's reign, a world in which only the most elderly of Marian writers had been formed.

If purgatory and intercessory prayer can be seen as enjoying a somewhat ambivalent relationship to the inner devotional core of Marian Catholicism, they played an important part in defining its exterior shape. Neglect of Christian duty towards the dead was a checklist attribute of unorthodoxy, serving to demarcate an essential boundary between the thought-world of true Catholics and that of libertine heretics. In his contribution to the *Profitable and Necessarye Doctryne*, Bonner's chaplain Henry Pendleton identified as a doleful effect of the schism 'the unshameles breakynge of the deade mennes testamentes and theyr mooste godly intentes or ordinances'. John Gwynneth similarly condemned the heretics' 'handlyng of the wyls and testaments of men'.[124] In the mid-1550s, practices that had once been an occasion for the communal celebration of memory were increasingly framed as a doctrinal test. In 1554 Bonner demanded to know whether any in his diocese had spoken against 'burying of the dead, praying for them, specially saying of Diriges and Commendations'.[125] There were some who were clearly doing so; a number of arrests were precipitated by outbursts against purgatory and prayer for the dead. When solemn obsequies were commanded to be performed for the soul of Julius III at Easter 1555, a woman in the London parish of St Magnus announced, with marvellously unproveable irony, that she would not pray for him, 'for he nedeth not my prayers: and seeing he could forgive all our sins, I am sure he is clean himself'. In consequence, she was incarcerated for a time to 'cool herself'. Less fortunate was John Maundrel of Keevil in Wiltshire, who responded to the vicar's reading of the bede-roll by crying out in church, 'that was the pope's pinfold'. Two other parishioners were burned with him in March 1556 having asserted that 'the blood of Christ had purged their sins...so that they nothing feared the pope's purgatory, nor esteemed his pardons'. A year earlier, a man called John Tooley had gone to the gallows asserting that he trusted to be saved only by the merits of Christ's passion 'and not by any masses or trentals'; the authorities in the diocese of London had his corpse exhumed and burned. The efficacy of prayer for the dead was debated

[122] Duffy, *Altars*, 537–43.
[123] A point I owe to William Wizeman.
[124] *A Profitable and Necessarye Doctryne* (1555), 41ᵛ; J. Gwynneth, *A Declaration of the State wherin all Heretikes doe Leade their Lives* (1554), 45ᵛ.
[125] *VAI* ii. 348–9.

between Bishop Bonner and the Essex gentleman Thomas Hawkes in 1555, and between Bonner's chancellor and Elizabeth Young in 1558. Both Hawkes and Young took their stand on the question of scriptural warrant, provoking the chancellor to exclaim 'Why, ye have nothing but the skimming of the Scriptures. Our ancient fathers could find out in the bottom of the Scriptures that there is a purgatory.' Nonetheless, at least another nine lay martyrs were reported by Foxe to have denied purgatory or prayer for the dead.[126] A generation's-worth of evangelical propaganda had made these defining issues for the self-consciously godly. The confession of faith produced by the imprisoned Protestants Bradford, Saunders, and others in May 1554 to demonstrate their unity of doctrine laid down

that as a man departeth this life, so he shall be judged in the last day generally, and in the mean season is entered either into the state of the blessed for ever, or damned for ever; and therefore is either past all help, or else needeth no help of any in this life. By reason wherof we affirm purgatory, masses of scala coeli, trentals, and such suffrages as the popish church doth obtrude as necessary, to be the doctrine of antichrist.[127]

Some were pressured to recant these beliefs. The admission of grievous error over purgatory was a feature of the trials of William Barlow in 1554, and Richard Gybson in 1557.[128] Incarcerated in the Tower in May 1556 for his part in the Dudley conspiracy, Henry Peckham sought to ingratiate himself with the authorities by deposing that he had heard two fellow-prisoners reasoning of purgatory, and had himself interjected that 'there were two or three places in the scriptures that proved it, quoting St James: certain sins are not forgiven in this world, nor in the next'.[129] The issue also surfaced in the most notorious of Marian recantations, those of Thomas Cranmer in February and March 1556. In addition to affirming purgatory, Cranmer was made to confess to the endangering of souls by his abolition of requiem masses.[130] For Protestants in Marian England these were issues it was difficult to skirt or evade. Nicholas Ridley included the following as a compelling argument against the practice of Nicodemism on the part of his co-religionists: 'If any of the household die, if thou wilt not pay money for ringing and singing, for requiem, masses, *dirige*, and commendations... thinkest thou that thou shalt be reckoned for a catholic man, or for amicus Caesaris?'[131]

After three decades of growing religious division, the dead themselves had come to comprise two opposing camps, papists or heretics, each supposed by

---

[126] Foxe, vii. 37, 90–2, 103–4, 310, viii. 103, 311–12, 411, 491, 543.

[127] Bradford, *Writings*, i. 372. For Protestant difficulties in defining what constituted the experience of 'the mean season', see Ch. 5, below.

[128] Strype, *Ecclesiastical Memorials*, iii (1), 153, 407.

[129] C. S. Knighton (ed.), *CSPD Series Mary I 1553–1558* (1998), 424. Peckham's command of the Scriptures was imperfect: the passage he had in mind is Matt. 12: 23.

[130] MacCulloch, *Cranmer*, 586, 595, 599.

[131] N. Ridley, *Works*, ed. H. Christmas (PS, 1841), 66–7.

the living friends of the other to be the likely denizens of hell. In such circumstances the traditional imperative to venerate the memory of 'all the faithful departed' was increasingly selectively applied. It was a canonical requirement of long standing that heretics and excommunicates were to be denied burial in consecrated ground, and in Mary's reign the enforcement of this provision sharply focused the symbolic importance of the dead as a marker of religious disunity. In later recusant circles, it was persistently rumoured that Mary had ordered the exhumation and burning of the corpse of her own father.[132] Whatever the truth of this, the martyrologist John Foxe recorded a number of cases where godly people had been buried in fields or ditches because 'the manner of the papists was to deny their christian burial to such as died out of their popish antichristian church'.[133]

More shocking still to Protestant observers than that the papists might deny burial in consecrated ground was the practice of ritual disinterment, for which there was an unhappy precedent in the case of William Tracy. When the suspected heretic John Glover of Mancetter in Warwickshire died and was interred in the churchyard, the chancellor of the diocese of Coventry and Lichfield, Dr Draycott, was only dissuaded from ordering his immediate expulsion by the rector's protestations of how noisome the corpse would be after six weeks in the ground. But Draycott was prepared to bide his time: Glover was to be denounced in the pulpit as a damned soul, and after a year his bones were to be cast over the churchyard wall.[134] More imposing were the dramatic disinterments taking place in both Oxford and Cambridge in 1557. In Oxford, the body of the wife of the Italian reformer Peter Martyr Vermigli was dug up and buried in a dunghill. This was transgressive ritual in return for transgressive ritual. Not only was Mistress Vermigli that bugbear of the Catholics, a clerical wife, but she had been sacrilegiously buried in Christ Church close to the relics of St Frideswide. At Cambridge, the Marian authorities were able to get directly at the remains of two leading foreign reformers who had died in England in Edward's reign, Martin Bucer and Paul Fagius. These dead men were subjected to a formal process culminating in the exhumation and burning of their bones. According to Foxe – no dispassionate observer – the crowds in Cambridge on market day were alternately appalled by 'the extreme cruelty of the commissioners towards the rotten carcases' and amused by preparations involving the chaining of the corpses and the provision of armed guards, 'as though they were afraid that the dead bodies, which felt them not, would do them some harm'. There were very few, insisted Foxe, 'that liked their doing there'. The bodies which had been ritually cast out from their resting places under Mary

    [132] J. J. Scarisbrick, *Henry VIII* (1968), 497.
    [133] Foxe, vii. 38, 286, 401–2, 605. For parallel tensions over the issue in France, see P. Roberts, 'Contesting Sacred Space: Burial Disputes in Sixteenth-Century France', in *Place of the Dead*.
    [134] Foxe, vii. 400.

were ritually reinterred at the start of Elizabeth's reign, occasions that provided opportunities to denounce the unnatural proceedings of 1557. At the restoration of the bones of Peter Martyr's wife, Mr Rogerson denounced those 'which were not contented to practice their cruelty against the living, but that must also rage against one that was dead'. At the restitution of Bucer and Fagius to their Cambridge degrees in July 1560, James Pilkington 'blamed greatly the barbarous cruelty of the court of Rome, so fiercely extended against the dead'. An accompanying address by the University Orator George Acworth described the fate of the bodies of Bucer and Fagius as 'a thing surely incredible, if we had not seen it with our eyes'. Of course, such action did no harm to the dead, who were beyond feeling pain, 'yet it reproveth an extreme cruelness and unsatiable desire of revengement in them which offer such utter wrong to the dead'.[135]

By the end of Mary's reign, it had become part of the polemical instinct of both Protestants and papalists to accuse their opponents of cruelty and derogation in their demeanour towards the dead. From being emblems of continuity with a shared past, the dead had become susceptible to appropriations and politicizations of a quite unprecedented order. Their status mirrored the religious disputes of the living. In spite of a theological revolution that had attempted to displace and replace the dead, both in the afterlife and in the consciences of the living, their potency as a cultural symbol remained compelling. In terms of the social and cultural modes of memorializing the dead, Edward's reign was an undoubted climacteric—something fundamental had been loosened, broken, and reset. But Edwardian reformers were only too aware that they had not had time thoroughly to wean the people from 'superstitious' habits, habits to which in Mary's reign they had shown an alarming proclivity to revert. Not all contemporaries shared the scepticism of modern historians about the ability of intercessory practices to re-establish themselves at a popular level. Writing in 1562, Bishop Pilkington observed that there were many who 'would have not long ago said . . . have we not our altars, copes, masses, and trentals, that will bring us through purgatory for a little money'.[136] At the same time, Protestantism had recognized the need to formulate its own distinctive and pastorally effective idioms of commemoration and remembrance. A start had been made, but discernible fissures had already opened up about which forms and words were acceptable, and about what could legitimately be salvaged from the listing wreck of the popish past. Even among the supporters of the new regime that came to power in November 1558 reflection on the nature and extent of duties towards the dead evoked uneasy combinations of the feelings that there was much still to do, and that things had already gone too far.

[135] Ibid. viii. 261–97.
[136] J. Pilkington, Works, ed. J. Scholefield (PS, 1842), 77.

4

The Regulation of the Dead: Ritual and Reform in the English Church, *c.*1560–1630

THE death of purgatory was a slow and lingering business, and it left a debatable inheritance. The intention of this chapter is to follow two intersecting trajectories across the changing beliefscape of the Elizabethan and Jacobean Church. One is the long campaign on the part of bishops, theologians, and ordinary clergy to eradicate all traces of purgatory and intercessory prayer, a theme which has not been much studied, despite the current interest in the idea of 'long Reformation'. The other is the attempt at regulation in a complementary sense, the provision of new rules and a new framework for the liturgical and ritual commemoration of the dead. The two processes were complementary, but also sometimes contradictory, or so it might seem. Their conjunction constitutes a case-study in the difficulties over how to reconcile scriptural theology, pastoral practice, and social custom which were to bedevil the progress of the later Reformation as a whole.

THE HUNTING OF PURGATORY TO DEATH

The final annihilation of purgatory and prayer for souls represented a significant piece of unfinished business for the Elizabethan Church. At the start of the reign the topics were tackled in depth by the French exile and prebendary of St Paul's, John Veron, whose *The Huntyng of Purgatory to Death* (1561) was a lively dialogue recycling the familiar themes that purgatory was an unscriptural imposition by avaricious clergy, that the mass was no sacrifice for the dead, and that the souls of the dead could not return to the living.[1] A more high-profile opponent of purgatory was the new bishop of Salisbury, John Jewel, who to the chagrin of the conservative diarist

---

[1] Much of Veron's dialogue was lifted from the attack on purgatory in the Swiss reformer Pierre Viret's *Disputations Chrestiennes, touchant l'estat des trepassez, faites par dialogues* (Geneva, 1552). Cf. Viret, *The Christian Disputations*, tr. J. Brooke (1579).

Henry Machyn preached at a funeral at St Margaret Moses in January 1560, 'and ther he sayd playnly that ther was no purgatore'.[2] The denial of any efficacy in the mass for the souls of the dead was also a feature of Jewel's famous 'Challenge Sermon' of that same year, and in the 1560s Jewel was involved in controversies over the antiquity of purgatory and prayer for the dead with Thomas Harding, John Rastell, and others.[3] The most substantial contribution on the Catholic side was a 1565 work by the exile William Allen, *A Defence and Declaration of the Catholike Churches Doctrine touching Purgatory, and Prayers for the Soules Departed*. Allen was later to be made a cardinal by Sixtus V, and to attempt to orchestrate armed foreign intervention in England, but in the early years of Elizabeth's reign he seems to have been best known as the champion of purgatory. 'Alen, who wrote the late booke of Purgatory' heads the list of apostates due for arrest in a royal writ delivered to the High Sheriff of Lancashire in 1567, and a few years later William Fulke derisively termed him 'Master Allen of Purgatory'.[4] His defence of purgatory and intercession was traditional in many ways, applying the familiar proof-texts, and echoing More and Fisher with its evocation of poor souls crying out for assistance. But Allen supplied no graphic depictions of the torments of purgatory, and was noticeably cautious about advancing ghosts and visions as proof for the doctrine, preferring to cite the constant belief of the Church, and the theology of the communion of saints. This less 'medieval' and more 'Tridentine' tone was also a feature of the treatise defending Allen from the attacks of William Fulke by his fellow-Louvainist, Richard Bristow.[5]

In addition to Veron, Jewel, and Fulke, a number of other writers launched ino print against purgatory in the first half of Elizabeth's reign.[6] On the

---

[2] H. Machyn, *The Diary of Henry Machyn*, ed. J. G. Nichols, CS 42 (1847), 2.

[3] J. Jewel, *The Copie of a Sermon Pronounced by the Byshop of Salisburie at Paules Cross* (1560), B7^r–v, D8^r, E2^v–4^r; id., *Works*, ed. J. Ayre, 4 vols. (PS, 1845–50), ii. 742–5, 912, 920, iii. 559–69, iv. 844–5; J. Rastell, *A Confutation of a Sermon Pronouced by M. Iuell* (Antwerp, 1564), 36^r; P. Milward, *Religious Controversies of the Elizabethan Age* (Lincoln, Nebr., 1977), 1–24. This John Rastell was not the author of the *New Boke of Purgatory*, who had died in 1536.

[4] A. C. Southern, *Elizabethan Recusant Prose 1559–1582* (1950), 380; W. Fulke, *Fulke's Answeres to Stapleton, Martiall, and Sanders*, ed. R. Gibbings (PS, 1848), 104.

[5] W. Fulke, *Two Treatises Written Against the Papists* (1577); R. Bristow, *A Reply to Fulke in Defence of M. D. Allens Scroll of Articles, and Booke of Purgatorie* (Louvain, 1580). But cf. the more traditional treatment of the 'fearefull, and terrible paynes thereof' in J. Radford, *A Directorie Teaching the Way to Truth* (England, secret press, 1605), 309, 307–83.

[6] These include A. Anderson, *The Shield of our Safetie set Foorth* (1581); D. Fenner, *An Answere unto the Confutation of Iohn Nichols his Recantation... especially in the matters of Doctrine, of Purgatorie, Images, the Popes Honor, and the Question of the Church* (1583). More popular works satirizing purgatory, and Catholic funeral practices, include R. Burdet, *The Refuge of a Sinner* (1565) and R. Copland, *The Seven Sorrowes that Women have when theyr Husbandes be Deade* (1568). Stephen Bateman's *A Christall Glasse of Christian Reformation* (1569) supplied a woodcut of purgatory as a fishpond, into which monks and friars cast their lines (U3^r). The refutation of purgatory was also central to a number of translated foreign works: L. Lavater, *Of Ghostes and Spirites Walking by Nyght* (1572); Viret, *Christian Disputations*; P. Van Marnix, *The Beehive of the Romishe Churche*, tr. G. Gilpin (1580).

institutional front, purgatory, prayer, and sacrifice for the dead were condemned by the second book of *Homilies* of 1563, the Bishops' interim 'eleven
articles' of 1561, and the Thirty-Nine Articles of 1563. Article 22 of the latter
was essentially unaltered from the Forty-Two Articles of 1553, though purgatory was now described as 'the Romish doctrine' (*doctrina Romanensium*)
rather than 'the doctrine of school-authors' (*doctrina scholasticarum*) — a
reflection of its growing significance in the demarcation of hardening confessional identities.[7] As if in confirmation, at the end of that year purgatory was
formally endorsed in the last session of the Council of Trent.[8]

But anathemas and condemnations by themselves were no guarantee that
the English people had abandoned their trust in the false promises of popish
intercession. In parallel with the ongoing intellectual tussle with external
enemies, the Elizabethan authorities mounted a vigorous campaign against
internal backsliders. Given the substantial continuity of parish clergy from
Mary's reign to that of her sister, it was inevitable that some would continue
to perform those services towards the dead that had been such a large part of
their *raison d'être* under the old dispensation. In 1559 the vicar of New
Romney, Kent, was accused of reading 'place libera me' at the funeral of a
parishioner, while in 1561 the vicar of Romsey in Hampshire 'dyd fetche
forthe the corse to the churche with candles and tapers'.[9] In 1567 another
Hampshire vicar, of Odiham, was said to have buried a parishioner with
candles 'et ceteris ceremoniis papisticas', and in the same year over a dozen
ministers in Nottinghamshire and Yorkshire were discovered who 'useth the
Communion for the deade'.[10] In the same year, Bishop Parkhurst of Norwich was frustrated in his attempt to bar from institution to a rectory a
minister who in response to the question of 'whether their weare a purgatorie after this life' answered that 'it was for heigher learned men then he was
to aunswere that question'. More alarmingly, Parkhurst's own diocesan
chancellor, William Maister, was widely believed to be unsound on the
question.[11] Other clerical recidivists included a minster at Aylburton in the
Forest of Dean (1576), 'a mayntayner of popish purgatorie and other papis-
tries', and the vicar of Badsley in Warwickshire (1586), 'a secreat perswader
of the simple to poperie, one that praieth for the dead'.[12] Not all maintainers

[7] W. Haugaard, *Elizabeth and the English Reformation* (Cambridge, 1968), 240–2; *Sermons
or Homilies appointed to be read in Churches* (1833), 231; E. J. Bicknell, *A Theological
Introduction to the Thirty-Nine Articles of the Church of England*, 2nd edn. (1925), 347.
[8] H. J. Schroeder (ed.), *Canons and Decrees of the Council of Trent* (1960), 214.
[9] A. J. Willis (ed.), *Church Life in Kent, being Church Court Records of the Canterbury
Diocese 1559–1565* (1975), 14; HRO, 21M65/C1/7, 95ᵛ.
[10] HRO, 21M65/C1/11, 31ʳ; BI, V 1567–8 / CB 1, 5ʳ, 6ʳ, 28ʳ, 40ᵛ, 187ʳ, 194ʳ, 206ᵛ, 207ᵛ; CB 2,
36ʳ; J. S. Purvis, *Tudor Parish Documents of the Diocese of York* (Cambridge, 1948), 23, 30, 33.
[11] *The Letter Book of John Parkhurst Bishop of Norwich*, ed. R. A. Houlbrooke, Norfolk
Record Society, 43 (1974–5), 99, 32.
[12] C. Litzenberger, *The English Reformation and the Laity: Gloucestershire, 1540–1580*
(Cambridge, 1997), 131; A. Peel (ed.), *The Seconde Parte of a Register*, 2 vols. (Cambridge,
1915), ii. 169.

of purgatory were clergy: in June 1579 Ralph Cowley of Wath in North Yorkshire was ordered to declare in his parish church 'that he is sorry that it was his chance to speak anything defending planting and placing purgatory and defacing Mr Stubbs the parson of Wath who spake against the doctrine'.[13]

Such overt, defiant statements seem, however, to have been relatively rare in early and mid-Elizabethan England. Much more widespread was the continued use of funeral and commemorative customs whose clear rationale was a belief in the ability of the living to ameliorate the condition of the dead. A comprehensive itemization of such practices, 'wherin the papists infinitely offend', was supplied by Bishop Pilkington of Durham in 1562: 'masses, diriges, trentals, singing, ringing, holy water, hallowed places, year's, day's, and month's minds, crosses, pardon letters to be buried with them, mourners, *De profundis*, by every lad that could say it, dealing of money solemnly for the dead, watching of the corpse at home, bell and banner, with many more that I can reckon'.[14] Concerns about virtually all of these were regularly reflected in episcopal visitation articles of the 1560s, 1570s, and 1580s. Particularly emphatic were the injunctions issued by Archbishop Grindal in 1571 on taking over the notoriously recalcitrant archdiocese of York. There were to be 'no month minds, or yerely commendations of the dead, nor any other superstitious ceremonies [to] be observed or used which tend to the maintenance either of prayer for the dead, or of the popish purgatory'. Furthermore, no one was to say *De profundis* for the dead, or stop to rest at any cross in carrying the corpse to its place of burial, 'nor shall leave any little crosses of wood there'.[15] Like a number of his episcopal colleagues, Grindal identified a danger-point in the propensity of conservative laity, unable perhaps to dictate the order of the funeral service itself, to utilize the procession to the church for intercessory purposes. This was clearly happening at Tilston in Cheshire in 1578, where 'Rafe Leche useth praier for the deade and willeth the people to praie for them and saie a paternoster and *De profundis* for the dead when the people do rest with the dead corps'.[16]

It is a moot point whether such behaviour indicates a self-consciously oppositionist mentality, a post-Reformation Catholicism in the process of confessional formation, or whether it bespeaks rather an instinctive conservatism, deeply rooted in the social custom of local communities. Probably elements of both were present. In Nottingham in 1567 an alderman, John Gregory, pugnaciously 'commanded Brodshawe the Belman to praie for the dead as he was wont to doe, or els threateneth that he wold set him in the

---

[13] P. Tyler, 'The Administrative Character of the Ecclesiastical Commission for the Province of York 1561–1585', University of Oxford B.Litt. thesis (1960), 232.

[14] J. Pilkington, *Works*, ed. J. Scholefield (PS, 1842), 37.

[15] *VAI* iii. 286, 289.

[16] BI, V 1578 / CB 3, 8ʳ.

prison'.[17] On the other hand, in the town of Beaumaris in January 1570, when a corpse was buried with candles and singing of psalms, this was supposedly 'done of mere ignorance and a folishe custome there used'. A few months later, Bishop Robinson of Bangor wrote to the Council stating that he had now 'openly forbade all praiers and ceremionies over the deade not autorized by law of this realme', which suggests there had been some ambiguity, or perceived latitude, about this beforehand.[18] Parts of Wales, however, continued to be notorious blackspots for behaviour of this kind. In the aftermath of what was clearly an eye-opening visitation of his diocese of St Davids in 1583, Bishop Middleton produced a set of injunctions containing perhaps the most comprehensive attack on traditionalist funeral rituals issued in the period. There were to be no wooden crosses erected 'where they used to rest with the corpses', or about the grave, nor were the clerk or his deputy to go about town with a little bell called 'the bell before the burial' in a superstitious popish manner. No offerings were to be made at burials, or at month's minds or twelve-months' minds, 'as superstitiously they have been termed'; there was to be no prayer for the dead in the house or on the way to church, a practice which 'hath been frequented and tolerated by the ministers'. Only the clerk and one or two others were to throw earth upon the corpse, and no candles were to be placed on it while it was in the church; no bells were to be rung at burials, save one short peal before the burial and another after.[19] Declarations of this sort suggest the prevalence, or at least the persistence, of the practices they proscribe. It is worth pursuing the connection by examining in more detail one of the most recurrent complaints of Elizabethan reformers: the ringing of bells on the eve of All Souls.

RINGING AGAINST THE CHANGES

As we have seen, Hallowe'en ringing was nearly abolished at the end of Henry's reign, was emphatically so in Edward's, and was widely restored in Mary's. Reformers regarded the practice as particularly egregious: its association with an abrogated Catholic festival and its orientation towards the collective category of souls 'abiding the mercy of god' made it seem ideologically assertive as well as 'superstitious'. One of the 'Articles for ecclesiastical government' put before the 1563 convocation was that 'the superstitious ringing at All Hallows tide and All Souls day, with the two nights next before and after, be prohibited'. The proposal was not formally adopted at this time, but in 1571 convocation passed a canon instructing churchwardens not to suffer 'the bells to be rung superstitiously, either in the feast of All Souls or the day after All Saints (which day not long since was kept holy for the souls of the dead), neither at any time at all, whereas the

---

[17] BI, V 1567–8 / CB 1, 19ʳ.   [18] PRO, SP 12/69/14, 53.   [19] *EEA* iii. 142–3, 149.

custom of ringing shall seem to incline to superstition'.[20] In the interim, the puritan emissary Percival Wiburn had confessed to his Swiss hosts the continuing abuse of 'tolling of bells at funerals and on the vigils of saints; and especially on that of the feast of All Saints', and in 1572 'your ringing at Hallowtide for all Christian souls' was condemned in a sermon by the former Genevan exile William Kethe.[21] The first mention of the abuse in episcopal visitation articles appears to be in Parkhurst's for Norwich in 1569, a relatively late appearance which suggests it had emerged as a serious disciplinary problem over the course of the decade.[22] Through the 1570s and 1580s questions about ringing for the dead at All Saints or All Souls were a regular feature of visitation articles from all parts of the realm.[23] The last explicit inquiries into the practice were made by Bickley of Chichester and Westfaling of Hereford in 1586, but the canons of 1604 stipulated that churchwardens were not to tolerate ringing on days not authorized by the Book of Common Prayer, and Jacobean visitation articles for the northern province showed a continuing concern with bells being rung 'superstitiously upon hollidayes or daies abrogated by law'. There were echoes of the issue in some northern and western areas into the 1630s. Mathew Wren's articles for Hereford in 1635 asked if there were any 'superstitious or any unseasonable ringing', and a similar inquiry was made in the Archdeaconry of Northumberland as late as 1639.[24]

This chronology and geography of the problem suggested by the episcopal visitation articles broadly mirrors what can be reconstructed from the records of ecclesiastical justice. It is likely that a significant number of cases of illicit ringing remain undiscovered in local archives, and that the range of examples which follows is incomplete. But it serves to illustrate that the problem, particularly in the first two decades of Elizabeth's reign, was a general not a localized one. In Kent in 1561, for example, six parishioners of Wye were prosecuted for ringing after evening prayer on All Saints' Day.[25] A visitation by the archdeacon uncovered ringing at twelve parishes in Essex in 1563, and further cases of the practice were discovered in the county in 1564, 1565, 1569, 1585, and 1587.[26] In Sussex, a visitation by commissaries of Archbishop Parker in 1569 found that 'they use in many places ringing between morning and the litany, and all the night following All Saints' day,

---

[20] G. Bray (ed.), *The Anglican Canons 1529–1947*, Church of England Record Society, 6 (1998), 752, 195.

[21] H. Robinson (ed.), *Zurich Letters... during the early part of the reign of Queen Elizabeth I*, 2 vols. (PS, 1842–5), ii. 361; D. Cressy, *Bonfires and Bells: National Memory and the Protestant Calendar in Elizabethan and Stuart England* (1989), 8.

[22] *VAI* iii. 209.

[23] Ibid. 256–7, 286, 309, 334, 343, 383; *EEA* ii. 59, 72, 93, 118, iii. 142, 191.

[24] *EEA* iii. 214, 228; Bray (ed.), *The Anglican Canons*, 383; *VAIESC* i. 11, 35, 59, 61–5, 70, 182, ii. 143, 215.

[25] Willis (ed.), *Church Life in Kent*, 32.

[26] F. G. Emmison, *Elizabethan Life: Morals and the Church Courts* (Chelmsford, 1973), 136–7.

as before in time of blind ignorance and superstition'.[27] Cases also regularly
came before the courts from parishes in Norfolk throughout the 1560s and
into the 1570s.[28] In Hampshire, there was All Saints ringing at Bighton and
Eling in 1561, at Alton, Southsea, and Weyhill in 1567, at Cheriton,
Micheldever, and Popham in 1568, and at Kings Worthy in 1573.[29] In
Worcestershire it was reported at Halesowen in 1578, and in Oxfordshire
at Loncombe in 1584.[30] The practice of Hallowe'en ringing was equally, if
not more, prevalent in the north of England, where from the start of
Elizabeth's reign the Ecclesiastical Commission at York worked hard to
eradicate it.[31] In Yorkshire All Souls ringing took place at Hull in 1563
(and again in 1570), Kirkby Overblow, Hemingborough, and Snainton in
1564, Ripon in 1568, Skipton in 1571, Burnsall in 1573, Bingley in 1577,
Bulmer in 1585 and 1586, and Birkin in 1586. In Nottinghamshire there was
ringing at Gedling and Nottingham in 1564, at South Leverton in 1583, and
at Hickling in 1587. In Cheshire illict nocturnal ringing took place at
Sandbach in 1564, and at Middlewich and Weverham in 1578.[32]

   This activity has a good claim to be, as Ronald Hutton has suggested, 'the
ritual which the Elizabethan reformers found most tenacious'. It is worth
considering why this should be so. Hutton himself suggests solid practical
reasons for the longevity of the custom: it was the one Catholic seasonal rite
'which could be carried on without the use of illegal ornaments or the
participation of a priest, and after dark'.[33] But it is unlikely that the persistence of this particular calendar custom was primarily fortuitous; it needs to
be set alongside a phenomenon we have already identified—the marked
reluctance of conservative-minded laypeople to give up traditional practices
pertaining to the well-being of the dead. Nor in fact did such ringing
typically take the form of a secret nocturnal raid. Admittedly, the churchwardens of Woodham Mortimer in Essex in 1563 protested that they
'cannot tell who did ring', but it is clear that in a number of parishes,
particularly in the 1560s, All Hallows ringing was far from a furtive or
surreptitious exercise undertaken by a small group of anonymous individ-

---

[27] R. B. Manning, *Religion and Society in Elizabethan Sussex* (Leicester, 1969), 46.

[28] R. Houlbrooke, *Church Courts and the People during the English Reformation 1520–
1570* (Oxford, 1979), 249; *Letter Book of John Parkhurst*, 257.

[29] HRO, 21M65/C1/7, 99ᵛ, 104ᵛ; 21M65/C1/11, 11ᵛ, 15ʳ, 22ᵛ, 27ᵛ, 30ʳ; 21M65/C1/12, 49ʳ,
54ʳ, 116ʳ, 122ʳ; A. J. Willis (ed.), *Winchester Consistory Court Deposition Books 1561–1602*
(Winchester, 1960), 51.

[30] Cressy, *Bonfires and Bells*, 30; E. Brinkworth (ed.), *The Archdeacon's Court: Liber
Actorum 1584*, 2 vols., Oxfordshire Record Society, 23–4 (1942), ii. 155.

[31] P. Tyler, 'The Ecclesiastical Commission for the Province of York 1561–1641', University
of Oxford D.Phil. thesis (1965), 335.

[32] BI, HC CP 1563/4; 1564/2; 1570/3; HC AB 1, 194ᵛ, 208ʳ, 208ᵛ; AB 4, 33ᵛ–34ʳ, 39ᵛ; Purvis,
Tudor Parish Documents, 174–5; R. Hodgkinson (ed.), 'Extracts from the Act Books of the
Archdeacons of Nottingham', *Transactions of the Thoroton Society*, 30 (1926), 29; K. R. Wark,
Elizabethan Recusancy in Cheshire (Manchester, 1971), 7; BI, V 1578 / CB 3, 30ʳ, 31ʳ.

[33] R. Hutton, *The Rise and Fall of Merry England: The Ritual Year 1400–1700* (Oxford,
1994), 106.

uals. On All Hallows Day at Kings Worthy, Hampshire, in 1573 there was said to have been 'much talk in the church by divers of the parishioners there about the ringing of the bells that day'.[34] At Kirkby Overblow in 1564, it was the rector Richard Poole who commanded the clerk to ring the bells, and a group of parishioners reportedly 'went . . . about to dyvers others to provoke and styrr them to ring'.[35] In the parish of St Mary's, Nottingham, the same year, the vicar and the churchwardens were accused of causing the bells to be rung from eight till ten, 'and did gather money for that purpose'.[36] A collection was also taken at Ripon in 1568, where the proceedings seemed to bespeak a genuinely communal festivity. Here Thomas Buck and Thomas Shipperd (undersexton) went from door to door 'to the most parte of the house of Rippon', begging money and candles for the ringers. They then 'drunk ayle in the said churche with parte of the money they gott and the reaste they and the said ringers dyd bestow of good chere abrode in the towne the said nyght'.[37] This sounds very much like direct continuation of established practice. The impression of a firm local consensus to uphold ancient custom comes across even more strongly from Weaverham in Cheshire in 1578, where it was reported apologetically to the visitors that 'the people will not be staied from ringing the belles on all saintes daie'.[38]

The impression may, however, be misleading. The ritual of tolling the community's bells to bring succour to the souls of all the faithful departed was designed to express the aspiration for a perfect charitable unity, both among the living, and between the living and the dead, but in the parishes of Elizabethan England such an aspiration was a hollow one. It is possible that there were parishes of a sufficiently uniform conservative frame of mind for Hallowtide ringing to be kept from the attention of the authorities, but in several of those where we know it did take place it had become a symbol of division. At Holy Trinity, Hull in 1563 the attempt to maintain ringing descended into farce, an unseemly scuffle in the dark, and the vicar, the irascible Melchior Smith, having to defend himself from a charge of drawing blood in the parish church. Smith recounted how when a group of 'disorderlie persons' began ringing the bells for all Christian souls on All Saints night he had commanded them to cease, and when they refused, he went with the mayor and officers into the church to effect their arrest. At this the ringers began to run away, the church 'at that tyme being verey dark', and Smith found himself 'with others runyng abrode in the darke to apprehende the said disordered persons, one runyng against an other, amonges which . . . Nicholas Laborne was hurt and bled at the nose', an injury Smith

---

[34] Emmison, *Elizabethan Life*, 136; Willis (ed.), *Winchester Consistory Court Depositions*, 51.

[35] BI, C CP 1564/2; HC AB 1, 112ᵛ, 141ʳ, 169ʳ.

[36] BI, HC AB 1, 208ʳ.

[37] BI, HC CP AB 4, 33ᵛ–34ʳ.

[38] BI, V 1578 / CB 3, 30ʳ.

insisted was inflicted 'by chance in the darke'.[39] There was violence also at Henham, Essex, in 1587, William Glascock alleging that 'he and others, being ready to ring a peal after evening prayer about Allhallowtide, Thomas Measaunte churchwarden there by force did take the bell out of his hands and striking him offred to trip up his heels'. At Hickling in the Vale of Belvoir the same year, William Fearnebarne was accused of having 'used violence agaynst the parson at that tyme to mayntayne theire ringing'.[40] By the late 1580s the final manifestations of a pious ancestral custom seem to have been turning into an aggressive assertion of religious difference.[41] It is nonetheless remarkable that, a full generation after the accession of Elizabeth, a custom so quintessentially parochial and communitarian in its symbolism and rationale should still have been performed on behalf of the souls in purgatory.

THE PERISHING OF PURGATORY?

The last echoes of Hallowtide ringing in episcopal injunctions and court records in the late 1580s help to crystallize an important question: when did belief in purgatory finally die out among the population as a whole? This is not a question susceptible to a simple answer. There are distinct dangers in reifying so nebulous a concept as religious belief, as well as in privileging a model of the impact of Reform which supposes a merely attritional operation on traditional mentalities, and does not allow for their creative and gradual mutation. Contemporaries, however, did think in a binary and dialectical way about the hold of purgatory on men's minds. Veron concluded his 1561 treatise with a mock epitaph: 'Now all ye, that this way do travaylle, / Stay a whyle, and say a morfundis / For hym, I praye, that there he maye in helle / Broyle with the Pope, whose broude and sonne he is.'[42] At this early date, purgatory might well have responded that reports of his death were greatly exaggerated, but it was characteristic of Elizabethan writers, especially from the middle part of the reign, to assert that the ancient error had lost its tenancy. In a biblical commentary, John Jewel posed the rhetorical question, 'now where is purgatory? who regardeth it? who careth for it? Children scorn it in the streets, and know it is a fable.'[43] Writers

---

[39] HC CP 1563/4.

[40] Emmison, *Elizabethan Life*, 137; Hodgkinson (ed.), 'Act Books of the Archdeacon of Nottingham', 29.

[41] For the view that parish bell-ringers tended in any case to form a potentially disorderly fraternity, see D. Cressy, *Travesties and Transgressions in Tudor and Stuart England: Tales of Discord and Dissension* (Oxford, 2000), 176. The godly minister Richard Greenham had problems with 'some yong men in his chardg vainly disposed to ring bels' rather than come to be catechized: K. L. Parker and E. J. Carlson, *'Practical Divinity': The Works and Life of Revd Richard Greenham* (Aldershot, 1998), 204.

[42] Veron, *The Huntyng of Purgatory*, 396^v–97^r.

[43] Jewel, *Works*, ii. 920.

against purgatory sometimes apologetically suggested that their endeavours were hardly necessary in this time of the gospel. In 1593 Philip Stubbes described purgatory as 'so foolish a thing that I am ashamed to bestow anie labour in confuting of it'.[44] A few years later, James I dismissed it as 'not worth the talking of'.[45] William Fulke in 1577 explained that he had delayed in responding to Allen because he had thought people 'sufficiently disswaded from that blasphemous heresie'. The opinion of purgatory 'we have utterly removed and digged up even from the very foundations'.[46] John Foxe decided not to engage with the arguments of More's *Supplication* 'because John Frith hath learnedly and effectuously overthrown the same', and Richard Sheldon remarked vis-à-vis indulgences that 'there can be no more said concerning this abuse now adayes, then our fore beeres have said many yeares agoe'.[47] In numerous accounts, purgatory was designated an 'old wives' tale', an example of gendered (and generationed) discourse designed to stress its marginality and redundancy.[48] There was, of course, an element of disingenuity about all this: polemicists professed to regard the arguments for purgatory as beneath their notice even as they continued to commit considerable resources to their confutation. In 1581 Anthony Anderson dismissed trentals, masses, and pardons as 'pelfe yong babes can scoffe, and saye in these dayes. *Come tye the Mare Tomboy. A cake, a cake for all christian soules, De profundis, salve Regina* Godfather.' But in a funeral sermon published the same year, Anderson felt the need earnestly to warn his audience, 'as for the gainefull and painefull preaching of poperie, and her purgatorie, as a most venemous serpente, flee from it'.[49]

Establishing any kind of reliable chronology for shifts in popular attitudes towards purgatory is a highly uncertain business. The apparent stamping-out of All Souls ringing by the later 1580s suggests there may be something significant about this decade, one in which historians are in general inclined to see the Reformation starting to bed down.[50] But in spite of triumphalist claims, reformers did not drop their guard in the last years of the sixteenth

[44] P. Stubbes, *A Motive to Good Workes* (1593), 122.
[45] James I, *An Apologie for the Oath of Allegiance* (1609), 43.
[46] Fulke, *Two Treatises*, ii^r, 26.
[47] Foxe, iv. 666; R. Sheldon, *A Survey of the Miracles of the Church of Rome* (1616), 51.
[48] Veron, *The Huntyng of Purgatory*, 173^v; Jewel, *Works*, iii. 559; J. Calfhill, *An Answer to John Martiall's Treatise of the Cross*, ed. R. Gibbings (PS, 1846), 89; B. Rich, *The True Report of a Late Practise enterprised by a Papist with a Yong Maiden in Wales* (1582), Ei^r; R. Scot, *The Discoverie of Witchcraft* (1584), 533; W. Fulke, *The Text of the New Testament of Iesus Christ* (1589), 481; A. Willet, *Synopsis Papismi* (1592), 312; W. Walker, *A Sermon preached at the Funerals of . . . William, Lord Russell* (1614), 36. In using this topos, reformers were adapting a long-established synonym for worthless matter: A. Fox, *Oral and Literate Culture in England 1500–1700* (Oxford, 2000), 174–6.
[49] Anderson, *Shield of our Safetie*, G1^v; id., *A Sermon of Sure Comfort, preached at the Funerall of Maister Robert Keylway Esquier* (1581), 76.
[50] P. Collinson, *The Birthpangs of Protestant England: Religious and Cultural Change in the Sixteenth and Seventeenth Centuries* (Basingstoke, 1988), p. ix; D. MacCulloch, *The Later Reformation in England, 1547–1603*, 2nd edn. (Basingstoke, 2001), 113–15.

century, and with reason. In 1597 it was being reported that 'the King of Scots talks carelessly about religion, saying that if St Augustine believed in purgatory, it matters not if the papists believe it'.[51] Moreover, in spite of the more measured tone of some Catholic writings on purgatory, papists on the ground were still energetically fanning its flames. Sara Williams, one of the group involved in the infamous series of exorcisms performed by the Jesuit William Weston at Denham, Buckinghamshire, in the 1580s, was reportedly tempted by the devil to say that there was no purgatory.[52] Yet more dramatically, purgatory played a central role in the ecstatic (and, as the authorities claimed, counterfeit) visions experienced by Elizabeth Orton, a teenager in Flintshire in February 1580. Elizabeth supplied a remarkably graphic description of the nature of purgatory fires: these reached no higher than her waist, but were excruciating beyond earthly imagination, fuelled by pitch, resin, grease, brimstone, and boiling lead, all contained within a large furnace. Moreover, the flames were blue in colour, and burned vehemently, 'faster boyling than any water seethyng... casting like mountaines greate waves, not forward as the sea, but upward, especially when there laie any soule tormented'. In their local context, Elizabeth's visions were of more than abstract theological interest: she claimed to have communed directly with departed souls—her grandmother Mistress Conway, and a young woman named Alice Iova, buried earlier the same day. Alarmingly, these events took place in a milieu that was by no means insularly papist. Elizabeth herself was a conforming churchgoer, though persuaded into recusancy by her purgatorial experience. During her agonies, it was no seminarist priest but the local minister who, in an apotropaic gesture, tied a copy of St John's gospel around her neck. The same onlookers who were reportedly 'very desirous to understande the colour and nature' of purgatory, were at least nominal Protestants; when she began to rail against the established Church, this was said to have 'wearied the eares of the hearers'.[53]

The Orton case was an exceptional one, but 'superstitious' beliefs and customs concerning the afterlife long continued to register on the radar of concerned reformers. In around 1590 a group of zealous Lancashire ministers complained (either to the Privy Council or York High Commission) of 'manifolde popish superstition used in the buriall of the dead'. Before the body was brought to church, popish rites were used at home, the corpse 'all garnished with crosses, and sett rounde abowte with tapers and candelles burninge night and day'. During this time neighbours would

[51] M. A. Everett Green (ed.), *CSPD Series of the Reign of Elizabeth 1595–7* (1869), 391.

[52] F. W. Brownlow, *Shakespeare, Harsnett, and the Devils of Denham* (London and Toronto, 1993), 324, 353.

[53] Rich, *True Report of a Late Practise*, B1ʳ–D3ʳ. For an earlier case of a Lancashire Catholic placed in the pillory for publishing false revelations of a vision of Christ, and a bodily journey through heaven and hell, see W. P. M. Kennedy, 'A Declaration before the Ecclesiastical Commission, 1562', *EHR* 37 (1922), 256–7.

visit, each saying paternoster or *De profundis* for the soul, and being 'made partakers of the ded manse dowle or banquet of charitie.' On the way to church, the coffin would be set down at every cross on the way, 'and there all of them devoutly on theire knees make prayers for the dead'. Many then ignored or impeded the official burial service, making private prayers for the dead:

All the day and night after the buriall they use to have excessive ringinge for ye dead as also at the twelmonethes day after, which they calle a minninge day. All which time of ringinge, their use is to have theire privat devotions at home for the soule of the dead. But while the partie liethe sicke, they will never require to have the belle knowled, no, not at the pointe of deathe; whereby the people showld be sturred up to prayer in due time.[54]

Even allowing for hyperbole, ministers in the north-west clearly faced a real problem. At Leigh in 1601 there were those who 'desired the people to pray for a dead corpse'.[55]

Lancashire undoubtedly deserves its reputation as the 'wild west' of the Tudor Protestant world, but similar problems seem to have plagued the authorities in other highland and northern regions at the turn of the seventeenth century. In the spring of 1590 charges were brought against John Mynet, a lay reader in the parish of East Drayton, Nottinghamshire, for preaching a traditionalist sermon which turns out to have been lifted from Mirk's *Festial*. It included the claim that 'they that died in charity shall have part of all good prayers'.[56] In Yorkshire in 1592 a High Commission order complained of 'a generall abuse at burialles not onely by excessive ringinge of belles but allso by a rydiculus and popish custome of tyinge a cross maid off napkins or other clothes upon the bear over the dead corpes and burienge a staffe or metwande together in the grave with the dead body'.[57] That these problems persisted into the seventeenth century is suggested by the checklist of superstitious customs contained in Archbishop Toby Matthew's 1607 visitation articles: 'superfluous ringing, superstitious burning of candles over the corse in the day time, after it bee light. Or praying for the dead at crosses or places where crosses have beene, in the way to the church, or any other superstitious use of crosses with towells, palmes, metwands, or other memories of idolatry at burialls.' The article was reissued by other bishops of the northern province through the first three decades of the century.[58] In 1613 a new minister in the parish of Colwich, Staffordshire, was appalled to

---

[54] F. R. Raines (ed.), 'A Description of the State, Civil and Ecclesiastical of the County of Lancaster about the year 1590', Chetham Society, 96 (1875), 5–7.

[55] C. Haigh, *Reformation and Resistance in Tudor Lancashire* (Cambridge, 1975), 220.

[56] Cressy, *Travesties and Transgressions*, 162–70.

[57] R. W. Hoyle, 'Advancing the Reformation in the North: Orders from York High Commission, 1583 and 1592', *Northern History*, 28 (1992), 225.

[58] *VAIESC* i. 59, 61–5: William James (Durham 1607, 1613); Henry Robinson (Carlisle, 1612); Barnaby Potter (Carlisle, 1629); Thomas Morton (Chester, 1617).

find burials being carried out with processions, prayers for the dead, and a 'popish bagpiper'.[59]

When such behaviour was reported there was a determination to deal with it in exemplary fashion. In December 1612 eighteen parishioners from Dishforth and Thornton-le-Beans in the North Riding were brought before York High Commission and convicted of 'superstitious prayinge for the dead at crosses'. They were sentenced to perform public penance in a sheet 'with inscriptiones written upon sheetes of paper in capitall lettres on everie of their heads', the Dishforth offenders declaring the offence on the pavement at York, Topcliffe church, and at the market cross at Northallerton, and those from Thornton doing the same in the Minster and the pavement, at Otterington church, and at the market cross at Thirsk. Here the requirements of punishment and public persuasion went hand in hand; it is significant that the recantations were to take place at open-air crosses, those lightning conductors of illicit prayer for the dead.[60]

Many of the practices of which High Commission and Archbishop Matthew complained—the setting up of candles, excessive ringing, prayer at crosses—are already familiar. Others deserve some more attention here. The laying of crosses upon the coffin or corpse may once have been commonplace. The puritan *Admonition to the Parliament* of 1572 complained that it was a thing 'used of custom and superstition' that 'a cross white or black must be set upon the dead corpse'. Eighteen years later, the separatist Henry Barrow could still refer, as if it were a normal part of funeral ritual, to 'the linnen crosses wherwith the corps[e] is dressed'.[61] The diocesan authorities in Yorkshire, however, had no tolerance for the practice. At the visitation of 1615 two women of Aldfield cum Studley in the liberty of Ripon were charged with laying a cross with towels over the corpse of one Wood. When James Singleton of Markington (another parish in the liberty) pinned a cross to his dead child, the minister Mr Tailor reported with satisfaction that 'he pulled the same off the said corpes himselfe'. The practice continued, however, well into the 1620s.[62] Another 'ridiculus and popish custome' which proved difficult to eradicate in Yorkshire was that of placing a metwand or measuring rod in the grave along with the corpse. The precise symbolism of this act is obscure. Bishop

---

[59] Marie B. Rowlands (ed.), *English Catholics of Parish and Town 1558–1778*, Catholic Record Society (1999), 61. Anxieties of this sort were not confined to those exercising their ministry in the north. A petition published in 1606 by a group of London ministers observed that 'people are too much addicted to superstitious vanities about their dead, as *crosse towels, candles burning over them, A met wand, Ringing, &c.*': *A Survey of the Booke of Common Prayer, by way of 197 quaeres grounded upon 58 places, ministring iust matter of question, with a view of London ministers exceptions* (Middelburg, 1606), 141.

[60] BI, HC AB 16, fos. 10ᵛ, 11ʳ, 13ʳ.

[61] *An Admonition to the Parliament* (Hemel Hempstead(?), 1572), C3ʳ; *The Writings of Henry Barrow 1587–1590*, ed. L. H. Carlson (1962), 458.

[62] BI, V. 1615 / CB, 162ʳ; C. Gittings, *Death, Burial and the Individual in Early Modern England* (1984), 45.

Pilkington thought people originally believed that it could be used as a rod to drive away wild beasts or devils. More plausibly, it may have functioned as a sympathetic token of salvation, connected to the text of Revelation 22: 17 where the angel measures the wall of the heavenly Jerusalem, 144 cubits 'according to the measure of a man'.[63] At any event, the practice was thriving at Thirsk in 1615, where William Jackson and a number of other parishioners were charged with 'puttinge the metwande into the windinge shete in superstitious manner'.[64]

Here we begin to touch the fluid boundaries between overt Catholicism and apotropaic folk custom.[65] Not all 'superstitious' practices concerning the bodies of the dead can simply be regarded as tenacious continuations of pre-Reformation funeral ritual. In the later seventeenth century, John Aubrey recalled that 'when I was a boy (before the Civil-warres) I heard 'em tell that in the old time they used to putt a penny in dead persons mouth to give to St Peter: and I thinke that they did soe in Wales and in the north countrey'.[66] Was this a piece of protective magic, designed to ward off revenancy and safeguard the living from the unwanted attentions of the dead? If so, can the placing of metwands in winding sheets and the laying of crosses on coffins and corpses be regarded in the same light? Such questions exemplify the difficulties of distinguishing 'religion' from 'magic' and elucidating the motivations of 'popular religion'.

Similar problems surround the well-attested tradition of distributing 'soul-cakes' and the related custom of 'sin-eating'. A thumbnail sketch of the practice was provided by Philip Stubbes in 1593: it was the habit of papists 'to give soule-cakes (for so they shame not to cal them) or rather foole-cakes agaynst all soules daie, for the redemption of all christen soules, as they blasphemously speake'.[67] The origins of the practice are obscure, but it was already well established in the fifteenth century, when the homilist John Mirk described it as a custom of 'old tyme' and complained that it was in decline.[68] Yet in parts of England the custom survived into the later seventeenth century and beyond. In 1674 Thomas Blount described 'soul mass cakes' as a kind of oat cake that wealthy papists in Lancashire and Hertfordshire would distribute to the poor on All Saints, the latter responding 'God have your soul bones and all'. Aubrey noted it as a custom in Shropshire in his own time for 'a high heap of soule-cakes' to be set on the table at All Souls for visitors to take, and associated it with the old rhyme 'A soule-cake, a soule-cake, Have mercy on all Christen soules for a

---

[63] Pilkington, *Works*, 317; F. White, *A Replie to Iesuit Fishers Answere* (1624), 318.

[64] BI, V. 1615 / CB, 282ᵛ.

[65] For the reluctance of Protestants to recognize the distinction, see E. Cameron, 'For Reasoned Faith or Embattled Creed? Religion for the People in Early Modern Europe', *TRHS* 6th ser., 8 (1998).

[66] J. Aubrey, *Remaines of Gentilisme and Judaisme*, ed. J. Britten (1881), 159.

[67] Stubbes, *A Motive to Good Workes*, 124.

[68] T. Erbe (ed.), *Mirk's Festial*, EETS ES 96 (1905), 270.

soule-cake'.[69] In the later sixteenth century the distribution of cakes seems to have been a feature of funerary practice as well as an annual para-liturgical activity. A list of 'popish abuses' compiled in 1572 included 'cakes sent abrode to frendes' as one of the many superstitions at burials 'used bothe in countrey and Citie'.[70] This seems also to have been what the Lancashire ministers had in mind in 1590 when they complained that neighbours were 'made partakers of the ded manse dowle or banquet of charitie'.[71] The line here between receiving the charity of the deceased and performing an intercessory ritual on behalf of the deceased was an extremely fine one. In terms of the logic of reciprocity that underscored Catholic notions of inter-cession, the distinction was in any case false. Aubrey, once again our source for funeral customs of the early seventeenth century, records an old custom at Herefordshire funerals to hire poor men to take upon themselves the sins of the deceased. Sixpence, a loaf of bread, and a bowl of beer were delivered to the sin-eater over the corpse 'in consideration whereof he took upon him...all the sinnes of the defunct, and freed him (or her) from walking after they were dead'. Aubrey admitted that this was a custom 'rarely used in our dayes', but held that it had been continued by some 'even in the strictest time of the Presbyterian government'. For good measure, he threw in the observation that 'Methinkes, doles to poore people with money at funeralls have some resemblance of that of the sinne-eater', a perception shared by puritan critics of funeral charity.[72]

As Ronald Hutton has argued, it is likely that such practices became in the long run detached from the purgatorial theology which provided their original rationale.[73] But in the case of soul-cakes the association with popery and prayer for the dead was still quite apparent to observers in the later seventeenth century. This was true also of another burial custom that in-trigued the first generation of folkloric collectors, the recital of the funeral song known as the 'Lykewake Dirge'. An early account of this occurs in a letter of around 1600 to Sir Thomas Chaloner from his business agent in the Cleveland area:

when any dieth certaine women singe a songe to the dead body, recitinge the iorney that the partie deceased must goe, and they are of beliefe (such is their fondness) that once in their lives yt is good to give a payre of newe shoes to a poore man, forasmuch as after this life they are to passe barefoote through a greate launde full of thornes and furzen, except by the meryte of the almes aforesaid, they have redeemed their forfeyte; for at the edge of the launde an aulde man shall meet them with the same

---

[69] R. Hutton, 'English Reformation and the Evidence of Folklore', *PP* 148 (1995), 106–7; Aubrey, *Remaines*, 23.

[70] *Admonition*, C3^r.

[71] Raines (ed.), 'A Description of the State...of the County of Lancaster', 5.

[72] Aubrey, *Remaines*, 35–6; J. Brand, *Observations on Popular Antiquities*, ed. H. Ellis, 3 vols. (1841–2), ii. 152–3. There seems to be a reference to an analogous practice in M. Day, *Doomes-day: or, a Treatise of the Resurrection of the Body* (1636), 13.

[73] Hutton, 'English Reformation and the Evidence of Folklore'.

shoes that were given by the partie when he was lyving; and, after he hath shodde them, dismisseth them to go through thick and thin without scratch or scalle.[74]

According to John Aubrey, the dirge was sung at Yorkshire funerals 'till about 1624'. Aubrey also provides a version of the text, which illustrates the association between the folkloric and more explicitly Catholic elements:

> This ean night, this ean night,
>   every night and awle:
> Fire and Fleet and Candle-light
>   and Christ receive thy Sawle
>
> When thou from hence doest pass away
>   every night and awle
> To Whinny-moor thou comest at last
>   and Christ receive thy silly poor sawle.

Those who had given shoes and hose to the poor in this life now receive them again, providing protection from the sharp gorse bushes of Whinny-moor, while the uncharitable are pricked 'to the bare beane'. Thence souls pass across the 'brig of Dread', 'no brader than a thread', until 'to Purgatory fire thou com'st at last'. For those who gave away milk and drink the fire holds no terror; the others find 'the Fire shall burn thee to the bare bene'.[75] Here the visionary traditions of the Middle Ages are rooted in a recognizably northern landscape, and the relationship between good works and posthumous reward is firmly asserted. It is noticeable that the dirge was said to be 'sung of certain women', most probably a reflection of the traditionally important role played by women in mourning rituals. A gendered aspect is apparent in some other cases of 'superstitious' mortuary customs. When William Barton, a vicar choral of York Minster, was charged with allowing candles (in daylight) around the coffin of his wife, he placed the blame on two women, Elizabeth Dales and Isabella Lockwood, for placing them there and bringing him discredit. Women were prominent in the clutch of offenders found burning candles and laying crosses in the vicinity of Ripon in 1615, and even more so in the group from Dishforth and Thornton-le-Beans praying for the dead at crosses in 1612. The accused comprised two men and sixteen women.[76]

The failure totally to eradicate superstitious beliefs about the dead adds poignancy to a literary debate about the doctrines of purgatory and intercessory prayer which continued through the first decades of the seventeenth century. The principal catalyst was a treatise on purgatory by Rome's leading controversialist, Robert Bellarmine, first published as part of his *De Controversiis Christianae Fidei Adversus Huuis Temporis Haereticos*. Though Bellarmine may have had a reputation among English Protestants as

---

[74] BL, Cotton Julius F. vi. 461ᵛ.
[75] Aubrey, *Remaines*, 31–2.
[76] BI, HC AB 10, 195ᵛ; V. 1615 / CB, 161ᵛ–62ʳ; HC AB 16, 10ᵛ, 11ʳ, 13ʳ.

'the mildest and most modest childe of that crue',[77] that did not stop them queuing up to take potshots at his *Liber de Purgatorio* with the full armoury of scriptural and patristic arguments.[78]

While refutations of Bellarmine continued to emerge from the English presses, a parallel controversy was sparked by the defection to Rome of the minister Theophilus Higgons in 1609. In a work explaining his *First Motive . . . to suspect the integrity of his Religion*, Higgons claimed that the misrepresentations of Lawrence Humphrey, Richard Field, and Thomas Morton over the scriptural and patristic evidence for purgatory had induced him to leave the Church of England.[79] Higgons was refuted by Sir Edward Hoby and Richard Field, the latter seen by the Catholic Sylvester Norris as heir to Fulke's role as the most avid hater of purgatory and intercession among the heretics.[80] Hoby was subsequently entangled in further controversies over purgatory with the Jesuit John Floyd,[81] though in the meantime Higgons had turned direction again, apologizing at Paul's Cross in March 1611 for 'that *Purgatory*-discourse, which, in the heate of my *ignis fatuus*, and popish zeale, I sent back into my countrey'.[82] Other contributions to the early Stuart debates included a translation of a book against purgatory by the Huguenot Pierre Du Moulin, and an otherwise unknown work, *The Proofe of Purgatory*, included in a catalogue of popish books by the pamphleteer John Gee, and dated to 1621.[83] John Donne took the occasion to preach against purgatory at Paul's Cross on 21 May 1626, and again on 21 June.[84]

It would be disingenuous to pretend that controversial writings about purgatory and prayer for the dead represented more than a small fraction

---

[77] A. Willet, *Testrastylon Papisimi* (1599), 20.

[78] Willet, *Synopsis Papismi*, 307–19; M. Sutcliffe, *Adversus Roberti Bellarmini de Purgatorio disputationem* (1599); J. Hall, *The Peace of Rome* (1609), 39 ff.; T. Morton, *The Encounter against M. Parsons* (1610), 116–57; W. Guild, *Ignis Fatuus. Or, the Elf-fire of Purgatorie* (1625); J. Ussher, *An Answer to a Challenge made by a Jesuit in Ireland*, in *Whole Works*, 17 vols. (Dublin, 1829–64), iii. 177–277; W. Laud, *Works*, ed. W. Scott and J. Bliss, 7 vols. (Oxford, 1847–60), ii. 385 ff.

[79] T. Higgons, *The First Motive of T.H. Maister of Arts, and lately Minister to suspect the Integrity of his Religion* (Douai, 1609). See M. C. Questier, *Conversion, Politics and Religion in England, 1580–1625* (Cambridge, 1996), 86–7.

[80] E. Hoby, *A Letter to Mr T.H.* (1609); R. Field, *The Fifthe Booke of the Church* (1610), pt. 1; S. Norris, *An Antidote or Treatise of Thirty Controversies* (St Omer, 1622), 'The Epistle to the Reader'.

[81] J. Floyd, *Purgatories Triumph over Hell* (St Omer, 1613); E. Hoby, *A Counter-Snarle for Ishmael Rabshacek* (1613); id., *A Curry-Combe for a Coxe-Combe. Or Purgatories Knell* (1615). The latter work was presented by Hoby to the king as a New Year's gift: *The Letters of John Chamberlain*, ed. N. McClure 2 vols. (Philadelphia, 1939), i. 568.

[82] T. Higgons, *A Sermon preached at Pauls Crosse the third of March 1610* (1611), 45.

[83] P. Du Moulin, *The Waters of Siloe. To Quench the Fire of Purgatory*, tr. I.B. (Oxford, 1612); J. Gee, *The Foote out of the Snare* (1624), 96; id., *New Shreds of the Old Snare* (1624), 66–8.

[84] J. Donne, *Sermons*, ed. G. R. Potter and E. M. Simpson, 10 vols. (Berkeley and Los Angeles, 1953–62), vii. 164–89, 190–214.

of the total volume of Jacobean and early Caroline religious polemic. But it would be equally wrong to suppose that, nearly a century after the dissolution of the chantries, these had become peripheral or trivial issues in the minds of Protestant reformers. The unrelenting war of words with Rome and its apologists, and the painfully slow progress in eliminating superstition at home, provided Protestant writers with the incentive to continue to reflect on the relationship between the living and the dead, and how it should be articulated in ritual and religious terms. Debates about what the living might legitimately do, say, or think in the process of commemorating the dead were at the same time debates about a range of resonant contemporary issues. They touched upon introspective issues of human psychology, and the obligations of individuals in society one to another, as well as more politic questions about the nature of authority, the Church's relationship to its own past, and its freedom of manoeuvre in determining its future development.

CHARITY AND THE ORIGINS OF ERROR

In his *Defence and Declaration*, William Allen bullishly claimed that whoever Protestants might say began the practice of prayer for dead, he could name 'an other before him'.[85] Theophilus Higgons professed himself singularly impressed that he could not find a single author or council that had introduced it; it could not be a false doctrine as the Protestants claimed, as 'heresy doth alwaye spring from some certayn *Person, Time,* and *Place*'.[86] The fact that the practice of praying for the dead was so evidently to be found in the first centuries of Christianity posed problems for a Protestant ecclesiastical polity representing itself as a return to early Church purity. As Lawrence Anderton pointed out in 1633, 'What more generally disliked by Protestants then our Catholick doctrine of *Purgatorie*, and our charitable practise of *Praying and Sacrificing for the dead*? And yet what more generally confessed by Protestants to have been the beleef and custome of the Primitive Church?'[87] The response of Elizabethan and Jacobean divines was to attempt to separate prayer for the dead from purgatory, and to articulate a view of Church history in which their conjoining exemplified a highly cautionary falling from grace. Yet this was no uncomplicated narrative to construct, and distinguishing prayer for the dead from purgatory raised the question of whether the former might in fact be rehabilitated—a sensitive and highly divisive issue.

---

[85] Allen, *Defence and Declaration*, 243ʳ.

[86] Higgons, *First Motive*, 17.

[87] L. Anderton, *The Progenie of Catholicks and Protestants* (Rouen, 1633), 50. See also Norris, *An Antidote*, 329.

It was a shibboleth of early modern English Catholicism that purgatory and prayer for the dead were inextricably linked in mutual dependence.[88] On occasions, Protestants seemed prepared to concede the point, the Jacobean bishop Gervase Babington describing prayer for the dead as an action that 'proppeth up that lewd opinion of purgatorie, so derogatorie to the truth of God'.[89] But more commonly they demurred. In 1580 William Fulke insisted that 'prayer for the deade doth not necessarily draw purgatorie after it', and half a century later James Ussher could claim that it was only prayer for the dead as used in the Church of Rome that 'doth necessarily suppose purgatory'.[90] There was an easy point to be scored in reminding readers that the Greek Church, while practising prayer for the dead, had always rejected the doctrine of purgatory.[91]

If prayer for the dead did not presuppose its object as relieving the souls in purgatory, then what on earth was it for? The most usual Protestant approach identified its origins in a thanksgiving and praising of God for the departed. It was significant, thought Bishop Pilkington, that the ancient Church of Rome had included the singing of alleluia at funerals while modern papists forbade it.[92] Thomas Bell maintained that the early Fathers 'praied for the dead, to insinuate their hope in the resurrection, to mitigate their own sorrow, and to declare their affection towards the dead', and William Guild argued that they did so 'for declaration of their love to them, and not doubting that the soules notwithstanding were in blisse already'.[93]

Yet this pristine period when post-mortem prayer had equated to thanksgiving had clearly come to an end. For polemical purposes, Protestants sometimes contended that purgatory was 'but founde out of late', the creature of the Councils of Florence and Trent.[94] But it was more usual to

---

[88] Higgons, *First Motive*, 19; Norris, *An Antidote*, 316; R. Persons, *A Quiet and Sober Reckoning with M. Thomas Morton* (St Omer, 1609), 218.

[89] G. Babington, *Workes* (1622), iii. 124. See also G. Downame, *A Funerall Sermon preached at Watton in Hertfordshire, at the Buriall of... Sir Philip Boteler* (1607), 57.

[90] Fulke, *Reioynder to Bristows Replie*, 80; Ussher, *An Answer to a Challenge made by a Jesuit in Ireland*, 198

[91] J. Pilkington, *The Burnynge of Paules Church in London in the yeare of oure Lord 1561* (1563), H2ᵛ; T. Cooper, *An Answer in Defence of the Truth against the Apology of Private Mass*, ed. W. Goode (PS, 1850), 96; W. Alley, *The Poore Mans Librarie* (1571), ii. 45ʳ; Jewel, *Works*, iii. 563; Fulke, *Two Treatises*, 249; id., *Reioynder to Bristows Replie*, 80; Viret, *Christian Disputations*, 190ʳ; T. Rogers, *The Catholic Doctrine of the Church of England*, ed. J. Perowne (PS, 1854), 213; Willet, *Synopsis Papismi*, 310; Hoby, *A Letter to Mr T.H.*, 77; Field, *The Fifthe Booke of the Church*, 25; Morton, *Encounter against Mr Parsons*, 120–1; Ussher, *An Answer to a Challenge made by a Jesuit in Ireland*, 196–7.

[92] Pilkington, *Works*, 320.

[93] T. Bell, *The Survey of Popery* (1596), 308; Guild, *Ignis Fatuus*, 47. See also Fulke, *Text of the New Testament*, 480; Sheldon, *Survey of the Miracles of the Church of Rome*, 68; W. Ford, *A Sermon preached at Constantinople, in the Vines of Perah, at the Funerall of the vertuous and admired Lady Anne Glover* (1616), 71–2.

[94] C. Carlile, *A Discourse concerning Two Divine Positions* (1582), 38ᵛ; T. Beard, *A Retractive from the Romish Religion* (1616), 413.

recognize that it had a long pedigree, and that its rise was intimately bound up with the corruption of the Church as a whole. In his controversy with Harding, Jewel warned his adversary to take no comfort from the fact that 'we confess this imagination of purgatory is no new fancy'.[95] William Fulke admitted it was 'an aunceint errour'.[96] To a generation that knew its classical sources, the most obvious *fons et origo* was in the 'fantasies' of pagan philosophers: Homer, Pindar, Plato, Ovid, and Virgil were variously described as purgatory's first begetter.[97] The rise of purgatory was sometimes perceived as the price of syncretist compromises made by the early Church with pagan converts, who in Hoby's words, 'were of opinion that Christian religion should not derogate any thing from their wonted kindness to their deceased friends'.[98] John Donne regarded the embarrassing inclusion of commendations of prayer for the dead in the book of Maccabees as a result of the influence on the Jews of their gentile neighbours 'who were ever naturally enclined to this mis-devotion, and left-handed piety, of praying for the dead'. The Church Fathers were indulgent to new converts and loath to deter them from the faith, and so 'did not oppose it with any peremptory earnestnesse'.[99]

This, however, was a slippery slope. Ussher noted that the early Church's 'prayers of praise and thanksgiving' were supplemented with petitions that God would keep the deceased from hell, intercessions which were at first well meant, 'yet in time an occasion of confirming men in divers errors'.[100] The Huguenot Pierre Du Moulin insisted that prayer for the dead was not an apostolic tradition, but stemmed from the early, and at first harmless, custom of naming the martyrs during the celebration of the sacrament, and inscribing the names of the deceased on tablets in churches. Parents and friends began to give alms on the day of commemorating the deceased,

[95] Jewel, *Works*, iii. 560.

[96] Fulke, *Two Treatises*, 39; *A Reioynder to Bristows Replie*, 6.

[97] Jewel, *Works*, iii. 560; Stubbes, *A Motive to Good Workes*, 122–3; Viret, *Christian Disputations*, 28ʳ–30ʳ, 61ʳ; Van Marnix, *Beehive of the Romishe Churche*, 151ᵛ; Anderson, *Sermon of sure comfort*, 66; Sutcliffe, *Adversus Roberti Bellarmini de Purgatorio disputationem*, 1–2; W. Barlow, *A Defence of the Articles of the Protestants Religion* (1601), 137; Hoby, *A Letter to Mr T.H.*, 79; Guild, *Ignis Fatuus*, A2ᵛ; G. Wither, *A View of the Marginal Notes of the Popish Testament* (1588), 2; T. Morton, *A Catholike Appeale for Protestants* (1609), 498; W. Leygh, *The Soules Solace agaynst Sorrow* (1612), 33; Donne, *Sermons*, vii. 176; id., *Ignatius His Conclave*, ed. T. S. Healy (Oxford, 1969), 9; *The Sermons of Henry King (1592–1669), Bishop of Chichester*, ed. M. Hobbs (Aldershot, 1992), 206.

[98] Hoby, *A Letter to Mr T.H.*, 89. See also Leygh, *The Soules Solace agaynst Sorrow*, 33.

[99] Donne, *Sermons*, vii. 170. See also the view of Veron, *Hunting of Purgatory*, 151ʳ that singing, bearing of lights, and other ceremonies used at funerals were originally introduced 'to abolish and drive away the superstition and idolatry of the heathen'.

[100] Ussher, *An Answer to a Challenge made by a Jesuit in Ireland*, 298. He further noted (pp. 229–30) that prayers for deliverance from hell were retained in the Roman offices; curiously so, as those in purgatory had already escaped hell. A number of other writers made the point that the ancient texts used in the canon of the Roman mass seemed oddly unsynchronized with the theology of purgatory: Veron, *Huntyng of Purgatory*, 95ʳ⁻ᵛ; Viret, *Christian Disputations*, 81ʳ–82ᵛ; Field, *The Fifthe Booke of the Church*, 8; Du Moulin, *The Waters of Siloe*, 6.

and 'prayers for the succour of the dead soon after came to be adioned'. The final lapse, however, did not come until the sixth century, when learning was smothered by Barbarian invasion and there were no more Basils, Cyprians, or Augustines to uphold true teaching.[101]

Purgatory's perversion of commemorative rites for the dead slotted neatly into the eschatological framework of sacred history whereby Antichrist had arisen in the form of the papacy. In the view of William Fulke, 'the error of praying for the dead, was not damnable, while it continued in the Church of Christ, the Church of Antichrist by derogating full satisfaction from the bloud of Christ, hath made it damnable'.[102] Exactly when this had happened was uncertain. Gregory the Great was often chief suspect,[103] but, as Jewel recognized, the superstition of intercessory prayer was used 'both in Gregory's time and also long before'.[104] Fulke thought that there had been no prayer for the dead 200 years after the death of Christ.[105] But he and others could not but concede that prayer for the dead was advocated by Ambrose, Chrysostom, Cyprian, Jerome, and Augustine. Edmund Grindal thought petitionary prayer for the dead in Chrysostom and Ambrose rather 'figures of eloquence and exornation of their style and oration, rather than necessary grounds of any doctrine'. Chrysostom advised that worship at the eucharist should be offered for patriarchs, apostles, and the Blessed Virgin, figures who could hardly be in purgatory.[106] Grindal's episcopal confrères, Jewel, Thomas Cooper, and William Alley, similarly noted that Ambrose had celebrated for the soul of Emperor Valentinian, while believing his soul to be in heaven—not a propitiatory sacrifice, but one of thanksgiving.[107] Alley further noted that Chrysostom, Augustine, and Jerome believed that prayers were able to mitigate the sufferings of the damned in hell. The point was that prayer for the dead, as understood and practised by the Fathers of the Church, 'might be done, and was done without any conceit of purgatory'.[108] The placing of Augustine in these discussions had a special resonance; his totemic value to Catholics and Protestants alike was supreme. While some Protestants were prepared flatly to assert that the authority of Augustine unambiguously overthrew the Romish doctrine of purgatory,[109] it was more

[101] Du Moulin, *The Waters of Siloe*, 388–93.

[102] Fulke, *Reioynder to Bristows Replie*, 347.

[103] Calfhill, *Answer to John Martiall's Treatise*, 89; Foxe, vi. 379; E. Grindal, *Remains*, ed. W. Nicholson (PS, 1843), 25; Ussher, *An Answer to a Challenge made by a Jesuit*, 189; Du Moulin, *The Waters of Siloe*, 393; Donne, *Ignatius His Conclave*, 498; Laud, *Works*, ii. 392.

[104] Jewel, *Works*, ii. 743.

[105] Fulke, *Two Treatises*, 39.

[106] Grindal, *Remains*, 25–7.

[107] Cooper, *Answer in Defence of the Truth*, 96; Alley, *Poore Mans Librarie*, ii. 45ᵛ; Jewel, *Works*, ii. 742 (see also iii. 561).

[108] Beard, *Retractive from the Romish Religion*, 412–13. The foregoing refutes the view of M. McLaughlin, *Consorting with Saints: Prayer for the Dead in Early Medieval France* (Ithaca and London, 1994), 9, that 'whether they accepted or rejected prayer for the dead, the sixteenth-century reformers assumed that it had always been what it was in their own day'.

[109] J. Northbrooke, *Spiritus est Vicarius Christi in terra* (1571), 15ᵛ.

usually conceded that his writings were ambivalent about the idea of a third place.[110] In a manner analogous to the way in which Protestant exegetes approached apparent contradictions in Scripture, it was argued that the passages where Augustine seemed to admit purgatory were to be interpreted in the light of those where he did not.[111] In the view of the puritan preacher William Leygh, Augustine, rather like one of the elect undergoing a temporary falling-away, showed himself 'resolute at the last' on this issue.[112] Catholics of course took a diametrically opposing view. While Du Moulin noted that there was not a word about purgatory in the whole of Augustine's *De cura pro mortuis*, a secret translation was printed in England in the 1630s specifically to show that 'they who refuse to pray for soules in purgatorie, ar no such Christians as ancient S. Austin'.[113]

Debates about the licitness of prayer for the dead were matters not merely of historical, but of moral theology, and of conflicting interpretations of neighbourly duty and Christian charity. Catholic polemicists argued that, in setting their face against intercessionary prayer, Protestants were suppressing a normal human impulse.[114] A Catholic libel circulating in England at the start of the seventeenth century charged that Protestants had deprived the souls in purgatory of 'that Christian charitie, which charitable compassion, and mercifull pittie requireth, and by mutuall affection the members of one bodie helpe one another'.[115] Writing in the early 1620s, Sylvester Norris defended Bellarmine for showing that belief in a place of purgation was common to Jews, gentiles, and Turks. This was done not to credit their authority, but to demonstrate that 'this doctrine sprang out of the bowels of nature, and not from the private policy or invention of man'. Those who had neglected the prayers due to patrons and founders had revealed their 'uncharitable and savage harts'.[116] It was a shrewd polemical thrust when Theophilus Higgons remarked that by misrepresenting the teaching of the Church Fathers, Field was 'traducing the *Testaments* of the dead'.[117]

Protestants agreed that a natural human inclination was involved. The Elizabethan homilies warned people not to deceive themselves into thinking they could help the departed by their 'good and charitable prayers'.[118] To

---

[110] Jewel, *Works*, iii. 565–6; Fulke, *Two Treatises*, 161, 382, 386; id., *Reioynder to Bristows Replie*, 249 ff.; Viret, *Christian Disputations*, 194ʳ–197ᵛ; Guild, *Ignis Fatuus*, 47; R. Field, *Of the Church Five Bookes* (1606), 99; Hoby, *A Curry-Combe for a Coxe-Combe*, 10–11; King, *Sermons*, 207; Laud, *Works*, ii. 391–2.

[111] Alley, *Poore Mans Librarie*, ii. 45ᵛ.

[112] Leygh, *The Soules Solace agaynst Sorrow*, 38.

[113] Du Moulin, *The Waters of Siloe*, 320; *Saint Austins Care for the Dead* (England, secret press, 1636), 6.

[114] Allen, *Defence and Declaration*, 135ʳ; Higgons, *First Motive*, 19.

[115] Quoted in Barlow, *A Defence of the Articles*, 136.

[116] Norris, *An Antidote*, 308–9, 333.

[117] Higgons, *First Motive*, 105.

[118] *Sermons or Homilies*, 231

Alley, it was axiomatic that 'men be moved and as it were impelled with a certayne naturall love toward their frendes that be dead, to wish them well to do, and to breake out sometime into prayers for them'.[119] John Donne's anthropology similarly discerned a 'generall disposition in the nature of every man, to wish well to the dead'.[120] The early Church tolerated the pagan custom of prayer for the dead because 'it had a shew of pietie', a 'pretence of charitie'.[121] It sprang from 'a kind of excessive love and reverence of them that lived, towards their friends that were dead'.[122]

The impulses behind prayer for the dead, though understandable, were hardly admirable. Rather they pointed to the refractory moral condition of fallen man, a natural predisposition to superstition, and worse, idolatry. To Bishop Gervase Babington, intercessionary prayer was the manifestation of a 'preposterous love to the dead', which sought to 'presume in zeale and affection above any warrant of the Word of God'.[123] In a revealing passage in his influential *Christian Disputations*, Pierre Viret suggested how easy it was for men 'yea, the most sage and wysest' to fall into superstition 'by reason of an affection and love that wee doe beare unto our parentes and friendes, whome we cannot forget'. People were unable to restrain themselves, inclined to accept or invent anything they thought might be able to help the departed. The consequence was the origin of all idolatry, as images and sumptuous sepulchres were constructed to honour the dead.[124] John Donne was similarly convinced that 'a great part of the *Idolatry* of the *Nations*, flowed from that; an *over-amorous devotion*, an *over-zealous celebrating*, and *over-studious preserving* of the *memories*, and the *pictures* of some *dead persons*'.[125]

It was not the case that the memory of the dead should be abandoned, or that the living had no obligations towards them.[126] To pray for the dead, however, was not merely 'superfluous' but a positively uncharitable act. Andrew Willet argued that 'charitie bindeth not one to pray for another, because we knowe not one the particular needes of another. Nay, to pray for any departed, is against the rule of charitie... in praying for them, wee presuppose they are in miserie, and so neede our prayers', a position earlier espoused by William Fulke.[127] The doctrine of the Catholics was in fact

---

[119] Alley, *Poore Mans Librarie*, ii. 46ᵛ.
[120] Donne, *Sermons*, vii. 181.
[121] Fulke, *Two Treatises*, 386; Northbrooke, *Spiritus est Vicarius Christi*, 14ʳ.
[122] W. Whitaker, *An Answere to the Ten reasons of Edmund Campian the Iesuit*, tr. R. Stocke (1606), 306. The view that praying for the dead originated in an understandable desire 'to give some attestation of their love to the dead' was also Calvin's: *Institutes of the Christian Religion*, tr. H. Beveridge, 2 vols. in 1 (Grand Rapids, Mich., 1989), ii. 581.
[123] Babington, *Workes*, iii. 124–5.
[124] Viret, *Christian Disputations*, 180ᵛ–181ʳ.
[125] J. Donne, *Devotions upon Emergent Occasions*, ed. A. Raspa (Montreal and London, 1975), 93.
[126] For Protestant perceptions of duty towards the dead, see below, 266–70.
[127] Willet, *Synopsis Papismi*, 313; Fulke, *Reioynder to Bristows Replie*, 156–7.

further inimical to true Christian charity as 'they doe make great difference betweene the rich and the poore'.[128] Stout defenders of the existing social order they may have been, but most reformers were professed egalitarians with regard to the afterlife. It was invidious that the rich could accumulate obits, anniversaries, and private masses while 'the poore must be content with the generall praiers'.[129] In the Catholic scheme of things, Joseph Hall concluded, 'purgatory can have no rich men in it, but fooles and friendlesse'.[130] Well into the seventeenth century, Protestant authors continued to rehearse the polemical topos that if the pope and clergy actually had the power to deliver souls from torment, it was an extraordinary abrogation of charity on their part to fail to do so.[131]

Theologically, the hub around which these debates about charitable imperatives revolved was a disputed interpretation of the doctrine of the communion of saints. To William Allen, prayer for the dead was a natural expression of 'the unity and knotte of that holy felowship, in wich, the benefite of the heade perteynethe to all the membres...called in oure crede *communio sanctorum*'. This communion was a society 'by love and religion so wrought and wrapped together, that what any one membre off this fast body hath, the other lacketh it not'. People on earth and 'the chosen children that suffer chastisement in purgatorye' were linked by a perfect bond of unity. Anticipating a precept later enunciated by Karl Marx, Allen saw a system in which 'as one abundeth, redy to serve the other, as one lacketh, to crave of the other'. It was a characteristic aim of Protestantism 'utterly to break the band of peace betwixt theyme and us, as they have cursedly shaken thunytie of the living emongest theime selves'.[132] Protestants, of course, also subscribed to the communion of saints affirmed in the creed, and denied as a slander the Catholic charge that they had repudiated the doctrine.[133] But they meant something different by it. To Calvinists in particular, 'saints' were not 'dead men inrolled in the popes calendar, but all that are sanctified by the blood of Christ, whether they be living or dead', 'the whole company of them which are from everlasting predestinated to

[128] Willet, *Synopsis Papismi*, 318.

[129] Du Moulin, *The Waters of Siloe*, 143. See also Veron, *Huntyng of Purgatory*, 187ʳ; Jewel, *Works*, ii. 920.

[130] Hall, *Peace of Rome*, 29.

[131] Pilkington, *Works*, 21; Willet, *Synopsis Papismi*, 319; Viret, *Christian Disputations*, 62ᵛ; A. Wooton, *An Answere to a Popish Pamphlet* (1605), 40; A. Cooke, *Worke, More Work, and a Little More Worke for a Masse-Priest*, 3rd edn. (1630), 76–7. Edward Hoby added a novel twist to the argument: if the pope really cared for the souls in purgatory he would not have allowed the French king to overthrow the Templars, or Cardinal Wolsey to dissolve lesser monasteries: *A Curry-Combe for a Coxe-Combe*, 260.

[132] Allen, *Defence and Declaration*, 132ʳ–135ʳ. See also Bristow, *A Reply to Fulke*, 377; L. Vaux, *A Catechism of Christian Doctrine*, ed. T. G. Law, Chetham Society, NS 4 (1885), 16–17; Radford, *Directorie Teaching the Way to Truth*, 380; Floyd, *Purgatories Triumph over Hell*, 197.

[133] See e.g. Wooton, *An Answere to a Popish Pamphlet*, 36.

eternall life'.[134] There was indeed a spiritual bond between Christians in this life and the next, a 'knot of fellowship betweene the dead Saints and the living'.[135] But the negative aspects of this association were sometimes more clearly spelt out than the positive. According to Willet, the saints departed and the faithful living were members of the same body, and so bound in love one to the other, 'yet it followeth not that one should pray for the other'.[136]

In the course of opposing popish concepts of purgatory and intercession, Protestant writers sought to articulate their own ideal-typical relationship with the dead. For purposes of polemical advantage, as well as for more fundamental reasons of Protestant self-identity, it was often argued that purgatory and Romish prayer for the dead were not of such antiquity as their proponents claimed. Moreover, it was an imperative of anti-Catholic polemic to uncouple the concept of praying for the dead from the notion of a penal estate in the next life. Protestants of most complexions could agree that purgatory was not a necessary corollary of prayer for the dead. But did this mean that certain forms of prayer for the dead were acceptable, and if so, how, if at all, were they to be assimilated into a reformed polity? Protestant accounts stressed the compromises the early Church had made with the customs and expectations of pagan converts. A thousand and more years later, how much accommodation could or should there be with the 'tender consciences' of recent and perhaps reluctant converts to the gospel? There was a widespread recognition on the part of Protestant writers that deeply human desires to remember and to do good to the dead lay close to the source of the Church's historic apostasy from the teachings of Scripture. Those desires were no less strong in the reformers' own day. All of these issues would feed into the Reformation's attempt to build its own structures of ritualized commemoration for the dead—structures intended to exclude popish notions of intercession, but to give the dead their due. The task involved a finely calibrated balancing of the demands of theological probity against a recognition of deep-rooted tradition, and social and psychological needs. Unsurprisingly, there was to be no consensus about the outcome.

LITURGICAL REMEMBRANCE

Commemoration in the pre-Reformation Church had been inextricably bound up with the liturgy. The form of intercession which Protestants

---

[134] W. Perkins, *A Golden Chaine* (Cambridge, 1600), 499; E. Parr, *The Grounds of Divinitie* (1614), 241. I. Green, *The Christians' ABC: Catechisms and Catechizing in England c.1530–1740* (Oxford, 1996), 334–6, notes that, in dealing with the concept, 'godly' catechisms tended to stress spiritual fellowship of the elect with God; conformists the intercommunion of believers through offices of piety and charity.

[135] John Boys, *An Exposition of all the Principal Scriptures used in our English Liturgie* (1610), 46.

[136] Willet, *Synopsis Papismi*, 313. See below, 210–13.

found most offensive was the requiem mass, with its suggestion that the merits of Christ's passion could be applied selectively towards the dead. The Edwardian reforms had punched a hole through the system, and aimed at its replacement with a liturgy from which all traces of intercession had been totally expunged. Whether there should be any relationship at all between the communion service and the office of burial remained a vexed issue in Elizabethan England, many reformers feeling that to celebrate communions at that time was, at best, highly inappropriate. Thomas Becon remarked that 'they serve not for the burials of them that are departed, but for the exercises of them that be alive'.[137] Among the proposals at the 1563 convocation was 'that no manner of ecclesiastical person from henceforth minister or suffer to be ministred the holy communion at any burial, for avoiding of abuses that may thereof ensue'.[138] This perception that a funereal performance of even the most reformed eucharistic rite represented an open invitation to pray for the dead was widely shared by Elizabethan bishops. An unidentified set of episcopal interrogatories of 1560 enquired 'whether they keep any communion for the dead, the morrow after the burial, as they were wont to keep their requiem mass, or no?'[139] In 1565 Bishop Bentham of Coventry and Lichfield admonished the clergy in his diocese not to 'make the communion a mass of requiem for lucre and gain, persuading the people to pray for the dead', and in 1577 Bishop Barnes of Durham insisted 'that no communions or commemorations (as some call them) be said for the dead, or at the burials of the dead'.[140]

Yet the severance of the order of burial from the celebration of the Lord's Supper was neither sudden nor total. The diary of Henry Machyn reveals that communions were celebrated at elite funerals in the capital throughout 1559 and into 1560.[141] This was not necessarily a token of religious disaffection. At the lavish funeral obsequies performed at St Paul's in September 1559 for the recently deceased Henry II of France, *dirige* was sung and communion celebrated. The preacher on the occasion, Bishop Scory of Hereford, sought to vindicate the services that had been performed against two extremes, the one party thinking 'how the ceremonies used for burial were too many, that none at all ought to be used for the dead; the other thinking them to be too few'. In accordance with the practice of the primitive Church, the primary purpose of the obsequies for Henry II was to praise God for the deceased.[142] The issues resurfaced at the commemorative celebrations for another foreign Catholic prince, the Emperor Ferdinand, on 2–3 October 1564. Again, communion was celebrated, though on this occasion

---

[137] T. Becon, *The Sick Man's Salve*, in *Prayers and Other Pieces*, ed. J. Ayre (PS, 1844), 125.
[138] Bray, *The Anglican Canons*, 751.
[139] *VAI* iii. 88.
[140] Ibid. 167; *EEA* ii. 72.
[141] Machyn, *Diary*, 183, 184, 187, 188, 189, 221, 222.
[142] J. Strype, *Annals of the Reformation*, 3rd edn., 4 vols. (1735–8), i. 127–9.

'to the offatory and no farthor'.[143] This time the sermon was made by the bishop of London, Edmund Grindal, and like Scory, he endeavoured to put the appropriate gloss on the day's events: 'here is no invocation or massing for the dead; nothing else done, but that is godly: first, singing of the psalms; afterwards, reading of the scriptures, which put us in remembrance of our mortality and of the general resurrection, with doctrine and exhortation. All which things tend to edifying of the living, not benefiting of the dead.'[144] Behind the triumphalist tone one senses an underlying anxiety about participation in liturgical commemoration for a papist monarch.

The celebration of communion at funerals in places of public worship seems to have been abandoned after the early 1560s, but specific provision for it continued to be made by the official liturgy of the Church. The Latin version of the Book of Common Prayer, authorized by letters patent in April 1560 for use in college chapels, contained an appendix with texts for both a service commemorating benefactors and a 'celebratio coenae Domini in funeribus'.[145] The potentially controversial character of these additions was recognized in the letters patent, Elizabeth singling them out for special authorization: 'We have commanded to be appended certain special things fit to be repeated at the funerals and obsequies of Christians, the aforesaid Statute of the rite of public prayer...promulgated in the first year of our reign, to the contrary notwithstanding.' To see these services as evidence of the retention of crypto-Catholic practices at the heart of the Elizabethan establishment would be a misrepresentation. The appendix was prefaced with a familiar quotation from St Augustine to the effect that funeral ceremonies were about the comfort of the living, not the relief of the dead, and the rubric stipulating that the communion was to be celebrated if friends and neighbours of the deceased wished to communicate was very much in line with this perception. The service of commemoration was careful to frame all its references to benefactors in terms of giving thanks for their munificence, and to exclude any suggestion of intercession on their behalf. But in a number of respects the Latin Prayer Book was out of step with the vernacular liturgy of the Elizabethan Church. The 1560 translation (the work of Walter Haddon) was loosely based on Alexander Alesius's Latin version of the First Edwardian Prayer Book, and it betrayed a number of indications of its parentage, including the propers (collect, epistle, and gospel) for a requiem celebration of the eucharist which were dropped from the 1552 revision. The fact that a eucharistic service for burials was being authorized at a time when several bishops were insisting that no such

[143] J. Gairdner (ed.), *Three Fifteenth-Century Chronicles*, CS NS 28 (1880), 129.
[144] Grindal, *Remains*, 27–8.
[145] The following account draws on F. Proctor and W. H. Frere, *A New History of the Book of Common Prayer*, 3rd edn. (1905), 118–25; R. Boggis, *Praying for the Dead: An Historical Review of the Practice* (1913), 181–2; Haugaard, *Elizabeth and the English Reformation*, 113–17.

celebrations might take place in the parishes seems to constitute a distinctly mixed signal. Given the conservatism of the 1560 Prayer Book, criticism of its use seems surprisingly limited, though in 1568 students at Corpus Christi College and Gonville Hall, Cambridge, rejected it as 'the Pope's dregs'.[146] In 1571 a new Latin Prayer Book was produced, removing many of the distinctive features of the 1560 version, though the latter was never officially revoked. The limited scope of controversy over the funeral offices in the Latin liturgy reflects their restricted application, as well as a feeling that Oxbridge dons could in the main be trusted to understand the theological niceties. But it was otherwise with the burial service in the vernacular Book of Common Prayer, which was to excite continued if sporadic controversy throughout our period.

The fact that the 'Order for the Burial of the Dead' in the Prayer Book of 1559 was unchanged from that of 1552 did not stop some from finding it theologically objectionable.[147] The first high-profile criticism of the reformed burial order came in the 'View of Popish abuses yet remaining in the English Church' appended to the *Admonition to the Parliament* drawn up by the puritan activists John Field and Thomas Wilcox in 1572. This castigated the authorities for instigating 'a prescripte kinde of service to burie the deade', and for making a clerical monopoly out of a duty that pertained to every Christian. Much of the authors' ire was reserved for popular burial customs ancillary to the service itself, but the charge against the Prayer Book was an intentionally shocking and provocative one. The prominence of the minister, and the petition that 'we with this our brother, and all other departed in the true faithe of thy holy name, may have our perfect consummation and blisse' meant that 'prayer for the dead is maintained'.[148] The *Admonition* was attacked by John Whitgift, then Master of Trinity College, Cambridge, and defended by the presbyterian Thomas Cartwright, who charged that the burial rites were employed 'without any example either of the churches under the law, or of the purest churches under the gospel, that is, of the churches in the apostles' times'.[149]

The requirement of all ministers to subscribe to Archbishop Whitgift's Three Articles of 1583, accepting that the Prayer Book 'containeth nothing in it contrary to the Word of God' served further to crystallize puritan objections to the burial service. A set of 'questions to be awnswered concerning the archbishops urginge of subscription' hoped that it would be possible to add to the articles 'somewhat of prayer against the dead', an

[146] Haugaard, *Elizabeth and the English Reformation*, 116.

[147] The text is most conveniently found in J. E. Booty (ed.), *The Book of Common Prayer 1559* (Charlottesville, Va., 1976), 309–13.

[148] *Admonition*, C3ʳ. See also the rejoinder to a no longer extant reply to the *Admonition*, in W. H. Frere and C. E. Douglas (eds.), *Puritan Manifestos* (1907), 142–3.

[149] W. Whitgift, *Works*, ed. J. Ayre, 3 vols. (PS, 1851), iii. 365. The definitive study of the 'Admonition Controversy' is P. Lake, *Anglicans and Puritans? Presbyterianism and English Conformist Thought from Whitgift to Hooker* (1988).

unfortunate but intriguing Freudian slip.[150] Increasingly, however, the objection was not so much that the burial service sanctioned a proxy form of intercessionary prayer as that it undercut both the godly discipline and the doctrinal coherence of the Church by making a promiscuous promise of eternal life to all departed souls. The same document asked rhetorically 'whether it be not absurd, whensoever the mynister burieth Protestant, Papist or Atheist, Heretique, Usurer, or Whoremonger, good or badde, to say that he is his brother, as the booke appointeth, and that he committeth him to the grounde . . . in sure and certain hope of the resurrection to eternall life?' In 1584 a petition of Suffolk ministers stated bluntly that 'it is impossible to commit notorious sinners to the grave in sure and certain hope of resurrection to everlasting life'.[151] In 1586 Robert Cawdry, rector of Loughnam in Rutland, admitted before the High Commission that he had omitted parts of the burial service 'because he believes that the words "In sure and certain hope &c." tend to superstition'. In another Rutland parish in 1589, it was preached that the Book of Common Prayer was full of abominations, one being the burial of the dead.[152] Across the country as a whole in the last two decades of the sixteenth century, it is possible to multiply examples of ministers criticizing or editing the prescribed order, and of some godly laity dispensing with clerical services altogether in burying their family dead.[153] Even godly ministers whose instincts were conformist found their consciences troubled. Richard Greenham, the minister of Dry Dayton, Cambridgeshire, 'being asked his opinion of the burial of the dead', responded that 'wee read no prescript order of it'. Both 'prophain casting of the body' and 'superstition' should be avoided, and he thought it 'not inconvenient to read the word and to leave out the praying'.[154]

Pressure against the burial service did not end with the political defeat of the presbyterian movement in the early 1590s. The first years of the seventeenth century witnessed concerted campaigns by groups of ministers in various parts of the country to expound their reasons for refusing to subscribe 'willingly and *ex animo*' to the Three Articles of 1583, as they were required to do by the canons of 1604.[155] Puritan ministers in the diocese of Exeter voiced familiar objections: it could not be consonant with the Word of God to inter a notoriously wicked man 'in sure and certain hope of the resurrection', and it was mendacity to call him a 'dear brother'. In peremp-

[150] Peel (ed.), *Seconde Parte*, i. 198.

[151] Ibid. 201, 242.

[152] Ibid. ii. 204; W. J. Sheils, *The Puritans in the Diocese of Peterborough 1558–1610* (Northampton, 1979), 63.

[153] Sheils, *The Puritans*, 113; Peel (ed.), *Seconde Parte*, i. 132, 259, ii. 45, 222; P. Collinson, *The Elizabethan Puritan Movement* (1967), 370–1; Emmison, *Elizabethan Life*, 172–3; Cressy, *Birth, Marriage, and Death*, 404–7.

[154] Parker and Carlson, '*Practical Divinity*', 249.

[155] On Jacobean subscription, see K. Fincham, *Prelate as Pastor: The Episcopate of James I* (Oxford, 1990), 213–31.

torily affirming that 'god hath taken to him the soul of the departed', the Church was implicitly advancing the heresy of universalism: '*Origens* grosse error, that saith al shalbe saved'.[156] A 1606 *Survey of the Booke of Common Prayer*, purporting to represent the views of ministers in London, agreed that this was too 'confident', and like the *Admonition*, took distinct exception to the prayer concluding 'that we with this our brother...', demanding 'whither this be not prayer for the dead?' The reasoning here was logically impeccable: the petition seemed to desire 'perfect consummation of bliss' for all who had died in the true faith, but such happiness was assured for them, and impossible for all who had not. If words had to be appointed to be said at the grave, then it should be something 'less scandalous'. Moreover, the prominence of the minister, and especially his meeting the corpse at the church stile, tended to 'the confirmation of simple people in a superstitious opinion of burying the dead'. Burial of the dead more properly pertained to the clerk, ministers being ordained for the service of the living. The requirement to preside at burials was a potentially all-consuming one, threatening to enervate the ministry as an instrument of spreading the gospel, 'seeing the mortalytie of the last plague, 1603, was such, that if in some parishes in and about London the minister had buried all the dead him selfe, there had bene litle service, much lesse preaching some Sundayes togither'.[157]

Attacks on the burial service came not just from semi-conformists who wanted reform from within, but increasingly from those who had given up on the Church of England as irredeemably corrupt. In his *Brief Discoverie of the False Church* (1590), the imprisoned separatist leader Henry Barrow launched a ferocious attack on the burial service, alleging that when the corpse was laid to earth 'dirge and trental is read over him', the priest pronouncing 'that almightie God hath taken the soule of that their brother or sister unto him, be he hereticke, witch, conjurer, and desiring to meete him with joy in the resurrection'.[158] The refrain was taken up by a Brownist tract of the early seventeenth century, which similarly diagnosed malignant popery infecting the body of an ostensibly reformed liturgy: the Church of England might deny the doctrine of purgatory, 'yet how wel your practise sutes with it'. The prayer for God to hasten his kingdom so that 'we with this our brother' might have perfect consummation in body and soul amounted to prayer for the dead.[159] Through the 1620s and 1630s the separatist Church at Amsterdam continued to sneer at the burial rites performed in

[156] T. Hutton, *Reasons for Refusal of Subscription to the Booke of Common Praier, under the hands of certaine ministers of Devon and Cornwall* (Oxford, 1605), 18, 20, 28–9; id., *The Second and Last Part of Reasons for Refusall of Subscription to the Booke of Common Prayer* (London, 1606), 1–19.
[157] *A Survey of the Booke of Common Prayer*, 141–5. See also T. Webster, *Godly Clergy in Early Stuart England* (Cambridge, 1997), 198.
[158] *Writings of Henry Barrow*, 458.
[159] J. Hall, *A Common Apologie of the Church of England against the Unjust Challenges of that Over-iust Sect commonly called Brownists* (1610), 104.

England. Though the language may have been more intemperate, the objections did not differ in substance from those of earlier non-separatist puritans, the Brownists recycling the arguments of Cartwright and the *Admonition*.[160]

A more subtle charge than that the burial service was blatant popery was that its theological and liturgical sloppiness allowed it to be twisted to that end. In his controversy with Archbishop Whitgift, Cartwright denied that the *Admonition* suggested that prayers for the dead were being offered in the full popish sense, but the fact that prescribed prayers were being said at all maintained 'an opinion of prayer for the dead in the hearts of the simple'.[161] There was anxiety in puritan circles about the potential for mischief-making the ambiguities and errors of the liturgy afforded to the Church's enemies. In 1584 John Edwine, vicar of Wandsworth, claimed that if all learned men had subscribed to the litany, there would be no reply to the charge of the papists that the English Church prayed for the dead.[162] Remarkably, Catholics (who usually insisted that Protestants had heinously and uncharitably abandoned all prayer for dead) were sometimes prepared to make this charge as well. In 1617 the Catholic exile Richard Broughton took a leaf out of the puritans' book in claiming the doctrines of purgatory and praying for the dead to be 'proved out of their publickly allowed and reconfirmed *Communion Booke*'. Pointing to the text in the burial service beginning 'that wee with this our Brother...', Broughton argued that 'if this prayer, that people deceased may come to heaven bodie and soule...is not to pray for the dead, nothing can be called praying for the deade, and for their salvation'.[163]

The Prayer Book, of course, did not lack defenders from the attacks of both right and left. In his response to Cartwright and the *Admonition*, Whitgift represented as nonsensical the charge that the 'prescript service' maintained prayer for the dead. The prayer that 'we with this our brother' would receive bliss at the resurrection was not a petition for the dead, but for ourselves (this underlining the importance of the syntactic shift between 1549 and 1552). Cartwright's fear that the service might delude the simple into believing prayer for the dead acceptable was similarly implausible; it would have the opposite effect:

whereas in times past the minister used to say mass and *dirige* for the souls of the dead, and sundry times move standers by to pray for the dead, at the time of burial; now doth he read most wholesome scriptures, declaring the misery of the

---

[160] J. Canne, *A Necessity of Separation from the Church of England*, ed. C. Stovel (1849), 112–13; A. Leighton, *An Appeal to the Parliament; or Sions Plea against the Prelacie* (Amsterdam, 1629), 29.

[161] Whitgift, *Works*, iii. 366.

[162] Peel (ed.), *Seconde Parte*, i. 250. The problem with the litany was most probably the petition for God to deliver us 'in the hour of our death, and in the day of judgement': Booty, *Common Prayer*, 69. Another minister objected to the litany at Durley, Hants., in 1586: HRO, 21M65/C1/23/1, 39[r].

[163] R. Broughton, *The English Protestants Recantation* (Douai, 1617), 377–8.

life of man, the shortnes of his days, the happiness of those that die in the Lord, and the certainty of the resurrection. And who can hereof gather any prayer for the dead?[164]

In an anti-Brownist tract of 1610, Bishop Joseph Hall expressed similar exasperation that anyone should conflate the collect of the burial service with popish intercessory prayer: 'wee make account of an heaven, of a resurrection; not of a purgatory... To pray for the consummation of the glorie of all Gods elect: what is it, but Thy Kingdom come?'[165]

A more difficult charge for conformists to refute was that the comforting language of the burial service, its emphasis on the 'sure and certain hope of the resurrection' was theologically deeply flawed. In his reply to the non-subscribing ministers of Devon and Cornwall, the Oxford divine Thomas Hutton argued that just as the Church in preaching the gospel 'delivereth it pell mell in the hearing of elect and reprobate', so its directions for the burial of the dead applied in general something which 'in special belongs to them that die in the Lord'. Hutton reminded his readers that there was no requirement for the burial service to be used in the case of those (for example, traitors and suicides) who had been formally cut off from the fellowship of the visible Church, but there was no reason why the wicked should all be denied decent burial—even Jezebel had been properly interred. Hutton suspected that those who objected to the words spoken at the graveside in fact resented any prayer being used there at all, and he rejected the appeal to the discipline of Geneva, 'whose slender performance of this solemn duetie is noe sufficient rule to direct us'.

A crucial part of Hutton's defence of the established phraseology was his insistence that the elect and reprobate are not certainly knowable in this life, reiterating William Perkins's opinion that the damned were often esteemed to be true Christians. Indeed, Hutton sought to turn the tables on those who accused the Church of pre-empting the judgement of God, by asserting that it was precisely they who were doing so by their desire to withhold expressions of hope in salvation from some of the departed. He denied that the order of burial implied a universalist soteriology, supplying an inventive gloss on the text that 'it hath pleased God of his great mercy' to take the soul of the deceased. If the dead person was one of the reprobate, this referred to God's 'mercy toward the Church, in disburdening the world of him'. Most importantly, however, Hutton stressed the importance of charity and social obligation in the commemoration of the dead. He was particularly critical of the unwillingness of the non-subscribers to extend the phrase 'dear brother' indiscriminately to the dead, a discourtesy which seemed to him deeply socially divisive. 'The phrase of our countrie, the guise of civill conversation, the outward appearance, the rule of charitie all iustifie this appellation.' Burial was a ritual of social inclusion: 'we come foorth as his

---

[164] Whitgift, *Works*, iii. 364–6.   [165] Hall, *A Common Apologie*, 106–7.

brethren, not as his iudges . . . notwithstanding such a one (thus charitablie thought of) may in the ende receive his portion with the devill and his angels'.[166]

Hutton's emphasis on the imperative to think and hope the best was echoed in Joseph Hall's attack on the Brownists: 'Goe and learne how much better it is, to call them our brothers, which are not, in an harmelesse overweening, and over-hoping of charity: then to call them no brother, which are in a proud and censorious uncharitablenesse.' Passing up the opportunity for a thoroughgoing theological defence of the controversial phrases in the burial service, Hall went on the offensive, accusing his opponents of pharisaical hypocrisy: 'let all the world know, that the English Church at Amsterdam professeth nothing which it practiseth not: we may not be so holy, or so happy'.[167] In the view of its defenders, one of the virtues of the 'prescript' burial service was that it irreproachably put into practice that duty of charity towards the dead which was so compelling a theme in contemporary controversies. Concordant problems and opportunities sounded forth from another clerically performed instrument of commemoration: the funeral sermon.

PREACHING OVER THE DEAD

According to the 1572 *Admonition*, burial sermons 'are put in place of trentalles, whereout spring many abuses, and therefore in the best reformed churches are removed'.[168] The best reformed churches in this case meant those of Switzerland. In a letter of August 1573 to Bishop Richard Cox, the Zurich reformer Rudolph Gwalter outlined the reasons why 'funeral sermons are not usual among us'. Men being naturally inclined to superstitions 'and those especially, which are thought to aid the salvation of the deceased', it was safest to abstain from anything that might give the impression that what was being done was for the sake of the departed. The whole popish traffic in purgatory and chantry masses had arisen from 'sermons of this kind, which we know to have been religiously instituted by godly fathers of old time'.[169]. The problem with the funeral sermon, thought Cartwright, was that 'it nourisheth an opinion that the dead are the better for it; which doth appear in that there are none more desirous of funeral sermons than the papists, which although they

---

[166] Hutton, *Second and Last Part of Reasons for Refusall*, 1–19, quotes at pp. 3, 17, 4, 7, 14, 11.

[167] Hall, *A Common Apologie*, 104–7.

[168] *Admonition*, C3ʳ.

[169] Robinson (ed.), *Zurich Letters*, ii. 234. At Mary Queen of Scots' funeral in Peterborough Cathedral in 1587, it was reported that all bar one of the Scots in attendance, having processed from the bishop's palace, then departed 'and would not tarry at sermon or ceremonies'. V. Staley (ed.), *Hierurgia Anglicana*, 3 vols. (1902–4), ii. 210.

cannot abide the doctrine which is preached, yet they will have such sermons'. He conceded Whitgift's point that Calvin had tolerated their use by the English Church in Geneva, but this was because 'there being no papists in all the city, and all being well instructed, there was no danger in a funeral sermon there, as is here amongst us, where there be many papists and more ignorant'.[170] Again, Cartwright's views were echoed in a cruder form by Henry Barrow. Rich men who showed no love for sermons in their lifetime 'will be at cost to get some learned priest or other to preach over him at his burial: and that shalbe much more wholesome for him than a paltrie masse'.[171]

To some, the argument that funeral sermons encouraged lingering belief in purgatory and intercessory prayer seemed one of the sheerest perversity. In his *Answer to the Admonition*, Whitgift fulminated 'with what face of brass dare you liken them to trentals? What similitude is there betwixt a godly sermon and the wicked mass?...When is there a more meet time to beat down trentals, sacrificing for the dead, prayers for the dead, purgatory, and such like, than that wherein they were accustomed to be most used?'[172] Whitgift had a point. Anti-purgatorial polemic is central to the few extant Edwardian funeral sermons, and common in Elizabethan ones, particularly in the first half of the reign.[173] At the funeral of a member of the Skinners' Company in 1560, Henry Machyn noted that Bishop Jewel preached 'and ther he sayd playnly that ther was no purgatore'. Four years later, at the exequies for Ferdinand, Grindal asserted that 'purgatory gaineth nothing by this day's action or such like, but rather receiveth a blow; for at such times there is always just occasion ministered to speak against that foolish fable'.[174] Attacks on the doctrine featured prominently in Edwin Sandys's commemorative sermon for Charles IX in 1574; Richard Davies's sermon for the earl of Essex in 1577; Anthony Anderson's for Robert Kelway in 1580, and Thomas Sparke's sermons for the earl of Bedford in 1585, and Lord Grey of Wilton in 1593.[175] In James's reign, when a much greater number of funeral sermons were printed, proportionately fewer concerned themselves with explicit attacks on Roman doctrine. But side-swipes at the

---

[170] Whitgift, *Works*, iii. 372, 378.

[171] *Writings of Henry Barrow*, 459–61.

[172] Whitgift, *Works*, iii. 371.

[173] J. Hooper, *Early Writings*, ed. S. Carr (PS, 1843), 561–72; R. King, *A Funerall Sermon that was prepared to have bine preached...for a certein honourable lady then almoste deade, but afterward recovered* (1552), E1ᵛ– 2ʳ, E7ᵛ–F3ʳ.

[174] Machyn, *Diary*, 224; Grindal, *Remains*, 28. The same point was argued by Francis Dillingham in 1609: E. Carlson, 'English Funeral Sermons as Sources: The Example of Female Piety in Pre-1640 Sermons', *Albion*, 32 (2000), 570.

[175] E. Sandys, *Sermons*, ed. J. Ayre (PS, 1851), 161 ff.; R. Davies, *A Funerall Sermon...at the Buriall of the Right Honourable Walter Earle of Essex* (1577), C3ʳ, F1ʳ; Anderson, *A Sermon of sure comfort*; T. Sparke, *A Sermon preached at Cheanies at the Buriall of the...Earle of Bedford* (1585); id., *A Sermon preached at Whaddon in Buckinghamshire...at the Buriall of the Right Honorable Arthur Lorde Grey of Wilton* (1593), 83–4. See also T. White, *A Godlie Sermon preached the xxi. day of Iune 1586 at Pensehurst in Kent* (1586), B8ᵛ.

popish theology of purgatory and penance remained regular features of the
genre, and a few preachers, for example George Downame in 1607, or
Richard Carpenter and William Leygh in 1612, launched sustained broad-
sides against the papists' teachings.[176]

The utility of the funeral sermon as a vehicle for inculcating right doctrine
undoubtedly helps to explain its popularity with a wide spectrum of Protestant opinion. The response of Bishop James Pilkington in 1562 to the suggestion that there might be too many funeral sermons in the city was to exclaim
'God grant us some more in the country!'[177] In fact, from the very beginning
of Elizabeth's reign the idea of the funeral sermon as a Trojan horse for
popish intercession seems to have been a minority position, even among the
godly themselves. The diary of Henry Machyn shows how rapidly sermons
became de rigueur at the funerals of London mercantile society in the early
1560s, with evangelical preachers such as Pilkington, John Veron, and
Thomas Becon much in evidence.[178] Funeral sermons were also warmly
recommended in Becon's best-selling treatise on the art of Protestant
dying, *The Sick Man's Salve*.[179] Proponents of funeral sermons on the 'left'
of the Elizabethan Church occasionally adopted a somewhat defensive tone.
The godly preacher Anthony Anderson began a funeral sermon in 1580
noting that

it hath beene from auncient time received, and verie long used in the Church of
God... at the funerals of the godly to have the word preached to the people: not
thereby to profite the deade (which no way after life can chaunge this departing state)
but by it to instruct the lyving... why may not the godly preacher, take occasion at
funeralls to preach the worde of God?[180]

A few years later the moderate puritan writer Andrew Willet pronounced
there to be no reason 'why it is not lawfull now among Christians, at
funerals and burials, to have some godly sermon and exhortation, to put
the people in mind of their end, and to comfort them with the hope of the
resurrection'.[181] The perspective here was little different from that of his
(distinctly un-puritan) contemporary Richard Hooker, who defended fu-

---

[176] Downame, *A Funerall Sermon preached at Watton in Hertfordshire*, 57 ff.; R. Carpenter,
The Soules Sentinel (1612), 29, 38 ff.; Leygh, *The Soules Solace agaynst Sorrow, passim*;
R. Welcome, *The State of the Godly both in this life and in the life to come* (1606), 8; Walker,
Sermon preached at the Funerals of... William, Lord Russell, 35–6; J. Cleland, *A Monument of
Mortalitie upon the Death and Funeralls of the... Duke of Richmond and Lenox* (1624), 10; J.
Phillips, *The Way to Heaven* (1625), 39–40; W. Sclater, *A Funeral Sermon preached at the
Buriall of the Right Worshipfull Mr John Colles* (1629), 10–11. Further examples in J. L.
McIntosh, 'English Funeral Sermons 1560–1640: The Relationship between Gender and
Death, Dying and the Afterlife', University of Oxford M.Litt. thesis (1990), 87–9.
[177] Pilkington, *Works*, 321.
[178] Machyn, *Diary*, 212, 216, 225, 226, 231, 234, 248, 254, 255, 257, 263, 284.
[179] Becon, *Sick Man's Salve*, 119, 191.
[180] Anderson, *Sermon of Sure Comfort*, 3–4.
[181] Willet, *Synopsis Papismi*, 317.

neral sermons against the *Admonition* on the grounds that 'the known benefit hereof doth countervail millions of such inconveniences as are therein surmised'.[182] Less temperate than either, the lay puritan writer Philip Stubbes condemned those who saw funeral sermons as taking the place of popish *diriges* as 'phantasticall spirites...a great deale more curious than godlie wise'.[183]

By the latter part of Elizabeth's reign, one can see the emergence of a distinctly puritan tradition of funeral preaching, which was to bloom into full flower in the seventeenth century. There is a sense of a chapter closing in 1603 when, irony of ironies, the eminent puritan divine John Dod preached a sermon at the interment of Thomas Cartwright.[184] But even in the second half of Elizabeth's reign some still had qualms. In 1586 the preacher at Kingston upon Thames, John Udall, was reported to refuse to preach until after the burial service was concluded, observing that 'many loved to have sermons at the funerals of themselves and their friends who did not love sermons much otherwise'.[185] In his will of 1588 a London girdler, Richard Walters, displayed a full-blooded Cartwrightian attitude, insisting that there be no sermon at his funeral, 'not for that I do not allow of preaching...but for that the funeral sermons are commonly used for custom, which in time may grow to superstition rather than for any profitable edification'.[186] Other testators were not so self-denying, but could feel the need to wire their requests with theological trip-switches. An Essex gentleman left money for six sermons in 1585, specifying 'there shall be no other ceremonies', and a townsman of Elizabethan Bury St Edmunds paid 10s. for a sermon 'not for that I looke for anye good myselfe from that sermon when once I am ded but for his labour then in exhortinge those that are alive'.[187] Well into the seventeenth century, preachers of

[182] R. Hooker, *Of the Laws of Ecclesiastical Polity*, ed. C. Morris, 2 vols. (1907), ii. 403–4.

[183] P. Stubbes, *The Anatomie of Abuses*, ed. F. J. Furnivall, 2 vols. (1877), ii. 86. I hold to the traditional designation of Stubbes as a 'puritan' despite the scepticism expressed in A. Walsham, '"A Glose of Godliness": Philip Stubbes, Elizabethan Grub Street and the Invention of Puritanism', in S. Wabuda and C. Litzenberger (eds.), *Belief and Practice in Reformation England* (Aldershot, 1998).

[184] F. B. Tromly, '"Accordinge to Sounde Religion": The Elizabethan Controversy over the Funeral Sermon', *Journal of Medieval and Renaissance Studies*, 13 (1983), 293–312, at p. 309. See also P. Collinson, '"A Magazine of Religious Patterns": An Erasmian Topic Transposed in English Protestantism', in id., *Godly People: Essays on English Protestantism and Puritanism* (1983).

[185] Peel (ed.), *Seconde Parte*, ii. 43.

[186] D. Hickman, 'From Catholic to Protestant: the Changing Meaning of Testamentary Religious Provisions in Elizabethan London', in N. Tyacke (ed.), *England's Long Reformation 1500–1800* (1998), 124.

[187] D. Cressy, 'Death and the Social Order: The Funerary Preferences of Elizabethan Gentlemen', *Continuity and Change*, 5 (1989), 108; J. Craig, 'The Bury Stirs Revisited: An Analysis of the Townsmen', *Proceedings of the Suffolk Institute of Archaeology and History*, 37 (1991), 21.

funeral sermons felt impelled to defend their profession as a legitimate practice of the primitive Church.[188]

From one perspective, Protestant theological objections to funeral sermons can seem hard to understand.[189] After all, they had been closely associated with early evangelical critics of purgatory and post-mortem prayer such as Humphrey Monmouth, Hugh Latimer, and Edward Crome, and historians tracing the development of Protestantism in local communities through testamentary evidence have been inclined to regard the appearance of the first bequest for a funeral sermon as an early swallow of the Reformed faith.[190] Yet it is by no means clear that those who saw in the funeral sermon a potential for syncretist abuse were simply being silly. The pattern of requests for funeral sermons in a number of Elizabethan wills is sometimes noticeably redolent of the etiquette for endowing intercessory masses: multiple numbers of sermons, requests for them to be preached within a specified period after death, or at the 'month's' end, distributions of charity to take place at them.[191] In general, however, funeral sermons can reasonably claim to represent a success story in the campaign to Protestantize mortuary ritual. They showed it was possible to have public (and indeed ritual) commemoration of the dead, which fulfilled the twin duties of praising God, while comforting survivors, and performing the office of charity towards the dead. Though they were not a post-Reformation innovation, their much greater social diffusion in the second half of the sixteenth century

[188] Walker, *Sermon preached at the Funerals of ... William, Lord Russell*, 3; C. Fitz-Geffry, *Elisha His Lamentation* (1622), 32; R. Parr, *The End of the Perfect Man. A Sermon preached at the Buriall of the Right Honourable Sir Robert Spencer* (Oxford, 1628), 21; R. Bolton, *The Foure Last Things* (1632), 2. It may be significant that the godly archbishop of York, Tobie Matthew, whose preaching diary provides evidence of his prodigious sermonizing (727 sermons from 1606 to 1622), appears to have delivered only two funeral sermons, for 'Bess of Hardwick' in 1608 and her stepson the earl of Shrewsbury in 1616, most likely occasions of public responsibility rather than personal commitment: W. J. Sheils, 'An Archbishop in the Pulpit: Tobie Matthew's Preaching Diary 1606–1622', in D. Wood (ed.), *Life and Thought in the Northern Church c.1100–c.1700: Essays in Honour of Claire Cross* (Woodbridge, 1999), 385, 389–90.

[189] The argument that sermons typically constituted a form of hypocritical praise-mongering was rather different: see below, 268–9.

[190] S. Wabuda, 'The Provision of Preaching during the Early English Reformation: With Special Reference to Itineration, c.1530 to 1547', University of Cambridge Ph.D. thesis (1992), 201–7; K. Wrightson and D. Levine, *Poverty and Piety in an English Village*, 2nd edn. (Oxford, 1995), 155; C. Cross, 'The Development of Protestantism in Leeds and Hull 1520–1640: The Evidence from Wills', *Northern History*, 18 (1982), 234; id., 'Religion in Doncaster from the Reformation to the Civil War', in P. Collinson and J. Craig (eds.), *The Reformation in English Towns* (Basingstoke, 1998), 59; G. Mayhew, 'The Progress of the Reformation in East Sussex 1530–1559: The Evidence from Wills', *Southern History*, 5 (1983), 53; J. S. Craig, 'Reformation, Politics and Polemics in Sixteenth-Century East Anglian Market Towns', University of Cambridge Ph.D. thesis (1992), 154.

[191] Gittings, *Death, Burial and the Individual*, 38; Houlbrooke, *Death*, 127; R. Greaves, *Society and Religion in Elizabethan England* (Minneapolis, 1981), 706. Andrew Willet felt compelled to deny any significant parallels between the calendrical and cyclical patterns of anniversary masses and endowed commemorative sermons: Carlson, 'English Funeral Sermons', 570.

made them appear in practice a new instrument of commemoration, through
which it was relatively easy to articulate approved messages. Yet the successful disentangling of old and new was not always so easy. The problems
reformers faced are particularly exemplified in two ancillary aspects of
funeral observance which were deeply imbued with the mentality of popery,
and yet not without utility or an acceptably Protestant rationale: the ringing
of bells, and the distribution of alms.

DEATHLY RATIONING: BELLS AND DOLES

In the minds of some Protestants bells were deeply suspicious objects. To
John Veron they served no purpose but 'to bringe the peopell unto super-
sticion, and to confirme them in the opinion of purgatory'. There was no
mention of bells in Scripture, yet papists did not shame to assert that they
could drive away devils, and even baptized them. All of this was seductive to
the ears of 'foolishe and ignoraunte people, whiche is alwayes geven to such
vayne toyes and gugas'.[192] The association between bells and prayer for the
dead was recognized by polemicists such as Andrew Willet and Edward
Hoby, and at a more demotic level by the balladeer Robert Copland, envis-
aging a widow whose 'heart erned' at the tolling of a bell, sighing 'I am
bounde for hym dayly to pray'.[193] As we have seen, Elizabethan bishops
battled long and hard to eradicate the practice of ringing bells for the repose
of All Souls. Yet it was never likely that bells per se would be comprehen-
sively rejected by the Protestant establishment, banished from the parish
churches along with altars and images of saints. Instruments of very considerable social and political utility, bells were firmly woven into the social and
temporal fabric of sixteenth-century English communities.[194] More surprisingly, however, there was only limited support for moves to deprive bells of
any part in the ritual management of death. They had their role to play in the
commemoration of the dead, but with distinct provisos. As with a thera-
peutic drug dangerous to the patient's health if taken in too large a dosage,
or on the wrong occasions, the spiritual physicians of Elizabethan England
attempted to regulate the intake of funerary bells, reproving both those
liable to overdose and those who refractorily refused to take the medicine
at all.

The rules on what kinds of ringing were permissible, even required,
were both remarkably simple and disconcertingly ambiguous. The broad

[192] Veron, *Huntyng of Purgatory*, 49ᵛ, 60ᵛ, 62ᵛ. For a contemporary Catholic account of the apotropaic function of bells, see Vaux, *Catechism of Christian Doctrine*, 87–8.
[193] Willet, *Synopsis Papismi*, 316; Hoby, *Curry-Combe for a Coxe-Combe*, 101; Copland, *Seven Sorrowes*, Bi4ʳ.
[194] On the symbolic and communal importance of bells, see Cressy, *Bonfires and Bells*, 68–80.

parameters were set in the early 1560s when the 'Interpretations of the Bishops' provided that bells were to be rung for the dying, and that there was to be 'but one short peal' after a person's death, and two others before and after the burial. This formula (derisively referred to by critics as the 'threefold peal') was repeated in Archbishop Parker's Advertisements of 1566, and became normative for the rest of the period (a peal represented the ringing of a set, as opposed to the tolling of a single bell).[195]

In the meantime there had been attempts to circumscribe practice more closely. At the convocation of 1563 there was a proposal to limit the peal after death to one hour, and at the burial to half an hour, and another that 'there be no solemn peal rung after the death of any person, but one bell as hath been heretofore. And that not passing three quarters of an hour at the most, and to give warning to the burial not passing half an hour.'[196] These acquired no legal status, however, and ecclesiastical authorities did not in the main attempt to define too precisely what constituted excessive ringing. Bishop Thomas Bentham of Coventry and Lichfield was unique in insisting in 1565 'that you suffer no ringing of bells for the dead, but only to knoll a bell at the hour of death for the space of half an hour and ring one short peal a little before the burial', though a half-hour rule was also enforced by the authorities at Wells Cathedral in 1612.[197] More commonly, episcopal articles enquired in a generalized way if parishes stuck to observing the three short peals, and if there had been any other 'superstitious', 'superfluous', 'vain', or 'unnecessary' ringing. Occasionally, concern was expressed over the ringing of bells during times appointed for prayer, and over the use of handbells, which traditionally entreated prayers for the departed.[198] In October 1561 the authorities in Hampshire specifically admonished the churchwardens and parishioners of Bighton that 'there shall no bedeman go ... [ringing] any bell before any cors ne pray in the stretes openly for the deade with a bell tynkynge'.[199] The recidivist potential of the practice was dramatically exemplified during the Northern Rising of 1569 when, after the death of a Durham goldsmith, the shoemaker Henry Hutcheson went forth 'with the hand bell to byd any man come to saul masse and *dirige*'.[200]

A uniform order in the matter of bells was supplied after a fashion by the canons of 1604, though this merely restated the long-standing requirement for there to be no more than three short peals: after the death, and before and

---

[195] Haugaard, *Elizabeth and the English Reformation*, 163–4; Bray, *The Anglican Canons*, 167.

[196] Bray, *The Anglican Canons*, 729, 752.

[197] *VAI* iii. 170; Cressy, *Birth, Marriage, and Death*, 425.

[198] *VAI* iii. 91, 98, 105, 159 (time of prayers), 256, 285 (handbells), 309, 383; *EEA* ii. 72, 93, 132, iii. 149 (handbells), 190–1, 214, 228, 293.

[199] HRO, 21M65/C1/7, 99ᵛ.

[200] J. Raine (ed.), *Depositions and other Ecclesiastical Proceedings from the Courts of Durham*, SS 21 (1845), 163.

after the burial.[201] Concern over whether canon 67 was rightly observed was a regular feature of subsequent visitation articles, but like their Elizabethan predeccessors, Jacobean bishops did not attempt to regulate funeral ringing any more closely.[202]

The potential for confusion, conflict, and dispute in this area was considerable. In the absence of prescriptive allocations of time, interpretations of what constituted a 'short' peal were bound to be subjective, and the point at which ringing became 'excessive' or 'superstitious' was a matter of opinion. As the frustrated reformers of 1563 correctly feared, the imprecision of the rules allowed conservatives scope to attempt to maintain traditional custom under the guise of the new dispensation. Diocesan courts felt that the line had been crossed in several Essex and Hampshire parishes in the 1560s.[203] In a number of Cheshire parishes in the late 1570s, practice went far beyond what the authorities were able to tolerate, even if the nature of the offence could only be described in terms of spirit and degree. At Holy Trinity, Chester, 'Randall Griffeth ther parishe clerke being oftentymes forbydden ringeth mo peales at the funeralles of the dead than is decent'; similarly at Manchester there was 'more rynginge at buryalles then is decent'; at Walton 'more rynginge after buryalles then is required'; at Middlewich simply 'to much ringing for the deade'.[204] On the other side of the country, the parish clerk of Hull was charged in 1570 that 'at burialls he maketh such busyness with ringinge that the minister cannot be heard of the people'. But the elasticity of the law allowed him to offer the legalistic (if not entirely convincing) defence that 'according to lawfull order prescribed in the metropoliticall articles or Iniunctions he dothe rynge but one shorte peall before the buryall of any dead corpses and one shorte peall after the buryall'.[205] In 1620 three parishioners of Carlton in Nottinghamshire, despite a warning by their minister, 'did notwithstandinge unceasonablie jangle the bells contrarie to the 67 Canon'.[206]

If some (particularly in the north and west) came to the attention of the authorities for suspicious profligacy in their ringing of bells, others did so for over-precise parsimony. At the end of Elizabeth's reign, John Todde, vicar of Great Bentley in Essex, was cited because he 'would not let the bell be tolled or knell rung when the corpse of Humphrey Searles' wife was brought to be buried'. In another Essex parish (Goldhanger) in 1591, the sexton refused to

---

[201] Bray, *The Anglican Canons*, 359.
[202] VAIESC i. 17, 59, 61–5, 76, 182, 207. See S. A. Peyton (ed.), *The Churchwardens' Presentments in the Oxfordshire Peculiars of Dorchester, Thame and Banbury*, Oxfordshire Record Society, 10 (1929), 251, 293–4.
[203] Emmison, *Elizabethan Life*, 136; HRO, 21M65/C1/7, 99ᵛ; 21M65/C1/12, 86ᵛ; 21M65/C1/13/1, 36ᵛ.
[204] BI, V 1578 /CB 3, 19ᵛ, 37ʳ, 46ᵛ; Purvis (ed.), *Tudor Parish Documents*, 73.
[205] BI, HC CP 1570/3.
[206] Hodgkinson (ed.), 'Act Books of the Archdeacon of Nottingham', 31. See also the concerns about contravention of canon 67 in *A Survey of the Booke of Common Prayer*, 145.

ring for a man lying on his deathbed, while at Great Bardfield in 1585 the churchwardens were termed 'knaves and fools' for restricting the ringing at the burial of one Sergeant Benlowe.[207] Flowing throughout the period was a stream of opinion distrustful of all ringing linked to the dead and dying, even if it rarely surged as strongly as at Tarporley, Cheshire, in 1640, where the rector Nathaniel Lancaster struck a man as he tolled the bell for a passing soul.[208] At Paul's Cross in 1563, a preacher called for an end to bells for the dying, and the tolling of bells at funerals featured on the lists of continuing abuses in the Church drawn up by Percival Wiburn in the late 1560s, the *Admonition* authors in 1572, and Anthony Gilby in 1581.[209] From the 1560s to the 1630s a smattering of testators, clerical and lay, insisted that their funerals were to take place 'without singing or ringing', 'the jangling or ringing of any bells', 'popish pomp, vain compliments and ringing'.[210] This was regarded as characteristic enough of the precisian mentality to be caricatured in the anti-puritan tract, *Martins months minde*, in which Martin Marprelate requests burial 'without bell, pompe, or any solemnitie'.[211]

Predictably, separatist critics of the Church of England regarded any ringing at deaths and funerals as further evidence of its inherent corruption, and harped on the common linguistic linkage of bells and souls. Henry Barrow noted that for money anyone could have 'a soule-peale on all the hallowed belles for his soule'. Responding to a Brownist accusation of 'your ringing of hallowed bels for the soules', Joseph Hall protested that 'we call them soule-bels, for that they signifie the departure of the soule, not for that they helpe the passage of the soule'.[212] The usage, however, invited confusion, even among those who ought to have known better. The compilation *A Garden of Spiritual Flowers*, whose authorship–Richard Rogers, William Perkins, Richard Greenham, Mathew Mead, George Webbe–comprised a roll-call of distinguished Calvinists, included 'A godly meditation to bee had in mind, at our going to bed'. This contained the extraordinary verse: 'The nightly bell which I heare toule / When I am laid in bed, / Declares that bell which for my soule, / Shall sound when I am dead.'[213]

[207] Emmison, *Elizabethan Life*, 174–5.

[208] J. Maltby, *Prayer Book and People in Elizabethan and Early Stuart England* (Cambridge, 1998), 57.

[209] Gairdner (ed.), *Three Fifteenth-Century Chronicles*, 125; *Admonition*, C3ʳ; Robinson (ed.), *Zurich Letters*, ii. 361; A. Gilby, *A Pleasaunt Dialogue betweene a Souldior of Barwicke and an English Chaplaine* (Middelburg(?), 1581), M4ʳ.

[210] R. C. Richardson, *Puritanism in North-West England: A Regional Study of the Diocese of Chester to 1642* (Manchester, 1972), 30; Gittings, *Death, Burial, and the Individual*, 50; Greaves, *Religion and Society*, 701.

[211] Mar-phoreus (Thomas Nashe(?)), *Martins months minde* (1589), F5ᵛ.

[212] *Writings of Henry Barrow*, 462; Hall, *Common Apologie*, 104, 107.

[213] Quoted in H. C. White, *English Devotional Literature (Prose) 1600–1640* (Madison, Wis., 1931), 211.

Despite such occasional lapses, the function of bells in the overall scheme of mortuary ritual was largely clear to Protestant churchmen. The passing-bell urged hearers to pray for the sick person in their last moments, and after they were dead the ringing served first to announce the departure of the soul, and at the funeral to 'gather the people together to hear the word of God and the thanksgiving'.[214] But in society at large ringing for the deceased served other, less overtly didactic purposes. It represented a stream of parochial income as well as 'a significant marker of the status of the deceased'.[215] In the parishes of early modern England, urban as well as rural, there was no more public acknowledgement of the loss sustained by the community than the protracted ringing of the bells in the church tower. As the contemporaries of John Donne knew well, it was an instinctive response to ask for whom the bell was tolling.[216] The sensitivities involved here were sharply lampooned by an anecdote in a Jacobean jest book. A 'rich churle and a beggar' were buried on the same day, 'and the belles rung out amaine for the miser'. The rich man's son, however, hired a trumpeter to stand in the belfry, and between each peal to blow and proclaim 'Sirres, this next peal is not for R., but for Maister N., his father.'[217] Yet, as the story itself suggests, arranging the appropriate level of aural commemoration for the departed was a serious business. When in around 1570 the children of John Pentland in County Durham met the night before his burial to discuss the will and their inheritance, 'they had talk of ringing the bells for their fayther'.[218]

Wills, probate, and churchwardens' accounts show great variety in payments made for the bells, with individual churches setting their own scales of charges. Fees varied according to the number of bells rung, the gender and age of the deceased, and where they were to be buried. While charges levied for the ringing of the passing-bell were typically a shilling or less in the late sixteenth and early seventeenth centuries, payments for funeral peals were often five, six, or ten times this amount.[219] Where payments of 6s., 12s., or more were being made for ringing, it is hard to see on what reasonable reckoning this could have constituted a 'short peal'. Indeed, it is clear that ringing at funerals often went on far longer than the half-hour godly reformers grudgingly regarded as an acceptable maximum. In the London parish of St Peter Cornhill in James's reign, the ringing of the great bell for six hours was not uncommon. In 1632, payment was made from the estate of William

---

[214] Becon, *Sick Man's Salve*, 125.

[215] D. Beaver, '"Sown in Dishonour, Raised in Glory": Death, Ritual and Social Organization in Northern Gloucestershire, 1590–1690', *Social History*, 17 (1992), 405–6.

[216] Donne, *Devotions*, 216: 'never send to know for whom the *bell* tolls; It tolls for *thee*'.

[217] Cited in Brand, *Observations on Popular Antiquities*, ii. 132.

[218] Raine (ed.), *Depositions and other Ecclesiastical Proceedings from the Courts of Durham*, 103.

[219] M. L. Rifkin, 'Burial, Funeral and Mourning Customs in England, 1558–1662', Bryn Mawr College Ph.D. thesis (1977), 50–52; Houlbrooke, *Death*, 276; Beaver, '"Sown in Dishonour, Raised in Glory"', 406.

Stanshall of Nottingham for bells ringing 'all the day of his funerall'.[220]
Despite the authorities' apparent success in eradicating All Souls ringing,
extended and extensive peals at burials represented an area of distinct
continuity with the mortuary culture of pre-Reformation England. In
one particular manifestation, the continuities were remarkable. Despite
the conviction of bishops like Grindal that handbells were a suspiciously
popish artefact, some towns in the early seventeenth century retained ringers
whose job was to tour the streets with a handbell to announce the death
of local noteworthies. The fees of the bell-man employed by the city of
Oxford were scaled in accordance with the rank of the deceased, and were
to be paid 'albeit any man or woman being executrix shall be unwilling to
have him go abroad'. In a particularly retarditaire touch, the university's
bell-man went from college to college wearing the cap and gown of the
deceased don.[221]

What all of this suggests is that the process of expunging Catholic associations from the commemoration of the dead was slow, messy, and never
entirely successful. Of course, it would be a mistake to suppose (as some
puritans clearly did) that the symbolic resources of post-mortem bell-ringing
(or of funeral ritual more generally) were somehow fixed and immutable,
unsusceptible to reinvention and creative transformation in a Protestant
context. One thinks here of David Cressy's work demonstrating how the
traditional role of church bells in marking out the cycle of the Catholic
liturgical year was subsumed into the articulation of a new, secularized
Protestant festive calendar of Armada celebrations and Gunpowder
Plot.[222] It is very likely that, as the seventeenth century progressed, anxiety
was receding on the part of ecclesiastical authorities that prolonged ringing
at funerals was desired primarily to secure prayer for the dead. Yet as the
expression 'soul-bell' might indicate, the suggestion of a linkage between
ritualized bell-ringing and the spiritual fate of the deceased was probably
never entirely broken. In the 1640s Thomas Fuller complained of the ringing
taking place at London funerals: 'men's charity herein may be suspected
of superstition in praying for the dead'.[223] Fuller was right to suppose that
bells could evoke atavistic responses. Even so resolute (if idiosyncratic)
a Protestant as the physician and philosopher Thomas Browne might

---

[220] G. W. Gower (ed.), *A Register of all the Christninges, Burialles and Weddinges within the
Parish of St Peter upon Cornhill*, Harleian Society (1877), 169, 172–3, 176; Houlbrooke,
Death, 276 n. Of significance here is the introduction of three-quarter bell-wheels and conse-
quent casting of new bells and strengthening of church towers from the latter part of Elizabeth's
reign. See A. Woodger, 'Post-Reformation Mixed Gothic in Huntingdonshire Bell Towers and its
Campanological Associations', *Archaeological Journal*, 41 (1984).

[221] Gittings, *Death, Burial, and the Individual*, 134–5. As recently as 1556 Cordwainer-
Street ward in London had begun to employ a bell-man whose remit was to tour the streets at
night giving warning of fire hazard, as well as to encourage prayer for the dead: Strype,
Ecclesiastical Memorials, iii(1), 311.

[222] Cressy, *Bonfires and Bells*.

[223] Brand, *Observations on Popular Antiquities*, ii. 133.

wistfully note that he 'could scarce containe my prayers for a friend at the ringing of a bell'.[224]

A parallel set of anxieties and paradoxes attends another component of pre-Reformation mortuary ritual which survived in Protestant England, the distribution of doles of money or bread to the poor at funerals. Charitable giving to the poor was of course deeply inscribed in Protestant patterns of piety, but reformers were sometimes distinctly uneasy about the resonances of post-mortem charity. In an Edwardian funeral sermon, Robert King conceded that such giving to the poor was allowable, but warned that if men waited till they were dying to give 'god shall thanke us therafter... nothyng at all'.[225] A more robust line was taken by the puritan preacher Anthony Anderson in a funeral sermon of 1580. Anderson fulminated against the covetousness and 'greedie desire' of those who 'are come in hope to have a dole to day'. Such doles were unacceptable because they lent themselves to being 'abused by the wicked, to father their popish prayer for the deade, uppon your charitable devotion to the poore'. Feeding the poor was a laudable act of charity, but should not take place on the day of the burial. Instead he advised setting aside some other occasion 'and give them with warning, that you meane no procuring of prayer for the dead'.[226]

A few testators clearly concurred. In 1604 the London alderman Richard Goddard refused to provide a distribution of alms at his burial 'for I conceive that to be but a popish imitation of such as were desirous after their death to have their soul prayed for'.[227] But many other Protestants, particularly in the early part of Elizabeth's reign, did not accept the logic here and regarded their burial as a perfectly appropriate context for fulfilling the exhortations towards charity which they were hearing from the preachers. A Southampton apothecary whose will preamble in 1571 claimed the merits of Christ 'as a sufficient propitiation and satisfaction for all my sins' (a fairly explicit repudiation of purgatory) nonetheless provided 40s. for distribution to the poor at his funeral. The same bequest was made by a butcher of the town two years later, who also trusted to be saved by the blood of Christ 'and by none other ways nor means'.[228] Funeral doles were a fixture of the Elizabethan mortuary scene, a significant status-marker in the exequies of gentry and nobility. In her study of probate accounts Clare Gittings found them to be 'by far the most frequent deathbed request'.[229] Their persistence through

---

[224] T. Browne, *Religio Medici*, in *The Major Works*, ed. C. A. Patrides (Harmondsworth, 1977), 68.

[225] King, *A Funerall Sermon*, F2ᵛ.

[226] Anderson, *A Sermon of Sure Comfort*, 27, 43–4.

[227] Hickman, 'Catholic to Protestant', 124.

[228] E. Roberts and K. Parker (eds.), *Southampton Probate Inventories 1447–1575*, Southampton Records Series, 35, 2 vols. (1992), ii. 290, 334.

[229] Gittings, *Death, Burial and the Individual*, 161–4, 241. Over half of the sampled accounts contained them in the 1580s. See also Greaves, *Society and Religion*, 717–22; Cressy, 'Death and the Social Order', 108–9.

the second half of Elizabeth's reign cannot plausibly be attributed to a widespread vestigial belief in the likelihood or efficacy of the poor's prayers for the donor's soul, though, as Anderson testifies, a perceived connection was never fully dissolved. Into James's reign, there was certainly an atavistic feel to some patterns of charitable giving. A Suffolk rector in 1615, for example, left 40s. to the poor of his parish with the instruction that half was to be distributed 'at the day of my buriall, and thother 20 that day twelvemonth after'.[230] There was nonetheless a clear distinction between this and the overtly Catholic gesture of the Teeside woman who in the following year left 'unto the powre of Cokkerton 5s to praie for me'.[231]

From the third decade of the seventeenth century funeral doles seem to have been waning, the percentage of probate accounts mentioning them in Berkshire, Lincolnshire, and Kent falling to less than half of what it had been a generation earlier.[232] By the 1620s it was becoming more common for testators, like the Suffolk yeoman Robert Hawes, to provide detailed prescriptions for the distribution of charity through churchwardens and parish overseers 'so that there shall be no concourse of poor people at [my] funeral and no dole to be then given'.[233] Such concerns were likely not so much about theology as about good order and the claims of the 'deserving' poor. They may also point to a more general dissociation of sociability between governors and governed in the local context.[234] Nonetheless, both bells and doles exemplify the ways in which issues of social status, local custom, piety, and doctrine were inextricably intertwined in the practice of commemoration. Paradoxically, this compound of the social, ritual, and spiritual may have eased transitions even as it raised anxieties about the pace and meaning of religious change. This was even more marked in contemporary debates about another commemorative issue: the function and utility of funeral monuments.

TOMBS: DEFACERS AND DEFENDERS

The tolling of bells and distribution of bread were the most ephemeral instruments of posthumous memory; the erection of a brass or stone monument the most enduring. As an aspect of a reformed order of commemoration, they evoked, as we have seen, distinctly ambivalent attitudes within

---

[230] S.H. (ed.), *Shotley Parish Records* (Bury St Edmunds, 1912), 105.

[231] J. Atkinson *et al.* (eds.), *Darlington Wills and Inventories 1600–1625*, SS 201 (1993), 141.

[232] Gittings, *Death, Burial and the Individual*, 241.

[233] M. Allen (ed.), *Wills of the Archdeaconry of Suffolk 1620–1624*, Suffolk Records Society, 31 (1989), 363. See also ibid. 423. This was not an entirely new departure. The poor-law legislation of 1536 had criticized 'commen and open doolis', and even before this some testators had ruled out indiscriminate giving at their burial: Duffy, *Altars*, 362–4, 510–11.

[234] K. Wrightson, *English Society 1580–1660* (1982), 223–4.

the Edwardian Church. In the minds of some later commentators, the royal commissioners of 1559 picked up pretty much where their Edwardian predecessors left off, interpreting their iconoclastic brief to include tombs and encouraging amateur enthusiasts to follow their lead. John Weever's 'barbarous rage against the dead' supposedly continued 'untill the second yeare of the raigne of Queene *Elizabeth*'.[235] The Laudian historian Peter Heylin depicted the reformers moving frenetically from the destruction of images of Christ and apostles to 'the tearing off of all the brasses on the tombs and monuments of the dead, in which the figures of themselves, their wives or children, their ancestors, or their arms, had been reserved to posterity'.[236] Whatever level of indignity monuments suffered in the first two years of the reign, Queen Elizabeth determined to put a stop to it by proclamation on 19 September 1560.[237]

It is not clear if there was an immediate trigger for this. The preamble began conventionally, the queen 'understanding... there hath been of late years spoiled and broken certain ancient monuments', though Cecil at one point considered correcting this to read 'partly by credible report, partly by her owne knoledg'.[238] One possibility is that it was prompted by events at Bures, Suffolk, in the latter part of 1559. Here the arrival of the royal commissioners in September had encouraged local radicals to hack down the screens, and destroy the Easter Sepulchre canopy in the parish church. In the process they damaged the splendid monuments of the Waldegrave family, inducing the current head of the family, William Waldegrave, to have the iconoclasts successfully indicted at the Bury general sessions, and to complain to the Privy Council. The affair made a mark at the very highest level. In 1561 when the queen was on progress in Suffolk and staying with the Waldegraves in Bures, Sir William Cecil was invited to come to the church to see the monuments. Cecil was suitably appalled by the damage 'and thought the Reavers therof worthy to make it ageyn at their own charges'.[239] On the other hand, it is possible that events in the capital were a catalyst. Writing in 1584, Thomas Bentley, a former churchwarden of St Andrew Holborn, recorded how in the second year of the reign the church-wardens there had taken up copper and brass from the gravesones, selling it

[235] J. Weever, *Ancient Funerall Monuments* (1631), 50–1.
[236] C. Dodd, *The Church History of England*, ed. M. Tierney, 5 vols. (1839–43), ii. 148. On the thoroughness of the 1559 visitors in general, see M. Aston, *England's Iconoclasts* (Oxford, 1988), 298–303.
[237] *TRP* ii. 146–9.
[238] Cf. a draft of the proclamation: PRO, SP 12/13, 77ʳ.
[239] D. MacCulloch, *Suffolk and the Tudors: Politics and Religion in an English County 1500–1600* (Oxford, 1986), 182–4. Visiting the church around 1618, Robert Reyce found the Waldegrave tombs 'now within these thirty yeares since I first knew them much decayed and worne outt': R. Reyce, *Suffolk in the XVIIth Century: The Breviary of Suffolk*, ed. F. Hervey (1902), 204. Surprisingly, John Weever's description of the Waldegrave tombs in 1631 made no mention of the Elizabethan iconoclasm, noting that 'this church of Buers is very neatly kept': *Ancient Funerall Monuments*, 757.

for 7s. 6d., 'which defacing of monuments in the church in this parish and elsewhere, in others, was at the length complained of to her majesty, whereupon she presently... caused a very godly proclamation to be published through her realm, against defacing of monuments'. Bentley thought the proclamation 'meet to be set up in all churches'.[240]

The proclamation itself characterized deliberate damage to funeral monuments as 'barbarous disorder', and admitted that commissioners in the past had sometimes gone beyond their brief, which was only 'to deface monuments of idolatry and false feigned images in churches and abbeys'. This description did not apply to funeral monuments, tombs, or graves of kings, princes, nobles, or others 'set up for the only memory of them to their posterity in common churches and not for any religious honor'. Responsibility for enforcement was placed on both secular and ecclesiastical authorities. Offenders were to be imprisoned pending the arrival of the assize judges, and then to be punished by fine or further imprisonment. Further, bishops and other ordinaries were at their visitations to enquire what damage had been done in churches, and by whom, and to enjoin offenders to repair it under pain of excommunication. The bishops were also authorized to recover compensation from executors, and to employ surplus revenue from cathedrals and collegiate churches to the re-edification of damaged monuments. A draft of the proclamation with corrections in the hand of William Cecil reveals the fine-tuning that preceded promulgation. Cecil's changes stipulated that the penalties only pertained to offences committed since the start of the reign (thereby indemnifying colleagues associated with Edwardian iconoclasm). In other ways, however, he widened the scope, making it clear that it aimed to offer protection to 'ancient' monuments, and those 'in any manner of place'. Cecil also sharpened its teeth by inviting the presentation of offenders to Star Chamber, and he imputed an ideological as well as financial motive to the iconoclasts, who were said to be seeking 'a slanderous desolation of the places of prayer'.[241]

The secular and political impulses behind the issuing of the proclamation seem relatively clear. Attacks on funeral monuments not only extinguished 'the honorable and good memory of sundry virtuous and noble persons deceased', but also threatened to confuse 'the true course of inheritance' by interfering with the recording of genealogy, lineage, and descent. Disrespect for the sepulchral monuments of the landed elites implied an impugning of the social and political personae the tombs enshrined. The proclamation asserted an unproblematically secular concept of 'memory'—there was a

---

[240] T. Bentley, 'Some Monuments of Antiquities worthy memory, collected and gathered out of sundry old Accounts', in E. Griffith, *Cases of Supposed Exemption from Poor-rates, claimed on grounds of extraparochiality, with a preliminary sketch of the ancient history of the parish of St Andrew, Holborn* (1831), p. xxi.

[241] PRO, SP 12/13, 77ʳ–79ʳ.

world of difference, it seemed to be saying, between the abused shrines of saints and the honourable monuments of the nobility and gentry. But in reality, of course, the issues were not so clear-cut. Monuments erected in the clear light of the gospel might conceivably conform to the new paradigm, but no one could realistically deny that a primary purpose of 'ancient' monuments was to function as a focus for intercessory prayer. This begged the question of whether the commemorative and intercessory aspects of pre-Reformation tombs were identifiably separable—might requests for prayers for the soul, for example, be carefully and respectfully excised? The proclamation seemed to imply not: it forbade the defacing of 'any parcel of any monument', and specifically made mention of inscriptions. This made the designation of the purpose of monuments as being 'the only memory of them to their posterity' somewhat disingenuous, to say the least. The government was willing to tolerate a reminder of popish superstition in pursuit of broader social and political aims. Not all considered this a price worth paying.

Assessing the impact of the proclamation is an extremely uncertain exercise. Later antiquarians hailed it as a magnificent step, but there is also some evidence for a warm reception at the time. Charged with promulgating the proclamation along with one devaluing base coins, the earl of Bedford wrote to Cecil from Exeter at the end of September 1560 proposing 'to proclayme first thon for the monumentes, to take awaye thereby or at the least to aswage the hote noyse of the fall of money'.[242] Yet evidence for the actual enforcement of the proclamation over the succeeding decades is extremely sparse.[243] Prosecutions do not seem to have been taking place at assizes, and given the presently uncatalogued state of the Elizabethan Star Chamber records, finding cases there, if they exist at all, is likely to be a needle-and-haystack operation.[244] Either very little injury to monuments was taking place, or there was no particular rush to stamp it out, an impression that might seem to be confirmed by the extraordinarily lax episcopal reaction to this governmental policy initiative. Although the proclamation specifically charged the episcopate with enquiring into the destruction of monuments, only one Elizabethan bishop, Guest of Rochester in 1571, included a charge to this effect in his diocesan visitation articles.[245] The only other recorded

---

[242] PRO, SP 12/13/48, 127.

[243] In early 1590s, however, it was reported that William Fleetwood, recorder of the city of London 'being commissioner amongst others for the visitation of causes Ecclesiastical' had imprisoned certain persons for defacing the monument of 'Queen Katherine Dowyger' (Catherine of Aragon) at Peterborough: W. Wyrley, *The True Use of Armorie* (1592), 25.

[244] The offence does not appear in the indexes of any of the Elizabethan *Calendars of Assize Records* edited by J. S. Cockburn. P. Sherlock, 'Funeral Monuments: Piety, Honour and Memory in Early Modern England', University of Oxford D.Phil. thesis (2000), 84, conjectures that a 1615 case relating to the destruction of a church window in Wellington, Somerset, 'may be the only instance of monumental defacement brought to Star Chamber as suggested by the Proclamation of 1560'.

[245] *VAI* iii. 335.

response comes in Bancroft's articles for St Paul's Cathedral in 1598: the bell-ringers were to look that 'no idle nor evil disposed persons do break up any pavements or gravestones, or the brasses or monuments upon the gravestones of the Reverend Fathers the bishops who lie buried in the body of the church'.[246] Some bishops indeed seemed more concerned with the threat posed by, rather than to ancient monuments. Grindal's archiepiscopal visitation in 1576 elicited a report from one Gloucestershire parish that there was still 'idolatrie in the church windows and on tombes'.[247] Weever reported that the 1560 proclamation was followed by another to the same purpose in 1571–2, charging Justices of Assize to provide severe remedies, but that 'these proclamations tooke small effect'.[248]

There is scattered evidence to confirm Weever's pessimism. In 1563 a Colchester butcher's wife attacked the archdeacon John Pulleyn and other preachers 'for they had preached such good sermons that they had preached away all the pavements and gravestones in St Martin's church'.[249] Similar expulsions took place at Durham Cathedral, after William Whittingham became dean there in 1563, events recalled at the end of the sixteenth century by the anonymous author of a manuscript known as 'the rites of Durham'. At the east end of the chapter house was the 'centry garth', where monks and priors lay buried along with 'divers gentlemen of good wourship'. But these tombs 'ar now defaced and gone'. Whittingham pulled up the stones on the priors' graves, breaking and defacing those which had any pictures or chalices wrought on them, and carrying the residue away to his own use. He 'dide make a washinge howse of many of them for women landerers to washe in'. The chronicler commented that the dean 'could not abyde anye auncyent monumentes nor nothing that apperteyned to any godlie religiousness or monasticall liffe', and a later continuator added, 'by which act hee shewed the hatred that he bore to the memories of his predecessors in defacinge so rudely their ancient and harmlesse monuments'.[250]

Not all depredation was so ideologically driven, but churchwardens' accounts show a number of parishes selling off old brasses after 1560: Yeovil

---

[246] *EEA* iii. 312. There were reported to be no monuments pulled up or stolen since the last visitation: W. S. Simpson (ed.), *Registrum Statutorum et Consuetudinum Ecclesiae Cathedralis Sancti Pauli* (1873), 274.

[247] C. Litzenberger, 'Responses of the Laity to Changes in Official Religious Policy in Gloucestershire 1541–1580', University of Cambridge Ph.D. thesis (1993), 173 (Compton Abdale).

[248] Weever, *Ancient Funerall Monuments*, 54.

[249] M. Byford, 'The Birth of a Protestant Town: The Process of Reformation in Tudor Colchester, 1530–80', in Collinson and Craig (eds.), *Reformation in English Towns*, 41.

[250] J. T. Fowler (ed.), *The Rites of Durham*, SS 107 (1902), 59–60. Authorship of the 'rites' has recently been ascribed to the Durham gentleman, and friend of Stow and Camden, William Claxton: A. I. Doyle, 'William Claxton and the Durham Chronicles', in J. P. Carley and C. G. Tite (eds.), *Books and Collectors 1200–1700* (1997), 335–55.

received 8s. for 23 lbs of brass in 1566.[251] At St Andrew Holborn, the chronicler Thomas Bentley, who recorded the loss of monumental brasses from the church in 1547, 1548, and 1560, noted that there had been further depredations in 1574–5, the churchwardens 'like ill husbands for the church' selling eleven gravestones. In Bentley's view this was probably illegal 'since therein they do great injury to the dead', would discourage future benefactors to the church, and disregarded 'her Majesty's special commandment, as appeareth in her proclamation for this cause'.[252] Similar developments at St Leonard Shoreditch in the 1580s elicited an equally censorious response from John Stow. For covetousness of the brass, the vicar, Meredith Hammer, plucked up 'many plates fixed on the graves, and left no memory of such as had beene buried under them: a greate iniurie both to the living and the dead, forbidden by publike proclamation, in the raigne of our soveraigne Lady Queene Elizabeth'. But, Stow added, this prohibition was 'not forborn by many, that eyther of a preposterous zeale, or of a greedy minde spare not to satisfie themselves by so wicked a meanes'.[253] Antiquarians of Stow's generation tended to paint a depressing picture of how much destruction of tombs had taken place by the end of Elizabeth's reign. Stow gave details of thirty London churches where funeral monuments had been defaced 'by bad and greedy men of spoyle'.[254] In 1592, after a recent journey 'through some countries of this land', William Wyrley described finding 'many monuments both of burials and in glasse . . . broken and defaced', the work of men 'that taken upon them to be reformers . . . and onely look but into the abuses of things, and do not see into the grounds and depth of the reasons and causes for which good ordinances are made'.[255] Other commentators shared the disapproving diagnosis. Sir John Harington ascribed the stripping of the pavement in a Coventry church to 'a zealous fellow with a counterfeit commission, that for avoiding superstition, hath not left one pennyworth nor penny-breadth of brass upon all the tombs of all the inscriptions, which had been many and costly'.[256] An anonymous writer in November 1600 spoke of 'our own eyes daily beholding the miserable defacing of epitaphs and monuments', and in 1618 the Suffolk antiquary Robert Reyce agreed that tombs 'doe yett remain subject to envy, bitternesse of malice'.[257]

---

[251] A. B. Connor, *Monumental Brasses in Somerset* (repr. Bath, 1970), 81.

[252] Bentley, 'Some Monuments of Antiquities worthy memory', pp. xxxi–xxxii.

[253] J. Stow, *A Survey of London*, ed. C. L. Kingsford, 2 vols. (Oxford, 1908), ii. 75. Weever also recounted this 'by relation of the Inhabitants', adding that Dr Hammer 'ashamed belike of such a detestable act, went over into Ireland, and there ignominiously ended his dayes': *Ancient Funerall Monuments*, 427.

[254] Stow, *Survey*, i. 131, 135, 195, 197, 198, 204, 207, 208 (quote), 212, 220, 224, 229, 235, 243, 253, 257, 260, 261, 262, 269, 274, 284, 294, 314, 319, 322, 327–8, 330, 333, 347, ii. 6, 75, 109.

[255] Wyrley, *True Use of Armorie*, 24–5.

[256] Cited in E. W. Badger, *The Monumental Brasses of Warwickshire* (Birmingham, 1895), 22.

[257] T. Hearne (ed.), *A Collection of Curious Discourses written by Eminent Antiquaries upon several Heads*, 2 vols. (1775), i. 236; Reyce, *Breviary of Suffolk*, 158.

Of all the late Elizabethan and early Stuart cataloguers of tombs and
epitaphs, John Weever was the most thorough, as well as the most pessimistic, never failing to note the churches where he found monuments 'most
shamefully defaced'.[258] Weever contrasted the care taken to preserve the
memory of the dead in other realms with the situation in England, where
monuments were so often 'broken downe, and utterly almost ruinated, their
brasen inscriptions erazed, torne away, and pilfered'. He feared that shortly
there would be nothing left to continue the memory of the deceased to
posterity: 'pilfery and the opinion some have, that tombes, and their epitaphs, taste somewhat of poperie, having already most sacrilegiously stolne,
erazed, and taken away, almost all the inscriptions and epitaphs, cut, writ,
inlaid, or engraven upon the sepulchres of the deceased'.[259] This was hyperbole of the highest order, and Weever's own text suggests a patchy rather
than comprehensive loss. Monuments in towns may have been more vulnerable than those in country churches.[260] But even in London there were
churches, like St George Botolph Lane, where, as Stow approvingly noted,
'the monuments for two hundred yeares past are well preserved from
spoyle'.[261]

There is, moreover, a distinct irony in the fact that the same antiquarian
collectors who bewailed the extent of the destruction provide an invaluable
source illustrating just how much managed to survive. A compelling picture
of the balance of loss and retention for one county at the start of the
seventeenth century is provided by the anonymous *Chorography of Suffolk*,
compiled in around 1602. Unlike some other county historians, whose
interest in tombs was limited to heraldry, the author provided detailed
transcriptions of epitaphs wherever they survived, and noted too where
epitaphs had been 'reaved' (i.e. defaced). Of fifty-one Suffolk churches for
which details of the monuments are recorded, deliberate damage is noted to
have occurred in only ten, in six cases it being specified that inscriptions had
been erased. In most of these places damage was far from comprehensive: at
Fressingfield, Stoke by Nayland, Letheringham, Campsea-Ashe, and Ken-
ton, some epitaphs had been reaved, but others requesting the mercy of God
had been left in place. At Dennington, the author was able to read a
medieval epitaph which had been removed from the tomb 'but reserved at
the sextens house'.[262] Alongside this evidence of apparently limited and

[258] Weever, *Ancient Funerall Monuments*, 286, 294, 373, 424, 427, 430, 534, 539, 548, 550,
628, 637, 655, 658, 730, 755, 756, 773, 820, 825, 826.
[259] Ibid., A1^r, 18.
[260] Weever remarked apropos of Thaxted and Braintree that neither there 'nor scarcely in any
other Church seated within a Market Towne, shall you finde either Monument or Inscription':
ibid. 628.
[261] Stow, *Survey*, i. 210. He made similar remarks about St Olave Upwell and St John
Zachary: i. 281, 305.
[262] D. MacCulloch (ed.), *The Chorography of Suffolk*, Suffolk Records Society, xix (1976),
75, 76, 79, 81, 84, 85, 91, 93, 96, 102.

circumspect iconoclasm, the *Chorography* provides descriptions of no fewer than seventy-eight epitaphs in thirty-two churches containing traditional Catholic petitions for the welfare of the soul of the deceased. Only some half-dozen of these survive *in situ* today, the others casualties of later iconoclasm, or, more likely, of subsequent theft, neglect, and Victorian enthusiasm.[263] This is impressive evidence for the restraining influence of the 1560 proclamation, or for an absence of zealous iconoclastic impulses, and the strength of local social pressures acting to protect ancestral monuments. The pattern is replicated elsewhere: a comparison of the Norfolk *Chorography* of 1605 with an antiquarian collection of the early eighteenth century similarly suggests that present-day survivals represent only a fraction of the epitaphs remaining in the churches throughout the seventeenth century.[264] Between 1619 and the early 1630s, 152 churches in Yorkshire and Nottinghamshire were visited by the antiquary Roger Dodsworth, and for no less than 122 of them (79 per cent) he recorded the presence of pre-Reformation intercessory inscriptions, often in abundance, and on windows as well as tombs.[265] Nor was this a state of affairs unique to out-of-the way country churches. The many visitors to St Paul's could peruse pre-Reformation epitaphs with the characteristic suffix 'cujus animae propicietur Deus'.[266] It is a circumstance worth reflecting on, that great numbers of Elizabethan and Jacobean Protestants met weekly to recite divine service in parish churches, which, though they might have been stripped of their roods, and statues of the Virgin and saints, were still replete with monuments requesting prayers to expedite the progress of souls through purgatory. In East Anglia there were certainly plenty of 'popish inscriptions' surviving into the 1640s for the parliamentary commissioner, William Dowsing carefully to strip away. At Orford he removed eleven such brasses; at All Hallows, Sudbury, some thirty 'brazen superstitious inscriptions, ora pro nobis, and pray for the soul &c' awaited his attention.[267]

---

[263] I have used the notes to MacCulloch's edition to calculate the survival rate of epitaphs.

[264] J. Finch, *Church Monuments in Norfolk before 1830: An Archaeology of Commemoration* (Oxford, 2000), 130. More impressionistically, one can note that the 871 pages of Weever's *Ancient Funerall Monuments* are stuffed with references to 'ora pro anima', 'of your charity, pray for the soul of' etc. See also C. R. Councer (ed.), 'A Book of Church Notes by John Philipot, Somerset Herald', *A Seventeenth Century Miscellany*, Kent Records, 17 (1960).

[265] J. W. Clay (ed.), *Yorkshire Church Notes 1619–1631*, YASRS, 34 (1904). These figure may underestimate the total, as in some churches Dodsworth concerned himself solely with the recording of heraldic detail. Only rarely, as at Spofforth, did he note 'the brasse taken away' (p. 97). The point about windows is underlined by C. R. Councer (ed.), *Lost Glass from Kent Churches*, Kent Records, 22 (1980), which provides numerous examples of intercessory inscriptions in glass extant in the seventeenth century. At Aylesford, the Jacobean herald John Philipot recorded a window inscription urging 'Orate pro animabus Robti a Rowe & Catherine uxori suis', while noting of the Rowe tombs there that 'the scochins and inscriptions are torne from the gravestone' (*Lost Glass*, 7). On the practical imperatives behind survivals of glass, see Aston, *England's Iconoclasts*, 330.

[266] H. Holland, *Monumenta Sepulchraria Sancti Pauli* (1614), B4^v, E3^r.

[267] Norris, *Monumental Brasses*, i. 262.

Theologically dubious sentiments on tombs were not just pre-Reformation and Marian survivals, but continued to be inscribed on monuments throughout the reign of Elizabeth. These usually took the traditional form of a postscript to the biographical detail of the inscription, such as 'on whose soul God have mercy', 'whose soul Jesus pardon', 'cuius animae propitietur Deus', or the like. Such formulas were understandably most common on inscriptions from the 1560s, but did not die out abruptly thereafter.[268] Later examples include tombs at Hornby, Yorkshire (1572); Hambledon, Buckinghamshire (1572); Wetherden, Saterly, and Brampton, Suffolk (1574, 1578, 1585); Coughton and Withibroke, Warwickshire (1588, 1602); Bunny, Nottinghamshire (1603); Brewood, Staffordshire (1606); Turvey, Bedfordshire (1612). In places this must have been facilitated by sympathetic seigneurial patronage (Coughton was the seat of the conservative Throckmortons). The connection is evident in the series of inscriptions executed *c*.1585–95 for the monuments of the Catholic Gage family, which still dominate the church of West Firle, Sussex, each unrepentantly proclaiming 'quorum animabus propicietur Deus'.[269] A late example of the genre is found at Wraxall in Somerset where the epitaph for John Tynte Esq. (d. 1616) noted that he had been succeeded by his brother, the husband of Ann Gorges, 'Quibus omnibus propitietur Deus'. At the time of composition, this may have been technically a prayer for the living, but in context it appears a barely disguised traditional formula.[270] In employing such forms of words on their monument, some individuals were consciously asserting a connection with ancestors or predecessors buried in the same place. The request for God's mercy on the 1566 brass of John Fenton, vicar of Coleshill, Warwickshire is identical to that on the brass of a previous vicar interred there in 1500. The entreaty 'on whose soulls ihesu have mercy amen' on the 1544 monument to Sir Walter Luke and his wife at Cople, Bedfordshire,

---

[268] Examples of this type of epitaph from the first decade of the reign are given by H. W. Macklin, *The Brasses of England*, 3rd edn. (1913), 284; Badger, *Monumental Brasses of Warwickshire*, 13, 48, 53; H. R. Mosse, *The Monumental Effigies of Sussex*, 2nd edn. (Hove, 1933), 120, 121; G. Isherwood, *Monumental Brasses in the Bedfordshire Churches* (1906), 23; *Hierurgia Anglicana*, iii. 155–7; MacCulloch, *Chorography of Suffolk*, 84, 97; Clay (ed.), *Yorkshire Church Notes*, 10, 74. David Hickman calculates that such formulae were present on 30% of Leicestershire and Nottinghamshire tombs from the 1560s: 'Wise and Religious Epitaphs: Funerary Inscriptions as Evidence for Religious Change in Leicestershire and Nottinghamshire, *c*.1500–1640', *Midland History*, 26 (2001), 117. An Essex clergyman in 1561 asked that 'ora pro me' be inscribed on his gravestone: F. G. Emmison (ed.), *Essex Wills (England)*, 3 vols. (Washington, DC and Boston, Mass., 1982–6), i. 306.

[269] Clay (ed.), *Yorkshire Church Notes*, 231; N. Llewellyn, *Funeral Monuments in Post-Reformation England* (Cambridge, 2000), fig. 194; *Hierurgia Anglicana*, iii. 157–9; MacCulloch, *Chorography of Suffolk*, 83, 81; D. Hickman, 'Reforming Remembrance: Funerary Commemoration and Religious Change in Nottinghamshire, 1500–1640', *Transactions of the Thoroton Society*, 103 (1999), 115; Ravenshaw, *Antiente Epitaphs*, 53; Mosse, *Monumental Effigies of Sussex*, 81–7.

[270] Connor, *Monumental Brasses in Somerset*, 162.

was reiterated verbatim in the inscription to Nicholas Luke Esq. and his wife in 1563.[271]

A handful of Elizabethan monuments even retained explicit invitations for bystanders to pray for the soul of the deceased, for example, that of Thomas Ellis of Doncaster in 1562, or Alice Wagstaff of Harbury, Warwickshire in 1563.[272] The inscription on the monument to Thomas Oken (1573) in St Mary's, Warwick, displays at best a confused syncretism in asking readers to 'Of your charyte give thankes for the soules of Thomas Oken & Jane his wyff, on whose soules Jesus hath mercy'.[273] More robust was the 1592 epitaph to John Morgan at Knook, Wiltshire: 'Of your cheriti praye for ye soule of Iohn Morgan Gentleman and Elinor his wife with all thaire progenitors and all Christians amen'. An inscription at Iton, Somerset, gave the instruction, 'Pray for the soule of Nycholas Wadham, which depted oute of this world in the yere of our Lord 1603, on whose soul Jhesu have mercy', and a similar request graced the brass of Rowland Eyre and his wife at Great Langstone, Derbyshire, as late as 1624.[274] Morgan, Wadham, and Eyre were consciously Catholics, but in its final manifestation theirs was a Catholicism that impinged, that imposed itself on the religious sensibilities of Protestant neighbours in the parish church itself, and that provided an uneasy reminder of how all funeral monuments were potentially monuments of superstition.

There was a difference of degree but not fundamentally of kind between inscriptions asking for prayers and those imprecating God to have mercy on the soul. The two formulas were traditionally linked on pre-Reformation monuments, and the latter conveyed an at least implicit acknowledgement of purgatory with its suggestion that the state of the departed soul was capable of amelioration. In an unusual, but nonetheless revealing, case in 1589, Hugh Birde of Burythorpe in East Yorkshire was charged by High Commission with having 'caused a superscription in popish maner to be ingraven upon a stone over his wife as followeth— "Jesu have mercy on the soule of Mary Bird the late wife of Hughe Bird", to the great offence of the godly, hurtfull to the simple, greatly derogatory to the lawes in this time of the gospell and to the evil example of others'.[275] Nonetheless the hope that God would pardon the soul of the departed was a pious thought that seems to have come naturally to the lips of many in late Tudor and early Stuart England. When the corporation of Wisbech in Cambridgeshire began a

[271] Badger, *Monumental Brasses of Warwickshire*, 12–13; Isherwood, *Monumental Brasses in the Bedfordshire Churches*, 22–3.
[272] Cross, 'Religion in Doncaster', 56; Badger, *Monumental Brasses of Warwickshire*, 26.
[273] Badger, *Monumental Brasses*, 44.
[274] Ravenshaw, *Antiente Epitaphs*, 38; *Hierurgia Anglicana*, iii. 158.
[275] BI, HC CP 1589/3. This was not a unique case of the policing of monuments. In 1633 Lady Wotton was fined in High Commission for a 'bold epitaph' on her husband's tomb in Boughton Malherbe church, Kent, stating that he had died a true Catholic of the Roman Church: L. E. C. Evans, 'The Wotton Monuments', *Archaeologia Cantiana*, 87 (1972), 25.

new book to record their acts in November 1567, they noted without embarrassment that the corporation existed as the result of a grant from 'the late kyng of most famous memorye Kyng Edward the sixt whose soule god pardon'.[276] Nearly half a century later, the burial of a Durham Cathedral chorister was recorded in the register of St Oswald's parish with the postscript 'whose soule the Lord Jesu have mercye upon. Amen.'[277] The propensity of people to use this sort of language at the death of a friend was a source of frustration to the Jacobean bishop Gervase Babington, 'a bad custom' which 'seeketh to come upon our tongues so readily'. Optimistically, he suggested as alternatives 'God hath had mercie on him, I trust', 'he is at rest from his labours', or 'hee hath finished his course'.[278] Yet the custom seems to have been endemic. An Elizabethan preacher at St Paul's Cross complained of supposed Protestants who saw no harm in charitable imprecations for the dead: 'What will you have me say, The devil go with them?'[279] Queen Elizabeth herself sent a condolence letter after the death of the Portuguese pretender Dom António in 1595, 'whose soul may God pardon'.[280]

Those whose vocation it was to record the funeral monuments of past generations were well aware that their labours involved handling what some regarded as harmful substances. In a number of places in his *Survey of London*, John Stow noted simply that an individual was buried 'with an epitaph', or gave a partial text of the epitaph ending with an elliptical '&c.' In each case, a complete transcription in Stow's original manuscript reveals the inscription to have ended with a request for prayers.[281] It may be that Stow, from whose house popish books were confiscated in an official raid in 1569, felt a special need to be circumspect.[282] But an apologetic tone is to be found in the work of other antiquarians. William Camden represented the intercessory purposes of pre-Reformation inscriptions as of merely incidental and historical significance. As the Romans had begun their epitaphs with 'D. M.' for 'Diis manibus', so many Christians had written 'according to the doctrine of the time, *Ora pro, &c.*, Of your charity, &c'.[283]

---

[276] Wisbech Museum, Wisbech Corporation Records, 1566–99, unpaginated. I owe this reference to Chris Marsh.

[277] J. Barmby (ed.), *Churchwardens' Accounts of Pittington and Other Parishes in the Diocese of Durham*, SS 84 (1888), 149 n. (Myles White, 1611).

[278] Babington, *Workes*, iii. 124. A generation earlier, John Hooper had similarly objected to people saying 'God have mercy upon his soul' ('as the most part of men doth'), and advocated alternatives: *Early Writings*, 572.

[279] Strype, *Annals of the Reformation* ii. 492.

[280] S. Doran, 'Elizabeth I's Religion: The Evidence of her Letters', *JEH* 51 (2000), 714.

[281] Stow, *Survey*, i. 207, 248, 251, 297, 298, 305, 306, ii. 309, 326, 327, 338, 399, 341, 342. I am grateful to Patrick Collinson for alerting me to this. It may also be significant that references to foundations of chantries were nearly all inserted for the first time in the second edition of 1603: i, p. xxxvii.

[282] A. Kinney and D. Swain (eds.), *Tudor England: An Encyclopedia* (New York, 2001), 675.

[283] W. Camden, *Remains Concerning Britain*, ed. T. Moule (1870), 390.

Robert Reyce cheerfully transcribed 'orate pro animabus' inscriptions in full, but insisted that his interest in recording the details of 'honourable monuments' was not 'for that they doe conferre any profitt to the immortality of the soul ... butt onely to continue the reverend opinion and memory of the departed'.[284] In describing the methodology of his *Ancient Funerall Monuments*, Weever affirmed that 'I conclude the epitaphs and funerall inscriptions ... as I finde them engraven, with a *cuius anime propitietur Deus*: or with God pardon his soule'. He admitted some might say they could have been as well left out, but he hoped his practice would not 'seeme any way offensive to my intelligent reader'.[285] In spite of themselves, such protestations underlined the historic connections between funeral monuments and intercessory prayer.

While Elizabethan bishops generally ignored the question of what was happening to funeral monuments in their dioceses, much greater interest was shown by some of their early Stuart successors, principally, though not exclusively, by those who came to be associated with 'Arminian' questioning of Calvinist orthodoxies about predestination, and with Archbishop Laud's campaigns for 'beauty of holiness'. In visitation articles for Norwich in 1619, John Overall demanded to know 'whether hath any in your parish defaced, or caused to be defaced any monuments or ornaments in your church', an interrogatory repeated by Francis White at Norwich in 1629, John Davenant at Salisbury in 1622 and 1628, and John Howson at Durham in 1629. In his articles for Lincoln in 1634, Laud enquired 'whether have any ancient monuments or glasse windows beene defaced, or any brasse inscriptions, lead, stones, or any thing else belonging to your church or chappell beene at any time purloyned', and similar investigations were launched by Mathew Wren at Hereford in 1635, John Owen at St Asaph in 1637, and Richard Montagu at Norwich in 1638.[286] It is hard to say whether this was in response to a perceived upsurge of iconoclasm, or a belated determination to enforce the law, but it is remarkable that in the first decades of the seventeenth century—the golden age of English tomb sculpture—anxieties about the attention of iconoclasts were far from dissipated. The epitaph (sometimes attributed to Shakespeare) on the early seventeenth-century monument to Sir Edward Stanley at Tong, Shropshire, boasted that his memory would outlive 'marble and defacers' hands'.[287] An attempt to make sure that the monument itself would defeat defacers' hands was made by the archbishop of York, Samuel Harsnett, in 1631, his will stipulating that his tomb was to have 'a plate of brasse moulten into the stone an ynche thicke ... the brasse to be soe rivited and fastened cleane throughe the stone as sacrilegious handes maye not rend off the one withoute breakinge

---

[284] Reyce, *Breviary of Suffolk*, 158, 168–9.
[285] Weever, *Ancient Funerall Monuments*, A2ʳ⁻ᵛ.
[286] *VAIESC* i. 161, 170, 172, 173, 174, ii. 86, 132, 174, 193.
[287] E. A. J. Honigmann, *John Weever* (Manchester, 1987), 70.

the other'.[288] Harsnett had reason to be concerned. The image he chose for his brass was deliberately provocative, the first post-Reformation episcopal monument depicting a bishop fully vested with mitre and crozier. But in the same year an incised slab commemorating members of the Poyntz family at Iron Acton, Gloucestershire was defaced.[289] Also in 1631, Weever published his *Ancient Funerall Monuments*, reporting that people could be heard nowadays 'swearing to pull downe crosses, and to deface or quite demolish all funerall monuments; swearing and protesting that all these are remaines of Antichrist, papisticall and damnable'.[290]

The smouldering set of issues surrounding the permissibility of funeral monuments, their inscriptions and decorations, seems to have quietly re-ignited as the general theological temperature in the English Church rose from the late 1620s. Like the universalist language of the Prayer Book burial service, 'superstitious' monuments represented an itch on the godly conscience which could be tolerated in the medium term, but was likely to be addressed when the opportunity for radical treatment presented itself. The fate of funeral monuments in the civil war years is beyond the chronological scope of this book, but prescient contemporaries were aware of their potential vulnerability as the political and social order shifted. In 1640 as the Long Parliament assembled, William Dugdale foresaw that 'destruction of monuments in churches' might be back on the political agenda, and, following Weever's example, he departed on a tour to record as many tombs and inscriptions as he could.[291] As he did so, the logic of funeral monuments as a target for godly enthusiasts was being strengthened by the suspicion that moves were again afoot to sanction prayer for the dead in the Church of England.

PRAYING FOR THE DEAD

Writing in the mid-1630s, Thomas Browne confessed that his 'greener studies' had been polluted with ancient heresies. One of these 'I did never positively maintaine or practice, but have often wished it had been consonant to truth, and not offensive to my religion, and that is the prayer for the dead . . . 'Twas a good way me thought to be remembered by posterity, and farre more noble then an history'.[292] Browne's wistful renunciation of

---

[288] Cited in Brownlow, *Shakespeare, Harsnett, and the Devils of Denham*, 161. A visitor to Chichester Cathedral in 1635 reported that the brasses were 'pickt out and stolne away' from all the monuments and gravestones there: L. Wickham Legg (ed.), 'A Relation of a Short Survey of the Western Counties Made by a Lieutenant of the Military Company in Norwich in 1635', *Camden Miscellany XVI*, CS 52 (1936), 34.

[289] Lewellyn, *Funeral Monuments*, 261.

[290] Weever, *Ancient Funerall Monuments*, 37–8

[291] G. Parry, *The Trophies of Time: English Antiquarians of the Seventeenth Century* (Oxford, 1995), 216.

[292] Browne, *Religio Medici*, 66–8.

praying for the dead points towards an area of considerable pastoral sensitivity for the Reformed Church of England.[293] Popish prayer for souls was anathema, but speaking to God on behalf of the departed was a deep-rooted human impulse from which good Protestants were not immune. The following section examines the efforts of reformers to find acceptable ways of locating the dead in the language of prayer. As the controversies over the Prayer Book burial service demonstrated, this was a task which required great precision in its execution. 'Prayer for the dead' was a phrase almost guaranteed to raise Protestant hackles—could there be any place for it at all in a reformed order of commemoration?

Remarkably, the Elizabethan primer of 1559 appeared to sanction prayers for the repose of the dead. A collect at the conclusion of Lauds contained a petition 'to grant unto the living mercy and peace, to the dead pardon and rest', and a version of the *dirige* was included, calling on the Lord to 'give thy people eternal rest, / and light perpetual shine on them', and concluding with a prayer for mercy for 'the souls of thy servants, being departed from this world in the confession of thy name, that they may be associate to the company of thy saints'. All of this reflected a much closer reliance on the Henrician primer of 1545 than on the radical revision of 1553, though there were some significant revisions: no prayer for the souls of specified individuals, and no references to the 'remission of sins' nor 'purging of all sins'. The primer was reprinted twice in 1560, again in 1565, and once more in 1575: it took some considerable time for the realization to dawn that these devotions hardly accorded with the soteriology of the Elizabethan Church.[294]

But the degree of scope within that soteriology for some form of praying for the dead remained an open question. The general admission that prayer for the dead had been practised in the early Church could not but prompt contemporary reflection. It was possible, of course, to gloss the collect of the burial service as a prayer not for the departed, but for the living ('that *we* with this our brother'), thus refuting the charge that the Church of England sanctioned any prayer for the dead, but a remarkable number of divines did not wish to follow this path of least resistance. In his 1598 work *A Reformed Catholike*, William Perkins aimed to clarify the points of agreement and disagreement between good Protestants and their papist opponents. On the question of prayer for the dead, Perkins conceded that it was allowable, but

---

[293] Note here that it was the desire to pray for his wife Venetia's soul that seems to have prompted Kenelm Digby's reconversion to Catholicism: C. Gittings, 'Expressions of Loss in Early Seventeenth-Century England', in P. C. Jupp and G. Howarth (eds.), *The Changing Face of Death* (1997), 22, 31.

[294] W. K. Clay (ed.), *Private Prayers put forth by Authority during the Reign of Queen Elizabeth* (PS, 1851), 33, 57, 59, 67; T. W. Drury, *Prayers for the Dead: An Historical Review of Church of England Formularies from A.D. 1536 to A.D. 1662* (1909), 10. On the conservative tone of the Elizabethan primers in general, see E. Duffy, 'Continuity and Divergence in Tudor Religion', in R. N. Swanson (ed.), *Unity and Diversity in the Church*, SCH 32 (Oxford, 1996), 171–205.

within firmly prescribed limits: 'We praie...in generall manner for the
faithfull departed, that God would hasten their joyfull resurrection, and
the full accomplishment of their hapiness'. To Perkins's mind, the non-
specific character of this prayer was a safeguard against abuse: 'to pray for
particular men departed: and to pray for their deliverance out of purgatorie,
we thinke it unlawfull'.[295] A similar stance was taken by Edward Hoby in
his controversy with Higgons: 'we pray even in our churches, for the faithful
departed, *that God would hasten their ioyfull resurrection*, and the full
accomplishment of their happinesse...This is as much as the scripture will
warrant.' Interestingly, Hoby allowed himself to conjecture the result of this
prayer on its objects: 'by which they are not a little relieved'.[296] That prayer
for the dead was a godly act if its focus was the resurrection was reiterated
by another of Higgons's opponents, Richard Field.[297] To James Ussher also,
the commendable practice of praying for the dead in the early Church had
reference to the day of the resurrection, 'that the whole man (not the soul
separated only) might receive public remission of sins, and a solemn acquit-
tal in the judgement of the great day'.[298]

At one level, these validations of prayer for the resurrection of the dead
might seem merely an adjunct of polemical discourse, a hypothetical case to
wrong-foot the papists. But there are echoes of it in the actual practice of
Protestantism. As the language of the Prayer Book burial service slowly
penetrated the consciousness of the Elizabethan laity, so supplications for
the glorious resurrection of the individual dead began to find expression. An
entry in the parish register of St Oswald's Durham for 1592 recorded the
burial of the vicar, Charles Moberly, 'a grave and discreet man...to whom
the Eternal God send a joyful resurrection, and to bee of His elect children in
Christ Jesus his Saviour'.[299] The theological qualifications of this prayer
seem unimpeachable, though it is questionable whether Perkins would have
approved its overtly *ad hominem* character. It is intriguing too to note a new
fashion in the inscriptions on funeral monuments, taking hold in different
parts of the country from the 1570s. This was the conclusion of epitaphs
with such imprecations as 'to whose soul God graunte a joyfull resurrection',
'unto whom the Lord give a joyful Resurrection', 'God grant him a glorious
resurrection'.[300] These phrases fulfilled precisely the same structural role in
the epitaphs as requests for God to pardon the soul of the deceased, raising
the question of whether they provide evidence for the internalization of
Protestant teaching, or for the tenacious hold of traditional ways of thinking
about the dead. To suppose some combination of the two is not necessarily

[295] W. Perkins, *A Reformed Catholike* (Cambridge, 1598), 278.
[296] Hoby, *A Letter to Mr T.H.*, 71.
[297] Field, *The Fifthe Booke of the Church*, 3–4.
[298] Ussher, *An Answer to a challenge made by Jesuit in Ireland*, 216–28.
[299] *Hierurgia Anglicana*, iii. 145.
[300] I. M. Roper, *The Monumental Effigies of Gloucestershire and Bristol* (Gloucester, 1931),
547; *Hierurgia Anglicana*, iii. 157–9.

paradoxical. Either way they give the lie to the suggestion that Protestantism and the abolition of purgatory offered absolutely no scope for an active religious interest in the happiness of the dead.[301]

By the early seventeenth century, however, a number of 'avant-garde' theologians were seeking to go beyond the lowest common denominator of prayers for the hastening of the resurrection.[302] In the van here, as elsewhere, was Lancelot Andrewes, Jacobean bishop of Ely. His private devotions contained 'Heads of Intercession', which asked for 'refreshment and light' for those fallen asleep, petitioned God to grant them rest, and to 'set them in the tabernacles of the just'.[303] In public, Andrewes was more circumspect, but not markedly so. His preferred form for the consecration of a church asked God to 'grant to such bodies as shall be here interred, that they with us, and we with them, may have our perfect consummation and bliss, both in body and soul, in Thine everlasting kingdome', and a similar petition figured in his form for consecration of a cemetery.[304] These prayers for living and dead inverted the customary order of precedence, restoring the form 'they with us' of 1549 which was banished from the Elizabethan bidding prayers and burial service.

One of Andrewes's intellectual heirs, John Cosin, continued to experiment in the same direction. In a series of notes in an interleaved Prayer Book of 1619, Cosin developed an interpretation of the order of burial that would have confirmed the worst fears of Field, Wilcox, and Cartwright. In his view 'prayer for the dead cannot be denied but to have been universally used of all Christians, in the ancientest and purest times of the Church'. With regard to the petition 'that we with this our brother...', Cosin commented, 'the puritans think that here is prayer for the dead allowed and practised by the Church of England, and so think I'. The prayer was justified on the grounds that the dead still lacked their full consummation of bliss, and prayer for the resurrection, the coming of God's kingdom, was legitimate. Thus far many Protestants would have agreed, but more contentious was his view that souls already in heaven 'may have a greater degree of bliss by our prayers', and that (following Chrysostom) prayers for the damned were not necessarily impious. Furthermore, Cosin regretted the abrogation in Edward's reign of a celebration of the eucharist at the burial, which he attributed to 'Calvin's letter to the sacrilegious duke of Somerset'. He saw no reason why the custom should not be revived 'to shew that our Church is not to be ruled by Calvin', and also to 'apply the effect of Christ's sacrifice unto the party deceased for his resurrection again at the last day'. In a later

---

[301] This theme is explored in greater detail in the following chapter.

[302] A label originated by Peter Lake, 'Lancelot Andrewes, John Buckeridge, and Avant-Garde Conformity at the Court of James I', in L. Levy Peck (ed.), *The Mental World of the Jacobean Court* (Cambridge, 1990).

[303] Boggis, *Praying for the Dead*, 218–19.

[304] *Hierurgia Anglicana*, iii. 146.

set of notes in a Prayer Book of 1638, Cosin was slightly more agnostic about the precise benefits that might accrue to the dead through the living's prayers for them, but he firmly insisted that 'whatsoever the effect and fruit of this prayer will be ... hereby we shew that charity which we owe to all those that are fellow-servants with us to Christ; and in this regard our prayer cannot be condemned'.[305] Cosin's *A Collection of Private Devotions: in the Practice of the Ancient Church* (1627) included (pp. 392–3) a commendation for a departed soul that 'hee may escape the gates of hell, and the paines of eternall darkenesse: that he may for ever dwell with Abraham, Issac, and Iacob in the Region of light ... and may rise againe with the iust'.[306] He also brought his understanding of the burial collect into his funeral sermons. That for Dorothy Holmes in 1623 requested God in his mercy to bring us to everlasting joy in heaven 'that we with this our sister and all others departed in the faith of Christ, may have our perfect consummation there in soul and body'. Cosin's sermon for Lancelot Andrewes in 1626 similarly beseeched God 'to grant to him, and all the faithful and saints departed, and us all with him, a joyful resurrection to everlasting life'.[307]

These were suggestive but not unique irregularities in the conventional Protestant patterning of the commemorative sermon. In a sermon for the son of Lord Stanhope, John Wall, Oxford DD and student of Christ Church, ended with the petition 'Sweet Iesu ... raise our brother'.[308] There may have been something in the water at Christ Church, for a yet more overt and provocative expression of public prayer for the deceased was made by another Student of the college, Thomas Browne (not the philosopher), in a sermon in the university church of St Mary's in December 1633. Browne began with a prayer, giving thanks for the university's benefactors, and praying for the king, royal family, privy council, clergy, and university officers. He then invited his auditors to pray for all those 'which are departed hence from us with the signe of faith, and doe now rest in the Sleep of Peace. That it may please him, to grant unto them his mercy, and that at the day of the generall resurrection, we and all they, which be of the mysticall body of his sonne, may be set on his right hand all together.'[309]

In this climate cherished certainties might suddenly appear contingent and negotiable. The Caroline bishop of Edinburgh, William Forbes, regarded prayers for the dead as a 'most ancient and universal custom', approved of their retention in the 1549 liturgy, and blamed their subsequent abandonment on the malign influence of Bucer and other foreign Protestants. While

---

[305] J. Cosin, *Works*, ed. J. Sansom, 5 vols. (Oxford, 1843–55), v. 169–71, 375–7.

[306] Contrast this with the godly rectitude of Robert Hill, *The Path-way to Prayer and Pietie* (1609), 406, who included in his collection of prayers for various occasions 'A Thanksgiving for the faithfull departure of one after he or she is dead'.

[307] *Hierurgia Anglicana*, iii. 146–7.

[308] J. Wall, *A Sermon preached at Shelford in Nottinghamshire* (1623), D9ᵛ.

[309] T. Browne, *The Copie of the Sermon preached before the Universitie at S. Maries* (Oxford, 1634), 10–13.

Forbes did not believe there was any scriptural support for purgatory, he regarded the doctrine as an error of excessive zeal, rather than an impious heresy, a view anticipated by another Laudian bishop, Richard Montagu.[310] Perhaps the most 'avant-garde' statement on this issue was a sermon preached by William Page of All Souls College, Oxford, in 1635, arguing that 'we maie and ought to pray for the dead without any reference to a popish purgatory'. Page's arguments seem almost consciously designed to offend long-established Protestant sensibilities. He argued that prayer for the dead was scriptural, provocatively citing the second book of Maccabees, and he sailed equally close to the wind by seeming to endorse the 'opinion among the auntientes' that 1 Corinthians 3: 13 (a common proof-text for purgatory) suggested all must 'passe through a fire that shall trie and examine us' at the Day of Judgement. Even if prayer for the dead could not be proven from Scripture, it should be observed on the basis of 'the constant practice of the church of God for so manie hundered yeares even from the Apostles to these times of reformacon'. In more recent times, Page noted, the King's Book of 1543 recommended prayer for the dead, as did the Edwardian Injunctions of 1547, and he proceeded to assert that the litany and the burial service contained 'a plaine direct prayer for the dead in reference to the resurrecon'. Page's sermon concluded with some suggested brief forms of prayer for the dead, recommending 'God's peace be with him', or 'God rest his soule', blessings which were in any case 'the comon and comendable custom in most places' (something which, as we have seen, irritated the godly Bishop Babington). In a marvellously archaic flourish, Page urged that the warden and fellows of his college should resume their founder's injunction to pray for the souls of Henry V and 'all departed in the faith', ingeniously proposing that such a step would constitute an argument against purgatory, since 'all souls' comprehended the prophets, apostles, martyrs, and saints who could only be in heaven.[311]

A radical change of tone is also audible in the response of the authorities to the case of the delinquent cleric Richard Carrier, coming before Star Chamber in January 1632. Among the charges against him was that he had said several times since the start of the reign 'that there might be a purgatory for ought he knew, and that it was noe harme to pray for the dead'. Sir John Finch described this as 'a scandalous speech and full of ignorance and deserveth a great punishment', adding that Carrier seemed not to have read Scripture or the Fathers, nor to know that the Greek Church had always opposed purgatory. William Laud, soon to be archbishop of

---

[310] A. Milton, *Catholic and Reformed: The Roman and Protestant Churches in English Protestant Thought, 1600–1640* (Cambridge, 1995), 215–16; D. MacCulloch, *Tudor Church Militant: Edward VI and the Protestant Reformation* (1999), 219.

[311] Bodleian Library, MS Barlow 54, 29ʳ–35ᵛ. Page's sermon remained in manuscript, which explains why it did not become the focus of as much hostile attention as Browne's Oxford sermon of 1633. He had already antagonized the godly with *A Treatise or Justification of Bowing at the Name of Jesus* (Oxford, 1631).

Canterbury, was, however, notably more sanguine: 'there is some molifica-
tion to be had because this is pardoned, it is soe long since, and by way of
argument at table, when, if ever, men are ready to offend, I blame them that
make religion table talke'.[312]

The notions that prayer for the dead was a baby ejected with the bath-
water, and that purgatory was a debatable scholastic opinion, or an essentially harmless topic of dinner-table argument, rather than an egregious
popish heresy whose refutation lay at the heart of the Reformation's identity,
were not of course the only issues dividing the English Church in the reign of
Charles I. But they can be considered symptomatic of the unresolved ten-
sions over history and authority, ritual and meaning, which had hung over
English Protestantism for the best part of a century. By the late 1620s
'Laudians' were increasingly ready to be provocative over this issue, and
their opponents to take offence. The publication of John Cosin's book of
devotions in 1627 prompted puritan charges that he aimed 'to iustifie and
countenance the popish affection of prayer for the dead, which *the Church
of England and all her worthies* have hitherto opposed'.[313] William Prynne
noted with some satisfaction that the prayer for the departed to dwell with
Abraham, Isaac, and Jacob in the region of light had been 'rectified' in
Cosin's second edition 'after great exceptions taken to it and complaint
against it'.[314] Thomas Browne's Oxford sermon of 1633 was national
news. The godly diarist William Whiteway of Dorchester was outraged to
hear in February 1634 that 'one Browne a Master of Arts in Oxford in his
sermon praied for the dead' and got away with it.[315] The issue was not
forgotten seven years later when a committee of divines appointed by the
Lords sat down to consider 'innovations in the doctrine and discipline of the
Church of England, together with considerations upon the common prayer
booke'. The group, which included the veteran polemicist against purgatory
James Ussher, included in its list of unacceptable innovations that 'some
have *introduced prayer for the dead*, as Master Browne in his printed
sermon, and some have coloured the use of it with questions in Cambridge,
and disputed that *preces pro defunctis non supponunt purgatorium*'. The
latter suggestion—that prayer for the dead did not suppose purgatory—was,
as we have seen, a commonplace of Elizabethan and Jacobean anti-Catholic
polemic, but in the changed context of the early 1640s it had come to seem
an invitation to popish apostasy. Inevitably, the committee looked at the
Prayer Book's order of burial, and lighted upon a familiar point of conten-

---

[312] S. R. Gardiner (ed.), *Reports of Cases in the Courts of Star Chamber and High Commission*, CS NS 39 (1886), 91–92, 102, 104–5.
[313] W. Prynne, *A Brief Survay and Censure of Mr Cozen his Couzening Devotions* (1628),
25–6; H. Burton, *A Tryall of Private Devotions* (1628), K1ʳ–M1ʳ.
[314] Prynne, *A Brief Survay*, 26.
[315] *William Whiteway of Dorchester His Diary 1618 to 1635*, Dorset Record Society, 12
(1991), 140.

tion: where "'tis said, *we commit his body to the ground in sure and certain hope of resurrection to eternall life*, why not thus, *knowing assuredly that the dead shall rise again?*'[316]

In the two generations after the accession of Elizabeth I, English reformers sought to deconstruct a relationship of living and dead based on an erroneous theology of purgatory and intercession, and to reconstruct it on the basis of biblical faith. This was a project not peripheral but central to their vision, and it constituted a massive long-term exercise in social and cultural engineering. It also represented a significant intellectual challenge, as reformers were obliged continually to reflect on biblical and patristic sources to refute Catholic charges of 'novelty' and uncharity. The balance-sheet of success and failure here is, however, highly difficult to read. Whose criteria for success should we adopt? By the early decades of the seventeenth century, the Reformation had made significant if incomplete progress in eradicating traditional rituals and practices surrounding the dead, and in modifying or replacing the belief systems that sustained them. But the abolition of the social and ritual idioms of intercession and their replacement with a reformed order of commemoration was neither a swift nor a straightforward process, and it unerringly exposed latent divisions deep within English Protestantism. The weight of the dead pressed on the fault-line between those who felt that elements of past practice were retainable or reclaimable, and those who saw virtually all the media of post-mortem memory as potentially infected with the cloying miasma of popishness. Protestants varied in their willingness to recognize that reforming the relationship of the living with the dead was not just a disciplinary exercise, but one that involved negotiation and compromise with deeply embedded social, political, and religious values, values that structures and rituals of commemoration—such as tombs, bells, and alms-giving—both reflected and helped to sustain. In the process of regulating the dead, more perhaps than in any other aspect of the Reformation, theological absolutes met social and pastoral exigencies in an unavoidable encounter. The conjoining was sometimes confrontational, sometimes creative, and the outcomes did much to give shape to the social experience of religious change as a whole.

---

[316] *A Copie of the Proceedings of Some Worthy and learned Divines Appointed by the Lords* (1641), 2, 9.

5

The Estate of the Dead: The Afterlife in the Protestant Imagination

'ALTHOUGH we generally know that the saints in heaven are blessed, yet we know not their particular state, their actions, the manner and degree of their happiness . . . Christ reveiled to the saints on earth, heavenly things, but not what was done in heaven.'[1] This marginal note from the English translation of William Whitaker's refutation of the Jesuit Edmund Campion's *Rationes Decem* epitomizes Protestant disdain for the papists' fervid and unwarranted speculation about the agency of blessed souls in heaven, and the promiscuity of their association with the living. Yet it was not the case that Protestant theology and spirituality made no effort to penetrate the veil separating the world of the dead from this. In the late sixteenth and early seventeenth centuries English Protestant culture, both learned and popular, gave considerable thought to the 'estate of the dead', the imagined experience of the dead (collectively and individually) in the life to come. This process of orientation took place within an eschatological landscape transformed by the excising of purgatory from the spiritual map of the hereafter. It involved, therefore, a profound reimagining of the afterlife on the basis of a reading of scriptural and patristic sources conditioned by an allergy to concepts of imprecation, intercession and post-mortem purgation. It will be argued in this chapter that the abrogation of purgatory involved not just the relocation of the dead in terms of formal theology, and a concomitant reform of liturgical and ritual practice, but a far-reaching reconfiguration of the cultural and emotional nexus that bound the living to the dead, of the idioms in which feelings, anxieties, and aspirations about the dead could be expressed. The new dispensation threw up questions that were matters of concern well beyond the boundaries of academic theology. How many would now be saved? How would they be occupied in heaven? Did the dead know or care about the state of living friends? In what sense would human bonds of affection be articulated or enacted in the next life? Now

[1] W. Whitaker, *An Answere to the Ten Reasons of Edmund Campian the Iesuit*, tr. R. Stocke (1606), 106.

that the living were forbidden to pray for their dead, and could do nothing to alter their condition, what, if any, were the appropriate ways in which solicitude for the estate of the dead could be expressed?

THE TWO PLACES

In place of the five locations which late medieval Catholic theology regarded as constitutive of the hereafter (heaven, hell, purgatory, *limbus patrum*, *limbus infantium*), the Reformation posited a stark polarity of two places in the next life, often treated side by side in works whose titles promised to reveal 'hell's torment and heaven's glory', 'hell's horror, heaven's felicity'.[2] These were themes that evangelical reformers wanted to write about, but an obvious inference from the frequency with which they were broached in print is that people wanted to read about them too. The nature of the life to come was addressed in a broad range of works, from systematic Calvinist theology to short inspirational treatises and devotional verse.[3] How far it was handled in sermons which were never printed is now impossible to say.

Paradoxically, an almost unanimous conclusion of Protestant descriptions of heaven was that it was indescribable: 'transendent, infinite, ineffable, incomprehensible, and remote from our weak senses'.[4] Yet for the most part Protestant divines did not try to anticipate Wittgenstein's dictum that 'whereof we cannot speak, thereof we should remain silent'. Scripture, in

[2] S. Rowlands(?), *Hels Torments, and Heavens Glorie* (1601); J. Denison, *A Three-fold Resolution, verie Necessarie to Salvation. Describing Earths Vanitie, Hels Horror, Heavens Felicitie* (1608).

[3] A search of the online Short Title Catalogue, using subject terms 'heaven', 'hell', 'Judgement Day', 'Second Advent', and 'Revelation' (not including commentaries on individual books) produced ninety-seven works published in the period 1561–1634 (including multiple editions). This (certainly incomplete) figure, however, represents only a small fraction of the coverage the nature of the afterlife received, in funeral sermons, catechisms, theological and controversial works, and other sources.

[4] J. Rogers, *A Discourse of Christian Watchfulnesse* (1620), 356. See also A. Hume, *A Treatise of the Felicitie of the Life to Come* (1594), 2; J. More, *A Lively Anatomie of Death* (1596), F1ᵛ; I.S., *Two Treatises, one of the Latter Day of Iudgement: the other of the Ioyes of Heaven* (1600), 95–8, 118; C. Sutton, *Disce Mori: Learne to Die* (1600), 104–5; Rowlands, *Hels Torments, and Heavens Glorie*, E1ᵛ; R. Welcome, *The State of the Godly both in this Life and in the Life to Come* (1606), 35, 39; Denison, *A Three-fold Resolution*, 437, 535–8; T. Tuke, *The High-way to Heaven* (1609), 187; W. Walker, *A Sermon preached at the Funerals of . . . William, Lord Russell* (1614), 29; J. Moore, *A Mappe of Mans Mortalitie* (1617), 161; B. Robertson, *The Crowne of Life. containing the Combate between the Flesh and the Spirit* (1618), 372–3, 377; J. Vicars, *A Prospective Glasse to Looke into Heaven* (1618), B5ʳ; L. Bayly, *The Practise of Piety* (1619), 141; S. Crooke, *Death Subdued* (1619), F8ᵛ; W. Drummond, *A Midnights Trance: wherin is discoursed of death, the nature of the soules, and estate of immortalitie* (1619), 91–2; J. Andrewes, *A Celestiall Looking-glasse: to Behold the Beauty of Heaven* (1621), A7ʳ, 19; C. Aslakssøn, *The Description of Heaven*, tr. R. Jennings (1623), 7–8; J. Donne, *Sermons*, ed. G. R. Potter and E. M. Simpson, 10 vols. (Berkeley and Los Angeles, 1953–62), vii. 137; J. Cole, *Of Death a True Description* (1629), 142; R. Bolton, *The Foure Last Things* (1632), 111, 119; G. Strode, *The Anatomie of Mortalitie* (1632), 313.

particular St John's vision of the heavenly Jerusalem in Revelation 21–22, provided some important clues to the nature of the future life. There was a widespread recognition, even insistence, however, that scriptural descriptions of heaven must be understood as metaphors which 'openeth but a little window, through the which wee may see a little glance'.[5] The Holy Ghost chose to describe heaven 'by such things as are most precious in the estimation of man', allowing men to 'conceive of these ioyes of heaven, by taking a view of the inferour beauties'.[6] The Christian paradise was not to be like that of the Koran, in which 'sensual men have imagined the ioyes of heaven, according to their sensual delights'.[7]

A number of writers preferred a systematic exposition. The Scot Alexander Hume thought heaven best considered under four heads: its situation, fabric, and beauty; the company and fellowship we shall enjoy; the pleasures and delectation to be had; the time and space in which the company shall endure.[8] In the more scholastic approach of Bishop Lewis Bayly these were represented as the place, the object, the prerogatives of the elect, and the effect of those prerogatives.[9] But a systematized appraisal of the attributes of heaven ran the risk of bathos: John Andrewes's reflections on its magnitude delivered the thundering conclusion that 'as heaven is a most glorious kingdome, so it is a most spacious and large place'.[10] The difficulties of conveying any concrete sense of the interiority of heaven persuaded some commentators to adopt the technique of the *theologia negativa*, to put across an impression of what heaven was like by stating what was not to be found there—death, disease, weariness, mourning.[11] One of the most cited (and plagiarized) passages in Protestant writings on heaven was St Augustine's evocation of it as a place of youth without age, health without sickness, knowledge without ignorance, security without fear, and so on.[12] Beyond this, Christians were expected to some extent to take the perfections of heaven on trust: 'the saintes would not so earnestly have longed after heaven had they not beene assured of the surpassing ioyes thereof'.[13]

[5] Roberston, *Combate between the Flesh and the Spirit*, 378.
[6] Bayly, *Practise of Piety*, 142; Bolton, *The Four Last Things*, 318. See also Denison, *A Three-fold Resolution*, 541–2.
[7] I.S., *Two Treatises*, 98–9.
[8] Hume, *Felicitie of the Life to Come*, 23.
[9] Bayly, *Practise of Piety*, 142.
[10] Andrewes, *A Celestiall Looking-glasse*, 13.
[11] Denison, *A Three-fold Resolution*, 538; Tuke, *High-way to Heaven*, 188; Andrewes, *A Celestiall Looking-glasse*, 10–11, 19; Aslakssøn, *The Description of Heaven*, 62–3. See C. A. Patrides, *Milton and the Christian Tradition* (Oxford, 1966), 283.
[12] I.S. *Two Treatises*, 114; Tuke, *High-way to Heaven*, A4ᵛ; Walker, *Sermon at the Funerals . . . of William, Lord Russell*, 29; J. Preston, *A Sermon preached at the Funerall of Mr. Iosiah Reynel* (1615), C2ʳ⁻ᵛ; W. Ford, *A Sermon preached at Constantinople, in the Vines of Perah, at the Funerall of the Vertuous and Admired Lady Anne Glover* (1616), 57; Moore, *Mappe of Mans Mortalitie*, 162; Drummond, *A Midnights Trance*, 93; Aslakssøn, *The Description of Heaven*, 76; Strode, *Anatomie of Mortalitie*, 333.
[13] Welcome, *The State of the Godly*, 48.

In general, Protestant writers found hell less of a challenge—an eternity and extremity of torment was easier to evoke, to relate to the real experiences of early modern people, than one of bliss. Many of the same caveats were supplied: the human mind was incapable of comprehending, as the human tongue was incapable of expressing, the horrors of eternal damnation.[14] Some authors insisted that the scriptural language of retribution—fire, brimstone, darkness, the worm that never dies—was to be understood figuratively.[15] Nevertheless, there was a concreteness and specificity about this imagery that encouraged a more literalist approach than was the case with the jewelled city of Revelation. In the Jacobean Church opinions differed over whether hellfire was best understood as a spiritual, corporal, or material fire, but there was a general agreement that it was no mere allegory.[16] Orthodox opinion held that it was the loss of the Beatific Vision that was the greatest punishment of hell,[17] but it was the intensity, and particularly the eternity, of hellish pains that brought forth the most arresting images: the damned would desire death but never get it, like a man being pressed with weights calling (fruitlessly) for more to dispatch him.[18] A further element of the misery of the damned was the finality of their separation from human society, 'solitary in regard of all good and glad company'.[19] Not the least of the horrors awaiting the reprobate at the Day of Judgement was that they would be pulled from the presence of parents, spouses, friends, 'who shall then justly and deservedly abandon them with all detestation and derision'.[20] As we shall see, the translation of social relationships to the next life remained a poignant, if problematic, theme in many contemporary constructions of the estate of the dead.

In many respects, the versions of heaven and hell on offer in later Reformation England can seem highly traditional. As Tessa Watt has shown,

[14] M. Coverdale, *Remains*, ed. G. Pearson (PS, 1846), 205; A. Dent, *The Plaine Mans Pathway to Heaven* (1605), 363; Roberston, *Combate between the Flesh and the Spirit*, 385; Bolton, *The Four Last Things*, 95, 99.
[15] T. Tuke, *A Discourse of Death, Bodily, Ghostly, and Eternal* (1613), 100; Rogers, *Discourse of Christian Watchfulnesse*, 334–5.
[16] H. Jacob, *A Treatise of the Sufferings and Victory of Christ* (1598), 81; T. Bilson, *The Survey of Christs Sufferings* (1604), A3ᵛ, 39–44; R. Parkes, *A Brief Answere unto Certain Obiections and Reasons Against the Decension of Christ into Hell* (1604), 8; Denison, *A Three-fold Resolution*, 397–8; H. Greenwood, *Tormenting Tophet: or a Terrible Description of Hel* (1615), 53–62.
[17] Greenwood, *Tormenting Tophet*, 64–6; Bolton, *The Four Last Things*, 95; Denison, *A Three-fold Resolution*, 386.
[18] Rowland, *Hels Torments, and Heavens Glorie*, C3ʳ–4ʳ; Dent, *Plaine Mans Path-way*, 364–5; Denison, *A Three-fold Resolution*, 420–7; Greenwood, *Tormenting Tophet*, 10, 71–4; Moore, *Mappe of Mans Mortalitie*, 63; Roberston, *Combate between the Flesh and the Spirit*, 388–9; Bayly, *Practise of Piety*, 101; M. Day, *A Monument of Mortalitie* (1621), 68–81; Bolton, *The Four Last Things*, 107–8.
[19] Crooke, *Death Subdued*, E4ᵛ.
[20] Bolton, *The Four Last Things*, 94. See also Dent, *Plaine Mans Path-way*, 367.

descriptions of hell in ballads and chapbooks could be strikingly atavistic,[21] and the same tendency is discernible in more 'elite' sources. Protestant theologians regularly trotted out medieval *obiter dicta*, such as that, in comparison to hellfire, earthly fire was like a painted fire on a wall.[22] Some were not above recycling graphic medieval vision literature, or, like Odilo of Cluny in the tenth century, adducing the roarings of volcanoes like Vesuvius and Etna as evidence of the fate awaiting the damned.[23] Protestant preaching on hell sometimes resembled pre-Reformation preaching on purgatory to the extent that it overtly performed a similar didactic and preventative function: the evocation of hellfire was intended 'not to cast you in, but to make you to runne further from it'.[24] In some Protestant descriptions of the joys of heaven there was little to which Thomas Aquinas could have taken strong exception. Nonetheless, quite apart from the radical surgery which had been performed on the afterlife—the amputation of purgatory and the limbos—other subtler forms of treatment were being administered.

One of these was a growing fastidiousness about pronouncements on the 'geography' of the afterlife: where, in relation to the physical world, heaven and hell were located.[25] Protestant polemic regularly lambasted the papists for an absurd and specious precision about the whereabouts of purgatory and limbo, and it became a trademark of Reformed writings on heaven and hell to warn against 'curiosity' about where they might be situated. Some writers would not even commit themselves to the popularly accepted notion that heaven was 'above' and hell 'below', particularly during the so-called 'Decensus Controversy' when 'puritans' clashed with 'conformists' over whether the article in the Apostles' Creed stating that Christ 'descended into hell' was to be understood symbolically or literally.[26] But fastidiousness about these issues was no monopoly of puritanism. The reports provided for Bishop Neile on the conduct of his primary visitation of the diocese of

---

[21] T. Watt, *Cheap Print and Popular Piety 1550–1640* (Cambridge, 1991), 110–12, 171, 238–9, 312. See also D. Oldridge, *The Devil in Early Modern England* (Stroud, 2000), 66–7.

[22] Rowlands, *Hels Torments, and Heavens Glorie*, C6ᵛ; Dent, *Plaine Mans Path-way* 363; Greenwood, *Tormenting Tophet*, 60; Bolton, *The Four Last Things*, 100. Cf. the 'Sermon of Dead Men', in G. Cigman (ed.), *Lollard Sermons*, EETS 294 (1989), 231 (an orthodox rather than noticeably 'Lollard' text).

[23] Rowlands, *Hels Torments, and Heavens Glorie*, D3ʳ–5ʳ; Greenwood, *Tormenting Tophet*, 17. Cf. J. de Voragine, *The Golden Legend*, tr. W. Ryan, 2 vols. (Princeton, 1993), ii. 280; P. Sheingorn, '"Who can open the doors of his face?" The Iconography of Hell Mouth', in C. Davidson and T. Seiler (eds.), *The Iconography of Hell* (Kalamazoo, Mich., 1992), 2–3.

[24] Rowlands, *Hels Torments, and Heavens Glorie*, B1ᵛ; Greenwood, *Tormenting Tophet*, 'To the Christian Reader'; Day, *Monument of Mortalitie*, 69; *The Sermons of Henry King (1592–1669), Bishop of Chichester*, ed. M. Hobbs (Aldershot, 1992), 210; R. Horne, *Certaine Sermons of the Rich Man and Lazarus* (1619), 81 (quote). In this, Protestant preachers resembled their contemporaries of the Spanish Counter-Reformation: C. Eire, 'The Good Side of Hell: Infernal Meditations in Early Modern Spain', *Historical Reflections / Réflexions Historiques*, 26 (2000).

[25] I pursue this theme in greater detail in '"The Map of God's Word": Geographies of the Afterlife in Tudor and Early Stuart England', in *Place of the Dead*.

[26] Ibid. 118–20; D. Wallace, 'Puritan and Anglican: The Interpretation of Christ's Descent into Hell in Elizabethan Theology', *Archiv für Reformationsgeschichte*, 69 (1978).

Lincoln in 1614 commended the preaching at Luton of Mr Rawlinson on 2 Kings 2: 11, with the qualification that he had been 'too curious in assigning of the place of the abode of the body of Elias before the coming of Xt.'[27]

Another development was a decisive reinterpretation of the otherworldly destination identified in Luke 16: 19–31, the 'bosom of Abraham', where the beggar Lazarus was taken while the rich man went to hell. By the end of the Middle Ages, the dominant trend of Catholic theology was to identify this place with the *limbus patrum* harrowed by Christ, thus locating it within the macrocosm of the subterranean infernal world.[28] The reformers categorically rejected this, refuting vehemently the suggestion that Abraham's bosom could be any part of hell.[29] They often had to recognize, however, that patristic writers had distinguished it from heaven, seeing it as a kind of atrium of paradise where the faithful did not yet enjoy that full blessedness which would be theirs at the final judgement.[30] Some Protestant authorities retained something of this, John Veron writing that Abraham's bosom was a paradise, 'but yet not so perfect as it was afterwards'.[31] Yet such subtleties ran the risk of implying that the afterlife included some kind of 'third place', and English Protestantism was committed to an unremittingly binary construction of the other world. There were thus strong theological arguments for affirming Abraham's bosom as a straightforward scriptural synonym for heaven, and this is the line most Elizabethan and Jacobean divines followed.[32] In a devotional context, the identification of Abraham's bosom with heaven seems to have become almost entirely unexceptional. According to an early

[27] E. Venables (ed.), 'The Primary Visitation of the Diocese of Lincoln by Bishop Neile, A.D. 1614', *Associated Architectural Societies' Reports and Papers*, 16 (1881–2), 48.

[28] J. Le Goff, *The Birth of Purgatory*, tr. A. Goldhammer (Aldershot, 1984), 157–8; P. Binski, *Medieval Death: Ritual and Representation* (London, 1996), 210; P. Sheingorn, 'The Bosom of Abraham Trinity: A Late Medieval All Saints Image', in D. Williams (ed.), *England in the Fifteenth Century: Proceeding of the 1986 Harlaxton Symposium* (Woodbridge, 1987).

[29] The rich man in hell was noted to have 'lift up his eyes' and seen Lazarus 'afar off': J. Northbrooke, *Spiritus est Vicarius Christi in terra* (1571), 6ᵛ; W. Fulke, *Two Treatises Written Against the Papistes* (1577) 58; id., *The Text of the New Testament of Iesus Christ* (1589), 116–17; A. Willet, *Synopsis Papismi* (1592), 305, 609; id., *Testrastylon Papisimi* (1599), 158.

[30] Binski, *Medieval Death*, 183, J. Ussher, *An Answer to a Challenge made by a Jesuit in Ireland*, in *Whole Works*, 17 vols. (Dublin, 1829–64), iii. 291; E. Hoby, *A Curry-combe for a Coxe-combe* (1615), 153; T. Beard, *A Retractive from the Romish Religion* (1616), 414–15.

[31] J. Veron, *The Huntyng of Purgatory to Death* (1561), 314ᵛ. See also Bilson, *Survey of Christs Sufferings*, A6ʳ, 541, 550, 656.

[32] W. Fulke, *A Reioynder to Bristows Replie* (1581), 149; id., *A Defence of the Sincere and True Translations of the Holy Scripture*, ed. C. H. Hartshorne (PS, 1843), 285; T. Becon, *The Catechism*, ed. J. Ayre (PS, 1844), 394; A. Anderson, *The Shield of our Safetie set Foorth* (1581), G3ᵛ, H1ᵛ; C. Carlile, *A Discourse Concerning Two Divine Positions* (1582), 164ʳ; G. Gifford, *A Discourse of the Subtill Practises of Devilles by Witches and Sorcerers* (1587), E2ʳ; G. Wither, *A View of the Marginal Notes of the Popish Testament* (1588), 73; H. Smith, *Sermons* (1592), 536; W. Barlow, *A Defence of the Articles of the Protestants Religion* (1601), 140; W. Cowper, *A Defiance to Death* (1616), 3; T. Cartwright, *A Confutation of the Rhemists Translation* (1618), 191; Bayly, *Practise of Piety*, 113; Horne, *Certaine Sermons*, 60. R. King, *A Funerall Sermon that was prepared to have bine preached…for a certein honourable lady then almoste deade, but afterward recovered* (1552), D7ᵛ: 'Afore Christes comyng, that place was called the bosome of Abraham: but now it is called heaven'.

Jacobean funeral sermon by Robert Pricke, the souls of the faithful immediately 'meete with the Lord Iesus in Paradise: are gathered in the bosom of
Abraham'. A few years earlier, Nathaniel Gilby had told the dying earl of
Huntingdon that 'angels attended to cary his soule to the bosome of Abraham', a theme echoed in many funeral sermons.[33] The deathbed declaration
of faith which Philip Stubbes placed in the mouth of his teenage bride in 1591
included the comforting certainty that the blessed would recognize each
other in the life to come, as 'the riche man lying in hell, knewe *Abraham*
and *Lazarus* in heaven'.[34] The pastoral appeal of this elision of Abraham's
bosom and heaven might also be adduced from the knowing solecism of
Shakespeare's *Henry V*, where Hostess Quickly says of the dead Falstaff, 'sure
he's not in hell, he's in Arthur's bosom, if ever man went to Arthur's bosom'.[35]

All this suggests that it was not beyond the capacity of the reformers to
develop imagery about the afterlife that was accessible, comforting, and
adaptable, sometimes almost tangible in its physicality. A broadside epitaph
produced for Bishop John Jewel by the 'semi-professional ballad-writer'
William Elderton concluded: 'Abraham rendes his clothes, and bowells out
his brest / And sayth to Iuell iumpe in here, and take thye quiet rest.'[36]
Hardly less somatic was the image deployed by Robert Welcome in a funeral
sermon of 1605: as infants rest quietly in their mother's bosom, 'so heaven is
a receptacle and bosome for the faithfull, in which they take their quiet rest
and ease after the sturres of this tumultuary life'.[37] What these and other
descriptions convey is that Abraham's bosom was conceived pre-eminently
as a place of rest and quiet. Some of the implications of this semiology will be
considered later in this chapter.

THE POPULATION OF HEAVEN

Heaven was the most desirable of destinations, but this was to say nothing
about how easy it was to get there. The pre-Reformation dead had been

[33] R. Pricke, *A Verie Godlie and Learned Sermon* (1608), E1ʳ; M. C. Cross, 'The Third Earl of
Huntingdon's Death-Bed: A Calvinist Example of the *Ars Moriendi*', *Northern History*, 21
(1985), 102.

[34] P. Stubbes, 'A Christal Glasse for Christian Women', in *The Anatomie of Abuses*, ed. F. J.
Furnival (1877), 204; G. Downame, *A Funerall Sermon preached at Watton in Hertfordshire, at
the Buriall of . . . Sir Philip Boteler* (1607), 61; R. Carpenter, *The Soules Sentinel . . . A Sermon
preached at the Funerall Solemnities of . . . Sir Arthur Ackland* (1612), 109; J. Bowle, *A Sermon
preached at Flitton in the Countie of Bedford, At the Funerall of Henrie Earle of Kent* (1615),
D4ᵛ; S. Price, *The Two Twins of Birth and Death. A Sermon preached in Christs Church in
London . . . Upon the Occasion of the Funeralls of Sir William Byrde* (1624), 46.

[35] *Henry V*, II. iii. 9–19. For other references to Abraham's bosom used in this sense in
Shakespeare, see *Richard III*, IV. iii. 38; *Richard II*, IV. i. 94–5. See also Cressy, *Birth, Marriage,
and Death*, 384.

[36] W. Elderton, *An Epytaphe uppon the Death of the Right Reverend and Learned Father in
God, I. Iuell* (1571). On Elderton, see Watt, *Cheap Print*, 52, 54.

[37] Welcome, *The State of the Godly*, 34–5.

directed via appropriate channels through the immigration controls of the afterlife: martyrs, and other men and women of heroic sanctity, were fast-tracked into heaven; those who died unrepentant with mortal sins unconfessed were consigned to the fires of hell. More conscientious and repentant sinners who had sought the sacramental aid of the Church came to heaven slowly (perhaps very slowly), via the cleansing fires of purgatory. Infants dying unbaptized had their special permanent place in *limbus infantium*. This elaborate taxonomy was blown apart by the reformers' teaching on justification and election. After death all Christians went directly to either heaven or hell, enacting the divine decree of election or reprobation which, according to the Calvinist orthodoxy prevalent in the Elizabethan Church, had been made irrespective of individual merits before the creation of the world.[38] Moving from the abstractions of theology to the personal calculus of loss and bereavement, pre-Reformation Catholics could be fairly sure that dead friends languished in purgatory, where they could be assisted by the prayers of the living, but in the later sixteenth century the question of where a specific person had gone, and how likely it was that he or she was among the saved, was posed in a new and acute form.

Instinctively, of course, Protestants referred such questions to the rule of Scripture, and Scripture appeared to offer comforting words on this score. St John the Divine saw an 'innumerable multitude' standing before the throne of the Lamb (Rev. 7: 9), while at Capernaum Christ foretold that many would come from east and west to sit with Abraham, Isaac, and Jacob in the kingdom of Heaven (Matt. 8: 11). He also taught (John 14: 2) that his Father's house was comprised of 'many mansions'. Some writers adduced these texts to suggest the copious numbers of the elect,[39] but this was not the dominant exegetical trend. William Alley, the Elizabethan bishop of Exeter, took a depressingly minimalist interpretation of John 14: 2: when Christ said that there were many mansions in his Father's house, he meant merely that heaven was not prepared for him alone.[40] Alley was not alone in taking grim delight in deconstructing texts that seemed to promise open access to God's kingdom. To some Jacobean preachers it was a matter of absolute and relative numbers. According to Thomas Tuke, 'the elect, considered apart simply by themselves, are exceeding many...[but] in comparison of the reprobate and damned are but few'.[41] Henry Greenwood agreed: 'though

---

[38] For the theology of Elizabethan Calvinism, and in particular the growing dominance of the idea of 'limited atonement' (that Christ died for the elect only), see R. T. Kendall, *Calvin and English Calvinism to 1649* (Oxford, 1979).

[39] J. Veron, *The Overthrow of the Iustification of Workes and the Vain Doctrin of the Merits of Men* (1561), cited in E. Disley, 'Degrees of Glory: Protestant Doctrine and the Concept of Rewards Hereafter', *Journal of Theological Studies*, 42 (1991), 87; J. Barlow, *The True Guide to Glory. A Sermon preached at Plympton Mary in Devon, at the Funerals of the Lady Strode of Newingham* (1619), 44; Andrewes, *A Celestiall Looking-glasse*, 14–15.

[40] W. Alley, *The Poore Mans Librarie* (1571), 48ᵛ.

[41] Tuke, *High-way to Heaven*, 32–3. See also Cole, *Of Death a True Description*, 159–60, 174.

the number of the elect be great, by itselfe considered ... yet if it be compared to the number of those that shal glorifie Gods iustice in hell, Alas then a *remnant of Israel shall be saved*'. Greenwood had a clear, if approximate, idea of the order of the differential involved: 'where there is one that commeth to the profession of the truth ... there are ten, yea twenty, yea more, that walke in the way of sinne, in the road to *Tophet*'.[42] Such pessimism was by no means unique: John Denison feared that 'not one of ten, but rather nine out of ten are in danger of falling from the bridge of iniquitie into the pit of eternall destruction'.[43] Nicholas Byfield was sure that 'almost all that wee meete with, are malefactors, under sentence ... unquenchable fire kindled against them'.[44]

Puritan commentators habitually juxtaposed their conviction of the small number of the elect with the complacent presumption which they projected onto the ignorant multitude. The unpalatable facts of election had to be well pondered, thought Tuke, 'because some hath imagined that God hath elected all'.[45] In Arthur Dent's *Plaine Mans Path-way to Heaven* (1605), when the divine Theologus insists that 'there be few in heaven and many in hell', the cavilling Antilegon retorts, 'I am of the mind that all men shall be saved'.[46] Atheos, the simple rustic in George Gifford's *Country Divinity* (1581), is similarly deceived.[47] The Northamptonshire minister John Rogers parodied the reaction of the ungodly pressed to make serious preparation for death: 'this would bee able to fright a fearefull simple body out of his wits, and to draw honest neighbours to desperation ... Shall not wee be saved as our neighbours, and what doe wee desire more?'[48] Samuel Gardiner similarly despaired of the attitudes of 'the common careless people' who, when asked whether they thought they should be saved, 'will wipe their mouths with their handkerchiefe, and say, yea, without all doubt'.[49]

---

[42] Greenwood, *Tormenting Tophet*, 50–2.

[43] Denison, *A Three-fold Resolution*, 430.

[44] N. Byfield, *The Cure of the Feare of Death* (1618), 91–2. Further examples of this kind of extreme pessimism are cited by P. Collinson, 'The Cohabitation of the Faithful with the Unfaithful', in O. P. Grell, J. Israel, and N. Tyacke (eds.), *From Persecution to Tolerance: The Glorious Revolution and Religion in England* (Oxford, 1991), 52–4; J. Spurr, *English Puritanism 1603–1689* (Basingstoke, 1998), 42. Perhaps the hardest line of all was to assert that the 144,000 virgin followers of the Lamb referred to in Revelation 14: 1–4 represented all the elect of God throughout eternity, the view taken by John Cameron, Professor of Divinity at the university of Saumur: Disley, 'Degrees of Glory', 87.

[45] Tuke, *High-way to Heaven*, 34.

[46] Dent, *Plaine Mans Path-way*, 264–6.

[47] G. Gifford, *A Briefe Discourse of Certaine Points of the Religion, which is among the Common Sort of Christians which may be termed the Countrey Divinitie* (1581), 66ʳ.

[48] Rogers, *A Discourse of Christian Watchfulnesse*, 174. See also J. Barlow, *Hierons Last Fare-well. A Sermon preached at Modbury in Devon, at the Funerall of ... Samuel Hieron* (1618), 15, attacking those 'that thinke it the easiest matter of a thousand, to go to heaven'; Bolton, *The Four Last Things*, 26: 'How many ... go to hell with a vaine hope of heaven; whose chiefest cause of damnation is their false perswasion, and groundlesse presumption of salvation!'

[49] S. Gardiner, *The Way to Heaven* (1611), C6ᵛ–7ʳ.

Such comments undoubtedly tell us more about the mentality of puritanism than the mind of popular religion. Recent scholarship has promoted the useful and persuasive concept of a 'Calvinist consensus' in the 'Jacobethan' Church, but has also reminded us that there were Calvinists and Calvinists, and that it was possible to take a less restrictive view of the operation of God's saving grace than that espoused by Tuke, Greenwood, or Denison.[50] Moreover, there was a inclusionary impulse of sorts built into the mind-set of 'experimental predestinarianism' itself.[51] All Christians were urged to reform their lives and develop a sense of assurance of their own salvation; as Samuel Gardiner put it, 'every faythfull man standeth bound to beleeve that he is elected'.[52]

Nonetheless, the logical and semantic drift of the theology of grace to which the English Church formally subscribed made clear that access to heaven was limited to a predetermined group, the principle of selection implying, if it did not necessarily establish, the removal of the lesser out of the greater. As Patrick Collinson has remarked, the doctrine of election, particularly in its developed form as double predestination, was 'a mental structure of binary discrimination . . . It elevated to a cosmic and divine principle that gross over-simplification which reduced the teeming variety of human conditions and types to just two: elect and reprobate.'[53] The belief that the mercy of God would save all would have been regarded as an egregious heresy by churchmen who did not share the precisian instincts of George Gifford and Arthur Dent.

But to insist upon the general depravity of mankind was an entirely different matter from pronouncing upon the post-mortem condition of a specified individual. The sources that explicitly address the latter question, principally funeral sermons and epitaphs, were often markedly optimistic in tone, and display a desire (with varying degrees of ease and unease) to accommodate the ineluctable doctrine of election to a deep-seated social impulse to think well of the dead. It is clear from printed funeral sermons that preachers recognized that important theological issues were involved in speculating upon the present estate of the deceased, but the issue was rarely ducked or fudged. In these texts God's mercy was a prevalent theme. The Devon minister John Preston, in a funeral sermon published in 1615, insisted

[50] P. Lake, 'Calvinism and the English Church 1570–1635', *PP* 114 (1987); N. Tyacke, *Anti-Calvinists: The Rise of English Arminianism c.1590–1640* (Oxford, 1987).

[51] The distinction between 'credal predestinarians', who accepted predestination as a formal theological proposition, and 'experimental predestinarians', who set out to discover how they could know whether or not they were of the elect, is usefully made by Kendall, *Calvin and English Calvinism*.

[52] Gardiner, *The Way to Heaven*, A6ᵛ. Ian Green suggests that 'providing assurance of election was a particular hallmark of high Calvinism in England', citing, among others, the works of Perkins, Rogers, Greenham, and Bolton: *Print and Protestantism in Early Modern England* (Oxford, 2000), 313.

[53] Collinson, 'Cohabitation of the Faithful with the Unfaithful', 54.

that Christ 'came to open heaven gates, and what meant he but that we
should enter in?' Preaching that same year at the funeral of the earl of Kent,
John Bowle declared, 'I will be liberal on Gods part; I will promise heaven
assuredly to that sinner, that doth repent but *one day* before he dies.' A few
years earlier at another aristocratic interment, Thomas Sparke asserted that
everyone 'that walketh before God in righteousness . . . is sure immediately
uppon his death, to enter possession in soule of an everlasting and most
comfortable peace'.[54] Nonetheless Elizabethan puritans like Sparke or Anthony Anderson, even at funerals of the evidently godly, were sometimes
careful to eschew utter certitude in their verdicts: 'of which number (I hope)
you here present are fully perswaded, this honorable person . . . was one'; 'we
may pronounce of him, with good confidence, that his soule doth rest in
peace'.[55] A common homiletic device was to invoke the 'judgement of
charity' that the deceased was among the elect, without usurping the 'judgement of certainty' that belonged to the Lord alone. This sometimes involved
a forensic picking-over of virtues to bolster the case. George Downame's
sermon at the funeral of Sir Philip Boteler adumbrated the deceased's sobri-
ety, gravity, discretion, frugality, temperance, public calling as a magistrate,
and (from Downame's perspective the clincher) his respect for the ministry
('I doubt not to avouch, that the religion and devotion of men towards God,
may be discerned by no one signe better, then by the respect which they have
to Gods Ministers'). He surmised that 'wee may be bold to conclude
according to the iudgement of charitie, that hee is in the number of those
whom the holy Ghost in this place pronounceth blessed'.[56] In his 1622
sermon for Paul Cleybrooke, William Stone sounded even more like counsel
for the defence at the bar of divine justice: 'for besides that there is no
evidence to the contrary, and charity ever more iudgeth the best, we have
also sufficient evidence, wherupon to conclude according to the iudgement
of charitie, that he lived and died a saint'.[57] There was a fine line here

---

[54] Preston, *A Sermon preached at the Funeral of Mr Iosiah Reynel*, C3ᵛ; Bowle, *A Sermon
preached at Flitton*, D3ʳ; T. Sparke, *A Sermon preached at Whaddon in Buckinghamshire . . . at
the Buriall of the Right Honorable, Arthur Lorde Grey of Wilton* (Oxford, 1593), 2. Barnaby
Potter's funeral sermon for Sir Edward Seymour was highly unusual in drawing explicit
attention to 'the small number of such as shall be saved': *The Baronets Buriall* (1613), 18.

[55] T. Sparke, *A Sermon preached at Cheanies at the Buriall of the . . . Earle of Bedford* (1585),
A2ᵛ; A. Anderson, *A Sermon of Sure Comfort, preached at the Funerall of Maister Robert
Keylway* (1581), 87.

[56] Downame, *Sermon preached at Watton*, 61–72, quotes at pp. 64, 72.

[57] W. Stone, *A Curse become a Blessing. or a Sermon preached in the Parish Church of S.
John the Baptist, in the Ile of Thanet in the County of Kent, at the Funerall of . . . Mr Paul
Cleybrooke* (1622), 49. See also Welcome, *The State of the Godly*, 80; Carpenter, *The Soules
Sentinel*, 109; S. Smith, *A Christian Taske. A Sermon, preached at the Funerall of Maister Iohn
Lawson* (1620), 8; N. Guy, *Pieties Pillar: or, A Sermon preached at the Funerall of Mistresse
Elizabeth Gouge* (1626), 52; J. Cleland, *A Monument of Mortalitie upon the Death and
Funeralls of the . . . Duke of Richmond and Lenox* (1624), 23; E. Layfield, *The Mappe of
Mans Mortality and Vanity. A Sermon, preached at the Solemne Funerall of Abraham Iacob*
(1630), A1ʳ.

between strict theological probity and pastoral compassion, a line which some preachers felt needed to be negotiated with sensitivity and caution. Many other early Stuart funeral sermons, however, simply asserted without qualification that their subject was now a saint in heaven.[58] The separatist Henry Barrow sarcastically suggested that for money the deceased would not want for a preacher to 'to tell the people that his soule is assuredly with God'.[59]

If funeral sermons rarely agonized unduly about placing the departed in heaven, other commemorative media typically had even fewer scruples. The issue was unproblematic, for example, in the printed broadsheet epitaphs produced for prominent figures by hack writers in Elizabeth's reign, or in the rather more polished commemorative verse being produced by Thomas Churchyard, George Whetstone, and other public elegiasts.[60] Expressions of certainty also appear in condolence letters, dedicatory epistles, even works of polemic, Edward Hoby invoking the authority of Lawrence Humphrey, 'this worthie saint' who 'now resteth in peace', and Andrew Willet of 'that godly learned man Doctor [John] Reynolds, who is now at rest in the Lord'.[61] There were few more emphatic statements than that made by the London rector and royal chaplain Martin Day in 1621 in the course of a lavish volume commemorating the wife of the printer John Bill: 'The Church

---

[58] Sparke, *A Sermon preached at Whaddon*, ii^v; J. Leech, *A Sermon preached... at the Funerall of the Most Excellent & Hopefull Princess, the Lady Marie's Grace* (1607), 39; Pricke, *Godlie and Learned Sermon*, E1^v; R. Kilbye, *A Sermon preached in Saint Maries Church in Oxford... at the Funerall of Thomas Holland* (1613), 18; D. Price, *Spirituall Odours to the Memory of Prince Henry* (1613), 16–17; id., *Lamentations for the Death of the Late Illustrious Prince Henry* (1613), 4; T. Jackson, *Sinnelesse Sorrow for the Dead. A Comfortable Sermon, preached at the Funerall of Mr Iohn Moyle* (1614), 5; R. Stock, *The Churches Lamentation for the Losse of the Godly. Delivered in a Sermon, at the Funerals of... Iohn Lord Harington* (1614), 'epistle dedicatorie'; Walker, *Sermon at the Funerals of... William Lord Russell*, 61; Bowle, *A Sermon preached at Flitton*, F4^v; Ford, *Sermon preached at Constantinople*, 56–7, 73; T. Taylor, *The Pilgrims Profession. Or a Sermon preached at the Funerall of Mrs Mary Gunter* (1622), 125; T. Gataker, *Christian Constancy Crowned by Christ. A Funerall Sermon... preached at the Buriall of M. William Winter* (1624), 30–1; Price, *Two Twins of Birth and Death*, 39; W. Fuller, *The Mourning of Mount Libanon* (1628), 35–6; R. Parr, *The End of the Perfect Man. A Sermon preached at the Buriall of... Sir Robert Spencer* (1628), A2^r; J. Buckeridge, *A Sermon preached at the Funeral of... Lancelot late Lord Bishop of Winchester* (1629), 22. See also R. Houlbrooke, 'Funeral Sermons and Assurance of Salvation: Conviction and Persuasion in the Case of William Lord Russell of Thornhaugh', *Reformation*, 4 (1999), 119–38.

[59] *The Writings of Henry Barrow 1587–1590*, ed. L. H. Carlson (1962), 461.

[60] F. Newport, *An Epytaphe of the Godlye Constaunte and Counfortable Confessor Mystres Darothye Wynnes whiche slepte in Christ the yere of grace. M.D.L.X.* (1560); R. M., *An Epytaphe upon the Death of M. Rycharde Goodricke* (1562); Elderton, *Epytaphe uppon the Death of... I. Iuell*; J. Philips, *An Epytaphe, or a Lamentable Discourse: wherein is bewayled the Death of... Sir William Garrat* (1571); id., *An Epitaphe on the Death of the Right Noble and Most Vertuous Lady Margarit Duglasis* (1578); N. Bourman, *An Epytaphe upon the Death of the Right Worshipfull, Sir William Garrat* (1571); id., *An Epytaphe upon the Death of the Right Reverent Father in God I. Iuell* (1571); D. Kay, *Melodious Tears: The English Funeral Elegy from Spenser to Milton* (Oxford, 1990), 17–19, 23–6.

[61] More, *A Lively Anatomie of Death*, A2^v; S. Doran, 'Elizabeth I's Religion: The Evidence of her Letters', *JEH* 51 (2000), 714–15; E. Hoby, *A Letter to Mr T.H.* (1609), 73; A. Willet, *Loidoromastix* (1607), A3^v.

may canonize Saints without a pilgrimage to *Rome*, or any such presumptive authoritie: In which confidence, I present the name and memory of this deceased Mistresse Anne Bill'.[62]

The place where the issue was most frequently adduced, however, was in the inscriptions attached to the tombs and monuments steadily accumulating in England's parish churches. A few epitaphs publicly recognized that the salvation of the one commemorated was not a matter of certainty, but of charitable hope and the balance of probabilities provided by a good life. A brass to Robert Chapman (1574) at Stone in Kent observed that 'his soule, wee hoope in heaven doth reste'. A 1579 inscription to a curate of Wakefield: 'Sir Christopher Stead / We wish with Christ'.[63] The epitaph to John Truslowe at Avebury, Wiltshire (1593) noted that, dying, he bequeathed his soul to heaven 'in sured hope to satisfie his debte'.[64] John Stansfield's monument in All Saints, Lewes, recorded that he 'hopefullye ended his mortall life, the 23 day of February Anno Domini 1626'.[65] An inscription on a marble tomb in the parish church of Brundish, Suffolk, echoed the rationalizing to be found in some funeral sermons:

If life in god, & like of good / If love of Christ & eke his word / If strife with vice as fire with wood / If death with fayth in th'only lord / Are tokens sure of endles blisse / Which god prepared hath for his / Then Thomas Glemham here doth lye / Who rest with Christ in heaven hye.[66]

Much more common, however, was for epitaphs to state without any reservation or qualification that the soul of the deceased had gone to heaven. The inscriptions which did this were conventional, but not formulaic. The sentiments in them ranged in expression from the prosaic ('his soul is gone to god / his bones lye in this grave'[67]), to the florid ('whose soule (no doubte) hath pearsed the cloudes & skalde thempire skies'[68]), to the unintentionally hilarious (a 1626 epitaph for the grocer John Jarret in St Saviour's, Southwark: 'To heaven he is gone, the way before / Where of Grocers there is many more'[69]). Perhaps the most common formulation was that, while the

---

[62] Day, *Monument of Mortalitie*, 64. The volume comprised five treatises on memento mori themes, along with illustrations of fanciful monuments, and eulogistic verses in English and Latin celebrating Anne Bill as a saint in heaven.

[63] H. W. Macklin, *The Brasses of England*, 3rd edn. (1913), 245; J. W. Clay (ed.), *Yorkshire Church Notes 1619–1631*, YASRS, 34 (1904), 48

[64] T. F. Ravenshaw, *Antiente Epitaphs* (1878), 39.

[65] H. R. Mosse, *The Monumental Effigies of Sussex*, 2nd edn. (Hove, 1933), 126.

[66] D. MacCulloch (ed.), *The Chorography of Suffolk*, Suffolk Records Society, 19 (1976), 101. Similarly, a late Elizabethan inscription in Hempsted, Gloucestershire, reported that a woman's godly life and blessed death 'were signes to us, & seales to her of Ioyful Resurrection': I. M. Roper, *Monumental Effigies of Gloucestershire and Bristol* (Gloucester, 1931), 333.

[67] F. A. Greenhill, *Incised Effigial Slabs: A Study of Engraved Stone Memorials in Latin Christendom c.1100 to c.1700*, 2 vols. (1976), i. 337 (Thomas Corbet, Nailstone, Leics., 1586).

[68] M. Norris, *Monumental Brasses: The Memorials*, 2 vols. (1977), i. 239 (Alice Walker, Barford St Martin, Wilts., 1584).

[69] Ravenshaw, *Antiente Epitaphs*, 73.

body lay here in the earth, the soul had gone to heaven.[70] Other epitaphs referred to the deceased being lifted into heaven,[71] called to heaven,[72] entering heaven's harbour,[73] going to God,[74] appearing before God in glory,[75] seated in glory,[76] crowned with a glorious crown,[77] inheriting heaven,[78] living with Christ for ever,[79] dwelling 'in endlesse blisse',[80] reigning with Christ and the just,[81] 'entombed in Abram's brest',[82] perpetually rejoicing in the company of saints,[83] 'sweetly paradis'd in Eternity',[84] or simply living or being with God or in heaven.[85] Inscriptions on tombs and monuments also regularly produced two themes which I will address in more detail later in this chapter: the eternal rest of the deceased, and the rising again to eternal life.

Despite the anxieties of some Calvinists, there appears to have been a broad cultural presumption in later Reformation England that salvation was widely accessible. To assert this, however, involves side-stepping a number of imponderables. We have no way of knowing how common it was for people to speculate or agonize deeply about the most likely whereabouts of a loved one's soul. The Elizabethan poet George Puttenham thought that the grief of bereavement was caused in part by 'our uncertainty and suspition of their estates and welfare in the places of their new abode'.[86] It is possible

---

[70] Greenhill, *Incised Effigial Slabs*, i. 337, 344; E. W. Badger, *The Monumental Brasses of Warwickshire* (Birmingham, 1895), 36, 44; J. Stow, *A Survey of London*, ed. C. L. Kingsford, 2 vols. (Oxford, 1908), ii. 357; A. B. Connor, *Monumental Brasses in Somerset* (repr. Bath, 1970), 118, 232, 241; Roper, *Monumental Effigies of Gloucestershire*, 62; Ravenshaw, *Antiente Epitaphs*, 38, 41, 45, 55, 58, 59, 69, 70, 78; Norris, *Monumental Brasses: The Memorials*, i. 239; Clay (ed.), *Yorkshire Church Notes*, 11, 82, 209; Houlbrooke, *Death*, 352.
[71] Ravenshaw, *Antiente Epitaphs*, 29.
[72] Badger, *Monumental Brasses of Warwickshire*, 22; Roper, *Monumental Effigies of Gloucestershire*, 646.
[73] Ravenshaw, *Antiente Epitaphs*, 64.
[74] Ibid. 46; Macklin, *Brasses of England*, 280.
[75] Badger, *Monumental Brasses of Warwickshire*, 44.
[76] G. Isherwood, *Monumental Brasses in the Bedfordshire Churches* (1906), 32.
[77] Macklin, *Brasses of England*, 274; Greenhill, *Incised Effigial Slabs*, i. 341; Clay (ed.), *Yorkshire Church Notes*, 203.
[78] Ravenshaw, *Antiente Epitaphs*, 63.
[79] Greenhill, *Incised Effigial Slabs*, i. 333, 338; Connor, *Monumental Brasses in Somerset*, 242; R. H. D'Elboux (ed.), *The Monumental Brasses of Essex*, 2 vols. (Ashford, 1948–51), i. 47.
[80] Ravenshaw, *Antiente Epitaphs*, 60, 34; Connor, *Monumental Brasses in Somerset*, 317; Clay (ed.), *Yorkshire Church Notes*, 161.
[81] Greenhill, *Incised Effigial Slabs*, i. 340; Ravenshaw, *Antiente Epitaphs*, 27; Connor, *Monumental Brasses in Somerset*, 32.
[82] Isherwood, *Monumental Brasses*, 18; Norris, *Monumental Brasses: The Memorials*, i. 240.
[83] Badger, *Monumental Brasses of Warwickshire*, 59.
[84] Ravenshaw, *Antiente Epitaphs*, 74
[85] Stow, *Survey*, i. 212, 283; Ravenshaw, *Antiente Epitaphs*, 27, 42, 47, 52, 53, 55, 59, 60, 69; Mosse, *Monumental Effigies of Sussex*, 169; Clay (ed.), *Yorkshire Church Notes*, 201; Greenhill, *Incised Effigial Slabs*, i. 343; MacCulloch, *Chorography of Suffolk*, 100.
[86] G. Puttenham, *The Arte of English Poesie*, ed. G. Willock and A. Walker (Cambridge, 1936), 48.

that optimistic assertions, in epitaphs and other places, of the blessed estate of the departed functioned to offset deep-seated anxieties on this score, but this seems an unnecessarily counter-intuitive reading of the evidence. Certainly, we know there were those who believed themselves to be damned, although, almost by definition, this was a pathological condition.[87] To despair of one's salvation was not the act of a faithful Christian; doubtfulness of salvation was presented as a characteristic of popery.[88] After all, the preamble concerning the soul which began nearly every will in this period ('I bequeath my soule into the handes of Almighty God my maker'[89]) was predicated on the belief that God would accept rather than reject it. The fact that such preambles were conventional or formulaic reinforces rather than undermines the impression of a religious culture that surmised that many were called, and many were chosen. It is almost certainly premature to speak of a 'decline of hell' in this period, but orthodox Protestantism clearly struggled to reconcile its conception of God's mercy with its insistence on God's justice. A paradoxical message was woven into the reformed liturgy itself, the burial rite of the Book of Common Prayer committing each body to the ground 'in sure and certain hope of the resurrection to eternal life'. As we have seen, the passage was deeply offensive to puritan sensibilities, as it appeared to promise salvation to 'Papist, or Atheist, Heretique, Usurer, or Whoremonger, good or badde'.[90] Here, not uniquely, pastoral imperatives coexisted in uneasy tension with the apparent logic of the Church's theology of grace.

In another area, however, theology took the lead in casting wider the net of God's mercy, bringing in a whole category of persons who before the Reformation had been ruled inadmissible as candidates for salvation: infants dying before they could receive baptism. There was no absolute agreement as to the purpose and effect of baptism in the Elizabethan and early Stuart Church. From a high Calvinist perspective, sacraments did not confer, but merely confirmed prevenient grace.[91] In the formulation of the Swiss reformer Pierre Viret, no man's salvation was tied to the visible signs, 'but

---

[87] Some of the patients of the proto-psychotherapist Richard Napier suffered from crippling anxiety about whether they could be saved, but their experience can hardly have been normative, any more than that of the London apprentice Nehemiah Wallington, author of ten suicide attempts because he took lustful feelings as a sign of reprobation: M. MacDonald, *Mystical Bedlam* (Cambridge, 1981), 220–1, 134; P. Seaver, *Wallington's World: A Puritan Artisan in Seventeenth-Century London* (1985), 22–3.

[88] T. Becon, *The Sick Man's Salve*, in *Prayers and Other Pieces*, ed. J. Ayre (PS, 1844), 174–5; J. Bridges, *A Sermon, preached at Paules Crosse on the Monday in Whitson weeke Anno Domini 1571* (1573), 33–6; T. White, *A Godlie Sermon preached the xxi. day of Iune 1586 at Pensehurst in Kent* (1586), B8ᵛ; Gardiner, *The Way to Heaven*, B3ᵛ.

[89] Will of Bray Rolfe, Sarratt, Hertfordshire (1606), typical of countless others: printed in W. Coster, *Family and Kinship in England 1450–1800* (2001), 119.

[90] A. Peel (ed.), *The Seconde Parte of a Register*, 2 vols. (Cambridge, 1915), i. 210, 242, ii. 204, 222. See also J. Maltby, *Prayer Book and People in Elizabethan and Early Stuart England* (Cambridge, 1998), 61–2.

[91] W. Perkins, *A Golden Chaine* (Cambridge, 1600), 152.

dependeth of the only election and grace of God ... for he may sanctifie them even in their mothers bellie'.[92] Some 'conformist' Protestants, however, worried about the devaluation of the sacrament implicit in such formulations and were more inclined to see baptism as possessing a regenerative role on its own account.[93] There was broad agreement, however, that while the salvation of unbaptized infants could not be guaranteed, it certainly could not *ipso facto* be disallowed.[94]

Few, of whatever shade of theological opinion, would have found much to object to in Richard Hooker's statement that, since grace was not absolutely tied to the sacraments, 'it is not to be misliked that men in charitable presumption do gather a great likelihood of their salvation'.[95] This position had been anticipated in the visitation injunctions of Bishop Barnes of Durham, who instructed ministers in his diocese to tell their parishioners that such infants were 'to be well hoped of', and were to be allowed burial in consecrated ground, though without ringing or other divine service.[96] As the Catholic John Brerely noted disapprovingly in 1620, 'it be now an ordinary opinion among Protestants that children borne of faithful parents dying without baptisme may be saved'.[97]

One advantage of this position was that it enabled Protestant controversialists to claim the moral high ground in their disputations with Catholics. In teaching that there could be no admission to heaven without the sacrament of baptism, Rome stood accused of gratuitous callousness: 'O cruell sentence, and bloudie decree'; 'a wicked and barbarous opinion'; 'this so presumptuous and cruel doctrine against children'; 'a cruell religion, that sends poore infants remedilesly unto the eternall paines of hell; for want of that which they could not live to desire'.[98] That *limbus infantium* was part

---

[92] P. Viret, *A Christian Instruction*, tr. J. Shoute (1573), 35. For other denials that baptism was a prerequisite of salvation, see Carlile, *Discourse Concerning Two Divine Positions* (1582), 95^{r-v}, 159^{r-v}; W. Hubbock, *An Apologie of Infants ... proving, by the revealed will of God, that children prevented by death of their baptisme, by Gods election, may be saved* (1595), *passim*; Whitaker, *Answere to the Ten Reasons*, 241.

[93] I. Green, *The Christians' ABC: Catechisms and Catechizing in England c.1530–1740* (Oxford, 1996), 532; Tyacke, *Anti-Calvinists*, 15–16; Cressy, *Birth, Marriage, and Death*, 114–15; Houlbrooke, *Death*, 49.

[94] During Neile's visitation of Lincoln in 1614, the clerical table-talk at Stony Stratford turned on 'whether children dying before baptisme might be saved? The affirmative was maintained—and the old distinction was aledged, viz. That baptisme was necessary only ex necessitate praecepti, and not ex necessitate medii': Venables (ed.), 'Primary Visitation of the Diocese of Lincoln', 48.

[95] R. Hooker, *Of the Laws of Ecclesiastical Polity*, ed. C. Morris, 2 vols. (1907), ii. 248–9.

[96] *EEA* ii. 73.

[97] J. Brerely, *Sainct Austines Religion* (n.p., 1620), 71.

[98] Hubbock, *Apologie of Infants*, 9; Whitaker, *Answere to the Ten Reasons*, 241; P. Du Moulin, *The Waters of Siloe. To Quench the Fire of Purgatory*, tr. I.B. (Oxford, 1612), 26; J. Hall, *The Peace of Rome* (1609), 33–4. See also P. Viret, *The Christian Disputations*, tr. J. Brooke (1579), 30^r. That 'children dying without baptism be damned' was one of the propositions a Catholic was called upon to renounce in conference with William White in the 1570s: Peel (ed.), *Seconde Parte*, i. 102.

of hell in a rather technical sense (there was loss of the Beatific Vision, but none of the torments) cut little ice. William Hubbock mocked the doctrine as 'some drop of mercie, an easie hell... a hell not so bad as for the actual sinners'.[99] John Northbrooke thought that the concept of limbo was 'not onely to the great derogation of Gods mercie, but also to the great discomforting of the poore seely parentes'.[100]

The attitudes of these bereaved parents to the theological changes associated with baptism (and its omission) are a moot point, and difficult to reconstruct with any degree of certainty. The earliest attempts of reformers to undermine popular faith in the popish efficacy of baptism met considerable resistance. The insistence of the first Edwardian Prayer Book that baptisms should not be celebrated on weekdays provoked the south-western rebels of 1549 to demand that they should.[101] It is likely that parental anxieties about the fate of unbaptized infants receded only slowly. A preacher at Paul's Cross in 1577 attacked fellow-Protestants who still held to 'patches of popery', such as 'that infants unbaptized and dead, cannot but be damned'.[102] As the researches of David Cressy and Judith Maltby have shown, Elizabethan and Jacobean ministers who were negligent in administering the sacrament of baptism, and who allowed children to die unchristened, could become the objects of considerable parochial opprobrium.[103] On the other hand, Will Coster's work on parish registers has identified suggestive changes in meaning associated with the term 'chrisom child', which implied innocence and purity. In the early sixteenth century, this signified a baby who had died after being baptized, but in some parishes from the middle of Elizabeth's reign it was coming to be applied to unbaptized infants.[104] Registers have also been used to show that in one London parish at least (St Peter Cornhill), the gap between birth and baptism was gradually widening towards the end of the sixteenth century.[105]

While anxieties about the salvation of unbaptized infants appear to have been slowly and unevenly assuaged in later Reformation England, there are indications that not many doubted that children surviving a few years longer were assured of a place in heaven. Effigial tombs of the early seventeenth century sometimes depict them (particularly those under 7) adorned with the martyr's palm, an iconographical token of their identification with the Holy

[99] Hubbock, *Apologie of Infants*, 38.
[100] Northbrooke, *Spiritus est Vicarius Christi*, 16ʳ.
[101] A. Fletcher and D. MacCulloch, *Tudor Rebellions*, 4th edn. (1997), 140.
[102] J. Strype, *Annals of the Reformation*, 4 vols. (1735–8), ii. 492
[103] Cressy, *Birth, Marriage, and Death*, 115–16; Maltby, *Prayer Book and People*, 52–6. See also Peel (ed.), *Seconde Parte*, ii. 45.
[104] W. Coster, 'Tokens of Innocence: Infant Baptism, Death and Burial in Early Modern England', in *Place of the Dead*.
[105] B. M. Berry and R. S. Schofield, 'Age at Baptism in Pre-Industrial England', *Population Studies*, 25 (1971), 462.

Innocents slaughtered by Herod.[106] Epitaphs on these and other memorials of young children often assert categorically that their souls have ascended to heaven.[107] The same is true of the very few printed funeral sermons which commemorate infants. George Jay's heart-rending account of Mary Villiers, eldest daughter of the earl of Anglesey, who died before her third birthday in 1626, sought to comfort her parents with the reflection that 'this blessed childe is not lost but prefferr'd, her soule hath exchang'd a house of clay for a kingdome of glory, and having broken prison, hath left an unquiet habitation to enjoy a perpetuity of rest'; they were not to mourn excessively: 'they know she lives, & triumphs in heaven'.[108]

DEATH, POPERY, AND THE ANCESTORS

In contemplating the place in the next life of children prematurely removed from this one, the theological interpenetrated the personal in the most intense way. Such infants must have represented individual bereavement of the sharpest kind, as well as a dashing of dynastic and familial aspirations, the broken shafts of that 'arrow of family history' spoken of by Natalie Zemon Davis.[109] But what of those who had pulled the bow-strings of family progress—ancestors, near or distant? Apart from anyone who could claim consanguinal as opposed to spiritual descent from that faithful remnant of the Lollards, all Protestant Englishmen and women sprang from papist stock. Elizabethan Protestants were likely to have grandparents, if not parents, who had lived and died in popery. Were these by definition damned souls tormented in hellfire, or could hope be reasonably expressed of their good estate in the next life? Would faithful professors be able to meet their ancestors in heaven?

This was a question on the table almost from the moment that Henry VIII broke with Rome. Writing in 1536 Thomas Starkey welcomed the enlightenment that had led his country to throw off the papal yoke, yet he insisted that it was wrong to suppose 'all our forefathers, whiche have ben obedient therto this. vii. C. yeres therfore be damned . . . caste into the depe pytte of

---

[106] J. Wilson, 'Holy Innocents: Some Aspects of the Iconography of Children on English Renaissance Tombs', *Church Monuments*, 5 (1990).

[107] Ibid. 57, 59; Mosse, *Monumental Effigies of Sussex*, 34, 123; Greenhill, *Incised Effigial Slabs*, i. 346, 347; W. Lack *et al.* (eds.), *The Monumental Brasses of Berkshire* (1993), 165.

[108] G. Jay, *A Sermon preacht at the Funerall of the Lady Mary Villiers* (1626), 24–5. See also the (unsurprising) affirmations of the child's salvation in Leech, *A Sermon . . . at the Funerall of the Most Excellent & Hopefull Princess, the Lady Marie's Grace*, 39 (appended elegies), A2ᵛ, E2ʳ.

[109] N. Z. Davis, 'Ghosts, Kin, and Progeny: Some Features of Family Life in Early Modern France', *Daedalus* 106/2 (1977), 103. The view of Lawrence Stone, *The Family, Sex and Marriage in England, 1500–1800* (1977), that early modern parents did not form emotional bonds with young infants, has been largely discredited. See Coster, 'Tokens of Innocence', 266–7.

hell'.[110] The evangelical author Nicholas Wyse came to a similar answer to the question 'Are all our fathers lost?' He had no doubt that many who did not know the straight path to Christ would in the end obtain his mercy.[111] But not all were so sanguine about this. In May 1537 there was an acrimonious exchange about religion in Rotherham, Yorkshire, between the conservative parish clerk William Ingram, and the radical schoolmaster William Senes. When Ingram protested that he believed as his father had done, Senes retorted, 'Thy father was a lyer and ys in helle, and so ys my father in hell also. My father never knewe scrypture and now yt is cum forthe.'[112] The Marian pamphleteer and polemicist Miles Huggarde aimed a shrewd blow in demanding of his opponents, 'Thynk you to be saved more then your parents, or doe you iudge them already condemped?'[113]

This was a question some Protestants preferred not to answer. Preaching at Stamford in November 1550, Hugh Latimer dismissed the issue of 'what is become of our forefathers' as 'a vain and unprofitable question...whatsoever they did, let us do well...God knoweth his elect, and diligently watcheth and keepeth them'.[114] Similarly, in 1577 William Fulke remarked, apropos of medieval intercessory institutions, 'whether the builders of such places, be saved or damned, it perteineth not to us to iudge, nor to enquire'.[115] Yet the regularity with which the issue crops up in contemporary sources suggests it was one that Protestant authorities could not afford to ignore or sideline. Across the spectrum of churchmanship, the topos was regarded as a matter of genuine engagement with popular concerns: 'What say you then of all our forefathers in the long time of popery? Are they all without peace?' 'Now if any man aske, what is then become of all those, that either now die, or in times past are dead in places where Popery is, or hath beene professed?'[116] The issue was recognized as a minefield for Protestant controversialists. Archbishop Toby Mathew believed that the enemies of the Church of England entangled people in no 'one quiddity, or cavil, more than in that particular'; Thomas Morton's experience with papists identified it as 'the greatest barre and hinderance unto us, for their conversion'.[117]

---

[110] T. Starkey, *An Exhortation to the People, Instructynge them to Unitie and Obedience* (1536), 6ᵛ, 17ʳ.

[111] N. Wyse, *A Consolacyon for Chrysten People to Repayre Agayn the Lordes Temple* (1538), E2ʳ.

[112] PRO, SP 1/123, 202ᵛ (*LP* xii (2), 435).

[113] M. Huggarde, *The Displaying of the Protestantes* (1556), 118.

[114] H. Latimer, *Sermons*, ed. G. E. Corrie (PS, 1844), 305.

[115] Fulke, *Two Treatises*, 341.

[116] Anderson, *Shield of our Safetie*, K1ʳ; M. Sutcliffe, *An Abridgement or Survey of Poperie* (1606), 327–8.

[117] A. Milton, *Catholic and Reformed: The Roman and Protestant Churches in English Protestant Thought, 1600–1640* (Cambridge, 1995), 285 and n. See Viret, *Christian Disputations*, 273ᵛ: 'the question which is made dayly, touching the salvation or dampnation of our predecessours which have lived in errour and ignoraunce'.

In spite of the difficulties the question posed, and the hostages to fortune it threatened to create, there was an emergent consensus in the Elizabethan and Jacobean Church that there was no fundamental reason why some, perhaps very many, of the natural forebears of its Protestant members might not have been saved, despite rather than because of their membership of a corrupt Church. God either forgave their invincible ignorance, or, in so far as they could, they actually evinced faith in Christ alone.[118] In his sermon at the Temple in March 1586, Richard Hooker preached that 'we may hope that thousands of our fathers living in popish superstitions might be saved'.[119] As Anthony Milton has shown, such apparent magnanimity was in part a polemical device against contemporary papist opponents. In the work of Jacobean divines such as Richard Field or George Carleton, the Council of Trent could be portrayed as the final triumph of a corrupting 'papalist faction' which had not so totally dominated the medieval Church that the means of salvation had been utterly unavailable within it. This also had the added bonus of providing a partial answer to the perennial charge 'Where was your Church before Luther?'[120]

Although a wide spectrum of Protestant opinion could agree that Catholics living and dying before the time of Luther might have been the recipients of God's mercy, much more controversial was the question of whether papists dying after the onset of the Reformation might be numbered among the elect. Logically, the corollary of allowing the possibility of salvation to pre-Reformation Catholics (who had no opportunity to discern the truth in religion) was to deny it to those of the Counter-Reformation.[121] Preachers at funerals sometimes took the occasion to put their auditors straight on this score. Speaking in 1585 at the funeral of the earl of Bedford on the familiar text of Revelation 14: 13 ('Blessed are they that die in the Lord'), Thomas Sparke anticipated that some will say that 'both Papist and Protestant may seeme to be such as die in the Lorde. For both professe faith in Christ, and labour to shew their faith by their works.' He conceded that 'it may seem so to a simple man', but it was far otherwise.[122] Twenty years later, at the funeral of Sir Philip Boteler, George Downame asserted that 'whosoever liveth and dieth a resolute and absolute Papist, acknowledging the Popes supremacie, professing the Antichristian faith, and practising the idolatris and superstitions of the apostatical Church of Rome; *He shall drinke of the*

---

[118] Anderson, *Shield of our Safetie*, K1ʳ; Sutcliffe, *Survey of Poperie*, 327–8; T. Gataker, *Abrahams Decease* (1627), 57–60. Haranguing his contemporaries for their lukewarmness in comparison to the charitable achievements of earlier centuries, Philip Stubbes thought it likely that 'our good forefathers . . . shall go before us into the kingdome of heaven': *A Motive to Good Workes* (1593), A5ʳ.

[119] Hooker, *Laws of Ecclesiastical Polity*, i. 39.

[120] Milton, *Catholic and Reformed*, 160–1, 285–9.

[121] Hooker's Temple sermon was denounced by the puritan Walter Travers on the grounds that it seemed to concede the possibility of salvation in the post-Reformation popish church: Milton, *Catholic and Reformed*, 286.

[122] Sparke, *Sermon preached at Cheanies*, 30–1.

wine of Gods wrath...whereby is meant everlasting damnation.' He
accepted that some might find it hard that men 'being either terrified by
the crueltie of Antichrist, or seduced by his craft, to ioyne with him, shal
everlastingly bee tormented in fire and brimstone', but the teaching of the
Holy Spirit was that it was impossible for the elect ever to be finally
seduced.[123] This hard line was ameliorated somewhat by Mathew Sutcliffe
in his *Abridgement or Survey of Poperie* (1606): 'We hope also, that many
there are among the papists now, which conform themselves to them in
outward ceremonies, and yet beleeve not the errors of Popery positively,
but hold themselves to the old Apostolike faith, and of these mens salvation
we have no cause to despaire.'[124]

While Protestants agonized over whether they could envisage papists, past
or present, securing a place in heaven, Catholic controversialists were happy
to engage in point-scoring on the theme. A chapter headed 'Our Auncestors
saved, and theirs damned' in Richard Bristow's purgatory treatise of 1580
argued that salvation was so certain in the Roman Catholic Church 'that the
Protestantes themselves dare not say, our people to have been damned for so
many hundred yeares as they lived and dyed in our side'.[125] The point was
developed by William Wright in *A Briefe Treatise in which, is made playne,
that Catholikes Living and Dying in their Profession, may be Saved, by the
iudgement of the most famous and learned Protestants that ever were* (St
Omer, 1623). Appended was 'A Note of fifty Kings & Queenes of Great
Britany, accounted Saints, & their memories celebrated for such, by our
Catholike Forefathers; and this by the testimony of Protestants themselves.'
The allusion to royal ancestors was a shrewd one, touching a point of
particular Protestant sensitivity. No one wished even to hint that the illustrious forebears of Elizabeth Tudor and James Stuart might be roasting in
hellfire, even when the latter's most immediate ancestor was that champion
of popery, Mary Queen of Scots.[126] Conversely, Protestant controversialists
were outraged when Catholic opponents insinuated that the late Queen
Elizabeth was unlikely to be in heaven with her Catholic ancestors.[127]

[123] Downame, *Sermon preached at Watton*, 2–3.
[124] Sutcliffe, *Survey of Poperie*, 327–8.
[125] R. Bristow, *A Reply to Fulke* (Louvain, 1580), 373. See also W. Allen, *A Defense and Declaration of the Catholike Churches Doctrine touching Purgatory* (Antwerp,1565), 214ʳ.
[126] Sir Edward Hoby asserted that on her deathbed Mary had put her trust in the merits of Christ alone, a claim he also advanced on behalf of the duke of Anjou, Henry III, and Stephen Gardiner: *A Letter to Mr T.H.... in Answere of his first motive* (1609), 106–8. Thomas Morton, *A Catholike Appeale for Protestants* (1609), 440–1, in response to Romanist claims that 'his Maiesties ancestors lived and died in that faith', similarly alleged that Mary in the last act of her life hoped to be justified only by faith in Christ.
[127] Hoby, *Curry-Combe for a Coxe-Combe*, 65–6; id., *A Counter-snarle for Ishmael Rabsha-cek* (1613), 17; J. Floyd, *Purgatories Triumph over Hell* (St Omer, 1613), 25. For the case of a young Hampshire girl imprisoned in 1593 for a vision in which she saw Mary Tudor and Mary Stuart in heaven, and Henry VIII and the earl of Leicester in hell: see A. Walsham, *Providence in Early Modern England* (Oxford, 1999), 210–11. Ibid. 236–7 for English Protestant reactions to a Jesuit play performed in Lyons in 1606 depicting Edward VI and Elizabeth in everlasting torment.

The question of whether there might be any papists in heaven was not an abstruse point of academic theology, but one which in a concrete and local application touched on issues of neighbourhood, charity, and community. This is made plain in the lengthy apologia appended by John Phillips, minister of Faversham in Kent, to the printed version of a funeral sermon he had preached for a parishioner, Edward Lapworth, one well known to be 'inclined to the Romish religion'. Some had denounced Phillips for laudatory remarks about Lapworth. But Phillips's gloss on his own words was that he had said no more than that 'a simple-hearted papist, not holding the whole mysterie of Romish iniquity, but only erring in some lesse points...may upon repentence in generall, of sinnes knowne and not knowne, find mercy with God'. Lapworth's manner of life (as well as his supposed ignorance of the most offensive popish doctrines and practices) justified a charitable presumption that he was such a one. Phillips concluded that 'we of the reformed Churches think and iudge charitably of our forefathers that lived in those blinde and darke times of Popery, and of such as yet that remain among them, or are intangled by them'. Phillips was no ecumenist in the modern sense, but he exemplifies what may have been a broader instinct in contemporary religious culture. Keith Thomas has suggested that the abrogation of purgatory meant that 'each generation could be indifferent to the spiritual fate of its predecessor'.[128] In a society so deeply imbued with the values of continuity and inheritance, however, it is unlikely that this was generally the case. A concern with the eternal destiny of ancestors dying 'in time of popery' can be inferred, not only from the regularity with which the question was handled in the writings of reformers, but also from the symbolism and conservatism of burial practices, particularly those whereby the landed gentry sought to have their bodies 'reincorporated amongst those of their ancestors', sometimes explicitly requiring interment 'in the usual place where my ancestors have been buried'.[129] Part of the defence of tombs and monuments articulated by the early Suffolk antiquary Robert Reyce in 1618 was that 'nature teacheth every one to perpetuate the reverend estimation and continuance of his ancestors'. His contemporary, the herald William Segar, agreed: the violation of sepulchral monuments was an intolerable indignity to anyone concerned to uphold 'the honour of his noble Ancestors'.[130] Like Camden before him, John Weever defended his interest in

[128] K. Thomas, *Religion and the Decline of Magic: Studies in Popular Beliefs in Sixteenth- and Seventeenth-Century England* (Harmondsworth, 1973), 721.
[129] N. Llewellyn, 'Honour in Life, Death and in the Memory: Funeral Monuments in Early Modern England', *TRHS* 6th ser., 6 (1996), 183.
[130] R. Reyce, *Suffolk in the XVIIth Century. The Breviary of Suffolk by Robert Reyce*, ed. Lord Francis Hervey (1902), 157; W. Segar, *Honor Military, and Civill, Contained in Foure Bookes* (1602), 255. This impulse, however, was not a universal one: at the end of the sixteenth century, the puritan iconoclast John Bruen undertook the destruction of some of his own family monuments in Tarvin church. M. Aston, 'Puritans and Iconoclasm, 1560–1660', in C. Durston and J. Eales (eds.), *The Culture of English Puritanism, 1560–1700* (Basingstoke, 1996), 101.

abbeys and priories with the reflection that 'our ancestors were, and we are, of the Christian profession'.[131] In the concern of these heralds and antiquaries with the preservation of sepulchral monuments, questions of the articulation of lineage and descent, and the social power and cultural capital they laid claim to, were clearly of the first order. But within and alongside this was a sense that the spiritual destinies of past and present generations remained inextricably bound. Below the level of the gentry, only a small minority of will-makers evinced an overt concern with the resting place of their ancestors, but instances of it can be multiplied from across the country. In the late sixteenth-century Tyneside parish of Whickham, a testator requested to be interred 'neer unto the burials of my auncestoures'; a man in Jacobean Kent desired 'to lie amongst his ancestors'.[132] In North Yorkshire a woman stipulated that her body was to be buried 'in Askrigg church yeard amongst my ancestors, trusting that I shall receve the same againe, not a corruptible, mortall and vile body, but an immortall, uncorruptible and a glorious body'. In his will of 1585, Thomas Andrew of Bury St Edmunds requested burial 'in the churche yarde nighe unto the southe syde of St James Churche wheare myne Auncestors lye buried, not for that I thinke any place better then other but to declare my hope and beleve that they and I shall ryse together in the last day throughe Jesus Christ our onely saviour and Redemer to lyfe everlasting'.[133] This expectation of reunion with the dead was a recurring subtext of contemporary thanatological discourses, and will be considered in more detail below. More immediately, however, it needs to be noted that reunion necessarily implies distance and separation, concepts at the heart of the Protestant understanding of the afterlife.

THE AMNESIA OF THE DEAD

If some people in Elizabethan and early Stuart England continued to show a concern about their ancestors, could they imagine that their ancestors were concerned about them? The commemoration of the dead in pre-Reformation England presupposed the offering of reciprocal prayer between living and dead, mutual exchanges between the members of a tripartite Church: militant, suffering, and triumphant. It was this reciprocity which Protestant reformers were determined to break. A recurrent and insistent refrain in the

---

[131] J. Weever, *Ancient Funerall Monuments* (1631), A1r.

[132] K. Wrightson and D. Levine, 'Death in Whickham', in J. Walter and R. Schofield (eds.), *Famine, Disease and the Social Order* (1989), 162; C. Gittings, *Death, Burial and the Individual in Early Modern England* (1984), 87.

[133] H. Thwaite (ed.), *Abstracts of Abbotside Wills 1552–1688*, YASRS, 130 (1968), 37; J. Craig, 'The Bury Stirs Revisited: An Analysis of the Townsmen', *Proceedings of the Suffolk Institute of Archaeology and History*, 37/3 (1991), 217. Other examples: M. Allen (ed.), *Wills of the Archdeaconry of Suffolk 1625–6*, Suffolk Records Society, 37 (1995), 176; Allen (ed.), *Wills of the Archdeaconry of Suffolk 1620–1624*, 122.

writings of late sixteenth- and early seventeenth-century divines was that the souls of the dead in heaven did not listen to the prayers of the living, indeed, could not hear them; that the dead on their own account could have no knowledge of what transpired in the created world.[134] These convictions were a conscious reaction to the unreformed Church's practice of invoking the aid of particular saints, and the saints' cults the practice sustained. The Elizabethan homily on prayer taught that true prayer comprised not the outward sound of words, but an inward crying of the heart to God, something no virgin, patriarch, or prophet among the dead could apprehend:

they have so little knowledge of the secrets of the heart, that many of the ancient Fathers greatly doubt whether they know any thing at all, that is commonly done on earth. And albeit some think they do, yet St Augustine, a Doctor of great authority and also antiquity, hath this opinion of them; That they know no more what we do on earth, than we know what they do in heaven.[135]

To suppose that saints could know the thoughts of men was a blasphemy: it was to make them gods.[136] Thomas Cartwright mocked the Jesuits for believing 'small and low voices to be heard of creatures removed... from other infinite spaces'.[137] 'Protestants expressely say', accused the Catholic exile Richard Smith (later namesake of the Henrician theologian), 'that saints know not what we doe, that they heare not our praiers, perceave not our necessities, know not our estate.'[138]

Among the texts to prove that the dead were unaware of the condition of the living, Protestant authorities pointed to Ecclesiastes 9: 5 ('the dead know not any thing') and to Isaiah 63: 16 ('Thou O God, art our Father: though

---

[134] Although there had been controversy about this in the Middle Ages, most theologians accepted the view of Aquinas (following Gregory) that 'those who see God know all that passes here below'. Cited in T. More, *Utopia*, ed. E. Surtz and J. H. Hexter (1965), 531.

[135] *Sermons, or Homilies, Appointed to be read in Churches* (1833), 223. See also J. Veron, *A Stronge Battery against the Idolatrous Invocation of the Dead Saintes* (1562), 27ʳ: 'Saint Augustine dothe plainely affirme that the soules of the saintes that be in Heaven do not know what the lyving doo heere in earth.' The authority of Augustine (*De cura pro mortuis*, ch. 13) was also appealed to by Willet, *Synopsis Papismi*, 338; P. Martyr, *The Common Places*, tr. A. Marten (1583), pt. i, 75; Coverdale, *Remains*, 218–21; W. Leygh, *The Soules Solace agaynst Sorrow* (1612), 25–8; S. Gardiner, *The Devotions of the Dying Man* (1627), 302.

[136] H. Bullinger, *The Decades: The Fourth Decade*, ed. T. Harding (PS, 1851), 211; Willet, *Synopsis Papismi*, 337; Bell, *Survey of Popery*, 340.

[137] Cartwright, *Confutation of the Rhemists Translation*, 192.

[138] R. Smith, *A Conference of the Catholike and Protestante Doctrine with the Expresse Words of Holie Scripture* (Douai, 1631), 153. Other statements that saints in heaven have no knowledge of events on earth: W. Perkins, *A Reformed Catholike* (Cambridge, 1598), 247, 250–6; Perkins, *Golden Chaine*, 503, 656; Sutcliffe, *Survey of Poperie*, 175; Veron, *Huntyng of Purgatory*, 207ᵛ, 240ᵛ; T. Bell, *The Survey of Popery* (1596) 338; Vicars, *A Prospective Glasse*, C6ʳ; J. Denison, *Heavens Ioy, for a Sinners Repentance* (1623), 11–12. Few early Stuart divines (not even William Laud) were in sympathy with the view of Richard Montagu that since it was technically impossible for the dead to hear the living, prayer to saints was merely ineffectual rather than impious or idolatrous: *A Gagg for the New Gospel? No. A New Gagg for an Old Goose* (1624), 229, cited and discussed by Milton, *Catholic and Reformed*, 206–7.

Abraham be ignorant of us').[139] Awkwardly, however, there were other scriptural passages which suggested that Abraham's ignorance might not be so total. The parable of Dives and Lazarus implied that Abraham was aware of the lives of the rich man and the beggar, as he also knew of Moses and the prophets who had come after him. Another passage in Luke (15: 10) stated that the angels rejoiced whenever a sinner repented on earth. There did not appear to be complete radio silence between this world and the next. To account for the apparent anomaly, Protestant exegetes were again prepared to follow the lead of St Augustine: the dead have no knowledge of worldly actions while they are being committed, but (God permitting) might hear of them from souls newly arrived in heaven, or from the angels who travel back and forth between the two worlds as executors of God's justice and mercy.[140] To concede this possibility, thought George Wither, did not amount to 'anie ordinarie knowledge of our affaires' by the saints in heaven.[141] Not all Protestants, however, were comfortable with this rather mechanistic model of how news might be transmitted between earth and heaven. William Fulke thought that here 'Augustine wandreth in his imaginations', missing the point that the story of Dives and Lazarus was a parable. Referring to other aspects of the story, Fulke remarked that one might as well say that souls have fingers and toes, or that water can quench hellfire, as that Abraham knew which books had been written after his death.[142]

By divine decree the dead were unable to perceive the needs of the living, but this was not intended to betoken an intrinsic lack of charity on their part, an extinction of their 'humanity'. In considering the sensitive question of whether the dead prayed for the living, William Perkins allowed that the saints 'doe in generall pray for the church militant upon earth...I say *in generall*, because they praie not for the particular conditions and persons of men upon earth considering they neither know, nor see, nor hear us: neither can they tell what things are done upon earth'.[143] This seems to have been a broadly consensual position among Elizabethan and Jacobean divines: the saints could be expected to evince an inclusive concern for the welfare and salvation of the elect in the world, but they did not pursue

---

[139] Bullinger, *Fourth Decade*, 211; Gardiner, *Devotions of the Dying Man*, 302.

[140] Wither, *View of the Marginal Notes*, 73–4; Bell, *Survey of Popery*, 338–41. Willet, *Testrastylon Papisimi*, 158, cited the authority of the Decretum ('your own canons') for the view that 'the dead know not the things here done, while they are in doing, but afterwards they heare them of those that depart unto them by death'.

[141] Wither, *View of the Marginal Notes*, 74.

[142] Fulke, *Text of the New Testament*, 117; King, *A Funerall Sermon*, E5ᵛ, had earlier insisted that we should not infer from the parable that 'thei that be in heaven...should bothe se and talke with them, that be in the place of dampnacion'.

[143] Perkins, *Golden Chaine*, 503. Cf. Whitaker, *Answere to the Ten Reasons*, 106: 'whether the martyrs and heavenly saints pray unto Christ for us or no, we know not: but certaine it is, that they are ignorant of those things we doe'.

individual cases.[144] 'Although the affection of charitie remaine in the deade', argued William Fulke, 'yet it is not shewed by looking to our earthly necessities, which they know are subiect to the providence of God.'[145]

Some writers suggested that to suppose the saints in heaven capable of hearing our prayers and having knowledge of our affairs on earth was not merely a derogation of the majesty of Christ, but an injury to the dead themselves, for how could they enjoy that blessed rest promised by the Scriptures if they were distracted by the strivings of the living? 'To say that the godly in peace should be troubled particularly, or in speciall manner about their friends affayres below; what were it, but much to derogate from their true rest?'[146] The theme was an appropriate one for funeral sermons. Preaching in 1601 at the exequies of the young Lancashire gentlewoman Katherine Brettargh, William Leygh posed the question

May we think them at quiet whom the troublesome sturs of this world may vexe? I trow no, for doe but suppose, that the saints in heaven did behold the miseries heere on earth; princes the subversion of their kingdomes; nobleman of their houses; gentlemen of their lands, line, and families; did fathers see the sinnes of their sonnes, and mothers the shame of their daughters... I say, if saints in heaven had a sense and feeling of these miseries, woes, and calamaties, small were their rest, little were their ease, and heaven were no hold for happiness.[147]

The Norwich minister Samuel Gardiner envisaged the dead 'sleep[ing] supinely in their lockers, careless and senseless of secular affaires', and the devotional writer James Cole believed that when we are dead 'our wives and children will then move us no more, then if wee never had loved them'.[148] In Timothy Oldmayne's 1636 funeral sermon for Edward Lewkenor, forgetfulness is presented as a defining condition of death: 'when a man is dead, hee remembreth no more the worke and labour of his hands... Hee knoweth not what hee hath done: and if you tell him, hee will not regard. Friend or foe are

---

[144] Willet, *Synopsis Papismi*, 334–5; R. Field, *Of the Church, Five Bookes* (1606), 111; Crooke, *Death Subdued*, F7ʳ; Horne, *Certaine Sermons*, 121: 'I will not deny but Christian charity abides in the Saints in glory, not by speciall rememberance of one more then another; for, such charitie in them extendeth it selfe indifferently and generally to all here, living, or yet unborne, whom they love as themselves'. The 'Anglican' Jeremy Taylor believed that the dead remained concerned about the welfare of their friends on earth and showed their affection by praying for them: Houlbrooke, *Death*, 41–2. This was clearly not a widely held position among pre-Caroline divines.
[145] Fulke, *Two Treatises*, 205.
[146] Horne, *Certaine Sermons*, 121. See also Willet, *Synopsis Papismi*, 338: 'The saints are at rest, they do cease from the affaires of this life'.
[147] Leygh, *The Soules Solace agaynst Sorrow*, 28–9. Leygh's purpose, however, was to set up a polemical sally against the invocation of saints: 'They see you not; they heare you not; nor have they feeling of your miseries. Your *ora pro nobis* is out at doores' (p. 30). The death of the godly Katherine (sister of the iconoclast John Bruen) was a minor cause célèbre, with local ministers determined to counter papist claims that she had died despairing of her salvation: R. N. Watson, *The Rest is Silence: Death as Annihilation in the English Renaissance* (Berkeley and Los Angeles, 1994), 306–15.
[148] Gardiner, *Devotions of the Dying Man*, 156; Cole, *Of Death a True Description*, 54.

all one to him: neither doth he care, whether his sonnes be honourable, or of low degree.'[149] In such accounts, death represents a radical and transformative dissociation of affinity: the living are obliterated from the consciousness of the dead. This life and the next are no longer linked by the potential for mutual assistance, but separated by mutual incomprehension: the estate of the dead is beyond the imagination of the living, as the estate of the living is beneath the notice of the dead.

There was a consolatory aspect to these notions, in so far as they were designed to bring home to survivors the calm and peace that characterized the experience of the elect. Yet there are scattered echoes in the sources to suggest that this image of complete impenetrability may have been emotionally unsatisfactory, even to those of impeccable Protestant orthodoxy. Writing to Peter Martyr in March 1551 to describe the recent exequies of Martin Bucer, and the honour done to him by the scholars and townspeople of Cambridge, Sir John Cheke allowed himself to hope that 'if there be any perception by those who rest in Christ of the transactions of this earthly scene, [he] may rejoice in the fruit of the labours which he bestowed in this world below'.[150] Over seventy years later, in a consolatory letter to Lady Kingsmill upon the death of her husband, John Donne advised that 'we are not bound to think that souls departed have divested all affections towards them whom they left here'.[151]

While some funeral sermons stressed the obliviousness of the dead, others employed affective language to suggest their continuing tenderness towards the living. Thus the dedicatory epistle to John Wall's 1623 sermon for John Stanhope encouraged his parents to imagine that 'hee behold you from the top of heaven, and seeme to speake unto your hearts in that sweet and gracious voice of our blessed Saviour on the Cross, Woman, behold thy sonne'.[152] Another Jacobean funeral sermon, preached by William Ford in, of all places, Constantinople, depicted the souls in heaven not in a state of complete emotional detachment from the living, but concerned for their salvation and in lively anticipation of seeing them again:

an infinite number of acquaintance expect us there: our parents, our brethren and sisters, our children, our kindred, our friends, that are alreadie secure of their own

---

[149] T. Oldmayne, *Lifes Brevitie and Deaths Debility* (1636), 71. Cf. Byfield, *Cure of the Feare of Death*, 109–10: 'when thou diest, all will be forgotten, there is no more remembrance of former things, nor shall there be any remembrance of things which are to come, with those that shall come after'. There is an echo of these assertions in the (unusual) 1619 epitaph of Elizabeth Leigh at Arreton, Isle of Wight: 'What friends, what children, what blest Marriage, / Dead I forgette ...'. Ravenshaw, *Antiente Epitaphs*, 64.

[150] G. Gorham (ed.), *Gleanings of a Few Scattered Ears, during the Period of the Reformation in England* (1857), 238–41.

[151] *No Man is an Island: A Selection from the Prose of John Donne*, ed. R. Scott (1997), 49.

[152] J. Wall, *A Sermon preached at Shelford in Nottinghamshire* (1623), A5ʳ. See also J.C., *A Handkercher for Parents Wet Eyes, upon the Death of Children* (1630), 64, advising a bereaved father to rejoice at his son's felicity: 'He sits aloft, and smiles at this *Emmet*-hill of Earth.'

immortalities, but yet sollicitous for our safetie, what ioy, what comfort will it be to see, to imbrace them.[153]

Ford's depiction of heaven involved, in some definite if unspecific sense, the reconstitution of earthly bonds of affinity and sociability. This seems a deeply attractive concept, a comfort both to the dying person and to the bereaved. Not surprisingly, it was one which intrigued the religious imagination of late sixteenth- and early seventeenth-century Protestant England.

MEETING AGAIN: SOCIETY IN HEAVEN

The nature of society in heaven, like the essence of heaven itself, might have seemed to be a subject beyond human imagination or comprehension, but it was one which surfaced repeatedly in contemporary discussions of the afterlife, and which for some Protestants raised extremely vexatious questions.[154] The paradox of attempting to say anything meaningful about society in heaven (perhaps the paradox of theology itself) was that theologians had to shape a discourse which made clear that what they were describing was not a mere sequel to or reconstruction of human companionship, while being able to bring to the task only familiar human concepts: knowledge, recognition, circumscribed networks of affinity and association. It was a theological axiom, and a social and cultural 'fact', that the dead were 'persons' with a past, a present, and a future (corresponding to their mortal life, their soul's abode in heaven, and their expectation of resurrection). But were the modes in which they could express desire, experience consciousness, or exercise will in any way cognate to those of living persons?

The literary scholar Robert N. Watson has claimed that Protestant theology 'by its particular emphasis on individual interiority, on the sinfulness of that interiority, and on the lack of any purgatorial process that could winnow out that sinfulness, must have made it virtually impossible to imagine satisfactorily the survival of full selfhood in heaven'.[155] Yet this seems too extreme a judgement. After all, Protestantism taught an individual judgement on souls after death, and the common insistence that there would be 'degrees of glory' in the afterlife, through which souls experienced beatitude according to their different capacities, implicitly affirmed the idea of the preservation of individual identity beyond death.[156] Moreover, the central

---

[153] Ford, *A Sermon preached at Constantinople*, 61. This is virtually identical to a passage in Ralph Jennings's 1623 translation of Aslakssøn's *Description of Heaven* (p. 82), suggesting Ford may have been familiar with the work in its original Latin form.

[154] The following section draws on my 'The Company of Heaven: Identity and Sociability in the English Protestant Afterlife, c.1560–1630', *Historical Reflections / Réflexions Historiques*, 26 (2000), 311–33.

[155] Watson, *Rest is Silence*, 6.

[156] A point made by Disley, 'Degrees of Glory', 104.

doctrine of the resurrection of the body was predicated upon the physical manifestation of an individuated existence for the elect in eternity.[157] Nonetheless, much of the language used to describe the experience of the elect was more eloquent on their unity of purpose, and their conformity to the will of God, than on their existential disaggregation from the mass of their fellows. A consensus seemed to be, not that individual identity was extinguished in heaven, but that heaven was a perfectly corporate and non-hierarchical society where 'the happinesse of one is the happinesse of the whole, as the happinesse of the whole is the happinesse of every one'.[158] In the more mystical language of John Donne, 'all soules shall be so intirely knit together, as if all were but one soule, and God so intirely knit to every soule, as if there were as many Gods as soules'.[159]

There seems little scope here for the expression of 'personality' or the development of 'relationships' in the senses with which we are familiar with the terms. Many Protestant writers clearly envisaged the pre-eminent activity in heaven to be a rapt contemplation and adoration of the godhead which left little room for any other association. The Devon minister John Preston believed that 'although the soule thorough death doeth not loose his faculties, notwithstanding she doth not exercise her operations. The actions of the godly after this life is a perpetuall fruition of eternall happinesse, put in the contemplation of divine glory.'[160] In striving for the metaphor which best expressed this face-to-face exaltation of the deity, writers recalled the congregational psalm-singing that was characteristic of developed Protestant worship: 'their time shall bee spent in singing the hymnes of prayses to the harpe of glory'; 'singing praise to God with the whole Church'; 'singing our ditty Allelujah, the quire Angels and Saints'.[161] It is no surprise to discover that to some puritans the most pleasing analogy was that of a perpetual sabbath.[162] Another characteristic note was an emphasis on the stilling of individual

---

[157] Cf. C. W. Bynum, 'Material Continuity, Personal Survival and the Resurrection of the Body: A Scholastic Discussion in its Medieval and Modern Contexts', in id., *Fragmentation and Redemption: Essays on Gender and the Human Body in Medieval Religion* (New York, 1991), 239–97; N. Z. Davies, '"On the Lame"', *American Historical Review*, 93 (1988), 602.

[158] Drummond, *A Midnights Trance*, 91. See also Walker, *Sermon at the Funerals of . . . William Lord Russell*, 29; Gardiner, *Devotions of the Dying Man*, 361.

[159] Donne, *Sermons*, vii. 139.

[160] Preston, *A Sermon preached at the Funeral of Mr Arthur Upton*, 32. See also Perkins, *Golden Chaine*, 142; Tuke, *The High-way to Heaven*,189; Walker, *Sermon at the Funerals of . . . William Lord Russell*, 29; Ford, *Sermon preached at Constantinople*, 56; Andrewes, *A Celestiall Looking-glasse*, 24. The English evidence broadly endorses the view of C. McDannell and B. Lang, *Heaven: A History* (New Haven and London, 1990), 178, that the Reformation preferred a 'theocentric model' of heaven.

[161] Denison, *A Three-fold Resolution*, 473; Pricke, *Godlie and Learned sermon*, E4ᵛ; Strode, *Anatomie of Mortalitie*, 333. See also Price, *Lamentations for the Death of . . . Prince Henry*, 4. On psalm-singing, see R. Zim, *English Metrical Psalms: Poetry as Praise and Prayer 1535–1601* (Cambridge, 1987). These ideas are echoed in the Jacobean epitaph to John Barker Esq. in St Werburgh's, Bristol. His soul was said to be 'where with the Saints and Angells thou dost sing Sweet Hallelujahs to Thy Glorious King': Roper, *Monumental Effigies of Gloucestershire*, 172.

[162] Bayly, *Practise of Piety*, 154–5; Gardiner, *Devotions of the Dying Man*, 383.

desires. 'In heaven', observed the Jacobean preacher John Bowle, 'there is *Desideriorum quies*, the verie center and quiet of desiring, where our desires shall not be satiated, but they shall be *satisfied*.'[163] Christ had made it clear that there was to be no marriage in heaven; indeed some commentators denied that souls possessed any distinction of sex or gender.[164]

On the other hand, most authorities did not mean to give the impression that souls were rapt in the contemplation of God to the extent that they were oblivious of the presence of others: the dominant model for activity in heaven was that of congregational worship, not private devotion. The question of whether we shall know one another in heaven was frequently posed, and invariably answered in the affirmative. The teaching of Scripture appeared to be definitive: Adam knew Eve in paradise; the apostles recognized Moses and Elijah during the Transfiguration; Jesus promised that the faithful would sit down with Abraham, Isaac, and Jacob in the kingdom of heaven; the rich man knew Lazarus in hell. This being so, 'much more shall the Elect know one another in heaven'.[165] This mutual recognition did not necessarily imply, however, a priority to the resumption of past relationships. The saints in heaven would know each other irrespective of whether they had ever met in this world, and a number of accounts stressed the joys of continual conversation with saints, angels, and prominent biblical figures, without much interest in the renewal of earthly bonds of sociability.[166] Indeed, some early seventeenth-century writers explicitly counterposed the social networks of this world with those of the next. In the view of Edward Vaughan, one of the reasons which should make us willing to die was

of our companie; as when we change the societie, fellowship, and companie of men, for the company and societie of angels; the company of whoremongers, drunkards, liers, swearers, oppressors, and such like, for the company of the saints; the company of children on earth, for the company of children in heaven, the company of husband or wife, for the company of Iesus Christe himself.[167]

To James Cole, the exchange seemed similarly beneficial: 'if heere wee depart from our earthly parents, we are entertained there of *our Heavenly*

[163] Bowle, *A Sermon preached at Flitton*, B3ᵛ. See also Roberston, *Combate between the Flesh and the Spirit*, 359; Aslaksson, *Description of Heaven*, 73.

[164] Matt. 22: 30; Roberston, *Combate between the Flesh and the Spirit*, 375; McDannell and Lang, *Heaven*, 24–32; H. Gamon, *The Praise of a Godly Woman. A Sermon preached at the Solemne Funerall of ... Ladie Frances Roberts* (1627), 3. The question of the gender of souls does not seem to have been much discussed, perhaps because it was widely accepted that the resurrected body would retain its sexual characteristics (if not habits).

[165] Gen. 2: 23; Matt. 17: 4; John 20: 20; Matt. 8: 11; Luke 13: 28, 16: 23. See H. Smith, *Sermons*, 2 vols. (1866), ii. 420; Perkins, *Golden Chaine*, 518; Gardiner, *Devotions of the Dying Man*, 363; Donne, *Sermons*, vii. 139; Bolton, *Foure Last Things*, 146–8; Bayly, *Practise of Piety*, 157 (quote).

[166] Hume, *A Treatise of the Felicitie of the Life to Come*, 32–4; R. Harris, *Samuels Funerall. Or a Sermon preached at the Funerall of Sir Anthonie Cope* (1618), 12; Crooke, *Death Subdued*, H4ᵛ; Donne, *Sermons*, vii. 139.

[167] E. Vaughan, *A Divine Discoverie of Death* (1612), 47.

father. If here wee leave our chiefest friends and kindred, wee meete there with our brethren in Christ.'[168] In fact, some theologians displayed a distinct unease about the anticipation of joyous reunions with the dear departed. William Fulke insisted that the love of the saints 'is not now carnal and special towards their friends in the flesh, brethren, kinsfolkes and other, but spiritual and generall toward all the elect of God'.[169] In the opinion of William Perkins, the question 'whether men shall knowe one another after this life or no' was 'oftener mooved by such as are ignorant, then by them that have knowledge'. He confirmed there would be recognition, 'but whether they shall know one other after an earthly manner, as to say, this man was my father, this was mine uncle, this my teacher &c. the word of god saith nothing: and therefore I will be silent'.[170] Perkins's agnosticism over whether relationships among the elect implied an awareness of consanguinity was reiterated by Samuel Gardiner, who regarded the question as 'curious', advising 'let our care be to knowe whether wee shal come to heaven, then to know whether we shall know one another in heaven'.[171] Another Calvinist luminary, Robert Bolton, expressed similar misgivings. While Bolton was in no doubt that there would be 'familiar acquaintance' in the life to come, he worried that the topic encouraged 'the curious *Quaere* of carnall people . . . feeding falsly their presumptuous conceits with golden dreames, and vaine hopes of many future imaginary felicities in the world to come'. 'Our mutual knowledge one of another in heaven', Bolton insisted, 'shall not be in outward and worldly respects, but divine and spirituall.'[172] In such qualifications we encounter a familiar puritan anxiety about the 'country divinity' of the common people, in their expectations of life after death looking merely for the reconstitution and amplification of the good and familiar things of this life, rather than reflecting on the utter transcendence of God and his kingdom.

Yet in addressing the highly poignant issue of reunion with the dead, Protestant writings were by no means univocal. In many pastoral works, consolatory treatises on death, and printed funeral sermons, theological caveats of the sort espoused by Perkins or Bolton were largely absent. The latter may have been concerned about the 'presumptuous conceipts' of the hoi polloi, but according to his biographer Edward Bagshawe, as he lay on his deathbed he summoned his wife 'and bad her make no doubt but shee should meete him againe in heaven'.[173] Another puritan minister, Samuel

---

[168] Cole, *Of Death a True Description*, 145. See also Crooke, *Death Subdued*, F6ᵛ; C. Fitz-Geffry, *Elisha his Lamentation . . . a Sermon, preached at the Funeralls of the Right Worshipfull Sir Anthony Rous* (1622), 30; Downe, *Certaine Treatises*, 53.

[169] Fulke, *Text of the New Testament*, 119.

[170] Perkins, *Golden Chaine*, 518.

[171] Gardiner, *Devotions of the Dying Man*, 364–5; id., *Doomes-Day Booke: or, An Alarum for Atheists* (1606), 108–9.

[172] Bolton, *Foure Last Things*, 144–50.

[173] E. Bagshawe, 'The Life and Death of Mr Bolton', prefixed to *The Foure Last Things*, C6ʳ.

Rogers, imagined heaven in the 1630s as a place where he would 'sit downe in companye, with Abraham, Paul, my grandfather [the renowned minister, Richard Rogers], and all other blessed saints, and angels'.[174] It was a cliché of pious literature and of funeral sermons that the dead had 'gone before us', and we would follow after.[175] In Thomas Becon's *ars moriendi* dialogue, *The Sick Man's Salve* (first published *c.*1560, but reprinted in twenty-five editions up to 1632), when the dying man expresses sadness at leaving the company of his friends, he is assured that 'if your friends live in the fear of God, and depart in the christian faith, they may be sure to come thither, where you shall be, even unto the glorious kingdom of God, where you shall both see them, know them, talk with them, and be much more merry with them than ever you were in this world'.[176] Just as they frequently sought to reassure their auditors that the subject of their oration was in heaven, preachers of funeral sermons encouraged the belief that they would meet them again: as Richard Stock put it in his 1614 sermon for Lord Harington, 'lead the same life with him, and you shal soone enioy his holy and comfortable presence'.[177]

Like Stock, some preachers envisaged a reunion of souls in heaven immediately consequent upon the death of the surviving friend, spouse, or child. Many other divines, however, preferred to imagine a meeting-again which would take place at the end of time, when the Lord returned in glory, and the bodies of the dead rose from their graves to rejoin their souls upon a new earth. According to John Rogers, 'then we shall see and know one another, the king his subjects, the pastor his people, the parents, their children, the husband his wife, the master his servants, and they him'.[178] A similarly

---

[174] T. Webster, *Godly Clergy in Early Stuart England* (Cambridge, 1997), 137 n., noting similar visions of reunions of the godly in heaven on the part of Richard Baxter, John Wilson, and John Barker.

[175] Sutton, *Disce Mori*, 275–6; G. Powell, *The Resolved Christian* (1603), 59; Welcome, *The State of the Godly*, 68; Price, *Spirituall Odours*, 49; Preston, *A Sermon preached at the Funeral of Mr Iosiah Reynel*, D3ʳ; Bowle, *Sermon preached at Flitton*, F4ᵛ; S. Denison, *The Monument or Tombe-stone: or A Sermon preached . . . at the Funerall of Mrs. Elizabeth Iuxon* (1620), A5ʳ; Price, *Two Twins of Birth and Death*, 34.

[176] Becon, *Sick Man's Salve*, 152–4. For the publishing history, see Green, *Print and Protestantism*, 360–1.

[177] Stock, *Churches Lamentation for the Losse of the Godly*, 102. See also Taylor, *Pilgrims Profession*,175. The motif also figured prominently with a number of German preachers: S. Karant-Nunn, *The Reformation of Ritual: An Interpretation of Early Modern Germany* (1997), 186; B. Gordon, 'Malevolent Ghosts and Ministering Angels: Apparitions and Pastoral Care in the Swiss Reformation', in *Place of the Dead*. But it is worth noting that Protestantism had no monopoly on the theme. John Fisher had painted one of the joys of heaven as 'to se there our speciall frendes and acquayntaunce whiche we had here before in this lyfe', and a generation later the Jesuit Robert Persons urged readers to 'imagine . . . what a ioye it shall be unto thy soule at that daye, to meet with all her godlie freendes in heaven, with father, with mother, with brothers, with sisters: with wyfe, with husband, with maister, with scholares: with neyghboures, with familiares, with kyndred, with acquayntance'. *A Critical Edition of Two Fruytfull Sermons of Saint John Fisher*, ed. M. D. Sullivan (Ann Arbor, Mich., 1974), 17; H. Davies, *Worship and Theology in England from Cranmer to Hooker 1534–1603* (1970), 413–14.

[178] Rogers, *A Discourse of Christian Watchfulnesse*, 238.

joyous scene was evoked by John Andrewes: 'fathers and mothers, husbands and wives, maisters and servants, brothers and sisters, parents and children, neighbours and friends, all shall meete together: what cryes and shouts will there be for ioy? What clapping of hands and sweete embracements one of another?'[179] John Donne reflected that 'though we part at divers daies, and by divers waies here, yet wee shall all meet at one place, and at one day...the day of the glorious *Resurrection*'.[180] The centrality of the Last Judgement and the resurrection of the body in the theology of Elizabethan and early Stuart Protestantism is striking, and is of considerable significance for how that religious culture constructed its view of the afterlife, and articulated its relationship with the dead.

SLEEP AND RESURRECTION

In the course of a funeral sermon in 1585, Thomas Sparke broke off from his discussion of rewards in heaven to make clear that 'I would not have it hereupon inferred that my meaning is that soules departed in faith have straight their consummation and ful crown of glorie that is prepared for them. For I know that shal not be before the general resurrection.'[181] Some years later, the Jacobean preacher Samuel Crooke tempered his fulsome account of the joyous state of elect souls with the tantalizing reflection that 'all this is but an *interim* of blessednes, a *morsell* to keepe the soule in appetite, till the great *day of the restitution of all things*'.[182] This was fully consistent with a Reformed theology which envisaged the salvation of the elect as a process leading from initial justification, through sanctification, to ultimate glorification. The justified sinner was sanctified in this lifetime to begin to conform him- or herself to the image of God, but this process was only finally consummated when the soul of the saint was reunited with its glorified body.[183] Thus John Denison's account of the steps of the godly into glory (starting with their sense of assurance in this life) could completely ignore the theme of the enjoyment of heaven without the body.[184] Calvin himself depicted the post-mortem condition of the elect as one of happy anticipation: 'the souls of the righteous, after their warfare is ended, obtain

---

[179] Andrewes, *A Celestiall Looking-glasse*, 27.

[180] Donne, *Sermons*, viii. 62. Other writers whose discussion of post-mortem reunion focused on the resurrection include Perkins, *Golden Chaine*, 518; R. Hill, *The Path-way to Prayer and Pietie* (1609), 260; T. Playfere, *The Pathway to Perfection* (1611), 222; Parr, *End of the Perfect Man*, A4^r; J.C., *Handkercher for Parents Wet Eyes*, 65; J. Gaule, *A Defiance of Death being the Funebrious Commemoration of...Baptist Lord Hickes* (1630), 46; Bolton, *Foure Last Things*, 144–5.

[181] Sparke, *A Sermon preached at Cheanies*, 85–6.

[182] Crooke, *Death Subdued*, H4^v–5^r.

[183] E. Hebblethwaite, 'The Theology of Rewards in English Printed Treatises and Sermons (c.1550–c.1650)', University of Cambridge Ph.D. thesis (1992), 175.

[184] Denison, *A Three-fold Resolution*, 439 ff.

blessed rest where in joy they wait for the fruition of promised glory'.[185] His English disciple William Perkins was of the same mind: 'soules being once in heaven, remaine there till the last day of iudgement, where they partly magnifie the Name of God, and partly doe waite, and pray for the consummation of the kingdome of glorie, and full felicitie in body and soule'.[186]

This being the case, it was incumbent upon Protestant theologians to find a convincing answer to the question posed in a 1614 catechism composed by Elnathan Parr: 'if the soules of the elect goe presently after their death to heaven, and the soules of the reprobate to hell, what neede a generall Iudgement?' Parr's own answer was a rather juridical one: 'there must be a general Iudgement notwithstanding, both that the iustnesse of such particular Iudgement may bee made more manifest to the glorie of God, and that the whole man, consisting of body and soule, may receive the due reward'.[187] Other Protestant writers, however, preferred to emphasize the 'soul's natural appetite and desire' to be reunited to the body.[188] There was a fine line to be trod here. The condition of the elect in heaven might be considered imperfect by God's standards, but most Protestants had no wish to imply that it involved actual sorrow or poignant longing on the part of souls who were still separated from their bodies. In a Jacobean dialogue between the flesh and the spirit, flesh asks 'Doth not the soule then long for the body, seeing it knoweth it is rotten in the cold ground?' The spirit replies that souls rest in a place where there is no unquietness or desire; they look forward to the resurrection, but without sorrow, persuaded that no mischance can befall their bodies 'but that they pleasantly and softly sleep and rest' until rising again.[189]

This imagery of sleep is highly significant, and pervades Protestant literature on death and commemoration of the dead to an extraordinary extent. The connection between sleep and death was not, of course, discovered for the first time in the mid-sixteenth century. In the judgement of the founding father of recent historical thanatology, Philippe Ariès, 'the idea of sleep is the most ancient, the most popular, and the most constant image of the beyond'.[190] Medieval liturgies included prayers for those sleeping in the sleep of peace, but the image in no sense dominated or shaped pre-Reformation

---

[185] J. Calvin, *Institutes of the Christian Religion*, tr. H. Beveridge, 2 vols. in 1 (Grand Rapids, Mich., 1989), ii. 267. There is a similar emphasis on the conscious and blessed (though imperfect) state of souls in the writings of Calvin's contemporary, the Lutheran scholastic Basilius Faber: R. B. Barnes, 'Prophetic Pedagogy: Basilius Faber (*c.*1520–1575) and Evangelical Teaching on the Last Things', *Historical Reflections / Réflexions Historiques*, 26 (2000), 280–1.

[186] Perkins, *Golden Chaine*, 142.

[187] E. Parr, *The Grounds of Divinitie* (1614), 237. See also H. Greenwood, *A Treatise of the Great and Generall Daye of Iudgement* (1606), 66–7; T. Draxe, *An Alarum to the Last Iudgement* (1615), 1–8.

[188] Drummond, *A Midnights Trance*, 68–9; Playfere, *The Pathway to Perfection*, 230; J. Donne, *Devotions upon Emergent Occasions*, ed. A. Raspa (Montreal and London, 1975), 96.

[189] Robertson, *The Crowne of Life*, 358–60.

[190] P. Ariès, *The Hour of Our Death*, tr. H. Weaver (1981), 24.

mortuary culture to the extent that it was to do later.[191] Reformers were drawn to it for a number of reasons. In the first place, it was or seemed to be profoundly scriptural. Both the Old and New Testaments abounded with references to the dead sleeping in the Lord.[192] The concept of the dead sleeping or resting was also believed to be inimical to the popish concept of purgatory: how could the blessed dead be said to be at rest if they were tormented with purgatory fire? To conceive of death and the state of being dead as a sleep was also regarded as a comforting doctrine for the dying and the bereaved. The congruences seemed to make the analogy a perfect one: 'nothing more like death than sleep'; 'nothing more like to the grave, then our beds'; 'nothing better resembleth death then our sleep'.[193] Indeed, it may be a measure of how deeply embedded the symbolism of sleep had become that by the 1630s a funeral sermon could feel obliged to labour the rather obvious point that people should not imagine death as 'properly to be asleep'; that death was called sleep 'in regard onely of a kinde of similitude and proportion that is betwixt them'.[194] The notion of death as sleep had enormous utility as an instrument of pious consolation, particularly in the literature of *ars moriendi*, and in the printed funeral sermon. It was constantly reiterated that the godly should not fear to die, nor should their loved ones mourn excessively for them, since, to the godly, death was but a sleep.[195] According to Samuel Gardiner, the thought of the dead merely having put off their clothes and gone to bed allowed us to 'sucke comfort from the iuyce of this grape, against the bitter death of such, as while they lived, were most deare and neere unto us'.[196] In his *Anatomie of Mortalitie*, George Strode remarked that Scripture's designations of death as bed, peace, rest, sleep was for 'the singular comfort of all God's children'.[197] The associations religious writers applied to the condition of the dead revolved around concepts of rest from wearisome labour, physical comfort, exemption from trouble and care, refreshment, and new starts. The frequency and

[191] R. J. E. Boggis, *Praying for the Dead: An Historical Review of the Practice* (1913), 149; Houlbrooke, *Death*, 256. Cf C. Zaleski, *The Life of the World to Come: Near-Death Experience and Christian Hope* (Oxford, 1996), 65: 'The Protestant tradition has tended, beginning with Luther, to reduce the repertoire of images for the interim period to the single image of sleep.'
[192] A selection only: Deut. 31: 16; 1 Kgs. 2: 10, 11: 43, 15: 8; Ps. 4: 8; Isa. 28: 20; Dan. 12: 2; John 11: 11; Acts 7: 60; 1 Cor. 15: 6; 1 Thess. 4: 13 (a key text); Rev. 14: 13 (an important prooftext against purgatory).
[193] H. Bull, *Christian Prayers and Holy Meditations* (Cambridge, 1842), 76; J. Norden, *A Progress of Piety* (Cambridge, 1848), 157; F. Rodes, *Life after Death* (1622), 21; Moore, *Mappe of Mans Mortalitie*, 233.
[194] Oldmayne, *Lifes Brevitie*, 71.
[195] J. Jewel, *Works*, ed. J. Ayre, 4 vols. (PS, 1845–50), ii. 866; Hume, *Felicitie of the Life to Come*, 21; Perkins, *Golden Chaine*, p. 141; Sutton, *Disce Mori*, 120; Denison, *A Three-fold Resolution*, 479; Kilbye, *Sermon... at the Funerall of Thomas Holland*, 11; Gaule, *Defiance to Death*, 30.
[196] Gardiner, *Devotions of the Dying Man*, 160.
[197] Strode, *Anatomie of Mortalitie*, 203–5.

enthusiasm with which the typology of sleep was adduced in these contexts suggests that there may well be scope for historians to investigate further the meanings of sleeping as a socially and culturally constructed experience in early modern England.[198]

For Protestants to make sleep the dominant image for death was not, in theological terms, an entirely risk-free strategy. To encourage the faithful to envisage their death as a falling asleep might embolden them to give credence to the doctrine of 'soul-sleeping', which in the early Tudor period had caused a nasty spat within the ranks of the English evangelical movement. Psychopannychism, the doctrine that the souls of the righteous sleep in expectation of an awakening at the Resurrection, was a doctrine associated with Luther in early Reformation England.[199] If the dead were not conscious, that dealt at a stroke with the doctrine of a purgatory where they would suffer and be purged. At the same time, maintaining that the dead did not experience blessedness in heaven immediately after their death might seem to restore soteriological meaning to a final judgement which could otherwise appear as a kind of eschatological rubber-stamping. For all these reasons, ideas about the sleep of the soul exercised an obvious appeal to early English evangelicals, who were regularly accused of holding it by Catholic opponents.[200] In the early 1530s the issue set at odds two leading reformers, William Tyndale and George Joye. Joye took exception to passages in Tyndale's *Answer to More*, which argued that it was an error (albeit a non-damnable one) to suppose that 'the souls were in heaven immediately'. Here and elsewhere Tyndale professed a sturdy agnosticism about what exactly, or where exactly, the condition of souls would be before the Last Judgement.[201] The issue was further publicized by that founding charter of English Protestantism, the testament of William Tracy, for which, as we have seen, both Tyndale and John Frith wrote commendatory prefaces. Tracy had looked forward to the 'resurrection of body and soul', a phrase that left him open to charges of denying the soul's immortality. Frith defended him from this, but glossed the phrase to refer to 'the soule

---

[198] In addition to the references already cited, see Sparke, *A Sermon preached at Whaddon*, 81–2; Pricke, *Godlie and Learned Sermon*, D3ʳ; Tuke, *A Discourse of Death*, 63; Cowper, *A Defiance to Death*, 91–2; R. Brathwaite, *Remains after Death* (1618), E7ʳ; Byfield, *Cure of the Feare of Death*, 34; Bayly, *Practise of Piety*, 113; Denison, *The Monument or Tombe-stone*, 12, 74; C. Fitz-Geffry, *Deaths Sermon unto the Living* (1620), 11; Stone, *A Curse become a Blessing*, 57; Bolton, *Foure Last Things*, 6. Further encouragement to compare death to a sleep was provided by the funeral service, which prescribed the reading of 1 Cor. 15: J. E. Booty (ed.), *The Book of Common Prayer 1559* (Charlottesville, Va., 1976), 310–12.

[199] N. T. Burns, *Christian Mortalism from Tyndale to Milton* (Cambridge, Mass., 1972), 29.

[200] Foxe, iv. 697; T. More, *The Apology*, ed. J. B. Trapp (New Haven, 1979), 101, 88; id., *The Confutation of Tyndale's Answer*, ed. L. A. Schuster *et al.* (New Haven, 1973), 288, 625, 702; R. Edgeworth, *Sermons very Fruitfull, Godly and Learned*, ed. J. Wilson (Cambridge, 1993), 129–30.

[201] W. Tyndale, *An Answer to Sir Thomas More's Dialogue*, ed. H. Walter, (PS, 1850), 127, 180–1; id., *Expositions and Notes . . . together with The Practice of Prelates*, ed. H. Walter (PS, 1849), 185.

whiche in the meane ceason semeth to lye secret'. According to the hostile
account of Germaine Gardiner, Frith stated during his last imprisonment
'that he thought no sayntes soule came in heven before the day of dome / but
in the meane season reposed hym selfe he wiste not where'.[202] In
the meantime, Joye sought to marshal evangelical opinion against the psy-
chopannychists. In a letter to Latimer from Antwerp in 1533, he claimed to
have proved 'that the sowles departyd slepe not nor lye ydle tyll domes daye
as Martin Luther and the Anabaptystes saye and as me thynkethe Frythe
and William Tyndall wolde'.[203] The following year, in preparing an unauthorized edition of Tyndale's New Testament, Joye made some twenty
changes of Tyndale's word 'resurrection' to 'the life to come', or 'the very
life', or other, his declared intention to frustrate the false opinion of
'anabaptists' that at the resurrection souls will be called from 'prevey lurking
places / in whiche they had ben hyd from the tyme of their departyng unto
the resurreccion of their bodies'. In a preface to his own revision of the New
Testament of November 1534, Tyndale denounced Joye, claiming that 'no
small nomber thorow his curiosite, utterly denye the resurreccion of the
flesshe and bodye, affirminge that the soule when she is departed, is
the spirituall bodye of the resurreccion'.[204] Joye retaliated, accusing Tyndale
of going beyond the words of Scripture by claiming that souls were not
in heaven.[205]

Despite Joye's guerrilla campaign, through the early part of the 1540s a
number of English evangelicals continued to claim that the souls of the dead
experienced no consciousness before the Last Judgement.[206] But mainstream
Reformed opinion in Europe was turning decisively away from the idea,
which was coming to be identified as an anabaptist tenet, opening the door
to mortalism (belief in the death of the soul) and annihilationism (the denial
there would ever be a resurrection of the body). In 1542 Calvin fulminated
against soul sleepers (though he avoided criticizing Luther) in his *Psycho-
pannychia*, an abbreviated translation of which appeared in English in 1549.
In the meantime John Veron had translated a dialogue against soul sleep by
Heinrich Bullinger, whose good opinion was generally highly valued by
Edwardian reformers.[207] The suggestion that the Edwardian bidding prayer
of 1547, with its hope that the departed 'may rest both body and soul' in
heaven, verged on psychopannychism is an unconvincing one; it specifically

---

[202] Burns, *Christian Mortalism*, 104–6; G. Gardiner, *A Letter of a Yonge Gentylman...
wherin Men may se the Demeanour & Heresy of John Fryth* (1534), 14ᵛ.

[203] PRO, SP 1/75, 183ʳ (*LP* vi. 402).

[204] Burns, *Christian Mortalism*, 107–8.

[205] G. Joye, *An Apology to W. Tindale 1535*, ed. E. Arber (1883), 15.

[206] G. R. Elton, *Policy and Police* (Cambridge, 1972), 117; J. F. Davis, 'Lollardy and the
Reformation in England', in P. Marshall (ed.), *The Impact of the English Reformation
1500–1640* (1997), 48; *LP* xviii (2), 546, p. 304.

[207] H. Quistorp, *Calvin's Doctrine of the Last Things* (1955), 81–9; Burns, *Christian Mortalism*, 19–24, 112–16; D. M. Loades, 'Rites of Passage and the Prayer Books of 1549 and 1552',
in M. Wilks (ed.), *Prophecy and Eschatology*, SCH Subsidia, 10 (1994), 208.

related this to 'the day of judgement'.[208] Nonetheless, in 1551 Bucer was anxious about the reference in the 1549 Prayer Book to the departed resting 'in the sleep of peace', which might 'give satisfaction to those who affirm that the dead in the Lord are asleep...until the last day'.[209] John Hooper was undoubtedly advancing the orthodox Edwardian view in his *Brief and Clear Confession of the Christian Faith* of 1550, which included as its penultimate article a repudiation of 'the fond opinion of the sleepers, which affirm that the spirits of the saints are not yet in heaven, but do sleep in a certain place unknown to us, until they shall receive their bodies at the last day'.[210] In 1553, amidst a clutch of articles condemning anabaptist doctrines, the Edwardian articles of religion laid down that 'the souls of them that depart this life do neither die with the bodies, nor sleep idly'.[211] As this excursus suggests, Protestants were generally on firmer ground when tearing up the Catholic map of the afterlife, than when filling in detail of their own.

Anxieties about the issue were receding in the second half of the sixteenth century. The Edwardian article was withdrawn from the Thirty-Nine Articles promulgated in 1563, though a number of authors of death treatises and funeral sermons continued to take side-swipes at the 'sleepy-heads', and to emphasize that the scriptural promises of sleep related to the body only and not to the soul.[212] In his 1629 treatise *Of Death a True Description*, James Cole noted that Scripture sometimes reported the dead to sleep, and sometimes to rest; he judiciously suggested that the one referred to the state of the body, the other to the soul.[213] It was for this reason, it was often rather pedantically noted, that the etymology of the word cemetery, from the Greek *koimeterion*, revealed a dorter or sleeping-place.[214]

---

[208] S. Wabuda, 'The Provision of Preaching during the Early English Reformation: With Special Reference to Itineration, c.1530 to 1547', University of Cambridge Ph.D. thesis (1992), 186.

[209] E. C. Whitaker (ed.), *Martin Bucer and the Book of Common Prayer*, ACC 55 (1974), 52.

[210] J. Hooper, *Later Writings*, ed. C. Nevinson (PS, 1852), 63.

[211] J. Ketley (ed.), *The Two Liturgies...in the Reign of King Edward VI* (PS, Cambridge, 1844), 537 (no. 40).

[212] Bullinger, *Fourth Decade*, 389–90; Veron, *Huntyng of Purgatory*, 31ʳ; Becon, *Sick Mans Salve*, 182; Anderson, *Shield of our Safetie*, G3ʳ⁻ᵛ; Sparke, *A Sermon preached at Cheanies*, 90–1; id., *A Sermon preached at Whaddon*, 83; Perkins, *Golden Chaine*, 515; Welcome, *The State of the Godly*, 53; Walker, *Sermon at the Funerals of... William Lord Russell*, 35; Robertson, *The Crowne of Life*, 370–1; Crooke, *Death Subdued*, F6ᵛ; Guy, *Pieties Pillar*, 34; Z. Boyd, *The Last Battell of the Soule in Death* (Edinburgh, 1629), 11–12; Houlbrooke, *Death*, 308. That there were no grounds for complacency about the potential of soul-sleeping ideas is suggested by their apparent revival from the 1640s, and their association with major figures such as Richard Overton, John Milton, and Thomas Hobbes: Burns, *Christian Mortalism*, ch. 4.

[213] Cole, *Of Death a True Description*, 34.

[214] Veron, *Huntyng of Purgatory*, 31ʳ; Viret, *Christian Disputations*, 67ᵛ; Cleland, *Monument of Mortalitie*, 36–7; Strode, *Anatomie of Mortalitie*, 94. See also Cressy, *Birth, Marriage, and Death*, 385–6.

By itself, however, the notion of the sleep of the body represented only half a concept; as a metaphor it made sense only in the context of the awakening of the Last Judgement, and the resurrection of the body that would accompany the Second Coming of Christ. According to Bullinger, it was to show that the body was not extinguished by death that 'holy men are said in the scriptures to sleep, not to die, that thereby the mystery of the resurrection of our flesh may be signified'.[215] A Jacobean funeral sermon by the Devon pastor Richard Carpenter reached the triumphal conclusion that 'it is but a sleep which is mis-called death, his grave is his bed, and he shall awake as sure as he lay downe, yea more fresh and glorious in the great day of resurrection'.[216]

The doctrine of the resurrection of the body has historically always been a cornerstone of Christian faith, but it seems particularly prominent in the mind-set of early modern English Protestantism.[217] To reformers of all types it was axiomatic, for example, that while funeral exequies and burial practices were of no spiritual help to the deceased, decent burial was meaningful as a token of faith in the resurrection.[218] John Donne, whose preaching was peppered with references to the resurrection of the body, insisted that 'as soon shall God tear a leaf out of the book of life and cast so many of the elect into hellfire as leave the body of any of his Saints in corruption for ever'.[219] The resurrected body itself exercised the imagination of Protestant theologians to a considerable degree, and a remarkably consistent picture was presented. At the sound of the Last Trumpet, souls would be restored to bodies, and the bodies of the living transformed 'in the twinkling of an eye'. These bodies would be perfect, agile, and luminous (like the transfigured body of Christ), having no need of food, sleep, or clothing. At the same time it was stressed that these were not new bodies, but glorified and perfected versions of the ones which had been laid in the grave, sometimes envisaged metaphorically as a furnace where the body was refined, or a bath where it was scoured and purged. Bodies would retain their distinctions of sex, but would lose all impediments, scars, and deformities. It was thought likely that

---

[215] Bullinger, *Fourth Decade*, 390.

[216] Carpenter, *The Soules Sentinel*, 110. See also Horne, *Certaine Sermons*, 74; R. Chambers, *Sarah's Sepulture, or a Funerall Sermon, preached for the Right Honourable and vertuous Lady, Dorothie Countess of Northumberland* (1620), 25; Strode, *Anatomie of Mortalitie*, 94, 203–4.

[217] Allusions to the resurrection in mid-sixteenth-century wills seem to be an indicator of Protestant sympathy: C. Litzenberger, *The English Reformation and the Laity: Gloucestershire, 1540–1580* (Cambridge, 1997), 42, 75, 79, 120, 153.

[218] J. Pilkington, *Works*, ed. J. Scholefield (PS, 1842), 320; T. Draxe, *The Earnest of our Inheritance* (1613), 60; Ford, *Sermon preached at Constantinople*, 71; Rodes, *Life after Death*, 214; G. Babington, *Workes* (1622), 124; Hooker, *Of the Laws of Ecclesiastical Polity*, ii. 401, 404; M. Day, *Doomes-Day: or, A Treatise of the Resurrection of the Body* (1636), 16.

[219] *No Man is an Island*, 161.

all (irrespective of the age at which they died) would rise at the prime of life, around the age of 33.[220]

Yet despite the enthusiasm with which they approached the subject, Protestant writers in the early seventeenth century regularly admitted that of all the doctrines of the faith, the resurrection of the body was the most difficult for people to accept, a consequence of 'our naturall incredulitie, and distrust in this point'.[221] To coin an unfortunate phrase, the devil was in the detail. Protestant writers on the Last Judgement imagined doubters rehearsing hypothetical objections familiar to their medieval scholastic predecessors: what if a man were eaten by a wolf, the wolf by a lion, the lion by birds, and the birds by other men; what of those eaten by cannibals?[222] The multiplication of detailed, practical questions about the mechanics of the operation was Satan's preferred strategy to make it 'bee thought a meere *dreame and fable*'.[223] Just as with the issue of post-mortem reunions, there was a concern in some quarters that the people would miss the point, approaching questions about the resurrection in a grossly material way.

In a good many orthodox Protestant accounts of the life to come, there was a distinct emphasis on deferred gratification, a privileging of the imagery of sleep and the joys to be experienced by the resurrected. Here was the ultimate revelation of God's majesty and infinite power. Rather less interest was displayed in the intermediate state, except in so far as reformers were concerned to steer a course between egregious errors: the Scylla of popish purgatory, and the Charybdis of soul-sleeping and mortalism.[224] The obsession of the medieval Church with negotiating the counterfeit demands of purgatory had engendered a crude foreshortening of the eternal perspective of Christianity. Many Protestant reformers refocused their own hopes on the end of time, an end which some at least did not believe to be so far

[220] This synthetic presentation is compiled from Perkins, *Golden Chaine*, 143, 519; Gardiner, *Doomes-Day booke*, 54–5; Denison, *A Three-fold Resolution*, 486–9; Draxe, *The Earnest of our Inheritance* A3ʳ, 48–57; Price, *Spirituall Odours*, 45; Barlow, *Hierons Last Fare-well*, 27; Byfield, *Cure of the Feare of Death*, 139; Harris, *Samuels Funerall*, 10; Bayly, *Practise of Piety*, 119–24; Crooke, *Death Subdued*, G11ʳ⁻ᵛ; Aslakssøn, *Description of Heaven*, 77; S. Denison, *Another Tombestone* (1627), 38; Gardiner, *Devotions of the Dying Man*, 385; Bolton, *Foure Last Things*, 129–40. See also Patrides, *Milton and the Christian Tradition*, 283–4; Houlbrooke, *Death*, 42–3. *Pace* N. Llewellyn, 'The Royal Body: Monuments to the Dead, For the Living', in L. Gent and N. Llewellyn (eds.), *Renaissance Bodies: The Human Figure in English Culture c.*1540–1660 (1990), 221–2, it would seem emphatically not the case that 'the sense of separation between the decaying body and the eternal soul had been increased by reformist attacks on the doctrine of purgatory and the prohibition on masses for the dead'.
[221] Moore, *Mappe of Mans Mortalitie*, 246. See also Draxe, *The Earnest of our Inheritance*, A2ʳ; Drummond, *A Midnights Trance*, 94; Cole, *Of Death a True Description*, 38.
[222] Barlow, *Hierons Last Fare-well*, 25; Gardiner, *Doomes-Day booke*, 47, 54. Cf. Bynum, 'Material Continuity', 243–4, 260, 282, 288.
[223] Day, *Doomes-Day*, 192.
[224] I dissent here from the conclusion of Houlbrooke, *Death*, 41, that most reformers were reluctant to dwell on the fact that the happiness of the saved would not be complete till after the resurrection, 'probably fearing that to do so might encourage a reopening of the question of the existence of purgatory'.

away.[225] Yet a more difficult question to assess is that of the extent to which these attitudes took root in religious culture more generally.

In the first years of James I's reign a convicted murderer and housebreaker, Robert Tetherton, was pressed to make a full confession before he faced the gallows, and was urged to reflect upon the Last Judgement. But Tetherton was reported to have brushed these urgings aside, and to have asked 'why there should be a generall iudgement, at the end of the world, if the soule passe a triall and receive reward forthwith upon the departure hence?'[226] It would be surprising if other, less extreme, sinners never posed themselves the same question.[227] In a study of wills from sixteenth-century Madrid, Carlos Eire reflects on 'the nearly universal tendency of Western Christendom' to overlook the orthodox teaching that Christ redeemed the whole human person body and soul: 'little mention is ever made of the promised resurrection of the body...It is the soul—and *only* the soul—that is created and redeemed by the blood of the Lord. The body simply dissolves into the earth and disappears.'[228] In broad terms, this characterization would seem to work for later Reformation England also. Ralph Houlbrooke's study of wills across the period 1558–1660 leads him to conclude that 'the great majority of preambles were concerned with the destination of the soul rather than the ultimate fate of the body'. A relatively small number expressed hopes of resurrection, and still fewer made explicit reference to the reunion of soul and body.[229] My own sampling of the testamentary evidence confirms Houlbrooke's intuition. Of 424 wills granted probate in the archdeaconry court of Suffolk in 1625 and 1626, for example, 251 (59 per cent) expressed an explicit assurance or hope of salvation, usually by the merits of Christ's passion, but of these only 48 (11 per cent) made any direct reference to the resurrection of the body.[230] Interestingly, when testators did so, they often echoed that most contentious phrase of the burial service, the 'sure and certain hope of the resurrection'.[231] Very rare indeed was the kind

[225] On this theme, see B. W. Ball, *A Great Expectation: Eschatological Thought in English Protestantism to 1660* (Leiden, 1975); R. Bauckham, *Tudor Apocalypse* (Appleford, Oxon., 1978); P. Christianson, *Reformers and Babylon: English Apocalyptic Visions from the Reformation to the Eve of the Civil War* (Toronto, 1978); K. R. Firth, *The Apocalyptic Tradition in Reformation Britain 1530–1645* (Oxford, 1979).

[226] *A True Report of the Horrible Murther which was Committed in the House of Sir Ierome Bowes* (1607), D2ᵛ–3ʳ. Tetherton was answered that, though there was an increase in joys for the elect, and pains for the damned, he should principally remember that the Last Judgement would be 'for a publique honour of the blessed, and for an open shame and contempt of the cursed', and that his shame 'should bee written on his forehead'.

[227] As we have seen, Elnathan Parr's catechism supposed that it would be.

[228] C. Eire, *From Madrid to Purgatory: The Art and Craft of Dying in Sixteenth-Century Spain* (Cambridge, 1995), 80–1.

[229] Houlbrooke, *Death*, 124.

[230] Allen (ed.), *Wills of the Archdeaconry of Suffolk 1625–6*.

[231] J. Atkinson *et al.* (eds.), *Darlington Wills and Inventories 1600–1625*, SS 201 (1993), 64, 83; Allen (ed.), *Wills of the Archdeaconry of Suffolk 1620–1624*, 74, 75, 300, 341, 349, 375, 442, 443.

of theological sophistication found in the will of Thomas Jonys, a Bristol timber merchant, in 1554. Jonys was confident that when he was loosed from the 'corrupte tabernacle' of the body, he would join those 'whiche alreadie ar revested with the first stole that is the glory of the soule', before in due course receiving 'the seconde stole whiche is the glorie of the bodie at the laste daie of iudgement'.[232]

Wills, of course, were concerned primarily with the immediate disposal of the goods of the deceased, and by analogy their spiritual concerns were with the imminent requirements of body and soul. One might expect the longer-term view to be more evident on tombs and monuments, structures which their patrons and builders clearly hoped would stand until the Last Judgement. Art historians have traced the process whereby the general resurrection gradually emerged as 'the great religious theme of English sculpture up to the Restoration and beyond'.[233] Inscriptions and epitaphs which alluded to the resurrection (often invoking Job 19: 25–6, 'in my flesh shall I see God') begin to appear with some regularity on brasses and stone monuments in Elizabeth's reign, particularly from the 1570s onwards.[234] After around 1600, the subject began to impinge on monumental sculpture. A handful of monuments in the second and third decades of the seventeenth century showed the body of the deceased rising from the grave, a form which allowed the representation of religious subject matter without involving the doctrinally sensitive issue of specifically religious imagery (angels were an optional extra). The fashion reached its artistic apogee in Nicholas Stone's famous 1631–2 monument to John Donne in St Paul's Cathedral, a sculpture in white marble depicting the poet standing erect, and beginning to emerge from his shroud.[235] By the time Donne's monument was completed, John Weever was complaining of the adorning of tombs with 'pictures of naked men and women; raising out of the dust'.[236] The characteristic form of these

---

[232] T. P. Wadley (ed.), *Notes or Abstracts of... the Great Orphan Book and Book of Wills* (Bristol, 1886), 189.

[233] A. White, 'Church Monuments in Britain c.1560–c.1660', University of London Ph.D. thesis (1991), 405–22 (quote at p. 416). See also K. Cohen, *Metamorphosis of a Death Symbol: The Transi Tomb in the Late Middle Ages and the Renaissance* (Berkeley Calif., 1973), 131–2; B. Kemp, *English Church Monuments* (1980), 165–6; J. Hurtig, 'Seventeenth-Century Shroud Tombs', *The Art Bulletin*, 64 (1982).

[234] Ravenshawe, *Antiente Epitaphs*, 36, 38, 44, 57, 59, 75; Badger, *Monumental Brasses of Warwickshire*, 4, 38; Macklin, *Brasses of England*, 274; Mosse, *Monumental Effigies of Sussex*, 24, 29; Connor, *Monumental Brasses in Somerset*, 90, 229, 242, 306, 313, 317, pl. xliv; D'Elboux (ed.), *Monumental Brasses of Essex*, ii. 83; Roper, *Monumental Effigies of Gloucestershire*, 166, 197, 332, 333, 477, 547; Greenhill, *Incised Effigial Slabs*, i. 333, 337; MacCulloch, *Chorography of Suffolk*, 90, 92; Lack *et al.* (eds.), *The Monumental Brasses of Berkshire*, 27, 49; Roper, *Monumental Effigies of Gloucestershire*, 28; White, 'Church Monuments in Britain', 405, 406, 408; J. Wilson, 'I Dote on Death: The Fractured Marriage in English Renaissance Art and Literature', *Church Monuments*, 11 (1996), 58; J. Finch, *Church Monuments in Norfolk before 1830: An Archaeology of Commemoration* (Oxford, 2000), 138–9.

[235] Conveniently reproduced in P. C. Jupp and C. Gittings (eds.), *Death in England* (Manchester, 1999), 168.

[236] Weever, *Ancient Funerall Monuments*, 11.

monuments—a shrouded demi-figure arising from the dead—had its antecedents in a form employed on late medieval brasses. There is an irony, though not necessarily a contradiction, in the fact that depictions of the resurrection on English tombs in the early seventeenth century may provide simultaneous evidence of the absorption of Protestant doctrine, and the re-emergence of a pre-Reformation iconographical tradition.

Yet it is striking that epitaphs which made reference to the reunion of loved ones after this life only occasionally did so in the context of the resurrection; more commonly they envisaged a meeting in heaven immediately after the death of the survivor.[237] Sometimes these showed scant regard for the biblical teaching that there would be no marriage in the life to come. The brass of the widow Elizabeth Alfraye at Battle in Sussex (1590) referred to her soul seeking out that of her husband 'among the saints above / And there in endless blysse enioye her long desired love'. A 1621 monument erected by Humphrey Gunter in memory of his wife Mary at Fawley in Berkshire states 'My mornefull soule doth wish it where tho art. / Till then farewell sweet saynt, my halfe, my hart'. The inscription to Dorothy Pytt at Ombury, Shropshire (1630), personified death as divorcing her from her husband's side, leaving him to grieve 'Till death, by striking him, weds her againe'. The 1635 tomb of Lady Margaret Throckmorton in the Lord Mayor's Chapel, Bristol, stated that she had left to her husband 'this sole pledge of love / Her statue toombe and hope in heavnly licht / To meete again his blessed Margarit'.[238] These monuments, like the many which affirmed the deceased to be alive in heaven, demonstrate an outlook which did not regard the soul's sojourn in heaven as merely an interim and provisional anticipation of full blessedness, nor one which consigned the dead to a realm beyond the limits of human knowledge, love, or longing. The clergy of the Church of England did not always discourage these deeply human hopes and yearnings.

It has become something of a truism among cultural historians that the commemorative culture of Elizabethan and early Stuart England was profoundly retrospective, its nodal points the articulation of social hierarchy and the celebration of secular achievement. The demise of the imperative to

---

[237] Connor, *Monumental Brasses in Somerset*, 241; Roper, *Monumental Effigies of Gloucestershire*, 563. Ravenshaw, *Antiente Epitaphs*, 28, 34, 55 , 69. The Jacobean epitaph composed by her husband for Lucy Bromfield at Titchfield, Hants., read: 'Here by him dead, I dead desire to lye, / Till, rais'd to life, wee meet no more to dye.' Ibid. 62. See F. Bamford (ed.), *A Royalist's Notebook: The Commonplace Book of Sir John Oglander* (1936), 83, where Oglander imagines his prematurely dead son advising his parents 'not to be so overgrieved with my travelling thither, where all happiness inhabits and where shortly I shall meet you both to our unspeakable comfort'.

[238] Mosse, *Monumental Effigies of Sussex*, 25; Lack *et al.* (eds.), *The Monumental Brasses of Berkshire*, 67; Ravenshaw, *Antiente Epitaphs*, 77; Roper, *Monumental Effigies of Gloucestershire*, 77. See also Greenhill, *Incised Effigial Slabs*, i. 340–1, 342; Connor, *Monumental Brasses in Somerset*, 257.

pray for the dead resulted in a kind of 'secularization' or at least 'naturalization' of their memory; the deceased were contemplated as exemplifications of past virtue rather than as persons with whom any kind of continuing relationship could be envisaged.[239] There is some truth to this, but the evidence in this chapter points to a culture in which supposedly more 'secular' habits of thinking about the dead continued to be shaded by a decidedly prospective interest in their 'estate' in the next life. There is no doubt that the abolition of purgatory was a huge cultural watershed, and brought with it a heightened sense of distance and separation between this world and the next, of the strangeness and 'otherness' of the dead. Yet at the same time these changes created their own counter-currents: a compulsion to affirm that the beloved dead were saints in heaven, and to express the expectation of meeting them again. Paradoxically, an insistence on the inability of the dead to know or care about living relatives may have added poignancy to the theme of post-mortem reunion. Clerical elites explored these themes in various ways, some downplaying the immediate beatitude of the dead to concentrate upon the joys of the elect following the Last Judgement; others demonstrating more concern with the society the saints would enjoy in the 'intermediate state'. In the process one can see Protestant eschatology functioning as a kind of applied science, addressing legitimate concerns about the nature of life beyond the grave. Of course it had to take account of profoundly theological absolutes—the absence of purgatory, the inability of the living to ameliorate the condition of the dead—but these were necessarily processed in intimate and pastoral contexts. It was not, however, a particularly smooth or coherent process, and it left in its wake a number of anomalous attitudes and impulses. These included notions about the dead who seemingly refused to remain fixed in their estate in the next life, a question to which attention must now turn.

[239] For suggestions to this effect, see Gittings, *Death, Burial and the Individual*, 144–9; R. Rex, 'Monumental Brasses and the Reformation', *Transactions of the Monumental Brass Society*, 14 (1990); N. Llewellyn, *The Art of Death: Visual Culture in the English Death Ritual c.1500–1800* (London, 1991), 28, 46–9; M. Neill, *Issues of Death: Mortality and Identity in English Renaissance Tragedy* (Oxford, 1997), 38–42, 48; N. Pounds, *A History of the English Parish: The Culture of Religion from Augustine to Victoria* (Cambridge, 2000), 497.

6

The Disorderly Dead: Ghosts and their Meanings in Reformation England

GHOSTS, revenants, spectres—perceived presences of persons perished—have been allotted virtually no role in conventional histories of the English Reformation. Nor, more surprisingly, have they featured much in the recent scholarship on the social history of death in England.[1] Ghostlore (the word itself an indicator of professional historians' inattention) has for decades been principally the preserve of folklorists, and of literary critics, the latter drawn to the topic by the fortuitous presence of a ghost at the heart of the greatest dramatic work in the English language.[2]

This neglect undoubtedly reflected, in the days before the advent of the new cultural history, a shared understanding of the kind of topics with which serious historians should concern themselves. But it also points to a methodological difficulty, for ghosts, appropriately enough perhaps, are for the period covered by this book peculiarly intangible and elusive in terms of their evidential traces. There are only very occasional references to them in the records of the secular or ecclesiastical courts. In a couple of Jacobean Star Chamber cases, for example, defendants were alleged to have fabricated appearances of spirits in order to terrify the plaintiffs into handing over property to them.[3] But it may be significant that spirits of the dead seem to have played very little part in English witchcraft cases in this period. English

---

[1] There is a single passing reference in Cressy, *Birth, Marriage and Death*, 402–3; two in Houlbrooke, *Death*, 40, 291.

[2] K. Briggs, *The Anatomy of Puck: An Examination of Fairy Beliefs among Shakespeare's Contemporaries and Successors* (1959), ch. 9; T. Brown, *The Fate of the Dead: A Study in Folk-Eschatology in the West Country After the Reformation* (Ipswich, 1979); H. Ellis Davidson and W. Russell (eds.), *The Folklore of Ghosts* (Cambridge, 1981); G. Bennett, 'Ghost and Witch in the Sixteenth and Seventeenth Century', *Folklore*, 97 (1986). For the extensive literature prompted by the 'ghost problem' in *Hamlet*, see below, n. 143. Among historical works, K. Thomas, *Religion and the Decline of Magic: Studies in Popular Beliefs in Sixteenth- and Seventeenth-Century England* (Harmondsworth, 1973), ch. 19, is the most significant contribution. R. Finucane, *Appearances of the Dead: A Cultural History of Ghosts* (1982) is a useful survey, but chronologically broad and pan-European in scope. There are some suggestive remarks in R. Hutton, 'English Reformation and the Evidence of Folklore', *PP* 148 (1995).

[3] C. L. Ewen, *Witchcraft in the Star Chamber* (1938), 15–16.

church courts were concerned with the orderly administration of canon law; they were no Inquisition monitoring and policing the beliefs of the populace. No one in Elizabethan or early Stuart England, it would seem, was put on trial simply for maintaining they had seen a ghost. In a handful of cases where central authority instigated inquiries into supposed hauntings we can see that the motive was a political one, the involvement of high personages. In the 1580s the Council was understandably interested in the spirit that appeared to Mary Cocker of Hertfordshire to warn her of a threat to the life of the queen, and it took seriously the defence of the 'apparition of souls after their departure out of this life' by Henry Caesar, vicar of Lostwithiel in Cornwall, because of his allegation that Sir Walter Mildmay had engaged a conjuror to summon up the ghost of Cardinal Pole.[4] In the late 1630s the Council pressed the magistrates to investigate an apparition in Minehead, Somerset, which was apparently casting aspersions on the morality of the Protestant bishop of Waterford.[5]

Printed evidence too looks at first glance unpromising. With the exception of a rather eccentric piece on *The Terrors of the Night*, penned by Thomas Nashe in the 1590s, there was nothing corresponding to a native English ghost treatise published in this period. A Latin work on spectres written at around the same time by an Oxford cleric, Randall Hutchins, remained in manuscript till the twentieth century.[6] The really significant work was imported. The treatise *De Spectris*, by the Zurich minister Ludwig Lavater, was translated by Robert Harrison in 1572, and a second edition appeared in 1596.[7] The *IIII Livres des Spectres* of Lavater's French Catholic opponent Pierre Le Loyer was translated in 1605 by Zachary Jones; or rather the first book only, dealing with demonic and delusory apparitions, was translated. When Le Loyer turned to 'the matter itselfe of Specters and Apparitions', i.e. the possibility of 'real' ghosts, Jones ended his work of translation with an abrupt 'Finis'.[8] In the period before the civil war, there was no extensive and fully developed genre of ghost treatises in English, and the ghost-hunting historian is obliged to sift painstakingly for references through a mass of works of theology and religious controversy, writings on witchcraft, sermons and pastoral treatises, literary and dramatic pieces, ballads, pamphlets, and tracts.

---

[4] PRO, SP 12/200, 65; 12/173, 114; 12/176, 46; A. L. Rowse, *Tudor Cornwall* (1941), 334–6.
[5] PRO, SP 16/383, 13^r–18^r; W. Laud, *Works*, ed. W. Scott and J. Bliss, 7 vols. (Oxford, 1847–60), vii. 301–2.
[6] T. Nashe, *The Terrors of the Night*, in *The Works of Thomas Nashe*, ed. R. B. McKerrow and F. Wilson (Oxford, 1958), i. 345–86; R. Hutchins, *Of Specters*, tr. and ed. V. B. Heltzel and C. Murley, *Huntington Library Quarterly*, 11 (1947–8).
[7] L. Lavater, *Of Ghostes and Spirites Walking by Night 1572*, ed. J. Dover Wilson and M. Yardley (Oxford, 1929).
[8] P. Le Loyer, *A Treatise of Specters or Strange Sights, Visions and Apparitions appearing sensibly unto Men*, tr. Z. Jones (1605), quote at p. 145^r. Jones's preface and marginalia offer occasional apologies for Le Loyer's popish opinions: A3^v, A4^v–5^r, 88^v.

But despite the difficulty of detection, no scholar interested in the Reformation as an agent of cultural change can afford to ignore what ghosts have to say. Commenting on the European scene as a whole, R. W. Scribner thought it distinctly curious that 'despite removing belief in purgatory and so dramatically reorientating attitudes to the dead, Protestantism was unable to abolish belief in the presence of the untimely dead, and ghosts and poltergeists plagued Protestants and Catholics with confessional indifference'.[9] The confessions, however, were hardly indifferent to ghosts. More than any other manifestation of popular religious culture, belief in ghosts challenged the Protestant maxims that the dead had no interest in the affairs of the living, and the living no role to play in securing the happiness of the deceased. According to Sir Keith Thomas (one of very few historians to give serious attention to the topic), belief in ghosts was 'a shibboleth which distinguished Protestant from Catholic almost as effectively as belief in the Mass or the Papal Supremacy'. Ghosts, thought Thomas, 'presented no problems' to reformers in the first century of the Reformation.[10] But this perception may need to be revised. In a particularly distilled form ghosts exemplify a theme and a paradox already articulated in this study. On the one hand, they point to the propensity of attitudes towards the dead to act as a motor of religious reform and a clear marker of confessional and cultural boundaries. On the other, they suggest the ways in which the emotional claims and cultural leverage exercised by dead ancestors could prove peculiarly intractable to the dictates of Protestant orthodoxy, and even encourage some of the self-proclaimed defenders of that orthodoxy to muffle the distinctive tones of their divinity.

GHOSTS, SCRIPTURE, AND POLEMIC

As we have seen, 'popular' and 'official' notions about the nature and motivation of revenants in the later Middle Ages existed in uneasy, and sometimes crooked, alignment.[11] But the perception that the appearance of a ghost demanded ritual action directed towards securing the quietude of the apparition was a fairly universal one. The doctrine of purgatory supplied a theological rationale which proved compatible with more 'folkloric', atavistic, beliefs. It is no surprise, therefore, that in the minds of many Elizabethan and Jacobean Protestant writers, ghosts were indelibly associated with the abrogated doctrines of purgatory and intercessory masses.[12]

[9] R. Scribner, 'Elements of Popular Belief', in T. Brady, H. Oberman, and J. Tracey (eds.), *Handbook of European History 1400–1600*, 2 vols. (Leiden, 1994–5), i. 237.

[10] Thomas, *Religion*, 703, 704.

[11] See above, 12–18.

[12] Much of what follows draws on my 'Deceptive Appearances: Ghosts and Reformers in Elizabethan and Jacobean England', in H. L. Parish and W. G. Naphy (eds.), *Religion and 'Superstition' in Reformation Europe* (Manchester, forthcoming).

Indeed, it was often alleged, ghosts were not some accidental waste-product of the popish purgatory, but the foundation of the whole edifice. In a sermon of 1564 the bishop of London, Edmund Grindal, claimed that the doctrine of purgatory was 'maintained principally by feigned apparitions, visions of spirits, and other like fables'.[13] No one would have heard of purgatory, according to Henry Smith, 'but for these spirites which walked in the night, and tolde them that they were the soules of such and such, which suffred in fire till their masses, and almes, and pilgrimages did raunsome them out'.[14] Stories about the appearance of ghosts encapsulated the ignorance, credulity, and corruption of papists, whereas the rejection of them by Protestants was symptomatic of a sober, scriptural faith. In a funeral sermon of 1552, Robert King contrasted the reliance of the spirit on the unadorned Word of God with the wayward craving of the flesh: 'it sekethe the trueth at the deade, it geveth credite to spirites'.[15] The Jacobean bishop Thomas Morton argued that Romanists displayed an 'infatuation' with 'ghostly apparitions, which Protestants dare not beleeve', and the view that Catholic authorities habitually and promiscuously appealed to the authority of ghosts to prop up their imaginary purgatory was a recurrent refrain throughout the period.[16]

In their efforts to discredit popish visions of the dead, Protestant authors turned instinctively to Scripture. While a huge array of scriptural texts could be deployed against purgatory, there were few places in the Bible that seemed to have a specific application to the question of ghosts. Mention was frequently made of the warnings to the Israelites in Deuteronomy and Isaiah not to consult with the dead,[17] but usually only two proof-texts were construed at any length, one from the Old Testament, and one from the New. The New Testament passage was Luke's parable of the rich man and

[13] E. Grindal, *Remains*, ed. W. Nicholson (PS, 1843), 24.
[14] H. Smith, *Sermons* (1592), 540–1.
[15] R. King, *A Funerall Sermon that was prepared to have bine preached...for a certein honourable lady then almoste deade, but afterward recovered* (1552), G3ᵛ–4ʳ.
[16] T. Morton, *A Catholike Appeale for Protestants* (1609), 428; J. Frith, *The Revelation of Antichrist* (1529), F8ʳ⁻ᵛ; M. Coverdale, *Remains*, ed. G. Pearson (PS, 1846), 475; T. Cranmer, *Miscellaneous Writings and Letters*, ed. J. E. Cox (PS, 1846), 63; J. Veron, *The Huntyng of Purgatory to Death* (1561), 201ᵛ; J. Calfhill, *An Answer to John Martiall's Treatise of the Cross*, ed. R. Gibbings, (PS, 1846), 90; H. Bullinger, *The Decades: The Fourth Decade*, ed. T. Harding (PS, 1851), 400; Lavater, *Of Ghostes*, 110; W. Fulke, *Two Treatises Written against the Papistes* (1577), 163–4; G. Wither, *A View of the Marginal Notes of the Popish Testament* (1588), 74; M. Sutcliffe, *Adversus Roberti Bellarmini de Purgatorio Disputationem* (1599), 101; E. Hoby, *A Letter to Mr T.H.* (1609), 42; S. Purchas, *Purchas his Pilgrimage* (1613), 179; T. Beard, *A Retractive from the Romish Religion* (1616), 414; R. Horne, *Certaine Sermons of the Rich Man and Lazarus* (1619), 135; R. Jenison, *The Height of Israels Heathenish Idolatrie* (1621), 143; J. Donne, *Sermons*, ed. E. M. Simpson and G. R. Potter, 10 vols. (Berkeley and Los Angeles, 1953–62), x. 145–6; A. Cooke, *Worke, More Work, and a Little More Worke for a Masse-Priest*, 3rd edn. (1630), 46.
[17] J. Frith, *Work*, ed. N. T. Wright (Oxford, 1978), 174–5; Calfhill, *Answer to Martiall*, 90; A. Anderson, *The Shield of our Safetie Set Foorth* (1581), H2ʳ; R. Scot, *The Discoverie of Witchcraft* (1584), 139; G. Gifford, *A Dialogue concerning Witches and Witchcraftes* (1593), F2ʳ; Horne, *Certaine Sermons*, 134.

Lazarus. The rich man in hell spies Lazarus afar off in 'the bosom of Abraham', and pleads with Abraham to send Lazarus to his father's house to warn his five brothers of the fate that awaits them if they do not mend their ways. Abraham replies that they have Moses and the prophets, and that if they will not listen to them they would not repent even if one were to rise from the dead.[18] To Protestants, the passage seemed an unambiguous assertion of the primacy of the word of Scripture as the sole source of revelation, over the visions, apparitions, and human traditions of their papist opponents. In the words of the Elizabethan bishop of Exeter William Alley, 'by this place it is most certaine, and evidently confuted that the soules have not, nor can not appeare after their death'.[19] The glosses of the Catholic Rheims New Testament of 1582, which argued that if damned souls showed such concern for their relatives on earth, the saints and saved souls would show much greater solicitude, called forth a new wave of attacks on 'extraordinarie instruction by the dead'.[20] In 1619 Robert Horne published a series of sermons on the parable, and concluded that 'wee learne that the doctrine of teaching man, by men from the dead, is a doctrine from hell'.[21]

More widely canvassed, however, was a text which, from the Protestant point of view, proved rather more problematic, the account in the first book of Samuel of Saul's encounter with the Witch of Endor. Saul asked God how he would fare in his battle with the Philistines, and when the Lord declined to answer him, he turned to 'a woman that hath a familiar spirit'. The witch summoned up the spirit of the dead prophet Samuel, who correctly foretold Saul's death in battle.[22] Laying aside miracles associated directly with the ministry of Christ, this was the the Scriptures' sole instance of the appearance of a dead soul, and it was a text to which Protestant commentators repeatedly turned in their determination to demonstrate that God had forbidden all forms of communication between the living and the dead. The crucial issue was stated by Thomas Bilson in 1599: this 'hath moved much question in the church of God, whether it were *Samuel* in deede that rose and spake, or whether it were the divell transforming himselfe into the likenesse of *Samuel* to drive *Saul* into dispaire'.[23] With some qualifications, the former interpretation was upheld by Catholic exegesis in the late sixteenth and early seventeenth centuries, the Douai Bible of 1609

---

[18] Luke 16: 23–31.
[19] W. Alley, *The Poore Mans Librarie* (1571), 53ᵛ. See also Cranmer, *Miscellaneous Writings*, 43; Bullinger, *Fourth Decade*, 401; Anderson, *Shield of our Safetie*, H2ʳ.
[20] Wither, *View of the Marginal Notes*, 74; W. Fulke, *The Text of the New Testament of Iesus Christ, translated ... by the Papists of the Traiterous Seminarie at Rhemes* (1589), 119; W. Perkins, *A Reformed Catholike* (Cambridge, 1598), 250; Sutcliffe, *Adversus Roberti Bellarmini de Purgatorio Disputationem*, 101; Jenison, *Height of Israel's Idolatrie*, 146; G. Strode, *The Anatomie of Mortalitie* (1632), 71.
[21] Horne, *Certaine Sermons*, 122.
[22] 1 Sam. 28: 1–19.
[23] T. Bilson, *The Effect of Certaine Sermons ... preached at Pauls Crosse* (1599), 204.

adding the marginal note 'soules sometimes appeare after death'.[24] Bilson, along with virtually all shades of opinion in the Church of England, was in no doubt that this reading was false. In their marginal annotations to verse 14—'And Saul perceived that it was Samuel'—both the Geneva and the Bishops' bibles explained, 'To his imagination, albeit it was Sathan in dede'.[25] As William Perkins helpfully put it, Scripture often speaks of things 'not as they are in themselves, but as they seeme to us'.[26] Henry Smith invoked the linguistic figure of metonymy to make the same point: the delusion was called Samuel 'as the bookes of Calvin are called Calvine . . . as he that playeth the king upon a stage, is called a king'.[27] Protestant exegetes adduced numerous reasons why Saul did not really see the soul of the prophet: the souls of the dead are at rest; the Lord had refused to answer Saul by ordinary means; the true Samuel would have reproved Saul for resorting with witches, and could not have prophesied that Saul (a reprobate) would be with him in paradise the next day.[28] Moreover, commentators noted that Saul had bowed down before the apparition: a true prophet would not have suffered himself to be worshipped, whereas what Satan desires most is for his followers 'to adore him as a

[24] R. Bellarmine, *Liber de Purgatorio*, in *De Controversiis Christianae Fidei Adversus Huuis Temporis Haereticos*, 5 vols. (Ingolstadt, 1601), ii. 791–2; *The Holie Bible Faithfully Translated into English . . . by the English College of Doway*, 2 vols. (Douai, 1609–10), i. 631–2; N. Taillepied, *A Treatise of Ghosts*, tr. M. Summers (1934), 152–7. A more agnostic attitude is evident in W. Allen, *A Defense and Declaration of the Catholike Churches Doctrine touching Purgatory* (Antwerp, 1565), 110ᵛ.

[25] *The Holie Bible* [Bishops' Bible] (1568), 50ʳ; the Bible [Geneva version] (1599 edn.), 109. The story is treated in some detail by I. Aepinus, *Liber de Purgatorio* (1549), 41ʳ–54ʳ; Lavater, *Of Ghostes*, 127–45; Anderson, *Shield of our Safetie*, H2ᵛ–I1ʳ; P. Martyr, *The Common Places*, tr. A. Marten (1583), 72–7; Scot, *Discoverie*, 139–52; G. Gifford, *A Discourse of the Subtill Practises of Devilles by Witches and Sorcerers* (1587), E1ᵛ–3ᵛ; H. Holland, *A Treatise against Witchcraft* (Cambridge, 1590), C1ᵛ–3ʳ; A. Willett, *Synopsis Papismi* (1592), 305–6; Hutchins, *Of Specters*, 424–6; J. Deacon and J. Walker, *Dialogical Discourses of Spirits and Divels* (1601), 120–26; W. Perkins, *A Discourse of the Damned Art of Witchcraft* (Cambridge, 1608), 108–20; T. Cooper, *The Mystery of Witchcraft* (1617), 151–4. Briefer mentions in Frith, *Work*, 175; J. Hooper, *Early Writings*, ed. S. Carr (PS, 1843), 326; King, *A Funerall Sermon*, G2ʳ; F. Coxe, *A Short Treatise declaringe the Detestable Wickedness of Magicall Sciences*, (1561), B2ʳ; Bullinger, *The Fourth Decade*, 403; Alley, *Poore Mans Librarie*, 54ʳ; P. Viret, *The Christian Disputations*, tr. J. Brooke (1579), 104ᵛ; W. Fulke, *A Defence of the Sincere and True Translations of the Holy Scriptures*, ed. C. H. Hartshorne (PS, 1843), 299–300, 313; Fulke, *Two Treatises*, 164; Smith, *Sermons*, 538–9; W. Covell, *Polimanteia* (Cambridge, 1595), O3ᵛ; James I, *Daemonologie*, ed. G. B. Harrison (1924), 79–80; A. Willett, *Testrastylon Papisimi* (1599), 159; W. Perkins, *A Golden Chaine* (Cambridge, 1600), 50; Horne, *Certaine Sermons*, 122; J. Cotta, *The Triall of Witchcraft* (1616), 31, 37; R. Bernard, *A Guide to Grand-Iury Men* (1627), 106. Medieval interpretations of the passage are discussed in J.-C. Schmitt, *Ghosts in the Middle Ages: The Living and the Dead in Medieval Society*, tr. T. L. Fagan (Chicago and London, 1998), 15–17; linguistic and exegetical issues in M. Summers, *The History of Witchcraft and Demonology* (1926), 177–81.

[26] Perkins, *Discourse of the Damned Art*, 113.

[27] Smith, *Sermons*, 538.

[28] Holland, *Treatise against Witchcraft*, C2ʳ; Perkins, *Golden Chaine*, 515; *Discourse of the Damned Art*, 109–10, 112, 115; Deacon and Walker, *Dialogical Discourses*, 121–2; Cooper, *Mystery of Witchcraft*, 151–2.

God'.[29] To Protestants, then, the utility of the story was clear: it provided a confutation, in the words of the Coventry minister Thomas Cooper, of 'that which the *Church of Rome* doates concerning the *walking of dead men*'.[30] It was also, suggested Perkins, a caveat to us 'not easily to give credit to any such apparitions. For though they seeme never so true and evident, yet such is the power and skill of the devill, that he can quite deceive us.'[31]

Yet the text in question was an ambivalent and potentially deceptive one. In the first place, Catholic controversialists could point out that another book of the Bible, Ecclesiasticus, made reference to the story, asserting unambiguously that Samuel prophesied after his death.[32] Protestants could of course respond that Ecclesiasticus was not a canonical book; in Perkins's view 'a very worthie description of Christian Ethicks... yet it is not scripture'.[33] To Henry Holland, this merely indicated that 'most Jews of those times did imagin ther might be some conference with spirits and soules of men'—the congruence of Catholic and Jewish superstition about ghosts was itself a polemical trope.[34] Yet the fact that the Book of Common Prayer sanctioned the use of such apocryphal books in public worship was a source of irritation and embarrassment to some Protestants. In December 1584 the issue was raised at a conference at Lambeth between Archbishop Whitgift and the puritans Thomas Sparke and Walter Travers, convened in the presence of the earl of Leicester, Lord Grey of Pirgo, and Sir Francis Walsingham. Whitgift was compelled to admit that the relevant chapter of Ecclesiasticus was appointed to be read in church, prompting Lord Grey to ask 'what error the people might be in daunger to learne by the hearing of this read, and by believing of it?' To this, in Travers's account, the archbishop had no satisfactory answer.[35]

At much the same time a yet more unsettling interpretative trajectory was discharging from the pen of Reginald Scot, who treated the story of Samuel and Saul at some length in his *Discoverie of Witchcraft*. Scot's interpretation shockingly broke ranks with the orthodox Protestant one in arguing that there was no manifestation of the devil, but merely 'an illusion or cousenage practised by the witch'. 'Samuel' was a role played by an accomplice kept in

[29] Willett, *Synopsis Papisimi*, 306; Perkins, *Discourse of the Damned Art*, 111; *Golden Chaine*, 50; Gifford, *Discourse of the Subtill Practises of Devilles*, E1ᵛ; Holland, *Treatise against Witchcraft*, C2ʳ.

[30] Cooper, *Mystery of Witchcraft*, 152.

[31] Perkins, *Discourse of the Damned Art*, 118

[32] Bellarmine, *De Purgatorio*, 792; Douai Bible, ii. 441; Taillepied, *Treatise of Ghosts*, 153.

[33] Perkins, *Discourse of the Damned Art*, 112; Willet, *Synopsis Papismi*, 305.

[34] Holland, *Treatise against Witchcraft*, C2ʳ; Purchas, *Purchas his Pilgrimage*, 179: 'poore Purgatorie with Jewes and Romists is preached by walking ghosts'.

[35] A. Peel (ed.), *The Seconde Parte of a Register*, 2 vols. (Cambridge, 1915), i. 279; P. Collinson, *The Elizabethan Puritan Movement* (London, 1967), 269. A later conformist response to puritan objections to this passage admitted that the verse reflected 'the general voice of those times, and the opinion of *Saul* and the Witch then generalie currant': T. Hutton, *Reasons for Refusal of Subscription to the Booke of Common Praier, under the hands of certaine ministers of Devon and Cornwall* (Oxford, 1605), 116.

the witch's closet, and the prophecies were supplied by the ventriloquist skills of the witch herself 'speaking as it were from the bottome of hir bellie'. In an objection remarkably similar to those made by Catholic commentators, Scot argued that 'if it had beene a divell, the text would have noted it in the same place of the storie'.[36] Scot's scepticism about the appearance of the devil to Saul was crucial to his argument that witches had no real power to harness or channel the powers of Satan. This was the central theme of his *Discoverie*, in which ghosts per se play a merely subsidiary role. Nonetheless, Scot had little hesitation in applying the template to all subsequent reported appearances of the dead: 'in all ages moonks and preests have abused and bewitched the world with counterfet visions'. The biblical prohibitions on seeking counsel of the dead, or attempting to raise them, did not signify that these things were possible, but that 'men beleeve they doo them, and thereby cousen the people...some one knave in a white sheete hath cousened and abused manie thousands that waie'.[37] Scot's thoroughgoing scepticism about the possibility of any intervention of supernatural forces in the created world made him pretty much unique among contemporary authors.[38] Nonetheless, there were echoes of his attitude to ghosts in later writers, most notably in Samuel Harsnett's *Declaration of Egregious Popish Impostures* (1603), which drew heavily on Scot for its chapter on 'the strange formes, shapes and apparitions of the devills'. Harsnett praised Chaucer for discerning that 'all these brainlesse imaginations of...house-hanting and the rest, were the forgeries, cosenages, imposturs, and legerdemaine of craftie priests and leacherous friers'.[39] In a discussion of whether the spirits of the dead walk upon the earth, Harsnett's fellow-bishop, Gervase Babington, accepted that devils might assume the shape of the deceased, but laid greater emphasis on the fact that 'many a thousand times have false iuggling hypocrites abused Gods people to establish their idolatry, superstition and error'.[40] As Harsnett's citation of Chaucer suggests, there was a considerable tradition to draw on here. Fraudulent apparitions featured in Erasmus's *Colloquies*, and monkish tricks of this sort were enthusiastically exposed by Continental writers such as Johan Weyer and Ludwig Lavater.[41] Even the Catholic writers Le Loyer and Taillepied accepted that many apparitions of the dead were the result of trickery, albeit committed by youthful practical jokers rather than avaricious priests.[42]

---

[36] Scot, *Discoverie*, 139, 142–50, 152.

[37] Ibid. 462, 139, 152.

[38] See S. Anglo, 'Reginald Scot's *Discoverie of Witchcraft*: Scepticism and Sadduceeism', in id. (ed.), *The Damned Art: Essays in the Literature of Witchcraft* (London, 1977), 106–39.

[39] S. Harsnett, *A Declaration of Egregious Popish Impostures*, repr. in F. W. Brownlow, *Shakespeare, Harsnett, and the Devils of Denham* (London and Toronto, 1993), 309.

[40] G. Babington, *Workes* (1622), bk. ii, 189.

[41] *The Colloquies of Erasmus*, tr. C. R. Thompson (Chicago, 1965), 230–7; J. Weyer, *De Praestigii Daemonum*, ed. and tr. G. Mora *et al.* as *Witches, Devils, and Doctors in the Renaissance* (Binghamton, NY, 1991), 439 ff.; Lavater, *Of Ghostes*, chs. 5–9.

[42] Taillepied, *Treatise of Ghosts*, ch. 6; Le Loyer, *Treatise of Specters*, 75^v–79^v.

If for Scot the encounter between Saul and the Witch of Endor was the pattern and precursor of popish trickery and fraud, for many other Protestant writers it was no less than the archetype of demonic witchcraft. It is a measure of how corrosive Scot's theory was to the prosecution of witchcraft that over the succeeding decades English demonological writers turned again and again to attack the idea that the appearance of Samuel to Saul was 'a meere cosenage of the witch'.[43] If the one scripturally attested ghost was in fact the devil, then it followed that subsequent appearances of ghosts served a satanic agenda. Here indeed the devil took a more direct and personal role than in any other manifestation of popish superstition, for to many Protestants it was axiomatic that he, or his demons, took on 'the similitude of some person, that was lately, or had been long dead' to deceive the ignorant.[44] The book of Deuteronomy seemed to identify seeking counsel of the dead as a species of witchcraft, and while the term 'necromancy' in this period may have been a loose synonym for demonic magic of all sorts, in the taxonomies elaborated by Elizabethan and Jacobean demonologists, it retained its specific sense of a means of divining by attempting illicit communication with the dead.[45] The account of the Witch of Endor might represent a key to unlock the pattern of demonic heresy which underpinned popish devotions. The fact that Saul had worshipped the apparition was particularly significant. As perhaps the most potent symbol of the inversion of all right religion, idolatry firmly fixed the link between feigned ghosts, demonic witchcraft, and popish practice and belief. In the influential *Christian Disputations* of the Swiss reformer Pierre Viret, translated into English in 1579, it is the ultimate indictment of Catholicism that priests and monks had

set up and erected a necrolatrie ... an adoration and worshipping of the dead, and the most greatest Idolatrie that ever was upon the earth: And have made the bodies of men to serve the divell, and have made him to be worshiped, under the name and title of them, even as Saul worshiped him under the name of Samuel.[46]

It is significant, too, that the dedicatory epistle to James I which Zachary Jones prefixed to his 1605 edition of Le Loyer's ghost treatise justified the translation on the basis of the king's admirable track-record on witchcraft, and because Le Loyer too was 'a professed foe to all these damned artes'.[47]

---

[43] Perkins, *Discourse of the Damned Art*, 118 (quote); *Golden Chaine*, 50; Gifford, *Subtill Practises of Devilles*, E3^{r-v}; Holland, *Treatise against Witchcraft*, C2^r; Cooper, *Mystery of Witchcraft*, 154; Deacon and Walker, *Dialogical Discourses*, 125–6 (though here Scot's view is given a slightly more sympathetic airing than elsewhere).

[44] Strode, *Anatomie of Mortalitie*, 205. See also P. Du Moulin, *The Waters of Siloe. To Quench the Fire of Purgatory*, tr. I.B. (Oxford, 1612), 395; Hutchins, *Of Specters*, 426.

[45] Deut. 18: 10–11; R. Kieckhefer, *Magic in the Middle Ages* (Cambridge, 1989), 152; Holland, *Treatise of Witchcraft*, D4^r; Perkins, *Discourse of the Damned Art*, 107–8; *Golden Chaine*, 50; Cotta, *Triall of Witchcraft*, 37.

[46] Viret, *Christian Disputations*, 104^v. The charge of 'necrolatrie' against the papal Church had earlier been made by John Bale, *A Mysterye of Inyquyte* (Geneva, 1545), 54^v.

[47] Le Loyer, *Treatise of Specters*, A3^r.

For many Protestant writers, the theories that visitations of ghosts were elaborate frauds perpetrated by popish priests, and that they were personal appearances by the devil or one of his minions, were by no means mutually exclusive. Thomas Beard, for example, argued that all the 'strange stories . . . touching walking ghosts' to be found in old popish books belonged in one of two categories: 'eyther they were jugling tricks of imposters to deceive the simple, or deceits of devils to delude the learned'.[48] Another Jacobean writer equally hedged his bets: 'if they be not popish which make such false apparitions for gaines sake, they are certain evil spirits'.[49] In a sermon preached at St Mary's in Cambridge towards the end of James's reign, Robert Jenison similarly asserted that many apparitions were feigned popish miracles, but that 'many also have the devill, who is false and a lier, for the chiefe author of them; by which, the supposed miracle-workers his instruments, doe not only delude others, but are deluded themselves'.[50] Papists were thus both perpetrators and victims of the delusions and falsehoods which apparitions fathered upon the world.

Despite the fact that it is difficult to identify a discrete corpus of texts which could be said to embody an English 'ghost controversy' in the Reformation period, ghosts clearly had their role to play in the parallel processes of theological debate and confessional formation. They came within the purview of a range of reformers with differing priorities and concerns, and they lent themselves to a variety of constructions, and the validation of a spectrum of anti-Catholic views. While to some critics ghosts did no more than epitomize the credulity and knavery of papists, to others they conveyed more transcendent meanings. Papist endorsement of demonic apparitions (starting with that of 'feigned Samuel') could be made to slot effortlessly into that system of antithesis, contraries, and inversion which permeated early modern intellectual thought, and by which popish religion as a whole could come to be associated with the antitype of God, Satan, and with Satan's worship on earth, witchcraft.[51] As Richard Bernard remarked in a witchcraft treatise of 1627, Satan is ever ready 'to further popish idolatry', and 'sorcery is the practice of that whore, the Romish synagogue'.[52] A rather different conclusion was drawn, however, in one of John Donne's sermons of

---

[48] Beard, *Retractive from the Romish Religion*, 437.

[49] J. Preston, *A Sermon preached at the Funeral of Mr Arthur Upton Esquire in Devon* (1619), 33.

[50] Jenison, *Height of Israel's Idolatrie*, 141.

[51] On inversion and witchcraft, see the work of Stuart Clark: 'King James's *Daemonologie*: Witchcraft and Kingship', in Anglo (ed.), *The Damned Art*, 156–81; 'Inversion, Misrule and the Meaning of Witchcraft', *PP* 87 (1980); *Thinking with Demons: The Idea of Witchcraft in Early Modern Europe* (Oxford, 1997), ch. 6.

[52] Bernard, *Guide to Grand-Iury Men*, 34, 99. See also Cooper, *Mystery of Witchcraft*, 22; J. Napeir, *A Plaine Discovery of the Whole Revelation of Saint John* (Edinburgh, 1593), 46; N. Jones, 'Defining Superstitions: Treasonous Catholics and the Act Against Witchcraft of 1563', in C. Carlton, R. L. Woods, M. L. Robertson, and J. Block (eds.), *State, Sovereigns and Society in Early Modern England* (Stroud, 1998), 187–204.

the same year, finding connections between 'the easiness of admitting revelations...and apparitions of spirits, and purgatory souls' of papists on the one hand, and the 'super-exaltation of zeale, and...captivity to the private spirit' characteristic of puritan schismatics on the other.[53]

SPECTRES OF CATHOLICISM

Ghosts did not exist, and so the papists had found it necessary to invent them. But what were Catholics saying in response to the Protestant polemic that disparaged defenders of ghostly visions as fools, knaves, and instruments of the devil? Ronald Finucane has suggested that the later sixteenth century was a time when 'more than ever Catholic apologists appealed to apparitions to prove the existence of purgatory'.[54] But, at least as far as England is concerned, this seems a difficult claim to substantiate. Indeed, English Catholic writers were sometimes anxious to deny that the doctrine of purgatory rested on the testimony of ghosts. In his book on purgatory of 1565, William Allen did not deny that the souls of the dead had appeared to the living, but he stressed that such occurrences 'follow not the ordinary course of nature', and that it was not his job to defend 'every peculiar mannes phantasy'.[55] Shortly before Allen wrote, the Council of Trent's decree on purgatory had warned against 'things that tend to a certain kind of curiosity or superstition', and ghosts found no mention in treatises defending purgatory and prayer for the dead by Richard Bristow in 1580, Theophilus Higgons in 1609, or John Floyd in 1613.[56] Even the Continental Catholic treatises by Le Loyer and Noel Taillepied, which did allege the appearance of souls as evidence for purgatory, hedged their assertions with qualifications and disclaimers.[57]

But if in their formal polemical engagement with Protestant opponents English Catholics displayed a distinct wariness about invoking the testimony of ghostly apparitions, a rather different attitude becomes apparent in some of their inward discourses. Accounts of miraculous appearances of souls from purgatory continued to be recorded, to edify the faithful, and to

---

[53] Donne, *Sermons*, vii. 168, viii. 135. Echoes of a conformist anti-puritan rhetoric are also audible among the anti-Catholic trumpetings of Harsnett's *Declaration of Egregious Popish Impostures*. See Brownlow, *Devils of Denham*, 74–5.

[54] Finucane, *Appearances of the Dead*, 113.

[55] Allen, *Defense and Declaration*, 110ᵛ–111ʳ, 115ʳ.

[56] H. J. Schroeder (ed.), *Canons and Decrees of the Council of Trent* (1960), 214; R. Bristow, *A Reply to Fulke, in Defense of M. D. Allens Scroll of Articles, and Booke of Purgatorie* (Louvain, 1580); T. Higgons, *The First Motive of T.H...touching the question of Purgatory, and Prayer for the Dead* (1609); J. Floyd, *Purgatories Triumph over Hell* (St Omer, 1613).

[57] Taillepied insisted, for example, that 'we must not too easily believe all that we see at night in the dark, nor take every apparition to be a spirit or a soul from purgatory': *Treatise of Ghosts*, 34. Le Loyer developed at great length the idea that the senses are often deceived and natural things taken for ghosts: *Treatise of Specters*, chs. 7–11.

confirm them in their recusancy. If some of these manifestations were purely mystifying—like the 'three loud knocks' on a table heard by Sir Thomas Tresham while a book of devotion was being read in the 1580s[58]—others served a clear didactic purpose. The Jesuit John Gerard recorded in his memoir for 1591 the appearance of a strange light to the widow of a schismatic gentleman who had died before he could be reconciled to the faith. After a trental of masses had been said for him 'according to the old custom of the country', the light was seen to ascend to heaven.[59] At around the same time another deceased schismatic, John Lord Stourton, was said to have appeared and requested masses from the Jesuit John Cornelius.[60] In 1612 a letter from the archpriest George Birkhead to his agent in Rome relayed news concerning a Herefordshire man who was in great doubt whether he should take the Jacobean oath of allegiance. The night before he was due to swear, his old confessor, the martyred priest Roger Cadwallader, 'appeared to him holding a chalice full of water in his hand, and said: John, yf there be made never so little an hole in this chalice, all that is in yt will runne out'. The man took the point, 'and resolved never to take that oath'.[61] Another clerical letter of the same year excitedly reported recent events at a Catholic house in Lancashire, where a young woman had been visited by the troubled soul of a priest who had received money for saying masses, but not performed them. When the woman arranged for the masses to be said, he was seen (in the form of a child) to ascend into the chalice and thence to heaven.[62] In 1635–6 the ghost of John Sherman appeared to an English nun, Aloyza Garman, in the convent in Ghent. Sherman was a church papist, whom Aloyza had known in England, and whose deathbed reconciliation to the Church she had helped to arrange (not least by dispatching his 'puritan sonne' on an errand to Cheapside to fetch some herbs). Preceded by mysterious sets of three knocks (like those heard by Tresham) every time Aloyza began her nightly prayers, John Sherman's disembodied voice anounced that he had been sent by the Virgin to request five masses to be said for his soul. As the final mass was being said, Aloyza perceived 'the soule of John Sherman with a verie pleasing countenance in a loose whit garment standing at the Altar at the Epistle side'. After promising that the convent was so pleasing to God 'that none in it shall not die a happy death', he vanished.[63] Such accounts seem more redolent of the ethos of the *Golden Legend* than of the Tridentine decree on purgatory, as does a contemporary Catholic account of the vengeful spirit of Thomas Pilchard, a priest

[58] Finucane, *Appearances of the Dead*, 108.
[59] J. Gerard, *The Autobiography of an Elizabethan*, tr. Caraman (1951), 38–9.
[60] R. Challoner, *Memoirs of Missionary Priests*, ed. J. H. Pollen (1924), 198–9.
[61] Archives of the Archdiocese of Westminster, A series, XI, no. 25.
[62] M. C. Questier (ed.), *Newsletters from the Archpresbyterate of George Birkhead*, CS, 5th ser. 12 (1998), 178–9.
[63] BL, Additional MS 21203 no. 9, 24^r.

quartered at Dorchester in 1587. Pilchard returned from the grave to take
the life of the officers who had carried out his execution, the keeper of the
prison where he was kept, and, for good measure, a pregnant Catholic
prisoner who died in childbirth—a grisly story which seems to reflect a
blend of counter-Reformation propaganda and atavistic acquaintance with
the behaviour of folk revenants.[64]

Some Elizabethan and early Stuart 'Catholic' ghosts appeared in a more
overtly proselytizing context. Reginald Scot charged that papists had faked
the appearance of walking spirits at Canterbury in 1573, and at Rye in
1577.[65] The visions of the ecstatic Flintshire girl Elizabeth Orton, which
included sightings of Christ, the Virgin, and saints Anne and Mary Magdalen, as well as recently deceased neighbours, were relayed, as we have seen,
to a fascinated audience of local conformists.[66] A tract of 1624 by the anti-
papist pamphleteer John Gee, recounted two recent cases in London. In the
first of these a group of Jesuits had attempted to brainwash Mary Boucher, a
young Protestant gentlewoman, by staging a series of interviews with her
deceased godmother. In the second they deployed a vision of St Lucy to
suborn another young Protestant woman, Frances Peard, into becoming a
nun and parting with her inheritance. Gee had little doubt that these hauntings had less to do with satanic intervention than with paper lanterns,
transparent glasses, and the high-pitched voice of 'some nimble handed
Novice Jesuitable Boy'. As entertainment, he thought popish apparitions
displayed poor production values: always a woman 'arrayed in white, white,
white... white from heaven, and white from purgatory... Apparitions from
the dead might be seen farre cheaper at other Play-houses. As for example,
the ghost in Hamlet, Don Andreas ghost in Hieronimo.'[67] Yet Gee's sarcasm
fails to disguise a back-handed compliment to the effectiveness as a missionary strategy of invoking departed souls. An openness to the messages of
returning spirits was no peculiarity of a die-hard Catholic remnant, but
rather a shared cultural assumption with many of their conforming neighbours. The point is made in a ghost story recorded by the Jacobean Cornish
Catholic gentleman Nicholas Roscarrock, in his manuscript compilation of
'Lives of the Saints'. In the parish of Newlyn East, Roscarrock noted there
had been a chapel yard with four large stones in it, on which were laid the
relics of local saints during rogation week, a custom observed up until the
reign of Mary. In around 1580, one of the stones was 'taken from thence and
turned into a cheese-presse... by a gentlewoman named Mistresse Burlace',

[64] J. H. Pollen (ed.), *Unpublished Documents Relating to the English Martyrs*, Catholic
Record Society, 5 (1908), 288–9.
[65] Scot, *Discoverie*, 152.
[66] B. Rich, *The True Report of a Late Practise enterprised by a Papist with a Yong Maiden in
Wales* (1582), title page, D2^{r-v}. See above, 134.
[67] J. Gee, *New Shreds of the Old Snare* (1624), 1–25. This was a topical best-seller which
went through four editions in 1624 alone: I. Green, *Print and Protestantism in Early Modern
England* (Oxford, 2000), 174–5.

but after her death the stone was returned when her ghost appeared to an unspecified person and willed them to replace it. There was a clear Catholic point here about sacrilege, but the circumstances were not narrowly denominational: Roscarrock knew of the event from 'such as were of her kinsfolkes and friends', presumably Protestants. It is interesting too that Roscarrock was cautious about authenticating the apparition as the soul of Burlace: it was her or 'some thing assuminge her personage'.[68] This is unlikely to have been a concession to Protestant sensibilities, but rather a quite traditional recognition that the didactic impact of such stories was weakened rather than reinforced by a completely unfiltered credulity. Elizabeth Orton had reportedly feared that her visions 'might be some wicked sprites or Goblines', and initial scepticism or anxiety on the part of percipients about the true nature of an apparition had been a marked feature of several medieval accounts.[69] Hamlet's famous dilemma—'spirit of health or goblin damn'd'—was not, as some commentators seem to assume, an existential perplexity unique to educated Protestants.

PROTESTANTS AND THE PERSISTENCE OF GHOSTS

Though some papists might continue to fake hauntings, Protestant reformers liked to pretend that the advent of true religion had effectively closed the book on ghosts. As early as 1543, the Henrician reformer Robert Wisdom, defending his opinion that 'sowles departed do not come again and play boo peape with us', added that 'thankes to god, ever since the word of god cam in thei be nether herd nor senne'.[70] Under Elizabeth, a number of authorities were keen to confirm Archbishop Sandys's emphatic assurance that 'the gospel hath chased away walking spirits'.[71] The theme was a recurrent one of Lavater's ghost treatise: 'there were farre more of these kindes of apparitions and myracles seen amongest us, at such tyme as we were given unto blindnesse and superstition ... The clere light of Gods word driveth away al such spirits.'[72] Unsurprisingly, given his view that apparitions were typically monkish tricks, one of the most emphatic assertions came from Reginald Scot. Thanks to the preaching of the gospel, the sighting of apparitions was much reduced, and would shortly vanish away completely. In Germany, he reported on good authority, spirits had ceased to appear since the time of Luther. Enlightened and triumphalist, Scot declaimed that

---

[68] N. Roscarrock, *Lives of the Saints*, ed. N. Orme, Devon and Cornwall Record Society, NS 35 (1992), 94, 160.

[69] Rich, *True Report*, D2ᵛ; P. Barnum (ed.), *Dives and Pauper*, EETS 275 (1976), 171; C. Horstman (ed.), *Yorkshire Writers*, 2 vols. (1895), i. 383–4; E. Arber (ed.), *The Revelation to the Monk of Evesham* (1901), 55.

[70] BL, MS Harleian 425, 4–7.

[71] E. Sandys, *Sermons*, ed. J. Ayre (PS, 1841), 60.

[72] Lavater, *Of Ghostes*, 89, 183.

through ignorance of late in religion, it was thought, that everie churchyard swarmed with soules and spirits: but now the word of God being more free, open, and knowne, those conceipts and illusions are made more manifest and apparent . . . Where are the soules that swarmed in times past? Where are the spirits? Who heareth their noises? Who seeth their visions? Where are the soules that made such mone for trentals, whereby to be eased of the paines in purgatorie? Are they all gone into Italie, bicause masses are growne deere here in England?[73]

Here he was again echoed by Samuel Harsnett, who scoffed that in the time of 'popish mist' children, old women, and maids were afraid to cross a churchyard, and if tithes or Peter's Pence were unpaid 'people walked in fear of spirits'.[74] The claim that ghosts were more common when popery held sway was made by other early Stuart anti-Catholic writers, including John Donne, Richard Bernard, and Edward Hoby, the latter referring contemptuously to those night-ghosts 'which the world hath now for many yeares since forgotten to believe'.[75]

There is no meaningful test we can apply to discover whether ghost sightings were less frequent in 1600 than in 1500, and the vanishing of spirits was in any case less an empirical observation than a rhetorical and polemical trope in the campaign against Catholicism. In other contexts, Protestant writers were quite ready to affirm that popular belief in ghosts was far from moribund. In 1571 the preacher John Northbrooke took occasion to deny that the souls of the dead appeared to the living 'as foolishly is furnished'.[76] Such admonitions against backward and superstitious beliefs were perhaps to be expected in the early years of Elizabeth's reign, but the refrain is constant throughout our period. In less complacent mode, Reginald Scot complained that while his contemporaries now gave no credit to the schoolmen's tales 'of soules condemned to purgatorie, wandring for succour and release by trentals and masses said by a popish preest', 'yet we credit and report other appearances, and assuming of bodies by soules and spirits; though they be as prophane, absurd and impious as the other'.[77] In the 1590s Randall Hutchins saw such beliefs as characteristic of 'the unskilled multitude'.[78] Similarly, the Calvinist theologian William Perkins ascribed the idea that the souls of the dead 'wandreth here on earth among men' to 'the common people' and to 'many ignorant persons among us'.[79] The error was, according to the Jacobean moralist George Strode, 'still in the

---

[73] Scot, *Discoverie*, 152–3, 463. He was ill informed about the situation in Germany, where, Luther or no, ghosts continued to appear: see S. C. Karant-Nunn, *The Reformation of Ritual: An Interpretation of Early Modern Germany* (1997), 185–6.

[74] Harsnett, *Declaration*, 306–7.

[75] Donne, *Sermons*, x. 145–6; Bernard, *Guide to Grand-Iury Men*, 99–100; Hoby, *Letter to Mr T.H.*, 42.

[76] J. Northbrooke, *Spiritus est Vicarius in Terra* (1571), 15ʳ.

[77] Scot, *Discoverie*, 531–2.

[78] Hutchins, *Of Specters*, 410.

[79] Perkins, *Golden Chaine*, 515; *Discourse of the Damned Art*, 115–16.

mouth and faith of credulous superstition at this day'.[80] In the theophrastic dialogues beloved of puritan writers, bucolic characters are sometimes made to confess their desire to communicate directly with the dead. In Veron's *Huntyng of Purgatory to Death*, Dydimus, who describes himself as 'a poore simple and ignoraunt person', confesses that he doesn't know what to think about purgatory 'except peradventure, I shoulde chaunce too mete with some of those spirits and soules, which (as our priests wil make folkes to believe) arte wont to appeare after their deathe, for to crave good deedes'.[81] Four decades later, in Arthur Dent's dialogue *The Plaine Man's Path-way to Heaven*, the character of Antilegon refuses to accept assurances about the small number of the elect, unless, 'there should come two soules, one from heaven, and another from hell, and bring us certaine newes how the case stood'.[82]

Didymus and Antilegon were of course straw men, literary stereotypes whose dialectical function was to underscore true doctrine by articulating objections that could easily be disposed of. But in expressing concern about popular ghost beliefs, many authors were not merely setting up an artificial 'other', that inversion of orthodoxy whose postulation provided the logical and philosophical basis for their own attitudes. Rather, they were speaking to and from experience, and directly confronting a pastoral reality. Underpinning the ghost treatise of the Swiss reformer Ludwig Lavater was the conviction that 'daily experience teacheth us that spirits do appear to men'.[83] His translator, Robert Harrison, justified turning the treatise into English on the basis of pressing pastoral need. Not only were there still superstitious persons who had been taught to believe that 'mens soules returne agayne on earth, cravyng helpe of the lyvyng', but there were also those 'otherwise well trayned up in religion' whose beliefs on the question were confused and uncertain. Like Lavater, Harrison confirmed that 'there be many also, even nowe a dayes, which are haunted and troubled with spirites'.[84]

Some leading reformers knew this at first hand. In around 1564 Bishop Pilkington of Durham wrote to Archbishop Parker about happenings in Blackburn where

there is a fantastical (and as some think a lunatic) young man, which says he has spoken with one of his neighbours that died four year since or more. Divers times he says he has seen him, and talked with him, and took him to the curate, the schoolmaster, and other neighbours, which all affirm that they see him too. These things be

---

[80] Strode, *Anatomie of Mortalitie*, 204–5.

[81] Veron, *Huntyng of Purgatory*, 197ᵛ–198ᵛ. See also King, *A Funerall Sermon*, F4ʳ⁻ᵛ.

[82] A. Dent, *The Plaine Mans Path-way to Heaven* (1605), 265–6.

[83] Lavater *Of Ghostes*, 71. For the view that Lavater's was essentially a pastoral treatise, see B. Gordon, 'Malevolent Ghosts and Ministering Angels: Apparitions and Pastoral Care in the Swiss Reformation', in *Place of the Dead*, 87–109.

[84] R[obert] H[arrison], 'To the Reader', in Lavater, *Of Ghostes*.

so common here, and none of authority that will gainsay it, but rather believe and confirm it, that every one believes it. If I had known how to have examined it with authority, I would have done it.[85]

Despite (or perhaps due to) this unsettling experience, Pilkington did not address the question of ghosts at any length in his writings. But some ministers who went into print on the issue clearly did so in response to actual sightings or reports among their parishioners. In a 1581 treatise on the *Nunc dimittis*, the puritan minister Anthony Anderson included a long discursus 'beating down to death this error... that the soules of the dead depart not so from us, but that after buryall they walke in the earth, and appeare unto men'. His motive for doing so was that even as he composed the work 'a most slanderous report is raysed of an honest and vertuous minister departed this lyfe, that hys soule nowe walketh at this daye in his parsonage house'.[86] In a printed funeral sermon of 1619, John Preston took occasion to reprove the 'many who affirme that they have seene and heard dead men to walke and talke, to frequent their premises, and to say, I am the soule of this man, or of that woman'.[87] Preachers sometimes imaginatively anticipated (or perhaps echoed) the scepticism of the people towards orthodox Protestant interpretations. 'Thou wilt say', remarked Anderson, 'what shall we say to this, there is much iumblyng in suche a house, and there is seene lyvely such a man walke before us, whome we cannot but say to be our friend departed, to all our sences judgement'. 'How then?', ventriloquized Henry Smith, 'What is this which I see in the night like such a man, and such a man?'[88] The renowned Elizabethan pastor Richard Greenham was asked by a parishioner if spirits might haunt a house, and replied that it was possible, but that 'it is not undoubtedly the soule of any departed, but the evil spirits in the ayer'.[89]

Some reformers made serious efforts not merely to denounce, but to explain to a lay audience why such apparitions could not be the souls of the dead. Smith patiently expostulated that such an entity could not be a soul, since souls are spirits and by definition invisible. Nor could it be a body, since a body cannot walk without a soul, and a look in the grave of a dead man would confirm his body to be still there. Rather it must be a dangerous delusion of the devil 'to draw us from the word of God, to visions, and dreams, and apparitions, upon which manie of the doctrines of the papists are grounded'.[90] In his *Exposition of the Catholike Faith*, Bishop Babington proceeded in a similarly syllogistic fashion to answer negatively the question whether 'spirits of the dead walke here in earth or no'. Such spirits could not

---

[85] M. Parker, *Correspondence*, ed. J. Bruce (PS, 1853), 222.
[86] Anderson, *Shield of our Safetie*, H1ᵛ.
[87] Preston, *Sermon preached at the Funeral of Mr Arthur Upton*, 33.
[88] Anderson, *Shield of our Safetie*, H2ʳ; Smith, *Sermons*, 537–8.
[89] K. L. Parker and E. J. Carlson, '*Practical Divinity': The Works and Life of Revd Richard Greenham* (Aldershot, 1998), 217.
[90] Smith, *Sermons*, 540.

come from hell, whence there is no escape, and if they came from heaven, 'who should send them there hence to wander on earth?' Not the devil, who has no rule in heaven; nor God 'for he hath thousands of angels to doe his will'. If the dead could return of their own volition, they would seek to be with us always 'they being not now deprived of love, and become cruel'. Like other commentators, Babington cited Augustine's remark that if the dead were able to return his loving mother Monica would never have left him alone. God, however, had expressly forbidden the living to have contact with the dead.[91]

Protestant preachers and writers could thus with great confidence and clarity tell people that ghosts were not the souls of dead persons returning from heaven, hell, or a non-existent purgatory. Rather more problematic was the task of accounting for what they actually were, and about this there was no certainty or infallible test. The explanation often used to account for the proliferation of visions and apparitions in medieval times, namely that they were frauds engineered by the duplicity of popish priests and monks, obviously had more limited application after 1558. Very commonly, of course, ghosts were supposed to be devils, but this was not the only theory canvassed. Nor was it always clear with what aims and by whose authority such devils walked on the earth. In the process of telling the people what to think about ghostly apparitions, reformers were working it out for themselves, and the answers were not always clear and consistent.

To begin with the most esoteric of contemporary speculations, some reformers showed an awareness of the theory, propagated by the Renaissance magus Cornelius Agrippa, that apparitions of the dead represented a kind of temporary and natural projection from the body of the deceased, though they generally did so only to reject it.[92] The notion, however, had some wider cultural currency. It is almost certainly referred to in George Chapman's play *The Revenge of Bussy d'Ambois*, where on seeing the ghosts of Bussy and others, Clermont reflects that 'learned'st men hold that our sensitive spirits/ A little time abide about the graves / Of their deceased bodies, and can take / In cold condens'd air the same forms they had / When they were shut up in the body's shade.'[93] Ironically, here the postulations of learned natural magic may have overlapped with a long-standing popular intuition that the souls of the dead lurked for a transitional period near the places where they had been buried.[94] From

---

[91] Babington, *Workes*, bk. ii, 188–9; Anderson, *Shield of our Safetie*, H4ʳ.

[92] Scot, *Discoverie*, 141; Hutchins, *Of Specters*, 424. On Agrippa and ghosts, see R. H. West, *Shakespeare and the Outer Mystery* (Lexington, Ky., 1968), 58–9; id., *The Invisible World: A Study of Pneumatology in Elizabethan Drama* (repr. New York, 1969), 52–3.

[93] Cited in Briggs, *The Anatomy of Puck*, 133.

[94] N. Z. Davies, 'Some Tasks and Themes in the Study of Popular Religion', in C. Trinkaus and H. O. Oberman (eds.), *The Pursuit of Holiness in Late Medieval and Renaissance Religion* (Leiden, 1974), 333; R. Muchembled, *Popular and Elite Culture in France 1400–1750*, tr. L. Cochrane (Baton Rouge and London, 1985), 64: West, *The Invisible World*, 52.

neither angle did the idea recommend itself to the proponents of godly reformation.

One rather different approach to the problem was to imply that many sightings were not true apparitions at all, but rather the product of timorousness, over-active imaginations, and that characteristic Elizabethan malady, melancholy. It was a cliché of both English and Continental commentators those most likely to believe they had seen a ghost included the guilt-ridden, the sick, the aged, children, women (especially menstruating women), melancholics, madmen, cowards.[95] As Babington remarked, 'many times the corrupt humours that are in our heads will make us thinke we see formes, and faces and shapes and shadowes that indeed are not at all there'.[96] Scot put it more bluntly: on a dark night 'a polled sheepe is a perillous beast, and many times is taken for our fathers soule'.[97] There was, however, no necessary and intrinsic contradiction, and certainly no hard and fast dividing line, between subjective illusion and objective delusion, between 'natural' and 'supernatural' explanations for the phenomenon of ghosts.[98] Melancholics, like sinners and papists, were expected targets for the devil to insinuate himself upon, a truism reflected in contemporary theories of suicide, as well as in Hamlet's poignant concern that the devil 'out of my weakness and my melancholy—as he is very potent with such spirits—abuses me to damn me'.[99] The *locus classicus* of early modern treatments of melancholia, Robert Burton's *The Anatomy of Melancholy*, regarded it as axiomatic that 'melancholy men are most subject to diaboliical temptations and illusions, and most apt to entertain them'.[100]

The undoubted consensus of commentators was that at least a proportion of apparitions possessed some kind of objective reality, but did it follow that they were necessarily evil? 'Elizabethans believed that the world was vibrant with supernatural forces and invisible beings.'[101] These included God's servants, the angels; might they not manifest themselves visibly for the furtherance of God's purposes? The possibility was admitted by the pre-eminent Protestant ghost authority of the age, Ludwig Lavater, who began his treatise observing that spirits were 'not the souls of dead men... but

[95] Lavater, *Of Ghostes*, chs. 2–4; Scot, *Discoverie*, 152, 462; Taillepied, *Treatise of Ghosts*, chs. 3–5, 7; Hutchins, *Of Specters*, 412; Nashe, *The Terrors of the Night*, 348, 378; T. Lodge, *The Divell Coniured*, in *The Complete Works of Thomas Lodge*, ed. E. Gosse, Hunterian Club, 4 vols. (1883), iii. 33; Harsnett, *Declaration of Egregious Popish Impostures*, 304–5; Le Loyer, *Treatise of Specters*, 104ʳ–112ᵛ; Donne, *Sermons*, vii. 168; T. White, *The Middle State of Souls* (1659), 170.
[96] Babington, *Workes*, bk. ii, 189.
[97] Scot, *Discoverie*, 152.
[98] Clark, *Thinking with Demons*, 192–3.
[99] M. MacDonald and T. Murphy, *Sleepless Souls: Suicide in Early Modern England* (Oxford, 1990), 34–41; *Hamlet*, II. ii. 602–4. For discussion of the theme of melancholy in general, see M. MacDonald, *Mystical Bedlam: Madness, Anxiety, and Healing in Seventeenth-Century England* (Cambridge, 1981), 150–60.
[100] Cited in MacDonald, *Mystical Bedlam*, 169.
[101] Ibid. 157.

either good or evill angels'. But Lavater was also quick to insist that since all that was necessary for salvation was contained in the Word of God, 'good angels appeare to us more seldom in this oure tyme'.[102] A number of Protestants raised the possibility of angels appearing in bodily form only immediately to dash it. Predictably perhaps, Reginald Scot took this view: the age of miracles was past, and God no longer sent his 'visible angels' to men.[103] But Scot was here in good company. Elizabethan England's leading theologian, William Perkins, was of the opinion that angels 'appeare not nowe as in former times'.[104] The king of Scots agreed. In his *Daemonologie* of 1597, James denied that angels could appear in the forms of dead men, and insisted that 'since the comming of Christ in the flesh, and establishing of his Church by the Apostles, all miracles, visions, prophecies, and appearances of angels or good spirites are ceased'.[105]

Despite this authoritative testimony, the issue was not a closed one in the kingdom that James inherited in 1603. At Hidnam House near Launceston on the Cornwall–Devon border, the godly divine Daniel Featley was for a time house-guest to Sir Thomas Wise, who sounded him out on 'the truth of apparitions ... and notes of difference betweene good angels and bad'. Wise then confessed that about a month earlier his household had been troubled by a ghostly vision of a woman. This had first appeared in the bedchamber of his maids, whose screams had woken the house, and who told their master 'they were frighted with a walking spirit'. Sir Thomas initially suspected 'vaine fancy of womanly feare', but the following night the apparition appeared in his own chamber, standing at the foot of his bed for half an hour before gradually vanishing. Wise had previously been 'ever of the opinion that there were no such apparitions', and by his own account he had behaved in exemplary Protestant fashion, praying fervently, confessing his heinous and grievous sins, and charging the apparition 'in the name of the God of heaven to come no nearer'. After the event he had sought the counsel of the archdeacon [of Cornwall?], who 'held it to be an angellical apparition and not a diabolicall illusion', on the grounds that it did him no hurt, that he had the power to speak to it, and that it had appeared in white and shining raiment.[106]

---

[102] Lavater, *Of Ghosts*, B2ʳ, 145, 159–63, 193, 196, 199.

[103] Scot, *Discoverie*, 152, 462. Robert King had earlier insisted that spirits were invariably 'mockinges and deceiptes of the devel ... there is no revelation of Angels to be looked for': *A Funeral Sermon*, G2ʳ⁻ᵛ. Protestant insistence on the cessation of the age of miracles is explored by D. Walker, *Unclean Spirits: Possession and Exorcism in France and England in the Late Sixteenth and Early Seventeenth Centuries* (1981), 66 ff.; A. Walsham, *Providence in Early Modern England* (Oxford, 1999), 226–32.

[104] Perkins, *Reformed Catholike*, 247.

[105] James I, *Daemonologie*, 61, 65–6.

[106] Cf. here Scot, *Discoverie*, 534–5, citing the absurd views of 'witchmongers' (i.e. Aquinas, Gregory, Michael Andreas) that 'a damned soule hath a verie heavie and sowre looke; but a saints soule hath a cheerefull and a merrie countenance: these also are white and shining, the other cole black'.

Featley, however, judged 'rather it was an evill spirit'; firstly because 'miraculous revelations and angelicall apparitions are ceased', but also because angels were always sent with a message and this was just a dumb show, and because it was unheard of for an angel to appear in the form of a woman. He advised Sir Thomas not to enquire curiously about the apparition, 'but to examine his owne conscience, and give God thanks for his deliverance, but especially to sinne no more, lest a worse thing befell him'.[107]

The Hidnam haunting opens for us a range of perspectives on the same event: those of the terrified servants, of the educated Protestant layman, Sir Thomas, and of the learned divines he consulted about the affair. Even when the latter had had their say, the happening remained murky and perplexing. The remaining part of this chapter will attempt to explore how cultural constructions of the ghost in Reformation England were refracted through dialogues between elite and popular culture (albeit less literal ones than at Hidnam) and how in the process long-standing ideas helped to shape, and at times to dent, the clear-lined demonic apparition of Protestant orthodoxy.

EXEMPLARY SPIRITS

Before and after the Reformation, ghostly apparitions served the didactic and exemplary purposes of Catholicism. But the Catholics had no monopoly on this. It was a commonplace of Protestant rhetoric that the devil and his minions 'can do us no harme be they never so desirous, excepte God give them leave thereto', and that on occasion they could be directly employed to execute the judgements of God.[108] Ghosts, therefore, might be subsumed into that mind-set of providentialism, which, as Alexandra Walsham has demonstrated, saturates the discourses of early modern England.[109] This could lead in practice to the expression of a certain amount of ambivalence towards the status and nature of ghosts, even in some surprising places. In the 1563 edition of his *Acts and Monuments*, for example, John Foxe retold a story from the medieval chronicle of Mathew Paris. Pope Innocent IV had excommunicated the bishop of Lincoln, Robert Grosseteste, for rebuking the pope's corruption, and, two years after his death, the bishop appeared in the night to Innocent and beat him up with his staff. In the second (1570) edition, Foxe repeated the story in much greater detail, though this time adding 'a note to the reader concerning the appearing of dead men'. Images of things unseen might through the permission of God come to men in their sleep, but 'certaine it is, that no dead man materially can ever rise againe, or

---

[107] Bodleian MS Rawlinson D 47, 42^r–43^v. Randall Hutchins insisted it was unheard of 'that a good spirit has been seen in woman's form...but invariably in the aspect of a man': *Of Specters*, 419.

[108] Lavater, *Of Ghostes*, 175, 191; James I, *Daemonologie*, 58.

[109] Walsham, *Providence, passim.*

appeare, before the judgement day'.[110] Despite this delayed disclaimer, the moral and dramatic force of the story clearly lay in the idea of the dead acting as instruments of God's justice in avenging wrongs committed against themselves, an idea commonly found in the popular sermon collections of the late Middle Ages.[111] A 1581 pamphlet by the moralist Philip Stubbes told a similar, if more homely, cautionary tale. An avaricious Leicestershire woman who refused to remit the debt of a dying poor man was visited by the devil in the guise of the pauper, who struck her and turned her body black as pitch.[112] Stubbes at least was clear that the visitant was the devil in appropriate disguise. The issue was less clear-cut in another providential pamphlet, *A Strange and Fearful Warning to all Sonnes and Executors*, appearing in 1623. As the title suggests, this concerned a dutiless son, the heir of John Barefoote, a tailor of Sunning in Wiltshire, who held back legacies intended for his sisters. In consequence his house and belongings were repeatedly wrecked by a poltergeist until he finally relented. In recounting these events, the pamphlet displayed considerable ambiguity about the identity of the supernatural force at work. It is described initially as the work of the devil and an 'evil spirit', but later as 'Gods Angel and no evill'. Moreover, the author reported that certain children of the town had seen old Barefoote 'walke in the churchyard in a most strange and fearefull manner'. To account for this, the pamphlet offered the somewhat convoluted hypothesis that

it may be, that they might see some vision or representation of him, for some spirit (through Gods sufferance) might assume an apparant likeness of him: a thing only appointed to make men know and beleeve, that he was shewed in the likenesse of a Spirit, as a cause of all these present evils, in regard that he being wronged, that all these things (for his sake) happened to the wronger.[113]

Remarkably, there were some Protestant tellers of providentialist anecdotes in early Stuart England who didn't even go this far in attempting to conform to orthodox doctrine about ostensible appearances of the dead. A work by the Scottish writer David Person, published in London in 1635, unselfconsciously related the tale of a man who broke a promise to bury his wife in the churchyard. As a result, 'this woman's ghost... did so incessantly both haunt and affright, both him, his children, and family, that there was no resting for them at any time'.[114] Undoubtedly, there was a popular appetite in early seventeenth-century England for portentous messages from beyond

---

[110] J. Foxe, *Actes and Monumentes* (1563), **I*v; *Actes and Monuments* (1570), 409–10. I owe these references to Tom Freeman. Foxe was not the first English Protestant to retell the story: Thomas Swinnerton, *A Mustre of Scismatyke Bysshoppes of Rome* (1534), B4ᵣ.

[111] T. Erbe (ed.), *Mirk's Festial*, EETS ES 96 (1905), 270; J. de Voragine, *The Golden Legend*, tr. W. Ryan, 2 vols. (Princeton, 1993), ii. 290.

[112] P. Stubbes, *Two Wunderfull and Rare Examples of the Undeferred Judgement of God* (1581).

[113] *A Strange and Fearful Warning to all Sonnes and Executors (that fulfill not the will of their dead Fathers)* (1623).

[114] D. Person, *Varieties: or a Surveigh of Rare and Excellent Matters* (1635), 165.

the grave. A week after the death of Prince Henry in November 1612, a young man arrived stark naked at St James's 'sayeng he was the Princes ghost come from heaven with a message to the king'. It was reported that thousands came to see him incarcerated in the porter's lodge there.[115]

In exemplary cases of spirits (in the likeness of identifiable dead individuals) haunting malefactors of various kinds, it is possible to see Protestantism involved in a kind of dialogue with more perdurable elements of popular beliefs about the behaviour and rationale of ghosts. This is a pattern for which we have been prepared by the work of Walsham on providential literature more generally, of Peter Lake on murder pamphlets, and of Tessa Watt on cheap print and godly ballads.[116] In the field of ghostlore, this seems to have been a distinctly two-way traffic. The writings of reformers on this topic not only sought to engage with the beliefs of the people, but were themselves structured by them. It may not be going too far to suggest that English Protestant typologies of the demonic apparition were in fact substantially shaped by traditional expectations about the ghostly revenant.

In the first place, there was the question of what was considered to be the characteristic, even defining, activity of apparitions and spirits. In attacking Catholic traditions and superstitious popular beliefs about ghosts, reformers almost invariably typified them as 'walking' or 'wandering' spirits.[117] These rather aimless-sounding activities seem somewhat at odds with official Catholic teaching, which held that ghosts appeared by special permission of God for highly specific reasons, but they undoubtedly reflected a widespread popular sense about the conduct of restless, troubled spirits.[118] As we have seen, the maidservants of Sir Thomas Wise were 'frighted with a walking spirit', and looking back from the later seventeenth century, John Aubrey remembered how 'when I was a child (and so before the Civill Warres)... the fashion was for old women and mayds to tell fabulous stories nightimes of sprights and walking of ghosts'.[119] Protestants knew of course

---

[115] *The Letters of John Chamberlain*, ed. N. McClure 2 vols. (Philadelphia, 1939), i. 391–2.

[116] Walsham, *Providence*; P. Lake, 'Deeds against Nature: Cheap Print, Protestantism and Murder in Early Seventeenth-Century England', in K. Sharpe and P. Lake (eds.), *Culture and Politics in Early Stuart England* (Basingstoke, 1994); T. Watt, *Cheap Print and Popular Piety 1550–1640* (Cambridge, 1991).

[117] BL, MS Harleian 425, 6ᵛ; Northbrooke, *Spiritus est Vicarius Christi*, 15ʳ; Sandys, *Sermons*, 60; Bullinger, *The Fourth Decade*, 404; Anderson, *Shield of our Safetie*, H1ᵛ-2ʳ; Martyr, *Common Places*, 326; Scot, *Discoverie*, 462; Smith, *Sermons*, 525, 541; Hutchins, *Of Specters*, 426; Perkins, *Golden Chaine*, 515; id., *Discourse of the Damned Art*, 33; R. Pricke, *A Very Godlie and Learned Sermon* (1608), D4ᵛ; Harsnett, *Declaration of Egregious Popish Impostures*, 306; Purchas, *Purchas his Pilgrimage*, 179; Beard, *Retractive from the Romish Religion*, 437; Cooper, *Mystery of Witchcraft*, 152; Babington, *Workes*, bk. ii, 188–9; Strode, *Anatomie of Mortalitie*, 205. Cf. S. Greenblatt, *Hamlet in Purgatory* (Princeton, 2001), 108: 'the wandering of ghosts, like the wandering of vagabonds, was central to the fear they aroused'.

[118] Taillepied, for example, condemned the opinion those who believed the souls of the dead go wandering about on earth: Finucane, *Appearances of the Dead*, 100.

[119] Bodleian MS Rawlinson D 47, 43ʳ; Finucane, *Appearances of the Dead*, 124. See also the title of Fletcher and Shirley's play involving a supposed ghost, *The Night Walker*: Briggs, *Anatomy of Puck*, 142.

that the souls of the dead did not walk; it was the devil who simulated this to deceive the unwary. The logical corollary, however, was that in Protestant demonology one of the most direct and overt forms of satanic activity in the world was patterned after the folk-beliefs of medieval Catholicism. As Sir Thomas Browne had it, 'those apparitions, and ghosts of departed persons are not the wandring soules of men, but the unquiet walkes of Devils, prompting and suggesting us unto mischiefe, bloud, and villany'.[120]

A similar structural congruence between learned Protestantism and un-learned opinion relates to the places where this walking was most likely to take place. John Bossy has written that the traditional ghost 'was personal not real; he haunted people not places'.[121] In fact, this is probably only half-true. There is considerable evidence to suggest that the favourite haunt of late medieval and early modern ghosts was undoubtedly the parish church-yard. Jean-Claude Schmitt asserts that 'countless tales of apparitions' were linked to cemeteries.[122] Scot sarcastically noted that in the past 'every churchyard swarmed with souls'.[123] Certainly those accused, by Scot and others, of faking apparitions were often supposed to have played out their imposture in the churchyard.[124] In the early eighteenth century, the anti-quarian Henry Bourne was in no doubt that previous generations feared that the churchyard was 'more frequented with apparitions and ghosts than other places are', and therefore tended to avoid it at night.[125]

There was no particular reason in Catholic theology why souls from purgatory should have manifested themselves pre-eminently in churchyards. That ghosts were seen there was probably linked to a more naturalistic popular conception of the dead which associated their spirits with the places where their bodies were buried. In the folkloric world evoked in Shake-speare's *Midsummer Night's Dream*, the graves at night 'all gaping wide / Every one lets forth his sprite / In the churchway paths to glide', while at dawn 'ghosts, wand'ring here and there / Troop home to churchyards'.[126] Nor was there an obvious rationale for the devil to make the churchyard his base of operations, other than the fact that he appeared to do so. Inventive reasons were sometimes advanced by Protestant writers to account for this. Thomas Nashe stated that 'if anie aske why [the devil] is more conversant and buysie in churchyards and places where men are buried, than in anie other places', this was because he wanted to make us believe that 'the bodies

[120] T. Browne, *Religio Medici*, in *The Major Works*, ed. C. A. Patrides (Harmondsworth, 1977), 108.
[121] J. Bossy, *Christianity in the West 1400–1700* (Oxford, 1985), 29. Cf. Greenblatt, *Hamlet in Purgatory*, 41: 'the spectral voice is not for strangers; it is for those who awake at midnight and think about the dead person whom they have loved'.
[122] Schmitt, *Ghosts in the Middle Ages*, 137. See also pp. 80–1, 136–9, 179, 182–4.
[123] Scot, *Discoverie*, 462.
[124] Lavater, *Of Ghostes*, 22; Ewen, *Witchcraft in the Star Chamber*, 15; Le Loyer, *Of Specters*, 77ᵛ–78ʳ, 79ᵛ; Beard, *Retractive from the Romish Religion*, 437.
[125] H. Bourne, *Antiquitates vulgares* (Newcastle, 1725), 76.
[126] V. i. 10–12; III. ii. 382–3.

and soules of the departed rest entirely in his possession', and that 'the boanes of the dead, the divell counts his chiefe treasure, and therfore is he continually raking among them'.[127] According to Thomas Browne, the reason that phantoms 'doe frequent cemiteries, charnall houses, and churches, it is because those are the dormitories of the dead, where the Devill like an insolent Champion beholds with pride the spoyles and trophies of his victory in *Adam*'.[128]

Some echoes of genuine popular concerns may also be audible in discussions of whether the *bodies* of the dead were ever disturbed from their rest. As Nancy Caciola has recently demonstrated, belief in the power of the malevolent dead to reanimate their corpses was characteristic of non-learned culture in parts of medieval northern Europe. It was a particularly prominent feature of the series of ghost stories recorded by a monk of Byland Abbey in Yorkshire in the early fifteenth century.[129] Whether or not the devil had the power to automate the bodies of the dead was a question that genuinely divided Protestant divines in the sixteenth and early seventeenth centuries. Some authors, including Lavater, denied it outright.[130] Others were more agnostic, but thought it unlikely that the devil could do so.[131] The champion of the contrary view was James VI and I, who argued that if demonic possession of the living was permitted by God, appropriation of corpses certainly would be. As a consequence the devil could become visible to men 'and as it seemes unto them naturallie as a man converses with them'.[132] Significantly, the Jacobean witchcraft statute of 1604 added to the list of capital offenders those who dug up the bodies of the dead to use for any kind of sorcery.[133] In his 1596 treatise *The Divell Conjured*, Thomas Lodge agreed that evil angels can 'appeare in assumpted bodies, appropriat to their intents'. Furthermore, he endorsed the popular (and erroneous) belief that the hair, beards, and nails of the recently dead could continue to grow.[134] These were issues that resonated outside the world of theological

---

[127] Nashe, *Terrors of the Night*, 348–9.

[128] Browne, *Religio Medici*, 108.

[129] N. Caciola, 'Wraiths, Revenants and Ritual in Medieval Culture', *PP* 152 (1996).

[130] Lavater, *Of Ghostes*, 171; Veron, *Huntynge of Purgatory*, 245ᵛ; Deacon and Walker, *Dialogical Discourses*, 101–2, 104; Cotta, *Triall of Witchcraft*, 37; *No Man is an Island: A Selection from the Prose of John Donne*, ed. R. Scott (1997), 169.

[131] Cooper, *Mystery of Witchcraft*, 151; Preston, *Sermon preached at the Funeral of Mr Arthur Upton*, 33. See also Whitgift's admission at the 1584 conference at Lambeth that it was 'a question among the learned' whether witches had power to raise the bodies of the dead: Peel (ed.), *Seconde Parte*, i. 279, a comment wrongly attributed to Travers by Thomas, *Religion*, 706.

[132] James I, *Daemonologie*, 59, 67, 73; Hutchins, *Of Specters*, 416. For an example of a Catholic holding this view, see J. Helt, 'The Dead Who Walk: Materiality, Liminality and the Supernatural World in François Richard's "Of False Revenants"', *Mortality*, 5 (2000), 7–17.

[133] G. L. Kittredge, *Witchcraft in Old and New England* (New York, 1929), 312.

[134] Lodge, *Divell Coniured*, 23, 30. For the very long-standing popular intuition that the corpses of the dead continued to possess some degree of sentience or life-force, see Caciola, 'Wraiths, Revenants and Ritual'; R. Richardson, *Death, Dissection and the Destitute* (London, 1987), ch. 1.

polemic and demonological scholarship. In *The Vow Breaker* (1636) by the provincial playwright William Sampson, the ghost of a scorned lover returns to haunt his false sweetheart. However, the apparition is held by one of the other characters to be the result of sorcery: 'Hell can put life into a senseless body /And raise it from the grave, and make it speake / Use all the faculties alive it did, To worke the Devill's hellish stratagems!'[135]

As *The Vow Breaker* reminds us, ghosts in Reformation England were not just a topic of theological discourse, or an occasional and exceptional facet of genuine experience. They were also a cultural type affording the opportunity for imaginative representation. Ghosts, of course, made regular appearances on the Elizabethan and Jacobean stage. It has been calculated that in the period 1560–1610, fifty-one ghosts were featured in twenty-six plays.[136] They were also a mainstay of the genre of 'news' or 'letters from hell' which was in vogue in the 1590s and early 1600s, the ghosts here usually acting as mouthpieces for satire or social criticism.[137] In the light of Protestant emphasis on demonic delusion, it is ironic that 'ghosts' were ideal for this role due to their ascribed status as disinterested 'truth-tellers'.[138] Occasionally, representations of ghosts in literary works did carry rather self-conscious health warnings. When the spirit of the actor Richard Tarleton appears to the narrator at the start of the late Elizabethan burlesque *Tarleton's News out of Purgatory*, the latter starts back, crying '*In nomine Jesu*, avoid, Satan, for ghost thou art none, but a very devil. For the souls of them which are departed (if the sacred principles of theology be true) never return into the world again till the general resurrection . . . Upon these conclusive premises depart from me, Satan, the resemblance of whomsoever thou dost carry.' The ghost, however, is unimpressed, responding, 'Oh there is a Calvinist'.[139] The appearance of a ghost in John Marston's *Sophonisba* prompts a character to declare, 'What damn'd ayre is form'd / Into that shape?'[140] Yet in Cyril Tourneur's *Atheist's Tragedy*, when the supposedly dead Charlemont proclaims himself to be a ghost, it is the hypocritical puritan chaplain Languebeau Snuffe who declares, 'No. 'Tis profane. Spirits are invisible. 'Tis the fiend I' the likeness of Charlemont.'[141] Most dramatists who placed ghosts on the stage did not unduly agonize over their precise ontological status, or they evaded sensitive theological issues by

---

[135] Cited in Briggs, *Anatomy of Puck*, 137. The storyline was supplied by an enduringly popular ballad, *The Fair Maid of Clifton or Young Bateman*: Walsham, *Providence*, 111–12.

[136] E. Prosser, *Hamlet and Revenge* (Stanford, Calif., 1967), 255. General treatments of ghosts in Elizabethan drama are provided by Briggs, *Anatomy of Puck*, ch. 9; West, *Invisible World*, ch. 9.

[137] J. Belfield, 'Tarleton's News out of Purgatory (1590): A Modern-spelling Edition, with Introduction and Commentary', University of Birmingham Ph.D. thesis (1978), 116–33.

[138] See here the perceptive comments of A. E. Bakos, 'Images of Hell in the Pamphlets of the Fronde', *Historical Reflections / Réflexions Historiques*, 26 (2000), 339–52.

[139] Belfield, 'Tarleton's News out of Purgatory', 284.

[140] Cited in A. McGee, *The Elizabethan Hamlet* (New Haven and London, 1987), 19.

[141] Cited in West, *Invisible World*, 186.

rationalizing them as spirits from Hades in the Senecan tradition. As R. H. West has noted, ghost and spirit scenes in contemporary drama are there to serve 'dramatic not expository ends'.[142] Shakespeare's *Hamlet* is highly unusual among Elizabethan and Jacobean plays in explicitly addressing the question of whether the apparition is really the spirit of Hamlet's father, or a demonic illusion, and making it central to the action of the play.[143] It does not by any means follow that the authors of literary works featuring ghosts necessarily questioned the orthodox view that the souls of the dead could not appear again to the living: even so fervent an opponent of walking spirits as John Donne could in verse imagine himself returning as a ghost to haunt a faithless lover.[144] Rather, it points to the distinctly limited utility of the Protestant demon-ghost as an embodiment of dramatic meaning. The cultural patterning of the ghost in English Renaissance theatre was a compounded one: it certainly recognized the ideas of the Reformation, and generally contained no hint (*Hamlet* is a possible exception) of Catholic notions of purgatory and intercession. Nonetheless, as literary ghosts seek revenge, torment the consciences of the guilty, or show solicitude for loved ones, the emotive and imaginative energy of the genre is shown to be predicated on assumptions other than the doctrinally sound one that the dead had no interest in the state of affairs left behind them, or the obligations and deserts of the living.

EVOLUTIONS OF BELIEF

If reformers periodically engaged in forms of dialogue with popular cultures, and if literary and dramatic representations of ghosts often inadequately reflected the tenets of orthodox theology, this still begs the question of whether, and how, popular beliefs about ghosts themselves changed over the course of the period. The evidential problems involved here are, to say the least, considerable. The experiences of the great majority of those who believed they had seen ghosts were never recorded, and those that were often come to us at least third-hand, filtered through the perceptions and prejudices of educated commentators. Historians who have attempted to recon-

---

[142] Ibid. 93.

[143] Among the works tackling this aspect of the play, with very different perspectives on how Shakespeare intended the ghost to be interpreted, are J. Dover Wilson, *What Happens in Hamlet* (Cambridge, 1951), ch. 3; M. Joseph, 'Discerning the Ghost in Hamlet', *Publications of the Modern Language Association of America*, 76 (1961), 493–502; C. Devlin, 'Hamlet's Divinity', in *Hamlet's Divinity and Other Essays* (1963); Prosser, *Hamlet and Revenge*; West, *Shakespeare and the Outer Mystery*, ch. 4; R. M. Frye, *The Renaissance Hamlet: Issues and Responses in 1600* (Princeton, 1984), 14–28; McGee, *The Elizabethan Hamlet*, chs. 1–3. Greenblatt, *Hamlet in Purgatory*.

[144] 'The Apparition', in J. Donne, *Selected Poems*, ed. J. Hayward (Harmondsworth, 1950), 52.

struct early modern popular ghost beliefs have generally been forced to rely heavily on the collections of incidents put together in the late seventeenth century by clergymen such as Richard Baxter or Joseph Glanvil, or on the compilations of the antiquarian and proto-folklorist, John Aubrey.[145] Less overtly mediated evidence from the period before the civil wars is extremely rare. But the archives can provide some scattered clues about how perceptions of ghosts may have been structured in the outlook of persons below the level of the elite. In a Star Chamber case of 1606, the enemies of John Mountford, minister of Radwynter in Essex, were accused of trying to dispossess him of his benefice, 'by coniuration, witchcraft or by some devise or sleight', procuring 'fearfull and uglie shapes and formes of evill spirittes or divilles sundrie tymes by day and night to haunt and walke about the church and churchyard'. These were said to take sometimes 'the shape of a man, sometymes of a dogg, catt or such like'.[146] The balance of traditional and reformist elements is difficult to assess here. The emphasis on 'evill spirittes or divilles' seems in line with Protestant expectations. But souls of the dead took animal form in several of the tales in the fifteenth-century Byland collection, and Reginald Scot cited the Catholic authority Michael Andraes as saying that while a good soul can take no shape but that of a man, 'a damed soule may and dooth take the shape of a blacke moore, or a beast'.[147] The impression of a belief in revenants combining traditional ideas about wandering souls and supernatural beasts, with a tinge of diabolical agency, perhaps applies also to the obscure slander offered by Maurice Harman to the minister of Bishopstrow in Wiltshire in 1626: 'when [he]...died he thought he should meet him riding on a black bull'.[148] In a Suffolk case from the 1630s, the minister was the slanderer, Francis Abbott of Postlingford taunting his churchwarden, 'Sirra, your black grandfather will come for you one of these days'—surely an invocation of the kind of vengeful spectre whose shape can be discerned beneath the theological folds of so many medieval sermon exempla.[149]

The theme recurrs in a detailed set of depositions collected by the Somerset JPs in Minehead in early 1637, documents which allow a much fuller reconstruction of some early Stuart ghost beliefs.[150] The case involved the appearances of one 'Old Mother Leakey', over a period of some months and

---

[145] Thomas, *Religion*, 707–11, 713–16: Finucane, *Appearances of the Dead*, ch. 5. See the strictures of Bennett, 'Ghost and Witch', 10–12.

[146] Ewen, *Witchcraft in the Star Chamber*, 15.

[147] M. R. James, 'Twelve Medieval Ghost Stories', *EHR* 37 (1922), 413–22; Scot, *Discoverie*, 535.

[148] M. Ingram, *Church Courts, Sex and Marriage in England, 1570–1640* (Cambridge, 1987), 110.

[149] D. Cressy, *Travesties and Transgressions in Tudor and Stuart England: Tales of Discord and Dissension* (Oxford, 2000), 158.

[150] PRO, SP 16/383, fos. 13^r–18^r (*CSPD*, 1637–8, 276). The case is noted en passant by Thomas, *Religion*, 708, though he did not go beyond the calendar entry which is sparse and inaccurate. I intend to write about Mother Leakey's ghost in greater detail elsewhere.

to at least six persons—four of whom were examined by the justices: the deceased's daughter-in-law, Elizabeth Leakey; a neighbour, Elizabeth Langston; Elizabeth Leakey's servant, Eleanor Fluellin; and Mr Heathfield, the curate of Minehead. Their depositions provide a great amount of circumstantial detail about the background to the appearances, the manner and places of the apparitions, and the words exchanged between the deponents and the ghost. The magistrates seem to have suspected a whiff of popery about the case, but Heathfield insisted that old Mrs Leakey 'was for ought he knew a Protestant, for she came ordinarily and duly to church'. The overall impression from the testimonies is of close layering of Protestant and traditionalist attitudes. The prelude to the hauntings was a sharp exchange between Elizabeth Leakey and her mother-in-law, during which the latter had threatened the ultimate sanction, to come again after her death. To this, Elizabeth retorted (like a good Protestant), 'What, will you be a divell?', and was told, 'No, but I will come in the divells likenesse.' About six weeks after Mother Leakey's death, knockings began in the house 'like a drove of cattle', and after a year 14-year-old John Leakey fell ill and 'in the tyme of his sicknesse he complayned that he could not be quiett for his Grandmother'. He died crying out that he saw the devil. Elizabeth initially claimed to have seen a handprint round his throat, but later asserted slightly less dramatically that he was 'somewhat black around the neck'. She added that 'her husband and she suspect all this to be witchcraft, because he hath had greate losses of late by sea, and that they suspect a woman to be the witch'.

Yet despite this overtly demonic frame of reference, Elizabeth Leakey and the other percipients all evidently accepted the apparition for what it claimed to be, the spirit of her mother-in-law. Elizabeth addressed the ghost in time-honoured fashion: 'Is there any thing left undone in your will that I can doe for you?' The ghost's reported wishes involved the delivery of a bond, and the return to her son of a gold chain in the possession of another daughter-in-law in Barnstaple (the latter rejoicing in the godly name of Lords-neare). Mother Leakey also charged Elizabeth with a secret message for her daughter, Joan Atherton, in Ireland.

The commissioners, who included the Laudian bishop William Piers, and the moderately puritan local dignitary Sir Robert Phelips, were resolutely unimpressed by all of this, the hints of Satan's involvement included. Their report to the Privy Council discredited the witnesses, pointing to inconsistencies in the testimony, and concluded that the haunting was an 'imposture' framed for some particular purpose they could not fathom. Whether or not they were right about this, the story as the deponents told it clearly contains elements of the malevolent revenant of folk tradition, as well as more specifically Catholic and Protestant ghost tropes. Mother Leakey was almost certainly the Susan Leakey, widow of Minehead, who was buried on 5 November 1634, and died owing substantial debts, noted to be the cause of 'much despute'. She may thus fulfil the long-established popular expectation that revenance was typically the fate of querulous persons who had made a bad end, particularly if she is to be identified with the Susan Leakey of Bridgwater, accused of using a 'taunting, brawling and quarrelling manner' in a pew dispute of 1618.[151] Elizabeth Langstone's claim to have seen the ghost 'in the shape of a little child shining very bright and glorious' is redolent of the above-cited Lancashire Catholic ghost of 1612, and it may be significant that the ghost appeared to her on Christmas eve, and to Elizabeth Leakey and Elinor Fluellin 'about Allhallow tide'—both were traditional folkloric moments of 'slippage' between the parallel worlds of the living and the dead.[152] Though the Leakeys and their neighbours seem to have been Protestants, they displayed attitudes towards the dead quite inimical to orthodox Protestant divinity.

The Reformation failed to eradicate a widely held belief in the possibility of the dead seeking communion with the living. In 1659, a full century after the Elizabethan Settlement, it could be asserted that examples of people returning as ghosts after their death were 'numerous and frequent in all mens mouths'.[153] Why was this? Not, I think, as Ronald Hutton would have it, because of an 'instinctive assumption on the part of Protestants' that folk beliefs about wandering spirits were 'essentially harmless', and a wise pastoral decision to leave the subject well alone.[154] The evidence cited in this chapter suggests that the continuing propensity of English people to believe the dead might linger in this world was a matter of concern not just to a handful of puritan zealots, but to a broad spectrum of Protestant opinion in the Elizabethan and early Stuart periods. Though ghosts and apparitions account for a fairly small proportion of the ink spilt in theological controversy in the Reformation period, they had important lessons to teach about the right interpretation of Scripture, and the deadly dangers of popish superstition.

Of course, ghosts had their uses. As we have seen, Protestant authorities sometimes problematized their own message as they attempted to press-gang ostensible appearances of the dead into a framework of providentialist justice, and Shakespeare, along with a host of other writers and dramatists, found quasi-traditional ghost figures too useful a resource to resist. That ghosts performed important social functions has been the key insight of most of the recent writers on the subject. Keith Thomas, in a characteristically vivid and persuasive chapter of *Religion and the Decline of Magic*, suggests that, before the Reformation, ghosts upheld the Church's moral teaching;

---

[151] E. Fry (ed.), *Calendar of Wills and Administrations in the Court of the Archdeacon of Taunton* (London, 1912), 272; Somerset Record Office, DD/SP 1634/41; DD/SAS PR 306.

[152] See above, 14–15. See also J. Briggs, *Night Visitors: The Rise and Fall of the English Ghost Story* (1977), 40.

[153] H. More, *The Immortality of the Soul* (1659), 286.

[154] Hutton, 'English Reformation and the Evidence of Folklore', 114.

thereafter they operated quintessentially to objectify and uphold moral standards and societal norms, identifying murderers, enforcing wills and safeguarding the transfer of property, preserving the stability of society through the enforcement of obligations towards dead ancestors.[155] But too determinedly functionalist an approach runs the risk of downplaying the extent to which the meanings of ghostly apparitions were open, hazardous, and uncertain, both at the level of official theory, and among those who actually found themselves confronted in the night with a 'questionable shape'. Though it may seem trite to insist upon the point, hauntings were numinous occasions inspiring confusion and dread. As Lavater observed, 'it is naturall unto us, to be amazed with feare when we see suche things'.[156] Fear and frightfulness were stressed by all the witnesses in the Minehead case, the servants of Sir Thomas Wise were 'frighted with a walking spirit', and Aloyza Garman was similarly 'much affrighted' by the knockings in her Ghent convent.[157] Such evidence as we have suggests that this was equally true before the Reformation, and scholars who contrast the terrifying modern ghost with its 'homely' medieval ancestor are probably fairly wide of the mark.[158] Alongside grief, anticipation, and the urges to commemorate and forget, there is a place for fear as one of the psychological building-blocks of pre-modern relations with the dead.

To the Reformation historian, ghost belief invites plotting somewhere on a graph whose axes are the 'revisionist' paradigm (stressing the resilience of traditional religious cultures and their imperviousness to reform) and the 'post-revisionist' one (pointing to the potential of Protestantism to shape and influence these cultures while not obliterating their ties to the past). David Cressy has recently suggested that belief in ghosts in post-Reformation society 'may be related to the incomplete eradication of purgatory from popular consciousness'.[159] But despite what Protestant polemicists often asserted, there may have been no absolutely necessary dependence of ghosts on purgatory. After all, ghost beliefs are to be found in a wide variety of cultures with very different conceptions of the afterlife, and it may be helpful to think of medieval popular perceptions of the behaviour of revenants as construed within, rather than constructed by, the doctrine of the theologians.[160] As was suggested in Chapter 4, belief in purgatory and in the efficacy of intercessionary prayer for the dead seems to have been withering

[155] Thomas, Religion, ch. 19 (pp. 701–24). See also Finucane, *Appearances of the Dead*, esp. p. 150; Schmitt, *Ghosts in the Middle Ages*, 3, defines his purpose as ' to show how beliefs and the imaginary depend above all on the structures and the functioning of the society and the culture at a given period in time'.
[156] Lavater, *Of Ghostes*, 191.
[157] BL, Additional MS 21203 no. 9, 24ʳ.
[158] R. Bowyer, 'The Role of the Ghost-Story in Mediaeval Christianity', in Ellis, Davidson, and Russell (eds.), *The Folklore of Ghosts*, 177–92; Bennett, 'Ghost and Witch', 5–6. See Gordon and Marshall, 'Introduction', in *Place of the Dead*, 7–8.
[159] Cressy, *Birth, Marriage and Death*, 403.
[160] See above, 15–17.

away outside of explicitly Catholic circles by the end of the sixteenth century, something patently not true of belief in ghosts.

Perhaps Protestant teaching in its purest form was simply too cruelly counter-intuitive ever fully to take root in the popular consciousness. Judith Devlin's study of attitudes towards the supernatural among the nineteenth-century French peasantry argues that ghost-beliefs 'diminished the sense of loss and helplessness caused by the death of a relative or friend'.[161] While apparitions in Reformation England were often threatening or baffling, it is unlikely that this element was entirely absent. Nocturnal spirits in the form of unknown persons, like the woman who appeared to Sir Thomas Wise, might more easily be rationalized as beguiling delusions, but it may have been much harder to do this when family members were involved. In his treatise of 1594, Thomas Nashe faced the question head-on:

It will bee demaunded why in the likenes of ones father or mother, or kinsfolks, [the devil] oftentimes presents himself unto us? No other reason can bee given of it but this, that in those shapes which hee supposeth most familiar unto us, and that wee are inclined to with a naturall kind of love, we will sooner harken to him than other-wise.[162]

This was an unpalatable doctrine indeed for anyone who believed they had seen the form of a loved one again in this world. When Thomas Browne insisted that devils assumed the likeness of departed persons to instil the false belief that 'the blessed souls are not at rest in their graves, but wander solicitous of the affaires of the world', he was of course paying indirect tribute to the emotional power of the notion that the dead were solicitous of the living. A few years after Browne wrote, the Cambridge Platonist Henry More complained of what seemed to him the fundamental implausibility of the orthodox Protestant position on ghosts. The habitual and accepted activities of ghosts appeared to More to consist 'in detecting the murtherer, in disposing their estate, in rebuking injurious executors, in visiting and counselling their wives and children, in forewarning them of such and such courses'. Surely such actions were 'unfit for a devil with that care and kindness to promote'. Conversely, angels would surely not stoop to lying, and yet these spirits professed to be the soul of this or that person.[163] More exemplifies, albeit in exaggerated form, that gradual retreat from the former hard line on the possibility of ghosts that seems to be characteristic of some Protestant clergy in the later part of the early modern period.[164]

An earlier generation of reformers was only too well aware that ghosts shamelessly flouted their prescriptions for well-managed relations between

[161] J. Devlin, *The Superstitious Mind: French Peasants and the Supernatural in the Nineteenth Century* (New Haven and London, 1987), 91.
[162] Nashe, *Terrors of the Night*, 348.
[163] More, *Immortality of the Soul*, 296.
[164] Thomas, *Religion*, 705–6.

the denizens of this world and the next. In a society obsessed with order, they constituted the disorderly dead, illegal immigrants across a border that was supposed to remain sealed and impermeable until the end of time. Protestantism's failure to stop the traffic is evidence not solely of the resilience and intractability of 'popular' culture, but also of the difficulties reformers experienced at all levels of society in reconciling their doctrinal mandates with that unstable compound of love, longing, and loathing which constitutes the livings' legacy from the dead.

7

Remembering the Dead:
Commemoration and Memory
in Protestant Culture

VIEWING his native land from exile in 1565, William Allen remarked scornfully that 'nowe there is no blessing of mannes memorie at all'.[1] But from any objective assessment, the conclusion was a partial and misleading one, which scarcely fits the 1560s, and seems less convincing with every passing decade. Despite the dissolution of chantries and fraternities, the proscription of requiem masses and intercessory prayers, the putting out of obit lamps, and abrogation of bede-rolls, Elizabethan and early Stuart England possessed a plethora of methods and occasions for memorializing the dead, and sanctifying their memory. Foremost among these, perhaps, was the preaching and printing of funeral sermons and other commemorative works, and the commissioning and placing of funeral monuments. As we have seen, there were some Protestants for whom these media remained potentially contaminated with the asbestos dust of intercessory prayer. But while previous chapters have discussed the efforts to suppress suspect rites, practices, and attitudes, and to replace them with doctrinally sound alternatives, the focus here will be on a more positive articulation of the place of the dead in the religious culture of Protestant England. We have attempted this already with regard to the 'estate' of the dead in the next life, but how did people speak about the dead, and how did the dead wish to be spoken about, as a remembered social presence in this world? Addressing these questions involves examining a number of paradigms favoured by cultural, literary, and art historians in order to search out the lineaments of distinctive Protestant modes of remembering. The hope is to arrive at a more balanced and nuanced understanding of the terms under which the living and the dead continued to coexist in post-Catholic society, and to see how this dynamic may help us better to understand the social and cultural impact of the Reformation as a whole.

[1] W. Allen, *A Defense and Declaration of the Catholike Churches Doctrine touching Purgatory* (Antwerp, 1565), 169ᵛ.

OBLIGATIONS TO THE DEAD

The living could do nothing to alter the condition of the dead, but this did not absolve them of responsibilities towards them. At the start of Elizabeth's reign, in Veron's *Huntyng of Purgatory to Death*, a Catholic character plaintively poses the question, how can we do good unto the dead, 'or how can we acquyte our selves towardes them', if prayers are taken away? In the manner of such theophrastic dialogues, Veron has his answer ready. Scripture teaches only two ways: decent burial, and the succouring of children, friends, and kin.[2] In the view of Bishop Pilkington, 'that comely order which Christian charity requireth' consisted of decent, unsuperstitious burial, and preachers of funeral sermons sometimes described the congregation as met together 'to perform the last office and duty of charity'.[3] Protestant divines like William Perkins might thus agree with their Roman adversaries that 'Christian charitie is to extend it selfe to the very dead', but it was to show itself 'in their honest burial, in the preservation of their good names, in the helpe and reliefe of their posteritie'.[4] Bishop Gervase Babington extended the list of 'fit and allowable' duties towards the dead to include moderate mourning, hope in their resurrection, and faithful performance of their testaments.[5] To Samuel Gardiner (moderate) mourning for the deceased, 'as members of one and the same body', was something 'charity itself requireth'.[6] Edward Vaughan's 'holy duties towards the dead' included doing good to those the deceased had loved in their lifetime.[7] Thomas Tuke answered the question 'What honour ought the living to performe unto the dead?' with moderate grief, honest burial, imitation of their virtues, praising of God for taking them to mercy, and maintenance of their credit.[8] Elizabethan and Jacobean preachers looking to justify the publishing of laudatory funeral sermons frequently did so in terms of an acknowledged 'dutie to the

[2] J. Veron, *The Huntyng of Purgatory to Death* (1561), 71^{r-v}.

[3] J. Pilkington, *Works*, ed. J. Scholefield (PS, 1842), 318; W. Sclater, *A Funeral Sermon preached at the Buriall of the Right Worshipfull Mr John Colles* (1629), G2^r.

[4] W. Perkins, *A Reformed Catholike* (Cambridge, 1598), 278–9. Decent and reverent burial was endlessly rehearsed as a duty which the living owed to the departed: A. Willet, *Synopsis Papismi* (1592), 319; R. Hooker, *Of the Laws of Ecclesiastical Polity*, ed. C. Morris, 2 vols. (1907), ii. 401; C. Fitz-Geffry, *Deaths Sermon unto the Living* (1620), 11; S. Smith, *A Christian Taske. A Sermon, preached at the Funerall of Maister Iohn Lawson* (1620), 2; M. Day, *A Monument of Mortalitie* (1621), 77–8; F. Rodes, *Life after Death* (1622), 213–14; J. Cleland, *A Monument of Mortalitie upon the Death and Funeralls of the...Late Duke of Richmond and Lennox* (1624), 37, 43–4. Traditionally, burial of the dead was one of the Seven Works of Corporal Mercy, though Protestant writers did not refer to it in these terms, perhaps because, while the first six works were derived from a canonical gospel (Matt. 25: 36–6), this one was an addition from the apocryphal book of Tobit (12: 12).

[5] G. Babington, *Workes* (1622), iii. 124.

[6] S. Gardiner, *The Devotions of the Dying Man* (1627), 327–8.

[7] E. Vaughan, *A Divine Discoverie of Death* (1612), 189.

[8] T. Tuke, *A Discourse of Death* (1613), 80.

dead'.[9] Here popular sentiment and ecclesiastical prescription must have converged. The parishioners of East Mersea, Essex, were outraged in 1581 when their curate refused to perform burials, uncharitably appropriating the words of Scripture, 'Let the dead bury the dead'.[10] In an Oxfordshire village in 1631, a woman was heard to remark, as if proverbially, 'God's blessing on them that buried the dead, it is fit the dead should be buried'.[11]

To remark the conventionality of such expression is to underscore rather than undermine its social significance. The language of piety towards the departed is a defining feature of the commemorative discourses of later Reformation England; all educated contemporaries were familiar with the classical aphorism *de mortuis, nil nisi bonum* (speak nothing but good of the dead).[12] In 1628, for example, an entry in Sir John Oglander's commonplace book on the assassination of the duke of Buckingham concluded with the reflection that 'he was the greatest subiect that England ever had. Of his contrary virtues I will say nothing: *de mortuis nil nisi bonum*'.[13] Writers castigated those who habitually spoke ill of the dead; they were 'very offensive', 'the worst sort', 'unseasoned satyrists', 'envious detractors', 'cursing shimeries and rayling Rabshakethes'.[14]

The impulse to speak well of the dead, or some of the dead, was sharpened by religious controversies. It was a shrewd polemical sally to accuse opponents of impiety on this score. William Harrison's funeral sermon for Katherine Brettargh was put into print 'to cleere her from the slanderous reports of her popish neighbors, who will not suffer her to rest in her grave, but seeke to disgrace her after her death'.[15] In a controversial work of 1590, William Whitaker defended from Catholic attacks 'Master Doctor Iewell, the late worthie Bishop of Sarisburie of blessed memorie', and during the 'Decensus Controversy', Andrew Willet claimed to have been stung into print by Richard Parkes's attack on Dr John Reynolds: 'had he staied here onely, in

[9] G. Abbot, *A Sermon preached at Westminster* (1608), A3[r]; R. Stock, *The Churches Lamentation for the Losse of the Godly* (1614), 'epistle'; T. Jackson, *Sinneless Sorrow for the Dead* (1615), A2[r]; W. Ford, *A Sermon preached at Constantinople in the Vines of Perah* (1616), A3[v]; P. Hodson, *The Last Sermon preached before His Majesties Funerals* (1625), 5–6; W. Crompton, *A Lasting Jewell for Religious Woemen* (1628), F1[r].

[10] F. G. Emmison, *Elizabethan Life: Morals and the Church Courts* (Chelmsford, 1973), 172.

[11] D. Cressy, *Travesties and Transgressions in Tudor and Stuart England* (Oxford, 2000), 125. The remark was an edged one, the context the irregular burial of an excommunicated Catholic within the parish church.

[12] M. Coverdale, *Remains*, ed. G. Pearson (PS, 1846), 109; Foxe, iv. 645; D. Kay, *Melodious Tears: The English Funeral Elegy from Spenser to Milton* (Oxford, 1990), 27; Mar-phoreus (Thomas Nashe?), *Martins months minde* (1589), E1[r]; R. Carpenter, *The Soules Sentinel* (1612), 101; Babington, *Workes*, iii. 300; W. Bathe, *Ianua Linguarum*, 8th edn. (1634), 10–11.

[13] F. Bamford (ed.), *A Royalist's Notebook: The Commonplace Book of Sir John Oglander* (1936), 41, though Oglander could not resist going on to add 'No man was more adored in life, and few less respected after death.'

[14] C. Fitz-Geffry, *Elisha His Lamentation* (1622), 33; R. Brathwaite, *Remaines after Death* (1618), E4[r–v]; Stock, *The Churches Lamentation*, 61–2; Day, *A Monument of Mortalitie*, 79–80; J. Preston, *A Sermon preached at the Funeral of Mr Arthur Upton* (1619), 36.

[15] W. Harrison, *Deaths Advantage Little Regarded* (1612), A3[v].

censuring the living, and not proceeded to taxe the memorie of the dead, it had been more tolerable . . . to rage against the name and memorie of the righteous departed is impious, and sacrilegious'.[16] Another deceased puritan luminary, Lawrence Humphrey, was passionately defended by Edward Hoby in controversy with Theophilus Higgons. Since Humphrey had bene-fited many in his lifetime, it was fit that 'he should be defended by manie being dead . . . And if your superstition teach you to pray for the dead, you cannot, I hope, blame my generous disposition, to patronize the *Dead*.'[17] The contrast here is a revealing one. It was precisely because the dead were beyond all human help that it seemed a kind of sacrilege to slander them. If the book of Leviticus taught that it was wrong to curse the deaf, then 'much lesse the dead: for who deafer then a dead man? Who further off? Who lesse able to answere for himselfe?'[18] Conversely, those who spoke well of the dead, it was sometimes suggested, could not be suspected of any base motive. Since the departed were totally insensible of what transpired in this world, 'we need not feare to be counted flatterers in yeelding them their due prayses'.[19]

The latter claim reveals a sensitivity, and a degree of special pleading. As the funeral sermon developed as the definitive Protestant instrument of commemoration, its practitioners remained alert to the charge that they engaged in a kind of mercenary praisemongering, like bad lawyers 'who for a fee will pleade and commend any cause'.[20] In response, preachers developed a rationale for a duty of praise, one that, naturally, was sanc-tioned by the example of Scripture. David had commended Jonathan; Paul had praised the patriarchs and prophets, and the (albeit uncanonical) book of Ecclesiasticus provided a generalized exhortation to 'let us now praise famous men'.[21] A few added the testimony of long-approved custom.[22] To praise the dead was not only lawful, but highly laudable. In making known the virtues of the godly, preachers were in fact praising God for them, while providing exemplary patterns of piety for the living; funeral sermons con-formed to the familiar Augustinian trope that mortuary ritual served for the comfort of the living rather than the dead.[23] Hyperbolic or rhetorical praise

---

[16] W. Whitaker, *An Answere unto a Certaine Booke* (Cambridge, 1590), 40; A. Willett, *Loidoromastix* (1607), A3ᵛ, 11. The trope was a well-established one: cf. the ballad controversy prompted by the execution of Cromwell in 1540: 'Small charyte and lesse wytte is in thy nolle / Thus for to rayle upon a Christen soule'. *LP* xvi. 423.

[17] E. Hoby, *A Letter to Mr T.H.* (1609), 73, 49–50.

[18] Tuke, *A Discourse of Death*, 80.

[19] Harrison, *Deaths Advantage Little Regarded*, 5; Fitz-Geffry, *Elisha His Lamentation*, 33.

[20] J. Barlow, *The True Guide to Glory. A Sermon preached at Plympton Mary in Devon, at the funerals of the Lady Strode of Newingham* (1619), 46.

[21] Harrison, *Deaths Advantage Little Regarded*, 77; Cleland, *A Monument of Mortalitie*, 49.

[22] H. Gamon, *The Praise of a Godly Woman* (1627), A3ʳ; J. Gaule, *A Defiance to Death being the Funebrious Commemoration of the Right Honourable Baptist Lord Hickes* (1630), 36–7.

[23] Fitz-Geffry, *Deaths Sermon unto the Living*, 25; id., *Elisha His Lamentation*, 29; J. Philips, *The Way to Heaven* (1625), A4ʳ; R. Hill, *The Path-way to Prayer and Pietie* (1609), 276–8.

for its own sake ought to have no place in such a schema. Preachers insisted that funeral sermons were not the same as funeral orations, and many would have concurred with a remark of the Wiltshire minister George Ferebe at a funeral in 1614: 'it ill becomes any man, either flatteringly to adde more, or iniuriously to give lesse to the dead then is due'.[24] Some sermons even hinted at a profligate life redeemed by a godly death.[25]

Yet while condemning the abuse of 'commending the dead contrarie to desert', preachers often insisted that their own subject deserved nothing but unstinting praise.[26] In some cases the dead were to be commended whether they wished it or not. Preaching in May 1625 at the burial of the merchant Richard Fishburne, Nathaniel Shute noted that in his sickness he had often spoken against 'the abuse of this custome of over-spicing the dead in large commendation' and begged that in the funeral sermon the preacher should 'speake nothing of him'. Shute, however, felt unable to comply: 'by my silence I should have maymed the common expectation'.[27]

Social convention, and the expectations of audience and readership, helped shape the genre. Along with the imparting of 'some good learning', the poet George Puttenham considered 'saying well of the departed' to be the essential point of funeral sermons.[28] 'If a man dispraise, though never so truly', complained Babington, 'every one cryeth out, that it is inhumanitie ... and the friends of the dead especially and greatly are offended'.[29] Some preachers discovered the truth of this to their cost. When Emmanuel Utie felt 'directed by the finger of the spirit' to reprove the habitual drunkenness of the deceased in a funeral sermon preached at St Stephens Walbrook in 1616, he was abused for having 'emblazon'd the dead contrarie to the rule of charitie'.[30] The experience was shared by Samuel Hieron in 1618. Returning home after preaching at a funeral, he was accosted by the sisters and daughters of the dead man: 'by them I was openly, and in the hearing of many, with great vehemencie accused and challenged as an uncharitable wronger and defamer of the dead'.[31] In 1591 charges brought by parishioners against

[24] R. Harris, *Samuells Funerall. Or a Sermon preached at the Funerall of Sir Anthonie Cope* (1618), A4^r; R. Parr, *The End of the Perfect Man. A Sermon preached at the Buriall of the Right Honourable Sir Robert Spencer* (Oxford, 1628), A4^v; G. Ferebe, *Lifes Farewell. Or a Funerall Sermon preached ... at the Funerall of John Drew Gentleman* (1615), 26.

[25] Carpenter, *The Soules Sentinel*, 101.

[26] R. Eaton, *A Sermon preached at the Funeralls of ... Master Thomas Dutton* (1616), 20; Crompton, *A Lasting Iewell for Religious Woemen*, E2^v–E3^r; J. Wall, *A Sermon preached at Shelford in Nottinghamshire* (1623), A5^v.

[27] N. Shute, *The Crowne of Charitie* (1626), 25–6.

[28] G. Puttenham, *The Arte of English Poesie*, ed. G. Willock and A. Walker (Cambridge, 1936), 49.

[29] Babington, *Workes*, iii. 300.

[30] E. Utie, *Mathew the Publican. A Funerall Sermon preached in St Stephens Walbrooke the 11 of March 1615* (1616), A2^r, A3^r, 35.

[31] S. Hieron, *The Worldlings Downefall* (1618), A2^v.

the puritan minister of Stradishall, Suffolk, included speaking uncharitably of persons he disliked at their burials.[32]

This was not a culture characterized by a lack of concern or respect for its dead. Its impulse to memorialize, to commemorate, the dead was both deep-rooted and inventive.[33] The beasts, observed the memorial preacher Nataniel Shute, possessed only a 'sensitive memory', an instinctive recollection of an object seen, heard, smelled, or tasted. But man's capacity extended to an 'intellective memory' which enabled him to reduce things into memory not merely by representations of them 'but by discourse... which the beasts cannot doe, therefore it is called in the beasts, memory, but in man *Reminiscentia*, that is remembrance'.[34] It is with these discourses of remembrance, the structures, language, and idioms in which Protestant memorialization was couched, that the rest of this chapter is concerned.

THE MEANINGS OF MEMORY

'Remember me.'[35] The anguishing ambivalence of the ghost's words to Hamlet brings into focus sharp differences between the meanings of memory in pre- and post-Reformation England. Once, to remember the dead was to pray for them, to recite their names over and again in a variety of liturgical and quasi-liturgical contexts. A full half-century after the dissolution of the chantries, these practices were remote for Shakespeare and his audience, but the act of remembering still involved negotiating an intricate nexus of emotional and social responses, private grief and public duty. And what did the dead themselves want?

The antiquarians who at the end of the sixteenth century devoted themselves to the recording of data from funeral monuments considered the desire to be remembered a natural human instinct. Arthur Agard spoke of 'man having an instincte of divinytye in him, that is, a desyre to atteyne to an everlasting contynuance and remembraunce of his name and worthynesse'. Robert Reyce attributed the ubiquity of tombs to the fact that everyone 'naturally doth foster in himselfe a secret longing, and silent desire for his ever continuance in this beautiful frame'.[36] The attitudes here seem to be born of Renaissance humanism, upholding the importance of the

[32] J. S. Craig, 'Reformation, Politics and Polemics in Sixteenth-Century East Anglian Market Towns', University of Cambridge Ph.D. thesis (1992), 26.

[33] For helpful discussion of commemoration as the public and social aspect of memory, see J. Fentress and C. Wickham, *Social Memory* (Oxford, 1992).

[34] Shute, *The Crowne of Charitie*, 3-4.

[35] *Hamlet*, I. v. 91.

[36] T. Hearne (ed.), *A Collection of Curious Discourses written by Eminent Antiquaries upon several Heads*, 2 vols. (1775), i. 246; R. Reyce, *Suffolk in the XVIIth Century. The Breviary of Suffolk*, ed. F. Hervey (1902), 2.

individual, and the 'fame' he or she would leave behind. They are, quite literally, a world away from the fear that neglect of memory would lead to the soul's suffering in the next life. If these are the wellsprings of memory in Protestant commemorative culture—this-wordly, 'secularized'—then their effluence takes us via a cultural watershed of very profound moment.

The most useful starting-point here is the changing nature of epitaphs and monumental inscriptions. Most pre-Reformation ones had an overtly intercessory purpose, and though these did not disappear overnight after 1558, the overwhelming majority of inscriptions produced thereafter did not invoke prayers for the soul. Indeed, as we have seen, increasing numbers of them asserted that it was already dwelling in heaven.[37] This aside, the most striking contrast between pre- and post-Reformation epitaphs is the growing discursiveness of the latter. From the surviving effigial tombs in Sussex, for example, it can be calculated that the median word-count of inscriptions in 1496–1515 was thirty-five; in 1596–1615 it was eighty-six, and in 1616–35, ninety-four. Other studies confirm this was a national trend.[38] To some extent the increase reflected the growing inclusion of poetic tributes and scriptural quotations, but mainly it was due to the provision of extra biographical information about the deceased, beyond bare details of dates and descent. In 1631 John Weever began his 'discourse of funerall monuments' by defining them as things 'erected, made, or written, for a memoriall of some remarkable action, fit to be transferred to future posterities'.[39] Heroic deeds and exploits had occasionally been recorded on early sixteenth-century monuments, but were more likely to appear after 1560, along with the more quotidian achievements of the moderately great and good: service at court, or in parliament, the captaincy of trained bands.[40] Another new development, from the early seventeenth century, was the presence of a more affective language of loss and bereavement, particularly in the monuments erected to deceased spouses by the surviving partner, though whether this constitutes evidence for an actual change in family

---

[37] See above, 200–1.

[38] H. R. Mosse, *The Monumental Effigies of Sussex*, 2nd edn. (Hove, 1933), *passim*; B. Kemp, *English Church Monuments* (1980), 83; R. Rex, 'Monumental Brasses and the Reformation', *Transactions of the Monumental Brass Society*, 15 (1990), 380–3.

[39] J. Weever, *Ancient Funerall Monuments* (1631), 1.

[40] Sir Marmaduke Constable's epitaph (1520) at Flamborough, east Yorkshire, is a notable pre-Reformation example of the type: N. Pevsner, *Yorkshire: York and the East Riding* (1972), 230. For later examples, see E. Mercer, *English Art 1553–1625* (Oxford, 1962), 236; H. Holland, *Monumenta sepulchraria Sancti Pauli* (1614), D4^r; Mosse, *Monumental Effigies of Sussex*, 149, 192; F. A. Greenhill, *Incised Effigial Slabs: A Study of Engraved Stone Memorials in Latin Christendom c.1100 to c.1700*, 2 vols. (1976), i. 337; Kemp, *English Church Monuments*, 71. There was undoubtedly (and unsurprisingly) a gendered aspect to the contents of epitaphs: men were represented more in terms of their public roles, women as exemplars of devotion and 'private' virtue. For this theme in relation to funeral sermons, see J. L. McIntosh, 'English Funeral Sermons 1560–1640: The Relationship between Gender and Death, Dying and the Afterlife', University of Oxford M.Litt. thesis (1990), 125–39.

relationships must remain open to question.[41] A recurrent refrain of Elizabethan and early Stuart epitaphs was the need for a lasting or permanent
memory of the deceased. This phraseology had once been associated with
the establishment of perpetual chantries, but it now acquired a more protean
character. It was sometimes suggested that people achieved immortality
through their children, that 'they that leave posteritie, / Live in their off-
springgs, dye not properlye'.[42] More commonly, however, post-mortem
'existence' was represented as a function of the lives which individuals
themselves had led. Epitaphs regularly emphasized the 'fame' of their subjects, which death could not extinguish.[43] Virtuous lives were often said to
'deserve perpetuall memory'.[44] But it was sometimes explicitly recognized
that a permanent physical memorial was needed to bring this about. As a
marble table to Lady Boynton (d. 1634) at Roxby, North Yorkshire admitted, 'mortalities doth deface the memorie of thinges'.[45] Thus, in 1609, John
Smyth of North Nibley, Gloucestershire, erected a monument to his wife,
Grace, 'thereby to make perpetual the memoryal of her vertues', and a tomb
was built for Richard Caryll (d. 1616) at South Harting, Sussex, 'to eternize
his name as long as marbles shall endure'.[46] The decision of the earl of Essex
to be buried in Wales in 1576 was celebrated in a particularly unctuous
sermon by the bishop of St David's, Richard Davies: 'thy Tombe shall be
with us in reverence, estimation and honour, the fame and name of they
Nobilitie, valiauntnesse, vertue and worthiness, shal never be forgotten, but
shall lyve and be kept with us in memorie from generation to generation
whyle the world standeth'.[47] The final phrase here directly recalls the terms
in which perpetual obits had been endowed two generations earlier.[48] But

---

[41] Mercer, *English Art 1553–1625*, 241–4; J. Wilson, 'I Dote on Death: The Fractured
Marriage in English Renaissance Art and Literature', *Church Monuments*, 11 (1996), 43–60;
C. Gittings, 'Expressions of Loss in Early Seventeenth-Century England', in P. C. Jupp and G.
Howarth (eds.), *The Changing Face of Death* (1997), 27–8.

[42] Wilson, 'I Dote on Death', 49. See also T. F. Ravenshaw, *Antiente Epitaphs* (1878), 47, 55;
H. W. Macklin, *The Brasses of England*, 3rd edn. (1913), 279–80; W. Lack *et al.* (eds.), *The
Monumental Brasses of Cornwall* (1997), 100. The point was also made in funeral sermons:
Parr, *The End of the Perfect Man*, A2ᵛ; Gaule, *A Defiance to Death*, A2ᵛ.

[43] J. W. Clay (ed.), *Yorkshire Church Notes 1619–1631*, YASRS, 34 (1904), 82; A. B.
Connor, *Monumental Brasses in Somerset* (repr. Bath, 1970), 257; Lack, *Monumental Brasses
of Cornwall*, 130; Ravenshaw, *Antiente Epitaphs*, 54; Mosse, *Monumental Effigies of Sussex*,
123. This was not an exclusively post-Reformation topos: see, for example, Greenhill, *Incised
Effigial Slabs*, i. 330.

[44] Mosse, *Monumental Effigies of Sussex*, 190; E. W. Badger, *The Monumental Brasses of
Warwickshire* (Birmingham, 1895), 26; Ravenshaw, *Antiente Epitaphs*, 42; Greenhill, *Incised
Effigial Slabs*, i. 345.

[45] A. White, 'Church Monuments in Britain *c.*1560–*c.*1660', University of London Ph.D.
thesis (1991), 535.

[46] I. M. Roper, *The Monumental Effigies of Gloucestershire and Bristol* (Gloucester, 1931),
429; Mosse, *Monumental Effigies of Sussex*, 102.

[47] R. Davies, *A Funerall Sermon ... at the Buriall of the Right Honourable Walter Earle of
Essex* (1577), F2ʳ.

[48] See above, 21.

the nature of the perpetual memory envisaged was quite different, relocated from a cyclical ritual enactment to a linear and cognitive constant.

Davies's sermon, and the fact of its being printed, reminds us that tombs and their inscriptions were by no means the only instrument for perpetuating 'fame' available to the elites of Protestant England. Funereal verses—elegies, odes, and laments—which were sometimes attached to hearses or placed on tombs and church walls, were increasingly finding their way into print.[49] The reign of Elizabeth saw the development of a tradition of publishing epitaphs and elegies to mark the passing of prominent public figures, the foremost exponent of which was the happily named Thomas Churchyard.[50] In the printed epitaphs by contemporaries of Churchyard's, such as Nicholas Bourman and George Whetsone, 'endless fame' was a recurrent theme. The latter boasted that he would make the life of the earl of Bedford appear like 'Dyamonds set in Bras'.[51] There was clearly a market for these products, and the genre was a capacious one, embracing simple rhyming broadside epitaphs and polished Latin verse.[52] The death of Elizabethan England's emblematic hero Sir Philip Sidney in 1586 prompted an outpouring of over 200 poetic elegies from admirers, collected and printed in multiple volumes, and the death in France a decade later of the royal ambassador Sir Henry Unton led to the publication of a volume of memorial verses in Latin by fellows of Oxford University.[53] Almost fifty separate memorial volumes were produced after the death of Henry, Prince of Wales in 1612.[54] In a society as suffused by the medium of print as Elizabethan and early Stuart England, it is unsurprising that published works assumed such a prominent commemorative function, or indeed that authorship itself was sometimes taken to provide a form of immortality. The anti-atheistical writer Jeremy Corderoy pointed to 'the goodly and learned writings of holy men' as evidence that 'the godlinesse and pietie of the good die not with them when they depart this life', and the point was made *ad hominem* in John Buckeridge's funeral

---

[49] For the placing of temporary scrolls or tablets with tribute verses, see G. C. Gorham, *Gleanings of Few Scattered Ears, during the Period of the Reformation in England* (1857), 240; Foxe, viii. 288; F. Burgess, *English Churchyard Memorials* (1963), 219; K. Esdaile, *English Church Monuments 1510–1840* (1946), 130. For a literary reference to the practice, *Much Ado About Nothing*, IV. i. 208–9.

[50] Kay, *Melodious Tears*, ch. 1; Houlbrooke, *Death*, 327–8.

[51] N. Bourman, *An Epytaphe upon the Death of the Right Reverent Father in God I. Iuell* (1571); *An Epytaphe upon the Death of the Right Worshipfull Sir William Garrat* (1571); Kay, *Melodious Tears*, 24.

[52] For the more demotic end of the market, see C. R. Livingstone, *British Broadside Ballads of the Sixteenth Century: A Catalogue of the Extant Sheets* (1991). On the literary end, see M. Greenfield, 'The Cultural Functions of Renaissance Elegy', *English Literary Renaissance*, 28 (1998).

[53] J. Buxton, 'The Mourning for Sidney', *Renaissance Studies*, 3 (1989), 51; Gittings, 'Expressions of Loss', 26. Unton was also the subject of an iconographically complex memorial portrait, on which see R. Strong, 'Sir Henry Unton and his Portrait: An Elizabethan Memorial Picture and its History', *Archaeologia*, 99 (1965).

[54] J. Woodward, *The Theatre of Death: The Ritual Management of Royal Funerals in Renaissance England, 1570–1625* (Woodbridge, 1997), 153.

sermon for Lancelot Andrewes, where it was suggested that his works of learning would be *'monumentum ore perrenius*; a monument more lasting than *brasse* and stone'.[55]

The funeral sermon itself, however, was the most conspicuous instrument of post-mortem reputation as the sixteenth century drew to a close. Not just ephemeral utterances on the day of burial, funeral sermons were being put into print in increasing numbers around the turn of the seventeenth century.[56] Their official rationale was the edification of the living, not the exaltation of the dead, and the bulk of the text generally comprised the exposition of a scriptural passage. But this was followed by remarks about the life and death of the dead person, and the dedicatory epistles prefixed to most printed funeral sermons added more biographical material. Thomas Jackson agreed to the printing of his sermon for the Kentish gentleman John Moyle, so that 'I might by dead letters ... preserve him in living fame', and John Wall's sermon for John Stanhope was printed 'that his memorie may have a perpetuall beeing'.[57] In his sermon for the minister Richard Stock, Thomas Gataker protested that his praises would add nothing to the 'reverent estimation of him remaining in the mindes of so many', and yet 'this may bide, when they are gone'.[58] Nathaniel Shute similarly averred of Richard Fishburne, that 'I could not obtaine rest of my selfe by erecting him a monument onely in mine own heart, but ... must present this walking monument of him in paper to all the world'. Published a year after Fishburne's death, the sermon was 'now consecrated as an anniversary to his Fame'.[59] The impulse may be seen in the very titles of Stephen Denison's published funeral sermons for John Juxon, and his wife Elizabeth: *The Monument or Tombestone* (1620); *Another Tombestone* (1627). Unlike tombstones, however, sermons eternalized the author as well as the subject, and a number of preachers felt compelled to disclaim any selfish motive. In a sermon for Mary Swaine (1611), Lancelot Langhorne insisted that 'I seeke not my

---

[55] J. Corderoy, *A Warning for Worldlings* (1608), 33; J. Buckeridge, *A Sermon preached at the Funeral of ... Lancelot late Lord Bishop of Winchester* (1629), 22. See also C. Aslakssøn, *The Description of Heaven*, tr. R. Jennings (1623), A1ʳ. A backhanded tribute to the potency of the idea can be found in the attack on it by the moralist William Drummond: 'That renowne by papers ... how slender it is, the very word of paper doth import ... How many millions never heare the names of the most famous writers? And amongst them to whom they are knowne, how few turne over their pages?' *A Midnights Trance: Wherein is Discoursed of Death* (1619), 52.

[56] Cressy, *Birth, Marriage and Death*, 572 n., provides the following breakdown: three funeral sermons printed in the 1560s; three (1570s); seven (1580s); eleven (1590s); twenty-nine (1600s); fifty-six (1610s); forty-nine (1620s). Slightly different figures are given by Houlbrooke, *Death*, 386–7, but following the same pattern of growth. These represented, of course, only a small fraction of the number of sermons actually preached; Ian Archer suggests a figure of around 500 per annum in London by the 1590s: 'The Arts and Acts of Memorialization in Early Modern London', in J. F. Merritt (ed.), *Imagining Early Modern London* (Cambridge, 2001), 103.

[57] Jackson, *Sinneless Sorrow*, dedication; Wall, *A Sermon preached at Shelford*, A3ᵛ.

[58] T. Gataker, *Abrahams Decease* (1627), A4ᵛ.

[59] Shute, *The Crowne of Charitie*, A1ᵛ–2ʳ.

selfe, but the continual remembrance of this vertuous Gentlewoman'.[60] Shute's sermon for Fishburne was 'rather to keep up his remembrance, then to spread mine owne'.[61] It was a cliché of dedicatory epistles that the author had been earnestly pressed to take his text to a publisher by the 'importunitie of living friends'.[62]

In sermons and other commemorative discourses, it was common for the 'memorial' or 'remembrance' of the dead person to take on an essentially reified quantity: 'her remembrance is now with us', 'his memoriall shall not depart away from us', 'having now no relike of him, but only his remembrance'.[63] The habit is exemplified in the wonderfully bathetic Jacobean inscription to the North Yorkshire woman, Jane Smythe: 'Heaven haith her soule, Selby her memory'.[64] At the same time, the dead were frequently reported to 'live in memory', to remain among the living 'in name and memory'.[65] Some early Caroline preachers urged an affective, almost Ignatian exercise of mental recollection. John Gaule's sermon for Lord Hickes proclaimed 'let us have him now in our mindes, while he is now no more before our eyes: having lost his presence, let us inioy him yet in his remembrance'. John Donne's anniversary sermon for Lady Danvers invoked the departed to 'appeare in thy *history*; appeare in our *memory*'.[66]

The growing concern which the epitaphs and sermons of this period display with the achievements and fame of their subjects, and with the perpetuation of their 'remembrance' among the living, has prompted scholars to discern the emergence and consolidation of fundamentally new social and cultural attitudes. In a distinction first elaborated by the art historian Erwin Panofsky, the funeral monuments of later Reformation England seem profoundly 'retrospective', designed solely to commemorate the past achievements of the dead, in contrast to the 'prospective' monuments of an earlier period, focusing on the fate of the deceased in the afterlife.[67] Recent writers, both historians and literary critics, have tended to identify two crucial trends caused by the Reformation and its abolition of

[60] L. Langhorne, *Mary Sitting at Christs Feet* (1611), A5ʳ.

[61] Shute, *The Crowne of Charitie*, A1ᵛ.

[62] Jackson, *Sinneless Sorrow*, dedication; Harrison, *Deaths Advantage Little Regarded*, A3ʳ; N. Guy, *Pieties Pillar: or A Sermon preached at the Funerall of Mistresse Elizabeth Gouge* (1626), A3ʳ⁻ᵛ.

[63] Day, *A Monument of Mortalitie*, 84; S. Price, *The Two Twins of Birth and Death* (1624), 47; Shute, *The Crowne of Charitie*, 25.

[64] Clay (ed.), *Yorkshire Church Notes*, 79.

[65] Crompton, *A Lasting Iewell for Religious Woemen*, A2ʳ⁻ᵛ; S. Crooke, *Death Subdued* (1619), F6ᵛ; R. Chambers, *Sarah's Sepulture, or a Funerall Sermon preached for...Dorothie Countess of Northumberland* (1620), A2ᵛ; T. Taylor, *The Pilgrims Profession. Or a Sermon preached at the Funerall of Mrs Mary Gunter* (1622), 122.

[66] Gaule, *A Defiance to Death*, 37–8; J. Donne, *Sermons*, ed. G. R. Potter and E. M. Simpson, 10 vols. (Berkeley and Los Angeles, 1953–62), viii. 85.

[67] E. Panofsky, *Tomb Sculpture: Its Changing Aspects from Ancient Egypt to Bernini* (1964), 62–76. For a suggestive critique of the dichotomy, see P. Ariès, *The Hour of Our Death*, tr. H. Weaver (1981), 214–15, 228.

intercessory prayer. One trajectory is a marked shift of emphasis from the collective to the personal, and the crafting of post-mortem personal reputation, a process some prefer to think of as a rise of 'individualism'.[68] Another is the refocusing of the quest for personal 'immortality' on the things of this life rather than the next. By promoting a sense of the absoluteness and finality of judgement at death, the Reformation sharpened an awareness of death as oblivion, as the inscrutable annihilator of worldly achievements and status, social attributes which needed to be celebrated and preserved. Alongside individualism, then, 'secularization'.[69]

But there are grounds for caution here. As we have already seen, a 'humanist' concern with post-mortem fame predates the Reformation and was compatible with spiritual motivations; and the interest that tombs in Protestant England frequently displayed in the 'estate' of the dead in the next life distinctly problematizes (in Michael Neill's phrase) 'the overwhelmingly secular significance of such edifices'.[70] Neat dichotomies of before and after, of religious and secular, become yet harder to sustain if we turn to consider in more detail the emblematic symbols and themes of post-mortem 'fame' in Protestant culture.

THE DEAD SPEAKING

Few passages seem better to encapsulate the essentially secularizing spirit of post-Reformation commemoration than the observation of a character in John Webster's *The Duchess of Malfi* (1612–13):

> ...Princes images on their tombes
> Do not lie, as they were wont, seeming to pray
> Up to heaven: but with their hands under their cheekes,
> (As if they died of the tooth-ache)—they are not carved
> With their eies fix'd upon the starres; but as
> Their mindes were wholly bent upon the world,
> The self-same way they seeme to turne their faces.[71]

---

[68] R. N. Watson, *The Rest is Silence: Death as Annihilation in the English Renaisssance* (Berkeley and Los Angeles, 1994), 5; A. Fowler, *Time's Purpled Masquers: Stars and the Afterlife in Renaissance English Literature* (Oxford, 1996), 108; C. Gittings, *Death, Burial and the Individual in Early Modern England* (1984), 39–40, 47, 147–8.

[69] Gittings, *Death, Burial and the Individual*, 146; L. C. Attreed, 'Preparation for Death in Sixteenth-Century Northern England', *SCJ* 13 (1982), 65; L. Gandhi, '"Gainst Death and all Oblivious Enmity": Monuments and Memorializing in some of Shakespeare's Works', University of Oxford D.Phil. thesis (1991), 45, 58, 61, 76; Kay, *Melodious Tears*, 7–8; C. J. Somerville, *The Secularization of Early Modern England* (Oxford, 1992), 88; M. Neill, *Issues of Death: Mortality and Identity in English Renaissance Tragedy* (Oxford, 1997), esp. pp. 3, 38–40, 48, 306. See also Rex, 'Monumental Brasses', 379–80, though here the expression 'naturalization of memory' is preferred to 'secularization'.

[70] Neill, *Issues of Death*, 306. See above, 23, 230–1.

[71] *Duchess of Malfi*, IV. ii. 153–9.

The image is a poignant one, as well as a sharp satiric swipe at a particular fad in Jacobean monumental sculpture, but the literal and symbolic downward gaze was by no means universally recognized by contemporaries. It was a prime purpose of monuments for the dead, thought the devotional writer Robert Hill, to put us in mind of our glorious habitation in heaven, a perception shared by the Suffolk antiquary Robert Reyce: they signified 'a supernaturall desire to aspire to that devine and blessed immortalitie'.[72] Though in the course of the sixteenth century tombs shed their specifically Catholic imagery, that hardly meant they were devoid of religious significance, as their placing inside churches surely indicates. There is no opportunity here to embark upon an extended survey of the iconography and symbolism of Elizabethan, Jacobean, and Caroline tombs, though it is at the very least worth noting that, in what Katherine Esdaile once called 'the conservative world of sepulchral art', stylistic links with the past remained very much in evidence.[73] Well into the seventeenth century, the standard medieval pattern—the tombchest with recumbent effigy—remained the most popular type of composition, and the persistence of established iconographical patterns was equally marked in the case of brasses. Here the depiction of the subject kneeling in an attitude of prayer continued to be extremely common, albeit achievements of arms now sometimes occupied the place in the schema previously reserved for depictions of the Virgin or the Trinity.[74] As Nigel Llewellyn has observed, some tombs self-consciously upheld the late medieval tradition of functioning as memento mori, replete with personifications of death or even representations of the decomposing corpse.[75] After 1600 the religious elements in tomb sculpture became once again more overt, though avoiding subjects offensive to mainstream Protestant sensibilities. Representations of the resurrection, either allegorical or with a depiction of the deceased rising shrouded from the tomb, became popular, and, remarkably, so did angels (the latter highly biblical, despite some unfortunate associations with popery).[76] These

---

[72] Hill, *The Path-way to Prayer and Pietie*, 271; Reyce, *The Breviary of Suffolk*, 157.

[73] K. A. Esdaile, *English Monumental Sculpture Since the Renaissance* (1927), p. x. Comprehensive accounts are provided by ead., *English Church Monuments*; J. Finch, *Church Monuments in Norfolk before 1830: An Archaeology of Commemoration* (Oxford, 2000); Kemp, *English Church Monuments*; White, 'Church Monuments'; P. Sherlock, 'Funeral Monuments: Piety, Honour and Memory in Early Modern England', University of Oxford D.Phil. thesis (2000); as well as the work of Nigel Llewellyn: 'John Weever and English Funeral Monuments of the Sixteenth and Seventeenth Centuries', University of London Ph.D. thesis (1983); id., *Funeral Monuments in Post-Reformation England* (Cambridge, 2000); 'Claims to Status through Visual Codes: Heraldry on post-Reformation Funeral Monuments', in S. Anglo (ed.), *Chivalry in the Renaissance* (Woodbridge, 1990), 145–60; 'Honour in Life, Death and in the Memory: Funeral Monuments in Early Modern England', *TRHS* 6th ser., 6 (1996),179–200; White, 'Church Monuments'.

[74] Llewellyn, *Funeral Monuments*, 77–81; Houlbrooke, *Death*, 348; M. Norris, *Monumental Brasses: The Craft* (1978), 79.

[75] Llewellyn, 'English Funeral Monuments', 97–8.

[76] Kemp, *English Church Monuments*, 165–76; Llewellyn, 'English Funeral Monuments', 110; White, 'Church Monuments', 411–30.

changes seem to reflect a more relaxed attitude to the permissibility of funeral monuments as images. A related development may be the trend in brasses and effigies from the end of the sixteenth century towards greater realism in the depiction of the human form, and in some cases towards actual portraiture of the deceased. The stiffness and stereotyped character of much Elizabethan figure sculpture, it is sometimes suggested, indicates not so much 'bad art', as an understandable nervousness about affective realism in the wake of the iconoclastic campaigns of the mid-century.[77] Elizabeth's proclamation of 1560 defended tombs 'set up for the only memory of them to their posterity... and not for any religious honor', but in a society which regarded the social order as divinely ordained, and a life of virtuous public duty as a possible indicator of election, attempts to disaggregate the 'secular' and 'religious' messages that monuments were designed to send out are likely to founder. In the early seventeenth century particularly, monuments were regularly noted to have been erected in 'sacred memory' of the deceased.[78] They were intended not only to celebrate the lives of good men and women, but to sanctify and consecrate their memory. Memorialization of the departed was a pious duty.

In this context it is important to recognize that the preachers who lauded the achievements of the dead had not the slightest inkling that they were the practitioners of a Renaissance or neo-pagan 'cult of fame'. The book of Proverbs (10: 7) taught that 'the memory of the just is blessed', and the Psalms (112: 6) that 'the righteous shall be had in everlasting remembrance', texts that were endlessly cited in memorial sermons.[79] Sanctifying the memory of the virtuous dead, 'the saints', served an essentially pious purpose, the edification of the living. In the words of the Elizabethan bidding prayer, the living praised the departed and prayed God 'that we may have grace for to direct our lives after their good example'.[80] Funeral sermons almost invariably made explicit what was already implicit in the three-way

---

[77] Llewellyn, 'English Funeral Monuments', 107–9; M. Norris, *Monumental Brasses: The Memorials*, 2 vols. (1977), i. 234; id., *Monumental Brasses: The Craft*, 79; J. Bertram, 'The Iconography of Brasses', in id. (ed.), *Monumental Brasses as Art and History* (Stroud, 1996), 63; Mercer, *English Art 1553–1625*, 238–9; Esdaile, *English Church Monuments*, 48; R. Greaves, *Society and Religion in Elizabethan England* (Minneapolis, 1981), 731.

[78] G. Isherwood, *Monumental Brasses in the Bedfordshire Churches* (1906), 30; Mosse, *The Monumental Effigies of Sussex*, 93; Clay (ed.), *Yorkshire Church Notes*, 111; W. Camden, *Remains Concerning Britain*, ed. T. Moule (1870), 390; D. Hickman, 'Wise and Religious Epitaphs: Funerary Inscriptions as Evidence for Religious Change in Leicestershire and Nottinghamshire, c.1500–1640', *Midland History*, 26 (2001), 115.

[79] Pilkington, *Works*, 651; T. Sparke, *A Sermon preached at Whaddon in Buckinghamshire ... at the Buriall of the Right Honorable Arthur Lorde Grey of Wilton* (1593), 2ʳ; Stock, *The Churches Lamentation*, 'epistle'; Crooke, *Death Subdued*, G2ᵛ; W. Walker, *A Sermon preached at the Funerals of the Right Honourable William Lord Russell* (1614), A2ʳ; Jackson, *Sinneless Sorrow*, 3; J. Warren, *Domus Ordinata. A Funeral Sermon preached in the Citie of Bristol* (1618), A4ʳ; Day, *A Monument of Mortalitie*, 77; Price, *The Two Twins of Birth and Death*, A2ʳ; Crompton, *A Lasting Iewell for Religious Woemen*, A2ʳ⁻ᵛ; R. Bolton, *The Foure Last Things* (1632), 1.

[80] R. J. E. Boggis, *Praying for the Dead: An Historical Review of the Practice* (1913), 192.

relationship between clerical author, subject, and audience. According to the Kentish minister Thomas Jackson, it was 'the maine use of the commemoration of the vertuous lives of the godly; that they may be patternes to them that live'.[81] A Jacobean funeral sermon by George Ferebe used a striking analogy to underline the importance of this for a distinctively Protestant pattern of piety: 'as the papists say images are *laicorum libri, lay-mens books*: so may I say, that these dead images are *vivorum libri*, living mens bookes'.[82] The demands of commemoration and edification were seen to dovetail seamlessly: 'I desire so to preserve the memorie of the dead, as that I may also edifie the living'.[83]

Collectors of epitaphs sometimes justified their interest on precisely these lines. It was undoubtedly the case, argued Richard Brathwaite, that 'by the very inscriptions or titles engraven upon the tombes of the deceased, some have beene mooved to imitate their memorable lives in actions and attempts of like nature'.[84] In Weever's opinion, 'the often reading, serious perusall, and diligent meditation of wise and religious epitaphs' was an effective means for bringing men to repentance.[85] An epitaph, thought William Segar, 'should remember the name of the defunct and his progenie truly, his countrey and quality briefly, his life and vertues modestly, and his end christianly, exhorting rather to example then vaine glory'.[86] Late Elizabethan epitaphs often conformed to this typology, a 1599 inscription in the choir of Thornhill church, Yorkshire, declaring 'Here lyeth the body of Nicholas Radcliffe, whose constant religious lief, together with his godly ende, God grant they may move others to imbrace true piety'.[87] At Okehampton, Devon, Thomasin Petre was 'a mirror for all wyves to veiwe'; Ann Sewell of Coventry was 'a worthy stirrar up of others to all holy vertues'.[88] It would seem strange in this context to persist in locating changes in idioms of commemoration primarily within a paradigm of 'secularization'. Doubly so, when further thought is given to the specifics of the 'holy virtues' the living were expected to emulate. For there is little doubt that the most clamorous

---

[81] Jackson, *Sinneless Sorrow*, 3.

[82] Ferebe, *Lifes Farewell*, 25.

[83] Fitz-Geffry, *Elisha His Lamentation*, A3ᵛ. See also R. Welcome, *The State of the Godly both in this Life and in the Life to Come* (1606), 82–3; Abbot, *A Sermon preached at Westminster*, A3ʳ; A. Nixon, *Londons Dove: or a Memoriall of the life and death of Maister Robert Dove* (1612), A3ᵛ; Walker, *A Sermon preached at the Funerals of ... Lord Russell*, A2ᵛ; Barlow, *The True Guide to Glory*, A3ʳ; Crooke, *Death Subdued*, F7ʳ⁻ᵛ; Day, *A Monument of Mortalitie* , 65, 76; Price, *The Two Twins of Birth and Death*, 40; Fitz-Geffry, *Deaths Sermon unto the Living*, 12; Gamon, *The Praise of a Godly Woman*, A2ᵛ⁻³ᵛ; Sclater, *A Funeral Sermon preached at the Buriall of ... Mr John Colles*, G2ʳ; Crompton, *A Lasting Iewell for Religious Woemen*, F1ʳ.

[84] Brathwaite, *Remaines after Death*, C4ʳ⁻ᵛ, D5ᵛ⁻6ʳ, E4ʳ.

[85] Weever, *Ancient Funerall Monuments*, 9.

[86] W. Segar, *Honor Military, and Civill, contained in Foure Bookes* (1602), 256.

[87] Clay (ed.), *Yorkshire Church Notes*, 69.

[88] Ravenshaw, *Antiente Epitaphs*, 47; Badger, *Monumental Brasses of Warwickshire*, 20 (see also ibid. 25); Greenhill, *Incised Effigial Slabs*, i. 335; White, 'Church Monuments', 535.

theme in commemorative texts of the late sixteenth and early seventeenth centuries is that of charitable giving, and charity, greatest of the three theological virtues, flies uncomfortably as a banner of either 'secularization' or 'individualism'.

As we have seen, the question of whether praying for the dead itself represented a charitable act went to the heart of polemical debates over purgatory and intercession, and Protestant anxieties about the traditional links between alms-giving and intercessory prayer were slow to assuage in some quarters.[89] Catholics claimed that a decline of charity was the inevitable consequence of the abandonment of purgatory, and Protestants sometimes came close to conceding the point. Philip Stubbes regarded it as a cause of shame that men living 'in the times of superstition' should 'so farre passe us in good workes'. It was an occasion for 'the enemy to barke against us, as if our religion were nothing else but playne talking'.[90] In a sermon of 1578, Laurence Chaderton similarly conceded that 'the papists always cast in our teeth the great and famous hospitals of their nobility and clergy, the building of abbeys, monasteries, and nunneries, cathedral churches, colleges, with many other outward works which indeed are such as do stop our mouths and put us Protestants to silence'.[91]

Yet such concessions were intended as calls to arms, rather than admissions of defeat, and the more usual thrust of Protestant writing was that the Reformation had nothing of which to be ashamed. In his *Description of England*, William Harrison admitted that people sometimes made invidious comparisons, yet 'if you look unto these our times you shall see no fewer deeds of charity done'.[92] Some went considerably further. In 1614 Andrew Willet drew up a massive catalogue to establish that in sixty years the Gospel had brought forth many more good works than popery had managed in a period twice as long, a claim endorsed by Edward Hoby.[93] Moreover, the motivation behind works of charity was as important as their volume, Hoby scorning the achievements of 'a *Benefactor* called *Satisfactory Pennance*'. The papists' works of charity, remarked the preacher Ralph Tyrer, were but a means 'whereby they indeavour to merit their salvation, and get worldly commendation'. Popish piety, claimed Richard Sheldon, was always undertaken 'with conceit of merit; to cause friers to pray for

---

[89] See above, 141–8, 167.

[90] P. Stubbes, *A Motive to Good Workes* (1593), A3ᵛ, A4ʳ, 44–56, 72, 86.

[91] I. Archer, 'John Stow's *Survey of London*', in D. L. Smith, R. Strier, and D. Bevington (eds.), *The Theatrical City: Culture, Theatre and Politics in London, 1576–1649* (Cambridge, 1995), 31. See also L. Wright, *A Summons for Sleepers* (1589), 27–8.

[92] W. Harrison, *The Description of England*, ed. G. Edelen (Ithaca, NY, 1968), 37.

[93] Archer, 'John Stow's *Survey of London*', 31; E. Hoby, *A Curry-Combe for a Coxe-Combe. Or Purgatories Knell* (1615), 39. The desire to show that the Church of England surpassed the Church of Rome in charity continued well into the eighteenth century: J. Gregory, *Restoration, Reformation and Reform, 1660–1828. Archbishops of Canterbury and their Diocese* (Oxford, 2000), 165 n.

themselves, or the souls of their friends departed'.[94] By contrast, Protestant charitable works managed to commemorate their founders in a way untainted by such rank self-interest, being, in Harrison's phrase, 'better grounded upon the right stub of piety'.[95] In a sermon of 1627 extolling 'the uncounsum'd Bounty' of the City of London, Thomas Goffe challenged superstition and idolatry to 'open their eyes, and see what houses of charity the true and cleere *knowledge that he is the Lord*, hath built in this Kingdome, which shall ever remaine honourable monuments, in the memory of all that live, and attend their founders, as glorious trophees, when their easie dust shall give way to them, that they may come up out of their *Graves'*.[96]

Printed funeral sermons, particularly those of London mercantile elites, frequently made the charitable largesse of their subjects the centrepiece of the text, sometimes advertising this in the very titles of the works, as in Anthony Nixon's *Londons Dove: or a Memoriall of the Life and Death of Maister Robert Dove, Citizen and Marchant-Taylor of London, and of His Severall Almesdeeds and Large Bountie to the Poore* (1612) or Nathaniel Shute's *The Crowne of Charitie: a Sermon Preacht in Mercers Chappell, May 10 1625 at the Solemne Funerals of his Ever-renowned Friend, of Precious Memory, the Mirror of Charitie, Mr Richard Fishburne* (1626). John Gaule's 1630 sermon for Baptist Lord Hickes, Viscount Camden, contained as an appendix 'a iust and necessary catalogue', which minutely itemized charitable gifts to the town of Chipping Camden, Gloucestershire, to the City of London, and to other godly uses from Pembrokeshire to Northumberland, the effect being of a kind of one-man bede-roll.[97] The prominence of charity as a commemorative theme is even more marked in epitaphs than in funeral sermons, increasingly so in the early seventeenth century.[98] In some cases, the level of detail suggests that the purpose of the inscription was not merely to commemorate the piety of the benefactor, but to provide a quasi-legal record of the terms of the benefaction. The tomb of Richard Leche (d. 1596) at Fletching in Sussex claimed to have been put up

---

[94] Hoby, *A Curry-Combe for a Coxe-Combe*, 39; R. Tyrer, *Five Godlie Sermons* (1602), 304–5; R. Sheldon, *A Survey of the Miracles of the Church of Rome* (1616), 321.

[95] Harrison, *Description of England*, 37.

[96] T. Goffe, *Deliverance from the Grave. A Sermon preached at Saint Maries Spittle* (1627), 40.

[97] Gaule, *A Defiance to Death*, C4^r–6^v. See also Eaton, *A Sermon preached at the Funeralls of ... Master Thomas Dutton*, 22; Welcome, *The State of the Godly*, 76; Abbot, *A Sermon preached at Westminster*, 17; W. Fuller, *The Mourning of Mount Libanon* (1628), 29–30.

[98] The list could be expanded almost endlessly, but for good examples of the conspicuousness of charity in epitaphs, see W. Lack *et al.* (eds.), *The Monumental Brasses of Berkshire* (1993), 75, 85, 127; Connor, *Monumental Brasses in Somerset*, 317; Roper, *Monumental Effigies of Gloucestershire*, 29, 162, 510, 543, 563, 608, 690; Ravenshaw, *Antiente Epitaphs*, 74; Badger, *Monumental Brasses of Warwickshire*, 4, 58; Isherwood, *Monumental Brasses in the Bedfordshire Churches*, 30, 55, 68; Greenhill, *Incised Effigial Slabs*, i. 342; Clay (ed.), *Yorkshire Church Notes 1619–1631*, 46, 94, 98; Mosse, *Monumental Effigies of Sussex*, 180.

'for a perpetual memory of divers...charitable deedes' in Fletching and adjoining parishes, and it itemized these in great detail.[99] The stone of Richard Townend (d. 1605) in the choir of Worsborough church, Yorkshire, recorded the details of an annuity (to be paid at Pentecost and Martinmas) to the poor of the township.[100] The inscription on the Jacobean table tomb of William and Annis Whitbye in the churchyard of Mudford, Somerset, supplied only one detail beyond their names and date of death: 'which William / Gave 5ll. per annum ; for ever: to ye poore / of the parish; isshuing out of his lands / of Coxham, in ye parish of Yeavil'. For good measure, the inscription was duplicated on a stone placed inside the church.[101] In all these cases it is likely that the charitable sums mentioned were intended for distribution in the church where the monument was sited. A connection between the two was sometimes explicitly made. The mercer Peter Symonds left money in 1586 for a weekly distribution of bread in Winchester Cathedral, the loaves to be placed on a table under a slab depicting Symonds kneeling in prayer.[102] In 1612 the haberdasher Florence Caldwell endowed a similar weekly dole at St Martin Ludgate, to take place at the spot in the church 'where I have lately caused a little monument of me and my wives and daughter to be...sett up'.[103] In such cases, there was, as Ian Archer has written, 'a very strong performative element in acts of commemoration, the very act of distributing charity serving to inscribe the benefaction in the minds of both those distributing and receiving it'.[104] In late Elizabethan London, there were at least sixty-two separate distributions of bread to the poor every Sunday, which in their recital of the names of benefactors preserved something of the ethos of pre-Reformation charity. Charitable benefaction, and its monumental record, was often linked with the institution of commemorative sermons. The slab commemorating the brewer Charles Langlie (d. 1602) in St Giles Cripplegate itemized his gifts to the poor of the parish, along with his institution of a yearly sermon that 'others might be wonne thereby to follow Langlies waies'.[105] Annual sermons accompanying charitable distributions often prescribed that the benefactor be mentioned by name, and that they should be delivered on the anniversary of his funeral. Here again, there are clear structural congruences

---

[99] Mosse, *Monumental Effigies of Sussex*, 90.

[100] Clay (ed.), *Yorkshire Church Notes*, 70.

[101] Connor, *Monumental Brasses in Somerset*, 314. See also the 1605 bequest of a Nottinghamshire yeoman that the inscription on his tomb should describe 'what I have done by a deede to feofees in trust for the yerely releef of fower poore folkes': Hickman, 'Wise and Religious Epitaphs', 121.

[102] D. Hickman, 'From Catholic to Protestant: The Changing Meaning of Testamentary Religious Provisions in Elizabethan London', in N. Tyacke (ed.), *England's Long Reformation 1500–1800* (1998), 125.

[103] D. Hickman, 'Religious Belief and Pious Practice among London's Elizabethan Elite', *HJ* 42 (1999), 948.

[104] Archer, 'Arts and Acts of Memorialisation', 105.

[105] Greenhill, *Incised Effigial Slabs*, i. 338–9.

to earlier patterns of commemoration. The nineteen annual commemorative sermons at St Botolph Aldgate in the early seventeenth century recall the obits which punctuated the round of urban parishes at the end of the fifteenth century.[106]

The motivation and meanings were of course very different, but in all of this we find evidence of a continuing link, one might even say a symbiotic relationship, between commemoration and benefaction. Jacobean parishes had long abandoned their bede-rolls, but some did maintain a public record of the charitable donations of their parishioners. At St Michael Cornhill in 1608, a 'Table of Remembrance' was set up, listing the parishioners who had given to the poor, and intended to motivate 'such others as shall here after accordingly to their good examples bestowe any further charitable benevolences'. There was a similar table at St Christopher le Stocks, and elsewhere in London boards were erected to record individual gifts.[107] The corporation of Banbury ordered the setting up of a table of charitable benefactors in the church in 1603, and at Pittington, County Durham, the early Stuart vestry book scrupulously recorded for posterity 'the names of such as have given money to the stocke of the poore of Pittington parish, and to other pious and charitable uses'.[108]

The charitable giving which expected and received grateful memorialization might aim to benefit not just the poor but the community as a whole. The association, so very marked in the late Middle Ages, between commemoration and the equipping and beautification of parish churches resurfaced in the early seventeenth century. At Burnsall in North Yorkshire, the Jacobean antiquary Roger Dodsworth found verses from 1612 freshly painted on the chancel walls: 'This church of beawty most, repaired thus so bright / 200 poundes and more did cost Sir William Craven, Knight.' Craven was a local boy made good, a former lord mayor of London. A few miles to the east, Dodsworth came across further striking examples of signature-benefaction in the more imposing setting of Ripon Minster. Here he took special note of 'the church windowes which have all lately beene new glased by the liberality of sundry gentlemen'. In 1608–11 some twenty-seven windows had been reglazed and inscribed with the names of donors: 'Edward Kirby, draper, and John Mason, lateley deceased, to the praise of God, repaired this window, 1609'; 'Thomas Burton, of Ingerthorp, esquire, to the honor of the Holy Trinitie, repaired this window, 1611'. Among the higher south windows, a dozen panels emblazoned with the names of contemporary benefactors

---

[106] Archer, 'Arts and Acts of Memorialisation', 107–8. See above, 20–1.

[107] C. Schen, 'Women and the London Parishes', in K. French, G. Gibbs, and B. Kümin (eds.), *The Parish in English Life 1400–1600* (Manchester, 1997), 266; Archer, 'Arts and Acts of Memorialisation', 99.

[108] J. S. W. Gibson and E. R.C. Brinkworth (eds.), *Banbury Corporation Records*, Banbury Historical Society, 15 (1977), 80; J. Barmby (ed.), *Churchwardens' Accounts of Pittington and Other Parishes in the Diocese of Durham*, SS 84 (1888), 8.

nestled alongside a surviving pane from 1416, urging bystanders 'Orate pro animabus Mathei Batte et Johanne, uxoris sue'. At Long Preston in Ribblesdale the merchant James Knowles not only founded a hospital for the poor of the town in 1615, but paid for two stalls for them in the parish church, each embellished with the legend 'Though I be dead in name, / I do hope to live by fame'.[109] The desire of Jacobean parishioners (like their early Tudor grandfathers) to leave their visible mark on the fabric and furnishings of the parish church was no backward-looking peculiarity of the north. At the turn of the seventeenth century, in the London parishes of St Mildred Bread Street, St Stephen Walbrook, St Lawrence Jewry, and Holy Trinity Duke Place, the glazing of windows was funded by wealthy parishioners, whose names, arms, and occasionally even likenesses were recorded in the glass.[110] Rebuilding programmes in London parish churches often generated the display of boards listing contributors to the work, and, in London and elsewhere, it was common for churchwardens to place their names or initials on plate, new bells, or fabric improvements commissioned during their year of office, indulging what W. E. Tate once termed a 'mania for immortalizing themselves'.[111]

Charitable giving was a universal Christian obligation, but its representation as the primary motif of remembrance was undoubtedly particularly appealing to mercantile elites, for whom the celebration of lineage posed considerably more problems than it did for the landed gentry. The fields on which the philanthropy of merchant oligarchs might be inscribed were limited neither to the funeral monument, nor to the parish church, but encompassed printed works (both commemorative sermons and more ephemeral broadside epitaphs) as well as the public and corporate spaces of the livery company halls.[112] In this context, the development of civic portraiture is worth noting also, not least for its cousinage to the depiction of benefactors in monumental brasses.

In parallel to lingering anxieties about tomb sculpture, some Tudor Protestants were suspicious of portraits as potential vehicles of idolatry. But more commonly it was allowed that they performed a legitimate memorial function, William Perkins conceding that they could 'serve to keep in

---

[109] Clay (ed.), *Yorkshire Church Notes*, 238, 213–15, 38.

[110] Archer, 'Arts and Acts of Memorialisation', 100, 102; J. F. Merritt, 'Puritans, Laudians, and the Phenomenon of Church Building in Jacobean London', *HJ* 41 (1998), 941, 946.

[111] Merritt, 'Puritans', 945; W. E. Tate, *The Parish Chest*, 3rd edn. (1983), 100; C. Marsh, 'The Gravestone of Thomas Lawrence Revisited', in M. Spufford (ed.), *The World of Rural Dissenters 1520–1725* (Cambridge, 1995), 231.

[112] For epitaphs, see H. E. Rollins, *An Analytical Index to the Ballad-Entries in the Stationers' Registers: 1557–1704* (Chapel Hill, NC, 1924), nos. 725–71; Archer, 'John Stow's *Survey of London*', 17, 27, 31–2.

memory friends deceased whom we reverence'.[113] Peter Symonds, the wealthy Elizabethan mercer whose dole to the poor we have noted above, left a further bequest for his portrait to be hung in Haberdashers' Hall and Winchester Town Hall, noting that, 'although this may seem to smell of vainglory, yet being better construed it may be thought to a better purpose'.[114] The better purpose was the encouragement of others to emulate his generosity. By the early seventeenth century, the London livery companies' halls were cluttered with large collections of portraits of benefactors, along with their coats of arms, tables of their benefactions, collections of plate inscribed with their names, even statues and busts of them.[115] Symonds's demur notwithstanding, there is a distinct whiff of vainglory about all this, but the overall impression is of group solidarity as much as of individual glorification. As Robert Tittler has recently observed, the civic portrait 'seems intended to contribute to the reconstruction and preservation of a particular community', its aim to invite 'a frequent recollection of public achievement and an exhortation to respect the heritage of wise and weighty governance'.[116] In the same way, the presence of the monuments of the munificent dead sanctified the social structure of the City. Through Elizabeth's reign, the Fishmongers' Company preserved in good repair the tomb of one of their pre-Reformation brethren, Mayor William Walworth, who had been knighted by Richard II for slaying Wat Tyler. Its restoration was first undertaken in 1562, 'nuwe frest and gyld, and ys armes gyltt, with the pyctur all in alebaster lyung in ys armur gyltt, at the cost of Wylliam Parys fysmonger…a goodly rememborans for alle men of honor and worshype'.[117]

---

[113] R. Strong, *The English Icon: Elizabethan and Jacobean Portraits* (1969), 3; M. Aston, *England's Iconoclasts* (Oxford, 1988), 433, 448–51. Though note the somewhat censorious reaction of Richard Greenham to a woman who told him that out of regard for a certain deceased minister 'shee reserved his picture, in her sence to bee but in mind of him'. Greenham admonished her that the face was no commendation of the man, and that the appropriate way to keep his image was by calling to mind 'the sweet promises hee hath comforted you in the points of doctrine': K. L. Parker and E. J. Carlson, *'Practical Divinity': The Works and Life of Revd Richard Greenham* (Aldershot, 1998), 180.

[114] Hickman, 'From Catholic to Protestant', 125. The Elizabethan composer Thomas Whythorne, who had his likeness painted twice in his lifetime, similarly denied self-glorification. Portraits served as a reminder of virtues to friends and children left behind, that 'they may embrace and follow the same': *The Autobiography of Thomas Whythorne*, ed. J. M. Osborn (1962), 116.

[115] Archer, 'John Stow's *Survey of London*', 31–2; 'Arts and Acts of Memorialisation', 96–9; J. P. Ward, 'Religious Diversity and Guild Unity in Early Modern London', in E. Carlson (ed.), *Religion and the English People 1500–1640* (Kirksville, M., 1998), 94–5.

[116] R. Tittler, *The Reformation and the Towns in England: Politics and Political Culture, c.1540–1640* (Oxford, 1998), 297–303, quote at p. 303. See also id., *Townspeople and Nation: English Urban Experiences 1540–1640* (Stanford, Calif., 2001), ch. 3.

[117] *The Diary of Henry Machyn*, ed. J. G. Nichols, CS 42 (1847), 285, which anachronistically credits Walworth with the killing of Jack Cade.

The commemorative culture shaped by the English Reformation cannot unproblematically be regarded as either secular or individualistic, in sharp contradistinction to a spiritually orientated and corporate late medieval model. But the recurrent association of commemoration with generous benefaction raises another issue, that of whether a result of the changes in mortuary culture consequent upon theological change was to make post-mortem commemoration increasingly a prerogative of the socially import-ant, and thus narrow the circle of community, and increase social diver-gence.

THE STATUS OF THE DEPARTED

We commence here with a sense here of déjà vu. Like their medieval prede-cessors, Protestant preachers often claimed that the grave was a great leveller, where there was no difference between rich and poor.[118] But the opportunity to have one's voice heard from beyond the grave, in 1600 as in 1500, was hardly a universal right. Though the book of Ecclesiasticus exhorted the praising of famous men, it also noted that there were some who 'have become as though they had not been born'. Preaching at a funeral in 1623, John Cosin observed that most who die 'are clean forgotten and out of mind as soon as they are gone, as though they never were'.[119]

Of all the forms of commemoration, arguably the most emblematic of social status, hierarchy, and degree were monuments in parish churches. Contemporary theorists saw them as tokens of the love and affection which survivors felt for the deceased, and which encouraged the former to emulate the piety of the latter.[120] It was also sometimes insisted that their validation was essentially a moral one, early Stuart moralists such as Robert Hill or George Strode maintaining that the 'stately sepulchres' of the wicked did no more than proclaim 'his very dust and corruption'.[121] Yet at the same time Hill tempered his moralism with a matter-of-fact recognition that monuments 'distinguisheth betwixt person and person: for, though all die alike, yet all must not be alike buried'.[122] To the antiquary John Weever,

---

[118] E. Grindal, *Remains*, ed. W. Nicholson (PS, 1843), 7; Abbot, *A Sermon preached at Westminster*, 11; H. Greenwood, *Tormenting Tophet: or a Terrible Description of Hel* (1615), 33–4; Eaton, *A Sermon preached at the Funeralls of... Master Thomas Dutton*, 3; J. Moore, *A Mappe of Mans Mortalitie* (1617), 37; Barlow, *The True Guide to Glory*, 48; Cleland, *A Monument of Mortalitie*, 33–4; Gardiner, *Devotions of the Dying Man*, 80–1; Strode, *Anatomie of Mortalitie*, 72.

[119] Ecclus. 44: 9; E. Carlson, 'English Funeral Sermons as Sources: The Example of Female Piety in Pre-1640 Sermons', *Albion*, 32 (2000), 573.

[120] Hearne (ed.), *A Collection of Curious Discourses*, i. 222; Brathwaite, *Remaines after Death*, D5ʳ; Hill, *The Path-way to Prayer and Pietie*, 271; W. Wyrley, *The True Use of Armorie* (1592), 21

[121] Hill, *The Path-way to Prayer and Pietie*, 271; Strode, *Anatomie of Mortalitie*, 74.

[122] Hill, *The Path-way to Prayer and Pietie*, 271.

it was axiomatic that 'sepulchres should be made according to the qualitie and degree of the person deceased, that by the tombe every one might be discerned of what ranke hee was living'.[123] When Weever's predecessor William Camden produced a guide to the tombs in Westminster Abbey, he listed the monuments according to the social status of their subject, rather than by their location in the building. Nigel Llewellyn comments, 'the very structure of Camden's book suggests that his scholarship was controlled by the sense of social hierarchy generated by tombs'.[124] This was characteristic of the antiquarian outlook: when the herald William Segar spoke about the need to protect tombs from ruin and violation, he made it clear that he had in mind those 'of noble princes, and other great personages'.[125]

There is now a considerable body of scholarship which has addressed the significance of tombs for articulating messages about the social order in Elizabethan and early Stuart England. We have been taught to think about the structure and iconography of monuments as interlocking sets of systems for perpetuating the 'social body' or 'monumental body' of the deceased, and for preserving it as a permanent part of the parochial scene.[126] The fact that the parish church served as the primary setting for the display of the 'monumental body' had the effect, consciously or unconsciously, of asserting that asymmetries of power were sanctified by religion and sanctioned by God. For many of the gentry, assertions of virtue and godliness aside, what gave primary conceptual shape to the monumental body were the lines of lineage and dynastic continuity. The main instrument for the demonstration of these qualities was heraldry, and it has been claimed that 'many tombs in this period are designed to appear almost solely as vehicles for heraldic display'.[127] At the same time, it is increasingly recognized that monuments did not simply reflect a fixed social order, but were themselves part of the process whereby status was asserted, negotiated, and ascribed.[128]

---

[123] Weever, *Ancient Funerall Monuments*, 10.

[124] Llewellyn, 'English Funeral Monuments', 10.

[125] Segar, *Honor Military*, 254–5

[126] N. Llewellyn, 'The Royal Body: Monuments to the Dead, for the Living', in L. Gent and N. Llewellyn (eds.), *Renaissance Bodies: The Human Figure in English Culture c.1540–1660* (1990), 222–4; Llewellyn, 'Honour in Life, Death and in the Memory', 180–92; *The Art of Death: Visual Culture in the English Death Ritual c.1500–c.1800* (1991), chs. 7, 16, 17; F. Heal and C. Holmes, *The Gentry in England and Wales 1500–1700* (1994), 338–9; D. Cressy, 'Death and the Social Order: The Funerary Preferences of Elizabethan Gentlemen', *Continuity and Change*, 5 (1989), 112. Influential in formulations of the notion of the monumental body is E. H. Kantorowicz, *The King's Two Bodies: A Study in Medieval Political Theology* (Princeton, 1957).

[127] Llewellyn, 'English Funeral Monuments', 17. See also id., 'Claims to Status through Visual Codes'. I have benefited greatly here from reading two unpublished papers by Richard Cust, on 'Funeral Monuments' and 'Gentry Honour and Lineage'.

[128] Finch, *Church Monuments in Norfolk*, 184; Cust, 'Funeral Monuments'.

The question of location is a crucial one here.[129] Both before and after the Reformation, intramural burial was in itself a significant marker of local status, and within many of England's parish churches a well-understood zoning system was in operation. Burial within the chancel rails was usually seen as the most prestigious, followed by aisles and chapels, then the body of the church. Scales of charges for burial, graded according to location, were becoming increasingly standard for churches in the early seventeenth century, though it is unlikely that in many places there was a simple equation between ability to pay and the fact of burial in a requested location. Local gentry (particularly patrons of the church) often had prescriptive rights to certain places, and others may have been rationed and apportioned in ways that are now hard for us to reconstruct. Historians have begun to investigate how the allocation of seating in parish churches refracted concerns about precedence and order in local communities, and disputes over rights to pews, and over places of intramural burial, were often linked in the minds of contemporaries.[130] A petition of Lancashire ministers in 1590 complained that services were often disturbed 'by contentions... abowte seates, and places of buriall in the churche'.[131] The herald Arthur Agard similarly testified in 1600 that patrons in some parishes sought to restrict special places of burial to themselves and their kin, 'and I have known great stirre and sutes at law bothe about that, and for pewes in churches'.[132] According to John Donne, 'ambitious men never made more shift for places in court than dead men for graves in churches'.[133] In one such Jacobean case coming before Star Chamber, an uncle was said to have plotted to entitle himself to a particular 'seate and buriall place', thereby dispossessing his nephew 'being one of the best men in the sayde parishe'.[134] Throughout the period, a number of testators requested to be buried near or under the pew where they sat in church; in doing so they were more probably asserting what they saw as their rightful place within the community than expressing a whimsical preference.[135]

---

[129] For what follows, I draw on V. Harding, '"And One More May Be Laid There": The Location of Burials in Early Modern London', *London Journal*, 14 (1989), 112–29; K. Wrightson and D. Levine, 'Death in Whickham', in J. Walter and R. Schofield (eds.), *Famine, Disease and the Social Order* (1989), 162; D. Beaver, '"Sown in Dishonour, Raised in Glory": Death, Ritual and Social Organization in Northern Gloucestershire, 1590–1690', *Social History*, 17 (1992), 406–8; Llewellyn, *Funeral Monuments*, 146 ff.; Cressy, 'Death and the Social Order', 10.

[130] On pew disputes, see the forthcoming doctoral work of Catherine Wright of the University of Warwick.

[131] F. R. Raines (ed.), 'A Description of the State, Civil and Ecclesiastical, of the County of Lancaster about the year 1590', Chetham Society, 96 (1875), 6.

[132] Hearne (ed.), *A Collection of Curious Discourses*, i. 214.

[133] *No Man is an Island: A Selection from the Prose of John Donne*, ed. R. Scott (1997), 161.

[134] PRO, STAC 8/287/31.

[135] T. P. Wadley (ed.), *Notes or Abstracts of... the Great Orphan Book and Book of Wills* (Bristol, 1886), 230, 235, 263; Hickman, 'From Catholic to Protestant', 121; Wrightson and Levine, 'Death in Whickham', 162. The link between pews and place of burial was not an exclusively post-Reformation development: Duffy, *Altars*, 332; R. Dinn, '"Monuments Answerable to Mens Worth": Burial Patterns, Social Status and Gender in Late Medieval Bury St Edmunds', *JEH* 46 (1995), 248.

Competition over places of burial might involve a literal appropriation. In 1597 Robert Catton of St Peter Permountgate, Norwich, was charged with 'breaking upp the churche porche grounde and takinge upp a stone and break-inge the same whereon have been an epitaph, not havinge the consent of the churchwardens'.[136] More dramatic were events at Hallaton, Leicestershire, in 1611, when William Dent was accused of violently impeding the digging of a grave in the parish church. The case against him was dropped when it tran-spired that 'his father was buryed in the same place where the said grave was made . . . his corpes not consumed, namely the heyre of his head was freshe and his braynes evidently to be seene'.[137] For the gentry in particular, since tombs were accepted in law as evidence of ancestry, there was an obvious interest in demonstrating continuity through the location, as well as through the iconog-raphy, of series of family monuments. Some gentlemen constructed tombs for their ancestors replete with conscious archaism, or even in a few attested cases appropriated and falsified monuments in pursuit of a suppositious lineage.[138]

There are some indications that, from the end of the sixteenth century, monuments in churches were being constructed to commemorate a wider social range of subjects than had previously been the case. The overall number of monuments being placed in parish churches rose quite dramatic-ally in the first two decades of the seventeenth century, peaking in the 1620s. Francis Bacon was almost certainly correct when he wrote in 1592 that 'there was never the like of beautiful and costly tombs and monuments, which are erected in sundry churches in honourable memory of the dead'.[139] Rather more caustically, John Donne, in a sermon of 1619, condemned those who showed more concern for the church after their death than in their lives, 'in an affectation of high places and sumptuous monuments', and who neglected the needs of the poor while leaving large annuities 'for new painting their tombs, and for new flags and scutcheons every certain number of years'.[140] Perhaps he had a point: among the aristocracy, the proportion of the estate being spent on monuments was rising while that devoted to the expense of the funeral fell back.[141] Upon his sister's death in 1614, Sir Arthur Chichester reflected that 'a fayre monument to be erected upon her and her husbande . . . will make them memorable to posterities, when other temporarie expencies . . . will sone vanish'.[142] At the same time,

[136] J. F. Williams (ed.), *Diocese of Norwich: Bishop Redman's Visitation 1597*, Norfolk Record Society, 18 (1946), 35.
[137] Leicestershire Record Office, 1 D 41/13/35, 67. I owe this reference to Bernard Capp.
[138] Norris, *Monumental Brasses: The Craft*, 66; Heal and Holmes, *The Gentry in England and Wales*, 24–6, 34–7; Llewellyn, *Funeral Monuments*, 235–6, 301–2. For a 1586 case of a gentleman secretly exhumed from the church and reburied in the graveyard, see Emmison, *Elizabethan Life: Disorder*, 188.
[139] Cited in Llewellyn, 'English Funeral Monuments', 12.
[140] *No Man is an Island*, 109. For other examples of attacks on the vainglory of sumptuous tombs, see Llewellyn, *Funeral Monuments*, 247–8.
[141] Houlbrooke, *Death*, 368.
[142] W. Trevelyan and C. Trevelyan (eds.), *Trevelyan Papers*, CS 105 (1872), 127.

the growing popularity of hanging wall monuments, often involving a half-length effigy of the subject, seems to betoken a widening of the circle of patronage to include greater numbers of lawyers, lesser gentry, and particularly clergy, who aspired to join the 'community of honour' in the parish church.[143] Happily, greater pressure on space within the parish church was met by more space becoming available, the whitewashing of murals in Elizabeth's reign creating blank walls on which the new-style hanging monuments could be placed.[144]

Nonetheless, funeral monuments in Elizabethan and early Stuart England remained what they had always been, the preserve of a minority. Though wills do not provide a complete record of monuments arranged by executors, it is revealing to note that of the 1,050 Essex wills abstracted by F. G. Emmison (1558–77), only five make any reference to a stone or funeral monument. Similarly, of 1,208 wills proved in the Suffolk archdeaconry court between 1620 and 1626 only two made any bequest for a permanent grave marker.[145] Will-makers were themselves a socially advantaged group, the very poor having no property to bequeath. Just as before the Reformation, the majority of Christians had no permanent memorial over their place of burial.[146]

The linkage of commemoration with displays of social power and the articulation of hierarchical relations was emphatically not a purely post-Reformation development.[147] But the dissolution of fraternities and putting down of bede-rolls arguably removed opportunities for memorializing, if not the poor, then at least the 'ordinary', for which the new commemorative media of Protestant England, printed sermons, eulogies, and broadside epitaphs, provided little compensation.[148] Protestant polemicists had often argued that the doctrine of purgatory was inherently exclusive and divisive, a get-into-heaven-quick theology for the wealthy. But Catholic opponents were able to reverse the charge, suggesting it was the heretics who cared only for the memory of the rich. The Catholic Church, boasted William Allen,

---

[143] The expression is Nigel Llewellyn's: 'Honour in Life, Death and in the Memory', 187. See also id., 'English Funeral Monuments', 12–15; White, 'Church Monuments', 521–5; Kemp, *English Church Monuments*, 75.

[144] N. Pounds, *A History of the English Parish: The Culture of Religion from Augustine to Victoria* (Cambridge, 2000), 496.

[145] F. G. Emmison (ed.), *Essex Wills (England)*, 3 vols. (Washington, DC and Boston, Mass., 1982–6), i. 128, 246, 306, iii. 436, 463; M. Allen (ed.), *Wills of the Archdeaconry of Suffolk 1620–1624*, Suffolk Records Society, 31 (1989), 137, 241. The proportions here are not dissimilar to the 1,181 wills proved in the sacrist's court of Bury St Edmunds, 1439–1530, and analysed by Robert Dinn: only twelve testators mention memorials: '"Monuments Answerable to Mens Worth"', 251.

[146] There is some evidence for the practice of laying wooden planks with painted or engraved inscriptions in churchyards, though it is difficult to say how common the practice was: Burgess, *English Churchyard Memorials*, 28; Cressy, *Birth, Marriage and Death*, 469–70; London Guildhall Library, MS 9064/16, 95.

[147] See above, 33–5.

[148] Even unpublished funeral sermons were a mark of status. Eric Carlson notes that the price, typically 10s., put them well out of most people's reach: 'English Funeral Sermons', 574.

supplicated 'even for those whose frendes have forgotten theyme: whose paines and travell worldely men remembre not: whose obscure condicion of life or poverty would not suffer theime to procure prayers'. This showed an essential difference between 'oure own tender natural moother, and the cursed steppe dame . . . [that] hath theim no longer in mind then they be in sight'.[149]

There was no commemoration of All Souls in Protestant England, no rationale for creating structures or rituals to 'remember' the anonymous dead. But the sixteenth century did see the introduction of one important new means for providing a lasting record of the lives of even the humblest people: the parish register. Instituted in 1538 as an administrative record, the register (through its list of burials) was literally an obituary, a book of deaths, and it was often more than a bare listing.[150] The parish register kept from 1600 by Thomas Hassall, vicar of Great Amwell in Hertfordshire, regularly provided notes on the deceased. Nicholas Thurgood was a man 'of good accoumpt and estimation'; William Warner 'a man of good yeares and of honest reputation, by his profession an atturnye'; Thomas Gissy 'an honest and upright man who all his life had binne a servant to the church of Amwell'. On the distaff side, Mary Kingsland was 'a woeman too well deserving, too dearely beloved to bee soone forgotten' and Alice Blimely 'an honest olde woman of good reporte'. These were real assessments not pious platitudes, and Hassall was noticeably less charitable about Philip Winchly, 'an owld notorius bedlam roge', or Dorothy Andrew, 'neyther mayde nor mother, wife nor widdowe'.[151]

It would be wrong to regard these proto-biographical sketches as a 'secularized' form of memorialization, any more than the parish register itself was a purely secular and administrative document. To a number of entries, Hassall appended Latin scriptural tags or appropriately pious mottoes: *Memoria justi benedicta, Justis in morte vita est, Statutum est omnibus mori semel*, even, atavistically, *Requiescit in pace*.[152] Several parishioners were noted to be 'awaitinge the resurrection of the just'; 'expecting the resurrection'; lying 'there to sleape still untill the general Resurrection'. When his own son, Thomas, 'a youthe of hope', died aged 15 in 1629, Hassall recorded that 'hee lyeth in the middle of the chancell under the preist's stone awaitinge the Resurrection of the Just to lyfe eternall'.[153]

---

[149] Allen, *A Defence and Declaration*, 220ʳ–221ʳ.

[150] On the richness of parish registers as a source for social (as opposed to demographic) historians, see W. Coster, 'Popular Religion and the Parish Register 1538–1603', in French, Gibbs, and Kümin (eds.), *The Parish in English Life*, 94–113. See also Houlbrooke, *Death*, 329.

[151] S. G. Doree (ed.), *The Parish Register and Tithing Book of Thomas Hassall of Amwell*, Hertfordshire Record Publications, 5 (1989), 78, 86, 92, 94, 105–6, 95, 100.

[152] Ibid. 92, 100, 118, 95: 'the memory of the just is blessed'; 'for the just there is life in death'; 'it is appointed unto all once to die'; 'rest in peace'.

[153] Ibid. 94, 102, 113, 117.

The Great Amwell register was not unique. Though most provide only the requisite names and dates of burial, a good number of Elizabethan and early Stuart parish registers record considerably more information.[154] One such was that kept by Robert Leband, vicar of Rolleston, Nottinghamshire between 1583 and 1625, who regularly enlivened his record of burials with notes on the departed, even a poem about the darts of 'dreadfull death'.[155] The Rolleston register is a fortunate survival. The canons of 1597 ordered that registers henceforth be written on parchment, and that a parchment copy be made of entries from earlier paper registers for the reign of Elizabeth.[156] Usually, only the copy survies, but at Rolleston the paper original was kept alongside the parchment copy, and a comparison reveals that much additional material was omitted from the latter. For example, an eighty-one-word entry detailing the qualities and alms-giving of the centenarian Joane Caley was rendered in the transcript a lapidary: 'Joane Caley an ould woman'.[157] It may well be that the impulse to employ the parish register as an instrument of local memory was more widespread than the record can now show.

Perhaps most remarkable in this respect is the register of St Peter Cornhill, London, which was kept by William Averell, parish clerk and schoolmaster, from the 1590s up to his death in 1605. Like Hassall and Leband, Averell turned many of the burial entries into miniature epitaphs: 'a vertuous yong woman, religious, and good to the poore'; 'this yong man by his fruites showed his faith'; 'an upright and iust man'; 'a vertuous maiden'; 'old yet devout in often hearing the word'; 'a good benefactor to our poore'; 'a youth composed and framed out of the mould of vertu'; 'a pretty and modest woman'.[158] Averell also included commemorative verses of his own composition in English and Latin, whose style and content closely conform to those found on contemporary funeral monuments.[159] That Averell perceived the parish register itself to have a vital commemorative function for the community he served is clear from the 'certain verses upon this register' he added to the new book 'bought at the charge of the parish' in September

[154] For example, G.W. Loder (ed.), *The Parish Registers of Ardingly, Sussex 1558–1812,* Sussex Record Society, 17 (1913), 149; J. Barmby (ed.), *Churchwardens' Accounts of Pittington and Other Parishes in the Diocese of Durham,* SS 84 (1888), 149 n.; S. O. Addy, 'A Contribution towards a History of Norton in Derbyshire', *Journal of the Derbyshire Archaeological and Natural History Society,* 2 (1880), 17; S.H.A.H. (ed.), *Denham Parish Registers 1539–1850* (Bury St Edmunds, 1904), 53; S.H.A.H. (ed.), *Shotley Parish Registers 1571–1850* (Bury St Edmunds, 1911), 130, 211; Tate, *Parish Chest,* 65–6, 77–8.

[155] T. M. Blagg and K. S. Train (eds.), 'Extracts from the Paper Book of Robert Leband, Vicar of Rolleston, 1583–1625', *Thoroton Society Record Series,* 14 (1950), 1–20.

[156] G. Bray (ed.), *The Anglican Canons 1529–1947,* Church of England Record Society, 6 (1998), 252–4.

[157] Blagg and Train, 'Paper Book of Robert Leband', 17–18.

[158] G. W. G. Leveson Gower (ed.), *A Register of all the Christninges, Burialles & Weddinges within the Parish of Saint Peeters [sic] upon Cornhill,* Harleian Society Registers, 1 (1877), 138, 140, 141, 146, 152, 156, 159.

[159] Ibid. 139, 144, 145, 156, 158.

1598. Using the conventional imagery of memento mori, Averell portrayed the register as a crystal mirror, in which men might view the vanity of this world and the inevitable course of nature. He also compared the parchment register with its 'names of mortall men', and that other book 'not writ with incke, with pensill or with pen' wherein the names of God's elect were enrolled. The reader was exhorted to labour to be entered in the Book of Life, 'before this booke hath once registered thee'. The parallel seems intended to extol rather than belittle the importance of the latter. Averell's epigraph to the volume was the couplet: 'Though in the grave mens bodies soone bee rotten; Yet heare theyr names will hardlie bee forgotten'.[160]

For the pre-Reformation period, Eamon Duffy has suggested that the bede-roll was 'the parochial document par excellence', fixing the departed members of the community in the consciousness of the living.[161] It would be glib to evoke too exact a parallel here, yet one can hear a delayed echo of the weekly recital of the bede-roll in the 1597 instruction that, for the avoidance of fraud, registers 'shall be read openly and distinctly by the minister on Sundays, after morning or evening prayer, with the day and month on which particular events took place'.[162] It is hard to say how assiduously the practice was carried out, though the complaint of one Sussex parish in 1604 that the rector 'doth not rede publicly in the Church the Register of Marriages, Christenings, and Burials' suggests that it must have been happening elsewhere.[163] The order for a weekly recital from the register was dropped by the canons of 1604, but the standing requirements for careful recording and storage, and for the regular sending of transcripts to the diocesan bishop, may have helped to impress upon communities the utility of the register as a repository of local memory. Where registers were neglected or mismanaged, this could trigger a genuine parochial unease, as at Lancing in Sussex in 1624, where the vicar was said to keep the register to himself 'and hath not at any tyme called us to ioyne with him for the registring any names for this yeare past'.[164] Paying attention to the commemorative potential of the parish register points us towards the local and communal aspects of memory in Protestant culture. The following sections explore this theme further, reflecting on the presence of the physical remains

---

[160] Ibid., pp. ii, v, vii. Interestingly, St Peter Cornhill was a parish of which Stow remarked 'Monumentes of the dead in this church defaced': J. Stow, *A Survey of London*, ed. C. L. Kingsford, 2 vols. (Oxford, 1908), i. 195.

[161] Duffy, *Altars*, 153.

[162] Bray (ed.), *The Anglican Canons*, 255. Arguably, there is an even sharper resonance of the pre-Reformation bede-roll in the Elizabethan ordinance of the Grocers' Company that the names of benefactors should be read out 'once in a year at the least as time shall seem at the discretion of the wardens', though this included living as well as dead givers: Ward, 'Religious Diversity and Guild Unity', 94.

[163] W. J. Pressey, 'The Records of the Archdeaconry of Essex and Colchester', *Transactions of the Essex Archaeological Society*, 19 (1927–30), 13.

[164] H. Johnstone, *Churchwardens' Presentments (17th Century) Part 1: Archdeaconry of Chichester*, Sussex Record Society, 49 (1948), 93.

of the dead, and their memorials, in locations not set aside totally for that purpose, but occupied and employed by the living as well. If we want to conceive of the abolition of purgatory as a kind of divorce between the living and the dead, then we have to consider the implications of the couple continuing to live under the same roof.

LIVING WITH THE DEAD

In churches and churchyards throughout England, the dead impinged upon the living and the living upon the dead. Their enduring physical proximity represents a striking source of continuity, and a powerfully formative cultural statement. Yet it was not always an easy relationship. Though the proclamation of 1560 had (gradually and incompletely) provided monuments of the dead with protection from would-be iconoclasts, casual treatment of tombs was a fact of life. To John Weever, it was a cause of scandal that in London and elsewhere 'many monuments of the Dead . . . are covered with seates or pews, made high and easie for the parishioners to sit or sleepe in, a fashion of no long continuance, and worthy of reformation'. There were places too, he noted, where the construction of rails around the communion table had led to the pulling down of tombs.[165] In the London parish of St Dunstan's-in-the-West in 1630, efforts to introduce 'more commodious seating' involved the removal of brasses from the church floor.[166] Reconstruction work following the collapse of the tower at Astley in Warwickshire around 1600 led to the removal of tombs from the church and their storage in 'an old out-house amongst lime and rubbish'.[167]

If the monuments of the dead, particularly those of the longer-term dead, were sometimes vulnerable to the effects of collective improvement, they might also be at risk from individual depredation. At St Paul's in 1598, the verger was worried that continual walking on the graves had loosened the brasses, and that repairs needed to be made 'to avoyde the stealing of them awaye'. Brasses were stolen from Hereford Cathedral in the early seventeenth century, and systematic theft took place at Lavenham in Suffolk, Robert Reyce reporting in a letter of 1636 the actions of 'olde Arthure, an olde knave who covering his thefte with devotion came every hally daye very early to church & at lengthe was taken stelinge of ye brasses'.[168] When tombs came up for discussion by the newly formed Society of Antiquaries in

---

[165] Weever, *Ancient Funerall Monuments*, 701, 821, 856.

[166] Norris, *Monumental Brasses: The Memorials*, i. 273.

[167] J. R. Broadway, 'Antiquarianism in the Midlands and the Development of County History 1586–1656', University of Birmingham Ph.D. thesis (1998), 231.

[168] W. S. Simpson (ed.), *Registrum Statutorum et Consuetudinum Ecclesiae Cathedralis Sancti Pauli* (1873), 280; Norris, *Monumental Brasses: The Memorials*, i. 260; BL, MS Harleian 376, 149.

November 1600, the opinion was that grave-robbing was a thing of the past: 'it now being generally reputed a most vile acte, no man will presume to transgresse these lawes', but this was a rather premature judgement.[169] At South Petherton, Somerset, in 1637, a group of parishioners including the parish clerk and one of the churchwardens, secretly arranged for the digging up of a coffin in the church 'contayninge therein the relicks or the corpse of a person of qualitie longe since deceased', so that the lead could be melted down and sold. This 'would doe good and save the parishe charges'. Word, however, got out. For their 'sacrilegious violacon', the grave robbers were sentenced to public penance by Bishop Piers, who remarked that 'all men that heard of it detested it, sayinge that if the offenders were not severly punished; they feared hereafter they should not lye quiet in their graves'.[170] This was a particularly egregious case, but it exemplifies a phenomenon we have already encountered in a late medieval context, a utilitarian attitude to the monuments of the long-term dead. Christopher Marsh has shown how in 1609 a group of members of the sect known as the Family of Love in the Cambridgeshire village of Balsham appropriated the grave and gravestone of a fourteenth-century priest in the churchyard to bury one of their number, and argues that in doing so 'they may not have been breaking any pro-foundly important taboo'.[171] In 1638, a Leicestershire vicar was in trouble for digging up an ancient tombstone in the church and engraving new verses on it to lay upon his own son's grave.[172]

Irreverence or indifference were hardly the characteristic response of English parishioners to their departed neighbours. Yet the inconvenience of sharing their churches with the dead might be considerable, if seldom as dramatic as at St Lawrence Jewry in 1578, when the south aisle roof col-lapsed during the excavation of a vault for Sir John Langley's tomb.[173] More common was the dilatoriness of executors in repaving church floors after the ground had been broken to lay a corpse.[174] Parishes sought to regulate the disruption caused by intramural burial by setting fees, by insisting on prior permission from the churchwardens, and, as at Boxford, Suffolk in 1608, by demanding that anyone breaking ground in the church was to cover 'the said grave with pavement or gravestone within six weekes'.[175]

---

[169] Hearne (ed.), *Collection of Curious Discourses*, i. 228.

[170] PRO, SP 16/383, 6ʳ–8ᵛ.

[171] Marsh, 'The Gravestone of Thomas Lawrence Revisited', 226–8.

[172] Leicestershire Record Office, 1 D 41/13/65, 9ᵛ.

[173] Holland, *Monumenta Sepulchraria Sancti Pauli*, 28.

[174] A. J. Willis (ed.), *Church Life in Kent, being Church Court Records of the Canterbury Diocese 1559–1565* (1975), 62; Hussey (ed.), 'Visitations of the Archdeacon of Canterbury', 223; Williams (ed.), 'Bishop Redman's Visitation', 54; Emmison, *Elizabethan Life: Morals*, 170–1; Cressy, *Birth, Marriage, and Death*, 463–4; 'Act Book of the Archdeacon of Taunton', in T. F. Palmer (ed.), *Collectanea II*, Somerset Record Society, 43 (1928), 55.

[175] Barmby (ed.), *Churchwardens' Accounts of Pittington*, 213; M. L. Rifkin, 'Burial, Fu-neral and Mourning Customs in England, 1558–1662', Bryn Mawr College Ph.D. thesis (1977), 46–9, 53; Suffolk Record Office FB77/E2/3. I owe this reference to Steve Hindle.

The making and covering of graves inside the church was a far from rare event. At St Peter Cornhill, for example, an average of nine parishioners a year were buried inside the church in the ten years from 1595 to 1604.[176] In the 1630s, some Laudian churchmen worried about the cluttering effect intramural burial might have on the good ordering of prayerful space. Mathew Wren's Hereford visitation articles of 1635 demanded to know whether there were

any tombes or monuments for the dead, suffred to be erected, without the good licence and approbation of the ordinary first shewed to the church-wardens? Are there any so made, that they cumber some roome which may not well be spared; or trouble any seat or passage; or hinder the prospect of the church or chancell, or the light of any window; or be inconvenient to the minister in executing any part of the divine offices.[177]

In one Norfolk parish in 1633, the instruction to reposition the altar beneath the east window had not been carried out because 'the grave of Elizabeth Garmish was made and she interred nigh unto the same window a year since'.[178] When a second edition of Henry Holland's guide to the monuments in St Paul's appeared in 1633 at the time Laud was planning restoration work there, the author expressed his concern that 'in repairing the same, some Monuments of the dead might be defaced, if not quite razed'.[179]

The cohabitation of the living and the dead within English parish churches was not without its problems. Yet this cohabitation—a striking continuity across the vicissitudes of the sixteenth century—was long to remain a distinctive feature of English religion in its local setting. In this, Protestant England stood out from a number of its its sister Reformed Churches. Burial inside churches, its original rationales a desire for proximity to the relics of saints and for benefiting from masses and prayers, was understandably an object of some suspicion throughout the Protestant world. Hostility to the practice was perhaps most marked in Scotland, where enactments against it were passed at General Assemblies in 1588, 1597, 1638, and 1643. 'Defyle not Christ's kirk with your carrion' was the uncompromising message inscribed on a purpose-built mausoleum at Halhill in Fife in 1609.[180] In many places there was growing pressure not only against burial within churches, but against the very idea of a close proximity between the worshipping

[176] Gower (ed.), *St Peter Cornhill Register*, 144–60. This, of course, was a metropolitan parish, but an average of nearly 5.5 per annum were buried inside St Neot's, Cornwall in the seventeenth century (J. C. Cox, *Churchwardens' Accounts* (1913), 169), and 7.6 per annum at Holy Trinity, Chester (Will Coster, personal communication).
[177] *VAIESC* ii. 154.
[178] Cressy, *Travesties and Transgressions*, 193.
[179] G. Parry, *The Trophies of Time: English Antiquarians of the Seventeenth Century* (Oxford, 1995), 213.
[180] H. Colvin, *Architecture and the Afterlife* (New Haven, 1981), 296–303; A. Spicer, '"Defyle not Christ's Kirk with your Carrion": Burial and the Development of Burial Aisles in Post-Reformation Scotland', in *Place of the Dead*, 149–69.

community of the living, and the dead lying in parish graveyards. Across large swaths of Germany and Switzerland, throughout the period covered by this book, church graveyards were being closed and relocated outside town and city walls.[181] The main drives behind this process, which in some places had begun in the fifteenth century, were often practical rather than religious ones, concerns about overcrowding and the 'foul air' that was believed to be a cause of infectious disease, but the issue rapidly acquired and continued to carry a sharp theological charge. The displacement of the bodies of the departed, it has been argued, paralleled the spiritual separation of living and dead effected by the abrogation of purgatory; Luther was an ardent opponent of traditional churchyard burial, regarding it as a threat to the piety of the living.[182] There was, moreover, a clear biblical prototype. When Christ came to the city of Nain, he encountered 'a dead man carried out, the only son of his mother... and much people of the city was with her'.[183]

Such considerations undoubtedly struck a chord with some sixteenth-century English reformers. In a sermon of 1552, Latimer praised the 'good and laudable custom' of the citizens of Nain, and marvelled that London 'being so rich a city, hath not a burying-place without', particularly in view of the risks posed by epidemic disease there.[184] At the start of Elizabeth's reign, Bishop Pilkington insisted that it was clearly the practice of Christ's own time that 'they buried not in hallowed churchyards by any bishops, but in a several place appointed for the same purpose without the city; which custom remains to this day in many godly places'.[185] Pilkington's concern that the Church of England should not be suspected of teaching 'that one place is more holy than another to be buried in' was a standard attitude of Elizabethan reformers.[186] But by the end of the sixteenth century a serious desire to abolish churchyard burial was largely confined to the separatists, Henry Barrow condemning it as 'a thing never used until popery began... neither comly, convenient, nor wholsome'.[187] The mainstream puritan

---

[181] C. M. Koslofsky, *The Reformation of the Dead: Death and Ritual in Early Modern Germany, 1450–1700* (Basingstoke, 2000), 40–78; S. Karant-Nunn, *The Reformation of Ritual: An Interpretation of Early Modern Germany* (1997), 178–9. The relocation of cemeteries in Germany was often a contentious issue. For protests at Lübeck in 1629, see J. Beyer, 'A Lübeck Prophet in Local and Lutheran Context', in B. Scribner and T. Johnson (eds.), *Popular Religion in Germany and Central Europe, 1400–1800* (Basingstoke, 1996), 166–82.

[182] Koslofsky, *Reformation of the Dead*, 53, 76–7.

[183] Luke 7: 12.

[184] H. Latimer, *Sermons and Remains*, ed. G. E. Corrie (PS, 1845), 66–7.

[185] Pilkington, *Works*, 64.

[186] Veron, *The Huntyng of Purgatory to Death*, 26ᵛ–27ʳ, 30ᵛ–31ʳ; W. Fulke, *Fulke's Answers to Stapleton, Martiall, and Sanders* (PS, 1848), 105; Willet, *Synopsis Papismi*, 316; W. Perkins, *A Golden Chaine* (Cambridge, 1600), 80; T. Becon, *The Sick Man's Salve*, in *Prayers and Other Pieces*, ed. J. Ayre (PS, 1844), 124; J. Whitgift, *Works*, ed. J. Ayre, 3 vols. (PS, 1851–3), i. 535.

[187] *The Writings of Henry Barrow 1587–1590*, ed. L. H. Carlson (1962), 460. See also J. Canne, *A Necessity of Separation from the Church of England*, ed. C. Stovel (1849), 113. Such attitudes were mocked in *Martins months minde*, F4ᵛ: 'he would not be buried in eny... churchyard; for that they had been prophaned with superstition: but in some barne, outhouse, or field'.

conscience had largely reconciled itself to this fundamental sinew of continuity in burial practice. Asked his opinion on the matter, Richard Greenham
replied that while 'hee could wish the place to bury the dead in some other
place, then in the church yard, yet hee would desire whersoever it were, that
it should bee kept decently and reverently in no other respect, but beecaus it
was appointed for that use'.[188] Bishop Joseph Hall's pronouncement on the
matter was a pithy masterpiece of ecclesiastical double-speak: 'wee have
learned to call no place holy in itself (since the Temple) but some more holy
in their use, then others'.[189] To a limited extent, London did follow the
Continental pattern: a 'New Churchyard' was established outside Billings-
gate in 1569 as a response to the terrible plague of 1563, and a handful of
parishes with particular pressures on space established new graveyards
unattached to the church in the early seventeenth century.[190] But the vast
majority of people dying in the late sixteenth and early seventeenth centuries
were buried in the same ground where their late medieval ancestors had been
placed. If the physical separation of the living and the dead in the course of
the German Reformation can be regarded as 'one of its most profound
consequences',[191] then the failure of the English Reformation to bring
about a similar disengagement demands to be treated with equal seriouness.

In the seventeenth century, in fact, Protestant writers were increasingly
coming to regard the close proximity of the dead in churchyards not as an
embarrassing relic of the papist past, but as a powerful tool of memento
mori, the Jacobean writer Francis Rodes commending the practice of Christians 'who have their churchyards neere their temples and other publike and
frequented places, that men might alwayes bee put in minde of Death'.[192]
The fact that in going about their daily business Christians inevitably trod
upon legions of the dead became a favourite motif of preachers and moralists.[193] In a funeral sermon of 1591 Bartholomew Chamberlayne praised
those who 'to remember death do go every morning into the churchyeard
and behold the graves', and a little later George Strode recommended
churchyards as 'places to which we may resort to be put in minde of our

---

[188] Parker and Carlson, '*Practical Divinity*', 171.

[189] J. Hall, *A Common Apologie of the Church of England* (1610), 106.

[190] Harding, '"And One More May Be Laid There"', 117–19. Nationally, the Reformation
seems to have had remarkably little impact on urban burial space (which had always been under
pressure). An extramural churchyard was acquired at Bath, where the cathedral priory became
the parish church, but at Exeter, despite pressing need, a new municipal cemetery was not
established until well into the seventeenth century: Pounds, *English Parish*, 147–8; W. J.
MacCaffrey, *Exeter 1540–1640* (1958), 201. See also J. Barrow, 'Urban Cemetery Location in
the High Middle Ages', in S. Bassett (ed.), *Death in Towns: Urban Responses to the Dying and
the Dead, 100–1600* (1992).

[191] Koslofsky, *Reformation of the Dead*, 41.

[192] F. Rodes, *Life after Death* (1622), 74.

[193] Abbot, *A Sermon Preached at Westminster*, 3; Eaton, *A Sermon Preached at the Funeralls
of . . . Master Thomas Dutton*, 22; N. Byfield, *The Cure of the Feare of Death* (1618), 27; Fitz-
Geffry, *Deaths Sermon unto the Living*, 11; Warren, *Domus Ordinata*, 4; Bolton, *Foure Last
Things*, 24; Cressy, *Birth, Marriage, and Death*, 380.

mortalitie'.[194] Late medieval preachers would heartily have agreed: it was in a churchyard that the 'Three Living' experienced their life-changing encounter with the 'Three Dead'.[195]

Whether very many early modern English people were in fact in the habit of going Hamlet-like among the graves to contemplate their own mortality must be regarded as a distinctly open question. Clerical observers were quite apt to claim that these were places treated with too little rather than too great reverence. In a sermon preached in 1634, the Suffolk minister Timothy Oldmayne demanded rhetorically 'why doe wee not make more account of church-yards, and places of buriall, then we see usually is done; seeing that they are the dormitories and sleeping places of the bodies of the Saints'. A few years earlier, Robert Hill had wryly noted that the papists had 'divers good canons' against those who abused churchyards, and wished it were the same among his own co-religionists.[196] The visitation articles of Elizabethan and early Stuart bishops perennially enquired whether churchyards were decently fenced and kept from wild beasts, whether markets, tippling, brawling, or other forms of misrule had taken place there, and, less frequently, whether excommunicates or suicides had been granted burial within them.[197] As David Dymond has recently demonstrated, before and after the Tudor Reformations, the public space of the churchyard was employed for a variety of secular uses which the ecclesiastical authorities had only very limited success in controlling.[198] The good English yeoman, thought Sir Thomas Overbury, 'allows of honest pastime, and thinks not the bones of the dead anything bruised or the worse for it though the country lasses dance in the churchyard after Evensong'.[199]

Yet there are few real signs here of an irreverent popular culture at odds with the norms of official Christianity. Visitation evidence suggests that parishioners often had clear ideas about what constituted acceptable uses of the churchyard, and what did not. The churchwardens of Bourton in Oxfordshire in 1584, for example, confessed 'that sume tymes they doe use to boole in the churcheyard, especialle in the Whitson weeke', but they vehemently denied that there had been any dancing there.[200] It

[194] McIntosh, 'English Funeral Sermons', 71; Strode, *The Anatomie of Mortalitie*, 70–1.
[195] See above, 22n.
[196] T. Oldmayne, *Lifes Brevitie and Deaths Debility* (1636), 73; Hill, *The Path-way to Prayer and Pietie*, 272.
[197] *VAI* ii. 294, 345–6, iii. 136, 170, 222, 225, 227, 267–8, 271, 287, 291, 310, 323, 341, 381, 384; *EEA* ii. 58, 96, 110, iii. 143, 164, 209, 227, 228, 264, 317, 326, 342; *VAIESC* i. 21, 31, 43, 58, 59, 70, 101, 106, 113, 130, 161, 178, 183, 207, ii. 86; A. C. Wood (ed.), 'The Nottinghamshire Presentment Bills of 1587', *Thoroton Society Record Series*, 11 (1945), 7.
[198] D. Dymond, 'God's Disputed Acre', *JEH* 50 (1999), 464–97. See also Cressy, *Birth, Marriage, and Death*, 465–7.
[199] Cited in P. Levi, *The Life and Times of William Shakespeare* (1988), 7.
[200] E. Brinkworth (ed.), *The Archdeacon's Court: Liber Actorum 1584*, 2 vols., Oxfordshire Record Society, 23–4 (1942), i. 55. Bowling in the churchyard was clearly contentious at Stogumber in Somerset in 1623, one of the participants being charged with tripping up a neighbour who tried to stop the game: 'Act Book of the Archdeacon of Taunton', 82.

is unlikely that neighbours were willing to condone the behaviour of Alice Sundell of Porlock in Somerset in 1623, 'abuseing herself in the churchyard by easing herself in open shew'.[201] Communities might sanction some games in the churchyard, but not the destructiveness of a 1621 Shropshire stool-ball player who 'in leaping...doth break the graves with his heels'.[202] The presence of livestock within the precincts was a regular source of resentments: particular unease was expressed where there appeared to be deliberate and intensive grazing, and the churchyard found itself 'very much annoyed' with cattle (often the rector's).[203] At Whitstable, Kent, in 1606, the parson's sheep and cattle were said to 'annoy and foul the churchyard with their dung'; eleven years later the parish clerk was foddering cattle there, 'whereby the graves are rooted down with their feet'.[204] Much worse, however, was if pigs were admitted or found their way into churchyards and followed their instincts by rooting among the graves. At Swalecliffe in Kent in 1567 the lack of enclosure meant that 'hogs dig up the graves there, which is not comely or meet'. At West Chillington, Sussex, in 1621, their disturbing of the graves was 'to the grief of many of the parishioners'.[205]

Another regular cause of resentment was the appropriation of the communal space of the churchyard for the purposes of individual profit. Thus at at Rushford, Norfolk, in 1597 Robert Cocke was charged with letting his threshers put their straw in the churchyard, and shearing his sheep there.[206] At King's Sutton in Oxfordshire in 1619 the minister and churchwardens complained that the vestry was being occupied as a private dwelling house 'which causeth much loathsome and noysome abuse in the churchyard; not fit to be suffred in the places of christian buriall'.[207] At St Peter's Canterbury in 1573, a parishioner was said to 'mysuse the churcheyarde with layinge therin wood and tymbre'.[208] There was similar misuse at Lancing, Sussex, in 1624, where the vicar had reportedly filled the churchyard 'with sawpits, logs and trees, so as it lieth more like a wood yard than the churchyard—

---

[201] 'Act Book of the Archdeacon of Taunton', 80.

[202] A. B. Somerset (ed.), *Records of Early English Drama: Shropshire*, 2 vols. (Toronto, 1994), ii. 561.

[203] For example, Williams (ed.), 'Bishop Redman's Visitation', 35, 38, 46, 63, 105, 113, 135, 143.

[204] A. Hussey (ed.), 'Visitations of the Archdeacon of Canterbury', *Archaeologia Cantiana*, 27 (1905), 226, 228.

[205] Ibid. 218; Johnstone, *Churchwardens' Presentments*, 19–20. See also Brinkworth (ed.), *The Archdeacon's Court*, i. 43, 51; HRO, 21M65/C1/23 1, 9ᵛ; Pressey, 'Records of the Archdeaconry of Essex and Colchester', 13–14; C. Jenkins (ed.), 'An Unpublished Record of Archbishop Parker's Visitation in 1573', *Archaeologia Cantiana*, 29 (1911), 282, 313; S. A. Peyton (ed.), *The Churchwardens' Presentments in the Oxfordshire Peculiars of Dorchester, Thame and Banbury*, Oxfordshire Record Society, 10 (1929), 254; BI, V 1586/CB, 126ʳ; Burgess, *English Churchyard Memorials*, 23; Emmison, *Elizabethan Life: Morals*, 270–1.

[206] Williams (ed.), 'Bishop Redman's Visitation', 98.

[207] Peyton (ed.), *Churchwardens' Presentments*, 293, 297.

[208] Jenkins (ed.), 'Archbishop Parker's Visitation', 276.

most unseemly'.[209] The rector of Sutton Bonnington in Nottinghamshire in 1602 was similarly reported to have appropriated part of the churchyard to private use and dug 'a deepe pitte for sawyers to sawe woode and timber therein'. In this case, the rector admitted the depradation, but said that his actions were confined to the north part of the churchyard where the parishioners 'never did nor would burie their dead', and he insisted that charges made by local enemies of 'the prophaning and abusinge of the churchyard' were hypocritical.[210]

Such cases bring out the ambiguous status of churchyards in Reformation England: they were places used for burial, but not systematically so; places for the quiet repose of the dead but also for the legitimate (and sometimes illegitimate) business of the living. The Reformation had relatively little effect on the parish churchyard as a physical environment, beyond the putting down of churchyard crosses, and the attempt to ensure that when graves were marked it was not done with wooden crosses. The Laudian bishop of Ely, Mathew Wren, objected *tout court* to the churchyard being 'pestered and cloyed with frames of wood, piles of brick, or stones', but this was not a usual episcopal concern.[211] It is likely that, before and after the Reformation, the majority of graves had no permanent marker, though temporary memorials of the sort Wren objected to may often have identified their location for a few years, allowing people to entertain the realistic hope of being buried near family members. Commenting on the graveyard scene in *Hamlet*, Michael Neill describes the early modern cemetery as 'the most paradoxical of locations: at once a place of oblivion, and a site of memory; a place which annihilates all distinction ... and a site of monumental record; a place that both invites narrative and silences it'.[212]

The reflection brings us back to a theme we considered near the beginning of this book, that of how a religious culture arbitrates between the requirement to remember the dead, and the temptation to forget them. The balance was particularly problematic in the decades either side of 1600, for going back beyond a generation or two, the memory of the dead was also the memory of the Catholic past. To neglect it too completely was a potentially dangerous form of cultural and social amnesia; to celebrate it too exuberantly an equally dangerous temptation to apostasy.

REMEMBERING AND FORGETTING

The memorial culture of Protestant England, like that of pre-Reformation England, was energized by an emphasis on being forgotten. Medieval

[209] Johnstone, *Churchwardens' Presentments*, 93.
[210] BI, CP H 103. The abuse here was long-standing, charges first being brought at the visitation of 1587: Wood (ed.), 'The Nottinghamshire Presentment Bills of 1587', 22.
[211] Cressy, *Birth, Marriage, and Death*, 470.
[212] Neill, *Issues of Death*, 234.

preachers had warned their congregations of the friendlessness of the dead to stir them to virtuous lives and more earnest preparation for death, and their successors employed similar techniques. 'No sooner gone, but to be as suddainely forgotten', warned Timothy Oldmayne, 'for oblivion and neglect, are the two principal handmaids of death'.[213] Death, wrote the Jacobean moralist William Drummond, is 'the intomber of Fame, the only cause of forgetfulness, by which men talk of them that are gon away, as of so many shadows, or ageworn stories'.[214] The unkindness of executors, apophthegmatic in fifteenth-century England, had lost little of its edge a century and more later, and was noted by writers such as John Stow and John Weever. According to the latter, it was the reason why so many people erected their funeral monuments during their own lifetime, and a decade later Thomas Fuller gave 'the negligence of heirs' as a compelling reason for following this course.[215] There is certainly a proverbial ring to Benedick's declaration in *Much Ado About Nothing* that 'if a man do not erect in this age his own tomb ere he dies, he shall live no longer in monument than the bell rings and the widow weeps'.[216] Just as with the chantry requests of fifteenth-century gentry, so the post-mortem demands of Elizabethan and Stuart elites might be heavier than their heirs were willing to countenance. None of the instructions for lavish monuments left by Henry, earl of Southampton, in 1581, George Lord Hunsdon in 1599, and Sir Anthony Mildmay in 1615 were executed in full.[217] As Ralph Houlbrooke has observed, 'monuments were conventionally seen as tributes by the living to the memory of the dead. In practice, however, many of them were set up by the people commemorated or in accordance with their detailed instructions'; Nigel Llewellyn estimates that at least 30 per cent of monuments in this period were erected in the lifetimes of their subjects.[218] This was the case, for example, with the monument erected in 1614 by and for William Sewell, 'late vicar of Hornbye', Yorkshire, whose epitaph somewhat incongruously itemized for posterity his considerable generosity to the poor of four parishes while insisting that 'he gave thes not because he desired the applause or praise of people'. When Roger Dodsworth visited the church in October 1622 he noted that Sewell 'is yet living, and haith beene 40 yeres vicar'. For eight years he had been celebrating divine service in close proximity to his own tomb.[219]

[213] Oldmayne, *Lifes Brevitie*, 61.

[214] Drummond, *A Midnights Trance*, 9.

[215] Stow, *Survey*, i. 115; Weever, *Ancient Funerall Monuments*, 18–19; White, 'Church Monuments', 528.

[216] V. ii. 69–72.

[217] White, Church Monuments', 528; Greaves, *Religion and Society*, 732.

[218] Houlbrooke, *Death*, 369; Llewellyn, 'Honour in Life, Death and in the Memory', 191.

[219] Clay (ed.), *Yorkshire Church Notes*, 230–1. See also M. S. Byford, 'The Price of Protestantism: Assessing the Impact of Religious Change on Elizabethan Essex', University of Oxford D.Phil. thesis (1988), 88, for the 1590 will of William Shepherd, vicar of Heydon, requesting burial in the body of the church 'in the place and under the marblestone which I have ther alredye provided'.

In counterpoint, a positive advocacy of oblivion can sometimes be heard enriching the polyphony of early Stuart commemorative voices. In 1627 the Norwich minister Samuel Gardiner warned against giving thought to 'fame and celebritie': 'mortall are they all, whom thou dost expect to be trumpeters of thy value: and mortall and transitory are all the meanes by which thou doest lay the foundation of thy fame'.[220] The theme was taken up a few years later by Thomas Browne, who regarded the search after perpetual memory as a (literally) monumental folly, 'to hope for Eternity by Ænigmaticall Epithets, or first letters of our names, to be studied by Antiquaries'. It was the fate of 'the greater part' to be 'as though they had not been, to be found in the Register of God, not in the record of man'. Browne himself declared that 'I meane to take a totall adieu of the world, not caring for a monument, history, or epitaph, not so much as the bare memory of my name to be found any where but in the universall register of God'.[221] Yet to make such claims in works intended for publication seems something of a conceit, and Browne himself would in due course be memorialized on a stone in Gardiner's church of St Peter Mancroft in Norwich. A monument in St Paul's bearing the single word 'Oblivio' caused considerable amusement at the antiquaries' meeting in November 1600. One noted that 'the writer said one thing and intended another; for it cannot be thought that he would have the dead man forgotten'. The presence of the dead man's arms on the monument, suggested William Camden, rendered it 'not unlike to philosophers, which prefixed their names before their treatises of contemning glorye'.[222]

There was in the culture of late Reformation England a somewhat schizophrenic attitude towards the techniques of post-mortem memory. A veritable cliché of epitaphs in the early seventeenth century was that the virtues of the deceased made any other monument entirely unnecessary, or that their worthy name would live on when the tomb itself had crumbled and decayed.[223] Funeral sermons, too, sometimes made the same claims. Robert Willan's 1630 sermon for Viscount Sudbury effused that 'no *Babylonian* Tower, no *Ægyptian Pyramis*, no *Rhodian Colossus*, no *Mausolian* Tombe, no Triumphall Arche, no life-counterfeiting Statua, can give such life of memory, as a life itselfe transacted in worthy designes'.[224] In 1624 Sampson Price had made the identical point, if considerably less floridly: 'The best monument is not in stately houses, strong walls, high towers, glorious sepulchers, but in righteous actions'.[225] Yet as their authors on some level

[220] Gardiner, *Devotions of the Dying Man*, 78–9.
[221] T. Browne, *The Major Works*, ed. C. A. Patrides (Harmondsworth, 1977), 309–12, 111.
[222] Hearne (ed.), *Collection of Curious Discourses*, i. 243, 232, 259–60.
[223] Ravenshaw, *Antiente Epitaphs*, 42, 48, 50, 52, 56, 61, 74; Roper, *Monumental Effigies of Gloucestershire*, 62; Clay (ed.), *Yorkshire Church Notes*, 11; Mosse, *Monumental Effigies of Sussex*, 151; White, 'Church Monuments', 534–6; Esdaile, *English Church Monuments*, 132.
[224] R. Willan, *Eliah's Wish* (1630), 19–20.
[225] Price, *The Two Twins of Birth and Death*, A2ᵛ. See also W.S., *A Funerall Elegye in Memory of the late Vertuous Maister William Peter* (1612), A3ʳ.

must have known, for epitaphs so insistently to proclaim their own redundancy was inherently paradoxical, a claim that in fact betrays an anxiety about the amorally contingent nature of social memory. A late Jacobean monument at Backenham, Suffolk, encloses 'one whose name and worthe / Can live when marbell falls to duste', yet his epitaph nonetheless took the form of an acrostic on 'Richard Swift', 'For feare thou shoud'st forget his name'.[226] Unusually honest in facing up to the fiction that a worthy or 'famous' life itself guaranteed remembrance was the brass of John Fuller (d. 1610) at Uckfield, Sussex: 'Now that I am deade and layde in grounde / And that my bones are rotten / By this shall I remembered be / Or els I am forgotten'.[227]

The hope was not necessarily a vain one. There is scattered evidence to suggest that monuments might function as significant markers of local pride and identity. In 1567 in the parish of North Cadbury, Somerset, the great bell fell from the tower 'and broke the marbell tombe in the bellfrye bearynge the picture in brasse or copper which sometymes was rectore of this paryish'. The current incumbent, Giles Russell, noted that the inscription was at that time 'pleynelye to be read', and he carefully recorded the wording in the parish register: 'Here lyeth the bodye of John Feroure sometyme person of thys place which builded this tower at his owne proper coste'.[228] When in 1598 the rector of High Ham in Somerset came to record a memoir of his church in the parish register, and to vindicate its claim to be chief parish church against the chapel of neighbouring Low Ham, he observed caustically that the latter had 'no auncient monumentes'. Of his own church, he enthused: 'what shall I speake of the goodly marble and stone sepulchres and monuments of the dead, as well to be seene in the church as churchyard of such as have bin buried there for almost an hunderth yeares'.[229] On his expeditions to record details of tombs and epitaphs, John Weever regularly relied on preserved and inherited local knowledge. At Upchurch in Kent, Weever found a monument decorated with acorns and oak-leaves 'wherein the parish-clerke told me (as he had received it by tradition from his predecessours) that one *Wood-okes*, an eminent man in this county should be entombed'. Though the fifteenth-century tomb of Thomas Carleton at Edmonton in Middlesex was 'shamefully defaced', 'the inhabitants deliver by tradition, that this *Carleton* was a man of great command in this countie'. At Thaxted in Essex, Weever similarly relied on what 'the inhabitants say' to augment the details on a fifteenth-century monument. In Bury St Edmunds

[226] Ravenshaw, *Antiente Epitaphs*, 65. For other examples of mnemonic devices based on the subject's name, see ibid. 36, 46, 75; Camden, *Remains Concerning Britain*, 419.

[227] Mosse, *Monumental Effigies of Sussex*, 181. It is not entirely clear whether 'this' refers to the brass itself, or the acts of charity it records. Either way it testifies to a recognition of the indispensability of the monument as the agent of memory.

[228] Connor, *Monumental Brasses in Somerset*, 318.

[229] C. D. Crossman (ed.), 'Adrian Schaell's Memoir of High Ham Church and Rectory, AD 1598', *Somersetshire Archaeological & Natural History Society*, 20 (1894), 120–1.

he took note of an old monument, under which 'as I was told, one *Ienkin Smith* Esquire, lieth enterred: a great benefactour to this church'.[230] Weever's fellow-antiquary Roger Dodsworth found on a visit to Sprotbrough church in October 1620 a stone monument 'the first part worne out'. But the parish clerk 'that hath beene there 40 yeres saith he haith readd itt very plainely, and that itt was: Here lyeth John Fitzwilliams . . . sometymes lord of Sprotbrugh'.[231] In all these cases we hear a powerful counter-narrative to the story of iconoclasm and vehement repudiation of a condemned popish past.

In some places, tombs might function not just as promptuaries of local history, but as focal points of ritual activity. At the end of the sixteenth century, a funeral monument in St Paul's Cathedral was the centrepiece of a curious set of festive and inversive rites, the details of which were recorded by the antiquaries John Stow, Henry Holland, and Anthony Munday. This was the fourteenth-century tomb of Sir John Beauchamp, though 'by ignorant people misnamed to be Humphrey Duke of Gloucester'. On St Andrews day, a company of men, 'no worse than citizens and tradesmen', presented themselves before the tomb as Duke Humphrey's servants, allocated offices among themselves, and proceeded to a breakfast or dinner. Sixth months later, on May Day, 'a certain rude company of tankerd-bearers' performed a similar ritual of office-taking under the duke, and strewed herbs and sprinkled water on the tomb. By the second decade of the seventeenth century, these customs seem to have come to an end, Holland reporting that the bell-ringers had taken to barring the doors to prevent 'any idle ceremonie at the monument', telling would-be supplicants at Duke Humphrey's tomb that 'they should go to S. Albans where indeed it is'.[232] Yet a similar, though rather more dignified, set of rites continued at another tomb in St Paul's, that of Richard de Gravesend, the bishop of London who procured the city's charter from William the Conqueror. At Christmas the mayor and aldermen had of old paraded about the monument, reciting the *De profundis*, a ceremony which continued, noted Holland, though 'the popish order is quite abolished'.[233] In their petrified state, Sir John and Bishop Richard were a bridge connecting the living and dead, the present and the past, across the chasm of religious change. A venerable, and venerated,

[230] Weever, *Ancient Funerall Monuments*, 278, 534, 628, 731. Weever's predecessor, the early Tudor antiquary Leland, had similarly relied on local knowledge to identify the subjects of tombs: *The Itinerary of John Leland*, ed. L. Toulmin Smith, 5 vols. (1964), i. 16, 35, 83, 117, 175, 248, ii. 37, 61, iv. 76.
[231] Clay (ed.), *Yorkshire Church Notes*, 135. Local attributions of funeral monuments were not always, however, reliable: see A. Fox, *Oral and Literate Culture in England 1500–1700* (Oxford, 2000), 42, 245–6, 250–1.
[232] Stow, *Survey*, i. 335–6, ii. 348–9; Holland, *Monumenta Sepulchraria Sancti Pauli*, E2ʳ⁻ᵛ.
[233] Ibid. E4ʳ. Procession by mayor and aldermen to the tomb of a long-dead civic benefactor was recorded late in Henry VIII's reign at Wells and at Canterbury: *The Itinerary of John Leland*, i. 145, iv. 69.

tomb could thus be not merely a marker of social distinction, but also, in Graham Parry's phrase, 'a contribution to the idea of community'.[234]

The Refomation did not obviate all notions of community which might embrace both the dead and the living. But no one living at the start of the seventeenth century could be unaware of how much the successive waves of religious reform had done to buffet and reshape the relationship between the living and the dead, to overturn the express wishes of the latter, and some-times to deface and destroy their monuments and very remains. Despite its Italian setting, Antonio's speech delivered in a ruined church in Webster's *Duchess of Malfi* (V. iii. 9–19) evokes a specifically English sensibility:

> And questionless, here in this open court
> (which now lies naked to the injuries
> of stormy weather) some men lie interr'd
> Lov'd the church so well, and gave so largely to it,
> They thought it should have canopied their bones
> Till doomsday.

Here, the awareness of religious change has itself become a memento mori. Writing in the 1630s, the antiquary and historian of Somerset Thomas Gerard observed that those who had so eagerly sought sepulture in the Carmelite house in Taunton 'are now dubble buryed, first in their graves and secondly with the ruines of the church and priory on them, for that fatall thunderclapp in Henry the eight's daies amongst the rest of religious houses overthrew this priory to the ground'. Of the ruined friary at Ivelchester, Gerard commented: 'I have seen many monuments of the dead in it, but soe defaced as not to be knowne whose they were.'[235] Commenting on the desire to 'leave to after-times a monument, that once thou wast', William Drum-mond invited his readers to reflect that 'arches and stately temples, which one age doth rayse, doth not another raze? . . . hath not avarice defaced that, which devotion did make glorious?'[236]

Feelings of loss relating to the wishes and memorials of the Catholic dead were neither ubiquitous nor unambivalent in the learned culture of late Elizabethan and early Stuart England. But the reflectiveness on display here invites us to recognize that the English Reformation was not merely a force acting externally to change the rituals, structures, and meanings of commemoration, but that the lived experience and inherited awareness of radical change could itself promote, in some quarters at least, a markedly

---

[234] Parry, *Trophies of Time*, 211. Rather more prosaically, the tombs in St Paul's, and even more so those in Westminster Abbey, functioned as tourist attractions in the early seventeenth century, drawing, according to Weever, a 'daily concourse of people': *Ancient Funerall Monuments*, 41. Guides were published by William Camden in 1600 and Henry Holland in 1614.

[235] E. H. Bates (ed.), *The Particular Description of the County of Somerset Drawn up by Thomas Gerard of Trent 1633*, Somerset Record Society, 15 (1900), 59, 206.

[236] Drummond, *A Midnights Trance*, 50–2.

heightened sensibility about the memory of the dead, and the need to protect it.[237] For the antiquarians Stow, Camden, Reyce, Weever, and others, a powerful incentive to undertake the painstaking recording of the details of tombs and epitaphs in English churches was their evident vulnerability to religious zealotry and the vicissitudes of official policy. Arthur Agard attributed the disappearance of many monuments and epitaphs to 'what happened almost within our memorye, to wit, the dissolution of our most ancient religious houses'. His fellow-herald William Dethicke believed that the monuments of great princes 'have been so shaken and spoyled...that I cannot challenge knowledge of any, but of such as have been of late revived at Westminster, for the princes there buried, and for others in London, by the painfull and pleasant pen of Mr Stow'.[238] There was a fascination, thought John Weever, in beholding the 'mournfull ruines' of religious houses, though their structures were destroyed, 'their tombes battered downe, and the bodies of the dead cast out of their coffins'.[239] To William Camden it was a source of grim satisfaction that Henry VIII, 'who subverted so many churches, monuments and tombs, lyeth inglorious at Windsor, and never had the honour either of the tomb which he had prepared, or of any epitaph that I now remember'.[240] The subversion of the monuments of the gentle dead seemed a kind of betrayal of a sacred trust, a contract between past and current generations. Thus Weever, beholding the defaced condition of the Tyrrel tombs at Great Thorndon, commented disapprovingly, 'These *Tirells* (me thinks) having been gentlemen, for so many revolutions of yeares, of exemplarie note, and principall regard in this countrey, might have preserved these houses of rest for their ancestors, from such violation.'[241] Such attitudes were not confined to the handful of published antiquarians. An anonymous military officer, who left a journal of a tour across the southern counties in 1635, was scandalized by the damage to tombs and brasses he found in Chichester Cathedral: 'which is not onely a malicious detriment to posterity; but an inhumane, sordid, and base sacrilegious act, to steale away and utterly to extinguish the memories or knowledge of many vertuous, religious, pious, and liberall benefactors'.[242] This, a generation on, was the outlook of John Stow. While appalled by damage to monuments in general, Stow was particularly indignant where the victims had been notable

---

[237] My argument here complements Margaret Aston's suggestions about the significance of monastic ruins in promoting nostalgia on the part of late Elizabethan and Stuart writers: 'English Ruins and English History: The Dissolution and the Sense of the Past', in Aston, *Lollards and Reformers: Images and Literacy in Late Medieval Religion* (1984).

[238] Hearne (ed.), *Collection of Curious Discourses*, i. 246–7, 258.

[239] Weever, *Ancient Funerall Monuments*, 41.

[240] Camden, *Remains Concerning Britain*, 414.

[241] Weever, *Ancient Funerall Monuments*, 658.

[242] L. Wickham Legg (ed.), 'A Relation of a Short Survey of the Western Counties Made by a Lieutenant of the Military Company in Norwich in 1635', *Camden Miscellany XVI*, CS 52 (1936), 34.

local benefactors. Of the fifteenth-century mayor Robert Drope and his wife
Jane at St Michael the Archangel, he commented bitterly, 'notwithstanding
their liberality to that church and parrish, their tombe is pulled down, no
monument remayneth of them'. At St Mary Aldermary another mayor,
Henry Keble (d. 1518), had given generously towards the repair of the
church 'and yet not permitted a resting place for his bones there'. A third
pre-Reformation mayor, John Shadworth, was a generous benefactor at St
Mildred Bread Street, yet 'notwithstanding, his monument is pulled
downe'.[243]

Stow was a Catholic sympathizer with a nostalgic vision of the old order
in general, but the antiquaries who followed in his wake and built on his
achievements in general were not. Their primary concerns were with the
clarification of pedigree and descent, and with the 'honorable memory' of
ancestors as a social duty conducive to the regulation of a well-ordered
society.[244] But part of this was a marked willingness to recognize that
medieval ancestors had been Christians too, that they had undertaken
genuinely admirable acts of piety and charity, and that their requests for
intercessory prayer, while clearly misguided, did not require expunging from
the historical record. The recording of their epitaphs and monuments in
dedicated collections, books of church notes, and county histories was itself
a form of memorialization, almost a surrogate for those unpronounceable
prayers. The county histories which were being produced in significant
numbers right across England in the middle years of the seventeenth century
have seemed to one historian to represent 'a retrospective ceremonial substitute for the perpetual chantry', enshrining a 'newly invented cult of the
gentle dead within its own traditionally bounded arena of local influence;
a collective recitation of distinguished forefathers; a hymn to the descent of
provincial property and office'.[245] In the antiquarian outlook of the early
seventeenth century, an outlook increasingly that of the country gentry as a
whole, the century-old campaign to restrict the claims the dead might make
on the living seems to have struck its natural limits.

---

[243] Stow, *Survey*, i. 197, 253, 347.

[244] See here Llewellyn, 'English Funeral Monuments', 7–8; Parry, *The Trophies of Time*,
12–13, 190, 194, 204; Broadway, 'Antiquarianism in the Midlands', 230, 281–3. It is a
considerable exaggeration to say that 'an interest in antiquity became almost synonymous
with recusancy': J. Evans, *A History of The Society of Antiquaries* (Oxford, 1956), 5.

[245] C. Phythian-Adams, 'Leicestershire and Rutland', in C. R. J. Currie and C. P. Lewis (eds.),
English County Histories (1994), 230.

Conclusion

JACOBEAN writers offering consolation to the bereaved sometimes urged them to imagine that dead friends were 'taking their journey into some strange countries', 'gone from his home to a strange countrey'.[1] The metaphor is a more subtle one than might first appear: the emphasis on distance and separation is softened by the hope of reunion at destination, by the commonality of a pilgrim journey which all ultimately must take. Yet the 'strangeness' of that world of experience beyond death strikes a note which is alien to the religious culture of the later Middle Ages evoked at the beginning of this book, with its mental maps of purgatory, hell, and paradise, and its well-developed 'strategies for eternity'.[2] Another Jacobean Englishman, whose own life spanned the period during which the Reformation was planted and took root, could imagine his contemporaries speaking anxiously of 'the undiscovered country from whose bourn / No traveller returns', or fearing 'to die, and go we know not where'.[3] Over the course of a century or so, attitudes towards the dead, and towards the conceptual spaces the dead inhabited, were unsettled and transformed in England. This was a seismic event, a revolution of sensibilities whose ramifications were not confined to the private world of grief and personal remembrance, but one which was a primary influence on the creation of new liturgies, and patterns of ecclesiastical organization; new forms of public and civic commemoration; new uses of ritual space; new possibilities of cultural expression. From the perspective of a person planning for death and hoping for remembrance in the first years of Henry VIII, the nation inherited by the Stuart kings would appear a 'strange country' indeed. For not just the world of the dead but the world of the living looked very different as a result of that long collective reimagining of humanity's posthumous destiny.

This study has attempted to trace the roots, growth, and flowering of English society's reimagined relationship with the dead, and to understand its importance in the hothouse of religious, political, and cultural change known as the English Reformation. The dead in later medieval society were an active, at times a controlling social presence, an 'age group' whose

---

[1] R. Horne, *Certaine Sermons of the Rich Man and Lazarus* (1619), 74; R. Brathwaite, *Remains after Death* (1618), K6ʳ. See also E. Vaughan, *A Divine Discoverie of Death* (1612), 20; S. Gardiner, *The Devotions of the Dying Man* (1627), 165–6.

[2] C. Burgess, 'Strategies for Eternity: Perpetual Chantry Foundation in Late Medieval Bristol', in C. Harper-Bill (ed.), *Religious Belief and Ecclesiastical Careers in Late Medieval England* (Woodbridge, 1991).

[3] *Hamlet*, III. i. 80–2; *Measure for Measure*, III. i. 118. On Shakespeare's life as a mirror of cultural and religious change, see P. Collinson, 'William Shakespeare's Religious Inheritance and Environment', in id. *Elizabethan Essays* (1994).

distinctive requirements for individuated and cyclically enacted memory influenced many aspects of life, from the shape of the liturgy to economic conditions of inheritance and tenancy. I accept the findings of modern revisionist scholarship that the late medieval English laity seem on the whole quite content with the religious culture into which they were born, that there was no obvious and looming crisis facing the English Church for which the political ambitions of Henry VIII acted as mere catalyst. But at the same time I have tried to suggest that the requirements of commemorating the dead within the framework and logic of post-mortem purgation imposed considerable burdens on late medieval society, and posed questions which some intellectuals were starting to find increasingly troublesome. Of all the pillars of pre-Reformation Catholicism, the intercessory system proved particularly vulnerable when from the 1530s onwards it was confronted with the twin challenges of a searching theological critique, and a suddenly hostile English Crown. Through the middle decades of the sixteenth century theological and political considerations were sharply entwined around these issues. Aversion to the doctrines of purgatory and intercessory prayer was an instinct crucial to the identity of the first generations of English evangelicals, and the focus of some of the earliest and most effective of their propaganda. This was an issue on which the Tudor monarchs (Mary excepted) proved eminently persuadable, partly because of the evident and particular association of these doctrines with the political authority of Rome and the priesthood, and partly because of the possibilities for ecclesiastical disendowment which the 'fraudulent' nature of purgatory was able to justify.

The formal dismantling of the despised intercessory system was completed in 1548, temporarily reversed, and recapitulated in 1559. Yet the campaign to suppress 'superstition' in practices and attitudes relating to the dead was not fought and won in the middle of the sixteenth century, but continued into the reign of James I and beyond. There is a growing consensus among scholars that the English experienced a 'slow' and 'long' Reformation, indeed a Reformation which so far as some of its protagonists were concerned was never brought close to a satisfactory conclusion. More than almost any other indicator, beliefs about the dead reveal the innate cultural conservatism of early modern English communities, anxious neither to omit the pieties due to the memory of departed members, nor to provoke their wrath.

Yet ultimately beliefs cannot be formed or sustained in a vacuum. They require transmission, expression, and validation through a range of cultural practices, social networks, and symbolic language. Approaches to the history of the Reformation which see 'the people' as somehow naturally impervious to the reforming initiatives of those with the power to shape and order their lives are in the end unconvincing, particularly since generational change was incrementally but inexorably moving the population away from the value-systems of the early sixteenth-century world.[4] Sincere and articulate converts to 'the gospel' were at a premium throughout most of the period covered by this book. But since the Protestant Reformation success-fully removed most of the structures which had given social meaning to the doctrine of purgatory (chantries, obits, bede-rolls, communal ringing) and provided in their place the new rituals and language through which remem-brance of the dead could be framed, there can be no doubt that over the longer term it was able permanently to alter the outlook of the English people. Beliefs were restructured, but not in all the ways or to the degree that reformers of the first generation might have envisaged or wished. An intense interest in the nature of life after death survived the Protestant reshaping of the geography of the afterlife. Though purgatory was in the end largely eliminated from popular consciousness, early Stuart laypeople resem-bled their late medieval predecessors in displaying more interest in the immediate fate of their souls and those of their loved ones, than in the clerically privileged eschatological narratives of the Last Judgement. Nor, unsurprisingly perhaps, do they seem to have been as swayed by the preachers' threats of hell as they were by their promises of heaven. In the area of belief in ghosts, Protestant orthodoxy was stretched to breaking-point by a deep-rooted popular conviction that the dead had not in all cases passed irretrievably beyond the realms of human apprehension (in both senses of the term).

None of this should be taken to mean that the Protestant Reformation 'failed' in England, but rather that it represented in practice a complex and protracted process of cultural exchange, in which the teachings of the reformers were adapted and internalized in sometimes unforeseen ways, and in which the concerns of the people helped to shape and direct the priorities of reformers who were also often pastors. The period certainly witnessed a sustained assault on aspects of customary practice, but there was more going on than an attritional eradication of proscribed values, and imposition of an approved set of replacements. At the same time, an ongoing confessional conflict served, ironically enough, as a further medium of productive exchange. Protestant theorists were forced to respond to Cath-olic charges of cruelty towards the dead and contempt for their memory, and in the process formulated a fuller rationalization of the duties of the living towards the deceased, which accorded both with biblical precept and with conventional social expectation. The outcome, as elaborated in the final chapter of this book, was a rich and complex Protestant culture of commem-oration. The claims sometimes advanced that an effect of the Reformation was to redraw 'the boundaries of human community' or to 'sever the

---

[4] Cf. here the evocative closing sentence of Duffy, *Altars*: 'By the end of the 1570s ... a gene-ration was growing up which had known nothing else, which believed the Pope to be Anti-christ, the Mass a mummery, which did not look back to the Catholic past as their own' (p. 593).

relationship between the dead and the living' represent provocative starting-points for discussion, but are hardly sustainable without the severest qualification.[5] English people of the later sixteenth and early seventeenth centuries continued to devote significant cultural and material resources to the memorialization of the dead, and to activating them as an instructive social presence in the calculations of the living. Their methods for doing so were partly adaptation of traditional commemorative strategies, partly utilization of new possibilities, especially through the medium of print. In this area it would certainly be possible to attempt to draw up a precisely calibrated balance sheet of 'continuity and change' either side of a putative Reformation divide. But arguably it is more important (and certainly more interesting) to try qualitatively to understand the lived experience of individuals and communities across decades of sometimes revolutionary, sometimes evolutionary, development.

'Pre-Reformation' and 'post-Reformation' are terms used in this book with a deliberate vagueness as to when precisely it was that the one shaded into the other, and in neither case is the intention to imply a completely unitary cultural bloc, or consensual social polity. Yet there is a pleasing symmetry in the fact that the chronological span covered here is almost exactly equally bifurcated by the promulgation of the Edwardian Forty-Two Articles of 1553, with their declaration that 'the doctrine of school authors concerning purgatory...is a fond thing, vainly feigned, and grounded upon no warrant of scripture, but rather repugnant to the word of God'.[6] A theological proposition (the non-existence of purgatory) underpinned a campaign of confiscation and disendowment, and of regulation of local and customary mortuary practice, which led in turn to a gradual and widespread reshaping of religious belief. The crux question of this book then is of the significance of the loss of purgatory, and the stemming of that endless upward flood of intercessory prayer.

Perhaps it did not matter so greatly at all. A number of scholars, from a variety of disciplinary backgrounds, have set themselves to look for signs of the 'displacement' of purgatory, to identify the substitutes or replacements for the doctrine which emerged in the course of the Reformation or in post-Reformation culture. Thus David Cressy and Ralph Houlbrooke have argued that the grieving energies once directed towards intercessory prayer were harnessed in Protestant England to propel a greater attention to the management of bereavement and the 'art' of dying.[7] Richard Wunderli

---

[5] Ibid. 475; Cressy, *Birth, Marriage, and Death*, 398. See also K. Thomas, *Religion and the Decline of Magic: Studies in Popular Beliefs in Sixteenth-and Seventeenth-Century England* (Harmondsworth, 1973), 721. N. Z. Davis makes the more nuanced claim that it abolished the dead's status as an 'age group' in society: 'Ghosts, Kin, and Progeny: Some Features of Family Life in Early Modern France', *Daedalus*, 106 (1977), 95.

[6] J. Ketley (ed.), *The Two Liturgies...in the Reign of King Edward VI* (PS, 1844), 532.

[7] Cressy, *Birth, Marriage and Death*, 395; Houlbrooke, *Death, Religion, and the Family*, 228.

and Gerald Broce have detected 'a functional substitute for purgatory' in a supposedly growing concern with deportment on the deathbed and the 'final moment' which could redeem a sinful life.[8] Alexandra Walsham has described the retributive providences which afflicted the godly in this world as looking 'remarkably like a Protestant replacement for purgatory'.[9] The art historian Nigel Llewellyn suggests that 'to balance the traumatic effect of the loss of Purgatory, the Protestant churches gradually developed the theory of *memoria*, which stressed the didactic potential of the lives and deaths of the virtuous.'[10] Meanwhile, literary critics have been attracted by the idea that the impulses blocked by the abolition of purgatory and intercessory prayer became sublimated in the imperatives of the English Renaissance revenge tragedy: 'revenge tragedy exhibits a world in which the dead, precisely because they are now beyond the help of their survivors, have become practically insatiable in their demands upon the living', and the frenzies of the stage-revenger are best understood as 'a fantasy response to the sense of despairing impotence produced by the Protestant displacement of the dead'.[11] *Hamlet*, Michael Neill has observed, is a play dominated by a revenant 'whose most intense emotion is the dread of being forgotten'.[12]

There is lively insight in these approaches, but implicit in all of them is a rather functional view of religious belief-systems, in which purgatory served primarily to channel and resolve social and psychological needs which were capable of finding other outlets, indeed forced to do so. This book has approached beliefs about the dead by seeking to ask, not what they were for, but what they were like, and what they seemed to mean to those who espoused or questioned them. The doctrine of purgatory, and the customs and rituals it generated, represented a cultural construction of great intricacy and complexity, one which permeated late medieval religious and social organization to such an extent that it is difficult, if not impossible to reduce it to any one function or purpose. The dismantling of that construction, though slow and resisted, proved in the end complete and irrevocable, and

[8] R. Wunderli and G. Broce, 'The Final Moment before Death in Early Modern England', *SCJ* 20 (1989), 267.

[9] A. Walsham, *Providence in Early Modern England* (Oxford, 1999), 16. There are similar suggestions in E. Hebblethwaite, 'The Theology of Rewards in English Printed Treatises and Sermons (c.1550–c.1650)', University of Cambridge Ph.D. thesis (1992), 49–51, and in R. Fenn, *The Persistence of Purgatory* (Cambridge, 1995), 76, which identifies a seventeenth-century 'secularization' of the doctrine of purgatory: 'This life becomes the spiritual arena in which the soul is to be purified'.

[10] N. Llewellyn, *The Art of Death: Visual Culture in the English Death Ritual c.1500–c.1800* (1991), 28.

[11] M. Neill, *Issues of Death: Mortality and Identity in English Renaissance Tragedy* (Oxford, 1997), 46, 244–7. See also id., 'Remembrance and Revenge: *Hamlet, Macbeth*, and *The Tempest*', in I. Donaldson (ed.), *Jonson and Shakespeare* (1983); R. N. Watson, *The Rest is Silence: Death as Annihilation in the English Renaissance* (Berkeley and Los Angeles, 1994), 62; A. Welsh, 'The Task of Hamlet', *The Yale Review*, 69 (1980), 484–6.

[12] Neill, *Issues of Death*, 46.

its disappearance represents a significant dividing line in the history of
England. The people of early Stuart England could not easily imagine or
'remember' the dead in the ways their great-grandparents had done.[13]
Recent 'post-revisionist' scholarship has performed a valuable service in
alerting us to the presence of substantial continuities across the Reformation
divide, but we should be wary of over-reading the structural congruences
between pre-and post-Reformation religious practice, and of minimizing the
significance of articulated difference. When the authors of the 1572 *Admonition to Parliament* asserted that 'buriall sermons...are put in place of
trentalles', they were making an exaggerated polemical claim, and historians
should not rush to accept their logic.[14]

Yet if this was a world remade, it was not one transformed beyond
recognition. We should resist the temptation to see the post-Reformation
era as recognizably 'our' world, wellspring of modernity; that before the
Reformation as the transcendental 'other'. In particular we should be wary
of claims about the predominantly 'secular' nature of post-Reformation
mortuary culture.[15] Such assertions often rest on category distinctions which
are inappropriate to apply and impossible to sustain in the pre-industrial
world.[16] Though later sixteenth- and seventeenth-century English people
were barred from praying for their dead (other than under highly circumscribed conditions) this does not seem to have fostered a widespread loss of
interest in their state in the next life, nor to have brought about the straightforward replacement of a prospective language of remembrance by a retrospective one, concerned solely with worldly achievement. Protestant
England's most prominent commemorative media, its sermons, funeral
monuments, and memorial inscriptions, were scripted and read by contemporaries within overtly religious frames of reference and structures of meaning. Contrary to the perception of some literary scholars, the demise of
purgatory did not ring the death-knell for Christian culture in the British

---

[13] An observation which must hold true even for Catholics who consciously maintained
belief in purgatory, but were cut off from the public commemorative culture of their ancestors.

[14] *An Admonition to the Parliament* (Hemel Hempstead(?), 1572), C3ʳ.

[15] See above, 230-1, 275–86.

[16] These issues have been usefully focused in recent debates about whether early modern wills
should be considered primarily 'secular' or 'religious' documents: K. Wrightson and D. Levine,
'Death in Whickham', in J. Walter and R. Schofield (eds.), *Famine, Disease and the Social Order
in Early Modern England* (Cambridge, 1989); D. Beaver, ' "Sown in Dishonour, Raised in
Glory": Death, Ritual and Social Organization in Northern Gloucestershire, 1590–1690', *Social
History*, 17 (1992); C. Marsh, 'In the Name of God? Will-Making and Faith in Early Modern
England', in G. H. Martin and P. Spufford (eds.), *The Records of the Nation* (1990). See also the
long-running debate about 'secular' versus 'religious' motivation in the Pilgrimage of Grace, the
most sensitive treatment of which is C. S. L. Davies, 'Popular Religion and the Pilgrimage of
Grace', in A. Fletcher and J. Stevenson (eds.), *Order and Disorder in Early Modern England*
(Cambridge, 1985).

isles.[17] Nor did it in any demonstrably causal way bring about 'the decline of hell', though, as argued in Chapter 5, it may have encouraged a greater willingness to affirm the identity of 'saints' in heaven.[18]

Rather than unearthing the roots of secularization, a central theme of this book has been to trace an ongoing and almost universal concern with the sanctification of memory, and the variant possibilities for sacralizing death. Early modern England resembled most historical and contemporary cultures, and differed from our own, in expecting to find and express profound religious meaning in the death of its inhabitants and the reaction of survivors. Indeed, it is a measure of the importance of this impulse that those meanings were so hotly and exhaustively contested: between Catholics and Protestants, within Protestantism itself, and in the permeable spaces between clerical-elite and 'popular' mentalities. The 'reformation of the dead' which this book relates may not have activated or accelerated processes of 'secularization' or 'individualism', but it was a significant factor in the emergence of that *de facto* religious pluralism which was perhaps the most significant and enduring overall result of the Reformation in England.

A further finding of this study is the importance of beliefs about the dead in promoting among contemporaries a heightened awareness of, and reflectiveness about, the historical consequence of religious change. In an obvious sense the dead constitute 'the past'; historical subjectivity is formed by and expressed through remembrance of persons deceased. Repudiation of the past was an avowed goal of many Tudor reformers, who saw it as the abode of much darkness, idolatry, and superstition. The age of Reformation iconoclasm 'was an age of deliberate disrespect for the dead'.[19] But the first generations of Protestant English people were, quite literally, children of that past, and many of them baulked at the ideological certitude which would cast their ancestors out of heaven, and seek to dismantle the monuments to

---

[17] Robert Watson, for example, emphasizes the role of the Reformation in heightening the 'psychological burdens' of mortality, and argues that 'the inscrutable determinism and the systematic iconoclasm of Calvinist theology created a blank wall between the living and the dead, encouraging the ominous inference that all might be blankness or darkness beyond it': *Rest is Silence*, 5. See also Stephen Greenblatt's suggestion that the Protestant unmasking of purgatory as a 'fable' threatened in the end to expose the fictionality of all religious belief: *Hamlet in Purgatory* (Princeton, 2001), 47–9.

[18] Cf. D. P. Walker, *The Decline of Hell: Seventeenth-Century Discussions of Eternal Torment* (1964), 59: 'the Protestant rejection of Purgatory must be of great importance in attempts to discover why the doctrine of Hell began to be questioned when it did'. Walker, however, makes no substantive effort to follow up this insight. The same link has been made by Houlbrooke, *Death, Religion, and the Family*, 377, and W. M. Spellman, 'Between Death and Judgement: Conflicting Images of the Afterlife in Late Seventeenth-Century English Eulogies', *Harvard Theological Review*, 87 (1994), 49–65, though the fact that the existence of hell was not being widely called into doubt before the end of the seventeenth century makes any direct association with the abolition of purgatory problematic to trace or demonstrate.

[19] M. Aston, *England's Iconoclasts* (Oxford, 1988), 15.

their memory and achievements on earth. Thus it was that, though intense hostility to purgatory and to traditional intercessory practices were at the very heart of the Reformation movement, deeply held beliefs about the respect due to honourable forebears, and the debts of 'charity' due to the dead in general, along with firm intuitions about the role of commemoration in the articulation and preservation of the social order, did much over the longer term both to blunt radical iconophobic impulses and to soften rigidly predestinarian attitudes.

The Reformation in England is a phenomenon that can be convincingly characterized as either radical or cautious, recklessly destructive or profoundly conservative, a 'drastic caesura' or a 'gradual modification', 'an anemic substitute for the real thing' or a 'howling success'.[20] If we accept that the best way to make historical sense of the Reformation is as a unitive process of social and cultural transformation, rather than as a fortuitous conjoining of disconnected and politically driven 'reformations',[21] then close attention to long-term patterns in the commemoration of the dead turns out to be a rewarding exercise. It is the paradoxical argument of this book that profound concerns about the status of the dead were at once a powerful motor, and an effective brake, as English society journeyed uncertainly away from the medieval past. Studying those concerns from a variety of perspectives helps to reconcile more coherently the revolutionary and reactionary faces of the Reformation as a whole, or at least to understand the deeply ambiguous reactions that religious reform evoked among those who both experienced and participated in it. The religious and cultural odyssey that I will persist in calling the English Reformation was undertaken by the living, not by the dead. But the dead were treasured cargo that had to be carried along the way. The weight of the burden they imposed did much to determine both the length of the journey, and the sometimes unpredictable directions that it took.

---

[20] P. Collinson, 'The English Reformation, 1945–1995', in M. Bentley (ed.), *Companion to Historiography* (1997), 336; T. Watt, *Cheap Print and Popular Piety 1550–1640* (Cambridge, 1991), 327; C. Haigh, 'Introduction', in id. (ed.), *The English Reformation Revised* (Cambridge, 1987), 7; D. MacCulloch, 'The Impact of the English Reformation', *HJ* 38 (1995), 152.
[21] This is the approach suggested by C. Haigh, *English Reformations: Religion, Politics, and Society under the Tudors* (Oxford, 1993), 12–21.

Bibliography of Printed Primary sources

ABBOT, G., *A Sermon preached at Westminster* (1608).

'Act Book of the Archdeacon of Taunton', in T. F. Palmer (ed.), *Collectanea II*, Somerset Record Society, 43 (1928).

An Admonition to the Parliament (Hemel Hempstead(?), 1572).

AEPINUS, I., *Liber de Purgatorio* (1549).

ALLEN, M. (ed.), *Wills of the Archdeaconry of Suffolk 1620–1624*, Suffolk Records Society, 31 (1989).

—— (ed.), *Wills of the Archdeaconry of Suffolk 1625–6*, Suffolk Records Society, 37 (1995).

ALLEN, W., *A Defense and Declaration of the Catholike Churches Doctrine touching Purgatory* (Antwerp, 1565).

ALLEY, W., *The Poore Mans Librarie* (1571).

ANDERSON, A., *A Sermon of Sure Comfort, preached at the Funerall of Maister Robert Keylway Esquier* (1581).

—— *The Shield of our Safetie set Foorth* (1581).

ANDERTON, L., *The Progenie of Catholicks and Protestants* (Rouen, 1633).

ANDREWES, J., *A Celestiall Looking-glasse: to Behold the Beauty of Heaven* (1621).

ANGEL, J., *The Agrement of the Holye Fathers* (1555).

ARBER, E. (ed.), *The Revelation to the Monk of Evesham* (1901).

ASLAKSSØN, C., *The Description of Heaven*, tr. R. Jennings (1623).

ATKINSON, J., *et al.* (eds.), *Darlington Wills and Inventories 1600–1625*, SS 201 (1993).

AUBREY, J., *Remaines of Gentilisme and Judaisme*, ed. J. Britten (1881).

BABINGTON, G., *Workes* (1622).

BALE, J., *Yet a Course at the Romysh Foxe* (Zurich [i.e. Antwerp], 1544).

—— *A Mysterye of Inyquyte* (Geneva [i.e. Antwerp], 1545).

—— *Select Works*, ed. H. Christmas (PS, 1849).

—— *Complete Plays*, ed. P. Happé, 2 vols. (Cambridge, 1985–6).

—— *The Vocacyon of Johan Bale*, ed. P Happé and J. N. King (Binghamton, NY, 1990).

BARLOW, J., *Hierons Last Fare-well. A Sermon preached at Modbury in Devon, at the Funerall of . . . Samuel Hieron* (1618).

—— *The True Guide to Glory. A Sermon preached at Plympton Mary in Devon, at the Funerals of the Lady Strode of Newingham* (1619).

BARLOW, J., *The Burial of the Mass*, in E. Arber (ed.), *English Reprints* (1871).

BARLOW, W., *A Defence of the Articles of the Protestants Religion* (1601).

BARMBY, J. (ed.), *Churchwardens' Accounts of Pittington and Other Parishes in the Diocese of Durham*, SS 84 (1888).

BARNES, R., *A Supplicacion unto the Most Gracyous Prince H. the VIII* (1531).

BARNUM, P. (ed.), *Dives and Pauper*, EETS 275 (1976).

BARROW, H., *The Writings of Henry Barrow 1587–1590*, ed. L. H. Carlson (1962).

BATEMAN, S., *A Christall Glasse of Christian Reformation* (1569).

BATHE, W., *Ianua Linguarum*, 8th edn. (1634).

BAYLY, L., *The Practise of Piety* (1619).

BEARD, T., *A Retractive from the Romish Religion* (1616).

BECON, T., *Early Works*, ed. J. Ayre (PS, 1843).

——*The Catechism*, ed. J. Ayre (PS, 1844).

——*Prayers and Other Pieces*, ed. J Ayre (PS, 1844).

BELFIELD, J., 'Tarleton's News out of Purgatory (1590): A Modern-Spelling Edition, with Introduction and Commentary', University of Birmingham Ph.D. thesis (1978).

BELL, T., *The Survey of Popery* (1596).

BELLARMINE, R., *Liber de Purgatorio*, in *De Controversiis Christianae Fidei Adversus Huuis Temporis Haereticos*, 5 vols. (Ingolstadt, 1601).

BENTLEY, T., 'Some Monuments of Antiquities worthy memory, collected and gathered out of sundry old Accounts', in E. Griffith, *Cases of Supposed Exemption from Poor-rates, claimed on grounds of extraparochiality, with a preliminary sketch of the ancient history of the parish of St Andrew, Holborn* (1831).

BENTON, G. M. (ed.), *Essex Wills at Canterbury*, Transactions of the Essex Archaeological Society, 21 (1937).

BERNARD, R., *A Guide to Grand-Iury Men* (1627).

BILSON, T., *The Effect of Certaine Sermons…preached at Pauls Crosse* (1599).

——*The Survey of Christs Sufferings* (1604).

BLAGG, T. M., and TRAIN, K. S. (eds.), 'Extracts from the Paper Book of Robert Leband, Vicar of Rolleston, 1583–1625', *Thoroton Society Record Series*, 14 (1950).

BOLTON, R., *The Foure Last Things* (1632).

BOND, R. B. (ed.), *Certain Sermons or Homilies (1547)* (Toronto, 1987).

BONNER, E., *A Profitable and Necessarye Doctryne* (1555).

BOOTY, J. E. (ed.), *The Book of Common Prayer 1559* (Charlottesville, Va., 1976).

BOURMAN, N., *An Epytaphe upon the Death of the Right Worshipfull, Sir William Garrat* (1571).

——*An Epytaphe upon the Death of the Right Reverent Father in God I. Iuell* (1571).

BOWLE, J., *A Sermon preached at Flitton in the Countie of Bedford, At the Funerall of Henrie Earle of Kent* (1615).

BOYD, Z., *The Last Battell of the Soule in Death* (Edinburgh, 1629).

BOYS, J., *An Exposition of all the Principal Scriptures used in our English Liturgie* (1610).

BRADFORD, J., *Letters, Treatises, Remains*, ed. A. Townsend (PS, 1853).

BRAND, J., *Observations on Popular Antiquities*, ed. H. Ellis, 3 vols. (1841–2).

BRATHWAITE, R., *Remains after Death* (1618).

BRAY, G. (ed.), *The Anglican Canons 1529–1947*, Church of England Record Society, 6 (1998).

BRERELY, J., *Sainct Austines Religion* (n.p., 1620).

BRIDGES, J., *A Sermon, preached at Paules Crosse on the Monday in Whitson Weeke Anno Domini 1571* (1573).

BRINKELOW, H., *Complaynt of Roderyck Mors and The Lamentacyon of a Christen Agaynst the Cyte of London*, ed. J. M. Cowper, EETS ES 22 (1874).

BRINKWORTH, E. (ed.), *The Archdeacon's Court: Liber Actorum 1584*, 2 vols., Oxfordshire Record Society, 23–4 (1942).

BRISTOW, R., *A Reply to Fulke in Defence of M. D. Allens Scroll of Articles, and Booke of Purgatorie* (Louvain, 1580).

BROUGHTON, R., *The English Protestants Recantation* (Douai, 1617).

BROWNE, T., *The Copie of the Sermon Preached before the Universitie at S. Maries* (Oxford, 1634).

BROWNE, T., *Religio Medici*, in *The Major Works*, ed. C. A. Patrides (Harmondsworth, 1977).

BUCKERIDGE, J., *A Sermon preached at the Funeral of ... Lancelot late Lord Bishop of Winchester* (1629).

BULL, H., *Christian Prayers and Holy Meditations* (Cambridge, 1842).

BULLINGER, H., *The Decades: The Fourth Decade*, ed. T. Harding (PS, 1851).

BURDET, R., *The Refuge of a Sinner* (1565).

BURGESS, C. (ed.), *The Pre-Reformation Records of All Saints', Bristol: Part 1*, Bristol Record Society, 46 (1995).

——(ed.), *The Church Records of St Andrew Hubbard Eastcheap c.1450–c.1570*, London Record Society, 34 (1999).

BURTON, H., *A Tryall of Private Devotions* (1628).

BYFIELD, N., *The Cure of the Feare of Death* (1618).

CALFHILL, J., *An Answer to John Martiall's Treatise of the Cross*, ed. R. Gibbings (PS, 1846).

CALVIN, J., *Institutes of the Christian Religion*, tr. H. Beveridge, 2 vols. in 1 (Grand Rapids, Mich., 1989).

CAMDEN, W., *Remains Concerning Britain*, ed. T. Moule (1870).

CANNE, J., *A Necessity of Separation from the Church of England*, ed. C. Stovel (1849).

CARDWELL, E., *Documentary Annals of the Reformed Church of England*, 2 vols. (Oxford, 1844).

CARLILE, C., *A Discourse Concerning Two Divine Positions* (1582).

CARPENTER, C. (ed.), *The Armburgh Papers: The Brokholes Inheritance in Warwickshire, Hertfordshire and Essex c.1417–c.1453* (Woodbridge, 1998).

CARPENTER, R., *The Soules Sentinel* (1612).

CARTWRIGHT, T., *A Confutation of the Rhemists Translation* (1618).

CATHERINE OF GENOA, *Treatise on Purgatory*, tr. C. Balfour and H. Irvine, new edn. (1976).

CHALLONER, R., *Memoirs of Missionary Priests*, ed. J. H. Pollen (1924).

CHAMBERLAIN, J., *The Letters of John Chamberlain*, ed. N. McClure, 2 vols. (Philadelphia, 1939).

CHAMBERS, R., *Sarah's Sepulture, or a Funerall Sermon, preached for the Right Honourable and Vertuous Lady, Dorothie Countess of Northumberland* (1620).

CHAUCER, G., *The Riverside Chaucer*, ed. L. D. Benson, 3rd edn. (Oxford, 1988).

CIGMAN, G. (ed.), *Lollard Sermons*, EETS 294 (1989).

CIRKET, A. (ed.), *English Wills, 1498–1526*, Befordshire Historical Record Society, 37 (1956).

CLAY, J. W. (ed.), *Yorkshire Church Notes 1619–1631*, YASRS, 34 (1904).

CLAY, W. K. (ed.), *Private Prayers put forth by Authority during the Reign of Queen Elizabeth* (PS, 1851).

CLELAND, J., *A Monument of Mortalitie upon the Death and Funeralls of the... Duke of Richmond and Lenox* (1624).

COBB, C. S. (ed.), *The Rationale of Ceremonial 1540–1543*, ACC 18 (1910).

COLE, J., *Of Death a True Description* (1629).

CONNOR, A. B., *Monumental Brasses in Somerset* (repr. Bath, 1970).

COOKE, A., *Worke, More Work, and a Little More Worke for a Masse-Priest*, 3rd edn. (1630).

COOPER, T., *An Answer in Defence of the Truth against the Apology of Private Mass*, ed. W. Goode (PS, 1850).

COOPER, T., *The Mystery of Witchcraft* (1617).

A Copie of the Proceedings of Some Worthy and Learned Divines Appointed by the Lords (1641).

COPLAND, R., *The Seven Sorrowes that Women have when theyr Husbandes be Deade* (1568).

CORDEROY, J., *A Warning for Worldlings* (1608).

COSIN, J., *A Collection of Private Devotions: in the Practice of the Ancient Church* (1627).

—— *Works*, ed. J. Sansom, 5 vols. (Oxford, 1843–55).

COTTA, J., *The Triall of Witchcraft* (1616).

COUNCER, C. R. (ed.), 'A Book of Church Notes by John Philipot, Somerset Herald', *A Seventeenth Century Miscellany*, Kent Records, 17 (1960).

—— (ed.), *Lost Glass from Kent Churches*, Kent Records, 22 (1980).

COVELL, W., *Polimanteia* (Cambridge, 1595).

COVERDALE, M., *Remains*, ed. G. Pearson (PS, 1846).

COWPER, W., *A Defiance to Death* (1616).

COXE, F., *A Short Treatise declaringe the Detestable Wickedness of Magicall Sciences*, (1561).

CRANMER, T., *Writings and Disputations*, ed. J. E. Cox (PS, 1844).

—— *Miscellaneous Writings and Letters*, ed. J. E. Cox (PS, 1846).

CROMPTON, W., *A Lasting Jewell for Religious Woemen* (1628).

CROOKE, S., *Death Subdued* (1619).

CROSS, M. C., 'The Third Earl of Huntingdon's Death-Bed: A Calvinist Example of the *Ars Moriendi*', *Northern History*, 21 (1985).

CROSSMAN, C. D. (ed.), 'Adrian Schaell's Memoir of High Ham Church and Rectory, AD 1598', *Somersetshire Archaeological & Natural History Society*, 20 (1894).

DARLINGTON, I. (ed.), *London Consistory Court Wills, 1492–1547*, London Record Society, 3 (1967).

DAVIES, R., *A Funerall Sermon... at the Buriall of the Right Honourable Walter Earle of Essex* (1577).

DAY, M., *A Monument of Mortalitie* (1621).

—— *Doomes-day: or, a Treatise of the Resurrection of the Body* (1636).

DEACON, J., and WALKER, J., *Dialogical Discourses of Spirits and Divels* (1601).

D'ELBOUX, R. H. (ed.), *The Monumental Brasses of Essex*, 2 vols. (Ashford, 1948–51).

DENISON, J., *A Three-fold Resolution, verie Necessarie to Salvation. Describing Earths Vanitie, Hels Horror, Heavens Felicitie* (1608).

—— *Heavens Ioy, for a Sinners Repentance* (1623).

DENISON, S., *The Monument or Tombe-stone: or A Sermon preached ... at the Funerall of Mrs. Elizabeth Iuxon* (1620).

—— *Another Tombestone* (1627).

DENT, A., *The Plaine Mans Path-way to Heaven* (1605).

A Devout Treatyse called the Tree and xii Frutes of the Holy Goost, ed. J. Vaissier (Groningen, 1960).

DICKENS, A. G. (ed.), *Tudor Treatises*, YASRS, 125 (1959).

—— (ed.), 'Robert Parkyn's Narrative of the Reformation', in id., *Reformation Studies* (1982).

DONNE, J., *Selected Poems*, ed. J. Hayward (Harmondsworth, 1950).

—— *Sermons*, ed. G. R. Potter and E. M. Simpson, 10 vols. (Berkeley and Los Angeles, 1953–62).

—— *Ignatius His Conclave*, ed. T. S. Healy (Oxford, 1969).

—— *Devotions upon Emergent Occasions*, ed. A. Raspa (Montreal and London, 1975).

—— *No Man is an Island: A Selection from the Prose of John Donne*, ed. R. Scott (1997).

DOREE, S. G. (ed.), *The Parish Register and Tithing Book of Thomas Hassall of Amwell*, Hertfordshire Record Publications, 5 (1989).

DOWNAME, G., *A Funerall Sermon preached at Watton in Hertfordshire, at the Buriall of ... Sir Philip Boteler* (1607).

DRAXE, T., *The Earnest of our Inheritance* (1613).

—— *An Alarum to the Last Iudgement* (1615).

DRUMMOND, W., *A Midnights Trance: wherin is discoursed of death, the nature of the soules, and estate of immortalitie* (1619).

DU MOULIN, P., *The Waters of Siloe. To Quench the Fire of Purgatory*, tr. I.B. (Oxford, 1612).

DYBOSKI, R. (ed.), *Songs, Carols, and Other Miscellaneous Poems, from ... Richard Hill's Commonplace Book*, EETS 101 (1908).

EATON, R., *A Sermon preached at the Funeralls of ... Master Thomas Dutton* (1616).

EDGEWORTH, R., *Sermons very Fruitfull, Godly and Learned*, ed. J. Wilson (Cambridge, 1993).

ELDERTON, W., *An Epytaphe uppon the Death of the Right Reverend and Learned Father in God, I. Iuell* (1571).

ELVEY, E. M. (ed.), *The Courts of the Archdeaconry of Buckingham 1483–1523*, Buckinghamshire Record Society, 19 (1975).

EMMISON, F. G. (ed.), *Essex Wills (England)*, 3 vols. (Washington, DC and Boston Mass., 1982–6).

ENGLAND, G., and POLLARD, A.W. (eds.), *The Towneley Plays*, EETS 71 (1897).

ERASMUS, *A Playne and Godly Exposition or Declaration of the Comune Crede*, tr. W. Marshall (1533).

322 *Bibliography of Primary sources*

ERASMUS, *The Colloquies of Erasmus*, tr. C. R. Thompson (Chicago, 1965).

—— *Praise of Folly*, ed. A. Levi, tr. B. Radice (Harmondsworth, 1971).

ERBE, T. (ed.), *Mirk's Festial*, EETS ES 96 (1905).

EVERETT GREEN, M. A. (ed.), *CSPD Series of the Reign of Elizabeth 1595–7* (1869).

FENNER, D., *An Answere unto the Confutation of Iohn Nichols his Recantation ...especially in the matters of Doctrine, of Purgatorie, Images, the Popes Honor, and the Question of the Church* (1583).

FEREBE, G., *Lifes Farewell. Or a Funerall Sermon preached...at the Funerall of John Drew Gentleman* (1615).

FIELD, R., *Of the Church Five Bookes* (1606).

—— *The Fifthe Booke of the Church* (1610).

FINCHAM, K. (ed.), *Visitation Articles and Injunctions of the Early Stuart Church*, Church of England Record Society, 1/5 (1994–8).

FISH, S., *A Supplicacyon for the Beggers*, in T. More, *The Supplication of Souls*, ed. F. Manley *et al.* (New Haven and London, 1990).

FISHER, J., *Assertionis Lutheranae Confutatio* (1523).

—— *Treatyse concernynge the Fruytfull Sayings of Davyd* (1555).

—— *The English Works*, ed. J. Mayor, EETS ES 27 (1876).

—— *A Critical Edition of Two Fruytfull Sermons of Saint John Fisher*, ed. M. D. Sullivan (Ann Arbor, 1974).

FISHWICK, H. (ed.), *Pleadings and Depositions in the Duchy Court of Lancaster*, Lancashire and Cheshire Record Society, 32 (1896).

FITZ-GEFFRY, C., *Deaths Sermon unto the Living* (1620).

—— *Elisha his Lamentation...a Sermon, preached at the Funeralls of the Right Worshipfull Sir Anthony Rous* (1622).

FLOYD, J., *Purgatories Triumph over Hell* (St Omer, 1613).

FORD, W., *A Sermon preached at Constantinople, in the Vines of Perah, at the funerall of the vertuous and admired Lady Anne Glover* (1616).

FOSTER, C. W. (ed.), *Lincoln Wills 1505–1530*, Lincoln Record Society, 10 (1918).

FOWLER, J. T. (ed.), *The Rites of Durham*, SS 107 (1902).

FOXE, J., *Actes and Monumentes* (1563).

—— *Actes and Monuments* (1570).

—— *Acts and Monuments*, ed. S. R. Cattley and G. Townsend, 8 vols. (1837–41)

FRERE, W. H., and DOUGLAS, C. E. (eds.), *Puritan Manifestos* (1907).

—— and Kennedy, W. P. M. (eds.), *Visitation Articles and Injunctions of the Period of the Reformation*, 3 vols., ACC (1910).

FRITH, J., *The Revelation of Antichrist* (1529).

—— *A Disputation of Purgatory*, in *The Work of John Frith*, ed. N. T. Wright (Oxford, 1978).

FRY, E. (ed.), *Calendar of Wills and Administrations in the Court of the Archdeacon of Taunton* (London, 1912).

FULKE, W., *Two Treatises Written Against the Papists* (1577).

—— *A Reioynder to Bristows Replie* (1581).

—— *The Text of the New Testament of Iesus Christ* (1589).

—— *A Defence of the Sincere and True Translations of the Holy Scripture*, ed. C. H. Hartshorne (PS, 1843).

—— *Fulke's Answers to Stapleton, Martiall, and Sanders*, ed. R. Gibbings (PS, 1848).

FULLER, W., *The Mourning of Mount Libanon* (1628).

FURNIVALL, F. J. (ed.), *Ballads from Manuscripts*, Ballad Society (1868–72).

—— (ed.), *The Gild of St Mary, Lichfield*, EETS ES 114 (1920).

GAIRDNER, J. (ed.), *Three Fifteenth-Century Chronicles*, CS NS 28 (1880).

GAMON, H., *The Praise of a Godly Woman. A Sermon preached at the Solemne Funerall of ... Ladie Frances Roberts* (1627).

GARDINER, G., *A Letter of a Yonge Gentylman ... Wherin Men May Se the Demeanour & Heresy of John Fryth* (1534).

GARDINER, S., *Doomes-Day booke: or, An Alarum for Atheists* (1606).

—— *The Way to Heaven* (1611).

—— *The Devotions of the Dying Man* (1627).

GARDINER, S. R. (ed.), *Reports of Cases in the Courts of Star Chamber and High Commission*, CS NS 39 (1886).

GATAKER, T., *Christian Constancy Crowned by Christ. A Funerall Sermon ... preached at the Buriall of M. William Winter* (1624).

—— *Abrahams Decease* (1627).

GAULE, J., *A Defiance of Death being the Funebrious Commemoration of ... Baptist Lord Hickes* (1630).

GEE, H., and HARDY, W. J. (eds.), *Documents Illustrative of English Church History* (1896).

GEE, J., *The Foote out of the Snare* (1624).

—— *New Shreds of the Old Snare* (1624).

GERARD, J., *The Autobiography of an Elizabethan*, tr. P. Caraman (1951).

GERARD, T., *The Particular Description of the County of Somerset Drawn up by Thomas Gerard of Trent 1633*, ed. E. H. Bates, Somerset Record Society, 15 (1900).

GIBSON, J. S. W., and BRINKWORTH, E. R. C. (eds.), *Banbury Corporation Records*, Banbury Historical Society, 15 (1977).

GIFFORD, G., *A Briefe Discourse of Certaine Points of the Religion, which is among the Common Sort of Christians which may be termed the Countrey Divinitie* (1581).

—— *A Discourse of the Subtill Practises of Devilles by Witches and Sorcerers* (1587).

—— *A Dialogue Concerning Witches and Witchcraftes* (1593).

GILBY, A., *A Pleasaunt Dialogue betweene a Souldior of Barwicke and an English Chaplaine* (Middelburg(?), 1581).

GOFFE, T., *Deliverance from the Grave. A Sermon preached at Saint Maries Spittle* (1627).

GORHAM, G. C. (ed.), *Gleanings of a Few Scattered Ears, during the Period of the Reformation in England* (1857).

GOWER, G. W. (ed.), *A Register of all the Christninges, Burialles and Weddinges within the Parish of St Peter upon Cornhill*, Harleian Society (1877).

GREENE, R. L. (ed.), *The Early English Carols* (Oxford, 1977).

GREENWOOD, H., *A Treatise of the Great and Generall Daye of Iudgement* (1606).

—— *Tormenting Tophet: or a Terrible Description of Hel* (1615).

GRINDAL, E., *Remains*, ed. W. Nicholson (PS, 1843).

GUILD, W., *Ignis Fatuus. Or, the Elf-fire of Purgatorie* (1625).

GUY, N., *Pieties Pillar: or, A Sermon preached at the Funerall of Mistresse Elizabeth Gouge* (1626).

GWYNNETH, J., *A Declaration of the State wherin all Heretikes doe Leade their Lives* (1554).

HALL, J., *The Peace of Rome* (1609).

—— *A Common Apologie of the Church of England against the Unjust Challenges of that Over-iust Sect commonly called Brownists* (1610).

HANHAM, A. (ed.), *Churchwardens' Accounts of Ashburton 1479–1580*, Devon and Cornwall Record Society, NS 18 (1970).

HARRIS, R., *Samuels Funerall. Or A Sermon preached at the Funerall of Sir Anthonie Cope* (1618).

HARRISON, W., *Deaths Advantage Little Regarded* (1612).

—— *The Description of England*, ed. G. Edelen (Ithaca, NY, 1968).

HARSNETT, S., *A Declaration of Egregious Popish Impostures*, in F. W. Brownlow, *Shakespeare, Harnett, and the Devils of Denham* (London and Toronto, 1993).

HEARNE, T. (ed.), *A Collection of Curious Discourses written by Eminent Antiquaries upon Several Heads*, 2 vols. (1775).

HENRY VIII, *Miscellaneous Writings*, ed. F. Macnamara (1924).

Here begynneth a Lytel Boke that speketh of Purgatorye (?1531).

HIERON, S., *The Worldlings Downefall* (1618).

HIGGONS, T., *The First Motive of T.H. Maister of Arts, and lately Minister to suspect the Integrity of his Religion* (Douai, 1609).

—— *A Sermon preached at Pauls Crosse the Third of March 1610* (1611).

HILL, R., *The Path-way to Prayer and Pietie* (1609).

HOBHOUSE, E. (ed.), *Churchwardens' Accounts of Croscombe, Pilton, Yatton, Tintinhull, Morebath, and St Michael's, Bath, 1349–1560*, Somerset Record Society, 4 (1890).

HOBY, E., *A Letter to Mr T.H.* (1609).

—— *A Counter-Snarle for Ishmael Rabshacek* (1613).

—— *A Curry-Combe for a Coxe-Combe. Or Purgatories Knell* (1615).

HODGKINSON, R. (ed.), 'Extracts from the Act Books of the Archdeacons of Nottingham', *Transactions of the Thoroton Society*, 30 (1926).

HODSON, J. (ed.), 'An Agreement for the Construction of a Tomb in Wollaton Church, 1515', *Thoroton Society Record Series*, 21 (1962).

HODSON, P., *The Last Sermon preached before His Majesties Funerals* (1625).

HOLLAND, H., *A Treatise against Witchcraft* (Cambridge, 1590).

HOLLAND, H., *Monumenta Sepulchraria Sancti Pauli* (1614).

An Honest Godlye Instruction (1556).

HOOKER, R., *Of the Laws of Ecclesiastical Polity*, ed. C. Morris, 2 vols. (1907).

HOOPER, J., *Early Writings*, ed. S. Carr (PS, 1843).

—— *Later Writings*, ed. C. Nevinson (PS, 1852).

HORNE, R., *Certaine Sermons of the Rich Man and Lazarus* (1619).

HORSTMAN, C. (ed.), *Yorkshire Writers*, 2 vols. (1895).

HOYLE, R. W., 'Advancing the Reformation in the North: Orders from York High Commission, 1583 and 1592', *Northern History*, 28 (1992).

HUBBOCK, W., *An Apologie of Infants ... proving, by the revealed will of God, that children prevented by death of their baptisme, by Gods election, may be saved* (1595).

HUGGARDE, M., *The Displaying of the Protestantes* (1556).

HUGHES, P. L., and LARKIN, J. F. (eds.), *Tudor Royal Proclamations*, 3 vols. (New Haven and London, 1964–9).

HUME, A., *A Treatise of the Felicitie of the Life to Come* (1594).

HUSSEY, A. (ed.), 'Visitations of the Archdeacon of Canterbury', *Archaeologia Cantiana*, 27 (1905).

——(ed.), *Kent Obit and Lamp Rents*, Kent Records, 14 (1936).

HUTCHINS, R., *Of Specters*, tr. and ed. V. B. Heltzel and C. Murley, *Huntingdon Library Quarterly*, 11 (1947–8).

HUTH, H., and HAZLITT, W. (eds.), *Fugitive Tracts* (1875).

HUTTON, T., *Reasons for Refusal of Subscription to the Booke of Common Praier, under the hands of certaine ministers of Devon and Cornwall* (Oxford, 1605).

—— *The Second and Last Part of Reasons for Refusall of Subscription to the Booke of Common Prayer* (London, 1606).

The Interpretacyon and Sygnyfycacyon of the Masse (1532).

I. S., *Two Treatises, one of the Latter Day of Iudgement: the other of the Ioyes of Heaven* (1600).

JACKSON, T., *Sinnelesse Sorrow for the Dead. A Comfortable Sermon, preached at the Funerall of Mr Iohn Moyle* (1614).

JACOB, H., *A Treatise of the Sufferings and Victory of Christ* (1598).

JAMES I, *An Apologie for the Oath of Allegiance* (1609).

—— *Daemonologie*, ed. G. B. Harrison (1924).

JAMES, M. R., 'Twelve Medieval Ghost Stories', *EHR* 37 (1922).

JAY, G., *A Sermon preacht at the Funerall of the Lady Mary Villiers* (1626).

J.C., *A Handkercher for Parents Wet Eyes, upon the Death of Children* (1630).

JENISON, R., *The Height of Israels Heathenish Idolatrie* (1621).

JENKINS, C. (ed.), 'An Unpublished Record of Archbishop Parker's Visitation in 1573', *Archaeologia Cantiana*, 29 (1911).

JEWEL, J., *The Copie of a Sermon Pronounced by the Byshop of Salisburie at Paules Cross* (1560).

—— *Works*, ed. J. Ayre, 4 vols. (PS, 1845–50).

JOHNSTONE, H., *Churchwardens' Presentments (17th Century) Part 1: Archdeaconry of Chichester*, Sussex Record Society, 49 (1948).

JOYE, G., *The Subversion of Moris False Foundacion* (Emden, 1534).

——(?) *The Souper of the Lorde*, in T. More, *The Answer to a Poisoned Book*, ed. S. M. Foley and C. H. Miller (New Haven, 1985).

—— *An Apology to W. Tindale 1535*, ed. E. Arber (1883).

KEMPE, M., *The Book of Margery Kempe*, ed. S. B. Meech, EETS 212 (1940).

KENNEDY, W. P. M., 'A Declaration before the Ecclesiastical Commission, 1562', *EHR* 37 (1922).

——(ed.), *Elizabethan Episcopal Administration*, 3 vols., ACC (1924).

KETLEY. J. (ed.), *The Two Liturgies ... in the Reign of King Edward VI* (PS, 1844).

KILBYE, R., *A Sermon preached in Saint Maries Church in Oxford ... at the Funerall of Thomas Holland* (1613).

KING, H., *The Sermons of Henry King (1592–1669), Bishop of Chichester*, ed. M. Hobbs (Aldershot, 1992).

KING, R., *A Funerall Sermon that was prepared to have bine preached...for a certein honourable lady then almoste deade, but afterward recovered* (1552).

KNIGHTON, C. S. (ed.), *CSPD Series Mary I 1553–1558* (1998).

LACK, W. *et al.* (eds.), *The Monumental Brasses of Berkshire* (1993).

LANGHORNE, L., *Mary Sitting at Christs Feet* (1611).

LATIMER, H., *Sermons*, ed. G. E. Corrie (PS, 1844).

——*Sermons and Remains*, ed. G. E. Corrie (PS, 1845).

LAUD, W., *Works*, ed. W. Scott and J. Bliss, 7 vols. (Oxford, 1847–60).

LAVATER, L., *Of Ghostes and Spirites Walking by Night 1572*, ed. J. Dover Wilson and M. Yardley (Oxford, 1929).

LAYFIELD, E., *The Mappe of Mans Mortality and Vanity. A Sermon, preached at the Solemne Funerall of Abraham Iacob* (1630).

LEECH, J., *A Sermon preached... At the Funerall of the Most Excellent & Hopefull Princess, the Lady Marie's Grace* (1607).

LEIGHTON, A., *An Appeal to the Parliament; or Sions Plea against the Prelacie* (Amsterdam, 1629).

LELAND, J., *The Itinerary of John Leland*, ed. L. Toulmin Smith, 5 vols. (1964).

LE LOYER, P., *A Treatise of Specters or Strange Sights, Visions and Apparitions appearing sensibly unto Men*, tr. Z. Jones (1605).

LEVESON GOWER, G. W. G. (ed.), *A Register of all the Christninges, Burialles & Weddinges within the Parish of Saint Peeters [sic] upon Cornhill*, Harleian Society Registers, 1 (1877).

LEYGH, W., *The Soules Solace agaynst Sorrow* (1612).

The Lisle Letters, ed. M. St Clare Byrne, 6 vols. (Chicago, 1981).

LITTLEHALES, H. (ed.), *The Medieval Records of a London City Church (St Mary at Hill)*, EETS 128 (1905).

LLOYD, C. (ed.), *Formularies of Faith* (Oxford, 1825).

LODER, G. W. (ed.), *The Parish Registers of Ardingly, Sussex 1558–1812*, Sussex Record Society, 17 (1913).

LODGE, T., *The Divell Coniured*, in *The Complete Works of Thomas Lodge*, ed. E. Gosse, Hunterian Club, 4 vols. (1883).

MACCULLOCH, D. (ed.), *The Chorography of Suffolk*, Suffolk Records Society, xix (1976).

MACHYN, H., *The Diary of Henry Machyn*, ed. J. G. Nichols, CS 42 (1847).

MARSIGLIO OF PADUA, *The Defence of Peace*, tr. William Marshall (1535).

MARTYR, P., *The Common Places*, tr. A. Marten (1583).

MOORE, J., *A Mappe of Mans Mortalitie* (1617).

MORE, H., *The Immortality of the Soul* (1659).

MORE, J., *A Lively Anatomie of Death* (1596).

MORE, T., *Workes* (1557).

——*Utopia*, ed. E. Surtz and J. H. Hexter (New Haven and London, 1965).

——*Responsio ad Lutherum*, ed. J. M. Headley (New Haven and London, 1969).

——*The Confutation of Tyndale's Answer*, ed. L. A. Schuster *et al.* (New Haven and London, 1973).

——*A Dialogue of Comfort*, ed. L. Martz and F. Manley (New Haven and London, 1976).

—— *The Apology*, ed. J. B. Trapp (New Haven and London, 1979).

—— *A Dialogue Concerning Heresies*, ed. T. M. Lawler *et al.* (New Haven and London, 1981).

—— *The Answer to a Poisoned Book*, ed. S. Foley and C. H. Miller (New Haven and London, 1985).

—— *The Debellation of Salem and Bizance*, ed. J. Guy *et al.* (New Haven and London, 1987).

—— *The Supplication of Souls*, ed. F. Manley *et al.* (New Haven and London, 1990).

MORTON, T., *A Catholike Appeale for Protestants* (1609).

—— *The Encounter Against M. Parsons* (1610).

NAPEIR, J., *A Plaine Discovery of the Whole Revelation of Saint John* (Edinburgh, 1593).

NASHE, T., *The Terrors of the Night*, in *The Works of Thomas Nashe*, ed. R. B. McKerrow and F. Wilson (Oxford, 1958).

—— (?), *Martins months minde* (1589).

NEWPORT, F., *An Epytaphe of the Godlye Constaunte and Counfortable Confessor Mystres Darothye Wynnes whiche slepte in Christ the yere of grace. M.D.L.X.* (1560).

NICHOLS, J. G. (ed.), *Chronicle of the Grey Friars of London*, CS (1852).

—— (ed.), *Narratives of the Days of the Reformation*, CS 77 (1859).

NIXON, A., *Londons Dove: or a Memoriall of the Life and Death of Maister Robert Dove* (1612).

NORDEN, J., *A Progress of Piety* (Cambridge, 1848).

NORRIS, S., *An Antidote or Treatise of Thirty Controversies* (St Omer, 1622).

NORTHBROOKE, J., *Spiritus est Vicarius Christi in terra* (1571).

OGLANDER, J., *A Royalist's Notebook: The Commonplace Book of Sir John Oglander*, ed. F. Bamford (1936).

OLDE, J., *A Confession of the Most Auncient and True Christen Catholike Olde Belefe* (Emden, 1556).

OLDMAYNE, T., *Lifes Brevitie and Deaths Debility* (1636).

The Ordynare of Crysten Men (1502).

PAGE, W., *A Treatise or Justification of Bowing at the Name of Jesus* (Oxford, 1631).

PALMER, A. (ed.), *Tudor Churchwardens' Accounts*, Hertfordshire Record Publications, 1 (1985).

PARKER, M., *Correspondence*, ed. J. Bruce (PS, 1853).

PARKES, R., *A Brief Answere unto Certain Obiections and Reasons against the Decension of Christ into Hell* (1604).

PARKHURST, J., *The Letter Book of John Parkhurst Bishop of Norwich*, ed. R. A. Houlbrooke, Norfolk Record Society, 43 (1974–5).

PARR, E., *The Grounds of Divinitie* (1614).

PARR, R., *The End of the Perfect Man. A Sermon preached at the Buriall of the Right Honourable Sir Robert Spencer* (Oxford, 1628).

PAYNELL, T., *Certain Sermons of Sainte Augustines* (1557).

PEEL, A. (ed.), *The Second Parte of a Register*, 2 vols. (Cambridge, 1915).

PERKINS, W., *A Reformed Catholike* (Cambridge, 1598).

—— *A Golden Chaine* (Cambridge, 1600).

—— *A Discourse of the Damned Art of Witchcraft* (Cambridge, 1608).

PERSON, D., *Varieties: or a Surveigh of Rare and Excellent Matters* (1635).

PERSONS, R., *A Quiet and Sober Reckoning with M. Thomas Morton* (St Omer, 1609).

PERYN, W., *Spiritual Exercyses and Goostly Meditacions* (1557).

PEYTON, S. A. (ed.), *The Churchwardens' Presentments in the Oxfordshire Peculiars of Dorchester, Thame and Banbury*, Oxfordshire Record Society, 10 (1929).

PHILIPS, J., *An Epytaphe, or a Lamentable Discourse: wherein is bewayled the death of . . . Sir William Garrat* (1571)

—— *An Epitaphe on the Death of the Right Noble and Most Vertuous Lady Margarit Duglasis* (1578).

PHILLIPS, J., *The Way to Heaven* (1625).

PICCOPE, G. (ed.), *Lancashire and Cheshire Wills and Inventories from the Ecclesiastical Court, Chester*, Chetham Society, 33 (1857).

PILKINGTON, J., *The Burnynge of Paules Church in London in the Yeare of Oure Lord 1561* (1563).

—— *Works*, ed. J. Scholefield (PS, 1842).

PLAYFERE, T., *The Pathway to Perfection* (1611).

POCOCK, N. (ed.), *Records of the Reformation: The Divorce 1527–1533*, 2 vols. (1870).

—— (ed.), *Troubles Connected with the Prayer Book of 1549*, CS (1884).

POLLEN, J. H. (ed.), *Unpublished Documents Relating to the English Martyrs*, Catholic Record Society, 5 (1908).

POTTER, B., *The Baronets Buriall* (1613).

POWELL, G., *The Resolved Christian* (1603).

PRESSEY, W. J., 'The Records of the Archdeaconry of Essex and Colchester', *Transactions of the Essex Archaeological Society*, 19 (1927–30).

PRESTON, J., *A Sermon preached at the Funerall of Mr. Iosiah Reynel* (1615).

—— *A Sermon preached at the Funeral of Mr Arthur Upton Esquire in Devon* (1619).

PRICE, D., *Lamentations for the death of the late illustrious Prince Henry* (1613).

—— *Spirituall Odours to the Memory of Prince Henry* (1613).

PRICE, S., *The Two Twins of Birth and Death. A Sermon preached in Christs Church in London . . . Upon the Occasion of the Funeralls of Sir William Byrde* (1624).

PRICKE, R., *A Verie Godlie and Learned Sermon* (1608).

The Primer in English for Children, after the use of Sarum (1556).

PRYNNE, W., *A Brief Survay and Censure of Mr Cozen his Couzening Devotions* (1628).

PURCHAS, S., *Purchas his Pilgrimage* (1613).

PURVIS, J. S. (ed.), *Tudor Parish Documents of the Diocese of York* (Cambridge, 1948).

PUTTENHAM, G., *The Arte of English Poesie*, ed. G. Willock and A. Walker (Cambridge, 1936).

QUESTIER, M. C. (ed.), *Newsletters from the Archpresbyterate of George Birkhead*, CS 5th ser. 12 (1998).

RADFORD, J., *A Directorie Teaching the Way to Truth* (England, secret press, 1605).

RAINE, J. (ed.), *Depositions and other Ecclesiastical Proceedings from the Courts of Durham*, SS 21 (1845).

—— (ed.), *The Injunctions and Other Ecclesiastical Proceedings of Richard Barnes, Bishop of Durham*, SS 22 (1850).

—— (ed.), *Testamenta Eboracensia, V*, SS 79 (1884).

RAINES, F. R. (ed.), 'A Description of the State, Civil and Ecclesiastical of the County of Lancaster about the year 1590', Chetham Society, 96 (1875).

RASTELL, J., *A New Boke of Purgatory* (1530).

—— *The Pastyme of People and a New Boke of Purgatory*, ed. A. J. Geritz (New York, 1985).

RASTELL, J., *A Confutation of a Sermon Pronouced by M. Iuell* (Antwerp, 1564).

RAVENSHAW, T. F., *Antiente Epitaphs* (1878).

REDMAN, J., *A Reporte of Maister Doctor Redmans Answeres* (1551).

REYCE, R., *Suffolk in the XVIIth Century: The Breviary of Suffolk*, ed. F. Hervey (1902).

RICH, B., *The True Report of a Late Practise enterprised by a Papist with a Yong Maiden in Wales* (1582).

RIDLEY, L., *A Commentary in Englyshe upon Sayncte Paules Epystle to the Ephesyans* (1540).

RIDLEY, N., *Works*, ed. H. Christmas (PS, 1841).

R.M., *An Epytaphe upon the Death of M. Rycharde Goodricke* (1562).

ROBERTS, E., and PARKER, K. (eds.), *Southampton Probate Inventories 1447–1575*, Southampton Records Series, 35, 2 vols. (1992).

ROBERTSON, B., *The Crowne of Life. containing the Combate between the Flesh and the Spirit* (1618).

ROBINSON, H. (ed.), *Zurich Letters . . . during the early part of the reign of Queen Elizabeth I*, 2 vols. (PS, 1842–5).

—— (ed.), *Original Letters relative to the English Reformation* 2 vols. (PS, 1846–7).

RODES, F., *Life after Death* (1622).

ROGERS, J., *A Discourse of Christian Watchfulnesse* (1620).

ROGERS, T., *The Catholic Doctrine of the Church of England*, ed. J. Perowne, (PS, 1854).

ROSCARROCK, N., *Lives of the Saints*, ed. N. Orme, Devon and Cornwall Record Society, NS 35 (1992).

ROWLANDS, S. (?), *Hels torments, and Heavens Glorie* (1601).

RUPP, E. G., and DREWERY, B. (eds.), *Martin Luther* (1970).

Saint Austins Care for the Dead (England, secret press, 1636).

SANDYS, E., *Sermons*, ed. J. Ayre (PS, 1851).

SCHROEDER, H. J. (ed.), *Canons and Decrees of the Council of Trent* (1960).

SCLATER, W., *A Funeral Sermon preached at the Buriall of the Right Worshipfull Mr John Colles* (1629).

SCOT, R., *The Discoverie of Witchcraft* (1584).

SEGAR, W., *Honor Military, and Civill, Contained in Foure Bookes* (1602).

Sermons or Homilies appointed to be read in Churches (1833).

S.H. (ed.), *Denham Parish Registers 1539–1850* (Bury St Edmunds, 1904).

—— (ed.), *Shotley Parish Registers 1571–1850* (Bury St Edmunds, 1911).

—— (ed.), *Shotley Parish Records* (Bury St Edmunds, 1912).

SHELDON, R., *A Survey of the Miracles of the Church of Rome* (1616).

SHINNERS, J. (ed.), *Medieval Popular Religion 1000–1500* (Peterborough, Ontario, 1997).

SHUTE, N., *The Crowne of Charitie* (1626).

SIMPSON, W. S. (ed.), *Registrum Statutorum et Consuetudinum Ecclesiae Cathedralis Sancti Pauli* (1873).

SKEAT, W. (ed.), *Pierce the Ploughmans Crede*, EETS 30 (1867).

SMITH, H., *Sermons* (1592).

SMITH, R., *A Conference of the Catholike and Protestante Doctrine with the Expresse Words of Holie Scripture* (Douai, 1631).

SMITH, S., *A Christian taske. A Sermon, preached at the Funerall of Maister Iohn Lawson* (1620).

SMYTH, R., *A Defence of the Sacrifice of the Masse* (1546).

—— *A Bouclier of the Catholike Fayth* (1554).

SOMERSET, A. B. (ed.), *Records of Early English Drama: Shropshire*, 2 vols. (Toronto, 1994).

SPARKE, T., *A Sermon preached at Cheanies at the Buriall of the . . . Earle of Bedford* (1585).

—— *A Sermon preached at Whaddon in Buckinghamshire . . . at the Buriall of the Right Honorable Arthur Lorde Grey of Wilton* (1593).

STALEY, V. (ed.), *Hierurgia Anglicana*, 3 vols. (1902–4).

STARKEY, T., *An Exhortation to the People, Instructynge them to Unitie and Obedience* (1536).

—— *Life and Letters*, ed. S. J. Herrtage, EETS 57 (1878).

STOCK, R., *The Churches Lamentation for the Losse of the Godly. Delivered in a Sermon, at the Funerals of . . . Iohn Lord Harington* (1614).

STONE, W., *A Curse become a Blessing. or a Sermon preached in the Parish Church of S. John the Baptist, in the Ile of Thanet in the county of Kent, at the Funerall of . . . Mr Paul Cleybrooke* (1622).

STOW, J., *A Survey of London*, ed. C. L. Kingsford, 2 vols. (Oxford, 1908).

A Strange and Fearful Warning to all Sonnes and Executors (that fulfill not the will of their dead Fathers) (1623).

STRODE, G., *The Anatomie of Mortalitie* (1632).

STRYPE, J., *Ecclesiastical Memorials*, 3 vols. (1721).

—— *Annals of the Reformation*, 3rd edn., 4 vols. (1735–8).

STUBBES, P., *Two Wunderfull and Rare Examples of the Undeferred Judgement of God* (1581).

—— *A Motive to Good Workes* (1593).

—— *The Anatomie of Abuses*, ed. F. J. Furnivall, 2 vols. (1877).

—— 'A Christal Glasse for Christian Women', in id., *The Anatomie of Abuses*.

A Survey of the Booke of Common Prayer, by way of 197 quaeres grounded upon 58 places, ministring iust matter of question, with a view of London ministers exceptions (Middelburg, 1606).

SUTCLIFFE, M., *Adversus Roberti Bellarmini de Purgatorio Disputationem* (1599).

—— *An Abridgement or Survey of Poperie* (1606).

SUTTON, C., *Disce Mori: Learne to Die* (1600).

SWANSON, R. N. (ed.), *Catholic England* (Manchester, 1993).

SWINNERTON, T., *A Mustre of Scismatyke Bysshoppes of Rome* (1534).

TAILLEPIED, N., *A Treatise of Ghosts*, tr. M. Summers (1934).

TANNER, J. R. (ed.), *Tudor Constitutional Documents*, 2nd edn. (Cambridge, 1948).

TANNER, N. (ed.), *Kent Heresy Proceedings 1511–12*, Kent Records, 26 (1996).

TAYLOR, T., *The Pilgrims Profession. Or a Sermon preached at the Funerall of Mrs Mary Gunter* (1622).

THWAITE, H. (ed.), *Abstracts of Abbotside Wills 1552–1688*, YASRS, 130 (1968).

A True Report of the Horrible Murther which was Committed in the House of Sir Ierome Bowes (1607).

TUKE, T., *The High-way to Heaven* (1609).

—— *A Discourse of Death, Bodily, Ghostly, and Eternal* (1613).

TYNDALE, W., *Doctrinal Treatises and Introductions to Different Portions of the Holy Scriptures*, ed. H. Walter (PS, 1848).

—— *Expositions and Notes . . . together with The Practice of Prelates*, ed. H. Walter (PS, 1849).

—— *An Answer to Sir Thomas More's Dialogue*, ed. H. Walter (PS, 1850).

TYRER, R., *Five Godlie Sermons* (1602).

USSHER, J., *An Answer to a Challenge made by a Jesuit in Ireland*, in *Whole Works*, 17 vols. (Dublin, 1829–64).

UTIE, E., *Mathew the Publican. A Funerall Sermon preached in St Stephens Walbrooke the 11 of March 1615* (1616).

VAN MARNIX, P., *The Beehive of the Romishe Churche*, tr. G. Gilpin (1580).

VAUGHAN, E., *A Divine Discoverie of Death* (1612).

VAUX, L., *A Catechism of Christian Doctrine*, ed. T. G. Law, Chetham Society, NS 4 (1885).

VENABLES, E. (ed.), 'The Primary Visitation of the Diocese of Lincoln by Bishop Neile, A.D. 1614', *Associated Architectural Societies' Reports and Papers*, 16 (1881–?).

VERON, J., *The Huntyng of Purgatory to Death* (1561)

—— *A Stronge Battery against the Idolatrous Invocation of the Dead Saintes* (1562).

VICARS, J., *A Prospective Glasse to Looke into Heaven* (1618).

VIRET, P., *Disputations Chrestiennes, touchant l'estat des trepassez, faites par dialogues* (Geneva, 1552).

—— *A Christian Instruction*, tr. J. Shoute (1573).

—— *The Christian Disputations*, tr. J. Brooke (1579).

VORAGINE, J. DE, *The Golden Legend*, tr. W. Ryan, 2 vols. (Princeton, 1993).

WADLEY, T. P. (ed.), *Notes or Abstracts of . . . the Great Orphan Book and Book of Wills* (Bristol, 1886).

WALKER, W., *A Sermon preached at the Funerals of . . . William, Lord Russell* (1614).

WALL, J., *A Sermon preached at Shelford in Nottinghamshire* (1623).

WARREN, J., *Domus Ordinata. A Funeral Sermon preached in the Citie of Bristol* (1618).

WATSON, T., *Holsome and Catholyke Doctryne* (1558).

WEAVER, F. W. (ed.), *Somerset Medieval Wills 1501–30*, Somerset Record Society, 19 (1903).

WEAVER, J., and BEARDWOOD, A. (eds.), *Some Oxfordshire Wills Proved in the Prerogative Court of Canterbury, 1393–1510*, Oxfordshire Record Society (1958).

WEEVER, J., *Ancient Funerall Monuments* (1631).

WELCH, C. E., 'Three Sussex Heresy Trials', *Sussex Archaeological Collections*, 95 (1957).

WELCOME, R., *The State of the Godly both in this Life and in the Life to Come* (1606).

WEYER, J., *De Praestigii Daemonum*, ed. and tr. G. Mora *et al.* as *Witches, Devils, and Doctors in the Renaissance* (Binghamton, NY, 1991).

WHATMORE, L. E. (ed.), 'The Sermon against the Holy Maid of Kent and her Adherents', *EHR* 59 (1943).

WHITAKER, E. C. (ed.), *Martin Bucer and the Book of Common Prayer*, ACC 55 (1974).

WHITAKER, W., *An Answere unto a Certaine Booke* (Cambridge, 1590).

—— *An Answere to the Ten Reasons of Edmund Campian the Iesuit*, tr. R. Stocke (1606).

WHITE, F., *A Replie to Iesuit Fishers Answere* (1624).

WHITE, T., *A Godlie Sermon preached the xxi. Day of Iune 1586 at Pensehurst in Kent* (1586).

WHITEWAY, W., *William Whiteway of Dorchester His Diary 1618 to 1635*, Dorset Record Society, 12 (1991).

WHITFORD, R., *A Dayly Exercyse and Experyence of Dethe* (1537).

WHITGIFT, W., *Works*, ed. J. Ayre, 3 vols. (PS, 1851).

WHYTHORNE, T., *The Autobiography of Thomas Whythorne*, ed. J. M. Osborn (1962).

WICKHAM LEGG, L. (ed.), 'A Relation of a Short Survey of the Western Counties Made by a Lieutenant of the Military Company in Norwich in 1635', *Camden Miscellany XVI*, CS 52 (1936).

WILKINS, D., *Concilia Magna Britanniae et Hiberniae*, 4 vols. (1737).

WILLET, A., *Synopsis Papismi* (1592).

—— *Testrastylon Papisimi* (1599).

—— *Loidoromastix* (1607).

WILLIAMS, J. F. (ed.), *The Early Churchwardens' Accounts of Hampshire* (Winchester, 1913).

—— *Diocese of Norwich: Bishop Redman's Visitation 1597*, Norfolk Record Society, 18 (1946).

WILLIS, A. J. (ed.), *Winchester Consistory Court Deposition Books 1561–1602* (Winchester, 1960).

—— (ed.), *Church Life in Kent, being Church Court Records of the Canterbury Diocese 1559–1565* (1975).

WITHER, G., *A View of the Marginal Notes of the Popish Testament* (1588).

WOOD, A. C. (ed.), 'The Nottinghamshire Presentment Bills of 1587', *Thoroton Society Record Series*, 11 (1945).

WOOD-LEGH, K. (ed.), *Kentish Visitations of Archbishop William Warham and his Deputies, 1511–1512*, Kent Records (1984).

WOOTON, A., *An Answere to a Popish Pamphlet* (1605).

WRIGHT, L., *A Summons for Sleepers* (1589).

WRIGHT, T. (ed.), *Three Chapters of Letters relating to the Suppression of Monasteries*, CS 26 (1843).

—— (ed.), *Churchwardens' Accounts of the Town of Ludlow*, CS 102 (1869).

WRIGHT, W., *A Briefe Treatise in which, is made playne, that Catholikes Living and Dying in their Profession, may be Saved, by the iudgement of the most famous and learned Protestants that ever were* (St Omer, 1623).

WRIOTHESLEY, C., *A Chronicle of England*, ed. W. D. Hamilton, 2 vols., CS NS 11, 20 (1875–7).

W.S., *A Funerall Elegye in Memory of the late Vertuous Maister William Peter* (1612).

WYRLEY, W., *The True Use of Armorie* (1592).

WYSE, N., *A Consolacyon for Chrysten People to Repayre Agayn the Lordes Temple* (1538).

Index